Foundational Methods: Understanding Teaching and Learning

Third Edition

Edited by
Hilary Brown and Darlene Ciuffetelli Parker, Ph.D.

Taken from:

Models, Strategies, and Methods for Effective Teaching
by Hellmut R. Lang and David N. Evans

Classroom Management: Creating Positive Outcomes for All Students
by Lisa A. Bloom

Learning Theories: An Educational Perspective, Fifth Edition
by Dale H. Schunk

Teaching for Diversity in Canadian Schools
by Benedicta Egbo

Learning and Cognition: The Design of the Mind
by Michael E. Martinez

Understanding the Landscape of Teaching
by Irene Naested, Bernie Potvin, and Peter Waldron

*Authentic Classroom Management: Creating a Learning Community
and Building Reflective Practice,* Third Edition
by Barbara Larrivee

Becoming a Teacher, Third Canadian Edition
by Forrest W. Parkay, Beverly Hardcastle Stanford,
John P. Vaillancourt, and Heather C. Stephens

Custom Publishing

New York   Boston   San Francisco
London   Toronto   Sydney   Tokyo   Singapore   Madrid
Mexico City   Munich   Paris   Cape Town   Hong Kong   Montreal

Cover image: Courtesy of Images.com/Corbis

Taken from:

Models, Strategies, and Methods for Effective Teaching
by Hellmut R. Lang and David N. Evans
Copyright © 2006 by Pearson Education, Inc.
Published by Allyn & Bacon
Boston, Massachusetts 02116

*Classroom Management: Creating Positive Outcomes
for All Students*
by Lisa A. Bloom
Copyright © 2009 by Pearson Education, Inc.
Published by Merrill
Upper Saddle River, New Jersey 07458

Learning Theories: An Educational Perspective,
Fifth Edition
by Dale H. Schunk
Copyright © 2008, 2004, 2000, 1996, 1991 by Pearson
Education, Inc.
Published by Merrill

Teaching for Diversity in Canadian Schools
by Benedicta Egbo
Copyright © 2009 by Pearson Education, Inc.
Published by Prentice Hall
Toronto, Ontario

Learning and Cognition: The Design of the Mind
by Michael E. Martinez
Copyright © 2010 by Pearson Education, Inc.
Published by Merrill

Understanding the Landscape of Teaching
by Irene Naested, Bernie Potvin, and Peter Waldron
Copyright © 2004 by Pearson Education Canada, Inc.
Published by Prentice Hall
Toronto, Ontario

*Authentic Classroom Management: Creating a Learning
Community and Building Reflective Practice*, Third Edition
by Barbara Larrivee
Copyright © 2009, 2005, 1999 by Pearson Education, Inc.
Published by Merrill

Becoming A Teacher, Third Canadian Edition
by Forrest W. Parkay, Beverly Hardcastle Stanford,
John P. Vaillancourt, and Heather C. Stephens
Copyright © 2007, 2005, 1996 by Pearson Education, Inc.
Published by Allyn & Bacon
Toronto, Ontario

This special edition published in cooperation with Pearson Custom Publishing.

Printed in Canada

10 9 8 7 6 5 4 3 2 1

2009220138

DC/SA

**Pearson
Custom Publishing**
is a division of

www.pearsonhighered.com

ISBN 10: 0-558-37196-5
ISBN 13: 978-0-558-37196-8

Acknowledgements

We would like to extend our appreciation and our gratitude to the Methods Team at Brock University and to other special colleagues and students who took the time to support and consult on this custom-edited textbook. A special thank you to Lori Bittker and Lisa Gillis from Pearson Publishing for their flexibility and patience on this custom project.

Hilary Brown
Faculty of Education
Brock University

Dr. Darlene Ciuffetelli Parker
Faculty of Education
Brock University

Contents

1 Becoming a Teacher: Teacher as Reflective Practitioner

Reading A: Becoming a Reflective Practitioner

Today's classroom represents increasing diversity among students with a greater range of differences in ethnicity, socioeconomic status, developmental levels, motivation to learn, and achievement. Being responsive to this vast array of student needs requires teachers to reflect on their own behaviors and practices that may impede their potential for tolerance and acceptance, vital elements for meeting the needs of all students in a diverse society.

Reflection: A Vital Tool for Navigating Life in Today's Classroom

The explicit goal of reflection is to create deeper understanding and insight, forming the basis for not only considering alternatives, but taking continuous action to improve practice throughout one's teaching career. Reflective practitioners operate in a perpetual learning spiral in which dilemmas surface, constantly initiating a new cycle of planning, acting, observing, reflecting, and adapting (Larrivee, 2006a). Becoming a reflective practitioner means perpetually growing and expanding, opening up to a greater range of possible choices and responses to classroom situations.

There are many reasons for teachers to develop as reflective practitioners, but perhaps the most important is to help them respond more effectively to the inevitable dilemmas and tradeoffs involved in everyday decisions affecting the lives of students. Another benefit of developing as reflective practitioners is to free teachers from routine and impulsive acts enabling them to act in a more deliberative and intentional manner. Following routine helps teachers manage the task of teaching, but if teachers become slaves to routine they eventually come to feel powerless to influence their future careers. When teaching becomes so habitual that it is tantamount to a mechanical act it can be the path to teacher burnout. Routine action is dictated by circumstance, tradition, and external authority. On the other hand, reflective practice entails voluntarily and willingly taking responsibility for considering personal actions.

Growing demands on teachers of recently imposed federal and state mandates often lead to a sense of alienation and isolation, leaving teachers feeling like mere pawns in the system. However, teachers really can influence their practice much more than they may think by engaging in systematic reflection about their work (Larrivee, 2008). By taking control of their teaching lives they become empowered decision makers who can then begin to act on their world in ways that can change it. Reflective practitioners come to see themselves as change agents, capable of accepting what *is,* but also working to create what *could be.*

Historical Background

John Dewey (1910/1933, 1938) is generally credited with the foundational influence on reflection in education. He made the distinction between action that is routine and action that is reflective, contrasting reflective thinking with habits of thought that lack evidence and are based on faulty beliefs or unverified assumptions. Although Dewey first proposed his ideas nearly a century ago, the spirit of the concept remains essentially the same.

In the early 1980s the notion of reflective practice gained popularity through the work of Schön (1983, 1987) who challenged the reigning portrayal of teacher as technician, replacing it with teacher as committed, autonomous decision maker, or *reflective practitioner.* According to Schön, reflective practitioners continually learn from their experience, reconstructing experience through reflection.

Defining Reflective Practice

Reflective teaching, reflective thinking, reflective inquiry, reflection, and *reflective practice* are often used interchangeably. Reflection is a complex and multifaceted concept with many different dimensions. The term *reflective practice* is viewed as the culmination of all other forms of reflection. A teacher who engages in reflection in daily professional practice is referred to as a *reflective practitioner.*

Practice refers to one's repertoire of knowledge, attitudes, behaviors, and skills in specific areas of performance, including designing instruction, establishing assessment strategies, managing the classroom, and interacting with students, colleagues, and parents.

Some definitions of reflective practice focus only on the relationship between goals and outcomes:

- A process that helps teachers think about what happened, why it happened, and what else could have been done to reach their goals (Cruickshank & Applegate, 1981)
- The practice of analyzing one's actions, decisions, or products by focusing on one's process for achieving them (Killion & Todnem, 1991)

Others go further, characterizing reflective practice as a lifelong endeavor involving a commitment to ongoing learning:

- A critical, questioning orientation and a deep commitment to the discovery and analysis of information concerning the quality of a professional's designed action (Bright, 1996)
- A willingness to accept responsibility for one's professional practice (Ross, 1990)
- An inquiry approach that involves a personal commitment to continuous learning and improvement (York-Barr, Sommers, Ghere, & Montie, 2006)

- The capacity to think creatively, imaginatively, and, eventually, self-critically about classroom practice (Lasley, 1992)

Some extend their definition to include the ethical implications and consequences of their practices:

- Use of higher-level thinking, such as critical inquiry and metacognition, which allow one to move beyond a focus on isolated facts or data to perceive a broader context for understanding behavior and events (Hatton & Smith, 1995)
- An ongoing process of examining and refining practice, variously focused on the personal, pedagogical, curricular, intellectual, societal, and ethical contexts associated with professional work (Cole & Knowles, 2000)

At still another level, Osterman and Kottkamp (2004) define reflective practice as

- A systematic and comprehensive data-gathering process enriched by dialogue and collaborative effort

Aims of Reflective Practice

The aim of reflective practice is to think critically about oneself, one's assumptions, and one's teaching choices and actions (Cole & Knowles, 2000). The focus of reflection can be at the level of examination of classroom practices and behaviors, goals and outcomes, beliefs and values, or expectations and assumptions. Teachers bring into question their goals, encompassing desired aims, outcomes, and intentions. They can be general, such as creating the classroom as an authentic learning community, or they can be more specific, such as assessing the impact of task structures like cooperative learning groups and buddy or peer groupings.

Ten Attributes of a Reflective Practitioner
- Reflects on and learns from experience
- Engages in ongoing inquiry
- Solicits feedback
- Remains open to alternative perspectives
- Assumes responsibility for own learning
- Takes action to align with new knowledge and understandings
- Observes self in the process of thinking
- Is committed to continuous improvement in practice
- Strives to align behaviors with values and beliefs
- Seeks to discover what is true

Levels of Reflection

The term *reflection* is used to describe a vast array of practices ranging from mere thinking about a single aspect of a lesson to considering the ethical implications of teaching practice. The various definitions evolving over several decades most commonly depict three levels of reflection (Day, 1993; Farrell, 2004; Handal & Lauvas, 1987; Jay & Johnson, 2002; Larrivee, 2004; Van Manen, 1977) in which critical reflection represents the zenith or ultimate aim:

- An initial level focused on teaching functions, actions, or skills, generally considering teaching episodes as isolated events
- A more advanced level considering the theory and rationale for current practice
- A higher order in which teachers examine the ethical, social, and political consequences of their teaching, grappling with the ultimate purposes of schooling

Although there has been much discussion of the many different types and degrees of reflection, currently there is not any generally-accepted terminology to define the various levels in the development of reflective practice. The conceptual framework presented here represents a continuum of multiple levels adopting this author's terminology of surface reflection, pedagogical reflection, critical reflection, and self-reflection (Larrivee, 2006b, in press).

Surface Refection

At the first level, teachers' reflections focus on strategies and methods used to reach predetermined goals. Teachers are concerned with what works in the classroom to keep students quiet and to maintain order, rather than with any consideration of the value of such goals as ends in themselves. For this level, the term *technical* has been most widely used. The term *surface reflection* is used to depict a broader scope in this category.

Typical questions the teacher asks at the level of surface reflection are

Did I spend too much time on groupwork today?
How can I keep students on-task?
Did I have enough (too many) activities?

Pedagogical Reflection

At the next level, teachers reflect on educational goals, the theories underlying approaches, and the connections between theoretical principles and practice. This level has the least consensus in the literature, being variously labeled *practical, comparative, conceptual, contextual, theoretical,* and *deliberative.* The term *pedagogical* is a more inclusive term, merging all of the other concepts to connote a higher level of reflection based on application of teaching knowledge, theory, and research.

Teachers engaging in pedagogical reflection strive to understand the theoretical basis for classroom practice and to foster consistency between espoused theory (what they say they do and believe) and theory-in-use (what they actually do in the classroom). Teachers reflecting at this level can determine when there is dissonance between what they practice and what they preach (e.g., seeing themselves as humanistic yet belittling students when they persist in disobeying rules).

Typical questions the teacher asks at the level of pedagogical reflection are

How can I improve learning for all my students?
How can I increase individual accountability for cooperative learning tasks?
What strategies can I incorporate daily to give my students the opportunity to develop decision-making skills?
What else can I do to help students make connections to prior knowledge?
What can I do to better promote my students' self-management?

REFLECTION ON PRACTICE

Reflecting about a Teaching Practice

Activity Directions: Read the case study below. Then respond to the questions posed.

Mr. Clark had known for quite some time that a few of his particular teaching strategies weren't working very well. He had been teaching an elementary level special day class for 5 years and was beginning to think that he could do a better job. He wanted students to work together in his classroom, and he believed that when students learned together all of them could benefit.

For the last year, he had tried a variety of ways to gather his students into cooperative learning groups. He knew he had a knack for getting the students to feel like the classroom was theirs and that they were all part of "one big family," but when it came down to translating that feeling in specific learning situations, the achievement always seemed to elude him. So he signed up for a class on effective instruction. He learned that some of the research on collaborative learning indicated that (a) the teacher needed to plan the group work to align with the particular learning goals of the lesson in addition to a concern for the social interaction among group mem-

bers; (b) the teacher needed to identify what kinds of group talk would serve as evidence that learning was being achieved during the group sessions; and (c) the teacher should exercise caution when entering the group setting so as not to disturb the dynamics already in place.

Mr. Clark realized that he had to be much more strategic in his structuring of the groups to accomplish the learning goals he had for his students. Consequently, he changed the way he approached and structured group time with his class.

1. Describe a situation similar to Mr. Clark's in which new information or research caused you to make a significant change in a teaching practice.
2. What information, knowledge, or research findings would you like to have about a teaching method you are currently using or would like to use?

Reflective Questions
What is an aspect of your teaching that you would like to see working better?
What would you like to see that's not happening now?

Critical Reflection

At this level, teachers reflect on the moral and ethical implications and consequences of their classroom practices on students. They extend their considerations to issues beyond the classroom to include equity aspects of practice. Acknowledging that classroom and school practices cannot be separated from the larger social and political realities, critically reflective teachers strive to become fully conscious of the range of consequences of their actions. Few teachers get through a day without facing ethical dilemmas. Even routine evaluative assessment of students' work is partly an ethical decision, in that lack of opportunity to learn as well as impact on self-concept are ever-present considerations (Larrivee, 2000a).

Critical reflection involves examination of both personal and professional belief systems. Teachers operating at the level of critical reflection recognize that teaching is embedded within institutional, cultural, and political contexts and that these contexts both *affect* what they do and *are affected by* what they do. Teachers who are critically reflective focus their attention both inwardly, at their own practice, and outwardly, at the social conditions in which these practices are situated. These teachers acknowledge that their teaching practices and policies can either contribute to, or hinder, the realization of a more just and humane society. The focus of their deliberations is about issues of equity and social justice that arise in and outside of the classroom and on connecting their practice to democratic ideals.

The term *critical reflection* has the most consensus in the literature as a level of reflection examining the ethical, social, and political consequences of one's teaching. However, even within this category there is considerable debate regarding the inclusion of self-reflection. Some definitions of critical reflection include self-reflection. Some fail to acknowledge this category at all while others consider it to be embedded in the concept of critical reflection.

Typical questions the teacher asks at the level of critical reflection are

Do all students in my class have daily opportunities to be successful?
Who is being included and who is being excluded in this classroom practice?
How might the ways I group students affect each individual student's opportunity for success?
Does this classroom practice promote equity?
Do I have practices that differentially favor particular groups of students (e.g., males, females)?

Questions like these are in vivid contrast to questions generated by teachers engaging in surface reflection, who may question how to improve the behavior modification system they are using but may never question the larger issue of whether there are better approaches to behavior management (pedagogical reflection) or even if their management system limits the potential for some students with different cultural backgrounds to be successful (critical reflection).

Self-Reflection

Some models theorize more than three levels of reflection, generally singling out the concept of self-reflection as a separate entity. Day (1999), Hatton and Smith (1995), Valli (1997), and York-Barr, Sommers, Ghere, and Montie (2006) refer to this form of reflection as *intrapersonal, dialogic, personalistic,* and *reflection-within,* respectively, highlighting the dimension of dialogue with oneself. However, self-reflection as defined by this author is a broader concept.

Self-reflection is examining how one's beliefs and values, expectations and assumptions, family imprinting, and cultural conditioning impact students and their learning.

Based on the presumption that understanding oneself is a prerequisite condition to understanding others, self-reflection warrants distinction by itself.

The capacity for self-reflection is a distinguishing attribute of reflective practitioners. Considering how personal values, beliefs, attitudes, and vulnerabilities shape one's practice, inform one's judgments, and play out in one's teaching is at the heart of self-reflection. Self-reflection entails deep examination of values and beliefs, embodied in the assumptions teachers make and the expectations they have for students. Beliefs about students' capacity and willingness to learn, assumptions about the behavior of students, especially those from different ethnic and social backgrounds, and expectations formulated on the basis of the teacher's own value system drive teacher behavior.

Beliefs are convictions we hold dearly. They are enduring ideas about what is real. Although we have confidence in their truth, we acknowledge they are not susceptible to proof. A teacher's beliefs can be affirming or defeating, expansive or limiting.

Beliefs create the lens through which we view the world, shaping our identity. Thus, shedding a cherished belief can shake our very existence. For example, if a teacher tries to shed the belief that the teacher must be in total control to be effective, it means revealing uncertainty and vulnerability.

Values are deeply-held views about what we think is worthwhile. They steer how we behave on a daily basis to pursue educational goals and student outcomes. They also determine the lines we will and will not cross. Values are our ideals; thus, they are subjective and arouse an emotional response. In teaching, sets of values are often in conflict, challenging the teacher to weigh competing values against one another and play them off against the facts available. For example, a teacher who values being consistent while simultaneously valuing treating students justly may realize that there are times when to be fair is to be inconsistent.

As teachers develop the capacity to be self-reflective, they become increasingly aware of how they are interactive participants in classroom encounters rather than victims. By developing the practice of self-reflection teachers learn to

1. Slow down their thinking and reasoning process to become more aware of how they perceive and react to students
2. Bring to the surface some of their unconscious ways of responding to students

Typical questions the teacher asks at the level of self-reflection are

In what ways might I be modeling disrespect?
What is keeping me from trying to build a relationship with Darren?
Why am I so intolerant of Leroy's inappropriate behavior?

Inquiring about personal intentions and feelings is also included in this form of reflection. For example, teachers might question what is preventing them from taking action or keeping their perspective limited.

Here teachers may ask themselves questions like the following.

What were my intentions when I did that?
What triggered such an emotionally charged response?
Am I considering alternative explanations for what happened with Maria or am I fixed on my initial interpretation?

Cole and Knowles (2000) distinguish between *reflective inquiry* and *reflexive inquiry,* describing the latter as tantamount to self-reflection as defined here. Underpinning reflective inquiry is the notion that assumptions behind all practice are subject to questioning. On the other hand, *reflexive inquiry* is reflective inquiry situated within the context of one's personal history in order to make connections between personal life and professional career and to understand personal (including early) influences on professional practice.

An example of progression from surface to self-reflection is depicted below.

Moving through Surface Reflection to Self-Reflection
Surface Reflection: Are these good classroom rules for this group?
Pedagogical Reflection: Do my classroom rules represent reasonable expectations for my students?

Critical Reflection: Are the consequences for rule infractions just?
Self-Reflection: Do I overreact when responding to Derrick's behavior because of my own biases?

The Reflection on Practice task below was developed based on a want ad from *Reflective Practice for Educators* (Osterman & Kottkamp, 1993/2004).

REFLECTION ON PRACTICE

Qualities of Reflective Practitioners

Activity Directions: To identify key qualities of reflective practitioners, read the want ad below. Then reply to the questions posed.

WANTED
A Reflective Practitioner

A person who is inherently curious; someone who doesn't have all the answers and isn't afraid to admit it; someone who is confident enough in his or her ability to accept challenges in a nondefensive manner; someone who is secure enough to make his or her thinking public and therefore subject to discussion; someone who is a good listener; someone who likes other people and trusts them to make the right decisions if given the opportunity; someone who is able to see things from another's perspective and is sensitive to the needs and feelings of others; someone who is able to relax and lean back and let others assume the responsibility of their own learning. Some experience desirable but not as important as the ability to learn from mistakes.

List all the qualities that are sought in this want ad.

_____

_____

List the qualities you possess.

_____

_____

What one quality is your greatest strength?

_____

_____

What one quality is your biggest challenge?

_____

_____

Reflective Question
What could you do to begin to develop the quality that is your biggest challenge?

PRACTICES TO ENHANCE REFLECTION

Support Groups and Critical Friends to Enhance Reflection

Teaching is a complex and personal expression of multiple and varied forms of knowledge and knowing. Much of what teachers do is implicit, hidden from the practitioner, but observable by others. An individual teacher's thinking needs to be confirmed, modified, or stimulated to deeper levels of understanding by reflecting "aloud."

A major purpose of reflective practice is to test for the presence of assumptions and biases in the information one accesses. The checks and balances of peers' and critical friends' perspectives can help beginning teachers recognize when they may be devaluing information or using self-confirming reasoning, weighing evidence with a predisposition to confirm a belief or theory, rather than considering alternative theories that are equally plausible.

Reflective practice involves teachers questioning the goals, values, and assumptions that guide their work, entailing critical questions about the contexts, means, and ends of teaching. Engaging in such questioning is best accomplished in a supportive learning community, such as that provided in support groups or by critical friends.

Such support can help teachers keep from getting stuck in destructive habits to deal with the stress of teaching and can provide a buffer against the inevitable low points en route to becoming a reflective practitioner (Brookfield, 1995). Ideally, a support group or critical friend provides a safe haven so you can be vulnerable and ask for the help you need. Their function is not only to empathize with dilemmas but also to point out incongruencies in practice and fallacies in thinking. It often takes others mirroring back experiences and perceptions to open up a new way of seeing things.

Peer conversations help to break down the isolation many teachers feel. Colleagues' perceptions help teachers realize the commonality of their individual experiences. There is often much more that unites them than they realize. Collaborative dialogue helps teachers become aware of how much they take for granted in their own teaching and how much of their practice is judgmental.

Avoiding the Reflexive Loop

Argyris (1990) pointed out how our beliefs are self-generating and often untested, based on conclusions inferred from selected observations. In other words, from all the data available to us, we select data by literally choosing to see some things and ignore others. He coined the term *reflexive loop* to describe the circular process by which we select data, add personal meaning, make assumptions based on our interpretations of the selected data, draw conclusions, adopt beliefs, and ultimately take action. We stay in a reflexive loop where our unexamined beliefs affect what data we select.

Self-reflection involves a deep exploration process that exposes our unexamined beliefs, assumptions, and expectations and makes visible our personal reflexive loops. Becoming a reflective practitioner calls teachers to the task of facing deeply rooted personal attitudes concerning human nature, human potential, and human learning. Experience is culturally and personally sculpted. Experience is not pure—everything is contextually bound. We develop mental habits, biases, and presuppositions that tend to close off new ways of perceiving and interpreting our experiences (Argyris, 1990; Brookfield, 1995; Burbules, 1993; Knowles, 1992; Senge, 1990; Sokol & Cranston, 1998).

Being Authentic

Authenticity is a product of becoming a reflective practitioner. As teachers become more aware of the beliefs and assumptions that drive them, they become aware of the dissonance between what they say and what they do. With that awareness comes the capacity to change and become more authentic. To be authentic begins with being honest with yourself.

Understanding the brain's capacity to learn reveals that the gateway to accessing more of our potential lies in the emotions (Caine & Caine, 1997). Walking through that gateway means facing yourself. This journey through our own fears, limitations, and assumptions is essential for becoming more authentic.

Authenticity is acting without pretense. Brookfield (1995) describes authenticity as being alert to the voices inside your head that are not your own, the voices that have been deliberately implanted by outside interests rather than springing from your own experiences.

Palmer, in *The Courage to Teach,* similarly described this process as learning to listen to one's *inner teacher* and develop the authority granted to people who author "their own words, their own actions, their own lives rather than playing a scripted role at great remove from their own hearts" (1998, p. 33).

The opposite of authenticity is defensiveness. Authentic teachers, although not denying their fears, erect minimal barriers, have little to hide, and have nothing to lose that is worth keeping. Authentic teachers exude a powerful sense of inner authority and do not need to depend on others for their sense of well-being. Being authentic means not having to appear in control, or *look good*.

Ten Attributes of Authentic Teachers
Authentic Teachers . . .
Walk their talk

Know and trust who they are

Are aware of both their strengths and their weaknesses

Say what's on their mind without blame or judgment

Experience and display all their emotions

Are clear about their motives

Challenge others' inauthenticity

Are not afraid to be wrong

Admit their mistakes and try to correct them

Are always learning and changing

In Goleman's (1995, 1998) emotional competence framework, both self-awareness (knowing your internal state) and self-regulation (managing your internal state) are the cornerstone of the personal competencies needed to make your way in life as an "emotionally intelligent" being. To be authentic is to develop personal or *natural* authority by developing the capacity to be both self-reflective and able to respond *in-the-moment*. Having these two capabilities are the essence of authenticity.

Authenticity comes from aligning with your integrity. When you are authentic, you act with self-assurance, trusting your own capabilities so you don't need to use threats, gimmicks, or tricks in managing students. In effect, you manage yourself and the rest follows.

Authentic teachers share what's really going on with them. At the same time, they speak their truth without blame or judgment. They validate their right to the feelings they experience and respond honestly to students. Authentic teachers aren't afraid to be wrong and they communicate to their students that it's okay for them also to make mistakes. When teachers are authentic they create a climate in which their students feel safe enough to be authentic as well.

Authentic teachers use appropriate self-disclosure with their students. Self-disclosure that is appropriate in a classroom setting is used purposefully, that is, with the specific intent to extend a student's thinking about an issue or event. A teacher will need to assess the depth of disclosure that is called for and balance that with the teacher's own comfort level.

Essential Practices for Becoming a Reflective Practitioner

The process of becoming a reflective practitioner is a personal awareness discovery process. While it's not possible to prescribe a linear process or define a step-by-step procedure, there are actions and practices that are fundamental to developing as a reflective practitioner. The following three practices are essential.

1. SOLITARY REFLECTION. Making time for thoughtful consideration of your actions and critical inquiry into the impact of your own behavior keeps you alert to the consequences of your actions on students. Teachers also need reflective time to consider the inevitable uncertainties, dilemmas, and tradeoffs involved in everyday decisions that affect the lives of students. Any effort to become a reflective practitioner involves negotiating feelings of frustration, insecurity, and even rejection. Taking solitary time helps teachers come to accept that such feelings are a natural part of the task of teaching.

It's important to engage in systematic reflection by making it an integral part of your daily practice. Keeping a reflective journal is one vehicle for ensuring time is set aside for daily reflection. You might also want to take a few quiet moments in your classroom at the end of the day.

2. ONGOING INQUIRY. This practice involves unending questioning of the status quo and conventional wisdom by seeking your own truth. Becoming a fearless truth-seeker involves being open to examining the assumptions that underlie your classroom practices. It's a process of identifying and connecting patterns to form personal conceptions for understanding the complexity of what you observe and experience.

Engaging in ongoing critical inquiry is enhanced when you enlist collegial support. The support can be in the form of a support group, a "critical friend," or a mentor. The function of the support group or person is not only to empathize with your dilemmas but also to point out incongruencies in practice and fallacies in thinking.

3. PERPETUAL PROBLEM SOLVING. Becoming a perpetual problem solver involves synthesizing experiences, integrating information and feedback, uncovering underlying reasons, and discovering new meaning. Your *modus operandus* is solving problems, viewing the classroom as a laboratory for purposeful experimentation. A practice or procedure is never permanent. New insights, understandings, and perspectives can bring previous decisions up for reevaluation and consideration. You develop the capacity to reflect on your practices, coming to accept problems as natural occurrences and using them as opportunities to co-create better solutions, rather than enforce preset standards of operation. When you perpetually seek better solutions, you adjust the power dynamics to turn power *over* into power *with* learners.

Regularly engaging in these three practices helps teachers recognize their repetitive cycles and reflexive loops that limit their potential for tolerance and acceptance—the vital elements for effectively managing classrooms composed of students from different cultural and social backgrounds who have diverse beliefs and values. Reflective practitioners find a way to catch themselves when they try to unjustly impose their values or dismiss students' perspectives without due consideration.

Reflective teachers infuse their practice with a sense of excitement and purpose as they continually forge new ground. While they learn from the past, they thrive in the present. These teachers know that much of what occurs can't be predicted, but they also know that they are not victims of fate. Not to be reflective puts teachers in danger of what Freire (1993) calls "magical consciousness," viewing life in the classroom as beyond their control subject to whimsical blessings and curses.

There are many pathways to becoming a reflective practitioner, and each teacher must find his or her own path. Any path a teacher chooses must involve a willingness to be an active participant in a perpetual growth process requiring ongoing reflection on classroom practices. The journey involves infusing your personal beliefs and values into your professional identity. It results in developing a deliberate code of conduct that embodies who you are and what you stand for. Reflection is not only a way of approaching your teaching; it's also a way of life. The more you explore, the more you discover. The more you question, the more you access new realms of possibility.

Developing Awareness and Self-Reflection by Journal Writing

Journal writing is a reflective process that allows you to become more aware of your contribution to the experiences you encounter. This process is a useful tool for systematic self-reflection. Journaling can provide the clarification necessary for you to gain, or regain, a sense of meaning and purposefulness in your teaching. Finding personal meaning is the key to preventing burnout.

Journals can be instrumental in helping you unleash your creative powers as well as reduce daily tension. Making regular journal entries helps you remain clear and more aware of what is going on in both your inner and outer worlds. Most of all, a journal is a place where you can talk to yourself. The act of reviewing a journal over time can be a therapeutic tool.

Journal writing develops self-discipline. Attitudes about teaching and interacting with students are the result of attitudes and experiences gained over time. By making journal entries you can look more objectively at your behaviors in the classroom.

Having a record of your thoughts, feelings, concerns, crises, and successes provides a window of the past and a gateway to the future. When maintained over time, it can serve as a database offering both an historical perspective and information about patterns of thought and behavior.

Journals can serve several important purposes for teachers. They can provide a safe haven for

- Dumping all your daily frustrations
- Storing your most private thoughts and feelings
- Working through internal conflicts and solving problems
- Recording significant events and critical incidents
- Posing questions, naming issues, and raising concerns
- Identifying cause and effect relationships
- Seeing patterns of unsuccessful strategies over time
- Celebrating joys
- Experimenting with new ways of thinking and acting
- Tracing life patterns and themes

A journal can also be a place to set goals for yourself. Committing yourself in writing can be the impetus it takes to move you toward what is really important to you. Keeping a journal can help you map out where you want to be in your teaching 1, 5, or 10 years from now.

Journal writing is also an excellent tool for examining personal biases and prejudices that may unwittingly play out in your interactions with students whose backgrounds are significantly different from your own. Although you may not be conscious of inappropriate responses to students on the basis of culture, race, gender, or social class, there may indeed be areas where you unknowingly behave in insensitive ways. Making journal entries would allow you to look more objectively at your behaviors toward students from a variety of diverse settings.

The following questions can serve as a guide to beginning the process of making journal writing an integral part of developing the habit of reflection.

- What type of schedule would be manageable for you to keep a journal?
- When and where would you make entries?
- Would you do free-form reflection?
- Would you categorize entries?
- Would your entries be crisis or problem related?
- How would you use your journal to guide inquiry and decision making?

Teachers can also use journaling with students as a tool to provide them with a systematic opportunity to reflect on what they have read or studied. Teachers can use dialogue journals to create a vehicle for students and teachers to engage in authentic, interactive "conversation" about students' experiences, both inside and outside of the classroom.

REFLECTION ON PRACTICE

Daily Reflection

Activity Directions: One way to build reflection into practice is to take some time at the end of the school day and before you go home to reflect on the day. Based on what is important to you and the values you want to uphold in your classroom, write a few personal daily reflection questions. Below are some sample daily reflection questions.

1. Did I speak respectfully to all of my students?
2. Did I use fair and just discipline procedures?
3. Did I remain open to unusual or unexpected student responses?
4. Did I try to teach and reach all of my students?
5. Did I take time to interact with each student?

My personal daily reflection questions:

_____

_____

_____

Reflective Question
How can you make reflection an integral part of your daily practice?

Action Research as a Vehicle for Developing Reflective Practice

One widely recognized way to reflect on and improve practice is action research (Carr & Kemmis, 1986; Cochran-Smith & Lytle, 1993; Cole & Knowles, 2000; Dana & Yendol-Silva, 2003; Glanz, 2003; McFee, 1993; Mills, 2003; Osterman & Kottkamp, 2004; Parsons & Brown, 2002; Schmuck, 2006; Whitehead & McNiff, 2006). It is a systematic inquiry process conducted by and for those taking the action. Teachers assume the role of researcher in their own classrooms as part of a professional reflective stance.

Teachers use action research when they already recognize that they need to change something, such as a relationship with a student, or a task structure to enhance participation. Here the teacher entertains specific actions or interventions with students, the learning environment, or school community likely to produce more desirable results.

The process is similar to other reflection frameworks with the primary distinguishing feature being the emphasis on formalizing research questions and then collecting and analyzing data to take informed action. Action research is a form of disciplined inquiry ranging from simply raising a question about some educational practice and collecting information to answer the question, to doing statistical analyses to determine whether test results from an experimental group are statistically significant.

The purpose of action research is not the development of universal principles to be applied to all teaching situations. Rather each classroom is envisioned as its own unique social culture created by the teacher and students as they work together over a period of time.

Our Screening Process: Examining Our Personal Filtering System

Developing the practice of self-reflection allows you to recognize that what you see goes through a series of internal, interpretive filters reflecting your belief system. Perception is subjective—it is not pure and it can be distorted. When a student acts out, one teacher sees a cry for help, another a personal attack. It is our interpretation of the student's behavior, or the meaning we attach to the behavior, that determines how we will respond. Through self-reflection we can learn to see beyond the filters of our past and the blinders of our expectations.

The meanings we attribute to our experiences are influenced by various factors that effectively screen out some responses while letting others through. This screening process leads to differing perceptions of circumstances and events, resulting in different interpretations and, subsequently, in different responses. When we critically examine our screens, we can become more aware of how our screens may be filtering out potentially more effective responses to classroom situations and students' challenging behavior.

Our actions are governed by multiple screens that can be envisioned as a series of interpretive filters (see Figure 1.1). Each level of screen serves to eliminate some potential responses while allowing others to filter through. Our past experiences, beliefs, assumptions and expectations, feelings and mood, and our personal agendas and aspirations can either serve to limit or expand the repertoire of responses available to us in any situation. Beliefs about students' capacity and willingness to learn; assumptions about the behavior of students, especially those from different ethnic and social backgrounds; and expectations formulated on the basis of our value system can potentially be sources for responding inappropriately to students.

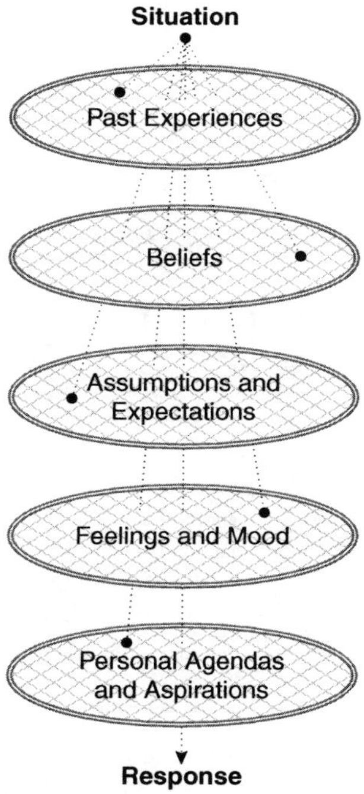

Certain responses can be eliminated by being screened through our past experiences. For example, a teacher may have tried putting students into cooperative learning groups, but soon abandoned the strategy rather than attempting adjustments to better accomplish desired goals.

Additional potential responses may be ruled out or in, on the basis of the beliefs we hold. Our beliefs can be affirming or defeating, expansive or limiting, rational or irrational. The assumptions that we make and the expectations that we have can make more responses available, or unavailable, to us. Our feelings, both those directly related to the immediate situation and those resulting from other experiences, can either serve to screen out responses or avail to us additional responses. And, finally, the agenda we set for ourselves and the aspirations we have act as still another filter. We may become driven by our personal goals and lose sight of what we stand for. For example, we might be so concerned about keeping our job that we go against our own values and keep the classroom quiet because that's what the principal values.

The way we respond is determined by this personal filtering system, which serves as a subjective mediating process. At the simplest level, there is an immediate reflexive response with no thought process occurring. A reflexive reaction, like removing your hand from a hot burner, is a reaction without conscious consideration of

FIGURE 1.1 *Personal Filtering System*

alternative responses. This type of response is often referred to as a "knee-jerk" response connoting that the response is automatic. Often we operate on "automatic pilot," closed off from entertaining a continuum of responses. When we do this in the complex classroom environment, we run the risk of responding to students in intolerant and disrespectful ways, which can easily escalate, rather than deescalate, student reactions.

Bringing your personal screens into awareness expands the intermediate thought process between a situation and your resulting reaction. By bringing a greater portion of the mediating process into awareness, you can increase your range of possible responses to the often difficult classroom situations you face daily.

As an example, consider your typical response to being criticized by a student. Suppose your reflexive reaction is to automatically offer a defense to the criticism. Let's say you usually respond with a "but . . ." rather than merely *taking in* the criticism or exploring it further. Becoming aware of your own resistance and asking yourself questions like, "Why am I being defensive?" or "What am I defending?" or "Why do I need to be right?" or "Why do I need to have the last word?" would represent challenging your screening process at the *assumptions-and-expectations* layer. By challenging your usual way of reacting, you allow a greater range of responses to filter through your interpretive screen.

Our cumulative layers of screens can lead to responding to situations in conditioned and rigid ways. To have the greatest freedom of choice and the capacity to respond uniquely to each classroom situation calls for constantly examining your choices to see how your personal screens are influencing your ability to respond in unconditioned ways.

As you take time to challenge your screens and consider alternate responses to reoccurring classroom situations, you become open to more possibilities and no possible response is automatically ruled out or in.

REFLECTION ON PRACTICE

Challenging Your Personal Screening Process

Activity Directions: To examine how your filtering screens may result in limiting responses to students, follow the steps below.

1. Think of an area in your teaching in which one of the five filters from Figure 1.1 is "clogged," keeping you from a more open response. Is it a bad past experience, a limiting belief, an expectation for how students should act?
   Clogged filter area:

   _____

   _____

   Describe the specific aspect of the filter area:

   _____

   _____

2. What types of responses are more likely because of this clogged filter?

   _____

   _____

   _____

3. What other ways of responding are being screened out?

   _____

   _____

   _____

4. List specific classroom actions you can begin to take to curtail your reflexive response.

   _____

   _____

   _____

5. Select one typical response that you want to begin challenging. Write a self-question that will help you.

   _____

   _____

   _____

Reflective Question
What can you do to remind yourself to become more aware of how your filters are screening out potentially more effective responses to students?

Examining Core Beliefs, Assumptions, and Expectations

Examining core beliefs is a critical aspect of self-reflection. A core belief is a fundamental belief about human nature, development, or learning. Our beliefs are adopted based on conclusions *inferred* from our observations and interpretations, and they often remain largely untested. Developing the practice of self-reflection involves observing our patterns of behavior and examining our behavior in light of what we truly believe. This process can be envisioned as flowing through several levels, from the level of core beliefs to the level of specific actions. Similar to a model developed by Shapiro and Reiff (1993) to examine the congruence between core beliefs and job performance, this process has four levels: philosophical, framework, interpretive, and decision making (see Figure 1.2).

Philosophy of life is the backdrop for all other levels and activities. The philosophical level embodies core beliefs and includes values, religious beliefs, ways of knowing, life meanings, and ethics.

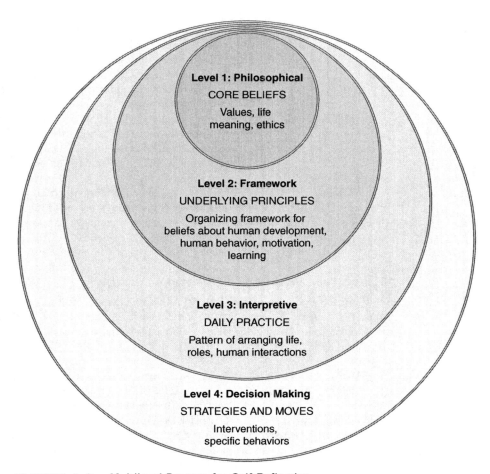

Level 1: Philosophical

CORE BELIEFS

Values, life meaning, ethics

Level 2: Framework

UNDERLYING PRINCIPLES

Organizing framework for beliefs about human development, human behavior, motivation, learning

Level 3: Interpretive

DAILY PRACTICE

Pattern of arranging life, roles, human interactions

Level 4: Decision Making

STRATEGIES AND MOVES

Interventions, specific behaviors

FIGURE 1.2 *Multilevel Process for Self-Reflection*

Level two represents our way of providing an organizational framework for these basic beliefs and includes the theories we espouse, such as theories of human development and human behavior, theories of motivation and learning, theories of organizational development, and chaos theory. It is our framework for attaching meaning to what's happening. These underlying principles serve as the basis for how we organize what we have learned and experienced.

The next level is how we interpret these underlying principles into our general approach to daily practice. This is where we link our beliefs and theories into a way of behaving. Our daily practice is an overriding stance, a pervasive attitude for how we approach life and the situations we encounter. It's a frame of mind.

From our attitude about daily practice evolves our momentary actions. It is our way of making real our ideals and translating them into thoughts, behaviors, and actions. This last level represents the translation into moment-by-moment decision making.

Core Belief	A fundamental belief about human nature
	• Each student is doing the best that he or she can at any given moment.
Underlying Principle	A principle that organizes our experiences and beliefs or our framework for interpreting experiences
	• We are all wounded by our unmet needs in childhood and our life experiences. Our wounds lead us to act in protective, and sometimes hurtful, ways toward ourselves and others.
Daily Practice	Linking of beliefs with a general plan of action
	• If I hold this core belief and understand that behavior is often driven by unmet needs, I will act in a way that accepts the student's limitations and refrains from judging the student.
Strategies and Moves	Linking of beliefs with moment-to-moment decisions
	• If I accept the student's behavior without judgment, then I will choose a behavior acknowledging that the student is not acting against me, rather to get unmet needs met.

Aligning Core Beliefs with Classroom Practice

Following are examples of core beliefs, one that is potentially affirming and one that is potentially limiting. For each type of belief, possible underlying principles, daily practice, and specific strategies are described. Some potential questions for reflection are also offered.

Affirming Core Belief	**Every student can be successful in my class.**
Underlying Principle	Students have different learning styles and intelligences that need to be addressed.
Daily Practice	Organize lessons to support multiple learning styles.
Specific Strategy	Allow students to select from three alternatives to demonstrate that they have learned the major concepts in the science unit on light.

Reflective Questions
- Have I given up on any students in my class because I have a limiting belief about their potential to learn?
- Do all students in my class have daily opportunities to be successful?

Limiting Core Belief	**Every student should show respect for the teacher.**
Underlying Principle	Adults have the best interests of children in mind.
Daily Practice	Have the following classroom rule: Treat everyone with respect.
Specific Strategy	When a student is disrespectful reprimand the student and apply a consequence.
Reflective Questions	

- Have some of the students in my class experienced adults who do not have their best interest in mind? If so, have they had an opportunity to learn respectful behavior?
- In what ways might I be modeling disrespect?
- Am I showing respect for all my students, or just those I think "deserve" it?

Often, reflection simultaneous with our actions is difficult because of the multiple demands we have to juggle in the classroom. For example, focusing our attention on completing a lesson may distract from paying attention to the way in which we interact with students. Thus, self-reflection often requires a perspective of a metaposition, a looking back after the action has taken place.

The self-reflective process raises our level of consciousness and this increased awareness provides an opportunity to spot incongruence or imbalance. Effective classroom management necessitates continual examining and revisiting of our core beliefs and assessing our actions against these beliefs.

Developing the practice of self-reflection keeps us coming back to our core beliefs and evaluating our choices in accordance with these beliefs. Change is an emergent process, requiring that we learn to become increasingly more aware. That consciousness is the source of our capacity to grow and expand, opening up to a greater range of possible choices and responses to classroom situations and individual student behaviors.

REFLECTION ON PRACTICE

Examining Core Beliefs

Activity Directions: To examine whether your actions in the classroom are congruent with what you believe, follow the steps below.

1. Write a belief you hold about education, students, classrooms, schools, learning, or human nature.

   Core Belief: _____

   _____

   _____

continued

2. List the principle(s) that underlie this belief. What are the theories of human development, human behavior, motivation, learning, or organizational development that frame this belief?

   Underlying Principle(s): _____

   _____

   _____

3. List specific ways of approaching classroom practice and the situations you encounter that support this belief.

   Daily Practice: _____

   _____

   _____

4. List specific classroom actions and behaviors that are consistent with this belief.

   Specific Strategies: _____

   _____

   _____

5. List any of your classroom behaviors and practices that are not in alignment with this core belief.

   _____

   _____

Reflective Question

What do you need to do to better align your moment-to-moment choices with this core belief?

Challenging Your Beliefs

In order to change, you have to challenge the underlying beliefs that drive your present behavior. If you merely try to change a behavior without attacking the belief that drives the behavior, the change is not likely to last long. However, the channel to changing beliefs is not direct; it is through perpetually examining your assumptions, interpretations, and expectations.

Because questioning assumptions and confronting limiting beliefs cause tension, the process inevitably leads to assaults on emotions. Arriving at a more examined set of beliefs and a more complex view of teaching practices creates a great deal of dissonance. Yet out of the discomfort comes invaluable learning and insight. Working through the challenges is essential to individual growth. Learning to be a reflective teacher requires a journey into the deep recesses of oneself, where both fears and hopes reside.

Your beliefs about the roles of the teacher and the learner, the nature and purposes of learning, and the teaching and learning environment best suited to these purposes will shape your management decisions. These beliefs disclose your operating principles related to how you view student potential, motivation, development, and growth. The following belief statements represent some possible beliefs that teachers may have.

- "I believe students learn best in an intellectually challenging learning environment."
- "I believe students misbehave when they feel defeated and become discouraged."
- "I believe students will thrive in a classroom environment where they enjoy each other's company."

REFLECTION ON PRACTICE

Aligning Beliefs and Practices

Activity Directions: To help you articulate some of your core beliefs about learning and examine practices that may not match your beliefs, complete the following:

1. Complete each statement.

   I believe my students learn best when I _____

   I believe my students learn best when they _____

2. For each of your core belief statements list some classroom practices and strategies that support the belief.

   _____

   _____

   _____

   _____

3. For each of your core belief statements list some classroom practices and strategies that are questionable when aligned with the belief.

   _____

   _____

   _____

   _____

4. Devise some alternative strategies that would be more in line with the belief.

   Alternative strategies: _____

   _____

   _____

Reflective Question
What questionable practice concerns you the most?

Challenging Limiting Expectations

Teacher beliefs are revealed in the expectations they have for students. There is much research to suggest differential teacher responses to students on the basis of their expectations. These expectations can, and often do, serve as self-fulfilling prophecies, when they are acted on with classroom interaction patterns that are discriminatory (Rosenthal & Jacobson, 1968). Limiting expectations can be based on gender, race, culture, social status, disability, or academic deficits, to name some. There is also research to suggest the teacher's mediating role in the attitudes that students develop toward their classmates as well (Larrivee, 1991).

There is a considerable body of research on the differing ways teachers treat and respond to students who are low-achieving versus students who are high-achieving. Good and Brophy (2002) list some of the following teacher behaviors that might communicate low expectations.

- Waiting less time for students who are low-achieving than for students who are high-achieving to answer questions before giving the answer or going to another student.
- Giving students who are low-achieving the correct answer rather than offering clues or rephrasing the question.
- Calling on students who are low-achieving less often.
- Asking students who are low-achieving only easy questions.
- Expecting less academic work from students who are low-achieving.
- Making fewer efforts to improve the performance of students who are low-achieving.
- Accepting and using fewer ideas of students who are low-achieving.

REFLECTION ON PRACTICE

Limiting Expectations

Activity Directions: Use the example of a particular student who is low-achieving to answer the following questions.

1. Describe the student's academic behavior.

   _____

   _____

   _____

2. Now read over your description. Does it reveal any limiting expectations? If so, list.

   _____

   _____

   _____

3. Which of the specific behaviors that communicate low expectations do you find yourself displaying with this student?

   _____

   _____

   _____

4. Are there any other behaviors you are engaging in with this student that might be communicating low expectations?

    _____

    _____

    _____

5. How does your experience relate to the research findings reported here?

    _____

    _____

    _____

6. What is one thing you want to change when responding to this student?

    _____

    _____

    _____

Reflective Question
What message is the student getting about your expectation for his or her performance?

Teacher Self-Efficacy Beliefs

A self-efficacy belief is your own estimation of your skill in handling some task. It's not a general belief about yourself; rather, it is a specific belief that is tied to a particular task (Watson & Tharp, 2007). What you believe about your ability to change affects how hard you will try to change, and that in turn affects your success. Research studies have shown that if people believe they can change difficult behaviors, they are more likely to be successful (Bandura, 1992, 1997, 2000; Bandura & Locke, 2003; Cervone & Scott, 1995; Maddux, 2002). When your self-efficacy belief about accomplishing something is high, you try harder, use better problem solving, are less distracted, persist longer, and are less likely to give up in the face of failure (Brown, 1991).

It is possible to increase one's self-efficacy beliefs. If people practice the behaviors necessary to reach some goal, their belief that they can do the things necessary to reach the goal increases. The belief that you can cope and can execute the process leads to greater effort in attempting to overcome difficulties and allows you to tackle problems with less emotionality. With self-efficacy, you can think of the specific skills you need to develop and put forth more effort when the going gets tough.

Teacher Self-Efficacy and Responding to Challenging Behavior

Teachers' notions of self-efficacy can play a part in perpetuating their reactions to certain types of student behavior. Self-efficacy refers to the teacher's perceived ability to be effective, find reasonable solutions to problems, and maintain a belief in their own capacity to effect positive change (Bandura, 1977, 1997). When teachers see students' actions as threatening their need for control and as intentional misbehavior, they are often pessimistic about their likelihood of producing positive results or any improvement (Brophy & Evertson, 1981).

Thus, teachers' notions of self-efficacy related to their lack of success with students exhibiting such behavior contributes to a sense of powerlessness in being able to effect change. That, in turn, often leads to a continuing pattern of ineffective, even increasingly more hostile, teacher responses.

In contrast, even frequent misconduct does not necessarily impair the teacher–student relationship if it is not disruptive or aggressive, provided the student responds well to the teacher's intervention. Apparently, even if they present behavior problems, students who defer to teachers' authority and respond positively to their interventions are treated with teacher concern and assistance, whereas students who fail to respond appropriately to teacher interventions are treated with rejection and hostility. These findings indicate an interdependence between the teacher's perceived effectiveness and resulting interaction pattern, and individual student's responses to teacher attempts to curtail inappropriate behavior.

Research findings support the contention that teachers tend to respond with rejection and an orientation toward control and punishment when students are disruptive or threaten the teacher's authority or control (Brophy & Evertson, 1981; Brophy & Good, 1974; Brophy & McCaslin, 1992). Teachers have been found to be especially rejecting and punitive when misbehavior is threatening rather than merely irritating. Students who persistently defy teachers' authority with sullenness or open hostility experience teacher rejection and punishment. Teachers react quite negatively to hostile–aggressive and especially defiant students and to any students who display a surly or insolent attitude. Responses typically depict negative expectations and are characterized by restricted language, often confined to terse demands for behavior change with little emphasis on shaping more desirable behaviors or improving coping skills. Demands are often accompanied by threat or punishment but seldom by rationales or offers of incentives for improved behavior.

Teachers' negative emotional response can trigger a need for control. When student behavior elicits feelings of frustration, irritation, or anger, teachers are more likely to respond with power assertion than to engage in problem-solving negotiations. On the other hand, teachers tend to respond supportively and attempt to help when student problems are purely academic or related to student anxiety or difficulty in coping with the demands of school. Similarly, responses to problems viewed as student-owned, where students are frustrated by people or events that do not include the teacher, are characterized by extensive talk designed to provide support and instruction, with frequent emphasis on long-term goals such as improving students' self-evaluations or teaching them coping techniques.

REFLECTION ON PRACTICE

Self-Efficacy

Activity Directions: Follow the steps listed.

1. Describe your emotional response to a student for whom your intervention tactics have been mostly ineffective.

_____

_____

2. What specific comment(s) do you find yourself making when you feel threatened?

_____

_____

3. What specific comments do you find yourself making when you fear losing control?

_____

_____

_____

4. What are the physical effects you experience when dealing with this student?

_____

_____

5. What are the mental effects you experience when dealing with this student?

_____

_____

6. How would you classify your usual comments (e.g., demands, threats, criticisms)?

_____

_____

7. How does your experience relate to the research findings reported here?

Reflective Question
What do you want to pay more attention to when dealing with this student?

Reading B: Becoming a Teacher

Integrating and Understanding Teaching

It is a story that has been told many times (Curtis, 1996). Four blind men chance upon an elephant. One man finds the trunk and, after touching it, concludes that elephants are like water hoses. A second man finds the tail and concludes that elephants are like brooms. A third man touches one of the elephant's legs and concludes that elephants are like telephone poles. The fourth man touches the elephant's side and concludes that elephants are like walls. Each man comes to a logical conclusion from his experience. Yet each man is wrong because he does not combine his experience with those of the other blind men. They do not integrate their conclusions. As a result, they do not have a complete and accurate picture of an elephant.

Recognizing the Influence of a Teacher's Worldview

I've had a lot of bad experiences in my life, and some of them actually happened.

—MARK TWAIN

The problem was not with the elephant. The problem was with the assumptions the men initially held and continued to hold despite their experience with the elephant. Perhaps in the same way, the problems that teachers encounter in teaching may not result from teaching, children, subject matter, schools, or society. The problem may be with the teacher's **worldview,** that mental model, that inner representation of the outer world, which is composed of the theories, beliefs, and assumptions about the big issues of life. A worldview is most influential in what teachers understand when they see children (brats or human beings), teaching (job or profession; work or calling), curriculum and subject matter (to be covered or to be constructed and discovered), and society (going to hell in a hurry or a beautiful place).

Teachers who are like the blind men might benefit from talking with the stakeholders in education—parents, teachers, school boards, professional associations, departments of education, and learners—people who have a legitimate interest in teaching, teachers, and public schools. These stakeholders would be able to warn them about what happens when people do not integrate their views of things. Unfortunately, the blind men were left to their own fragmented and partial view of elephants. Their initial assumptions, left unchallenged and unchanged, became the fences in the worldview that kept new and truthful ideas out.

Using a Worldview Approach to Understand Teaching

To understand the concept of worldview and how one's worldview influences one's teaching, we first need to understand three related concepts: integrated knowledge, schemata and shared praxis.

Integrated Knowledge

To **integrate** means to combine different ideas into one whole, non-fragmented, and coherent idea. It means that a person draws together all the facts about something, such as teaching, into an idea that makes sense. When ideas are integrated, a person can choose a deliberate, reflective, ethical response regarding a phenomenon such as teaching. **Integrated knowledge,** the combined knowledge from more than one source, is the key to understanding teaching. To have integrated knowledge about teaching means to weave into your worldview the needs and interests of teachers, learners, curriculum and subject matter, schools, classrooms, society, culture and history. Developing an integrated view of teaching will help you put together the puzzle of what it means to be an effective teacher. An integrated set of ideas about teaching will help you recognize more accurately what is really happening in classrooms with children. Integrated ideas will assist you when working with parents, administrators, and colleagues because you will have considered ahead of time, and woven into your own worldview, their interests, needs, and ideas.

Schemata

An integrated view of teaching means that you have schemata that are thoughtful and truthful. That word **schemata** (plural) can be thought of as self-organized clusters of particular information, attitudes, and possible behaviours about a concept. Your teaching schema (singular) is that cluster of information, attitudes, and possible behaviours related to teaching, organized in the mental file folder marked "teaching." We hope that after you read this book, when someone says "teaching," you will open that mental file folder and find that what is in there is integrated. The information about teachers will be sensibly integrated with schemata about learners, teachers, schools and classrooms, curriculum, and subject matter. Your teaching schema will have been threaded together by your understanding of the shared place of each stakeholder in education and in your teaching. You will know their respective vested interests in teaching and how their interests can be aligned with your interests. Your schema will have been formed through deliberate consideration to developing **teaching qualities**

CASE 1A.1

For Your Consideration

People acquire knowledge in five main ways: intuition, logic, experience, empirical/research, and revealed truth. How a person thinks about learners, teachers, schools, curriculum and subject matter, and society and culture depends on one's preferred way of acquiring the knowledge on which one's thinking is based.

1. Do you agree? Does it matter how a person comes to know about teaching?
2. Why is it preferable to think about children, let's say, using all five ways of knowing combined rather than just one way?

for effective teaching—qualities such as knowledge, thoughtfulness, diversity, authenticity, integrity, and relationships. Finally, your schema will have been put together as you examine, deliberately and intentionally, the commonplaces of teaching that influence the teacher's role.

Shared Praxis

The third concept to understand, as you develop a "worldview understanding" of teaching, is **shared praxis** (Groome, 1981). As you deliberately think about the specific interests of each commonplace, and integrate their interests into your teaching practice, you are engaging in praxis. When you share your reflections with practising teachers, principals, and professors, that praxis is shared reflection. This book helps you develop, through shared praxis, an integrated view of teaching, a thoughtful and truthful schemata that will make up your worldview.

To develop an integrated worldview, you will need to think in ways we believe are rarely asked of teachers in pre-service education. We hope that you will uncover the assumptions you already have regarding teaching and the five commonplaces, and will be prepared to engage in a *shared praxis* with your professor, your classmates, and your partner teachers and principals in the schools where you do your field experience. We invite you to identify, with your colleagues, what it is you actually do and why, regarding each aspect of teaching: what you do and why when you teach at your summer camp class or coach your community basketball team, and how you care for those with whom you work in your part-time job.

Be prepared to go even deeper than identifying your behaviours. We will guide you to uncover the theories, assumptions, and beliefs that give rise to that behaviour. Once both your assumptions and behaviours have been identified, we invite you to let the stories, research, assumptions, and experiences of others inform and, if necessary, call into question your behaviour and its assumptions. You should also be prepared to let your behaviours and assumptions affirm and, if necessary, disaffirm the research, assumptions, stories, and beliefs of others.

As you hear others' stories and others' hopes of the way they would like teaching to be, you will be invited to ask questions, inquiring into each story as to what insights are there. **Narrative inquiry** means reading and inquiring into a story for what insight it

Narrative inquiry is used to deepen and broaden understanding.

provides. Narrative inquiry characterizes this book. We believe that narrative inquiry may become for you a main way of deepening and broadening your understanding of teaching.

Finally, by the end of this book, we hope you will begin to choose a deliberate, reflective way of being a teacher. This choice begins with choosing a personally relevant world-view and a practice that will take you on to the next learning experience of what it means to be a teacher. This is a shared praxis way of becoming a teacher.

First Steps Toward Integrated Knowledge about Teaching

The first steps toward integrated knowledge about teaching include identifying and challenging your assumptions about teaching. Your worldview is made up of your assumptions and understandings about the essential nature of the world, which directly affect the degree to which you are able to make sense of your world. When they are left too long unchallenged, they are like walls a previous owner put up around a property. You might accept the wall but are not sure why it was put up in the first place. At the same time, if you take down a wall, before doing so it is good to ask why the wall was put up in the first place. We invite you to uncover old assumptions and understandings and then develop new ones. In the next section, we guide you on your first steps toward integrating your knowledge about teaching. We begin by examining the different ways teachers organize their knowledge about teaching.

Propositional Statements

How a person acquires knowledge affects a person's understanding of things. Eat all your meals at McDonalds, and you might understand fine dining to necessarily include Big Macs. If you teach only younger children, you might be hard pressed to understand how older children typically think and behave. People's knowledge of things ranges from simple to complex. It might be helpful for you to think about this range of **declarative knowledge** (an idea or concept that corresponds to the real thing) as a "food chain" of knowledge representations. People internally represent the external world in an increasingly complex, integrated way.

Propositional knowledge is the simplest knowledge representation. A proposition is a simple noun-verb relationship, such as "People eat food." In their language and behaviour, people present these forms of knowledge as "gists," or the essence of the thing. Teachers might comment that "teaching is hard work," or that "children are all different." Propositional knowledge can result in fairly simple and sweeping ways of behaving. Sometimes, this type of knowledge is called **macro-propositional** (Pressley, 1995). It would be simple and easy to behave toward the world of teaching in macropropositional ways. Have you ever heard someone say, "All children love to play?" That is an easy and quick way to represent the complexity of the external world of young people. Have you ever heard anyone say, "Teenagers are all sexually active?" That again, is an easy and quick way to represent the complexity of the world of adolescents and could lead to a simple and sweeping way of responding. Teaching, however, is more complex than what any proposition can handle.

Scripts

Scripts are a more complex knowledge representation in the food chain of knowledge representations (Pressley, 1995). These sequentially specify the steps to take in particular situations, such as ordering food from McDonalds. The script is clear and well-known.

Stand in line, wait your turn, approach the till, place your order, pay, wait for your food, and so on. You might be tempted to want to learn a "script" for being teacher. Unfortunately, teaching is far more complex than what a script might be able to handle.

Concepts

Concepts are more complex knowledge representations than scripts. A concept is like a set of rules that a person uses to determine what something means and where it fits in a person's understanding (Pressley, 1995). For example, if something has four legs, is furry, and meows, it is a cat. If a place that sells food looks like a McDonalds, it is likely that ordering food takes place in a certain way. If someone is physically smaller than an adult, enjoys games, and needs adult care, that someone is a child. Accurate concepts are helpful for teachers. However, conceptual knowledge alone is not sufficient for teachers to have integrated know-ledge and to become effective teachers.

Schemata

A more complex and integrated form of knowledge is a schema. A **schema** is a cluster of knowledge, attitudes, and proposed behaviour around a concept. (*Schemata* is the plural of *schema.*) For example, within one's "eating schema" are the eating behaviours, eating attitudes, and knowledge about food that characterize that person. Do you know any health-food zealots? That particular way of thinking about eating includes that person's attitude toward both junk food and good food, and that person's attitude and behaviour toward people who eat those foods. Teaching schema are helpful to teachers because they include concepts, scripts, and propositions, but also include attitudes and behaviours that ensure effective teaching.

Before we discuss the more complex knowledge representation, worldviews, we need to consider the profound ways that schemata, the building blocks of worldviews, affect our ability to think about teaching, learning, and schools.

CASE 1A.2

For Your Consideration

1. Draw a picture of a clock face. Put the numbers on the clock face, using roman numerals. Did you put IV for four o'clock? If you did, you were resorting to your "Roman numeral" schema. In fact, if you were to look at a clock face that uses roman numerals, you would see that all clocks use IIII and not IV. Your ability to think about clocks accurately was impaired, influenced more by your schema than by what Roman numeral clocks actually look like.

2. Think back a few years to your earlier school experience. Put a face and name together, if you can, as you do this activity. Think of a boy or girl in your elementary school who caused problems for teachers and students. Do you think that child turned out okay? If your first response was no, were you influenced to conclude that by your "what happens to bad kids" schema, or by another, more hopeful schema? For example, "There is hope for everyone," "People can be late bloomers," "If a child is loved, anything good can happen."

Worldviews

By far the most complex knowledge representation is worldview. We believe that teaching should be considered from the perspective of worldview because teaching is a complex activity, an ethical and moral way of being, one in which human beings and their well-being are at stake. Teaching deserves to be considered in the broadest and most profound ways possible. When worldviews are fragmented, and knowledge about the common-places of teaching is not integrated, teaching will be ineffective. When teaching is thought about only in terms of propositions, scripts, concepts, and schema, teaching is not well understood.

The Implications of Integrated Knowledge

A non-education professor once remarked that he couldn't understand why it took four or more years to prepare elementary school teachers because after all, he said, elementary school teaching isn't rocket science. He was right, of course. Elementary school teaching is far more complex and perhaps more demanding. The professor was speaking from a single perspective, the small, teaching worldview of a post-secondary professor, one whose teaching has consisted only of lecturing. He understands only one aspect of teaching. He does not have an integrated worldview of teaching. He is like the fisherman in an often-told story who fished in the ocean for fifty years with a net that had two-by-two-centimetre mesh. At his retirement party he stood up in front of the crowd, and with the certainty of fifty years of successful fishing behind him, stated emphatically that he knew, beyond a shadow of a doubt, that there were no fish in the ocean smaller than two by two centimetres. The net of our worldview can let all kinds of important and true ideas about teaching slip through.

A worldview provides a person with an inner representation of the world, one that spells out the answers to the big questions of life. What is most important? What is the role of human beings in history? What is most worth knowing? It is worldview that ultimately gives rise to, and most profoundly influences, a person's procedural knowledge—how to treat diversity in a classroom, for example, or how to engage in thoughtful reflection about a teaching problem. It is worldview that most profoundly influences a teacher's most important knowledge: knowledge about who children "really" are or what kind of relationship a teacher should develop with a child.

When a worldview is not integrated, when it consists of one or two perspectives only, it is like the fisherman's net. It is the premise of this book that to become an effective educator, one must have a view of teaching that is integrated.

CASE 1A.3

For Your Consideration

Think of a teacher whose worldview consists of the following outlooks:

Life is hard; then you die.

When it comes to life, no one gets out of it alive, so eat, drink and be merry.

1. How might those influence the teacher's relationship with learners?
2. Is hope necessary to be a good teacher?

Five Commonplaces of Teaching

To develop an integrated worldview regarding teaching, learning, and schooling, you will need to understand the five greatest influences in a teacher's work: learners and learning; teachers and teaching; schools and classrooms; curriculum and subject matter; and culture, society and history. It is toward an understanding of the five **commonplaces** and how you can integrate these into your understanding of teaching that we now go.

The notion of teaching "commonplaces" was introduced into the teaching field nearly twenty years ago and was evident in the writing of curriculum theorists like Joseph Schwab (1973). We believe it is a useful way for you to deepen and broaden your understanding of teachers, teaching, and schools, because the notion of commonplaces reminds us all that teaching is a practical, social, and complex activity. Theory alone, we believe, is of limited value in helping us understand teaching.

Theory, the plausible explanation for the way things work, might be helpful in understanding black holes in the universe or why birds migrate, but theory alone is not helpful in understanding teaching. A theory is a concept, and, as we discussed earlier, concepts can be limited in helping you become an effective teacher. Shared praxis is more helpful than theory.

It is also helpful to know **domain-specific procedural knowledge** (Pressley and McCormick, 1995), which is particular teaching skills wisely applied through judgments made about particular situations. Procedural knowledge develops over time, through reflecting with others, deliberately and systematically, on experiences. These experiences are often revealed in teachers' stories, in the language teachers use to tell their stories. We encourage you to listen closely to what teachers tell you about teaching.

Teachers do not work outside a social setting. You will hear teachers tell you this in their stories. Teacher's judgments about particular situations are influenced by principals, departments of learning, school boards, professional associations, parents, and by societal and cultural phenomenon such as media, violence, and family breakdown. Two very important issues to consider as you move toward developing an integrated worldview of teaching are

1. What influences do the commonplaces have on what it is like to be a teacher?
2. How might a teacher deliberately and reflectively make decisions regarding teaching through integrating the interests of each of the five commonplaces of education? How might a teacher make wise judgments about particular situations without compromising his or her own teaching worldview?

Learners and Learning

Learning is a profoundly complex activity. To understand learning and to teach with integrity means that you will need to understand the needs of children and youth, their developmental, psychological, and spiritual needs. You might not have expected that you will need to facilitate learning, guiding young people to be thoughtful, self-reliant, and self-directing, to be able to take risks, ask questions, and have real ownership over their learning. This is easier to write about than to do. Understanding learners and learning will be central to this book. We hope to convince you that understanding learning is central to your integrated understanding of what it means to be a teacher.

Teachers and Teaching

A lot more learning happens in a classroom than children learning to read, write, and do arithmetic. A look into classrooms may not reveal that right away. Reflection on your life and what teachers meant to you might be a better source of information regarding what else happens as a result of teachers and teaching.

Who has made an impact in your life? If you were to list ten people who were influential in your life, we suspect that a teacher would make the list. Why? What was it about that teacher that made a difference? We will look closely at your teachers who made a difference, the characteristics of great teachers, what those great teachers knew and did in order to be effective. For a hint of what is to come in Chapter 5, we invite you to look at For Your Consideration 1A.4, below.

CASE 1A.4

For Your Consideration

When you think of great teachers, even good teachers, what picture comes to mind? What does that great or good teacher look like? Make a list of these characteristics.

1. Did the list you create have more skills in it than attributes?
2. Did great teachers do something better than less great teachers, or were they better people than less great teachers? What was it about them that made a difference?

We suspect that your list contained words such as caring, enthusiasm, interesting, and respectful more than terms such as scholar, great teaching technique, or knowledge of physics. Not that we think a teacher shouldn't be these things too. It is evident that teachers who make a difference have some characteristics that are special.

You will not be a nobody when you become a teacher. Before you dismiss too quickly the significance you might one day have as a teacher, consider the following. Who taught today's great world leaders such as Nelson Mandela (South Africa) and Vaclav Havel (Czech Republic), and inspired their courage and motivated them to a life of public service and creative expression? Who influenced Mother Teresa at a particular point in her life to think about a life of service to the poor? Who was influential in creating the passion for music that drove the great musicians, the love of art to lift us up out of the daily drudgery. Who were those "nameless, anonymous people"? We might never know, but there were teachers in every life.

We believe that you can be a shaper of hopes and dreams, that you can ignite passion and insight. You can build or defeat a young person's hope in a better world. You can fill minds and hearts with love for what is best in the human situation, practices of love, hope, and justice.

Schools and Classrooms

We invite you to see schools and classrooms from the perspective of other stakeholders, from the point of view of teachers, parents, society, and administrators. It might surprise you when we suggest that it is a myth that schools are just for learners and learning.

Schools are for teachers, too. They are places where teaching careers are built, relationships are formed, skills are developed, and personal growth is experienced.

We will explore a number of other myths. We will look carefully at how schools are organized and governed, and how important it is that individuals who govern schools use leadership styles that are moral, civil, participatory, and empowering. You might have assumed otherwise. If you did, you are not alone. Many young teachers are surprised to learn that leadership and governance in schools involve more than just setting timetables and holding assemblies.

We invite you to look at classrooms from a different perspective, as well. We will pose some important and thought-provoking questions. For example, we will ask you to consider whether other settings than a classroom might be preferable for learning. We will ask you to consider how classrooms could be better connected to the school culture and the goals of the school.

CASE 1A.5

For Your Consideration

What was your favourite school subject? Consider the reasons you chose that subject. If you said gym class, why did you call it "gym class" and not "physical education"? If you said science class, was science taught primarily in a classroom? Outside?

Curriculum and Subject Matter

Curriculum is about all that a learner learns in school. It includes programs of study, subject guides, and school-specific policy decisions that affect the ways of working and general conduct of a school. Curriculum includes the goals of schooling, the outcomes intended or unintended, and all the experiences a learner has in school. The word *curriculum* comes from the Latin word *currere,* which means to run a course. Curriculum is very complex.

Many educators have raised the question, What do children really learn in school? When children come home from school and are asked what they learned, they may reply, "Nothing." Perhaps they should really be saying that they learned how to give teachers the answers they want rather than what they think is true. They learned how to be safe and quiet. They learned that other people can be mean if they want to, and they learned how to camouflage feelings of rejection and pain. They learned how easy it is to be bored, but learned how to hide boredom.

The **planned curriculum** is about what is intended that children learn in schools, the courses of study, the intended learning outcomes, and the teacher strategies.

The curriculum of a school includes the **null curriculum.** The null curriculum concerns what is not taught, perhaps about important issues such as death, sex, and love. The null curriculum is learned through what is not intentionally presented to learners.

We will look closely at the topic of curriculum later in this book. We will analyze what we mean by curriculum, how curriculum is developed, implemented, and assessed. We will look at various approaches for implementing curriculum, including on-line learning and other forms of distance education delivery.

CASE 1A.6

For Your Consideration

1. What were the most important lessons you learned at school? How did you learn those lessons?

2. What did schools not teach you that you now are convinced they needed to?

The other piece of this commonplace is subject matter. Subject matter in schools is organized according to the logic inherent in the subject matter and to what learners may be developmentally able to handle. Science, for example, lends itself to inquiry, therefore the subject matter of science in modern schools is inquiry-based and often hands-on. Learners in elementary schools can understand scientific concepts in very concrete terms. Learners in high school may be able to understand scientific concepts in more abstract terms. Your choice of subjects to teach may depend on your passion for a subject and your expertise developed in the subject matter. Physical education teachers, for example, often have a great deal of sport experience before attending teacher education programs.

Assessment, evaluation, measurement, and reporting are vast fields of study in education and are critical components to your profession.

Culture, Society, and History

We invite you to think about another commonplace, Canadian culture—the values, ideologies, and competing worldviews evident in Canadian history and society—that influence what it means to be a teacher in Canada. For now, we will give you a small illustration. The following are two debates that teachers can find themselves drawn into. We present these for you to initiate discussion with your classmates, professors, and partner teachers. Embedded in both stories are many cultural and ideological assumptions and understandings about what is most important to learn, whose interests are being served by education, and what is the role and place of religion in schools.

Students at Lakeview Elementary School won't be dressing up as witches or ghosts this year. In fact, they won't be dressing up at all. Paper witches on broomsticks no longer adorn classroom bulletin boards and windows. Complaints from various religious groups say the holiday is linked with the devil and several school violence situations have led many schools to tone down the Halloween celebration and replace them with neutral "fall festivals." The contemporary celebration of Halloween has its roots in Samhain, the Celtic harvest festival and New Year. On this day, the Celts believed the souls of those who died would wander and enter the land of the dead. ("U.S. Schools," 2000)

Students at Upper Gulch school will not celebrate Christmas this year. As a result of special interest groups, any reference to Jesus, Mary, and Joseph or to the traditional Christmas story will be removed from the school's December program. This decision was made despite the fact that most parents in the school either wanted the Christmas story told, primarily because it is a traditional part of their culture, or could not care less what happens at Christmas. The argument of the interest-group members was that public school should be neutral and should not be a place where people's beliefs are presented.

CASE 1A.7

For Your Consideration

1. What do the stories reveal regarding contemporary culture? Is a resolution possible in each story?
2. What assumptions, beliefs, and theories does each story reveal?

3. How can a teacher be neutral?
4. Is there a way to be a value-filled teacher and not offend religiously?

There are many other important issues to consider, including poverty, gender, race, and the media and their influence in schools and children's lives. The issues of society are not simple. Someone once remarked that the more complex the issue, the more people settle for simple answers. We will try not to do that in these chapters. Instead, whether we are discussing parenting, the rise in alternative schools, the social and economic struggles of cities, or the politicization of schooling, we will try to help you develop an integrated view, a worldview that will help you become the professional educator you want to become.

Creating Conditions for Insight

The one activity that most characterizes a teacher's role is creating conditions that promote learning. The more effective you become in creating conditions that promote learning, the more joyful and fulfilling will be your work as a teacher.

Stuart and Thurlow (2000) claim that pre-service teachers tend to be relatively passive in their student roles. They are reluctant to challenge the status quo after twelve or so years in classrooms as a student. "They have internalized, through an apprenticeship of observation, many of the values, beliefs, and practices of their teachers" (p. 114). Although pre-service teachers' beliefs and assumptions about teaching and learning are well-established, they are frequently simplified as well as unarticulated. If pre-service teachers do not uncover their beliefs and assumptions, examine them, and consider new understandings, "they will perpetuate current practices and the status quo will be maintained. This is unacceptable given that the student population has dramatically changed and many of the beliefs teachers and children hold are counterproductive to the teaching/ learning process. As pre-service teachers begin their careers, they will be in a position to break this cycle" (p. 119).

According to Finders and Rose (1999), "to best prepare the prospective teacher, a teacher education program must provide teaching experiences and tools for reflection on that experience. In order not to reinforce simplistic views of teaching, we must also provide opportunities to help students gain understandings of the complexities of classroom contexts" (p. 205).

Following are descriptions of some of methods we recommend that you engage in to uncover and articulate your assumptions of learning, school, and schooling. We hope that through the various processes you will affirm or disaffirm previous thoughts, beliefs, and assumptions on the topic under consideration and connect new theories of teaching, learning, and schooling.

Critical Reflection

The beliefs one holds about schooling are formed early; they tend to reflect traditional educational experiences, and they continue until they are reflected on critically which, according to Yost, Sentner, and Forlenza-Bailey (2000) is the highest level of reflectivity. Dewey (1916) felt that the "vision of teacher education postulated the development of future teachers empowered to improve upon the conditions of schools. The teacher quality Dewey believed most important is critical reflection" (Yost et al., 2000).

Reflection is an active, persistent, and careful consideration of any belief or supposed form of knowledge in light of the grounds supporting it. Reflection implies that something is believed or disbelieved because of evidence, proof, or grounds for that belief. The higher thought process involved in critical reflection involves "reflection on the assumptions underlying a decision or act and on the broader ethical, moral, political, and historical implications behind the decision or act" (Yost et al., 2000, p. 41). A reflective teacher is one who makes decisions on the basis of a conscious awareness and careful consideration of the assumptions on which the decisions are based, and the technical, educational, and ethical consequences of those decisions. We hope that you will practice critical reflection on your journey into the professional landscape of teaching. When you encounter a For Your Consideration section, please take time to consider the questions, discussions, reflections, surveys, or other tasks. This process is intended to assist you in developing your understanding of the teaching qualities and commonplaces.

Situated Performances

Finders and Rose (1999) wanted to teach reflective practice to pre-service teachers who had much experience as students and little experience as teachers. They conceived situated performance as a postmodern version of role-play.

Situated performances are role-playing activities in which the learners participate by assuming specific subject positions, where the performed actions, motives, and circumstances are subject to critical reflection. Vignettes contextualize teaching that freezes a moment in time in order to examine the options.

Situated performances view the classroom as a scene from a play where the participants are assigned roles. The scene is not highly scripted. Roles are given, and improvisation becomes the key. These performances enable pre-service teachers to imagine a variety of ways to respond to particular learning, teaching and classroom situations, define a problem, explore, examine and apply (Finders & Rose, 1999).

Co-operative and Collaborative Learning

Social constructionists such as Vygotsky (1987) assume that knowledge is socially constructed, that learning occurs among persons rather than between a person and a thing. The issues facing education today hinge on social relations, not cognitive ones, and knowledge involves people's assimilation into commun-ities of knowledgeable peers. "Liberal education today must be regarded as a process of leaving one community of knowledgeable peers and joining another" (Bruffee, Palmer, Gullette, and Gillespie, 1994, p. 40). Therefore according to the social constructionists, the more a pre-service teacher discusses issues and observations, the better prepared he or she will be to enter the professional landscape of teaching.

Co-operative learning is a learner-centred instructional process in which small, selected groups of three to five individuals work together on a well-defined learning task for the purpose of increasing mastery and or understanding of course content (Karre, 1994). According to Graves (1991), "academic controversy can be constructive and useful when the parties involved conduct a dialogue with the goal of understanding each other and arriving at a synthesis that takes all points of view into consideration" (p. 77). To be meaningful, co-operative learning requires listening carefully to each member in the group. Co-operative learning groups provide an immediate forum to talk through ideas and promote understanding through consultation. Members gain a diversity of perspectives and assist in the building of reflection, ownership, and relevance of information and ideas. Co-operative groups can be formed and used many ways. They include informal groups, brainstorming groups, response discussion groups, representative groups, master-learning groups, jigsaw strategies, and fishbowls. Guidelines for each must be followed for group learning to work. This includes both accountability as an individual and as a group. We hope you will collaborate with your peers and discuss the issues, stories, vignettes, and research found in this text.

Discussion and Debate

Brookfield and Preskill (1999) describe discussion as being more serious than conversation. Discussion requires participants to be mutually responsive to different views expressed and is primarily concerned with the development of knowledge, understanding, or judgment among those taking part. The purpose of the discussion should be to help participants reach a more critically informed understanding about the topic under consideration, to enhance participants' self-awareness and capacity for self-critique, to foster an appreciation among participants for the diversity of opinion that invariably emerges when viewpoints are exchanged openly and honestly, and to act as a catalyst to help people take informed action in the world (pp. 6–7). However, the main prerequisite for good discussion is that the participants be fully informed on the topic under consideration (p. 43). Therefore, the discussion participants need to have read or have access to relevant materials.

Materials presenting alternative perspectives need to be reviewed in advance. "Participating in discussion involves exposing oneself to a variety of alternative ideas and perspectives" (Brookfield & Preskill 1999, p. 47). We will provide relevant, topical information from alternative philosophies and pose questions for discussion and debate.

Jigsaw Strategy

In a jigsaw strategy, or representative groups of co-operative learning, participants are assigned to groups. Each group must have the same number of members. Each member of the group is assigned a subtopic to represent, investigate, or read about. They then meet with the members who explored the same subtopics in the other groups. They become a new group to discuss their subtopic. Following this discussion the team members go back to their original groups and share what they have discussed or learned in their subtopic groups.

Master-Learning

Master-learning, or expert, groups are similar to the jigsaw strategy. Here participants are given a topic or sub-topic to research and study. They then share their research and understanding with the members of their co-operative group.

Fishbowl

In a fishbowl discussion participants are divided into two groups that sit in a circle. The inner-circle group members are the observed and the outer-circle group members are the observers. The inner-circle members are assigned a topic to discuss while the outer-circle members observe and later give positive feedback or else feedback that is supported by concrete descriptors. The groups then change places and roles. This form of co-operative learning is helpful in enhancing individual and group observational and discussion skills (Barlow, Blythe, & Edmonds, 1999).

Brainstorming

Brainstorming is a useful way of generating a large number of alternative ideas for discussion and evaluation. It begins with the posing of an open-ended question. Members in a group work to generate and record a list of alternative ideas. Guidelines for brainstorming include the following: do no evaluation of ideas until after the brainstorming; consider the quantity of ideas as more important than quality; expand on others' ideas; and record all ideas. We will present various topics and issues that will require you to use this brainstorming technique to gain greater understanding or expose assumptions.

Mind-Mapping and Concept Mapping

"Inspiration is profoundly linked to memory" (Grudin 1990, p. 19). **Mind-mapping,** or concept mapping, is a technique to "link memory" for the learners by representing thoughts with pictures and colours. Mind, concept, or "knowledge maps are two-dimensional node-link networks that interrelate important concepts" (O'Donnell, 1994, p. 9). Mapping can be done by an individual or in small groups. The map is generally started in the centre of a page and is created as the learner reads, listens to a presentation, or watches a video. The act forces the learner to organize ideas and consider relationships between the ideas presented. Mapping can also be used to plan a lesson, presentation or story. The use of colour and symbols helps one to organize and make meaning of the idea under investigation and serves as an aid to memory. According to Margulies (1995), one does not have to be a great artist to draw symbols for mind-maps. It requires the creator to become a "visual thinker," and the more one creates mind-maps the better one will be at it. We invite you to use mind-maps while reading the chapters. Develop your own symbols and choose your own colours for the teaching qualities that are presented in Chapter 1, Reading B.

Questioning

Students and teachers ask questions; it is traditionally their stock in trade. Professional journals and textbooks tend to assume that questioning is a popular means of instruction, but few people believe that the questions teachers ask are the best questions—questions that go beyond simple recall or rote memory. Only thought-provoking questions can elicit thoughtful responses. The ability to ask this type of question is not inborn but can be learned. Bloom (1982) developed a taxonomy of higher-order questioning from recall of knowledge to application, analysis, synthesis, and evaluation. These five levels of questions have key verbs and can initiate learning processes and products. It is our intention to assist the pre-service teachers in a study of questioning patterns, practice in composing questions, and analysis of the responses the questions evoke.

How would you describe the learning taking place in each of these classrooms?

Narrative Inquiry, Case Studies, and Autobiographies

"Telling and writing stories have been identified as powerful ways for helping pre-service teachers understand how their world works." (Hunter & Hatton, 1998, p. 235) Narrative is sometimes called "poetic social science," the integration of anthropology and literature, which is one form of ethnography. Narrative inquiry in education, primarily used for research and professional development, has become a vehicle for pre-service teacher development (Conle, 2000). The purpose of self-narratives, according to Bochner (2000), "is to extract meaning from experience rather than to depict experience exactly as it was lived . . . to grasp or seize the possibilities of meaning" (p. 268).

Cases are narrative accounts and the field of teaching is essentially about a body of cases. Hunter and Hatton (1998) consider case writing to be an invaluable methodology that will help pre-service teachers and educators capture the complexity of practice and reflect on practice. Actual stories from pre-service teachers are seen as essential ingredients for professional preparation—serious learning and reflective tools (p. 236) that can focus attention on "the pedagogical moment," exposing its complexity, uncertainty, success, and failure, and provide a context for making meaning of school situations.

We suggest that during field experiences you capture a specific pedagogical moment related to a specific commonplace or teaching quality. Autobiographies are different from case studies in that they are stories written by individuals regarding their impressions of themselves as learners and teachers (D. Brown, 1999) and reflections on personal knowledge and history.

There is a human need for story as fundamental as the need for food and water. "Storytelling (including narrative song) was the principle medium for passing on a culture's knowledge and traditions" (Carroll, 1997, p. 1). Stories can create an emotional environment resulting in deeper meaning and understanding of an idea or issue. We hope our stories create "emotional environments" for you.

Reflection and Perspective on the Chapter

Teaching is a profoundly complex yet ethical and moral activity. Teaching involves decision making of the highest order, decisions that must be made with consideration to the influences that are common to teaching.

The task you will face as a teacher is indeed challenging. Your role will include creating conditions that promote learning, while aligning your teaching to the requirements and needs of others who have an interest in what happens in your classroom. The more knowledgeable and competent you become about creating those conditions, the more effective and joyful your teaching will become.

Key Terms

cases   15
commonplaces   7
concept   5
co-operative learning   12
curriculum   9
declarative knowledge   4
domain-specific procedural
   knowledge   7
integrate   2

integrated knowledge   2
macro-propositional
   (knowledge)   4
mind-mapping   14
narrative inquiry   3
null curriculum   9
planned curriculum   9
propositional knowledge   4

reflection   12
schema   5
schemata   2
scripts   4
shared praxis   3
situated performance   12
teaching qualities   3
worldview   1

Suggested Further Reading

Groome, Thomas. (1981). Some philosophical roots for praxis as a way of knowing are found in Chapter 8 of *Christian Religious Education.* San Francisco: Harper and Row. Providing a brief overview of the historical source of the word *praxis,* this chapter is a good introduction to a term that has been misused yet remains important and applicable in the Canadian classroom.

Reading C: Teaching Qualities

Chapter Focus

Teachers live in a complex universe. The professional teacher must visit many disciplines daily as the profession is practised. This complex array of knowledge may be vexing for those who are commencing professional studies. As one begins to engage in learning about the teaching profession there is, perhaps, a need for some frameworks, some benign structures, to provide guidance, reassurance, and utility, a need for something on which to "hang your hat" that will help make sense of this professional universe. Six teaching qualities serve in this capacity throughout the book. You will find that teachers consider and apply these qualities in the course of their practice. Figure 1B.1 presents the six qualities in visual format to illustrate how they are interconnected, providing a framework for a complex matter.

The qualities are not exclusive, but they are considered to be fundamental to reflection and action in teaching. We invite you to consider the teaching qualities when responding to questions in the text and learning opportunities presented as considerations throughout the book.

A teaching qualities symbol will appear in page margins throughout the book to draw your attention to particular teaching qualities addressed in the text.

Focus Questions

1. Of what value are teaching qualities to a practising teacher?
2. How could a teacher's strong relationships with young people contribute to successful learning?
3. In what ways do successful teachers understand the concept of diversity?
4. To what extent is authenticity in teaching and learning a prerequisite to success for teachers and students?
5. Why is it essential that thoughtfulness permeate all aspects of teaching and learning environments?
6. What dimensions of integrity contribute not only to success in learning and teaching, but also to feelings of personal efficacy and well-being?

The Teaching Qualities

This chapter discusses each quality in some detail, but the discussion is not intended to present a definition or prescription. You will provide meaning and understanding to the teaching qualities, based on your conversations about them, your use of them, and insights you gain as you embrace new knowledge. The meaning and understanding you gain will be constantly changing. And this is how it must be. Thoughtful teachers constantly

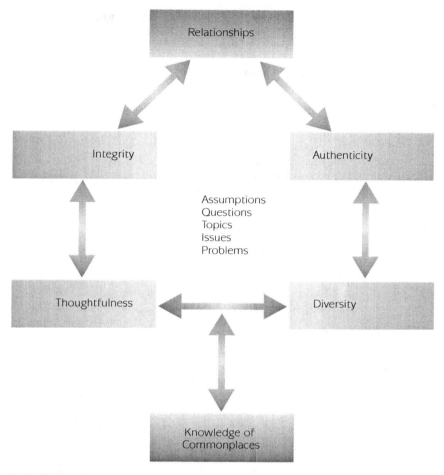

FIGURE 1B.1   *Teaching qualities for decision-making and praxis*

understand theory and practice differently as they are exposed to new knowledge, concepts, and ideas. Thoughtfulness is the hallmark of a good teacher.

Knowledge

Knowledge of commonplaces is given a position of prominence as a teaching quality in Figure 1B.1 because it is clearly the foundation for all the other qualities. As assumptions, questions, topics, and issues arise, we visit teaching qualities within the commonplaces of knowledge so that you can enrich your perspective and general worldview of learning, teaching, and schooling. These qualities are not discrete; they are not offered as an all-inclusive panacea for creating a "rose garden" in teaching. Rather, you should use them as fundamental areas for thought and reflection in decision making and praxis related to learning, teaching, and schooling. The qualities are not exclusive. Pre-service teachers

CASE 1B.1

For Your Consideration

Create your own symbol for the Teaching Qualities Model.

1. What colours would best describe each quality in this figure?

2. For each quality, visualize a symbol that taps into your understanding of that quality.

Substitute your own symbols and colours for the teaching qualities as they are introduced in the book.

may consider these teaching qualities as a useful foundation upon which to engage in reflection and contemplation about assumptions, questions, topics, issues, and problems related to learning, teaching, and schooling.

Relationships

Whether it is a relationship to one's own self, to others, or to the world, the experience of deep connection arises when there is a profound respect, a deep caring, and a quality of "being with" that honors the truth of each participant in the relationship.

Students who feel deeply connected through at least one such relationship are more likely to survive the "lure of risk" (Elias et al., 1997) and the damage of stress; they are more likely to discover and contribute the gift they are meant to bring to the world. (Kessler, 2000, p. 18)

What does the above quotation mean to you? Think back to your grade school experience. How important were relationships? What qualities did the teachers you really liked possess? We guess that, for most people, the common thread running through the responses would be one of connection. Typically, teachers whom you liked probably showed compassion, caring, sensitivity, maybe a sense of humour, along with clear professional competence. In short, the teacher was able to "connect" with the class.

A fundamental part of our human makeup is a profound need to belong. Even seemingly hardened souls, when their shells are uncovered, need to be wanted, need to be accepted, and need to belong. Many of us can probably think of situations in which people (of whatever age) presented an austere exterior marked by "in" language, rebellious clothing, overt expressions indicating pseudo-confidence, and a rejection of acceptable behav-

A principal welcomes students as they arrive at school.

iour. Many of these same individuals probably had a fragile inner self that was crying out to be wanted and included.

Secure relationships are at the heart of our human experience. Learning—all forms of learning—will prosper when it is founded on good relationships. Young people deserve to have bestowed upon them a humanness that is without degree.

> From the exalted statesman to the new-born child, we are equally human. To be human is to be competent, to have a view of the world, and to have ways of dealing with one's life. To interact with another human being is to accept the equality of humanness with humility. To know humanness is to know who a person is, to know how they see their world. (Waldron, Collie, & Davies, 1999, p. 52)

What, then, are the implications for learning, teaching, and schools? New learning very often entails taking a risk. Asking for help is easier when you know the person to whom your request is directed. Discipline takes on a different complexion when a good relationship exists between teacher and child. As you read the following story, think about how the outcome for Chris might have been different if he and Mr. Tanaka had had a good relationship.

> Chris was a lively boy who had difficulty with learning. His attention span was much shorter than one might expect for a boy of thirteen, and he couldn't apply himself very well to his work. One Friday Chris came to school in a seemingly bad mood. Even his friends were excluded from his company. Math was a particular problem for him. Even on a good day he struggled with its complexities. On this particular Friday, Chris couldn't understand what the teacher was saying. Mr. Tanaka stood at the blackboard with his piece of chalk, trying to explain the mysteries of quadratic equations. He wrote an example and demonstrated how to solve the equation when X equalled 3. Chris was completely confused, but he wouldn't think of asking for help. Mr. Tanaka looked dourly at the class, stating gruffly that he couldn't make things any clearer.
>
> "Anybody who can't understand this simple equation shouldn't be in Grade 8," he growled. "Take out your textbooks and complete questions 1 through 10 at the end of Chapter 6."
>
> Chris was making a nuisance of himself, bothering students around him to give him some paper, lend him a pen, or let him use a ruler. It wasn't long before Mr. Tanaka had had enough.
>
> "Get down to the office, Chris. Maybe you'll be of some use down there."
>
> So, after an extended visit to the bathroom, a visit to the gym, and a trip outside to waste more time, Chris arrived at the office, announcing that Mr. Tanaka had sent him.
>
> "Well," said the principal, "what can I do for you Chris?"

How would you describe Mr. Tanaka's general manner and disposition toward young people? What particular information in the story caused you to arrive at your conclusions? Do you think Mr. Tanaka's manner and disposition in any way contributed to Chris's learning difficulty and behaviour?

Young people who experience difficulties with their learning do so for myriad reasons, but their difficulties are often exacerbated by insensitive treatment from adults. Parents may be overly critical or may simply not care. Teachers often are more concerned with their lesson plans and covering the material; consequently they teach to the whole class, making disparaging comments to those who do not conform.

Confused and bewildered students act out their frustrations in ways that inevitably land them in trouble. Chris is a classic example of a frustrated learner. How might Mr. Tanaka have conducted himself differently so that Chris could have been helped? How might Mr. Tanaka's teaching approach have been modified so that Chris could have been helped? What role do relationships play in Mr. Tanaka's class? How might a more positive relationship between Mr. Tanaka and his class have helped Chris? And, finally, how do you think the principal should respond to Chris?

It is very important that students receive encouragement when making contributions to classroom learning, especially when their responses are incorrect. Students should always be left with their dignity intact after responding to a question or offering an opinion. Learning is not easy, and to learn successfully people must feel comfortable in their learning environments. New learning often involves risk-taking and it is only in environments where people feel safe and comfortable that they will easily take risks. Clearly, when a good relationship exists between teacher and students there is a positive correlation between this relationship and its effect on learning. Mr. Tanaka's relationship with his class was such that directing and telling marked his teaching style. His style also entailed an orientation toward teaching the whole class. A young man like Chris was simply one of the group and received attention only when Mr. Tanaka ventured down the rows of desks. What happens to young people like Chris when a teacher adheres to traditional forms of direct teaching, when flexibility in learning is at a minimum, and when individual help is cursory at best?

Diversity

Diversity, in our Teaching Qualities Model, assumes a broad context. We understand **diversity** to mean variety in the backgrounds and learning abilities of people, and in approaches to learning and teaching. Teachers must be constantly aware of diversity as they respond to learning needs in social and pedagogical contexts.

Diversity in People

Transience is a common feature of society today. People emigrate with increasing frequency. Many school districts comprise multicultural populations. The cultural traditions of recently arrived families present interesting challenges for school districts and teachers. Cultural and religious practices from distant countries must merge with those of the receiving culture in a harmonious way. Teachers must reflect upon the invitations to learning they offer to ensure that newly arrived young people will interpret the learning intentions in a positive manner.

Children from recent immigrant families are welcomed into school, where they must contend with values and social conventions that often conflict with their home culture. *Culture* is the way of life common to a group of people, consisting of the values, attitudes, and beliefs that influence their traditions and behaviours. *Ethnicity* is the quality of being a member of an ethnic group. Ethnic groups are identified by distinctive patterns of family life, language, recreation, religion, and other customs that differentiate them from others. "The concept of *race* is used to distinguish among human beings on the basis of biological traits and characteristic." (Parkay, Hardcastle-Stanford, & Gougeon, 1996, p. 135)

CASE 1B.2

For Your Consideration

Schools, more than any other institution in our society, assimilate persons from different ethnic, racial, religious, and cultural backgrounds and pass on the values and customs of the majority. (Parkay et al., 1996, p. 109)

Two concepts in that Parkay quotation may be controversial: the role of assimilation, and the passing on of values and customs of the majority. Should majority values and customs be honoured in schools? Should each student be expected to assimilate the values and customs of the majority?

Diversity also exists within the mainstream student population. You will often hear teachers express beliefs about diversity, using statements such as, "Children learn in different ways," "Young people learn at different rates," and "Every child is unique." You will appreciate the need to think deeply about the diverse needs of children and how you, as a teacher, must accommodate diversity in your ways of working with them.

Diversity also includes the range of ability levels, which can extend from gifted children, who are very capable of learning within the conventions of schooling, to children with diagnosed learning disabilities. Other children will have physical and mental conditions that do not fall within the learning disabilities classification. You will come across debates about "inclusion" with regard to this latter group of children. Your response to the inclusion question will be emotional and challenging.

Questions about diversity also concern teachers as a group. The majority of people entering the profession of teaching in Canada are white, middle-class females, who tend to hold middle-class values and attitudes, which they, consciously or unconsciously, impart to their students (Parkay et al., 1996; Solomon, 1997; Futrell, 1999).

Men and women tend to respond to the world differently. *Sex* refers to biological differences (Deaux, 1993), and *gender* usually refers to judgments about masculinity and femininity that are influenced by culture and context (Woolfolk, 1998, pp. 178–81). Gender–role stereotyping begins early in a child's life, though different treatment and expectations continue throughout a lifetime. Schools often foster gender bias in many ways—through textbooks, teachers' attitudes, assignments, roles, and responsibilities. It is important that teachers be aware of possible gender bias in their teaching and teaching resources to ensure that no students are excluded.

Diversity in Learning

The essential question regarding diversity in learning is this: How do you respond to the learning needs of a group of students? To answer this question fully you must examine your beliefs and assumptions about people generally. Do you believe that young people are all different? Do you believe they have different learning styles, different abilities, different intelligence levels, and different rates of learning? What was your grade school experience like? Did your teacher teach everyone in your class the same way? Traditional teaching methods see a great amount of time spent teaching the same way to the whole class. If you believe in the kinds of differences we have just discussed, do you see any problems with a teaching methodology that spends most of the time teaching to the whole class?

CASE 1B.3

For Your Consideration

- **Dimensions of Culture**
  List some ways that you as a teacher can learn more about the different cultures and values of your students.
- **Language and Culture**
  It is often said that language is culture and culture is language because the relationship between the two is so enmeshed. What implications does this statement have for school systems in terms of the teaching of more than one language?
- **Ethnicity and Race**
  According to Montagu (1974), "It is impossible to make the sort of racial classifications which some anthropologists and others have attempted. The fact is that all human beings are so . . . mixed with regard to origin that between different groups of individuals . . . 'overlapping' of physical traits is the rule" (p. 9). Some people limit their view of ethnicity to people of colour. Why is this so?
- **Schools and Diversity**
  Schools today must find ways to meet the needs of all students and parents, regardless of social class, gender, or ethnic, racial, or cultural diversity (Parkay et al., 1996, p. 112). What are the implications of this statement for you as you begin your teaching career? How can schools better address diversity?
- **Gender Discrimination in Classrooms**
  "One of the best-documented findings of the past 20 years is that teachers interact more with boys than with girls. This is true from preschool to college. Teachers ask more questions of males, give males more feedback (praise, criticism, and correction), and give more specific and valuable comments to boys. As girls move through the grades, they have less and less to say. By the time students reach college, men are twice as likely to initiate comments as women." (Woolfolk, 1998, p. 181) Why does this happen and what is the long-term effect of this pattern?

In a discussion group, have all members of your group complete the following stem anonymously:

"I appear to be _____ but really I am _____."

1. What is the common thread in the responses to "but really I am"?
2. What do the answers reveal about "the hardened shells" referred to at the beginning of the chapter, under "Relationships"?
3. What might you discover through this exercise about a class of grade school students?

Understanding this issue will be fundamental to your understanding of learning and your role as a teacher. Diversity has occasionally been conceptualized as a problem to be overcome through programs designed to reduce differences among learners. Ability grouping, in which children of differing abilities are segregated into different classes, is an example of an approach used to reduce differences among learners. This practice is also known as streaming, tracking, or banding.

Goodlad (1984) conducted on-site, longitudinal studies in many classrooms and schools, during which he surveyed secondary school teachers about their preferences and opinions about ability grouping. Just over eighty percent of those surveyed thought that ability grouping was a good thing. When asked if they would be prepared to teach the lower-ability groupings, only three percent said they would. What does this tell you? Do you think Goodlad would have obtained the same results if he had surveyed elementary school teachers? Why?

Ability grouping is not a common practice in schools, though some schools create same-ability groupings for short periods of time to meet specific student needs. Interestingly, Good and Brophy (2000) report the tendency of educators to see diversity as an asset rather than as a liability. They explain, for example, that "students with different backgrounds can interact with one another and learn how the same text material or concept can be interpreted differently by persons from different backgrounds" (p. 322). Since the days of the one-room schoolhouse, teachers with classrooms of varying ages, backgrounds, and abilities have used diversity through various forms of peer learning, in which students helped each other with their learning. The idea of students helping students may experience a renaissance in the context of today's diverse learning environments.

Diversity in Teaching

Teaching is, of course, inextricably tied to learning. One thing to remember is that your primary goal is to meet the learning needs of the students. In meeting these needs your responsibility is twofold. First, you must understand the students: their learning difficulties, their learning styles, their differing levels of skill development, and so on. Your second responsibility is to inject sufficient variety into your teaching approach to engage and motivate your students to learn. Can you see how diversity looms large in teaching? The astute connections you are able to make within these central responsibilities have much to do with your effectiveness as a teacher.

Authenticity

The word *authentic* is defined as "reliable, trustworthy, of undisputed origin, genuine" according to the Oxford Dictionary (Fowler & Fowler, 1954, p. 76). Webster's Dictionary (Woolf, 1979) is a little more expansive: "worthy of acceptance or belief as conforming to fact or reality. Not imaginary, false, or imitation. Being actually and precisely what is claimed. . . . Stresses fidelity to actuality and fact and may imply authority or trustworthiness in determining this relationship" (p. 75). We refer to dictionary definitions to show that our use of the term is grounded in everyday language. We use the word **authenticity** in the book to refer to professional behaviour that is genuine and sincere. In learning and teaching we understand *authentic* to apply to explicit connections between learning in school and in life beyond the classroom, and the opportunities afforded students to demonstrate their understanding of these connections.

The presence of authenticity in schooling takes many forms. A consideration of schooling uncovers five general areas where a discussion of authenticity is germane: relationships, leadership, learning and teaching, curriculum, and assessment.

Authenticity in Relationships

Relationships have already been discussed as a teaching quality, but we invite you to revisit this discussion in the context of authenticity. Consider the following scenario:

> September had finally arrived and teachers were assembling in the staff room, sharing stories about their summer experiences. Camping, house renovation, exotic holidays, hiking, and visits to relatives were typical topics of conversation. A number of teachers new to the profession were trying to mask their nervousness as they circulated around the room, introducing themselves to the veteran staff. Reassuring comments dominated these conversations, as experienced teachers offered encouraging words and willingness to share resources. The atmosphere was positive and an aura of enthusiasm permeated the room.
>
> Dan Brock had been teaching for about twenty years, during which time he had developed a way of dealing with students that he had changed little. His classes were

reasonably well disciplined. He kept control with his firm manner and intimidating presence.

On this first day of his twenty-first year, Dan found himself talking to Zinta, a twenty-two-year-old teacher in her first teaching job. After sharing stories about their summers, conversation turned to the practice of teaching and the inevitable questions a first-year teacher might have about managing students.

"What do you do, Dan, when the students enter the room for the first time? What kinds of things do you say to them?" Relishing the opportunity to flaunt his experience, Dan began to impart his views on kids, discipline, and control. After a lengthy monologue, Dan concluded with the advice, "Your best bet is to jump on them right away. Don't take any nonsense, don't give them an inch, and above all, don't smile 'til Christmas." At that point the PA announced that the staff meeting was about to begin, and staff began to make their way to the library. Zinta was left with Dan's pointed advice ringing in her inexperienced ears.

If Zinta followed Dan's advice, what image would she be presenting to the class? If Dan were to sustain that approach until Christmas, what would that say about Dan's character? Darling-Hammond (1997) reports research demonstrating that students experience much greater success in school settings that are structured to create close, sustained relationships between students and teachers. Could Dan Brock have a "close, sustained relationship" with his students? Brock's attitude of controlling students, not giving them an inch, and not allowing a smile until Christmas is hardly an example of getting to know his students as people. Would Mr. Brock's attitude toward his students be consistent with the definitions of authenticity presented earlier?

CASE 1B.4

For Your Consideration

Given the definitions of authenticity presented above and the research alluded to by Darling-Hammond, to what extent could we expect Mr. Brock to meaningfully engage his students in effective learning?

Authenticity in Leadership

There was a time when leaders ruled through power and autocratic behaviour. No doubt some still do. Increasingly, leadership in schools is becoming a shared responsibility. No longer do we assign leadership solely to those in administrative positions. Leaders are considerably more effective if they work with and through people in their enterprise. Trungpa (1988, pp. 159–160) speaks about "authentic presence," of being in an almost spiritual realm where we exhibit a genuine openness and honesty in the way we present ourselves to others. When leaders exhibit an authentic presence, they exert an enormous attraction over other human beings. Literature from many disciplines increasingly acknowledges the need for the relationship between the leader and the led to become less dependent on power and authority. Sergiovanni (1992) speaks of "moral leadership." Bender (1997) believes in "leadership from within," and Percy (1997), in his discussion of life and leadership, talks about "going deep." Kouzes and Posner (1999), on a practical level, espouse the merits of encouragement: "Expressing genuine appreciation for the efforts and successes of others means we have to show our emotions. We have to talk about our feelings in public. We have to make ourselves vulnerable to others" (p. 6). Clearly, this kind of expres-

CASE 1B.5

For Your Consideration

Discuss the following scenarios:

A. Arrowsmith Junior High School has a policy against throwing snowballs. Miguel and Tinisha, two Grade 8 students, are caught bombarding a group of Grade 7 girls with snowballs as they return to school from lunch. Mrs. Antonelli, on seeing the aggressors, herds them into the office, informs the secretary of what they were doing and leaves.

B. Jack Grogan had just finished doing some work in his classroom at the end of the day when he decided to head for the staff room. On his way he came across two Grade 6 boys who were shouting at each other angrily, and one boy was roughly pushing the other around. . . .

1. Complete the Jack Grogan scenario in the context of "authentic presence." If you were Jack, how would you deal with the altercation?

2. How did your completion of the Jack Grogan scenario differ from the action taken by Mrs. Antonelli? To what extent was Mrs. Antonelli demonstrating "authentic presence"?

sion of our inner self demonstrates who we really are, and not any pseudo role or act we might wish to offer. In short, it is a requirement that we exhibit authenticity.

Senge, Kleiner, Roberts, Ross, Roth, and Smith (1999), speaking from a business context, offer a useful message for schooling when they equate leadership-related relationships having to do with authenticity and "walking the talk." They write that leaders "who inquire effectively into their own values and behaviors . . . become more reflective and credible. In effect, they become models for the integrity and interpersonal trust needed to explore a host of organization-wide issues" (p. 564). In many of today's more enlightened schools, shared leadership is commonly understood in concept and action. Teachers are leaders in a very authentic sense.

Authenticity in Learning and Teaching

Schools are social institutions where teachers and young people work together with a common intention: learning. Young people attend school to learn. Learning helps them to understand their world, their life. And life for a youngster is immediate—it's now. The arrows in Figure 1B.2, below, illustrate the connection between young people, their learning, and their world.

The primary intention behind all activity in a school is to effect successful learning for all people, and this is represented in the centre of Figure 1B.2. As teachers work toward this central intention, fundamental considerations pertaining to the lives of people in learning contexts must influence and drive the teaching–learning process. It is very important that teachers understand the nature of the learners as they prepare to engage young people in learning. How long can six-year-olds remain still, for example? How would a class of young adolescents react to being talked to for most of a class just before lunch? What is the socio-economic background of the class?

A further consideration connected to the nature of people is the general question, How do people learn best? Young children, for example, are very inquisitive. Young teenagers tend to be kinesthetic; their bodies prefer to be active. People generally have preferred ways of learning; some through hearing, some through watching, and others through touching and doing. The peer group is a very strong influence in the lives of adolescents. Chapter 7 explores some aspects of social learning, which will have implications for successful learning for adolescents.

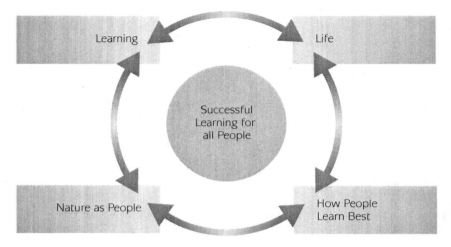

FIGURE 1B.2   *Reflection on authentic learning*

You have probably heard of deferred gratification. Simply put, this means that you do something that you may not find particularly interesting or enjoyable because it will be good for you at some time in the future. For young people in school this is seldom a useful practice. Because life for a youngster is now, successful learning is achieved when learning is connected to life, when it is meaningful and relevant.

A final consideration in Figure 1B.2 is learning, where we ask you to consider what and how students are being asked to learn. If, for example, you are asking students to learn quadratic equations, then in what ways would you take into consideration the nature of your students, how they learn best, and how quadratic equations are connected to their lives? If your intention is to effect successful learning for all students then all aspects of the illustration must be connected to thinking and praxis. Perkins (1999) says that, ". . . most students just plain forget most of what they have been taught. They often do not understand well what they do retain. And what they retain and understand, they often do not use actively" (p. 90). What are the implications of this for teaching?

Later chapters of this book will discuss learners, learning, and teaching, in which you should gain greater insight into the connections presented in Figure 1B.2.

This book addresses the concept of "transfer in learning," the ability of learners to apply their learning in different contexts. Life is the primary context for young people, and to the degree that is reasonable and possible, teachers should help young people to make connections between their learning and life.

CASE 1B.6

For Your Consideration

Authentic Learning

1. Discuss the meaning of the schema presented in Figure 1B.2 in the context of authenticity as it is defined on page 24 and of working in groups.

2. As a result of your discussion, write an explanation of your understanding of authentic learning.

Schools have a tendency to require students to learn skills and concepts for which the students see little or no purpose. Students often ask, "What do we have to do this for?" "What use is this to me?" Teachers may often struggle to provide justification for what they are teaching, and the essential message may be summed up by the term deferred gratification—in short, "You are doing it now because it will be good for you later." "Later" can mean anything from future grades to post-secondary education or some other time in life. Clearly, some things fit this justification. The question is, At what age can children understand this reasoning, and when is it appropriate?

When students perceive learning to be irrelevant to their lives, that is often a cue that the learning is not authentic; it is not real to them and they have difficulty becoming engaged in the learning. In cases such as this teachers often find themselves having to "make" students learn and "tell" them to learn. When these kinds of tactics are necessary, teaching and learning are hardly dynamic and effective. The challenge, then, for teachers, is to present learning to young people in ways that connect learning to their lives. Learning may then become real for students; it becomes authentic.

Authenticity in Curriculum

Our discussion of learning leads us to a consideration of curriculum and the need for authenticity. For now, however, let us understand curriculum as the programs of study, subject guides, and school-specific policy decisions that affect the ways of working and general conduct in a school.

Curriculum should be presented in meaningful ways. New information and learning in the classroom and the ways that behaviour and conduct are guided throughout the school should all be effected in ways that are appropriate to the ages of young people in question. When new information and learning are not connected to what is real for young people, when behaviour and conduct are not guided by age-appropriate understandings, then a lack of authenticity pervades the learning environment. In circumstances such as these teachers may rely on authority and control to effect learning. These kinds of power responses will have only limited effect. Nicholls and Hazzard (1993) remind us that "teaching requires the consent of students, and discontent will not be chased away by the

CASE 1B.7

For Your Consideration

In the discussion on authenticity in curriculum, you have read that new information and learning in the classroom and the ways that behaviour and conduct are guided throughout the school should all be effected in ways that are appropriate to the ages of young people in question.

Discuss the following questions pertaining to age-appropriateness, using your prior knowledge as the basis for your answer:

a) Why are young adolescents often restless during academic classes scheduled around 11 A.M.?

b) In elementary schools, where children tend to remain with the same teacher for most of their learning, why must recess be at the same time for all classes?

c) A characteristic of adolescence is that young people want to have some say in decisions that affect their lives. To what extent do schools respect this characteristic?

d) Is it a good idea for children in, say, Grade 3 to be sitting at desks, in rows, for much of their days in school?

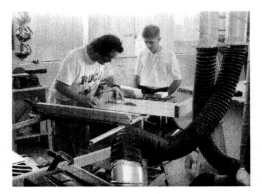

Curriculum is presented in authentic ways.

exercise of power" (p. 76). Authenticity in the presentation of curriculum will significantly contribute to contentment among learners.

Authenticity in Assessment

Assessment plays a significant role in a young person's schooling. Results from assessment activity are used as indicators of performance and progress on report cards, in communications with home, to demonstrate success at a grade level, and many other statements about students that responsible parties might have a right to know. In other words, assessment results are used to make rather profound decisions about (and for) a young person.

It is important that the methods used to assess students' performance in learning are such that students have a genuine opportunity to demonstrate or exhibit mastery of

CASE 1B.8

For your consideration

Vignette 1: Jenny and her friend Alena sit down on June 25 to write their final exams in social studies. The exam is a fifty-question, multiple-choice instrument, covering all aspects of the program. Jenny earns a score of 24 out of 50 and Alena scores 26 out of 50. Jenny fails the exam and Alice does not.

What could you speculate, from the scores the two girls received, about the degree to which they had learned successfully in social studies?

Vignette 2: Jaroslav has to deal with a form of assessment that is different from that used for Jenny and Alena, but one from which significant judgments will be made about his performance. Jaroslav is a boisterous boy who, from time to time, gives his Grade 4 teacher some difficulties with his behaviour. He comes from a single-parent home where he is left alone for extended periods of time until his mother

gets home from work. On Tuesday morning his mom had to leave in a hurry for work and Jaroslav was left to fend for himself for breakfast, not an infrequent occurrence. Later in the morning the teacher had planned a written test of largely short-answer questions that would provide a significant contribution to the upcoming report card mark. Jaroslav was restless and distracted throughout the test. On three occasions the teacher had to caution Jaroslav for turning around and generally distracting others. He did not score very well on his test.

1. What do you think Jaroslav's teacher might have said to his mother at parent–teacher interviews about his performance?
2. How might Jaroslav's life outside school affect his learning in school?

what they have learned. Assessment should be an authentic test of a student's ability. Sizer (1984) is of the opinion that "any exhibitions of mastery should be the students' opportunity to show off what they know and are able to do, rather than a trial by question" (as reported in Brandt [ed.], 1992, p. 86). Assessment methods that rely on questions to be answered on paper, either written or computer scored, tend to limit students' opportunity to demonstrate their mastery of learning. Not all people are at their best sitting at a desk with pen or pencil in hand, trying to respond to written questions within a specific block of time.

Accountability is the practice of holding people responsible for their behaviour. Provincial and territorial governments hold school systems accountable. School systems hold teachers and schools accountable for the effectiveness of learning and teaching. We're sure you agree that schools, like any other institution, must be accountable. The issue tends to be one of "how?" In what ways would accountability requirements be met such that young people are afforded opportunities to truly demonstrate their success in learning? How might young people demonstrate their learning in authentic ways? Sizer, in the quotation above, uses the term, "trial by question." What does this expression mean to you? Is he perhaps being sarcastic, even cynical? You probably know young people who are learning a sport, learning to dance, learning to act, learning to read, learning to drive a car. How do they demonstrate their success? They demonstrate success by actually doing the activity they are learning. The learning of skills could be viewed as rehearsal. They are rehearsing the parts that will eventually be put together for the ultimate goal of the learning—playing the sport, dancing, performing a role in a play, reading a book, driving a car. All these opportunities to demonstrate learning are in what we would call authentic, real, or free-form expression.

> In school our conventions determine success in learning using measures that are mostly unrelated to actual demonstrations of learning; they do not allow a young person the opportunity to demonstrate what has been learned in a real sense. Students are almost indoctrinated in the psychometric modes of learning measurement—short answer quizzes, multiple choice tests, fill-in-the-blanks, power tests, percentage-letter grades, computer-scored test sheets, and so on. (Waldron et al., 1999, p. 83)

You will hear these psychometric modes of measurement referred to as "pencil-and-paper" forms of testing. They are within what Sizer calls the "trial by question" form of

CASE 1B.9

For Your Consideration

1. How could you have demonstrated your learning in high school math, for example, in authentic ways?
2. Do you feel that the pencil-and-paper forms of testing, when used exclusively, allowed you to earn the best grade possible?
3. To what extent do your assumptions about testing govern your thoughts about authenticity?

4. Pick a unit or topic from your most recent high school experience in any subject you choose, and think of ways the assessment could have been more authentic, more real. Share these ideas with the rest of your class.

testing. It is important that authentic testing, or assessment, allows students to exhibit, or demonstrate, what they have learned in authentic tests of their ability.

Thoughtfulness

> If thought is awakened by a problem, not by the authoritative claims of a teacher or a text, then knowledge must be seen as the product of inquiry, as the answer to some set of pertinent questions that focuses inquiry and calls forth a search for knowledge. (Wiggins, 1987, p. 70)

Perspective essentially governs and determines all of our beliefs about the way we behave and the way things are. *Thought* is defined as the action or process of thinking (arranging ideas, new or old, turning something over in the mind), and being *thoughtful* is being absorbed in the process of thought, showing consideration for others. **Thoughtfulness,** therefore, is engaging in thought, reflection, and research, identifying and questioning assumptions, and thinking of others. It is in an environment of reflection, research, and questioning that thoughtfulness is evident.

In this book thoughtful learning and teaching are understood as a process of examining the beliefs and assumptions that constitute one's worldview. It is the unfettered application of knowledge—new and prior—to teaching practice, the genuine listening to the stories of other teachers, reflection on and in practice, and the elevation of the voices of young people to a level of eloquence.

Why is it important that teachers be thoughtful in their learning and teaching? What are the optimal conditions for thoughtfulness? Could these include situations that force an individual to think hard about something; an atmosphere conducive to questioning and inquiry; being around curious people who also inquire and question? Would it help one in becoming a more thoughtful learner and teacher to be in an environment where one was free to make mistakes, had time to reflect, and had opportunities to read, write, and discuss?

> Thoughtfulness requires close reading and disciplined debate about what has been read. It requires substantial writing—not just narrative writing but argumentative, analytical, and evaluative writing that is then closely read, discussed and rewritten. Thoughtfulness requires a great deal of time devoted to discussion—not just any discussion, but disciplined, Socratic dialogue. (R. Brown, 1987, p. 50)

Young people experience freedom of choice in their learning.

These children are thoughtfully analyzing a story.

Thoughtfulness, then, though ultimately a very personal process, is nurtured in social contexts. Wiggins reminds us that thought is a "product of inquiry." Brown states that thoughtfulness is making meaning by negotiating with others through disciplined Socratic dialogue. Social contexts for learning involve important processes for gaining understanding and making meaning. We will discuss social learning and some approaches to its application that you may encounter in schools in Chapter 7.

Integrity

To include integrity as one of our teaching qualities should intuitively make good sense to you. The word **integrity** has ethical connotations; it is typically used to refer to doing what is right and good. Teaching is like any activity that requires humans to work closely with each other. It is more effective when people are good to each other, when they do what is right. The word *integrity* also has another meaning, however, that raises a few more questions about how to be a teacher. The Oxford Dictionary (Fowler & Fowler, 1954) defines the word as "wholeness." The opposite word is fragmentation, or coming apart. A teacher who acts with integrity, then, acts in a way that corresponds to his or her thinking, beliefs, and assumptions. Let's look at this second understanding of integrity as a teaching quality for a moment.

There are some areas of teaching in which the value of teachers behaving with integrity is self-evident. Consider relationships, a teaching quality we have already discussed. From personal experience you know that when your relationships—with your parents, your spouse, or your friends—are whole, not fragmented or broken, you feel better and perform better. The same principle holds true for the staff in a school. If there is integrity on the part of the staff, then those involved feel that they are part of something bigger; they are more likely to enjoy one another; and they are better able to effectively deal with the stresses that inevitably rise when people work together in close proximity.

Your relationships with young people also require integrity. You will learn early in your teaching career that your students want to have a relationship with you, and want one that is good and healthy. You will also learn that they want this integrity on their own terms. Therefore, you will feel the fragility of this relationship, and will work hard at trying to preserve the relationships with your learners, both individually and as a class. You will want your learners to like you, and that is normal.

The value of having the quality of integrity is not always as evident in other areas of teaching. Teachers also need personal integrity; that is, they need to feel and experience

CASE 1B.10

For Your Consideration

Students want a relationship with you that is good and healthy and characterized by integrity.

1. Should a teacher like every learner in the classroom?

2. What if a teacher does not like a student? How can he or she show integrity toward that student? Is there a solution?

3. How might a teacher learn to value and respect each learner?

their own personal lives as being unfragmented. They need to be able to be themselves in the classroom and school. To behave in a way that is fragmented from who you really are tires you out and, sooner or later, produces stress. This expression of integrity is like the quality of authenticity that we discussed earlier.

You may also experience fragmentation with regard to curriculum. You will sometimes be concerned with integrating the goals of the curriculum with your own goals for learners. Another area concerns value systems. You may have a religious worldview and wonder how or whether you can have integrity in a public school setting in which religious views are to be treated in a purely objective, academic way. You may wonder if you are too fragmented in keeping your opinions about the key issues of life and death to yourself. Later chapters of this book will invite you to consider these ideas in more detail.

CASE 1B.11

For Your Consideration

In a discussion group, identify the aspects of teaching in which you might have the greatest struggle with integrity.

1. Why would this aspect be a struggle for you?
2. What is the most logical approach to handling this issue?

3. Is there a common theme among members of your group in the different struggles for integrity? If so, what does this reveal to you about the nature of integrity?

Reflection and Perspective on the Chapter

We hope you will keep these six teaching qualities in mind as you read the rest of the book. The qualities, as we have discussed them, are not exclusive; nor are they cast in concrete. Your understanding of them will constantly change as you gain new knowledge and form new meaning. The qualities are offered, however, as a useful framework within which to consider the assumptions, topics, issues, and ideas that you deal with as you "break from anchorage" on this exciting journey toward becoming a teacher.

You will read many times in this book that a good teacher is a thoughtful teacher. It is imperative that teachers constantly reflect on their practice. In professional circles you may hear the phrase "reflection *on* and *in* practice." Professional discussions outside the classroom—professional development days, staff meetings, planning sessions—would be situations where the practice of teaching and ways of responding to young people exemplify reflection *on* practice. Teachers talk about their work, sharing thoughts and ideas about learning, teaching, and schooling. Reflection *in* practice is less common, but equally important, because it entails thinking about professional actions and decisions at the time they occur. In-practice reflection is most effective when two or more colleagues are working together. However, since most teaching contexts are not designed to facilitate this kind of collaborative work, teachers must rely upon self-designed techniques for reflection *in* practice.

We now move on. Keep in mind the need to be reflective, to be thoughtful. The commonplaces of knowledge provide a structure for the book and each demands reflection and thoughtfulness, where new knowledge presented in the book is considered alongside your prior knowledge. During this process the assumptions that you hold will be identified, perhaps uncovered (some of them may be tacit), and profes-sionally challenged. Various contexts for discussion, debate, and conversation are presented throughout each commonplace of knowledge and it is within these contexts, particularly, that we invite you to apply the teaching qualities to your reflective actions. Whenever you encounter the following symbol for teaching qualities, it is a cue for you to reflect on the qualities as they apply to a particular discussion within the text. We will lead your thinking a little by listing the most pertinent teaching qualities each time the teaching qualities symbol appears, but we urge you not to allow your thinking to be limited by this list.

It is our hope that you will adopt this process for reflection into your way of being so that when you enter the profession you will model the very essence of a dynamic professional who responds to new knowledge and change in ways that benefit young people.

Key Terms

accountability   30

authenticity   24

diversity   21

integrity   32

thoughtfulness   31

Suggested Further Reading

Henderson, James G. (2001). *Reflective Teaching: Professional Artistry Through Inquiry* (3rd ed.). Upper Saddle River, NJ: Prentice-Hall Inc.

Hill, Linda D. (2001). *Connecting Kids: Exploring Diversity Together.* Co-published: Gabriola Island, BC: New Society Publishers; Duncan, BC: Building Bridges Consulting.

Kilbourn, Brent. (1998). *For the Love of Teaching.* London, ON: The Althouse Press.

Pike, G. and Selby, D. (2000). *In the Global Classroom.* Toronto, ON: Pippin Publishing.

Unrau, Norman J. (1997). *Thoughtful Teachers, Thoughtful Learners: A Guide to Helping Adolescents Think Critically.* Scarborough, ON: Pippin Publishing.

2 Education and Diversity: Framing the Issues

VIGNETTE

Gina had been teaching only a few months and, like all new teachers, she had already faced quite a few challenges, beginning with her initial conference with Mrs. Watkins the school principal. Gina had gone to the meeting with a list of "house-keeping" questions but had spent most of the hour asking about the challenges she was to expect in her culturally diverse urban classroom. Mrs. Watkins had done her best to allay her fears, and Gina had left the meeting feeling that her fears were probably unfounded. After all, she was now a professional and should, therefore, not allow her imagination to run wild (despite the stories she had heard from other teacher candidates who had interned in "multicultural" schools). Unfortunately, her fears came true. While Mrs. Watkins and her colleagues had been very supportive, Gina was experiencing difficulties managing her culturally diverse class.

She knew that she loved and cared for all her fifth graders (including Jimmy who some would consider for lack of a better word, a "nightmare"), but that was a different matter. Returning her thoughts to the noise and chatter of her students running around the playground, she wondered how her seemingly all-knowing foundations course professor would have handled an incident that occurred last week. It had culminated in racially offensive name-calling between a minority student and a White student during recess. She had done her best to resolve the conflict, but one of the parents had not been satisfied with the way she had handled the matter and had reported the incident, and her as well, to the principal. Why was she having so much trouble dealing with her students she wondered for the umpteenth time? Was it her own background? She prided herself in her ability to treat people fairly and equally, including those that are different from her. Besides, she mused, did she not pride herself for being "colour blind"? Was she trying too hard? Was it a case of self-fulfilling prophecy, or was it simply that she had not understood what she had learned during her training? Yes, she had learned a lot of theory. She wished now that she had had more opportunity to put some of that theory to practical use during her field experience. But that had been difficult since her cooperating teachers had remained in charge of maintaining discipline in almost every class she had been assigned to teach. What was it her professor had said about the connection between theory and practice? "Theory is to practice as practice is to theory". She wondered if there was any link at all between both concepts. Sometimes, the reality in the field seemed to suggest otherwise. Despite her misgivings, Gina knew that both are inextricably connected.

INTRODUCTION: SETTING THE STAGE

Gina's thoughts are not an unusual phenomenon among teachers, novice and veteran alike, who teach in culturally diverse contexts. Student diversity became a stable reality in Canadian schools as a result of demographic shifts that changed the country's ethnocultural landscape, which in turn, influenced social policy directions. Dealing with diversity in our schools remains as much a challenge today as it was decades ago. Then, as a matter of necessity, both the government and society at large began to address the issue of the changing "faces" of Canada, and its implication for education systems. Today, critical questions persist, such as what, why, and how to teach children in ways that reflect the rich tapestry of their diverse backgrounds.

Canada's challenges in dealing with diversity are part of a pattern of increasing student diversity in many Western countries because of massive global population shifts. To provide the conceptual base for analyzing the discussions that follow in the rest of the book, some of the theories and assumptions that dominate discussions of this phenomenon must first be clearly understood. In this chapter then, I explore some theoretical views of diversity and schooling: how they are interconnected; how taken-for-granted practices in schools are implicated in the marginalization and exclusion of some groups in society; and how the ways in which schools reproduce the existing social order further alienate and disenfranchise some groups. I also examine how, paradoxically, schools also hold the key to changing the status quo through policies and practices that are not only socially just but that also validate the identities of all students. Finally, I explore various perspectives on the linkages between diversity and academic achievement.

UNDERSTANDING DIVERSITY

In its simplest conception, diversity refers to difference. Thus, it is possible to speak of human diversity, bio-diversity, diversity of opinions, religious diversity, linguistic diversity, cultural diversity, etc. My concern in this book is more with this latter meaning — **cultural diversity** in its different theoretical conceptualizations. But cultural diversity cannot be properly understood without an understanding of the meaning of culture. As a social artifact, culture is a complex phenomenon that has different connotations depending on the context of use (Erickson, 2001). It is sometimes used in reference to aesthetic interests such as the arts or to describe the life-styles of groups and sub-groups within a society. It is also used in a sociological and anthropological sense to describe people's heritage, historical origin, and way of life. Bullivant (1989) distinguishes between two possible ways of looking at culture — as the heritage and traditions of a social group and as a group's strategy for adapting to, and surviving in its environment. Drawing on Bullivant's conception, Fleras and Elliott (1992) define culture as

> [a] shared system of meaning and symbols that account for patterned behaviour between individuals and among groups. This shared reality allows members of the community to make sense of the world they live in and to construct plans for adaptation and survival. Culture in the anthropological sense encompasses a complex range of beliefs and values that (a) define and generate behaviour, (b) contribute to the security, identity, and survival of community members, and (c) impart meaning and continuity during period of social change (p. 137).

As the above definition suggests, culture is acquired knowledge and as a result, does not exist outside a historical context. Rather, conceptions vary across time and space. However, while an understanding of what constitutes culture may vary temporally and across societies, it remains a primary component of individual and group identity formation. Because culture is embedded in language and language is an integral part of people's identities, it too features prominently in the conception of culture adopted in this book. Thus, culture is defined as the knowledge, values, customs, attitudes, language and strategies that enable individuals and groups to adapt and survive in their environment. Finally, culture is pervasive and "is in us and all around us, just as is the air we breathe. It is personal, familial, communal, institutional, societal, and global in its scope and distribution". (Erickson, 2001: 31).

In some societies cultural diversity—the different ways of knowing, perceiving, and interpreting reality, becomes a source of social conflicts as various groups struggle for survival and control of power. These conflicts can occur even within institutions such as schools. However, the extent to which cultural differences become problematic in schools (and society) depends on whether or not such differences are perceived as boundaries or borders. When cultural differences are treated as boundaries, there is a recognition that real differences exist between people but, these differences need not cause problems. However, when treated as borders, cultural differences become politicized and subsequently, become sources of dissention (Giroux, 1992). Differences aside, because each one of us identifies with at least two or more cultural affiliations, each person has his or her own cultural identity. This, in conjunction with some biological or inherited traits, becomes a marker of personal identity. The issue of how people's identities and differences are influenced by biology and social and cultural factors is one I develop in the sections that follow.

Biological and Social Factors Influencing Identity and Diversity

The construction of individual identity is a function of two variables, inherited genes and one's environment. Although our primary concern is with the social construction of identities, since inherited properties also contribute to our overall sense of who we are, it is necessary to briefly examine the biological influences on identity formation.

Biological factors are properties with which we are born. An obvious biological difference among people is sex since human beings are born either male or female (although emerging claims of the existence of more than two genders now challenge this belief). Other biological factors include race, skin colour, personality, and cognitive ability. These latter two also interact with the environment as people's identities evolve. For example, while we are born with certain cognitive abilities, our experience and interaction with the social context in which we are immersed may affect the extent to which these abilities develop. Interestingly, this perspective is the starting point both for theorists who subscribe to the belief that some groups in society are culturally deprived, as well as for scholars and practitioners who argue for empowering and inclusive educational policies and practices.

Unlike biological factors, social or cultural factors are those differences that emanate from our interactions with our environment. Social factors are often ascribed by society and are therefore temporal, depending on the prevailing social order. But, like biological factors, they too mediate the construction of individual and group identities. Examples of social and cultural factors which contribute to who we are include language, religion, social class, nationality, citizenship, and education.

The Individual and Cultural Identity

We are all cultural beings and our cultural backgrounds influence our perceptions of the world and, therefore, constitute an essential part of who we are. In theory, each individual belongs to at least one culture. Also, because a person simultaneously belongs to at least one macro-culture (the national culture), and one or more subcultures (functions of biology and the environment), we can say that in reality, as Figure 1.1 shows, human beings are fundamentally multicultural. For example, hypothetically, Gina in the opening vignette can be described as a White, middle-class, female, Christian, Canadian, teacher, of Scottish descent. She therefore belongs to one macro-culture (Canadian) and at least six different subcultures based on her race (White), social class (middle-class), gender (female), religion (Christian), profession (teacher), and ethnicity (Scottish). All these attributes, some of which were inherited and others socially assigned, contribute to Gina's identity. People's cultural identity (their perceptions of who they are on the basis of their race, ethnicity, gender, social class, religion, etc.), are inextricably linked to their historical experiences, their worldviews, and the extent to which they participate in the groups or subgroups with which they identify (James, 2003). In the words of Hall (1993: 394), " . . . identities are the names we give to the different ways we are positioned by, and position ourselves within the narratives of the past". However, this does not mean that people who belong to the same ethnic or cultural group should be considered as homogeneous. On the contrary, far from engaging in essentialist generalizations, we must be careful in our conceptualization of cultural

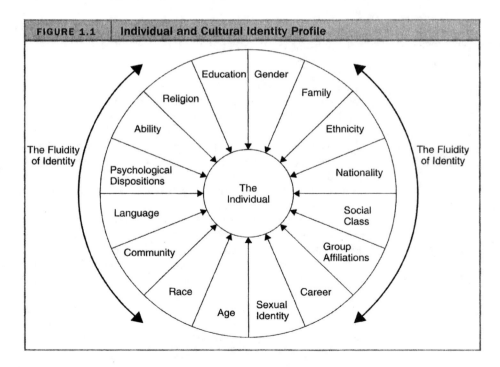

| FIGURE 1.1 | Individual and Cultural Identity Profile |

differences not to resort to **stereotyping** since membership in a culture or subculture is not an inevitable predictor of behaviour as Banks (2001) cautions:

> Although membership in a gender, racial, ethnic, social-class, or religious group can provide us with important clues about individuals' behaviour, it cannot enable us to predict behavior . . . Membership in a particular group does not determine behavior but makes certain types of behavior more probable (p. 13).

As will be established in the next section, schools, by their very nature as loci of social transmission, also contribute to the construction of individual and group identities through their **manifest** and **latent** functions, and their **explicit** and **implicit** curricula.

Our cultural background is our own personal possession and influences how we view ourselves. However, shared attributes link people to one another, and our perceptions of our selves and identities also change as our "spaces" change.

Certain social milieux influence our behaviour and perceptions of ourselves profoundly while others allow us to remain our authentic selves. Contexts where our identities are re-affirmed and legitimized will naturally contribute to higher self-esteem while the reverse is true in contexts where certain aspects of our identities are denigrated and stigmatized. For example, for many minority students, schools can be oppressive social arenas because of the devaluation of their worldviews, which are fundamental aspects of their identity. In making a case for the empowerment of minority students, Cummins (1996) argues that some minority students experience so much difficultly negotiating their identities that they begin to lose sight of who they are.

Race and Diversity

We have established above that several variables impact on diversity, and that identity can be fluid depending on one's environment or social positioning within a given space. One variable which contributes to our understandings of diversity and identity is the concept of *race*. Although there are biological bases for analyzing race, it is a deeply constructed phenomenon that is often shaped by social norms. This construct is then used by society to conveniently categorize groups of people who share similar physical features, including skin colour and other physiological differences (Chancer and Watkins, 2006). Race is therefore not a stable category; its conceptualization is dependent on the subjective interpretations of the dominant theory, often from the perspectives of the privileged group, during a particular historical period (Omi and Winant, 1993). Although the physiological distinction by skin colour may appear neutral, this is not so in reality because as Chancer and Watkins (2006: 50) posit, "[f]or many centuries, the Western world has accorded superiority to lighter skin types and relative inferiority to darker skin types, as biologically based shades of distinction came to reflect cultural and social prejudice".

How does this work in practice? Race becomes the basis of social discrimination when the dominant group, which considers itself the superior race, produces and distributes (but denies other groups or races) access to social rewards, thus placing the concept at the centre of discussions of power relations in society (Henry and Tator, 2006; Allahar, 1998; Omi and Winant, 1993). One question that is often asked within the Canadian context is "Does race matter?" The answer is a resounding yes. As Fleras and Elliott (2003) point out, even though Canadians are ambivalent about the concept, it will continue to count in everyday life and public policy:

> [N]ot because it is real, but because people respond as if it were real. Race matters not because people are inherently different or unequal, but because perceived differences may be manipulated as a basis for sorting out privilege and power. Race matters not because of biological differences, but because an exclusive preoccupation with genes detracts from scrutinizing those opportunity structures that are largely responsible for unequal relations. Race matters because reference to race has a controlling effect on those who are racially devalued (p. 52).

With regards to educational knowledge, there is indeed general agreement among critical writers that race is a variable which is commonly used to sustain inequality in schools, and subsequently in society (for example, Henry and Tator, 2006; Fleras and Elliott, 2003; James, 2003; Dei, 1996). But, in a reversal of this commonly held view of the link between race and inequality, educational and otherwise, Malik (1996: 39) argues that "it is not racial differentiation that has led to the denial of inequality but the social constraints placed on the scope of equality that has led to the racial categorization of humanity . . . it is not 'race' that gives rise to inequality but inequality gives rise to race".

This observation not withstanding, the fact remains as Ghosh (2002) points out, that the stratification of races is closely related to slavery and colonial processes, both of which were justified on the grounds of the superiority of the dominating race. Also today, sustained by the works of advocates of "scientifically-based" racial hierarchies, the belief in the superiority of certain races persists in Western societies such as Canada, the United States, the United Kingdom, and Australia, leading to **racism** and the continued oppression of minority groups. But, what is racism? James (2003: 136) describes racism as "the uncritical acceptance of a negative social definition of a colonized or subordinate group typically identified by physical features (i.e., race—black, brown, and yellow, red)". These groups are usually believed to be intellectually, physically, and culturally inferior, which gives oppressive groups "justifiable" reasons to dominate and oppress them by denying them power and privilege. Racism can be individual (operating at the level of one individual to another) or it can be institutional, structural, or systemic when "established policies, rules and regulations of an organization systematically reflect and produce differential treatment of various groups within that organization or institution and society more generally" (James, 2003: 137). This systemic, and most virulent, form of racism often denies subordinate and less powerful groups access to what society has to offer on the basis of their supposedly inferior skin colour. Institutional racism erects barriers that are sometimes insurmountable for nondominant groups.

Another variant of racism is cultural or ideological racism, which reinforces dominant group values by presenting them as normal and necessary for success in society and by practising them within social institutions such as the school. While all forms of racism are destructive, institutional racism is particularly inimical to the academic progress of children from non-mainstream communities. How does this happen? Henry and Tator (2006: 202) provide an outline of the ways through which racism is manifest within Canadian educational systems:

- racially biased attitudes of teachers and administrators
- Eurocentric curricula, and unfair and culturally biased assessment practices
- the construction of nondominant group children as "others"

- the harassment and excessive scrutiny of minority students
- the streaming of minority students into non-academic programs
- disciplinary policies that target minority students
- unrepresentative curricula, administration, and staffing
- the devaluation of nondominant group parents' and community involvement in schools

An example of how institutional racism operates in practice will illustrate the point. A school might, for instance, place a student with a limited knowledge of the English language in the same class as academically underperforming students even though he or she may, in fact, be an above average student. Similarly, schools sometimes (as a deliberate policy) place students whose first languages are variations of the English language, i.e., English as dialect students such as those from some parts of the Caribbean, in special needs classes. There is also the problem of the over-representation of minority students in vocational schools across the country.

Given the above argument, it is not surprising that progressive educators, in Canada and abroad who are committed to transformative change, have long argued that racism contributes in no small measure, to the tenuous relationship between minority students and educational systems. This is particularly true in contexts where there is cultural and racial incongruence between teachers and their students, and the latter are positioned as the "other" (Egbo, 2007; Delpit, 2006; Anyon, 2005; Razack, 1998; Ladson-Billings, 1994; Dei, 1996).

In her critically acclaimed book that analyzes the interplay between race and ethnicity in the classroom, Lisa Delpit (2006) argues that teachers can positively transform the lives of minority children if they dispense with prejudice, stereotypes, and cultural assumptions, which are in fact the consequence of miscommunications and miscues when primarily White educators teach "*Other People's Children*". Critiquing what she refers to as a "culture of power" which is operational at the micro-level of the classroom, she argues that because the culture of power emanates from the perspectives of those who already control power in society (the dominant group), navigating the culture that schools transmit is easier for children from such backgrounds. To elaborate her point, Delpit (2006: 24) identifies five key aspects of this culture of power as follows:

1. Issues of power are enacted in the classroom
2. There are codes or rules for participating in power
3. The rules of a culture of power are a reflection of the rules of the culture of those who have power
4. If you are not already a participant in the culture of power, being told explicitly the rules of that culture makes acquiring power easier
5. Those with power are frequently least aware of — or least willing to acknowledge — its existence. Those with less power are often most aware of its existence.

She goes on to argue that in the first instance, the issues include the curriculum, the resources, the power of the teacher over students, and the explicit and implicit functions of the school. The codes in the second constituent of power include linguistic codes, communicative competencies, ways of self-presentation, ways of writing, etc. In this case, success in school and society depends on the acquisition of the cultural values or culture-bases (as I argue later) of dominant society, specifically those who control the resources. Delpit's fourth constituent of the culture of power argues that since schooling is a culturally and ideologically mediated experience, teachers are morally compelled to teach their non-mainstream students the codes that are necessary to succeed in society. The fifth point, which Delpit suggests is often neglected in related discourses, underscores the fact that many people who have power in society either by virtue of their numbers, social positioning, or race, are the last to acknowledge it. For them, power becomes a taken-for-granted phenomenon that is recognized and alluded to only by those without it. Delpit's argument brings to mind the well-known treatise on the impact of power, *White Privilege* by Peggy McIntosh (1990), which provides compelling insights into the taken-for-granted advantages that accrue to "Whiteness" institutionally, systemically, and in everyday life. Such privileges grant her certain rights and freedoms, as well as participation in a culture of power, that are not available to non-White members of society. Also, this privilege tends to be invisible and even denied by members of the dominant group. This is true of Canada as it is of many Western societies that ideologically subscribe to democratic-liberalism. Ironically, while its control of power can be invisible to the dominant group, it can also be invisible to the dominated through **hegemony**, which is akin to "invisible" power.

Returning to Delpit's (2006) account of teaching and cultural conflict in schools, the issues she raises transcend the curriculum and pedagogy. They involve, in a deeply profound way, the **life chances** of racialized and minoritized children. Life chances are opportunities that are provided by social conditions within a given society, and are a function of two elements — options and ligatures (Dahrendorf, 1979). Options provide choices and have implications for the future, while ligatures are bonds and linkages that individuals develop through immersion in a social context or by virtue of their social positions and roles in society. In many parts of the world, access to education (especially the valued kind) is often associated with two sets of life chances: increased life options, which means a greater range of future choices as a result of the acquired knowledge, and increased ligatures, which means individuals develop a greater range of connection with one another as a result of their shared experience in education (Corson, 1998). Both types of life chances are critical to the empowerment of any group, particularly those that have historically been at the margins of their societies.

Hegemony and Diversity

Hegemony relates to the "invisible" process of maintaining power and social control by dominant groups through state and social institutions. Through the process of normalization, oppressed groups internalize and accept their subordinate condition while they are oblivious to the colonizing process that is actually at work. As a concept, it offers insights into the study of power and the ways in which domination becomes reproduced as common sense thinking (Kincheloe, 2005). In simple terms, hegemony is unobtrusive power and its potency lies in its invisibility and subsequent acceptance by those who are oppressed. When hegemony is operational, dominant groups are able to eliminate resistance and opposition by (re)presenting imposed ideology as normal.

This concept relates to the analysis of diversity in Canadian schools because many of the oppressive structures and practices in schools are inadvertently reinforced by those who are at the receiving end. For example, members of certain social groups can internalize and reinforce the dominant group's negative perceptions of their academic abilities by resisting educational "success". This kind of behaviour, or "self-fulfilling prophecy," is a classic case of hegemony at work. While many anti-oppression advocates work hard to transform the system, some minorities will uncritically accept oppressive and exclusionary practices that are accepted as "normal". However, like most kinds of power, hegemonic power can exist only through the consent of those who yield that power. When people become consciousness of disempowering social structures, they develop resistance and challenge the status quo, including unfair practices, ideologies, and attitudes that are transmitted through the school's explicit and hidden curricula as noted above.

The Hidden Curriculum

The explicit goal of schools to socialize and educate the next generation is generally stipulated in the formal curriculum. However, a substantive amount of what students learn is not openly stated, even though such implicitly conveyed knowledge (the **hidden curriculum**) underpins student and teacher behaviour. Generally defined as the behaviours, attitudes, and knowledge the school unintentionally teaches through its content selection, routines, and social relationships, the hidden curriculum provides additional space for spreading dominant ideologies in schools and consequently promotes institutional racism (Henry and Tator, 2006; Bennett and LeCompte, 1995). Traditionally, schools are organized around hierarchical and monolithic models of instruction that de-emphasize the values, learning styles, ways of knowing, and worldviews of dominated groups. It is through the hidden curriculum that schools convey messages about who controls power in society, as well as whose voices matter (through what is included and omitted in the formal curriculum). Moreover, learning in school is not only done through textbooks and teaching, but also through participation and interaction in various school activities that promote dominant group norms and ethos. Since children differ in class, race, and other social indicators, so too will their understanding of the messages that are being conveyed to them through the hidden curriculum.

Within the Canadian context, the hidden curriculum is manifest in such school arrangements, like the school calendar, social and religious celebrations, concerts and festivals, hallway displays, the collections in school libraries, Eurocentric values, and the tacit acceptance of racism and discrimination (Henry and Tator, 2006). Some writers have argued that the oppositional subcultures or "creative maladjustment" (Kohl, 1994) that minority students tend to develop in schools, is collective resistance to the negative messages that are conveyed to them through the formal and hidden curricula. For this reason, any attempt at understanding how schools perpetuate inequalities, discrimination, and prejudice, must examine and deconstruct the hidden curriculum since it has as much impact on the construction of identities as what schools explicitly teach students.

Prejudice, Stereotypes, and Xenophobia

Very often, misconceptions about other races and people can lead to **prejudice**—"a set of rigid and unfavourable attitudes towards a particular group or groups that is formed in disregard of facts" (Banks, 1988: 223). While most people have some form of prejudice, it becomes particularly harmful when it is used as a basis for oppression, discrimination, and stereotyping. When people stereotype, they make misleading and inaccurate generalizations about others. One problem with stereotypes is that they can never be uniformly applied to a group (Fleras and Elliott, 2003) because among all social groups, there is as much intra-group as inter-group diversity. Take, for example, the common misconception that women do not have a strong aptitude for mathematics and the sciences. In reality, this stereotyped view is not supported by the evidence since many women, both nationally and globally, have excelled in the sciences and have gone on to build distinguished careers in their chosen fields. Similarly, stereotypes usually do not stand the test of time. For instance, for the first half of the 20th Century African Americans (and Blacks in general), were supposedly not endowed with athletic skills and were consequently excluded from competitive sports in the United States and other Western countries. However, their current dominance in many professional sports has led to revisionist perceptions of their athletic prowess. Despite the role that segregationist and racist policies played in excluding Blacks from sports preceding the civil rights movement, they are now widely believed to have genetically superior athletic abilities. Also, the stereotypical beliefs about the biological and cultural basis of minority students' academic underachievement have been discounted now that structural, institutional, and ideological variables are considered important contributors to the schooling outcomes of minority students.

At school, prejudice and stereotyping can have devastating consequences on teaching and learning as well as on the academic success of minority students. How does this happen? First, teachers and students do not come to school as tabula rasa and their pre-existing misconceptions of different groups in wider society may find the school to be fertile nurturing ground. Like anyone else, teachers are prone to the influences of stereotyping, but the nature of their job places them in a unique position to put their views to work (Corson, 1998). Second, stereotypical beliefs about some students' race or heritage may affect how teachers teach certain subjects and their expectations of, and the nature of their interactions with the students. Conversely, a student who believes that a teacher holds negative views of his or her race, group, or gender, may react in ways that do not support their academic progress. Over time, both the teacher and the student will develop **mutual resistance**, which makes teaching and learning very challenging. Unfortunately, as Cummins (2000: 7) points out "classroom interactions between educators and students [are] the most direct determinant of educational success or failure for culturally and linguistically diverse students". He further argues that while for some students' resistance can result in concerted effort to succeed in order to disprove their teacher's low expectations, the typical reaction is mental withdrawal or disengagement from an apparently coercive relationship which in turn, results in negative academic, social, and material consequences.

As experts suggest, prejudice is difficult to reduce in schools because, by the time children get to school, their perceptions of various ethnic and cultural groups are already formed as a result of cognitive immaturity and the need for parental approval (Aboud, 1992). Unfortunately, this attitude is legitimated in schools by curriculum content and through the behaviour of educational personnel. In fact, school responses to prejudice tend to treat it as the by-product of a few "bad apples", whose deviant behaviour is symptomatic of deficient home socialization.

Finally, another reason why prejudice is difficult to combat is the fact that people are reluctant to admit to it — in part because they are not often aware that they are prejudiced in the first place. However, a simple test of prejudice as provided in Table 1.1 is a starting point for identifying a person's propensity towards prejudice and discrimination.

A different kind of prejudice which is not often given the attention it deserves in Canadian society is **xenophobia**. Originating from two Greek words *xenos* (foreigner or

TABLE 1.1	Sample Test of Individual Prejudice

What is the first thing that comes to mind when you see or hear these words (arranged in alphabetical order)? Write down your first thought in the middle column and a relevant score in the right-hand column.

Word(s)	First Thought	Score
Asians		
Blacks		
Christians		
First Nations Peoples		
Gays and Lesbians		
Immigrants		
Jews		
Moslems		
People with Disabilities		
Refugees		
Whites		
Women		

Scoring

For each "positive" thought you earn 2 points, and for each "negative" thought, 0 points. A "neutral" thought (i.e. I don't care) earns you 1 point. Add up your points; the highest possible score is 24 points. A total score of 12 points or less signifies that you have a prejudiced attitude towards those that are different from you. A score of 13 to 20 indicates that you have some prejudices although for the most part, you are accepting of those who are different from you. A total score of 21 to 24 points means that you have a positive attitude towards those that are different from you; you are therefore not prejudiced.

stranger) and *phobos* (fear), xenophobia is a persistent fear of foreigners or people who are different. Xenophobia, particularly towards new immigrants, is becoming prevalent in Western societies because of massive global population shifts, and especially in a post September 11 context, which has witnessed increases in previously existing inter-group tensions (Giroux, 2002). These tensions can easily spill into schools, and without proper understanding of what is at work, educators are likely to miss early warning signs of conflicts that originate from xenophobic attitudes among their students.

The "Colour-Blindness" Syndrome

It is ironic that in a racialized and multicultural society like Canada, people tend to claim colour blindness (in a metaphorical sense), as the ultimate evidence of their aversion to racism, prejudice, and discrimination. For instance, it is not uncommon to hear teachers make comments like, "Black, White, blue, or green, I love all my students", "I do not see colour", "I treat everyone equally", or "As far as I am concerned, everyone is the same". Even if we concede that some people are less prone to racial biases than others, the absurdity of this kind of comment is self-evident. Even in culturally homogenous educational contexts it would be unnatural to make such claims of equal treatment. First, by the very nature of human beings, it is impossible to "love" everyone equally. Second, it is not realistic to claim that every student can be treated equally since there are significant individual differences (such as learning styles, abilities, disabilities, cultural differences, and personal circumstances) that mandate differential treatment if teachers are to effectively meet the learning needs of all their students. Third, without denying that such a statement is probably well-intentioned, it is impossible not to notice racial differences among students in the closed confines of a classroom. Claiming colour-blindness then, is analogous to denying peoples' existence or a negation of their identities. Gina in the opening vignette is clearly guilty of this faux pas albeit the result of ignorance. Differences do exist among people as noted above. The problem arises when differences are used as markers for unfair categorizations, prejudice, and distribution of social goods. Once we recognize this fact, we are then able to accept and talk about it, and thereby challenge oppressive structures that lead to the exploitation of differences in the first place.

SCHOOLS, SOCIAL POSITIONING, AND PRIVILEGE: THEORETICAL VIEWS

That schools are agents of socialization that play an important role in people's lives is a matter of consensus. That social positioning, privilege, and the knowledge that is produced in schools (at least in Western and pluralistic societies such as Canada), intersect in complex ways that affect school success or failure is also a widely accepted premise. What remains a source of raging debate is the nature and extent that role plays in creating social hierarchies. In the vast literature that has accumulated over decades of research and debate on all three issues, two broad perspectives emerge which subsume other views — the consensus and interrogative perspectives.

Consensus Perspectives

I use the term *consensus perspectives* inclusively to describe **conservative** and **liberal-democratic** views of schooling that dominated educational thought up to the 1970s. Informed by **structural functionalism** as proposed by sociologists Emile Durkheim (1956), Talcott Parsons (1951, 1959) and Robert Morton (1957), consensus theories see society as organized systems and structures in which equilibrium, stability, order, and social cohesion are its prominent features while agreement is the most prevalent social force. Similarly, consensus views of schooling see education as a liberating and requisite force for individual and social progress, which provides equal opportunities for all regardless of race, socio-economic status, gender, and cultural background. Education is also seen as a means of providing skills training and knowledge transfer, as well as basic societal values. In this linear conception of the role of schools, society is seen as a **meritocracy** and schools as level playing fields where all students have equal chance to succeed regardless of their background or gender.

Despite more informed analysis of the links between schooling and society, consensus views of schooling continue to be adopted by neo-conservative reformists who advocate "back to basics" educational policies such as those recommended in *A Nation at Risk (1983)* and the *No Child Left Behind Act of 2002* in the United States. In Canada, the current accountability and competency-based educational reforms (such as standardized curricula and standardized tests) are implicitly aimed at providing students with what policy makers believe to be basic knowledge (Corson, 2001). Entrenched reformists generally see education as a public good that serves the interest of both the individual and the commonwealth by preparing children for meaningful existence in society (Sowell, 2002; Coulson, 2002). There is in effect a refusal to acknowledge schools as sites where intergroup and class distinctions are reproduced or as arenas that do not serve the interests of less privileged members of society. By adopting a neutral view of schooling, consensus accounts of schooling absolve society from any culpability in the educational failure of children from disadvantaged communities. In contrast, the complicity of both state and social structures remains a point of convergence for other theorists. They believe that in addition to their explicit function of educating the next generation, schools are sites that perpetuate social injustices and politicize knowledge. These "interrogative" theorists see an inherent connection between education, social positioning, and power in society.

Interrogative Perspectives

In his book *Changing Education for Diversity*, David Corson (1998) asks a seemingly straightforward but profoundly complex and important question concerning ways of dealing with student diversity in plural societies:

> The key question . . . is whether the differences that exist between . . . diverse students and the majority of students in a given setting *are* [emphasis in original] educationally relevant. If they are relevant, then some different type of educational provision is warranted (p. 1).

Some writers have sought to establish this relevance by questioning the explicit and in particular implicit functions of education systems (e.g., Bowles and Gintis, 1976; Giroux, 1983, 1992; Bourdieu, 1977; Bernstein, 1977; Freire, 1970; Apple, 1982; McLaren, 2007). Used in this context (as an umbrella term for a wide range of theoretical views that question the ostensibly neutral role of schools), interrogative perspectives see education as politics-laden, and as such, the nexus of power struggles in society. The vast majority of theorists in this category believe that understanding the intersections of class, power, and privilege is critical to understanding how schools carry out their mandate. Two of these views, **conflict** and **critical** theories, provide the theoretical framework on which the views in this book are grounded.

Conflict Theories

Conflict theorists question the assumed neutral and value-free views of schools and expose how they serve the interests of the dominant group. They further argue that as institutions of socialization, schools reproduce the values, ideologies, and worldviews of the dominant group, and in so doing, reinforce existing economic, political, and social inequalities resulting in **social reproduction**. Two of the most influential perspectives for examining this paradigm are the economic reproduction and the cultural reproduction theories.

Schools and Economic Reproduction

Originating from the work of Samuel Bowles and Herbert Gintis, the economic reproduction theory asserts that one of the essential functions of the school is to sustain the labour force and capitalism along the lines of class and gender, and as a consequence, reinforce existing class-based inequities. According to Bowles and Gintis (1976), schools achieve this goal through differential socialization, which systematically teaches youths the skills, attitudes, and values that correspond to their expected future roles and positions within the labour force:

> The educational system helps integrate youth into the economic system, we believe, through a structural correspondence between its social relations and those of production. The structure of social relations in education not only inures the student to the discipline of the work place, but develops the types of personal demeanour, modes of self-presentation, self-image, and social class identification which are the crucial ingredients of job adequacy (p. 131).

Their central argument rests on the "**correspondence principle**", which asserts that there is a relationship between the unequal treatment less privileged students receive in schools and the hierarchical structure of the labour force. In their analysis, middle and upper class children are educated to occupy leadership positions within the capitalist economy while working class children and those from other disadvantaged segments such as minorities, women, and immigrants (the latter within the Canadian context) are trained to occupy subordinate positions. How does this work in practice? In Canada, minority students predominate in "compensatory" and special needs programs. Just as they constitute the majority in special needs programs, ethnic minority students are more likely to take courses that are less academically challenging than their White peers. In many Canadian secondary schools, students' courses are organized on a hierarchical basis of presumed level of difficulty. These range from the least difficult to the most difficult streams namely, basic/general, advanced, and vocational or university bound. Students then choose or are assigned courses based on educators' perceptions of their abilities or motivation to do the associated work (Young, Levin, and Wallin, 2007). More often than not, students who are considered less able (or less motivated) are "streamed" towards courses that are deemed less academically rigorous. The socio-psychological consequences of such groupings are obvious, especially for those in the lower streams. Unfortunately, immigrant and minority students overwhelmingly populate the general, basic, or vocational streams. This "sorting" function limits their future prospects and life chances.

However, while the correspondence principle is helpful in understanding how schools perpetuate social division and subordination through its "tailoring" function, it is flawed by its determinist position, its passive view of human beings, and the implicit message of futility in changing the existing social order. Moreover, the theory's failure to explain the resistance and conflicts that are inherent in social relationships in schools has been criticized. As Giroux (1983) argues, people do not always remain passive; they do put up resistance against the forces of domination once they have achieved the level of consciousness that will enable them to initiate transformative action.

Schools and Cultural Reproduction

Developing out of the works of Pierre Bourdieu (1977, 1991), Bourdieu and Passeron (1977), and Basil Bernstein (1977), cultural reproduction theory examines the mediating role of culture in reproducing social inequalities in society through institutions such as the school. Critical of consensus views of education (which suggest that educational systems offer equal opportunities to all on a meritocratic platform), its emphasis is on how class-based differences are legitimated in schools under the guise of neutrality. Bourdieu (1977) explains:

> among all solutions put forward throughout history to the problem of the transmission of power and privileges, there surely does not exist one that is better concealed . . . than that solution which the educational system provides by contributing to the reproduction of the structure of class relations and by concealing, by an apparently neutral attitude, the fact that it fills this function. (pp. 487 – 488)

Bourdieu goes on to argue that the educational system in fact favours majority group children who possess the **cultural capital** and **cultural habitus** that are compatible with those demanded by schools. Cultural capital is the knowledge-base that individuals have including their patterns of language skills and overall ways of viewing the world, while cultural habitus refers to class-based predispositions that a person possesses. The cultural capital that is valued in schools depends on who controls power and resources in wider society (which in Canada is that of middle-class society of European ancestry). Elaborating on the importance of cultural capital and habitus in school success, Bourdieu (1977) contends that the educational system

> offers information and training which can be received and acquired only by subjects endowed with the system of predispositions that is the condition for the success of the transmission and of the inculcation of the culture. By doing away with giving explicitly to everyone what it implicitly demands of everyone, the educational system demands of everyone alike that they have what it does not give. This consists mainly of linguistic and cultural competence and that relationship of familiarity with culture which can only be produced by family upbringing when it transmits the dominant culture (p. 494).

Bourdieu's views are important in understanding how culture is reproduced in school while diversity among students and human experience is eschewed. His views also underscore the inherent political and social processes at work in education, especially in pluralistic societies such as Canada. Furthermore, it exposes how certain forms of knowledge are privileged and others de-valued, based on who participates in what Delpit (2006) refers to as "a culture of power". What does this mean in reality? Bourdieu's views suggest that in the classroom, children from privileged backgrounds are more likely to be found intellectually endowed while less privileged children are likely to be found less capable of learning, in part because schools reinforce the cognitive and affective skills which the former already possess leaving the latter at a definite disadvantage.

Developing similar arguments, Bernstein (1977) uses the notion of linguistic codes to demonstrate how social inequalities are linked to language and communication patterns in the family. Relating this to schools curricula and pedagogical practices, Bernstein proposes that schools embody an educational code that dictates how power and authority are to be mediated. Working class families, he believes, develop "restricted" or "particularistic" linguistic codes (which are structurally deficient and incompatible with the language of the school), often leading to academic failure. Meanwhile, middle class families impart to their children complex and abstract codes that are more compatible with those of the school, and therefore help to ensure their academic success. Since, all else being equal, academic success mediates future success, existing class structures and inequalities are thereby reproduced.

The cultural reproduction theory offers compelling insights into the pattern of discrimination, domination, and institutional prejudice that reinforce the marginalized status of students from diverse and working class backgrounds. It also underscores how schools are by no means level playing fields, nor sites that promote diversity in socally significant ways. However, like the economic reproduction theory, it too falls short of proposing strategies for meaningful change or for dealing with diversity in schools.

Critical Theory

Arguing against the accounts of schooling provided by conflict theorists, critical theorists propose an alternative view of society that offers possibilities for changing its social institutions such as school. With a focus on two issues (how schools help dominant groups maintain power and control, and how challenge and interrogation can interrupt the dominance), critical theory offers directions for change (McLaren, 2007; Kincheloe, 2005; Girous, 1983; Peters et al., 2003; Apple, 2003).

Rejecting the view of schools as sites where all interating variables are reducible to economics (or to uncontested wholesale transmission of dominant values and ideologies), critical theorists see schools as loci of power struggles between dominant and nondominant groups. However, while both conflict and critical theorists share the view that schools sustain hierarchies and unequal power relations in society, they diverge on one important point — the potential of schools as sites for transformative **praxis**. Critical theorists believe that if schools subordinate some groups in society, they therefore hold the key for change through just and inclusive practices that affirm diversity. Thus, critical theory offers a framework that is germane to any discussion of diversity in schools. It sees the curriculum not only as a complex medium that perpetuates domination, but also as one that holds **emancipatoy possibilities**.

Adherents of critical theory who are especially concerned about the role of schools in perpetuating social injustices (e.g., Giroux, 1983; Shor, 1992; Kincheloe, 2005a, 2005b; McLauren, 2007; Freire, 1970) advocate **critical pedagogy** that analyzes the relationship between knowledge and power in schools. Critical pedagogists emphasize how knowledge is constructed, situated, and contested within the context of power and marginality. They therefore critique, interrogate, and challenge educational practices that priviledge certain kinds of knowledge while devaluing others. Critical pedagogists see teaching as a politically charged, two-pronged activity that has the potential to either disempower students or raise their consciousness about unequal power relations in society. In the final analysis, critical theorists argue for transformative knowledge that would allow students to interrogate dominant assumptions about the social world, realign their worldviews, and gain a deeper understanding of the structures that impinge on their lives.

Post-modern Perspectives

Like critical theory, post-modern analysis of schooling tends to focus on the relationship between knowledge and power. Knowledge is seen as a site of struggle as the dominant group's control is challenged by less powerful groups in society. Postmodernists also critique dominant forms of analysis on which knowledge claims are based. They argue that such taken-for-granted **universal truths** should be challenged and deconstructed in order to reveal contradictions that are inherent in them. For postmodernists, knowledge is a fluid context-bound phenomenon wherein everyone's views matter. They also hold the view that because there are multiple realities and people construct knowledge differently, diversity should be celebrated rather than seen as a problem or inconvenience. Postmodernists therefore acknowledge differences (cultural, linguistic, racial, gender, sexual orientation, etc.), and emphasize the need to listen to previously silenced voices. Common criticisms advanced against postmodern theory are its relativistic stance (an implicit belief that "everything goes") and that it does not offer practical solutions for changing the unjust social and educational practices of which it is so critical.

DIVERSITY AND SOCIAL JUSTICE

One other perspective warrants examination in our analysis of the relationship between education and diversity. This is the commonly held view that valuing diversity in schools is a matter of fundamental human rights and **social justice** (Banks, 2006; Corson, 2001). Regardless of where on the political spectrum they are, theorists tend to agree on one point — social justice is a societal good worth aspiring to. Therefore, I briefly outline three dominant views of social justice that are relevant to the discussion here.

One common view of social justice is the account provided by John Rawls in his book *A Theory of Justice* (1971), which suggests that inequality in society is only justified if it benefits the disadvantaged. While belief in this perspective has traditionally produced liberal social policies that seek to ameliorate the condition of the less fortunate, Rawls' account of social justice has been criticized on two grounds: its predominant concern with economics and its view of the individual as the starting point for achieving a just society (Corson, 2001).

A second view (which is an improvement on Rawls' theory) sees social justice, or fairness, in terms of equal consideration of the claims of all stakeholders, even if the disadvantaged end up getting more than those who are better-off (Dworkin, 1978). In his analysis of individual and group rights in society, Dworkin makes a critical distinction between treating people equally and treating them as equals. In the former, everyone gets the same treatment regardless of their needs, while in the latter, everyone's needs are considered equally regardless of whether or not they get the same treatment. In other words, equality of treatment leads to injustice since equitable treatment means that the differences in peoples' needs are not taken into account during the distribution of social rewards (including fair access to educational opportunities). A hypothetical example will illustrate the point. Mark and Shane are two physically challenged grade 12 students in a high school that prides itself on its philosophy of "equal treatment for all". Both use motorized wheelchairs that double as their seats in class. While both students can write on regular desks, customized, adjustable desks would make their classroom experience less cumbersome and thus, increase their chances of having "equal" learning opportunities. While this would mean giving them differential treatment, the school would in reality, be living up to its pledge of equal treatment for all. Simply allowing the boys to write on the less-comfortable conventional desks amounts to social injustice. Another example will further explain the issue, and the concepts of equity and equality, which are implicit in the above example. To demonstrate how it is possible to have competing views of what constitutes equitable distribution of resources, Stone (1997) decides to share a mouth-watering chocolate cake in her policy class. She and the class decide to divide the cake into equal pieces before passing it around. It is instructive to note that, even though everyone had agreed to it, the students challenged the distribution strategy at the end of the exercise — on the grounds that what had been originally considered an equitable strategy for sharing the cake was, in fact, unfair. In all, there were eight different, but perfectly logical, reasons why the cake should not have been divided into equal slices. Taking stock of the cake-sharing experiment within the framework of "equality" meaning sameness, and "equity" denoting fairness, Stone concludes that sameness may in fact mean unfairness. Fair treatment may require unequal treatment, and the same distribution mechanism may be seen as equal or unequal, depending on one's point of view (p. 41).

Quite simply, in contexts of inequality, if one's goal is to achieve social justice, then fair treatment should result in differential treatment. Policies and programs (such as affirmative action in the United States and employment equity in Canada) that aim to improve the social and economic condition of traditionally disadvantaged groups (e.g., **visible minorities**, First Nations Peoples, women, and people with disabilities) were developed on the basis of such assumptions.

More recent perspectives have added other parameters to the constituents of social justice. In one such view, social justice is believed to transcend access to economic rewards and includes "relational and associational aspects — recognition and esteem of difference as cultural justice and equity of participation in social and political life" (Gamarnikow and Green, 2003: 210). An even more encompassing view of social justice is advanced by Young (1990; see also Gewirtz, 2001). Young's work provides a relevant analysis of social justice that is consonant with the discussion and ideas in this book. In Young's account of social justice, there are "five faces of oppression" as follows: **exploitation**, the transfer of the work of one group to another; **marginalization**, the exclusion of some segments of the society from access to social rewards; **powerlessness**, the lack of power, status, or authority of a group; **cultural imperialism**, the imposition of the culture of the dominant group on other less-powerful groups; and **violence**, unprovoked attacks on a perceived less-powerful individual (or group) for the purpose of humiliating the victim. Young's five dimensions of oppression are particularly important because they are congruent with the experiences of minoritized groups in many Western societies, including Canada.

The pluralistic accounts of social justice above recognize the fact that diversity is part of the human condition in which some groups are unfortunately marginalized. As such, they provide compelling reason why issues of cultural difference and schooling must remain at the core of public policy and educational discourse, certainly within the Canadian context. The need for such dialogue becomes even more urgent when we consider that racial and cultural differences are often used to explain differential levels of academic achievement among diverse groups.

DIVERSITY AND ACADEMIC ACHIEVEMENT

To fully appreciate the interplay between education and diversity, it is important to understand the key arguments that have been used to explain differential levels of school achievement between majority group children and children from minority backgrounds. Researchers, educators, and scientists have variously used biology, culture, and language-related factors to explain these differences.

GENETIC AND CULTURAL DEFICIT THEORIES

For much of the first half of the 20th Century, explanations of academic underachievement among students from certain ethnocultural backgrounds were bio-centric, i.e., the differences were believed to be the result of innate differences or a deficit in IQ (Jensen, 1969). In particular, scientifically racist explanations were drawn substantively from the field of psychology and from Darwin's theory of natural selection, which portrayed cognitive differences as a function of inherited traits (Winzer and Grigg, 1992). With regard to school achievement, the arguments were rather straightforward: students from certain races (e.g. Whites) were intellectually superior and therefore more likely to succeed academically, while the reverse was assumed to be true of racial and cultural minorities. The net result was that individual learners were considered solely responsible for their own success, and failure was attributed to a deficit in cognitive abilities. Such students (e.g., working class and non-White children) were accordingly labelled intellectually limited and subsequently treated in disempowering ways.

However, beginning in the 1960s, scathing criticisms of genetic deficit explanations, led to the emergence of a second framework for explaining the high rates of academic underachievement among students from non-mainstream backgrounds. According to the **cultural deficit** or **deprivation theory**, factors originating from students' home environment or cultural backgrounds (such as value systems, poor child-rearing practices, parental disinterest in their children's education, and lack of motivation on the part of the students), constrained their ability to achieve success in school. In many Western countries, the belief that academic failure among some racial and ethnic minority students was linked to culturally deprived environments led to the implementation of policies and programs that sought to remove (or at least minimize) the negative impact of the home environment on these students.

Unfortunately, deficit explanations of school failure persist in some quarters even though compelling empirical evidence has now challenged these assumptions. For example, Herrnstein and Murray (1994) and Rushton (1997) have re-insinuated the deficit argument into diversity and academic achievement discourse by making claims that by and large promote race-based explanations for differences in cognitive abilities. However, it cannot be emphasized enough that there is no evidence that biological or inheritable factors influence academic achievement in any significant way. Moreover, much evidence shows that factors such as racism, sexism, poverty, and homophobia have direct bearing on how well some groups perform in school. Although this will not necessarily end the controversy, some writers have suggested that it is more useful to speak in terms of ratios, i.e., how much of our cognitive abilities is the result of our genes, and how much is attributable to other factors. Finally, without discounting the fact that human beings differ from one another in their genetic make up, current knowledge clearly shows that factors that influence academic achievement are better explained by cultural differences and by structural inequalities that disadvantage students from poor and minoritized backgrounds.

Cultural Difference and Academic Achievement

One fact that seems to have gained acceptance among researchers in knowledge construction is the view of learning as an active and socially mediated experience. This means that in practice, as Levi Vygotsky (1962) asserts, the construction of knowledge is linked to how individuals interact with the world around them, both materially and socially. Therefore, in order to be meaningful, knowledge ought to be relevant to the experiences and meaning systems of learners, which should facilitate understanding and increase the chances of success. In a social constructivist view of learning, "learners create or construct their own knowledge through acting on and interacting with the world" (Woolfolk, 1995: 277).

A second noteworthy view of where cultural difference and school achievement intersect is the notion of schools as microcosms of society, in which (as I argued above), the majority group has a stranglehold on power. Consequently, practices within favour those who are already privileged in wider society, i.e., White students from middle-and upper-class backgrounds. Indeed, while much of the research over the last several decades emphasizes the importance of students' backgrounds in learning, students from subordinated groups are still expected to adapt to the monolithic culture that schools disseminate because of the devaluation of their cultural capital, including their first language (Cummins, 2000; Corson, 2001). The fact is that students from culturally different backgrounds often negotiate between two sometimes incommensurate worldviews or culture bases. I refer to these as a primary culture base (CB1) and a secondary culture base (CB2). CB1 is the worldview or cultural capital, including the first language (L1), that is acquired through home socialization. CB2 is the dominant culture, including mainstream language (L2), that minority students must acquire through immersion in the school culture in order to survive in wider society. The discontinuities between these two frames of reference not only create learning challenges for some minority students, they exacerbate inter-group tensions that may already exist outside the school (Bennett, 2007; Nieto, 2002; Erickson, 2001; Egbo, 2001).

Some researchers are convinced that much of the disadvantage and frustration that students from culturally different backgrounds experience in school invariably leads to feelings of disempowerment and alienation, which are precursors to dropping out. For example, in their study of dropouts among Black high school students in Toronto, Dei et al. (1997) link Black students' academic disengagement and readiness to drop out to school and structural variables that ignore their specific educational needs. To improve the chances of success among these students, Dei and associates propose (among other solutions), the establishment of **Afrocentric schools** that would impart African-centred knowledge to Canadian students of African descent. In a similar example, Bernhard and Freire (1999) discuss the case of a group of Latin American students in Toronto whose low academic performance was linked to teaching practices and educators' lack of knowledge (and attention to the perceptions, beliefs, and aspirations) of the students' community.

Besides micro-level educational practices, a host of writers has linked minority students' academic failure to discriminatory social policies in wider society. Cummins (1986: 32) sees the educational failure of minority students as "a function of the extent to which schools reflect or counteract the power relations that exist within broader society". In his discussion of the differences in rates of academic success among minorities Ogbu (1987, 1992) makes an interesting distinction between immigrant, or "voluntary", and native-born or "involuntary", minorities. He argues that what distinguishes (the more academically successful) voluntary minorities from (the less successful) involuntary minorities is neither genetic nor cultural environmental variables. Rather, the overriding factor is each group's perception of their status and place in society, which affects their perceptions of the value of education. A similar argument has been put forward to explain the low level of education and literacy among minority Francophones relative to Anglophones in Canada. For example, Wagner (1991, cited in Cummins, 2000) makes a distinction between two forms of illiteracy: illiteracy of oppression and illiteracy of resistance. In the latter, the minority groups (wishing to protect their language and culture), reject the kind of education that is provided by the dominant group. This resistance is a conduit to self-preservation. In contrast, illiteracy of oppression is the result of institutional processes that promote cultural assimilation with its resulting negative effects on identity.

Despite social obstacles, immigrants to countries such as the United States and Canada generally have a positive attitude towards their new country, and see the potential for better life chances in their adopted country as greater than that in their homelands. Thus, whatever problems they encounter are often perceived as temporary and surmountable through education and persistent hard work. On the flip side of the coin, involuntary minorities such as African Americans, Native Americans, and Canada's First Nations peoples, have no such recourse because their identities have been shaped within the context of a coercive and exploitative relationship with the dominant group. As Ogbu (1992: 8) puts it, "the more academically successful minorities [differ] from the less academically successful minorities in the type of cultural model that guides them. That is, in the type of understanding they have of the workings of the larger society and of their place as minorities in that working order".

There is some research evidence that immigrant minority students tend to aspire to lofty educational goals because education is highly valued in their families and communities. In a study of Punjabi Sikhs, Gibson (1987) found home support (parental attitude towards education) a significant factor in the considerable academic success of Punjabi immigrant high school students in Valleyside, California, because

> students are encouraged to excel academically and teased when grades and/or behaviour are poor. Parents remind their offspring that they have made great sacrifices for them and that the parents' lives would have been wasted if their children are not successful . . . Punjabis believe that they have the ability both to improve their lot economically, especially when they are well educated . . . (pp. 269, 271).

Hayes (1992), also reports positive attitudes towards education by a group of Mexican parents who believe in the power of education in improving one's life chances. In this case however, although there was an awareness of the value of education, a positive attitude did not appear to have produced academic success among the student sample. Ghuman (1980) and Ghuman and Wong (1989), in their studies of Punjabi parents and Chinese parents respectively, found that both groups value education very highly, both for education's sake and for the purposes of economic mobility. Similarly, Suarez-Orozco (1991) found that among Central American Hispanics in San Francisco, education is considered "the most significant avenue to status mobility in the new land" (p. 46). A Canadian study, *Youth in Transition Survey* (Statistics Canada, 2004), found that immigrant minority students have very high educational aspirations. According to this study, which examined the differences in the post-secondary aspirations of 15-year-old students, visible minority immigrant students had higher levels of education, reported higher grades, and were more engaged with school than their Canadian-born non-immigrant counterparts. The same study also reported that 79 percent of visible minority immigrant children aspire to acquire at least one university degree, compared with 57 percent of their Canadian-born nonimmigrant peers. In the same vein, 88 percent of visible minority immigrant parents and 59 percent of nonvisible minority immigrant parents respectively, shared the same educational aspirations with their children. Similarly, a study of Chinese parents' perceptions of their children's literacy, learning, and schooling in Canada (Zhang, Ollila and Harvey, 1998), found that parents from outside the mainstream (such as those in the study) have high expectations for their children's education, including a desire for their children to attend university.

If we accept Ogbu's claims and the findings of the studies cited above, then the link between diversity and academic achievement cannot be addressed outside the context of societal power relations. In effect, cultural difference per se may not necessarily lead to academic difficulties if students from culturally diverse backgrounds are treated inclusively, rather than as the "other", which is often the case.

Language Differences and Academic Achievement

Among educators, near-native proficiency in mainstream language (usually the formal language of the school), is often considered a correlate to academic success. As a consequence, there is a tendency towards discouraging students' use of their home languages in favour of the mainstream language. However, there is now sufficient anecdotal and empirical evidence that proves the importance of first language (L1) maintenance in the acquisition of a second language. In particular, researchers believe that substantive intellectual and cultural benefits accrue to minority students when active use of their first language is supported by educators (Corson, 1993, 2001; Cummins 2000, 2001; Ovando, 2001).

In Canada and other parts of the Western world, schools are no longer simply academic environments; they are also social sites where identities and power relations are negotiated and renegotiated with language issues featuring very prominently in the process (Cummins, 2000). Within this contested terrain, difficulties arising from limited proficiency in mainstream language often intersect with social positioning and access to social rewards. Those who have the requisite mainstream language tend to have more access to resources, whether one speaks of education or of other social capital. As Thompson (1991: 18) asserts, "The distribution of linguistic capital is related in specific ways to the distribution of other types of capital (economic capital, cultural capital, etc.) which define the location of the individual within the social space. Hence differences in terms of accent, grammar and vocabulary . . . are indices of the social positions of speakers . . . " Thompson's reference to accents delineates one language-related challenge that minority students face in school (which is not often given the attention it deserves in discussions of language and diversity) — accent-based discrimination.

Accent-based Discrimination

Accents are distinct manners of enunciation that are unique to an individual, group, or community of speakers. Quite often, as Lippi-Green (1997) asserts

> accent serves as the first point of gatekeeping because [people] are forbidden by law and social custom, and perhaps by a prevailing sense of what is morally and ethically right from using race, ethnicity, homeland or economics more directly. [People] have no such compulsions about language. Thus accent becomes a litmus test for exclusion, an excuse to turn away, to refuse to recognize the other . . . Accent discrimination can be found everywhere in our lives. In fact, such behaviour is so commonly accepted, so widely perceived as appropriate that it must be seen as the last back door to discrimination (pp. 64, 73).

A major rationale for accent-based discrimination is the perception that people who speak a dominant language (e.g., English or French), with non-native accents, have difficulties communicating meaning, and therefore are not easily understood. This attitude permeates interpersonal relations in schools (as it does in broader society), and as a result the greater burden of making sense in verbal exchanges is often placed on the party with the accent. Since schools have set notions of the "ideal speaker" of mainstream language, those who do not speak with conversational fluency are usually pathologized, and the chances of their success in school are questioned (as demonstrated in the discussion between the two teachers in the opening vignette in Chapter 3). Ironically, while it is not often consciously perceived as such, communication is a two-way process, with two or more participants subconsciously accepting the responsibility of mutually exchanging verbal or nonverbal cues as the case maybe (Burbules and Bruce, 2000). The "tune-out" that Lippi-Green describes above, accounts for some of the perceived language difficulties that immigrant students (who speak the mainstream language with accents) have in communicating meaning to their listeners. This is especially true for standard speakers who refuse to assume a fair burden of the exchange, even in school settings.

Admittedly, students, whose primary language differs from the formal language of the school sometimes experience difficulty when enunciating certain sounds as a result of mother tongue interference. For example, it is not uncommon to find speakers of academic (or standard) English, who are of Asian or African descent, mispronounce certain letters because their mother tongues have no corresponding sounds. However, even though these difficulties may not in any way hinder their academic progress, they are often treated as if their academic difficulties (where such exist) are directly linked to "imperfections" in speaking the mainstream language. This often results in accent-changing interventions that reinforce prejudicial attitudes and contribute to feelings of disempowerment among language minorities. It is not uncommon to find advertisements posted on notice boards on university campuses across Canada inviting "international students" to enrol in English conversational classes that would help them lose their accents (Dei, 1996). What those who write this kind of notice (who probably have the best of intentions) seem to miss is the fact that accents are integral attributes of a person's identity. Asking people to lose their accents through a deliberate or coercive effort in order to become successful in Canada (or any other country) is in essence asking them to lose a part of who they are. This has obvious socio-psychological implications. First, it is a way of saying to students who speak with accents that the way they (and their speech community) speak is not acceptable, thus taking the issue to the level of the negation of people's identities. Moreover, in time these students begin to internalize the messages of inadequacy, and therefore become unwitting partners in the perpetuation of linguistic hegemony (Egbo, 2001). Second, pathologizing the way such students speak, especially in elementary and secondary schools, may reduce their motivation to learn and precipitate a decision to drop-out of school.

Similar to accent-based discrimination is the issue of dialects — variations in mainstream language that sometimes provide a basis for language discrimination. For example, in Canada and the United States there is a belief that the English dialects spoken by some groups (e.g., First Nations peoples, Canadians of African and West Indian origin, Native Americans, Hawaiian Americans, African Americans, Hispanics, immigrants, and poor European-Americans) are all non-standard varieties that interfere with the acquisition of reading and writing skills and, perhaps, school success (Baron, 1997; Corson, 1995). Such perceptions among educators may lead to unfair assessments, and subsequent placement of dialect minority students in remedial education programs which may do more harm than good. In many ways, the extent to which minority students succeed in school depends on the extent to which their assessors consider them competent in written and oral language. Unfortunately, their inclusion or exclusion from certain programs and classroom activities also depends on such assessments. But, because the judgment of students' literacy skills, and thus their academic achievement, do not always depend on objective criteria (as we would like to think), assessment may provide widespread opportunity for language discrimination in schools (Corson, 1993). For example, as Edwards (1997) argues, teachers tend to react more unfavourably to reading miscues among dialect speakers than among standard speakers. Such attitudes may, in turn, lead to constant corrections that are detrimental because they send "a message to children that reading is concerned with word-for-word accuracy rather than meaning making" (p. 49). In the time-based environment of the classroom, constant interruptions may also reduce the amount of time students spend on reading and on learning in general.

Diversity and Preferred Learning Styles

There are countless studies that show that individuals vary in their approaches to learning. Some people learn visually, others aurally, still others learn experientially. Some prefer structured learning environments while others thrive in less organized environments. Another way of looking at learning styles is through the lens of the theory of multiple intelligences, which was developed by psychologist Howard Gardner. According to this theory, human beings possess several types of intelligence that enable them to solve problems in different contexts. Although Gardner originally proposed the existence of seven separate intelligences, he has since reformulated his theory to develop at least nine types of human intelligences (Gardner, 1999). These are linguistic intelligence, which is the ability to use language effectively (especially beyond everyday usage); musical intelligence, the ability to think in music; and logical/mathematical intelligence, the ability to understand causal links and manipulate numbers and quantities. Others include spatial intelligence, the ability to represent the spatial world in one's mind; naturalist intelligence, the ability to discriminate among living things and a sensitivity to other features of the natural world; and bodily-kinesthetic intelligence, the capacity to use the whole (or different parts) of the body to problem-solve or for certain kinds of production (as in athletics and the performing arts). Gardner's last three intelligences are intra-personal intelligence, or in-depth self knowledge; interpersonal intelligence, the ability to understand others; and finally, existential intelligence, the ability and tendency to ask critical questions about life, death, and what constitutes reality (see Table 1.2). Although not often interpreted as such at first glance, underpinning Gardner's influential theory is recognition of individual differences, which means that students should not be treated the same. In Gardner's own words

> I regard MI theory as a ringing endorsement of three key prepositions: We are not all the same; we do not all have the same kinds of minds (that is, we are not all distinct points on a single bell curve); and education works most effectively if these differences are taken into account rather

TABLE 1.2	Gardner's Multiple Intelligences
Type of Intelligence	**Ability to**
Linguistic	use language effectively, beyond everyday usage
Musical	think in music
Logical/Mathematical	understand causal links and manipulate numbers and quantities
Spatial	represent the spatial world in one's mind
Naturalist	discriminate among living things and a sensitivity to other features of the natural world
Bodily-kinetic	use the whole (or parts) of the body to problem-solve, or for production (as in athletics and the performing arts)
Intra-personal	acquire and consider in-depth self knowledge
Interpersonal	understand others
Existential	ask critical questions about life, death, and what constitutes reality

than denied or ignored. Taking human differences seriously lies at the heart of the MI perspective. At the theoretical level, this means that all individuals cannot be profitably arrayed on a single intellectual dimension. At the practical level, it suggests that *any* uniform educational approach is likely to serve only a small percentage of children optimally (1999, p. 91).

Just as learning styles differ from one individual to another, research has demonstrated that they also vary across cultures, although these differences may be subtle and variable (Parkay et al., 2005). For example, Au and Mason (1981) reported a substantial improvement in reading among a group of students at the Kamehameha Early Education Program (KEEP) in Hawaii when reading was taught in a manner that reflected the Hawaiian communicative style of cooperative story building. Based on their various researches, Ladson-Billings (1994), Dei (1996), and Ramirez (1982, cited in Scott, 2001), suggest that Black and African American students tend to prefer cooperative learning environments more than their White counterparts do. Similarly, Hampton and Roy (2002) in their study designed to identify ways in which university professors can facilitate the success of Canadian First Nations students, found that cooperative learning models are the most effective for engendering academic success among Aboriginal students.

Similarly, Grossman (1995) argues that there are significant ethnic differences in the extent to which students develop dependent or independent attitudes as a consequence of home socialization. He states that when compared to European American students, students from non-European American backgrounds (e.g. Hispanics, Filipino Americans, Native Americans, and South Asian Americans), are more likely to seek their teachers' direction and feedback.

In another study, May (1994) reports a positive learning environment, in a multiethnic and multilingual inner city school (Richmond Road) in New Zealand, through the revolutionary leadership of an educator who initiated a meaningful pluralistic classroom organizational structure. Through a complex system of vertical groupings, culturally inclusive curricula, and school/community partnerships, the school was able to accommodate the language and academic needs of all stakeholders.

La Escuela Inter-Americana in Chicago is another example of a school that has successfully incorporated cultural congruency into classroom activities (and education more generally), through the collaborative efforts of members of the community, educators, and students' families. According to a report by the National Coalition of Advocates for Students (NCAS, 1994), by adopting a philosophy of providing integrated education in a multicultural and bilingual setting (English and Spanish), this school has been successfully preparing students for harmonious existence in a culturally and linguistically diverse society.

Overall, the evidence seems to point to a preference for cooperative learning among nondominant group students. It should be noted, however, that learning-styles research has faced intense criticism. Woolfolk (1995) summarizes these arguments. First, the validity of some of the research has been called into question. Second, it may be arguably dangerous (e.g., racist and sexist) to identify learning styles and preferences on the basis of race and ethnicity. Indeed, it cannot be emphasized enough that learning styles are not racially or ethnically produced. Rather, they are culturally produced. The third point follows from the second. It should not be assumed that every member of a culture will learn best within one style since, as has already been established, individuals differ considerably even if they share a similar culture. One way of resolving this problem is to see learning style in terms of an individual attribute that is learned within a cultural context. The assumption that all members of a group have a preference for similar learning styles borders on stereotyping, which as argued earlier can produce very harmful consequences for those at the receiving end.

These criticisms not withstanding, adapting instructional strategies to the different learning styles of students has been found to be a useful means of optimizing academic success among diverse learners. In fact, in contexts of student diversity, this argument is one of the premises on which progressive theorists build their case for culturally relevant curricula and pedagogy. A similar argument is also often advanced by feminist scholars and activists in support of girl-friendly educational practices since, as the argument goes, schools reflect and reproduce male norms, values, and ways of viewing the world. Establishing learning contexts that are congruent with both boys' and girls' (and subsequently men's and women's) ways of knowing is also an important aspect of any attempt at effectively dealing with diversity in schools.

Gender-Based Differences

Gender, which is a socially constructed category based on sex or biological distinctions between men and women (Coates, 2004; Chancer and Watkins, 2006), is a significant marker of difference among individuals. Very early in life, children develop gender schemas — knowledge about what it means to be a male or female—that help them to mentally organize society's traditional expectations of them (Egbo, 2006). However, while men and women are physiologically different, research on the biological links between gender and achievement is inconclusive. In general, the evidence shows that while boys and girls achieve equally in mathematics and science during the early years of schooling, by the time they arrive in high school, boys have started to outperform girls in these areas. Girls on the other hand, appear to have a degree of superiority in language-related competencies.

It is, however, not clear whether innate qualities, socialization, or a combination of both, account for these differences (Egbo, 2006; Corson, 1993). It is no wonder then, that emerging knowledge on the link between gender and academic achievement cautions against the binary thinking that results in the over-simplification of a relationship that is far from being straightforward. To add to the confusion, the bulk of the research, including international assessments conducted by the Organization for Economic Cooperation and Development (OECD) through its Programme for International Student Assessment (PISA), suggests that many variables (such as modes of socialization, parental influence, sex-role stereotyping, individual motivation, and the school environment) contribute to any differential academic outcomes for boys and girls. Moreover, the argument that men and women have differentiated discursive norms, which in turn influence linguistic behaviour and practice both in and out of school, may have some significant implications for gender-based differences in schooling outcomes.

With particular reference to schools, the research findings tend to converge around several issues, the most salient being that pedagogical and classroom practices tend to silence girls. For example, for decades researchers have argued that prevalent classroom discourse, with teachers acting as enablers, tends to exclude girls, while boys tend to dominate classroom talk and initiate dialogue (Spender, 1982; Sadker and Sadker, 1986). However, during the last several decades, the language of education (and the classroom in particular) has taken an inclusive turn. This change has also shifted, to some degree, the language of texts and textbooks, which are now less stereotyped and paternalistic and more nuanced and neutral. Nevertheless, some writers have argued that the linguistic neutrality that now pervades educational texts simply masks the continued dominance of male norms under the pretext of egalitarian educational discourse (Bjerrum-Nielsen and Davies, 1997).

Besides biased language practices, a number of classroom observers have catalogued gender bias in the ways teachers interact with students. Boys appear to have more interactions with teachers, are called upon more often, and generally have more contact time with teachers. Teachers are also said to be more favourably disposed to boys' participation in class (Sadker, 2002; Shakeshaft, 1986; Sadker and Sadker, 1986). Taken together, these factors provide better outcome-oriented learning environments for boys.

But, not everyone agrees with the above assessment. There are views that suggest that the disproportionate attention that boys receive in class may be the result of teachers' frequently reprimanding their misbehaviour rather than deliberate discrimination against girls (Sunderland, 2000). Moreover, studies of classroom social interactions have shown that both genders sometimes behave in unpredictable ways. For example, based on the evidence from an **ethnographic study** of her own classroom, Gallas (1998) concludes that girls sometimes cross gender borders, put up resistance, and generally act in unpredictable ways. She also contends that while stereotypes may exist, heterogeneity may be more reflective of classroom interaction than is normally assumed. Also noteworthy are recent developments on the gender and achievement discourse. Emerging data suggest that girls are now catching up with, or doing better than boys in achievement levels as a result of long-standing advocacy for girl-friendly educational policies and practices (Murphy and Invinson, 2004). Indeed, the findings of a recent study conducted by the United States Department of Education (Freeman, 2004) concluded that

> [I]n elementary and secondary school and in college, females are now doing as well as or better than males on many indicators of academic achievement and educational attainment, and . . . large gaps that once existed between males and females have been eliminated in most cases and have significantly decreased in other cases. [However], women are still underrepresented in some fields of study . . . (p.1).

These new developments provide additional support to the social influences theory of the link between gender and academic achievement. In fact, any suggestion to the contrary remains extremely controversial. For example, in January 2005, the former president of Harvard University, Lawrence H. Summers, unleashed a firestorm of controversy when he suggested (at a conference on women and minorities in the science and engineering workforce) that males' apparent superior performance in the sciences and mathematics is the result of natural apititude (*Boston Globe*, January 17).

However, as with the case of the link between race-ethnicity and academic achievement, there is no conclusive evidence that shows that differences in cognitive abilities account for disparities between boys, and girls, academic achievement. Any gender-related differences that might affect how boys and girls learn, appear to be linked to patterns of socialization, which are context-dependent and therefore changeable. Indeed, seeing things this way (that school-based interventions can make a difference, as opposed to the natural aptitude padigm) should enable educational systems to develop and adopt policies and practical strategies for not only responding to gender inequalities but also to diversity in schools, more generally.

Summary

The purpose of this chapter was to establish a foundation and a theoretical base for analyzing and understanding the issues surrounding teaching for diversity in Canadian schools. Consequently, the chapter examined different views of the school as a social institution. Two broad paradigms, the consensus and interrogative perspectives, which subsume other views, were examined. In addition to exploring how schools contribute to sustaining the status quo in society, some commonly held views about the relationship between diversity and academic achievement were discussed. There seems to be no empirical evidence that shows that differences in academic achievement between culturally and racially diverse students and those from dominant backgrounds are attributable in any significant way to innate properties. Rather, a myriad of structural and contextual variables account for differential school achievement between various groups of students as well as that between boys and girls. Cognizant that there is as much intra-group diversity as there are intergroup differences, the chapter also examined the implications of learning styles for meeting the needs of all students, especially those from diverse backgrounds. Given that ethnocultural diversity is a stable Canadian reality, the chapter also examined the interactions between race, diversity, and education, as well as the concept of social justice (which should be the end result of transformative praxis).

Key Terms

Afrocentric schools

Cultural capital

Cultural habitus

Ethnographic study

Liberal-democratic
   ideology

Prejudice

Social reproduction

Universal truths

Critical pedagogy

Cultural deprivation
   theory

Hegemony

Life chances

Mutual resistance

Racism

Stereotyping

Visible minorities

Critical theory

Cultural diversity

Emancipatory possibilities

Hidden curriculum

Meritocracy

Praxis

Social justice

Structural functionalism

Xenophobia

Questions to Guide Reflective Practice

1. Before reading this chapter, what was your understanding of diversity?

2. What is the link between culture and diversity?

3. How are theory and practice connected?

4. What are your views on the interconnections between (a) culture and academic achievement, (b) language and academic achievement, and (c) gender and academic achievement?

5. Map out your own cultural identity profile. How does your cultural identity affect how you relate to people who are different from you?

6. In your opinion, is racism a pervasive problem in Canada?

7. What is your understanding of the concept of social justice? Should the distribution of social rewards be based on the principles of "equality" or "equity"?

Case Study Analysis: Chapter Opening Vignette

1. Analyze Gina's perception of herself as "colour blind". How do you treat people that are different from you?

2. Why do you think Gina is experiencing difficulties in managing her culturally diverse class? What would you do differently?

3. Is Gina's problem a case of self-fulfilling prophesy?

4. Should Gina have reported the incident between the two students to the school administration?

5. Assume that you are Gina's mentor. Develop strategies to help her meet the challenges of managing diversity in her classroom.

Test Your Knowledge

1. Studies have shown that Canadians have a certain attitude towards "race" and related issues. Research and identify these attitudes. What is the general attitude of Canadians towards those who are different from themselves?

2. Develop a hypothetical policy for achieving social justice in Canadian society. Distinguish between the concept of "equity" and "equality".

3. In this chapter, Ogbu (1987, 1992) talks about "voluntary" and "involuntary" minorities. Does Canada have involuntary minorities? Who are they and what is their status?

4. According to the United Nations, there are more than two races in the world, research and identify these races.

5. Racial minorities are often referred to as "ethnics". Is this an accurate description? Is there anyone who does not have a race, culture, or ethnicity? Research and outline the perspectives of various writers and theorists on this issue.

6. Do the school boards in your province include the principles of social justice in their guiding philosophy?

For Further Reading

Chancer, L., and Watkins, B. (2006). *Gender, Race and Class*. Malden: Blackwell Publishers.

Cook, V. (Ed.) (2003). *The Effects of the Second Language on the First*. Clevedon: Multilingual Matters.

Delpit, L. (2006). *Other People's Children: Cultural Conflict in the Classroom*. New York: The New Press.

Essed, P. (1991). *Understanding Everyday Racism: An Interdisciplinary Theory*. Newbury Park: Sage Publications.

Freire, P. (1970). *Pedagogy of the Oppressed*. New York: Herder & Herder.

Gardner, H. (1999). *Intelligence Reframed*. New York: Basic Books.

Giroux, H. (1983). *Theory and Resistance in Education. A Pedagogy for the Opposition*. South Hadley: Bergin & Garvey.

Henry, F. and Tator, C. (2006). *The Color of Democracy: Racism in Canadian Society*. Toronto: Thomson/Nelson.

Isajiw, W. (1999). *Understanding Diversity: Ethnicity and Race in the Canadian Context*. Toronto: Thompson Educational Publishing.

Kohli, W. (2005). What is Social Justice Education. In W. Hare and J. P. Portelli (Eds.), *Key Questions for Educators* (pp. 98–100). Halifax: Edphil Books.

Lippi-Green, R. (1997). *English with an Accent: Language, Ideology and Discrimination in the United States*. London: Routledge.

McIntosh, P. (1990). White Privilege: Unpacking the Invisible Knapsack. *Independent School*, Winter: 31–36.

McLaren, P. (2007). *Life in Schools: An Introduction to Critical Pedagogy in the Foundations of Education*, 5th Edition. Boston: Pearson Education.

Peters, M., Lankshear, C., and Olssen, M. (Eds.). (2003). *Critical Theory and the Human Condition*. New York: Peter Lang.

The Jossey-Bass *Reader on Gender in Education* (2002). San Francisco A: Jossey-Bass Vincent, C. (2003) (Ed.) *Social justice, Education and Identity*. London: RoutledgeFalmer.

Websites of Interest

www.socialjustice.org/ Centre for Social Justices

www.cfc-fcc.ca/socialjustice/index.cfm Community Foundations of Canada

www.oise.utoronto.ca/research/cld/diversity.htm Centre for Leadership and Diversity

www.cea-ace.ca/foo.cfm?subsection=edu&page=map Canadian Education Association – Multiculturalism and Diversity

www.crr.ca/ Canadian Race Relations Foundations

3 Lesson Planning: Microteaching, The Lesson Plan, and Lesson Preparation

It is the supreme art of the teacher to awaken joy in creative expression and knowledge. (Albert Einstein)

Being an educated person means being guided by values and beliefs and connecting lessons of the classroom to the realities of life. (Boyer, 1995, p. 16)

The Teacher Competence Profile criteria on lesson and unit planning can be found at the top of page 53. The key ideas are addressed in this chapter.

Planning Approaches

Teachers are accountable for lesson, unit, and yearly planning to district, state, and national standards, curriculum guides, and expectations of students, administrators, and parents. They think about how to attain the goals of education and student development.

Although effective teachers do not begin a course, unit, or lesson without careful planning, they realize that plans are not always followed to the letter. Changes occur because of emerging interests and needs. Good plans include alternative activities. Effective teachers are flexible and revise plans to help students achieve intended outcomes. They know subject matter, have a bank of instructional methods, and draw on a storehouse of activities. Content, and the mix of experiences, need to be carefully selected, well organized, and sequenced. They should motivate students and match their needs. Planning requires reflection and must be continuous.

OBJECTIVES

You will be able to:

1. Define each of the elements of a lesson and construct a simple lesson plan.
2. Describe the different kinds of set and closure.
3. Define *professional target* and plan a way of achieving a target.
4. Describe direct instruction and constructivist lesson models.
5. List the advantages of preparing instructional objectives and distinguish among the different kinds of objectives.
6. Prepare lessons that contain well-written and appropriate objectives.
7. Present a microteaching or classroom lesson with an effective set, development, and closure.
8. Describe the five kinds of stimulus variation presented in this chapter.
9. Teach a microlesson or school lesson with the professional target of stimulus variation.
10. Present the rationale for planning units, distinguish among the kinds of units presented in this chapter, and describe the elements common to most teaching unit structures.
11. Describe the teaching unit planning model and planning sequence presented in this chapter.
12. Prepare an effective concept map.
13. Prepare a practical unit plan.

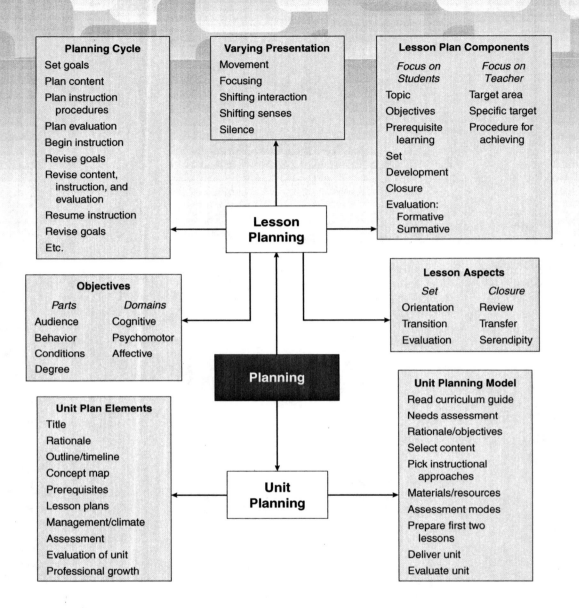

Planning Cycle

Set goals

Plan content

Plan instruction
   procedures

Plan evaluation

Begin instruction

Revise goals

Revise content,
   instruction, and
   evaluation

Resume instruction

Revise goals

Etc.

Varying Presentation

Movement

Focusing

Shifting interaction

Shifting senses

Silence

Lesson Plan Components

Focus on Students	*Focus on Teacher*
Topic	Target area
Objectives	Specific target
Prerequisite learning	Procedure for achieving
Set	
Development	
Closure	
Evaluation: Formative Summative	

Lesson Planning

Objectives

Parts	*Domains*
Audience	Cognitive
Behavior	Psychomotor
Conditions	Affective
Degree	

Lesson Aspects

Set	*Closure*
Orientation	Review
Transition	Transfer
Evaluation	Serendipity

Planning

Unit Plan Elements

Title

Rationale

Outline/timeline

Concept map

Prerequisites

Lesson plans

Management/climate

Assessment

Evaluation of unit

Professional growth

Unit Planning

Unit Planning Model

Read curriculum guide

Needs assessment

Rationale/objectives

Select content

Pick instructional
   approaches

Materials/resources

Assessment modes

Prepare first two
   lessons

Deliver unit

Evaluate unit

There are three interrelated levels of planning: (1) a year or semester course; (2) a sequence of instructional units or themes (a few days to two or three weeks); and (3) a series of lessons within a unit, from about twenty minutes to two or three classes.

Planning Phases

Planning and decision making usually occur during three phases: before, during, and after instruction.

During the *first phase* (preinstruction), teachers chose the content to be studied and a variety of teaching strategies, methods, and student activities. They think about the content, how rapidly to cover it, the time allocated to each topic, classroom management

TCP—LESSON AND UNIT PLANNING

Integrates skills common to all subjects and adapts curriculum to individual needs

In planning units and lessons, incorporates the skills common to all subjects; adapts curriculum plans to individual needs.

Unaware of common essential skills; does not incorporate skills common to all subjects; does not adapt curriculum plans to individual needs.

Plans varied learner-centered activities

Plans enable students to be actively involved in a broad range of motivating activities congruent with objectives and evaluation; development level and student needs and interests recognized; activities often learner selected; aware of the need to adapt to individual and group needs.

Prescriptive activities randomly chosen and sequenced or inappropriate to developmental level and student needs and interests; often incongruent with objectives and evaluation; activities always teacher selected; unaware of the need to adapt to individual and group needs.

Outlines long-range plans to guide student development

Logically sequenced; variety in presentation and student activities; addresses student readiness; plans adaptable to a variety of student needs; provides for evaluation; plans available prior to teaching.

Generally fails to plan units or drafts or series of lessons with little coherence, variety or attention to student needs; plans not available in advance.

Plans interdisciplinary thematic units

Plans units that focus on a specific theme/problem/issue, that integrate several areas; themes are realistic, relating to student interests and abilities.

Units always subject area specific.

Involves learners in the planning process

Learners are involved in planning units.

Students are never consulted or involved in unit planning.

Includes classroom management in plans

Unit plans contain detailed plans for classroom management.

Unit plans do not incorporate classroom management.

expectations, routines, and procedures. A key consideration is how to set a positive climate for learning and how to motivate while having high but achievable expectations.

In the *second phase* (the developmental or interactive), teachers make instructional decisions. They think about whether presentations and student activities are effective, how they can help students, whether transitions from one part of a lesson to another or from one lesson to another are smooth, and if pacing is appropriate. They are aware of classroom climate and the suitability of routines and procedures. Formative evaluation (on the progress students are making) is occurring continuously, and thoughts are given to summative evaluation.

In the *third phase* (postinstructional), summative tests or other measures are given and marks assigned, recorded, and reported. Testing may be through paper-and-pencil examinations, papers, projects, or portfolios (a combination technique). Tests provide feedback and an opportunity for teaching. Evaluation should inform students how they are doing—what they know well and what they still need to master. Follow-up is critical. Conscientious teachers provide guidance so students will be successful with work that was initially difficult and help turn deferred successes into successes. Importantly, *it is not just students who are being evaluated.* The effectiveness of the teacher's instruction and the appropriateness of evaluative measures also should be examined. The teacher needs to reflect on what went well during the teaching and learning process, what should be modified, and how it should be modified.

Linear and Nonlinear Approaches

Much research has been done on teacher planning. The traditional view is that the process is *rational-linear.* This begins by establishing goals and objectives, moves to planning instructional actions to promote achievement of objectives, and concludes with measurement of achievement. However, instructional planning is often nonlinear and teachers may, for good reason, deviate from plans. It is unrealistic to believe that a unit plan should consist of carefully preplanned lessons and be closely followed. The first lesson or two can be planned but may or may not be executed exactly as planned. It is more realistic to gather a selection of introductory, developmental, and culminating activities from which to choose in the light of what occurs from day to day. Of course, other activities may be added. Arends (2004, p. 99) claims the nonlinear approach is how many experienced teachers approach some of the aspects of planning.

As can be seen, there are four major sources for planning: (1) *goals and objectives* (examples of sources: department of education, school districts, and texts); (2) *subject matter* (i.e., knowledge of content; content-specific information, concepts, generalizations, skills, and processes; ordering of content for instruction); (3) *knowledge of teaching models, strategies, methods, and skills* (i.e., selection and use of these based on their effect on motivation, classroom management, and factors such as student motivation, at-task orientation, and rate of success); and (4) *learner characteristics and differences* (i.e., aptitude, past achievement, personality [anxiety, motivation, and self-concept], home life, and peer influences).

The Backward Design Approach

Wiggins and McTighe (1998) developed an approach called *backward design.* This, they note, is close to the way experienced teachers often plan. The backward design approach has three stages (pp. 9–13).

Stage 1. *Identify desired results.* What should students know, understand, and be able to do?

- Consider goals, examine established content standards (national, state, and district), and review curricular expectations.
- Make content choices. What is of enduring understanding (the big ideas and important understandings)? What is important to know and do (the facts, concepts, principles, and skills needed for students to accomplish key performances)? What is worth being familiar with? What do we want students to hear, read, view, research, and otherwise encounter?

Stage 2. *Determine acceptable evidence.* How will you know students have achieved the desired results and met standards? What will be accepted as evidence of student understanding and proficiency?

- Think like an assessor before designing units or lessons.
- Consider how you will determine whether students have attained the desired understandings.
- Consider the range of assessment methods to use.

Stage 3. *Plan learning experiences and instruction.* With clearly identified results (enduring understandings) and appropriate evidence of understanding in mind, educators can plan instructional activities.

- What activities will equip students with the needed knowledge and skills?
- What needs to be taught and coached? How should it be taught in the light of performance goals?
- What materials and resources are best suited to accomplish these goals?
- Is the overall design coherent and effective?

The Standards Movement

Many content areas now have standards that are helpful in planning content, strategies, and materials. Because most have web sites, unit planners can readily examine what subject councils and associations consider important.

"The standards address what should be taught, and the performance assessment indicates the level of performance that students should demonstrate. The goal of these new standards is to benchmark or match these assessments to those of other countries whose students achieve highly on international assessments" (Burden & Byrd, 2003, p. 30). What is essential can change over time and according to world events. They reflect national values, which in our postmodern society are subject to change. Learner and teacher expectations descriptors in this text are an excellent source of planning ideas.

- *Learner expectations.* The realities of global interdependence require learners to understand the increasingly important and diverse global connections among world societies. Analysis of tensions between national interests and global priorities contributes to the development of possible solutions to persistent and emerging global issues in many fields: health care, economic development, environmental quality, universal human rights, and others. Analyzing patterns and relationships within and among world cultures, such as economic competition and interdependence, age-old ethnic enmities, political and military alliances, and others, helps learners examine policy alternatives that have both national and global implications.

- *Teacher expectations.* Teachers of social studies at all school levels should provide developmentally appropriate experiences as they guide learners in the study of global connections and interdependence. They should guide learner analysis of the relationships and tensions between national sovereignty and global interests in such matters as territorial disputes, economic development, nuclear and other weapons deployment, use of natural resources, and human rights concerns.

WHAT DO CRITICS OF STANDARDS HAVE TO SAY?   Critics of standards tend to fall into three camps: one camp worries that standards force teachers to "teach to tests" and stress rote learning, not creative and individualized education. Another group worries that if standards are set too high, low achievers (particularly in disadvantaged communities) will become discouraged and drop out; if standards are too low, high achievers will not be challenged. The third group thinks standards should be set locally, not federally or by the state.

Those who object to "teaching to tests" say that this measures test-taking ability, not real-life skills, and is biased against those from disadvantaged backgrounds; it stresses memorization rather than creative thinking. Although these concerns do fit some standardized tests used as benchmarks, it should be noted that standards-based teaching does not rely only, or even primarily, on these kinds of tests. Achievement of standards can also be measured through writing skill or other assignments.

Fears about the levels of standards are common. For example, Richard Rothstein (1999) argued that holding schools with largely poor populations to the same standards as suburban schools penalizes students in disadvantaged districts for factors they cannot control and causes students in suburban schools to be insufficiently challenged. Also, holding students to standards—especially where promotion is the issue—will increase dropouts, especially in schools with heavy minority populations.

Planning Variables

Content

Content is more than facts, information, and motor skills. It includes concepts and generalizations, and interpersonal and social skills. It involves creative and critical thinking, problem solving, decision-making capability, attitudes, appreciations, and values. Content (and therefore objectives) can be declarative, procedural, or conditional and can be product or process. It can be cognitive, psychomotor, or affective.

Declarative content and objectives include the facts, concepts, or generalizations that students are to learn. *Procedural content and objectives* include the skills or processes—cognitive, affective, or psychomotor—that students are to learn and be able to do. *Conditional content and objectives* refer to the conditions and contexts associated with knowledge—knowing where, why, and when to apply declarative and procedural content. *Product objectives* ask that students acquire the knowledge, get the right answers, or acquire facts or information (what, where, or when); and *process objectives* ask students to acquire the processes of getting knowledge or knowing how to get the right answers or appropriate facts or information (how or why).

Cognitive objectives refer to information acquisition, comprehension, analysis, synthesis, and evaluation capability; *psychomotor objectives* refer to the manipulation and use of objects or the body; and *affective objectives* consider such things as attitudes, values, and emotions.

Objectives

IMPORTANCE OF CLEAR OBJECTIVES.   You, as the teacher, must have a clear idea of what students should know or be able to do as a result of a lesson, unit, or course. Student achievement can be improved if instruction is directed toward specific outcomes and if students know what is expected without sacrificing flexibility in the light of emerging contextual needs.

Although writing good objectives is hard work, the advantages are that (1) instruction is more focused; (2) learning is more efficient; (3) evaluation is fairer; and (4) students are better at evaluating themselves. To prepare good objectives, think about what the outcomes should be in keeping with the broad objectives of the unit and course under study. Consider the instructional procedures that can best help students achieve expected outcomes, and the kinds of evaluation suitable to see whether or not the hoped-for outcomes have been attained by students. Congruence is needed:

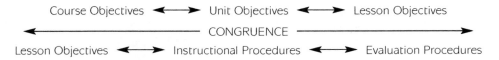

Objectives should specify the content students are to learn and the circumstances under which they are to show their learning. It is often more important to know how to do something than to get the right answer. Acquiring independent learning skills is also critical.

Initial planning involves setting goals and objectives, deciding on instructional approaches and activities, and devising evaluation congruent with objectives. Planning provides direction, should be continuous with preinstructional, during instruction, and postinstructional phases, and include the elements illustrated in Figure 3.1.

Professional teachers begin with aims or goals that may be adapted from a curriculum guide and from the school's statement of goals. Content and instructional approaches and student activities and evaluation schema are selected. How specific this planning is, and the sequence in which it occurs, varies by individual teacher and the school and district. However, effective teachers know, "Teachers who fail to plan, plan to fail."

If you want to be an effective professional, plan well ahead and think of adaptations that can be applied if needed. Many things can cause plans to change. A few examples are:

- You give a pretest and discover students either are more advanced than anticipated or do not possess the needed knowledge or skills.
- The time budgeted for a topic is either too short or too long.
- An activity you planned does not secure or hold student interest.
- A serendipitous happening provides a teachable opportunity to treat a topic out of the order planned.
- A golden, unanticipated opportunity presents itself (e.g., a television program is announced that is ideal for your language arts class; a surprise call for an election fits neatly into your social studies course).
- A resource you planned to use is no longer available or arrives too late. What resources are available? What adaptations can be made?

WRITING OBJECTIVES.   When students understand what they are to learn, they are more likely to have successful learning experiences. What are students to accomplish? What should students know, be able to do, or be like through their learning experiences? The success of programs, courses, units, or lessons depends heavily on how well thought out this is.

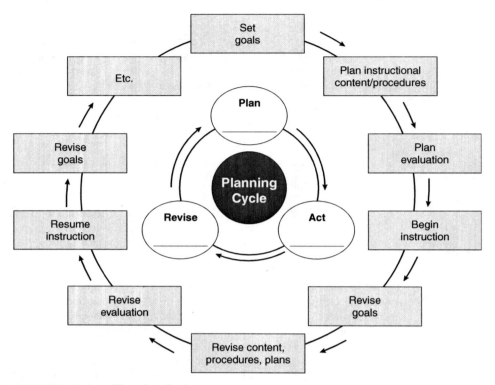

FIGURE 3.1   *Planning Cycle*

Teaching and evaluation of student progress is effective when there are clear and observable objectives that may be modified in the light of classroom events and student needs.

Well-thought-out objectives describe behavior you can observe. Compare the following. The first examples are vague and the second examples are clear.

Vague: Students will understand why Hamlet was called the melancholy Dane.
Clear: By referring to excerpts from *Hamlet,* students will be able to write a brief paper explaining why Hamlet has been called the melancholy Dane.

Vague: Students will be good at doing basketball set shots.
Clear: Each student will be able to sink at least seven out of ten set shots.

PREPARING LESSON OBJECTIVES.   Course or unit objectives are too general for specific lessons. Lesson objectives need to specify what learners are to know, be able to do, or value about what was learned. These express expected learner behavior. Objectives do *not,* for instance, include listening to a lecture, taking part in a discussion, or watching a film or demonstration—these are *activities* that may lead to the achievement of objectives.

When you prepare objectives, ask yourself, "How can students show me what they know or can do?" Objectives call for evidence of one of three things: (1) the *information* (concepts or generalizations) you want students to know or use; (2) the *skill or process* you want students to perform or display; or (3) the *value or feeling* you want students to experience.

ACTIVITIES VERSUS OBJECTIVES. *Activities* are the learning experiences in which students participate to achieve objectives. *Objectives* describe the knowledge, skills, or attitudes students should display as a result of participating in a lesson. That is, activities are the *means* to achieve objectives, whereas objectives are the *ends*. Try the following exercise.

> *Activity:* Students will view a filmstrip about the significance of nonverbal communication in a Native American culture.
>
> *Objective:* After viewing a filmstrip on the use of nonverbal communication by Northern Cree people, each student will be able to list five ways in which Canadian Northern Cree people may use nonverbal signals.

Which of the following are parts of good objectives that are activities?

1. Students will solve square-root problems.
2. Students will read Chapter 9 in the text.
3. Students will write a good business letter.
4. Students will take a field trip to the museum.
5. Students will practice cutting and pasting on computers.
6. Students will discuss the causes of pollution.
7. Students will name three advantages and three disadvantages of "free trade."

Items 1, 3, and 7 are parts of good objectives.

DESCRIBING STUDENT PERFORMANCE. Objectives specify the performance expected of students because of the lesson. Based on the objective, you should easily be able to evaluate the achievement or nonachievement of the objective. The key to describing performance is to use specific, observable verbs. The verbs should be active, not vague.

> *Vague (broad) verbs:* understand, know, comprehend, learn, remember, evaluate, feel, enjoy, value, and appreciate.
>
> *Action (specific) verbs:* list, name, select, write, draw, outline, match, pronounce, solve, and form.

Which of the following are good objectives because they include good verbs and observable student performance?

1. Students will list the countries through which the Danube River flows.
2. Students will appreciate the painting, *Mona Lisa.*
3. Students will be able to add two-digit numbers.
4. Students will match the names and pictures of Canadian animals.
5. Students will know the difference between the bass and treble clefs.
6. Students will remember what causes lightning.

Items 1, 3, and 4 are observable.

CONDITIONS OF PERFORMANCE.   Not only should the behavior expected be clear, the *conditions* under which it is to appear also should be clear and specific. Ask yourself, "Under what circumstances is the behavior to be performed?" Conditions often include materials or information students will be given. A common way to express conditions is to use the term "given."

> *Conditions included:* Given a three-page essay, students will be able to underline each simile and circle each metaphor.
> *Conditions absent:* Students will recognize the difference between similes and metaphors.

Which of the following identify the conditions (or givens)?

1. Students will know how to prepare a Caesar salad.
2. Given advertising slogans, students will be able to name the product being advertised.
3. Students will identify different figures of speech that writers can use.
4. Students will appreciate the complexities of the rules of baseball.
5. As they prepare the reference page of a manuscript provided, students will follow the rules in the APA style manual.
6. Students will underline each adjective in the list of words provided.

Conditions are identified in items 2, 5 and 6.

Following the "B, C, D's" will help you write good objectives. "B" is the *behavior* expected of students as they provide evidence of what they have learned—specific verbs are needed. "C" is the *conditions* (or "givens") under which the student behavior is to occur. "D" is the *degree* to which students are expected to achieve what they have been studying— it is an estimate of how well students will do or how many of the class will be able to do something. Consider the following.

1. *Behavior:*   Students will hit a golf ball into an area five yards in diameter,
   Conditions: on the practice range, using a nine-iron and the Vardon overlapping grip,
   Degree: seven out of ten times.
2. *Behavior:*   Students will name the pieces used to play chess,
   Conditions: when shown a diagram of a chessboard containing randomly arranged pieces,
   Degree: in ten minutes or less; 28 of 30 students will correctly identify all the pieces.
3. *Behavior:*   Students will be able to circle the capital cities of European countries,
   Conditions: when shown an outline map of Europe,
   Degree: and correctly identify at least 8 capital cities.
4. *Behavior:*   Students will write a paper explaining factors that led to the fall of the Third Reich,

Conditions: after viewing a sixty-minute film on PBS;
Degree: 25 of the 30 members of the class will satisfactorily describe at least four factors.

TAXONOMIES AND OBJECTIVES.   Objectives express educational intentions. The taxonomy approach developed by Benjamin Bloom and his colleagues (1956) has stood the test of time and is the most common. Bloom et al. classified learning intentions into three domains: *cognitive, psychomotor,* and *affective.* Each domain has levels of learning in a hierarchy from simple to complex. When you become aware that various levels exist, you will be sensitive to where learners are in their development. Understanding taxonomies helps you to adjust learning experiences to match learner needs.

Although you can write objectives for behaviors that are cognitive, affective, and psychomotor, in real life, behaviors from each domain often occur simultaneously. Considering each aspect separately sharpens your awareness of student progress and the experiences learners need.

It is not our purpose here to provide a detailed description of each taxonomy of Bloom et al. (1956), Krathwohl, Bloom, and Masia (1964), and Harlow (1972). You will be given information and practice with the cognitive taxonomy and information about the affective and psychomotor taxonomies. More information about the taxonomies is provided later. It is likely you will learn more about the other two elsewhere in your teacher education program.

The Cognitive Domain (Bloom et al., 1956).   Ms. Boyko teaches a unit on physical geology to her grade 7 students. Today's lesson is "rock families." She asks students the following:

- What are the names of the two main classifications of silicates?
- Can you think of an example of an igneous rock?
- What is one major difference between sedimentary rocks and metamorphic rocks?
- Look at samples of sedimentary rocks. What do they all have in common?
- What is a way we can make economic use of the rocks in this area?
- Can you think of new ways in which we could make use of the rocks in this area?
- What do you think of the practice of digging out and selling most of the rocks in an area?

Ms. Boyko's questions range from simple recall to requiring considerable understanding and thought. Bloom's cognitive taxonomy categorizes learning into six levels (below). Into which level do you think each of her questions fits?

BLOOM'S COGNITIVE TAXONOMY

Knowledge   Recalling information in the way it was presented, but not necessarily understanding it (i.e., recalling, recognizing, memorizing).

To learn and remember information (how many, when, who, where, locate, tell, name, list, point to, repeat).

continued

BLOOM'S COGNITIVE TAXONOMY *(continued)*

Comprehension:	Understanding, or ability to state content in your words, not necessarily applying or relating it to something else (i.e., describing, give an example, interpreting, why, explain, summarize). To understand information (reword, define, discuss, paraphrase, explain, give an example).
Application	Applying information to a new situation, or using a general concept to solve a problem (i.e., problem solving). To use information (try, employ, relate, put into action, follow steps).
Analysis	Breaking down, or subdividing, a situation into its parts (i.e., finding structure, identifying motives, discovering relationships). To take information apart or discover the parts or organization (dissect, test for, examine, inspect, "what makes it tick").
Synthesis	Coming up with something new, or organizing something in a new way (i.e., creating, inventing, composing, designing). *Note:* It need not be "new to humankind"; it may just be new to the learner. To create new ideas or things; doing something new with the information (build, make, create, formulate, develop, invent).
Evaluation	Judging using criteria, using a rationale or standards that decide the value of applying materials or methods (i.e., judging, resolving conflicts, reasoned choosing among alternatives). Based on criteria, making judgments about information (judge, appraise, assess, decide, rate, rank, evaluate).

The cognitive domain is the domain that is best known by teachers. It places ability in the sequence: knowledge, comprehension, application, analysis, synthesis, and evaluation. Though it is not rigidly followed, many teachers believe the cognitive taxonomy helps ensure that learning progresses well beyond memory work into the domain's higher levels, which are compatible with constructivist approaches to teaching and learning. Jill Slack (2002) notes that Bloom's taxonomy can be used to improve students' thinking and comprehension.

During the 1990s, Lorin Anderson (a former student of Benjamin Bloom) and a team reworked the cognitive taxonomy in an attempt to modernize it (OZ Teachers Net, 2004). The names of the six major categories were changed from noun to verb forms. The subcategories were replaced by verbs, and some were reorganized. This version (Anderson, Krathwohl, Airasian, et al., 2001) is preferred by some educators. A search of the literature reveals that extensive use is still made today of the original version of the cognitive taxonomy.

Instructional Variables

The effective instructor has a host of instructional approaches in his or her toolbox. These can be selected to match the context of any class or topic.

TCP—INSTRUCTIONAL VARIABLES

Demonstrates competence in basic instructional skills

Provides motivating lesson introduction (set); gives clear explanations; words questions clearly; provides for review and practice; checks for student understanding; provides lesson summary (closure).

Lessons introduced in unmotivating, vague ways; explanations are confusing; questioning skills are poorly developed; no effective closure.

Teaches for holistic development (physical, social, emotional, cognitive)

Lessons consist of activities that address physical, social, and emotional as well as cognitive needs.

Lessons are primarily cognitive.

Varies teaching approaches and activities

Consistently uses a variety of teaching strategies and methods appropriate for the content and students; experiments with a variety of ways of teaching.

Uses only one or two teaching strategies and methods; tries new methods only when urged to do so.

Ensures the participation and success of all

Assesses ongoing individual student development; modifies activities for active participation to ensure success of all students.

Little individual assessment; students expected to engage in the same activity regardless of level or ability.

Engages students in instructional dialogue

Engages students in dialogue about their experiences and learning; debriefs the processes of learning with students; teaches specific learning strategies, monitors the use of learning strategies.

Learning activities seldom debriefed; learning processes not taught to students; learning strategies not monitored.

Provides motivating set and closure

Always provides a motivating set for lessons and units that facilitates transfer from previous to new learning; always provides closure to lessons and units that reviews and provides transfer.

Begins lessons and units without a set; lessons end abruptly, without review or transfer.

Orders and sequences content to meet learner needs

Orders and sequences content to meet learner needs; recognizes when text organization is inappropriate. Uses advance organizers and in progress and post organizers well; fosters student capability in recognizing structures and patterns in content.

Rigidly follows the text or curriculum guide without consideration of learner needs; content is a smorgasbord of information; absence of use of organizers; students not helped to discover structures in patterns of content.

Provides for transfer of learning

Deliberate provision for transfer (bridging) within the subject, across subjects, and to life; examples used are relevant and interesting to students.

No attempt to bridge previous and new learning, or transfer learning within the subject, or to other subjects or life.

Varying the Presentation

Effective teachers, research suggests, make presentations varied and interesting (Good & Brophy, 1995, p. 283) so students pay attention, are motivated, and so they are more likely to learn and remember. The teacher appeals to a variety of senses, moves around the room, uses visuals, has students write or handle materials, varies speech, uses pauses, asks questions, and has students interact. In interesting lessons, stimulus variation occurs because of careful planning; at times it is spontaneous. Just using multiple senses—sight, touch, sound—has been shown to increase learning, as has greater involvement of, and participation by, learners (Diem, 1998). Shostak (1982) defines *stimulus variation* as teacher actions "designed to develop and maintain a high level of student attention during the course of a lesson by varying the presentation" (p. 121). A more complete definition would add that stimulus variation facilitates learning and retention.

Literature on learning styles, brain hemisphericity, learning mode preferences (visual, auditory, and kinesthetic), and multiple intelligences supports the need for variation in instructional approaches and learning activities. The skillful teacher uses stimulus variation techniques to direct and keep student attention on the lesson, emphasize key points or certain features, and provide a refreshing change of pace (Shostak, 1982, p. 123).

Why Vary the Presentation?

Varying the mode of presentation and choice of learning activities is important because students only tend to listen, watch, or do something, and remain interested for a limited time. Although this is particularly true of young children, it also applies to adults. A wise old sociology professor used to say, "If you can't strike oil after five or ten minutes, quit boring."

Information is received through all the senses. Murgio (1969) tells us that, of what we know, we have learned about 1 percent through taste, 2 percent through touch, 4 percent through smell, 10 percent through hearing, and 83 percent through sight.

Retention is increased if a multisensory approach is used. According to Murgio, of what we learn, we retain 10 percent of what we read, 20 percent of what we hear, 30 percent of what we see, 50 percent of what we hear and see, 70 percent of what we say, and 90 percent of what we say as we do. For several reasons, including previous experience and culture, we have preferred learning styles. Individual preferences vary. By varying the presentation, you reach more students.

Depending on the background of learners, at times presentations should be very concrete or "hands on," sometimes pictures or other visual representations can be used, and at still other times words (spoken or written) or other symbols may be sufficient. Keeping to a single mode of representation may be ineffective; using a symbolic mode before students have had concrete, or at least pictorial, previous experience may be a waste of time. These three "levels" of learning are similar to the learning processes (*enactive, iconic,* and *symbolic*) proposed by Bruner (1960), which are closely related to those described by Piaget (1929; see also Piaget & Inhelder, 1969).

Variety for the sake of variety is not productive in many life situations; however, when it comes to selection of teaching strategies, it pays dividends. Although research does not clearly demonstrate the superiority of one teaching strategy or method over another, use of a variety of strategies and method results in greater learning. Students are bound to get bored in an unchanging environment.

Techniques for Varying the Stimulus

How can you vary presentation in your lessons to attract and hold student attention? Shostak (1982, pp. 124–129) describes five *stimulus variation techniques* that should be part of your repertoire: (1) focusing, (2) kinesic variation, (3) shifting interaction, (4) pausing (silence), and (5) shifting senses. Descriptions of these techniques are presented below. We begin with focusing because it needs to be emphasized; as you will discover, all the other stimulus variation techniques are variations of focusing.

FOCUSING.   Learning takes place only through mental or physical activity. You use a stimulus so learners can focus on, and attend to, whatever is to be learned. Gain and hold attention to avoid boredom and loss of attention. Focusing can be done

- *Orally:* voice emphasis, variation, audio equipment and questions
- *Nonverbally:* gestures and pointing, physical movement, facial expressions
- *Visually:* variations in print, chalkboard or other visuals, films, etc.
- *With teaching materials:* blocks, rods, models, displays, and other teaching materials (many can be looked at, handled, smelled)
- *By varying interactions* (described below)
- *With silence* (described below)
- *By shifting senses* (described below)

The teacher who deliberately controls the direction of students' attention uses the skill of focusing. Among ways you can focus are

- *Using gestures.* Examples include pointing with your hand or an object, expressively motioning with your hands, nodding, raising your eyebrows or shoulders, and by smiling or frowning.
- *Making a statement.* Say things such as "Look at the map," "Listen for three main points," "Notice the differences in size," "Watch carefully when I add sulfuric acid," "Now, the next step is really important."
- *Supporting statements with gestures.* Examples include using a pointer on an overhead projector and saying, "This is the direction the water will flow"; holding up two fingers and saying, "There are two things you should remember"; tapping at a spot on a chalkboard diagram and saying, "This is where water will flow"; holding up two fingers and saying, "There are two things you should remember"; tapping a spot on a large map, saying, "This is where the attack took place"; bringing your hand gently down from above your head and saying, "The glider gently followed the air currents and eventually landed."

KINESIC VARIATION.   The eye tends to be attracted to, and follow, movement. Skillful directors make effective use of movement in plays or movies to draw attention, hold interest, and emphasize aspects of plot development. Good teachers move smoothly and freely and purposefully to various parts of the room. This is called kinesic variation. It causes students' attention to be focused on you.

SHIFTING INTERACTIONS.   Students are more actively involved when you use question and answer. They pay attention if they may be asked a question and can feel good about adding to the development of the lesson. Also, students like to interact with each other. Peers sometimes explain things to each other better than you can, and at-task socializing with peers can be motivating.

When you lecture without involving students, there is no overt interaction; when you ask a question of the group (rather than specific students), interaction is teacher centered; when you ask specific students questions to involve them in the development of the lesson, interaction shifts to being teacher directed rather than teacher centered; and when you redirect a response from one student to another, interaction shifts to become student centered.

PAUSING (SILENCE).   You have heard the expressions, "Silence is golden" or "Eloquent silence." Many teachers seem to feel they should not get paid if they don't constantly fill the air with words. People in the dramatic arts have long known the value of the dramatic pause. You may recall the story of the old couple in a small town where the train went through at 2:00 A.M. every morning. It never woke them. One night the train did not go through and the couple woke up, startled. The pause can be used effectively during the course of a lesson. Among the ways silence can be used are

- To emphasize an important point; to let it "sink in."
- To break a passage or information into smaller parts to promote comprehension.
- For dramatic effect, for instance, to create suspense.
- To provide time for students to think something through before they respond.
- To promote student participation through encouragement and opportunity to add comments or ask questions.
- To draw attention by contrasting speech with silence.
- To give a student time to think before finishing a response.
- To give students time to take notes before continuing with the lecture or dictation.
- To show disapproval of student misbehavior.
- To recognize the multicultural nature of the class. Some cultures make much more use of silence than white Americans, Canadians, or British.

SHIFTING SENSES.   Unfortunately, teacher talk is the dominant mode in most classrooms—about 70 percent of the time (Shostak, 1982, p. 128). Students' ability to take in and process information is increased significantly when the senses of sight and sound are used alternately (p. 127). We learn through all the senses and remember best when we use variety and combine senses.

Examples of ways that you can shift senses during the course of a lesson are:

- Explaining a dance step; demonstrating it; then having students try it.
- Showing a transparency on a screen; turning the projector off and commenting verbally; then, showing the transparency once more.
- Telling students about the difference in texture between wool and silk; having students feel actual samples of wool and silk; then, verbally clarifying the differences further.
- Flashing a slide on the screen; turning the projector off and commenting on the slide; turning the slide back on; then, after turning the projector off, having students draw what they have seen.

- Giving a lecture about sound; doing a demonstration using a tuning fork and a pith ball on a string; then, explaining the principle involved while pointing to a diagram on the chalkboard.

Use the data collection instrument in Appendix 3.1 to help you analyze the cases that follow. Your instructor may pose specific questions for your response.

CASE 3.1 Varying Presentation

Counting by Hand

Ms. Chadwick is teaching a lesson to a grade 2 class on counting by fives. She asks everyone to move to the carpeted area at the back of the classroom. There she has set up a stand that displays a 1–100 chart. She makes sure everyone can see the chart.

She tells the students what the lesson will be about and explains why it is important to know how to count by fives (telling time and counting money).

Ms. Chadwick checks to see if everyone can see the chart and shows how, when counting by fives, the fifth number is the one that is used. Pointing to the chart, she begins to identify the numbers by finding and circling each fifth number. She asks the children, "What number comes next? How do you know?" When the first several numbers have been identified, she says, "I'm going to ask you a question. I want you to think hard and put up your hands when you know the answer. Close your eyes and listen. Listen to me read the numbers we have circled. Listen to see if you can hear a pattern." She reads "5, 10, 15, 20, 25, 30, 35, 40, . . ." Hands begin to go up. After pausing a few seconds, Ms. Chadwick asks Manuel to identify the pattern. Manuel responds that the pattern is numbers ending in 5, then 0, then 5, then 0. "How many of you agree with Manuel?" The children raise their hands in agreement. Several also nod. "Can anyone guess what the next number will be?" Tanya is selected

from many raised hands to provide the answer. Then, the rest of the numbers to 100 are identified.

Ms. Chadwick asks the students to let their left hand be the "5 numbers" and their right hand be the "0 numbers." As they count by fives to 100, they raise their hands alternately, keeping time as they count in unison. Then the children are asked to move into a circle and each becomes a living part of a "counting by fives" procedure by putting up his or her left and right hand, in turn. One says "5, 10," the next says "15, 20," the next says "25, 30," etc., to 100.

Ms. Chadwick asks the children to form pairs. "I can see you can count by fives. In your pair, think of a way to count by fives so each partner is doing some counting. It's important to count correctly—help each other with that. See if you can think of a way to share the counting."

One pair alternates numbers, another does two numbers each, another pair does a pattern of three numbers, then one ("5, 10, 15," "20"; "25, 30, 35," "40") and so on. After a few minutes, Ms. C. asks children to show the class the ways they shared the counting.

As a final activity, the children work at their desks on a dot-to-dot activity that provides individual practice in counting by fives.

CASE 3.2 Varying Presentation

AttenSHUN!

Mr. Sargent, the grade 11 algebra teacher and a retired military man, was highly organized. Just by looking at his desk and the way he was dressed, you could tell. The school year was planned with precision. So much time, no more and no less, was devoted to each topic, and the pages to be covered in the text were identified in advance. His schedule of tests was strictly followed. Nothing could make him deviate from his schedule. His teaching was a study in the use of precise routines. Each day he would take up the last day's questions, going up and down the rows and beginning with the student after the one with whom he left off the previous day. This took twenty minutes. The next twenty minutes were used to present three (and always three) examples of the new material on the chalkboard. Next, questions for seatwork and homework were assigned. He would always have everybody do the first three questions and odd-numbered questions thereafter. Then Mr. Sargent circulated to help individuals as the students began their assignments.

Lesson and Unit Planning

Lesson Planning

In the following paragraphs you will be introduced to the elements of a basic lesson plan. Written plans are aids to teaching. First lesson plans should be detailed and in writing. Planning is not always linear. When you plan, you do not have to start with objectives and work your way down to the evaluation. Frequently, you will begin with the need to teach a certain topic or specific skill. Then you may ask yourself how you will know if students are learning what you hoped. Planning can start anywhere, for example, with information students need to learn or skills they need to develop, and then turn attention to writing specific objectives.

Lesson plan data collection instruments are given in Appendices 3.2 and 3.3. Elements of a lesson plan are shown in Figure 3.2.

LESSON PLAN MODELS.   Lesson plan models can range from an unstructured approach (going with what appears to meet the needs or interests of the students and teacher at a given time) to a rigidly structured and followed approach. The Gagné instructional model, Hunter direct instruction approach, and a constructivist approach are some popular models.

The Gagné Instructional Model.   The classic Robert Gagné (1985) nine-step model for lesson planning can be used for most models of instruction (Figure 3.3). Although some argue that it is not sufficiently learner focused, it is widely used. The Gagné model begins with gaining learner attention and motivation. Then, learners are told the objective of the lesson to provide a framework for what is to follow. Recall of prior knowledge is stimulated as a foundation for new learning. An appropriate amount of new material is then presented (Bloom's taxonomy can be used to sequence content). Following this, guidance for learning is provided, with the teacher simplifying and making the content easier to grasp. Next, learners practice using the new behavior, skills, or knowledge, followed by descriptive feedback using a test, quiz, or verbal comments. Performance is assessed to discover whether the lesson has been learned. Finally, provision for transfer of the learning to new contexts occurs.

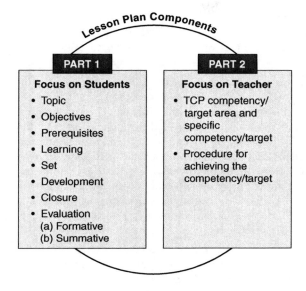

FIGURE 3.2 *Elements of a Lesson Plan*

The Hunter Direct Instruction Lesson Approach. Madeline Hunter's (1984) direct instruction lesson plan model may be considered a behavioral approach. Some authorities believe that behavioral approaches should be avoided. It was Hunter's intent, however, that lesson steps provide a useful structure for many kinds of lessons, including nonbehavioral lessons.

1. *Objectives (intentions).* The teacher decides what students are to know or be able to do as a result of a lesson. Decision making includes a determination of whether students have the needed prerequisite knowledge or skills.

2. *Standards.* The teacher needs to explain what will occur in the lesson, the procedures to be followed and what students are expected to do, what students will achieve through the lesson, and how they will demonstrate what they have learned.

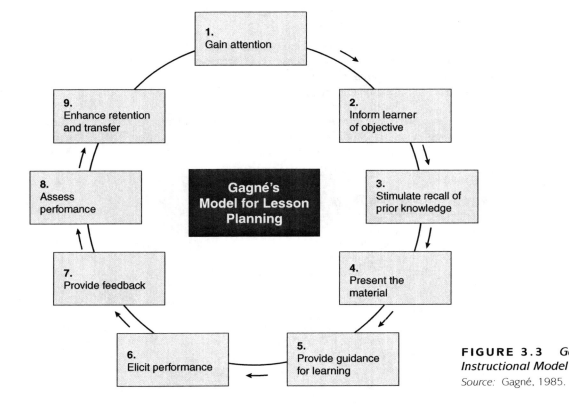

FIGURE 3.3 *Gagné Instructional Model*
Source: Gagné, 1985.

3. *Anticipatory set (set induction).* Students are told what will be done to secure student attention and put them in a receptive frame of mind for what is to follow. Set can include an "advance organizer" or framework for the content and activities that will be part of the lesson.

4. *Teaching/presentation.* Presentation includes three parts. The first is *input*—the information needed by students to gain the knowledge or skill is presented, whether by lecture, videotape, PowerPoint presentation, computer, or other means. The information could be drawn out of students through questioning or gleaned through research by the students. The second part is *modeling*—"how to do it" is modeled. Students are shown examples of what is expected and an end product of what their work will be like. Key aspects can be explained in a variety of ways. Students need to visualize what they will be expected to know (e.g., how to solve a problem or perform an operation). The third part of the presentation is a *check for understanding*—before students begin to work, a check is made to discover whether they understand what is to be done. They need to "get it" before they begin. If necessary, reteaching should occur.

5. *Guided practice/monitoring.* Students practice what was modeled. The teacher circulates to observe the level of mastery being achieved and, as appropriate, provides positive reinforcement for progress made, remediation, and encouragement.

6. *Closure.* The intent is to bring the lesson to an appropriate conclusion. Closure involves review and clarification and should consolidate or organize understanding—that is, make sense for students. In short, it should help students construct personal meaning and understanding. Furthermore, it lets students know they have achieved something important.

7. *Independent practice.* When the content or skill has been mastered, to ensure retention, a schedule is initiated for repeated reinforcement practice. This may be homework, or group or individual work in class. Provision for transfer to relevant situations, including other contexts, also needs to occur (pp. 175–176).

The Constructivist Approach.   In the constructivist approach (Table 3.1), students construct personal understanding and knowledge of the world by experiencing things and reflecting on their experiences. This approach can promote individual creativity and col-

---

TABLE 3.1   *A Constructivist Lesson Plan*

Invitation	Setting the stage—students' prior knowledge, ideas, and beliefs in the lesson surfaced and engaged using, for e.g., a question, demonstration, event, or interesting challenge. Includes objectives and materials needed.
Exploration	Describes the activities students will do to explore the concepts, phenomena, or ideas of the lesson.
Explanation	Students share. They discuss and reflect on findings, data, and analyses and compare ideas of peers and authorities on the topic.
Taking Action	Students take part in an activity to help them take personal or social responsibility for the ideas researched. They ask themselves what they learned and how this knowledge might help them solve a problem.

laboration if students are to discuss and exchange ideas. A lesson can contain activities and involve resources that require students to engage actively in the discovery process. If, in science, the teacher tells students how magnetism works, the approach is *explicit* or *direct*. If, on the other hand, learners discover they can use magnets and iron filings, are provided with these, experiment, observe, and prepare a description of how magnetism works, the approach is *constructivist*. They act on new information with the knowledge they bring to the activity. At this stage you are only introduced to constructivism; more will be said about it in Chapter 13. A useful description of constructivist theory and teaching practice you may want to read is by Fosnot (2005).

The role of the teacher, in the constructivist approach, is to pose questions and guide students to assist them in finding their own answers. A constructivist approach, though it may be more demanding on teacher planning and class time, allows learners to gain a deeper understanding and result in better recall. Students, it is said, are more motivated because they are actively involved and activities are "real world" (authentic) and social and communication skills are fostered.

A lesson plan template is provided to plan a constructivist lesson in Table 3.1. A constructivist lesson plan guide (author unknown) is provided on the following web sites: http://cied.gsu/Hassard/mos/con9.html, and www.gsu.edu ~ mstjrh/webbasedtemplate. html.

SET, DEVELOPMENT, AND CLOSURE. Instruction needs to be organized logically, normally beginning with an outline ("advance organizer") or preview, by pointing out connections (transitions) between parts, and by summarizing. Figure 3.4 reflects the theories of psychologist David Ausubel (1963, 1968, 1978), who helped develop the notion of constructivism, on concept mapping. Advance organizers (a concise structure or overview of what is to follow) are very useful. Post organizers (at the end of a lesson) also

1. Set: advance organizers or outline or general principles or questions	**4.** Frequent checks for student understanding to ensure mastery
2. Brief description of learning objectives and new or key concepts	**5.** Closure: review of main points
3. Presentation of material in small steps	**6.** Follow up with questions or provide assignment for understanding and application of learning

FIGURE 3.4 *A Lesson Plan That Reflects Ausubel's Theories*
Source: Good & Brophy, 1995.

can be useful. Organizers are particularly important in lessons that use an expository (direct) format, when the teacher presents information, concepts, and principles in a logical, sequenced manner. Post organizers may be particularly significant when lesson presentation is inductive (indirect), by which students are led to discover the ideas, concepts, or principles and how they are linked. Expository and inquiry teaching is discussed later.

Well-designed lessons usually have three parts: (1) they begin with a memorable focusing event and preview what is to come; (2) they logically present and link new materials, and check for understanding; and (3) they close with an event that summarizes, "pulls things together," and points out what students have achieved. We shall call the beginning event *set* and the ending event *closure* (Figure 3.4).

Set.   You want students to have favorable view, or positive set, for learning. In the context of a lesson, set is the predisposition to react in a certain way to the presentation and activities to follow. How you begin lessons (or lesson segments) has an important effect on the set that students will have.

Set has four purposes: (1) focusing student attention on the lesson; (2) creating a framework for the forthcoming information, ideas, concepts, or generalizations; (3) furthering understanding and application of abstract ideas by using examples or analogies; and (4) promoting student interest and involvement in what is to follow. The first purpose is likely a part of the other three.

There are three basic kinds of set (Figure 3.5) that teachers can use: orientation, transition, and evaluation (Shostak, 1977, p. 128).

1. *Orientation set.* Orientation set is used to introduce the lesson and leads to motivation. It focuses attention on new learning, using a motivating activity, event, puzzle, anecdote or joke, object, or something that students have interest in, or experience with. It can provide a structure to help students visualize the content or activities, or it can help clar-

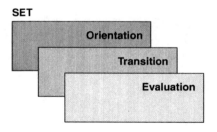

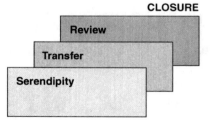

SET

- Orientation
- Transition
- Evaluation

Purposes:

Focus attention

Provide organizational framework

Provide examples/analogies for understanding

Promote interest and involvement

Bridge from past lesson(s)

CLOSURE

- Review
- Transfer
- Serendipity

Purposes:

Bring lesson to conclusion

Help bring things together and make sense of things

Provide repetition to aid retention

Bridge into next lesson

FIGURE 3.5 *Set and Closure and Their Purposes*
Source: Shostak, 1977.

ify the objectives of the lesson. Use can be made of orientation to ready students for the lesson.

2. *Transition set.* Transition set links what already is known or covered to that which is about to be learned. Reliance is on analogies, examples, or activities that students have interest in or with which they have had experience. It can also alert students about the content of future lessons.

3. *Evaluation set.* Evaluation set involves evaluation of students' understanding of previous material, or a review of previous material before going to new material. It relies on questions, examples, quizzes, and activities that are heavily student centered or generated, so the degree of understanding of previous content can be determined. Evaluation set also leads to a focus on the lesson ahead.

Development.   After the set, development of the lesson occurs. You provide experiences that guide and support students' efforts. For students to achieve planned or emerging instructional objectives, choose content that is meaningful, logically organized, and sequenced. Content should be challenging, not frustrating. During the lesson, students should be as actively involved as possible and should feel good about themselves and their accomplishments. Establish a warm, positive, but businesslike climate. So students can experience success, choose appropriate:

- Instructional skills
- Management procedures
- Resources and aids
- Teaching strategies and methods
- Student activities
- Checking-up procedures

Instructional skills, among others, include explaining and demonstrating, varying the stimulus (auditory, verbal, and tactile), and questioning technique. The teaching strategies chosen can be direct, indirect, interactive, experiential, or individual study. Teaching methods choices range from lecture to group problem solving, from seeking answers in a textbook to simulations requiring students to discover the answers. Choices include a variety of interaction patterns from independent study to small groups to the whole class. Teaching strategies are dealt with in detail later in the text. Examples of classroom management procedures are the establishment of routines and procedures, a positive climate, and ensuring that acts are followed by consequences. Student activities range from viewing a film to conducting an experiment, completing a project, playing a game, copying notes from the chalkboard, or doing seatwork. A wide range of resources and aids is available. Resources include texts, reference books, newspapers, laboratory equipment and supplies; aids are things such as flip chart paper and smart boards. Checking-up or assessment and evaluation procedures include asking questions, student reports, circulating around the room to view student work, worksheets, homework, and tests.

Closure.   Closure includes the statements or actions you use to "bring a lesson to an appropriate conclusion. . . . To help students bring things together in their own minds, to make sense out of what has been going on during the lesson" (Shostak, 1986, p. 128). Students should normally be actively involved in the closure. For example, they can be asked to recall the main ideas. Closure should highlight key ideas, reinforce, synthesize, and summarize. Good closures normally take at least ten minutes, particularly at the elementary level.

There are three kinds of closure.

1. *Review closure* concisely "ties up" a lesson or lesson segment. It uses techniques such as drawing students' attentions to a lesson's or segment's closing point; drawing attention to the major points, and their sequence; summarizing discussion that took place; or relating the lesson to the original concept or generalization can occur.
2. *Transfer closure* is used to reinforce or consolidate learning. Learning should be available for use in new contexts. Transfer closure draws students' attention to a closing point and facilitates transfer by reviewing the new learning, immediately practicing it, and asking students to extend the new learning to other contexts or to develop new knowledge from what has been learned.
3. *Serendipity closure* refers to a "natural" but unplanned opportunity for closure. You can take advantage of an opportunity to close that arises spontaneously near the end of a lesson. This might arise because of a student response, a key student question, an unusual event, or because of a sudden insight or idea.

The three major phases of the lessons that effective teachers follow—set, development, and closure—should flow naturally one to the other. This does not come about by accident. It requires planning. Smooth transition from one phase to the other is affected by the teaching methods and student activities chosen. Each time a group of students is being taught, whether for ten minutes or an hour, the elements of set, development, and closure should be present. A data collection sheet for microteaching lab and classroom lessons is shown in Appendix 3.4. You can use the data collection sheet to help you analyze the cases that follow. Your instructor may pose specific questions for your response.

CASE 3.3

Set and Closure

Mr. Jacobs was planning a learning experience on "pairs" for his first-grade class as preparation for counting by twos. He waited until all the children had returned to the classroom from physical education, then he entered the classroom, conspicuously wearing a shoe on one foot but just a sock on the other. He walked around the classroom busily as children got settled to give the children opportunity to notice his feet.

Soon there was snickering and whispered comments from many youngsters. Several asked questions: "Where's your other shoe, Mr. Jacobs?" "Did you forget something, Mr. Jacobs?" Mr. Jacobs pretended not to know what they meant. He asked, "What do you mean? What's the matter?"

Erin explained patiently, "Mr. Jacobs, you have a shoe on one foot and only a sock on the other. Teachers always wear two shoes, don't they?" "Yeah," added Sarah. "Two feet means you have to wear two shoes."

"Do shoes always come in twos?" asked Mr. Jacobs. Most children agreed. "What do we usually call a set of two shoes?" The children were thoughtful and several had ideas. "Boots." "Sandals." "Sneakers."

"Those are different kinds of footwear," said Mr. Jacobs. "But I'm still wondering what a set of two shoes is called. Two boots or two sandals or two sneakers would be a set or a . . . ?" "*Pair!*" shouted the youngsters. "A *pair* of sandals. A *pair* of sneakers."

"That's the word I was thinking of," said Mr. Jacobs. "So you think I should have a *pair* of shoes on, instead of just one?"

The activity proceeded with the children thinking of as many kinds of shoes as they could, telling where they might wear each pair. As a way of leading into counting by twos, Mr. Jacobs had the children put their gym shoes in a row, count them, and try to think of a counting pattern that would help them count

faster. There were several ideas for how this might be done, but Mr. Jacobs noticed it was just a few minutes before the children had to prepare for the noon break. "We'll work on this more tomorrow," he said. "But, before we stop today, someone explain what we were learning. Can you think of how to say it in a short way?" The children had been practicing summarizing (saying things in a short way), and several tried to summarize the discussion and activity. Mr. Jacobs encouraged responses, making sure, through questioning, that the idea of "pair" as two matching items and the fact that there are several ways to count pairs of things were mentioned. "Good summaries, and good thinking," he said. "Tomorrow we'll do more on finding a counting pattern to speed up our counting." Then Mr. Jacobs put on his second shoe.

CASE 3.4

Set and Closure

Ms. Holmberg began her lesson on stereotyping, discrimination, and racism in her grade 11 social studies class by writing the headings "Black," "Indian" (North American), "Japanese," "Spanish," and "White" on the chalkboard. Then the class was divided into five groups of six. She began, "You remember the rules for brainstorming. Just state whatever comes to mind. I am going to assign one of the headings on the chalkboard to each group. Your group will, for ten minutes, brainstorm all the characteristics that come to mind. These will be recorded under the appropriate chalkboard heading by the recorder in your group." Jason raised his hand and asked, "Should you avoid saying not nice things, like, uh, lazy or smelly?" "I'm glad you asked," Ms. Holmberg replied, "it shows you are a very sensitive person. At this stage you should not judge whether the characteristic is true or false or

good or bad. The next step, however, is to select the statements that are merely descriptive and those that are generalizations that do not apply to all, or even most, people in your category."

After students completed the initial stage of the exercise, Ms. Holmberg gave a presentation about beliefs, attitudes, stereotyping, discrimination, and racism. She reminded the class about what they had learned about critical thinking, particularly their learning about checking assumptions. She then asked the class to rejoin their groups to discuss the lists on the chalkboard, to see which of the characteristics they would now categorize differently. Then each group reported the characteristics they had placed under each category. Finally, with the help of the class, Ms. Holmberg summarized their learning about discrimination.

APPENDIX 3.1   *Stimulus Variation Professional Target*

PROFESSIONAL TARGET—VARYING PRESENTATION

Please describe what was said or done to vary the stimulus and how students reacted.

Presentation Skill	Descriptive Notes

Focusing
Pointing, gesturing, making statements
to draw attention to aids being used or
for emphasis

Shifting interaction
Using different interaction patterns:
teacher–class; teacher–student;
student–student

Pausing (silence)
Pausing to: gain attention; emphasize;
provide time to think; create suspense;
stop a minor disruption

Shifting senses
Having students use different senses:
looking; listening; feeling; tasting; smelling;
doing

Describe student reactions to the stimulus variations:

LESSON PLAN

Date _____   Subject _____   Name _____

Planning for Student Learning

(a) Topic:

(b) Content:

(c) Objectives:

  (1)

  (2)

  (3)

(d) Prerequisite Student Learning:

(e) Presentation (teaching methods and student activities):

  Set:

  Development:

  Closure:

(f) Materials and Aids:

(g) Evaluation:

Planning for Professional Development

Date _____   Name of Data Collector _____

(a) Target:

(b) Specific target:

(c) Descriptor elements:

(d) How I will go about trying to achieve the target:

(e) Data collection method: Check one.
    ____ Please use the attached sheet from the target topic.
    ____ Please use the attached sheet other than the target topic sheet.
    ____ Please collect data as described below.

APPENDIX 3.3   *Lesson Plan Elements Professional Target*

PROFESSIONAL TARGET—LESSON PLAN ELEMENTS

From your observations of the lesson presented, please describe what you perceive to be the lesson element or the things that were said and done.

Lesson Element	Descriptive Notes
Topic	
Content	
Objectives	
Set	
Development	
Closure	
Materials and aids	
Evaluation	
Professional target	
Plans for achieving the target	

APPENDIX 3.4 *Set and Closure Professional Target*

PROFESSIONAL TARGET—SET AND CLOSURE

Please describe how these were done: (a) *set* at the start of the lesson, and (b) *closure* at the end of the lesson.

Set and Closure Options	Descriptive Notes

A. Set:

Orientation Set (focusing attention through motivating activity)

and/or Transition Set (smooth transition from known to new material)

and/or Evaluation Set (determining what students know about previous material before going on to new material)

B. Closure:

Review Closure (reviewing material just taught)

and/or Transfer Closure (providing practice, and/or alerting students about future use of, or link to, material covered)

and/or Serendipity Closure (taking advantage of unique, unexpected situation that provides ideal closure)

On the reverse side of this sheet, please list and briefly describe each of the activities and instructional skills used in the development of the lesson.

4 Assessment and Evaluation

Introduction

Given the variety of assessment and grading practices in the field, the increasing importance of assessment, the critical role each classroom teacher plays in determining assessment and grades, and the trend toward greater accountability of teachers...there is a need to more fully understand assessment and grading practices. (McMillan, 2001, p. 20)

OBJECTIVES

You will be able to:

1. Describe ways teachers seek information about students.
2. Define key concepts in assessment and evaluation.
3. Describe alternative (performance/authentic) assessment and the range of possible techniques.
4. Describe the various methods of recording assessment data.
5. Describe ways of preparing good test items.
6. Differentiate between good and poor test items.
7. Describe alternative marking systems.
8. Recognize bias in tests and ways to address diversity when assessing.
9. Propose ways to achieve balance in the use of testing procedures.

Assessment and evaluation are important aspects of teaching and learning: (1) performance in school is used by society to sort people into occupational and other societal roles (for example, grades decide whether a person will be admitted to college); (2) grades are reward structures to motivate students; (3) parents want to know how their children are doing compared to others; (4) assessment can be used to judge the effectiveness of teachers and schools; and (5) other reasons for assessment will be explored in this chapter. Stiggins (2002) observes, "Politicians routinely ask, How can we use assessment as the basis for doling out rewards and punishment to increase teacher and student effort?" instead of the more important questions of: "How can we use assessment to help our students *want* to learn? How can we help them feel *able* to learn?" (p. 758). This is a critical part of assessment—not only assessment *of* student learning, but assessment *for* learning (assessment that helps students learn).

Teachers are responsible for assessing and evaluating students and reporting the results to school authorities, students, and parents. Material in this chapter will help you learn the basic concepts and skills. Later, the sections on Assessment and Evaluation from the Teacher Competence Profile are included for your convenience.

Key Concepts

Several concepts need to be understood before meaningful discussion can occur. Assessment and evaluation are used by teachers to better understand students—to discover their abilities and interests, and what motivates. *Assessment* usually means collecting a full

123

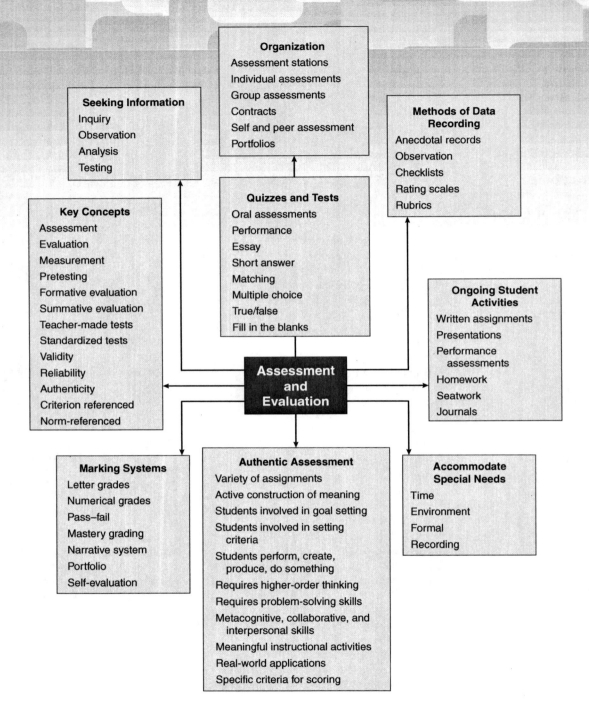

Organization
Assessment stations
Individual assessments
Group assessments
Contracts
Self and peer assessment
Portfolios

Seeking Information
Inquiry
Observation
Analysis
Testing

Methods of Data Recording
Anecdotal records
Observation
Checklists
Rating scales
Rubrics

Key Concepts
Assessment
Evaluation
Measurement
Pretesting
Formative evaluation
Summative evaluation
Teacher-made tests
Standardized tests
Validity
Reliability
Authenticity
Criterion referenced
Norm-referenced

Quizzes and Tests
Oral assessments
Performance
Essay
Short answer
Matching
Multiple choice
True/false
Fill in the blanks

Ongoing Student Activities
Written assignments
Presentations
Performance assessments
Homework
Seatwork
Journals

Assessment and Evaluation

Marking Systems
Letter grades
Numerical grades
Pass–fail
Mastery grading
Narrative system
Portfolio
Self-evaluation

Authentic Assessment
Variety of assignments
Active construction of meaning
Students involved in goal setting
Students involved in setting criteria
Students perform, create, produce, do something
Requires higher-order thinking
Requires problem-solving skills
Metacognitive, collaborative, and interpersonal skills
Meaningful instructional activities
Real-world applications
Specific criteria for scoring

Accommodate Special Needs
Time
Environment
Formal
Recording

range of information about students. It is gathered to make judgments about student progress and your instruction. *Performance assessment* provides information on the learning of tasks that require students to be actively engaged in a practiced behavior (e.g., playing a violin or taking part in a debate). *Evaluation* is the process of making judgments or

---

TCP—ASSESSMENT AND EVALUATION

Identifies student academic, personal, and social strengths

Uses formal and informal methods to identify students' strengths; shares assessment of strengths with students; incorporates knowledge of student strengths into planning for student assessment.

Tends to dwell on inefficiencies and weaknesses; does not assess student strengths or share them with students.

Assesses change in student development

Uses formal and informal methods to assess change in student development: maintains accurate and comprehensive records of each student's progress.

Does not document student development.

Involves students in assessment

Students are regularly given opportunities to set criteria for their work and to assess their progress; students are involved in individual conferences with the teacher; assessment is treated as a learning experience.

Students are not given the opportunity to assess their own work; no dialogue with students regarding progress.

Evaluates student progress

Various assessments are interpreted to evaluate student progress; the basis for evaluation is clearly and regularly reported to students and parents; evaluation is used to set goals for future growth.

Student evaluation is not based on regular formal and informal assessment; evaluation is reported as marks, with little or no reference criteria or interpretation.

Keeps thorough, well-organized records

Record keeping thorough, well organized, and accessible (e.g., attendance, marks, student progress, assignment and test schedules, record of professional targets, progress in essential learning).

Little or no evidence of usable record keeping.

Provides diagnosis and remediation

Uses and acts on standardized and teacher-made evaluation techniques for remediation or enrichment; refers to other professionals when appropriate.

Does not diagnose or provide remediation or enrichment.

---

decisions about achievement of learning objectives or the degree of value or merit of a particular program, activity, or approach. It usually involves assessing information against some standard. *Measurement* is the way data are provided for making judgments or decisions. It involves collecting data on the frequency or magnitude of something. When teachers take attendance, they engage in measurement; but assessment occurs when they decide that English usage is important in learning; evaluation occurs when teachers decide a test was too difficult or too easy.

Evaluation can be formative or summative. *Formative evaluation* happens before or during instruction and the learning process. It is used to plan and make adjustments to promote learning. It includes observation by the teacher of students and their work, questions during instruction, homework, pretests, and checkup tests. Formative evaluation should not be used to decide grades. Frequent *en route* (formative) evaluation may be used to increase comprehension and to provide repetitions to increase retention. *Summative evaluation* occurs after instruction, to discover the extent of student learning or the effectiveness of instruction. It is often used to decide grades. Summative evaluation may occur after an instructional unit has been completed or at the end of a course. It should measure student learning against the intended learning outcomes of a unit or course. It may include teacher-made, end-of-chapter or other tests, completed projects or papers, homework, portfolios, self-evaluation, and even standardized achievement tests. Summative evaluation is used to decide grades.

Tests can be teacher made or standardized. *Teacher-made tests* are created by the teacher to discover student achievement and teaching effectiveness. They should measure exactly what was taught *and only* what was taught. When built properly, test items reflect classroom objectives and the teaching methods and classroom learning activities used. *Standardized tests* are usually commercially designed. They sample performance under uniform procedures (directions, time limits, and methods for scoring), and they are usually meant for broad (often nationwide) use and include norms. *Pretesting* is used to discover students' knowledge or skill about a topic or performance before a lesson that requires these as prerequisites. If teachers are to design curricula and assessments appropriate for their classes and individuals within them, they need to take students from *where they are—not from where they a re supposed to be.* Discovering "where students are" in their development is the critical beginning point in the teaching–learning enterprise. Teachers can try to discover students' prior knowledge and capabilities both formally and informally. Formally, they can administer pretests, both teacher made and norm- and criterion-referenced standardized tests. Informally, pretesting can occur through observation, class assignments, person-to-person interactions, and class discussions.

How good is a test? Tests need to be valid, reliable, and authentic. *Validity* refers to the ability of a test to measure what it says it will measure. For example, if it is supposed to measure ninth-grade reading skills and does, then it is valid. *Reliability* refers to the consistency of a test (or another version of a test with similar items) to yield the same score or rank repeatedly when given to the same individuals under similar circumstances. *Authenticity* means the degree to which tests are congruent with reality—do they deal with important content, "real problems" that are transferable to life situations?

Evaluation may be criterion referenced or norm referenced. A *criterion* is a standard against which something is compared. *Criterion-referenced evaluation* involves comparing student performance to an absolute criterion (standard). It is used to help decide if a student needs more instruction or practice. For example, the criterion may be 7 out of 10 correct; or, to pass a course, students may have to score 80 percent or better on a test. *Norm-referenced evaluation* involves comparing each student's results to those of others in the group—either the class or another group. A norm-referenced test is a standardized test that evaluates a student's performance relative to that of a large representative sample of learners (called the *norm group*).

Assessment Techniques

Assessment techniques can be categorized into four groups: methods of organization, methods of data recording, ongoing student activities, and quizzes and tests. The discussion that follows uses this arrangement (Figure 4.1).

FIGURE 4.1 *Student Assessment Techniques*

Methods of Organization	Methods of Data Recording	Ongoing Student Activities	Quizzes and Tests
Assessment stations	Anecdotal records	Written assignments	Oral assessments items
Individual assessments	Observation checklists	Presentations	Performance test items
Group assessments	Rating scales	Performance assessments	Extended open-response items
Contracts	Rubrics	Homework	Short-answer items
Self- and peer assessments	Multiple-choice items	Journals	
Portfolios	True–false items		

Source: Adapted from Saskatchewan Learning (1991). *Student evaluation: A teacher handbook.* Regina, SK: Saskatchewan Department of Education.

Methods of Organization

ASSESSMENT STATIONS.   An assessment station is an area, in or outside the classroom, set by the teacher for assessment. Students, individually or in groups, go to this area to be assessed on academic or attitude achievement. Having such a spot allows students, during regular class time, to work with ideas or materials. At a station, they can, for example, demonstrate ability to use a zoology display to classify a specimen, prepare a chart on a computer, write a story, or perform a gymnastic skill.

INDIVIDUAL ASSESSMENTS.   Individual assessment involves examining individual student progress. In doing this, the teacher decides whether to use norm referencing (a group standard of students of the same age or grade), criterion referencing (a predecided standard), or self referencing (a student's previous level of achievement).

GROUP ASSESSMENTS.   Group assessment is a way to collect information about students working in groups; it accounts for group progress. The teacher awards the same mark to every member of the group, assigns individual marks, or uses a combination of group and individual marks. Each has advantages and disadvantages. The *individual* mark procedure is traditional, and some assessments are best done individually, but it encourages competition and it is difficult to measure an individual's contribution to a group project; the *group* procedure encourages cooperation and the teacher only has to assign one (not several) marks, but students and parents have come to expect individual marks. A compromise is to use a combination of individual and group assessments.

CONTRACTS.   A contract is an agreement between a student or group of students and the teacher about what is to be done, who will do it, how it will be done, when it is due, and how it will be marked. Students are involved in planning what the product is to be and how it is to be evaluated. Examples of products include written assignments, displays, models, and portfolios. Students may need to be taught how to plan contracts and encouraged to become self-directed learners.

SELF- AND PEER ASSESSMENTS.   When students evaluate their work, *self-assessment* occurs. When another student, or group students, evaluate a student's work, *peer assessment* occurs. Checklists or rating scales can be used for self- or peer assessment, though assessment can be written or oral. Self- or peer assessment is best used when student self-knowledge is important. Self- and peer assessments lend themselves to project work or group work. Ideally, students are involved in developing the criteria. When a teacher uses peer assessment, both the person being evaluated and the person doing it can benefit. Students should be taught how to assess peers in a descriptive, nonjudgmental way. It may involve the use of rubrics, which students may even help in designing.

PORTFOLIOS

> If you want to appear accountable, test your students. If you want to improve schools, teach teachers to assess their students. If you want to maximize learning, teach students to assess themselves. (Stiggins, 1993)

A *portfolio* is a chronological collection of student work over an extended period. Paulson, Paulson, and Meyer (1991) say it "is a purposeful collection of student work that exhibits the student's efforts, progress, and achievements in one or more areas. The collection must include student participation in selecting contents, the criteria for selection, the criteria for judging merit, and evidence of student self-reflection" (p. 60).

Teachers increasingly use portfolios of student work so that students gain the "real" information needed to assess progress and set learning goals. Portfolios can empower the teacher and learners. Achievement tests measure outcomes that can be tabulated or counted. Portfolios allow teachers to observe students in a more complete way and encourage students to be creative, take risks, and learn how to self-evaluate. A major purpose is to help students become self-directed learners. Portfolios, many teachers believe, are better ways to report student progress to parents or guardians.

Effective learning occurs when students have control over and take responsibility for learning. Doing a portfolio is a way to promote self-directed learning. It can have the added benefit of improving self-esteem, as students take pride in their work and share portfolios with others. Opportunities for sharing can occur during student-led conferences or as students share portfolios with peers. It occurs when portfolios are presented to the teacher and parents. By examining their children's work, parents form a clearer image of what occurs in classrooms. This can lead to genuine relationships with their children and the teacher. That is, portfolio assessment may be "authentic" in that it can communicate student learning in a very authentic way.

Regularly collected, dated, samples of student work provide an "image" of the learner over time. Because learning is continuous, standardized tests provide an imprecise snapshot of a student's knowledge on a given day. Assessment should reveal more. Students and teachers can jointly put together *a complete collection portfolio*. A *showcase portfolio, assessment portfolio,* or *parent conference portfolio* can be drawn from the student's portfolio.

Though using portfolios can have positive results, some educators cite disadvantages. Time and administration demands increase, and scoring and recording student performance is subjective and difficult. Critics add that deciding what should be included can be a problem.

Methods of Recording Data

Information about student progress, including tests and quizzes, or participation in ongoing activities, can be recorded in several ways. The technique selected should be easy to use, accurate, and represent fairly what occurred.

ANECDOTAL RECORDS.   Anecdotal records are written day-to-day accounts of student progress. They are based on observations of students and are usually collected in a folder or book. Most often, records consist of dated, descriptive, open-ended, and unstructured notes. The use of forms, with headings and space under which observation can be recorded, is common. *Formatively,* narrative records inform the teacher about how a student is progressing and areas that might require immediate attention. In the latter respect, they can be used for *diagnosis. Summatively,* anecdotal records detail student development over a period.

OBSERVATION CHECKLISTS.   Observation checklists focus on a teacher's observations of a student on critical behaviors or key things. They measure the presence or absence of desired concepts, skills, processes, or attitudes. They are usually completed during class time. Each entry is a formative picture. A longitudinal profile of progress may emerge if a checklist is used several times and evaluated. Examples of things recorded are problem-solving skills in mathematics, handwriting samples, spelling, ability to use information, an essay or report, attitudes and values about an issue, and participation in group or project work.

RATING SCALES.   Rating scales are used to judge the quality of performance or end product. They assess the extent to which students attain concepts, skills, processes, or attitudes. They provide a scale of values describing what is being evaluated whether a person, a group, or an object. We can, for example, use a 1–5 scale to rate students on nonverbal communication (facial expression, movement, gestures, mannerisms, eye contact, and use of silence) as they give presentations. Other examples are performance at a piano, doing technical work in a science laboratory, and a product in a woodwork shop (e.g., a bird house).

A variation is holistic rating scales. A *holistic rating scale* combines global and analytic scoring methods. Portfolios can be a good way to assess investigations reported in oral or written assignments in language arts and for long-term or extended problem solving in mathematics. Further discussion of rating scales is provided later in this chapter.

RUBRICS.   When we wish to assess how well a student has completed a task such as a performance, product, or something written, we look at two parts: the *task* itself and the *criteria* necessary to achieve the task. A *rubric* is a set of guidelines for assessment that states the characteristics being assessed with clear performance criteria and a rating scale (Scarborough Board of Education, 1997, p. 22). A rubric includes (1) the criteria or key elements of a piece of work, and (2) a scale or gradations of quality for each criterion. An example of a map rubric is given in Table 4.1.

Rubrics can be used to assess a wide range of work, including essays, presentations, portfolios of assignments, book talks, displays, projects, music performances, and physical education performances. As well as specifying expectations, they can be marking tools and make assessment *authentic.* A rubric form can be attached to student work and the degree of quality achieved for each criterion highlighted or circled. It is suggested that a *comments* section be added to the form, because the form alone may seem impersonal.

Rubrics are increasingly popular with teachers and students alike. Teachers like them because they provide a clear set of criteria or standards, and students like them because they clarify expectations. A rubric is learner centered. It openly lays out what the teacher expects

TABLE 4.1   *Criteria Descriptors*

	Excellent (4)	Very Good (3)	Good (2)	Fair (1)
Content	All labels included and accurately placed; details careful and accurate	All labels included, most accurately placed	All but one or two labels included, somewhat accurately placed	Several labels not included, many not accurately or carefully placed
Visual appeal	Very nicely colored, clean looking, labels easy to read	Some color, generally clean, a few labels not easy to read	Little color, labels somewhat difficult to read	Little or no color, labels very difficult to read
Map elements	Clear title, date, compass rose, scale key, source line, latitude and longitude lines	Most standard map elements, most accurate, easy to read	Several standard map elements are missing	Most standard map elements missing

and provides clear feedback to students about their achievement. Not only can a rubric be used by a teacher to assess student work, it can be used to do self-assessment or peer assessment. Parents like rubrics because they provide clear descriptions of what their child needs to do for a particular assignment (Goodrich, 1997). A rubric can reduce grading subjectivity. Huba and Freed (2000, pp. 170–171) give ways in which we can educate students by using rubrics:

- We can reveal to students the standards of our disciplines.
- We can inform students about the many qualities that comprise good—and poor—work.
- We can involve students in setting standards.
- We can involve students in describing the criteria in the rubrics.
- We can open channels of communication between us and our students.
- A variety of individuals give feedback to students about their work.

Goodrich (1997, pp. 14–15) gives five major reasons for the appeal of rubrics to students and teachers:

1. They are powerful tools for teaching and assessment—to improve and monitor student performance, make teachers' expectations clear, show students how to meet expectations.
2. They help students become thoughtful judges of their own and others' work.
3. They reduce the time teachers spend evaluating student work (teachers can circle an item in the rubric rather than write an explanation).
4. They can accommodate heterogeneous classes because of the range of quality in the descriptors (they also can accommodate gifted students and those with special needs).
5. They are easy to use and to explain to students and parents.

Although rubrics have much appeal, they have disadvantages. They are time consuming to design. Writing good criteria for each level of achievement is not easy. It is suggested that rubrics should be created by teacher teams and that students be involved. Involving students provides a sense of ownership in their assessment.

CASE 4.1   Assessment

Rubrics and Great Expectations

Mr. Polski's class is getting ready for the local history fair. The class has been divided into groups of two and three and each group has selected a history project to be researched and displayed. Sean and Hassim chose "The Oregon Trail," while Zillah, Maria, and Tiffany are doing "The Underground Railway to Canada." Mr. Polski is explaining the rubric by which work will be assessed.

Mr. Polski tells students there are four criteria: (1) originality of research, (2) quality of display, (3) clarity of writing, and (4) quality of interview with the judges. "What does 'criteria' mean?" Maria asks. Mr. Polski comments on the four criteria. Regarding research, he says there are four levels of quality and asks Hassim what they might be. "Well, the best would be 'excellent,' and the next . . . would be 'very good,' then 'good,' and then 'lousy' " says Hassim, grinning. The class laughs. "Not bad, Hassim," says Mr. Polski indulgently. "A better word might be

'poor.' " Mr. Polski reads the criteria for excellent research. "Students find high-quality evidence from several sources such as encyclopedias, textbooks, and a variety of print and audiovisual sources. All sources, including the Internet, are acknowledged. Primary sources such as print, pictorial, visual, and oral material will be considered." Mr. Polski asks Maria to explain what that all means. Maria thinks for a moment, knowing Mr. Polski waits for them to think their answers through. "It means that you just didn't get your stuff out of one encyclopedia or book, but took some trouble to find really interesting material." "Good, Maria, well thought out." Tiffany is asked what "primary" means. She answers, "For our project on the underground railway, we might find a photograph or a letter telling how some slaves fled to Canada." "Excellent," says Mr. Polski, pleased with the quality of his students' responses. "Let's discuss the other criteria."

Ongoing Student Activities

Students engage in a variety of activities during a school day, week, and term. Activities may involve the class as a whole, a group, or individuals, during a lesson, after a lesson, and in or outside of the classroom. Some activities are routine, others vary with the content and the judgment of the teacher.

WRITTEN ASSIGNMENTS.   Teachers can have students, individually or in groups, plan, complete, and submit a written product. The written product can be accompanied by an oral presentation. Examples of written assignments include essays, reports, journal entries, poetry, articles, short stories, interviews, analyses, observation reports in science, or research of some kind. Written assignments can be assessed with a rubric, checklist, or rating scale, or become part of a portfolio. Assessment may be done by the teacher or combined with self- or peer assessment.

PRESENTATIONS.   Presentations can be made by individuals or groups. They can be supplemented with audiovisuals or activities. A written report may accompany a presentation. Presentations can be used in any school subject and on a wide range of topics. For example, the class may be divided into groups to investigate topics that are part of a teaching unit on the environment. Different groups investigate different aspects (e.g., natural resources, pollution, conservation, energy sources, and land use and reform). Assessment can be at the end of a unit or course (summative) or as the course progresses (formative). The teacher can do the assessment or involve student self- or peer assessment. Stations, contracts, or portfolios can be used. Information can be sought, recorded, and assessed in various ways.

PERFORMANCE ASSESSMENTS.   Many things students should learn are more complicated than identifying, naming, or listing. *Performance assessments* are techniques to gather information about students as they actively engage in learning. Examples are manipulating materials (e.g., a basketball or a baton) or their bodies (e.g., dance or tumbling), doing a skill (embroidering or charcoal sketching), solving a complicated problem, giving a speech, or engaging in a debate. Some performances are assessed as they occur (e.g., operating a microscope); others by examining the product (e.g., a water color painting). The criteria used to measure achievement normally should be limited to important facets, and students should be informed about these.

HOMEWORK.   Homework is work students are to do beyond regular classroom presentations or activities. Frequent and systematic teacher monitoring of homework is important. It helps teachers identify students' strengths and weaknesses and the effectiveness of instruction. Homework can be teacher, self-, or peer assessed. Homework and seatwork are discussed in Chapter 10.

JOURNALS

> How can I know what I think until I read what I wrote? (Scotty Reston, Bureau Chief, *The New York Times*)

The use of journals for assessment is relatively recent. Journals are popular with many teachers. They can be a way to gain insight into student abilities and enhance student–teacher communication (Robinson, 1995). Teachers can use journals to help students construct concepts treated in class, promote critical thinking, and foster student self-assessment. Journals provide valuable information about the effectiveness of instruction. When they are done thoroughly, they make assessment an ongoing process for student reflection, teacher–student dialogue, continuous feedback, valuing of student ideas, encouragement, and they "enrich face-to-face interaction" (Heinmiller, 2000).

Students need to be taught how to use journals. They need to know why they are writing, and how to go about it. Journals provide opportunities for one-to-one conversations with their teacher, which helps the teacher monitor progress and enhance students' personal development. A conscious effort is needed to make journal writing nonthreatening. To encourage meaningful description, good analysis of learning, and expression of feelings, students need to know that there will be no undue emphasis on the quality of writing, grammar, and spelling. Rather, emphasis should be on good description, critical analysis, expression of feelings, and justification of responses. Students can be encouraged to express themselves in ways they feel comfortable. For example, some may wish to use pictures, diagrams, concept maps, or lists. A common format for journals is: (1) describe learning about what occurred in class, what was read, or experienced elsewhere, about an event, a lesson, or learning unit; (2) analyze the impact on personal understanding and feelings; and (3) propose what is intended to be done in the future as a result of what was learned and feelings about what was learned. With the increased use of computers, students may opt to submit journals by e-mail or as attachments. When it is done well, journal writing is a powerful way to construct meaning.

Although many teachers use journals extensively, some have stopped or cut back because: (1) they can consume much teacher time; (2) when several teachers assign journals, the workload for students may be too heavy; (3) students who are good at writing tend to like journals, but poor writers may dislike them; and (4) when journals are graded, free and honest expression may be inhibited.

Quizzes and Tests

Quizzes and tests present common situations to which students respond. Each quiz or test has common instructions and rules for grading. Quizzes differ from tests in that quizzes are usually shorter and limited to material studied in a lesson, a previous lesson, or recent lessons. Quizzes often are used to find whether students are ready to move to new material. The major use of quizzes and tests is to measure academic achievement. Most subject-matter quizzes and tests measure the degree to which students have achieved intended learning outcomes; they allow students to show what they know or can do at the time of the quiz or test.

PREPARING GOOD TESTS.   Good tests should be valid and reliable. They seek information about what was treated, and the way it was treated. Tests should consist of items appropriate for the learning outcomes to be measured. These may be recall, understanding, application, or higher-level outcomes that call for analysis, creativity, or reasoned judgments.

Testing and grading, particularly paper-and-pencil tests, have been fraught with controversy as long as they have been used. The arguments pro and con have changed little over the years. A summary of the criticisms and reasons for the use of testing are presented in Figure 4.2.

You, as the teacher, may know what you wanted to ask with a test item—students might not. Students need to understand what was asked and how to respond. Items should be free from clues, and the level of difficulty should be appropriate. Also, tests should be used to improve learning; though an important purpose is diagnosis of achievement and teaching effectiveness, *tests should also be teaching and learning tools.* Students deserve to receive clear feedback about how they did. This lets them check what they know and to turn "deferred successes" into "successes." In addition, tests should deepen understanding. Recall is enhanced because of this, and because material is reviewed while the test is written, and reviewed again when taken up. Tests can be learning experiences

FIGURE 4.2   *Testing and Grading: Criticisms and Reasons for Use*

Criticisms	Reasons for Use
• Dehumanizing	• To sort people for jobs and other roles
• Unduly emphasizes competition	• Used as rewards to motivate
• Promotes cheating	• To judge whether a teacher is or is not doing a good job
• An extrinsic reward system that discourages intrinsic interest	• So parents can judge how their children are doing compared to others
• Often tests the wrong things (recall rather than thinking and application)	
• Preparation and marking are very time consuming	

in themselves. They can be arranged so that less difficult items precede the more difficult ones. Short-answer questions in the early sections can provide knowledge that might be used in later long-answer sections. Initially, simple recall can be required, followed by questions that require analysis and synthesis. There are science and experience behind creating good test items. It is worthwhile to examine the testing approaches for Advanced Placement and The International Baccalaureate.

The types of test items you select should require the same performance of students, and the same conditions or "givens," identified in the instructional objectives, and be congruent with the activities students engage in to achieve the objectives. The types of test items available include: oral assessment, performance, extended open response (essay), short answer, matching, multiple choice, true/false, and variations of these. A first step is to decide what it is that you want to test.

ORAL ASSESSMENTS.   Oral assessment is done on what students say rather than write. It can be used when written assessment is not feasible or appropriate. It can supplement written assessment or check its validity. More questions can be asked, because written responses take longer than oral responses. Oral assessments can assess students' ability to express themselves orally or to check ability to "think on one's feet." Rating scales or checklists may be used to record judgments about student performance. If you use oral assessment, try to reduce the level of tension most students experience. Private sessions may be less stressful. The teacher can use oral assessment to recognize differences in culture or language background. Oral assessment may be used if a student has a physical handicap such as blindness or paralysis. When you use oral assessment, be wary of the tendency to provide prompts that are not available to every student. A variation is to use oral questions but require written responses. Oral assessments can be used in courses in which development of auditory comprehension skills is an objective. A major use of oral assessment can be to balance testing approaches and accommodate various learning styles.

PERFORMANCE TEST ITEMS.   Normally, performance tests are used to assess how well a student performs a behavior that has been practiced to achieve an objective or objectives. It include processes such as "working with others" or skills in physical education (e.g., tumbling). Usually, performance tests measure direct performance, such as operating a computer, giving a speech, playing a musical instrument, or operating a lathe. Assessment can occur on performance in simulations, for example, the simulated operation of an automobile. Clear criteria need to be set, and students need to be aware of them. The use of rubrics for grading has become common. Usually, both product (the "correct" answer) and process (how something is done) should be assessed. Avoid undue emphasis on product.

EXTENDED OPEN-RESPONSE (ESSAY) ITEMS.   Most people call extended open-response items *essay* items. Students are asked to compose a comprehensive, lengthy, or complex response on a topic. Students provide, rather than select, answers. No single response or pattern is correct. More than recall should be involved. Good items test complex cognitive processes or skills. Students have to "pull things together" (organize), use information to solve problems, express what they know, or be creative. Examples of outcomes that can be assessed through essay items are: seeking a solution to a problem, synthesizing data from two or more sources, comparing and contrasting, examining cause-and-effect relationships, developing an argument to support a position, and critically examining assumptions.

When items are prepared, be sure students know what is expected (e.g., to compare and contrast, to predict, to judge the merit of something using certain criteria, or to provide original examples). Avoid items that are "as broad as all outdoors," leave students guessing, require students to have memorized reams of information, and choices when you may want every student to write the same test. Importantly, *test only what was taught!*

Extended responses are time consuming to grade and the course content sampled is restricted, so important content may not be tested. Though only a few items have to be prepared and marked, marking may be long, laborious, and lack objectivity. Objective tests (e.g., multiple-choice) allow greater coverage of what was taught. Bluffing and writing skill can influence the score, so the test may not help you discover what students know. There is a tendency for teachers to grade essay items higher than objective items. Some authorities believe that extended response items should be restricted to term papers or take-home tests.

RESTRICTED RESPONSE (SHORT-ANSWER) ITEMS.   Restricted response items have students supply, or complete, short written responses to specific questions. Answers to short-answer items may be a single word, a phrase, or a paragraph or two. The question should specify response limitations, and evaluation criteria for scoring should be provided. Short-answer items are good for testing students' ability to recall. Many facts can be tested in a short time. Test construction is relatively easy. Fewer items are required than in other objective tests. Guessing is less than when other objective items are used, but less content can be surveyed than with, for example, multiple-choice items.

It is not easy to measure complex learning through restricted response items. As in other rapid response items, rote recall may be stressed and students may take time to memorize trivial details. It is difficult to construct clear, unambiguous items, and scoring can be difficult.

It is a good idea to develop a bank of short-answer and other items. If you want to use items in future tests, have tests returned. When you reuse items, make sure they are still appropriate.

MATCHING ITEMS.   When matching items are used, students are presented with two lists of items. Tell them to select an item from one list (the *premise* list) that most closely matches an item in the other list (the *response* list). Matching questions can test knowledge of facts, relationships, or associations. Arrange items in a list randomly and have the response list longer than the premise list. To avoid confusion, make sure the material is homogeneous (or related), avoid making the lists long, keep both lists on one page, and provide clear directions. Matching items are not suitable for assessing achievement of higher-level objectives. Constructing lists that are free from clues takes time and is difficult. Guessing may occur as the process of elimination takes place.

MULTIPLE-CHOICE ITEMS.   Multiple-choice items consist of a question or statement (the *stem*) followed by a list of possible *answers*. Provide four possible answers. Each answer should be plausible, and students should be told to pick the "best." Many think multiple-choice questions are the best type of objective test items. They are versatile and easy to mark. Learning at all cognitive levels can be evaluated, and items can be reliable and objective. A large knowledge base can be tested in a short time. Multiple-choice items probably should be used in conjunction with other testing formats.

Multiple-choice items, normally, are not suitable for measuring organization or composition capability. Measuring higher-level thought processes (though possible) is not easy. Constructing good items is time consuming and difficult. Great care must be taken to word items carefully and to avoid clues. It is hard to construct higher-cognitive-level items; therefore, tests sometimes include an inordinate number of low-level items. Many more items are required than in essay tests. Multiple-choice tests may promote guessing. Students with above-average reading ability may have an advantage, though students with less reading skill may know as much.

TRUE–FALSE ITEMS.   True–false (alternate response) items require students to indicate whether a statement is correct or incorrect. True–false items can test the most facts in the shortest time and are the easiest to score. They *seem* easy to prepare. While they are usually used to test recall, they can measure a range of thinking abilities. True–false questions should rarely be the sole testing technique in a test. A way to increase the value of true–false tests is to have a large number of items.

Guessing is a problem, so care must be taken to reduce the effects of guessing. A variation to reduce guessing is to have students explain their choice or to revise statements that are false (providing credit only if the revision is correct). Guessers tend to select "true" more often than "false," so have more "false" items than "true." True–false tests are good ways to pretest or diagnose. A short true–false test can be used as a set or preview of what will be learned.

ESSAY VERSUS OBJECTIVE TEST ITEMS.   A question you have may be whether to use essay or objective test items when you are testing. Table 4.2 may help you decide.

TABLE 4.2   *Whether to Use Essay or Objective Test Items*

	Essay	Objective
Competency measured	Ability to express oneself in own words using own background and knowledge. Taps high reasoning levels. Inefficient for measuring factual information.	Student selects answer from options provided, or supplies answer in one word or phrase. Can tap high reasoning levels. Efficient for measuring fact knowledge.
Content coverage	Only a limited field of knowledge in one test. Questions take long to answer. Good writers have an advantage. Questionable reliability measurement.	Broad field of knowledge can be covered in a test. Questions can be answered quickly, so there can be many questions. Broad coverage helps provide reliable measurement.
Encouragement to learn	Encourages students to learn how to organize ideas and clearly express them.	Encourages students to develop broad background and knowledge.
Preparation ease	Only a few questions per test. Tasks need to be clear, general enough for some leeway, specific enough to set limits.	Need to write many questions. Wording to avoid ambiguities and giveaways.
Scoring	Time consuming to score. Teacher can provide written feedback on test paper. Grade awarded.	Easily and quickly scored. Answer usually either right or wrong. However, scoring very accurate and may vary widely. Different markers may use different criteria.

Preparing Test Items

Writing Good Assessment Items

Make sure your assessment items measure the instructional outcomes intended. Good objectives specify behavior, conditions, and degree. Good assessment items measure the exact performance identified in the objectives. If assessment items ask for the same performance as the objective, and if the conditions or givens are the same as in the objective, the item will likely be good. Assessment items must not only be appropriate, they need to be well written. Consider the following good matches between the givens and the performances specified in instructional objectives and the performances required in assessment items.

1. (a) *Objective:* When presented with a newspaper or magazine advertisement, the student will be able to correctly identify the psychological influences on the consumer.
   (b) *Assessment item:* The teacher provides clippings of magazine and newspaper advertisements and students are asked to identify which psychological needs are being appealed to in each ad.
2. (a) *Objective:* Given a map of North America and a list of latitude and longitude coordinates, students will be able to identify the names of nine out of ten cities that match those coordinates.
   (b) *Assessment item:* Using their atlases, and given the coordinates for ten cities with a blank space beside each coordinate, students are to write the name of the city that matches. You will notice the performance in the objective is the same as that required in the assessment. Also, the way students are to do the performance is identical.

Now, look at examples of poor items.

1. (a) *Objective:* Given a mannequin, the student will demonstrate the correct procedure for mouth-to-mouth resuscitation.
   (b) *Assessment item:* The test item requires the student to, from memory, provide a written description of mouth-to-mouth resuscitation.
2. (a) *Objective:* The student will, for items in a list of foods, write the correct name of the food group to which each belongs.
   (b) *Assessment item:* Students are shown a picture that displays different types of foods and are asked, under the headings "milk," "meat," "vegetable," "fruit," and "bread–cereal," to name three foods that appear in the picture.

In the first poor example above, in the objective, a given was that a mannequin be present and the student was to simulate mouth-to-mouth resuscitation. However, in the assessment item, a mannequin was not present and the student had to describe, rather than do, mouth-to-mouth resuscitation. In the second poor example, in the objective, students were expected to name the food group to which items in a list belonged. The assessment item, however, asked students to select three examples for each food group, the names of which were provided.

If objectives specify, and learning activities involve, performance at one cognitive level, but assessment is at another, the assessment is inappropriate. Here is an example:

suppose the objective is for students to name different types of levers, a lecture is provided on different types of levers, and students then practice identifying levers. The test item, however, requires students to choose the types of lever to use in different situations and to justify their choices. A mismatch between objectives and learning activities and assessment has occurred. Students at all levels find mismatching objectives and testing to be unfair.

Writing Clear Assessment Items

Items should state clearly how students should respond. Avoid test items that allow more than one interpretation of the performance expected. Higgins and Sullivan (1981) say that lack of clarity occurs when directions are too complicated, or several answers may be correct, or students are asked to put things in sequence without telling them the sequence, or students are to describe something without knowing the kind of description expected. Examples of each of these follow.

1. *Unnecessary details*

   There are four factors of production, and combinations of these factors, that economists consider when they analyze the productive capacity of a geographic region. Name them.

   It takes too long to ask students to name the four factors of production.

2. *No basis for ordering things*

   In correct order, list the planets in our solar system.

   What order is wanted? Distance from the sun? Date of discovery? Size? Number and kinds of satellites? Alphabetical?

3. *Several correct answers possible*

   Geese migrate in _____ .

   Correct answers include: "the fall," "the spring," "flocks," "V-shaped formations."

4. *No basis for providing a description*

   Describe the cities, towns, and villages in Mexico.

   Students do not know whether to sort these by size, location, political status, goods produced, etc.

5. *Insufficient clues—the item is mutilated*

   The _____ calendar contains _____ and is based on calculation of the earth's orbit _____ .

   There are too many blanks and key information is missing—the missing words are "Gregorian," "365 days," and "around the sun."

6. *Confusing word choice*

   T   F   It is not correct not to fly the flag after sundown.

   This can confuse the student because of the double use of the word "not."

Avoid Prompted Items

Testwise students look for prompts or clues to correct answers. Tests laden with prompts are poor indicators of what students have learned. Instances of prompts are grammatical clues, equal-length lists in matching questions, specific determiners, and illogical alternatives in multiple-choice tests. Look at the prompted items below.

1. *Grammatical clues*

    Copper is an: (a) rare metal; (b) common metal; (c) alloy.

    The article "an" only fits the response, "alloy." Use "a/an." Avoid other prompts by, when appropriate, using combinations such as: "his/her," "is/are," and "was/were."

2. *Equal number of items*

    Match each metal with its category:
    ___ Gold   1. Alloy
    ___ Brass   2. Common
    ___ Aluminum   3. Rare

    The student who has two correct answers automatically will be correct on the third.

3. *Specific determiners*

    T   F   Aspirin should be taken with care because it always causes stomach problems.

    Test-smart students immediately circle "F" because words such as "always," "only," or "never" are usually false, and words such as "sometimes," "may," "could," or "usually" are normally true. In multiple-choice items, the longest response to a stem is most often the correct one.

4. *Illogical choice*

    A union may use a boycott as a tactic. A boycott is: (a) withholding of services; (b) a place where males sleep; (c) members don't buy the employer's product.

    Item (b) is ridiculous, so those who are unsure of the answer have a better chance of guessing the correct response.

More Ideas on Constructing Good Items

In true–false tests, every statement should be completely true or completely false. Statements should be concise, and trivial details should not cause a statement to be true or false. Normally, in true–false tests, there should *not* be a pattern of correct answers (e.g., every item false, every item correct, or a pattern of two correct answers followed by a false answer).

In multiple-choice tests, the stem items should clearly state the central problem. Choices should be grammatically consistent and concise, and repetition of lead words in possible answers should be avoided. Though a pattern of responses for multiple-choice items may ease scoring, avoid patterns (e.g., repetition of a pattern of "c," "b," "d," and "a" as correct responses). Test takers can tumble to the pattern. Each choice should be plausible. Begin with clear directions and keep the lists of premises and responses homogeneous.

For matching tests, the list of responses should not be too long nor too short (i.e., between five and fifteen).

No matter how well a test is written, unless students have learned how to take tests, it may not assess what was intended. After all, shouldn't you discover what each student knows? "Dry run" tests can be given and taken up to teach students how to read questions and provide appropriate answers. Students who have not taken many essay tests during their schooling may not know how to respond. They can, for example, learn to prepare and use an outline before they respond. Students can also be taught how to take objective tests.

After the Test Is Administered

After you have administered a test, before you file it, evaluate whether each item does the job for which it was designed. Examine the level of difficulty and the *discrimination index* of each item (the degree to which students who know the work answer the item correctly, more often than those who do not know the work well). Good items should be filed in a test bank; however, when you teach the course again, you probably will have to write new items to reflect how the course was taught. Many references describe how you can analyze test items. Examples include Stiggins's *Student-Involved Classroom Assessment* (2005) and McMillan's *Classroom Assessment: Principles and Practice for Effective Instruction* (2004).

Marking Systems

Grading and marking systems have long been sources of controversy. Differences of opinion exist on whether letter, percentage, or other symbols (e.g., stanine, which is a 9-point scale), or pass–fail systems should be used. More and more educators believe that alternative forms of assessment and reporting should supplement grades, even replace them. Some authorities prefer systems such as narrative reports, mastery reports, or portfolios, because these can make assessment more *authentic*. More and more authorities argue that instructional approaches such as cooperative learning, whole-language, outcome-based, or authentic instruction require approaches that are more flexible. To overcome objections to using a single marking system, some school districts have adopted multiple marking systems or *standards-based grading*. Though combinations, when used well, may be reasonable, the number of grades to report is doubled or tripled, and explaining the systems to parents is more difficult.

In any given school you may be required to use the marking system agreed upon, but you may have some flexibility. Whichever system or combination of systems is chosen, report cards should explain clearly what is used. Students and parents, not just school personnel, have a right to understand the method(s) chosen.

Letter Grade System

The letter grade system is the most widely understood. People are generally aware that A is the top mark, D denotes marginal performance, and F is failing. Letter grades that record and summarize performance over a period or a term are easy to record. The number of signs is as few as four or five, or as many as fifteen if plus and minus are used. Meaningless ranking of students is reduced (e.g., a student with a grade of 70 percent is ranked below a student with 71 percent); and unfair award decisions are less common (e.g., the student with an average of 96.29 percent does not get a scholarship because a classmate with an average of 96.56 percent is the winner). Some believe that letter grades (and for that matter, numerical grades) are needed as extrinsic motivation, arguing that students will not work hard enough if there are no objective grades.

The advantages of letter systems are balanced with disadvantages. Different school jurisdictions use different marking systems, so interpretation is difficult when a student moves from one school to another (e.g., performance awarded a B in one school may earn a C in another). Also, letter grades are arbitrary, gross indicators of a student's level of mastery—there may be much difference between a low C and a high C. For that matter, differences can occur between one teacher and another in the same school or department. Little information about a student's strengths and weaknesses is communicated. Some teachers think differentiation between the achievements of different students is necessary and so prefer a numerical system.

Numerical Grade System

The numerical grade system is not as widespread as the letter system. The most common numerical system uses percentages. Numbers are convenient ways to record a summary statement of work over a period or term. Scores or percentages are easy to average, and ranking is more discriminating. Many parents think numerical grades are meaningful and easy to understand, and some parents and teachers believe they are extrinsic motivators. Disadvantages include the impossibility of making, for example, 50 valid and reliable distinctions between 50 percent and 100 percent. Grading is arbitrary, and little information about student strengths and weaknesses is communicated. As with letter grades, numerical grades are not keyed to a common standard, so considerable differences occur in the meaning of the designations between one school or district and another (a grade of 88 percent in one jurisdiction may be 68 percent in another). And, remarkable differences occur between grades awarded by teachers in the *same* school or department.

It is not uncommon for school systems that use letter or numerical systems to supplement these with checklists or brief comments. Symbol systems do not describe a students' strengths or weaknesses, nor what a student can or cannot do. Checklists also may be used to describe nonacademic aspects such as social skills, responsibility, organization, or conduct.

Pass–Fail System

Another approach is the pass–fail system. Variations are *pass–fail–incomplete* and *satisfactory–unsatisfactory*. The pass–fail system is not as common as some other systems. It sometimes is used for subjects with a high performance or finished-product component. It can be argued that it is silly to use letter or numerical grades in performance-oriented, dance, drama, or visual arts classes or for products in vocational classes. An advantage is that the negative effects of competition and test anxiety are reduced, so students are not afraid to take risks and are more prone to help each other. Cheating on letter and numerical tests is more common than many educators care to admit. Some argue that students will do only what it takes to pass; others say that the opposite is true—students actually learn more and are more likely to improve interpersonal and social skills. Ranking and discriminating between one person's performance and others is difficult, but parents may want to know how their child did compared to other children.

Mastery Grading System

Mastery grading can be used for all or part of a course. Usually, the assumption is that virtually all students can master learning objectives if given enough instruction and time. Content is broken into parts with specific objectives and criteria for meeting objectives for each part. If, when tested, a student does not achieve a certain grade (e.g., 80 percent), more instruction and time are provided and, when a learner is ready, retesting takes place. Grading usually is pass–fail, but performance can be converted to marks. A variation of mastery grading, often used with individualized instruction, is *contract grading.* A contract, for example, specifies the type, quality, and amount of work required to earn an A, B, C, and D. Learners choose the grade they will work to achieve and will know exactly where they stand.

Narrative System

In the narrative system, teachers describe and comment on students' learning in writing. Narratives can provide much more information than letter or numerical grades. Diagnostic information can be included to help teachers consider how best to help students. Some believe that rubrics or checklists of competencies are easier to prepare and are as good as narrative reports. However, it is difficult to prepare checklists that adequately describe a student's level of performance or mastery. Narrative reports may be used for more than academic progress, such as work habits and level of effort, conduct, social skills, organization, and responsibility. *Anecdotal reports* may be included—brief, presumably objective descriptions of incidents or events involving students. Narrative systems can reduce test anxiety and the negative effects of competition. It is difficult to institute a narrative system, however, because of potential opposition from parents and politicians who use grades to rate teachers.

Portfolio System

Many school systems either use, or are considering using, portfolios as the major assessment tool or for use with other techniques. Many teachers are excited by the progress of their students and have become advocates of the portfolio approach.

Portfolios were described earlier. They are collections, in a binder or container of student work, to be reviewed and judged against preset guidelines. Ideally, students are involved in selecting work to be included, deciding how it should be rated, and evaluating it. This can motivate students. They can be useful for reporting to parents and to supplement report cards and standardized test results. "When using portfolios, students should be involved in deciding what will be included and how it will be evaluated" (Kauchak & Eggen, 2003, p. 412). The best portfolios contain evidence of student self-reflection, for example, through free-expression logs or journals. Common ways to check work are rubrics, checklists, and rating scales. Portfolios provide good information about students' strengths and weaknesses. They can reduce testing trauma, encourage cooperation, increase motivation, and free students to risk and be creative.

Teachers must not ignore parental, business and industry, and political objections to the use of portfolios, particularly if they are used as the main assessment technique. Critics, at least initially, object to portfolios, though they may be aware of the possible devastating effect of failing on some when a letter or numerical systems is used, sometimes with life long consequences. Portfolios can be very time consuming to examine and assess, record, and report results. Fine discriminations between the work of one student compared to others are difficult. In spite of criticisms, portfolio use is growing in popularity. This seems to parallel acceptance of the notion of *authentic instruction.*

Self-Evaluation

Increased emphasis is occurring in many school systems on self-directed learning. Self-evaluation is an important aspect. Students have input in determining their grades. This may be done through guidelines set by the teacher or by students in cooperation with the teacher.

Motivation may increase because students develop ownership and accountability for their learning. A potential shortcoming is that students may over- or underrate themselves.

Self-evaluation can occur in partnership with, or supplement, other grading techniques. It is argued that students are natural self-evaluators. If they are to learn to think critically and make sound judgments, they should have experience with self-evaluation (Bowd, McDougall, & Yewchuk, 1994). Self-reporting can occur on checklists, rating scales, self-report forms, or be included in a journal or log. Learning logs or journals, as self-monitoring aids, are increasingly popular, particularly in language arts. They are records, by students, of their reflections about themselves as learners, their learning, feelings, and goal setting. Teachers should encourage students to be constructively analytical about their successes and "deferred successes." Instruction on how to do meaningful reflection and self-evaluation is needed, as is frequent feedback on the process of reflection.

Other Forms of Assessment

Performance Assessment

The trend today, congruent with a desire for active learning and for student learning while being assessed, is the use of *performance assessment, alternative assessment,* and *authentic assessment.* Some educators use the terms interchangeably, saying students are required to perform a task rather than complete a paper-and-pencil test (Office of Educational Research and Improvement, 1993). Others distinguish between the terms. Arends (2004) says, in *performance assessment,* students are to demonstrate certain skills and behaviors, while in *authentic assessment* students go a step further, asking that the demonstration occur in a real-life situation (pp. 245–248). Another view is that performance assessment is an umbrella embracing both alternative and authentic assessment (Wangsatorntanakhun, 1997). Some use *alternative assessment* to differentiate between paper-and-pencil tests and most other tests. Regardless of the definition, students have to do something, whether over an extended time such as several weeks or a short time such as five minutes, for instance: write an essay, play a melody, paint a picture, prepare a report, interpret a problem, or demonstrate a ballistic stroke in badminton. Performance assessment has two parts: a clearly stated task and explicit criteria for assessing a product or performance. The purposes for using performance assessment are so (1) students will be better motivated because they must organize experiences and actively construct personal understanding, (2) teachers will glean valid information for improving teaching, and (3) learning will be improved because students perform better when they know the goals they are working toward and how their performance compares to criteria to be met.

Alternative Assessment

Alternative assessment methods can foster authentic learning; opportunity is provided to foster critical thinking skills, depth of knowledge, and to connect learning to student's daily lives (Muirhead, 2002). More and more educators use alternative assessment methods. The shift began because of frustration with the limitations of conventional evaluation. There are two main differences between traditional educators and those who use alternative assessment. The traditional educator depends on fewer assignments to evaluate performance, stressing tests and term papers (Muirhead, 2002). Teachers using alternative procedures use a variety of assignments requiring active construction of meaning, and moving beyond heavy reliance on passive recitation of information (McMillan, 2004). Critics of alternative assessments point out that they take much time to design and grade. Nevertheless, they offer opportunities for teachers to prepare relevant work so individualized learning opportunities can be provided and achievement promoted.

The shift in preference by educators from traditional paper-and-pencil testing has been made to increase relevance and meaningfulness for students as emphasis moves to contextualized problems without single correct answers. Individual pacing for student growth is a characteristic. In shifting attention to cognitive processes, how students learn is more important than the product. Active construction of meaning is the goal, aided by student self-monitoring. Emphasis is on the use or application of knowledge. Multiple approaches to assessment are used to recognize students' abilities and talents and to provide opportunities for students to develop, and demonstrate, diverse abilities. Assessments such as portfolios and journals provide an ongoing thermometer of developing understanding, skills, successes, and difficulties encountered, and students' feelings about their learning and themselves. Journals and portfolios encourage meaningful self-assessment. By including collaborative products to develop a profile of each individual's progress, the socioemotional dimension is included.

Several threads can be seen to link alternative assessments:

- Students are involved in setting goals and criteria for assessment.
- Students perform, create, produce, or do something.
- Tasks require students to use higher-level thinking and/or problem-solving skills.
- Tasks often provide measures of metacognitive skills and attitudes, collaborative skills, and interpersonal skills as well as the more usual intellectual products.
- Assessment tasks measure meaningful instructional activities.
- Tasks are often contextualized in real-world applications.
- Student responses are scored according to specified criteria, known in advance, which define standards for good performance. (Dietel, Herman, & Knuth, 1991)

Critics of alternative assessments point out that they take much time to design and grade. Nevertheless, they offer opportunities for teachers to prepare relevant work so individualized learning opportunities can be provided and achievement promoted.

Authentic Assessment

You likely will try to make your assessment *authentic,* as close to "real life" as possible. Proponents of authentic assessment argue that achieving fairness does not mean that assessment has to be impersonal and the same for every student. Instead, they say, assessment needs to be "appropriate." That is, it should be personalized and flexible to examine specific abilities and structured at the right level of difficulty. Authentic assessment is criterion referenced to identify strengths and weaknesses of students without comparing or ranking them. Students are asked to demonstrate their learning in a way *they* find appropriate. Authentic assessment is more labor intensive for a teacher but is nevertheless desirable. As you can understand after thinking about the various approaches to testing, each form has advantages and disadvantages. Differences of opinion exist and will continue to exist about the best approach. Some strongly favor the letter or numerical grade approach, others would jettison that approach and do away with standardized testing. The best approach may be a combination.

Educators who are reform minded should realize that meaningful contexts and authentic assessment can occur regardless of the technique or techniques used. That is, instruction and assessment contexts can be meaningful, authentic, and relate to the concerns and problems faced by students, as a combination of procedures is used. Jacqueline Brooks and Martin Brooks (1993) exhort us to "abandon the mimetic approach to learning and implement practices that encourage students to think and rethink, demonstrate and exhibit" (p. v). This can happen as we select a mix of assessment techniques and thereby reap the benefits of each.

Accommodating Special Needs Learners

Should students of different cultures, ESL learners, special needs learners, and learners with differing learning-style preferences be assessed in the same way as "mainstream" learners? If diverse learners should be treated differently, how can this reasonably occur? This is an issue you will face.

As a caring teacher you will try to understand all students in your class. What are their backgrounds? How proficient are they in the use of standard spoken and written English? Any physical or mental disabilities? Are any gifted? How do these factors affect how the students learn and how they can be meaningfully assessed? What are your students' sociocultural values, customs, and mores? Does gender or sexual preference affect performance? What stereotypes are typical for each diverse learner category? Maker, Nielson, and Rogers (1994) stress the need for a change in assessments within a diverse setting. To do this they rely on Gardner's theory of multiple intelligences. They designed a model to discover each student's particular problem-solving style and strengths. Each individual's preference is stressed while means for remediation are sought. Teachers need to be flexible in their formal and informal assessment practices so that every student can display what he or she knows and can do.

Have you ever heard someone say it is unfair for athletes, during competition, to wear eyeglasses or contacts? Glasses and contacts allow athletes with visual disabilities to perform as though they did not need help. The purpose is to reduce the influence of the disability on performance. Teachers need meaningful achievement information on *every* student and what might be done to help make assessment fair. Students with certain learning disabilities or physical limitations should have a "level playing field." They need the opportunity to show what they know and can do. "Let them wear glasses"— special arrangements, modified administration procedures, or the way students can respond to an assessment can provide a more authentic indication of achievement. Accommodations, however, should not compromise the validity of assessments.

Many school districts and departments of education have policies or guidelines regarding test accommodations for students with disabilities. The Wisconsin Department of Public Instruction (2001) provides examples of accommodations.

1. *Time accommodations*
   - Administer the test in shorter sessions with more breaks or rest periods.
   - Space testing over several days.
   - Administer the test at a time most beneficial to the student.
   - Allow the student more time to complete the test.

2. *Environment accommodations*
   - Administer the test at a time most beneficial to the student.
   - Allow the student to work in a study carrel.
   - Place the student in the room where he or she is most comfortable.
   - Allow the special education teacher or aide to administer the test.
   - Provide verbal praise or tangible reinforcers to increase motivation.
3. *Formal accommodations*
   - Use a Braille edition of the test for students with visual impairments.
   - Administer practice tests or examples before the date of the test.
   - Use sign language for directions and items for students with hearing impairments.
   - Allow use of equipment or technology that the student uses for other tests and school work.
   - Read directions and items for tests.
4. *Recording accommodations*
   - Have someone record the student's responses.
   - Use a computer board, communication board, tape recorder, etc., to record responses and then transfer these to the test booklet.

Assessment Issues and Trends

Bias

Teachers need to be fair and impartial, *and to be seen to be fair and impartial.* A huge range can occur in the grades awarded by different teachers on a test or assignment. Be aware of how easy it is, even with the best of intentions, for assessment to be biased. There has been extensive research on bias. The term *bias* refers to unequal treatment of students because of gender, culture, race, socioeconomic status, or other reasons. Each student is the product of his or her unique background. Previous experiences affect how students approach problems and how they respond to questions. Students from different cultural, linguistic, and socioeconomic backgrounds have different experiences and prior knowledge. Ask yourself whether students in your classroom have enough background knowledge to be successful in the assessment items you intend to use. Students should have had the opportunity to learn the test-taking knowledge and skills required for success.

Classrooms contain diverse populations—something to celebrate. Students are different by virtue of (1) learning style, (2) ethnic and cultural background, gender, and socioeconomic background, and (3) exceptionality. Because of diversity, it is easy to use biased tests. Kauchak and Eggen (2003) believe that bias can be reduced by accommodating diversity in assessment. Differences in background can be responded to, they say, by providing test-taking practice, teaching test-taking techniques, avoiding the use of language that may be confusing or unfamiliar, and making provision for non-native English speakers (p. 413).

Bias in content can occur in several ways. Consider a few examples. If you ask questions that include baseball or hockey illustrations, you may bias the test in favor of boys; if the illustrations include activities typically associated with girls, you bias the test in favor of girls. If you have items that speak of winter activities in the snow, you bias the test against recent immigrants who have never experienced winter snow. An item that speaks of a "touque" may be understood by a Canadian but not by an American, who would call the headgear a "stocking cap." If you ask students where the sun rises, the typical answer is "in the east." A student who was born near the North Pole would know that this is not always true, but the answer could be marked wrong.

Bias in testing procedures or test use occur because minority students, or those from another culture, respond to a test differently than expected. Metaphors and idioms common to people native to Canada may leave students who have recently immigrated totally confused. Severe problems with assessment procedures can occur with students who have limited command of English or who speak nonstandard English. Views of the role of testing can be another source of trouble. In North America, African American, Hispanic, and Indian heritage students, and in Britain certain ethnic group students, may have quite a different perspective of the role of testing and of the competitive nature of some assessment practices. Another problem can occur when students come from a culture that stresses oral rather than written communication. Tests with time limits may be a problem for people who believe it is best to do things when one is ready, rather than rushing through something and doing it poorly.

Discrimination can occur because tests do a poor job of measuring performance of students from minorities and nonstandard-English-speaking and non-English-speaking backgrounds. Inappropriate test scores can affect entrance into postsecondary programs or success in seeking employment. Problems such as the above provide a strong argument for using alternative methods of assessment. Students from minorities or nonstandard or non-English-speaking backgrounds should not be denied opportunities to achieve their potential. Some may come from cultures that emphasize testing and examinations and so may be more successful in taking tests than the majority school culture, especially tests that stress knowledge and recall.

Popham (1999) observes, "During the past couple of decades, educators have increasingly recognized that the tests they use are often biased against particular groups of students. As a consequence, students in these groups do not perform as well on a test, not because the students are less able, but because there are features in the test that distort the nature of the students' performances" (p. 67).

If you are aware your beliefs and practices are the products of your experience, and if you try to become more knowledgeable about the value systems and beliefs of other cultures, you can become a good cross-cultural teacher. Know where bias can occur and what you can do to make assessment less biased. Preparing students for tests, using problem situations and stems that are familiar to students, accommodating nonstandard-English or non-English-speakers (e.g., let a student who speaks Spanish answer questions in Spanish), taking up the tests in class, and use of alternative tests (e.g., an oral test), are among the things you can do.

Bias may be subtle, so teachers may not be aware of unintentional bias in the way they grade students. Marzano (2000), in discussing problems with the current approach to assessment, says, "Virtually all of the criticisms focus on one or more of three problem areas: (1) teachers consider many factors other than academic achievement when they assign grades, (2) teachers weight assessments differently, and (3) teachers misinterpret single scores on classroom assessments" (p. 3).

Assessment Trends

An examination of the literature on assessment reveals international trends: authentic assessment, emphasis on the cognitive rather than the behavioral view of learning, continuous assessment rather than written assessment, more student involvement and choice in assessment, self-assessment ability understanding of process at least as important as product assessment, use of technology in testing, use of multiple alternative assessments (including portfolios, journals, interviews, and documented observations), and group as well as individual assessment. A good source on international trends is provided by Brown, Bull, and Pendlebury (1997) in their book, *Assessing Student Learning in Higher Education.* An excellent U.S. reference is Stiggins's (2005) *Student-Involved Assessment for Learning.*

Assessment of and for Learning

If we want to foster improved student achievement in North America, says Stiggins (2002), we need to pay more attention to improving classroom assessment. He argues that the route to improvement lies in assessment, not only *of learning,* but also assessment *for learning.* While both are important, more attention is needed on the latter. He states, assessment *of learning* is done to seek evidence of achievement for reporting purposes; assessment *for learning* is done "to help students learn more" (p. 761). This involves gathering evidence to revise instruction and involving students. A continuous flow of information is needed to advance student learning. Teachers, Stiggins observes, do this by:

- understanding and articulating *in advance of teaching* the achievement targets their students are to hit;
- informing their students about those learning goals, *in terms that students understand,* from the very beginning of the teaching and learning process;
- becoming assessment literate and thus able to transform their expectations into assessment exercises and scoring procedures that *accurately reflect student achievement;*
- using classroom assessments to *build students' confidence* in themselves as learners and help them take responsibility for their own learning, so as to lay a foundation for life-long learning;
- translating classroom assessment results into frequent *descriptive feedback* (versus judgmental feedback) for students, providing them with specific insights as to how to improve;
- continuously *adjusting instruction* based on the results of classroom assessments;
- engaging students in *regular self-assessment* with standards held constant so that students can watch themselves grow over time and thus feel in charge of their own success; and
- actively involve students in *communicating* with their teacher and their families about their achievement status and improvement. (pp. 761–762)

An important part of assessment to help students learn is *formative assessment.* Formative assessment is increasingly important because of standardized testing and the pressure to have students succeed. Formative assessment "of learning," then, can be an enhanced, functional teaching and learning tool. Stiggins (1999), being interviewed on the theme of "assessment without victims," says for formative assessment to be most effective, teachers need to:

- Clearly state the achievement targets for students regarding knowledge, reasoning proficiency, performance skills, and product development capabilities
- Be confident, competent masters of the targets set for their students

- Transform valued achievement targets into quality, day-by-day indicators of achievement
- Provide evidence of things their students can now do they could not do before
- Ensure that formative assessment surfaces evidence that students are progressing
- Along with students, feel in control, not victimized

For formative assessment to be done well, teachers should be provided with, and take advantage of, an opportunity to increase what Stiggins calls their "assessment literacy." They need to know which assessment strategies to use in various situations, and how self-assessment and peer assessment can strengthen formative assessment. Students, he says, should be deeply involved in the assessment process (with no surprises, no excuses). Teachers, he adds, should build a portfolio of increasing competence with the use of formative assessment. Stiggins (2005) identifies three key factors in assessment. The teacher needs to articulate the standards of good assessment practice, meet these standards by accurately assessing student achievement, and have practical options for communicating assessment results. He stresses the importance of "the use of classroom assessment as a confidence builder for your students, as a motivator to keep them striving to learn, and as a strong foundation for unprecedented achievement gains for them" (p. 1). He adds, "We achieve excellence in classroom assessment when we balance a continuous array of assessments used to help students learn (assessment FOR learning) with periodic assessments used to verify that they did, in fact, meet prescribed academic achievement standards" (p. 1).

Technology and Assessment

"Technology can make the job easier and more efficient" (Heroman, 2003). You will want to enhance your proficiency and comfort with the use of technology in assessment. Kauchak and Eggen (2003) believe that technology (particularly computers) can provide important, time-saving functions. They can help you plan and construct tests, analyze data (particularly from objective tests), and keep student records (p. 422).

Most teachers have access to, and make frequent use of, computers in designing assessments and recording results. Computerized grading is common in many school systems. With this approach, a range of assessment items can be entered and weighted by importance in assessment of student progress. At the press of a button, the final mark can change significantly according to the weight given an item, but the programs do not make the grades generated "more accurate, honest, fair, or objective . . . in the end, teachers must still decide what grade offers the most accurate and fairest description of each student's achievement and level of performance" (Gusky, 2002, p. 780).

Integration

Assessment is a complex process that must be considered at all stages of the teaching process. Assessment, an aspect of learner-centered teaching, is the process of seeking information about student development. It is not just an add-on that happens after instruction—it is a key part of teacher decision-making and is closely integrated with instruction (McMillan, 2004).

Wiggins and McTighe (1998) present the idea of *backward design*. The implication of backward design for assessment is that we need to plan assessment early in the unit and lesson-planning process and not as an add-on at the end. Backward design involves the following stages:

1. *Identify desired results.* What should students know, understand, and be able to do? What is worthy of understanding? What enduring understandings are desired?
2. *Determine acceptable evidence.* How will we know the students have achieved the desired results and met the standards? What will we accept as evidence of student understanding and proficiency?
3. *Plan learning experiences and instruction.* With clearly identified results (enduring understandings) and appropriate evidence of understanding in mind, educators can now plan instructional activities. (pp. 9–13)

Assessment design should normally occur early during planning. "When planning to collect evidence of understanding, teachers should consider a range of assessment methods":

- Informal checks for understanding
- Observations and informal dialogue
- Traditional quizzes and tests
- Open-ended prompts
- Performance tasks and projects

"The assessment of understanding should be thought of in terms of a collection of evidence over time instead of an event—a single moment-in-time test at the end of instruction—as so often happens in current practice" (pp. 12–13).

CASE 4.2 Assessment

A Parent–Teacher Interview

It is parent–teacher interview night and Mr. Polski, the history teacher, is discussing Hassim's work with Hassim's parents, who, in looking at his report card, are surprised how well he has done. They note that English and history are not his best subjects. "I used to give a lot of written assignments," Mr. Polski says, "and most of my testing was done with essays and quizzes. I went to a workshop that opened my eyes. I realized, to be fair to every student, I had to assess in a variety of ways and provide more choices to students so I could discover their real ability." Hassim's mother looks puzzled. Mr. Polski, warming to the topic, explains that he always thought Hassim and several others were more intelligent and capable than his original testing revealed. He adds that Hassim is not a great writer, and has to work on that, but when he asks questions in class, Hassim knows what he's talking about. Hassim's parents smile at each other, knowing how much Hassim likes to talk. "We've been studying the American Civil War," continues Mr. Polski, "and usually I test through essays and a quiz. This time I included a portfolio, which includes all Hassim's class work and homework for the unit." He opens Hassim's portfolio. It includes written work, material found in different sources with a section on Civil War weapons, and maps of key battles, and Mr. Polski tells Hassim's parents that he is a very good artist. He explains that he gave credit for presentations and that Hassim did a great job on the significance of the Gettysburg Address. Hassim's parents smile even more proudly as they remember how excited their son was. Mr. Polski continues, explaining that in the final exam he tried several approaches, including an essay on the part that slavery played, and students could write an essay, journal, or a short play, as long as it answered the question. Hassim had written a remarkable imaginary diary of a freed slave—what a slave might have written if he could write. While there were style problems, it was very powerful. "We're very pleased, Mr. Polski," says Hassim's father, carefully folding away Hassim's report card. "We don't want any special treatment." "I understand," says Mr. Polski, "I think, this time, I found Hassim's true abilities. He needs to work on writing, but, as you can see in his portfolio, it's getting better and better. You have a very intelligent son."

LINKING PRACTICE TO THEORY

You have had much experience in being assessed. Now you are about to assess others. Try the approaches suggested in this chapter. Consider the difference between assessment of and for learning. What are the responsibilities and possibilities involved in assessment? What are the multiple perspectives in which assessment is used? How much do you have to conform to societal expectations? What are the possibilities?

Summary

Assessment is the process of seeking and obtaining information about student development and the effectiveness of instruction. Students' progress should be reported systematically from the beginning of the school term and be a regular professional activity. Student performance in a wide range of activities provides ample material for teachers to observe, record, and assess.

Assessment, evaluation, measurement, and testing are key aspects of promoting and recording students' performance. Inquiry, observation and analysis, and avoiding bias and discrimination are important characteristics. Assessment techniques can operate through an individual or group approach that involves teachers and students. Instruments of assessment vary widely and may be used singly or in combination. Data may be recorded in a variety of formats, from grading systems using letters or numbers to narrative reports and portfolios of student work. Bias and discrimination in testing, assessing, and grading students' work are not always easy to identify, but a strong and continual effort should be made to avoid them. Accommodations, when testing, can be made for special needs learners. Using a variety of approaches to testing, assessment, and grading probably is the fairest approach. Assessment should be considered early when planning lessons and units, and assessment needs to be continuous.

Activities

1. List things you liked or disliked about the way your performance was tested during your K–12 and post-high schooling.
2. In groups of four or five, identify what you consider the most important points a teacher should convey to parents when reporting student progress. Report the three or four most important points.
3. Ask your cooperating teacher (or other teacher) how he or she tests, assesses, and grades. Ask why this approach was taken and what alternative approaches he or she might take.
4. If, currently, you have a field experience in which you teach a short unit, construct a test to assess student performance. In groups of three, discuss your units and testing. Ask for questions about what you intend to do.
5. Pick a unit from a school subject you intend to teach. Assume you have taught that unit and now

must prepare the test. You wonder whether to make the test an extended response test, an objective test, or a combination. Agree on a solution.

6. Using the key terms in this chapter, have the class create an assessment and evaluation wall chart.

7. Have members of the class bring in a unit or a series of lesson plans they have designed. Using the principles in the chapter, have them attach effective assessment procedures.

8. In subject groups, discuss, then present to the class, the most common forms of assessment in their subject areas.

9. Present Gardener's multiple intelligences theory. Debate whether all students should have some choice in how they are assessed.

10. In subject groups, select a standard test item you have used before and redesign it giving choices based on multiple intelligences.

11. Get together in subject groups. Select an item of instruction for which you have a standard form of testing. Redesign the testing using a multiple intelligences approach.

5 Classroom Management

Reading A: Historical Perspective

> The classroom should be an entrance intothe world, not an escape from it.
>
> —*John Ciardi*

When I walk into Jonnie Walkingstick's classroom, I am always amazed at the comfort level in her room—the quiet happy buzz of students working together; the materials, learning centers, and books that reflect the Native American heritage of her students; and the displays of student work. I'm also amazed at the engagement, enthusiasm, and competence that she creates with her students. I hear her saying things to her students like "Do you think this is your best work?" You worked really hard to figure this out, can you show some of the others how you did it?" What are we learning from this activity?" and "Is this a good choice for you today?" Each day starts with a recitation of the classroom pledge: "We the peacekeepers promise to be truthful, respectful, caring, and responsible." All learners in her room, even those who had been unsuccessful the year before are successful, responsible, and caring.

When teachers begin their careers in the classroom, they often start with idealistic visions of their classrooms and their relationships with students. They envision inspiring learners and sharing their passion for their content area. Most teachers report entering teaching because of a desire to help young people learn and develop (Feistritzer & Haar, 2005).

Classroom management and discipline are among the most compelling demands of teachers' work. Some teachers tend to be "naturals" with regard to classroom management. Their classrooms are characterized by warm and caring relationships; inviting, positive classroom environments; and motivated students. For other teachers, the perceived apathy and irresponsibility of their students is a source of frustration and stress. Often new teachers are caught off guard by students who aren't motivated, who can't sit still, or who challenge their authority.

Never before has the role of the teacher been so complex. Today's teachers are driven by accountability and high stakes assessment. In most states, schools and teachers are held accountable for test scores of students through a system of rewards and sanctions. At the same time, schools and classrooms are becoming increasingly diverse, as are the needs of learners. Teachers identify dealing with issues of diversity, juggling multiple ability levels of learners, motivating students, and handling disruptions and distractions as challenges they face in classrooms (National Center for Education Statistics [NCES], 2005). Student discipline problems, lack of support from the school administration, poor student motivation, and lack of teacher influence over schoolwide and classroom decision making are reasons many teachers report for leaving the profession (Ingersoll & Smith, 2003; NCES, 2005). Many teachers identify student discipline as a source of stress (Lewis, 1999) and many teachers, especially new teachers, feel inadequately prepared for dealing with discipline in the classroom (Feistritzer & Haar, 2005). Bullying is one of the most frequently identified discipline problems identified by teachers, students, and administrators (U.S. Department of Justice, 2007). Teachers often leave their jobs in the first 5 years of teaching because of issues related to behavior problems in the classroom (NCES, 2005) and school violence (Smith & Smith, 2006).

In response to the increasing demands on teachers, in the last three decades, many systematic approaches to classroom management with the mission of bringing order to the classroom and creating safe schools have surfaced. While myriad approaches to classroom management offer teachers good strategies, the focus often centers on order and obedience. A comprehensive approach to classroom management considers multiple perspectives, intentionally sets goals for the development of caring classroom communities, utilizes relationships and strategies to achieve those goals, and engages teachers in critical evaluation and reflection.

Classroom Management and Teaching Variations

Current classroom management practices and teaching styles can be characterized by several traits, including whether the classroom is teacher centered or student centered, whether management is proactive or reactive, whether the predominant teaching style is authoritarian and unresponsive or authoritative and nurturing, and whether teacher knowledge is based on a linear model of research or a model where teachers are participants in research. Each of these characteristics is described below.

Teacher-Centered Versus Student-Centered Classrooms

Classrooms can be characterized with regard to the level of control, direction, and input from teachers and learners. In classrooms that are teacher centered, teachers set the curriculum, solve the discipline issues, and make decisions about how content will be delivered (Brown, 2003). In learner-centered classrooms, teachers take time to know students with regard to their culture, their areas of strength and weakness, their preferred approaches to learning, and their interests. The teacher engages learners in developing a learning community and solving problems that arise in the classroom. Their input regarding classroom practices, as well as the curriculum and how it is delivered, is sought and considered. Learner-centered classrooms foster student motivation and investment in learning (McCombs & Whisler, 1997). Jonnie Walkingstick's classroom can be described as learner centered. Decisions about instructional and management practices are informed by the characteristics of the individual learner's interests, talents, and culture, as well as academic, social, and emotional needs. Figure 5.1 summarizes the characteristics of teacher- and learner-centered classrooms.

FIGURE 5.1 *Teacher Centered Versus Learner Centered*

Teacher Centered	Learner Centered
Control for learning and behavior is in the hands of the teacher.	Students are active participants in creating rules and solving problems.
For the most part, instruction and management processes are the same for everyone.	Accommodate and modify for varying needs and abilities of students.
The teacher uses his or her expertise in content knowledge to impart knowledge.	Teachers provide a variety of instructional methods and techniques for helping learners construct their learning and develop a system for applying what they learn. Teachers create an environment where learners can make learning connections and learn from each other.
The effort to get to know learners and how they learn and what their strengths, talents, and interests are is secondary.	The student perspective is important. Teachers know individual learner cultures, preferred ways of learning, capabilities, strength, talents, and interests.
Classroom management processes and practices, for the most part, are static.	Classroom management processes and practices are dynamic and responsive to students' changing skills, interests, and needs.

Proactive Versus Reactive Discipline

Classroom management practices can differ with regard to their emphasis on proactive or reactive strategies. Proactive classroom management strategies are practices that are designed to prevent discipline problems. At the heart of proactive discipline is instruction that engages the hearts and minds of learners. When learners are actively engaged in learning, there is little time for mischievous behavior. Behavior is viewed as integrally connected to instruction and the climate of the classroom and school (Carpenter & McKee-Higgins, 1996). In addition, proactive discipline involves establishing classroom norms and expectations so that learners are aware of the behavior that is acceptable and unacceptable in the classroom. On the other hand, reactive strategies involve waiting for misbehavior to occur and then applying consequences or sanctions in reaction to the behavior. Teachers who employ reactive strategies often rely on threats and punishment to control their classrooms. Undesirable behavior is viewed as the problem rather than school or classroom instructional variables or climate (Carpenter & McKee-Higgins, 1996). Research indicates that the less teachers use dominance, threats, and punishments to control their classrooms, the more students demonstrate positive attitudes toward school and a commitment to learning (Lunenburg & Schmidt, 1989). Figure 5.2 summarizes proactive and reactive characteristics. Jonnie's style is proactive. By incorporating knowledge of learners in her instruction, communicating expectations, and teaching students to respect and care for each other, classroom disruptions are minimal.

FIGURE 5.2   *Reactive Versus Proactive*

Reactive	Proactive
Discipline is reactive in that consequences are applied on a misbehaving child.	Discipline is preventive in that the teacher uses engaging instruction and promotes a positive climate to motivate students.
Academic planning occurs without consideration of child factors such as interest and ability and waits until problems arise before responding.	Teachers plan well, and develop instruction to ensure maximum student engagement and motivation.
	Teachers predict how students will respond to certain activities or assignments to avoid problems.
The teacher decides what are good behaviors and bad behaviors and reacts accordingly.	Teachers act rather than react act—think through actions when problems occur instead of knee-jerk reactions that may lead to power struggles.
Classroom management processes and practices, for the most part, are static.	Classroom management processes and practices are dynamic and responsive to students' changing skills, interests, and needs.

Teaching Styles

Teaching style also comes into play in classroom management. As with the work of Baumrind (1971), who studied parenting styles along dimensions of responsiveness, level of demand, and authoritarian versus authoritative discipline, teaching styles have also been the subject of inquiry. Teaching dimensions that have been found to affect student performance and behavior include authoritarian versus authoritative discipline, control, level of demand, fairness, communication, support for autonomy, and responsiveness (Birch & Ladd, 1996; Rydell & Henricsson, 2004; Soenens & Vansteenkiste, 2005; Wentzel, 2002). In short, teachers who have high but reasonable expectations, are firm but fair and flexible, are warm and nurturing, use democratic communication, support student autonomy, and are responsive to student needs will have a positive classroom climate, little student conflict, and high student motivation. Jonnie's teaching style is evident in her warm and caring interactions with students. She promotes autonomy by allowing choices and decisions within limits. "You can choose to sit on the floor for this assignment as long as it helps you learn." In addition, she involves students in solving classroom dilemmas and predicaments. Students in her room know that *fair* means that everyone is not treated the same, rather, everyone gets what they need. Dimensions of teaching styles are summarized in Figure 5.3.

Research-Based Practices

According to Brown (2003), teacher-centered practices lend themselves to a linear view of research and a technical view of teaching. That is, research regarding best practices is handed down by school administrators and university research. Teachers are required or coaxed to implement those practices. On the other hand, in learner-centered classrooms, teachers act as professionals. They are researchers applying and investigating the effects of research-based practices and innovative ideas with regard to their unique classrooms and learners. Figure 5.4 summarizes two views of the teacher's role in research.

FIGURE 5.3 *Teaching Dimensions*

Authoritative, Demanding, Responsive	Authoritarian, Demanding, Unresponsive
Warmth and approval	Highly critical, negative feedback
Democratic communication—seeks and listens to learners' perspective	One-way communication, teacher's perspective is the only one that matters
Demands self-reliance and self-control	Demands obedience
Expectations to perform up to one's potential	High demands irrespective of student characteristics
Provides consistency and structure and firm limits, but flexible and considers learner's point of view	Inconsistent, inflexible, enforces rules through punitive measures
Autonomy supportive	Overly controlling

Popular Classroom and School Management Practices

There are many approaches to classroom management. The underlying premises of each approach reflect the teacher's philosophy, goals, and values. Two popular examples include positive behavioral support and assertive discipline.

Positive behavioral support represents a systematic approach for preventing inappropriate behavior and dealing with challenging behavior. It is widely used in many school systems in the United States. Positive behavioral support involves a three-tiered system for managing behavior. On the primary level, systems are put in place to increase the structure and support needed to promote prosocial behavior. School staff work collaboratively to determine schoolwide expectations that are then taught to all students, rewards for the performance of expected behaviors and consequences for rule infractions

FIGURE 5.4 *Linear View of Research Versus Teacher as Researcher*

Linear	Teacher Researcher
Classroom management and instructional practices are handed down from district mandates and published research. Classroom context and learner characteristics are secondary.	Information from published research and district agendae are reviewed within the context of classrooms and characteristics of learners in mind.
Professional development involves in-service training on best practices for teachers.	Professional development involves teachers' engagement in critical reflection and action research to address predicaments in the classroom.
Evaluation of classroom practices is completed by administrators.	Teachers assess classroom practices from multiple perspectives and with multiple sources of data. Evaluation is a collaborative process, including teachers and administrator.
Classroom management processes and practices, for the most part, are static.	Classroom management processes and practices are dynamic and responsive to students' changing skills, interests, and needs.

are put in place, and data are collected to evaluate the system (Sugai & Horner, 2002; Taylor-Greene et al., 1997). Office discipline referrals are typically used to determine the success of schoolwide positive behavioral support (Irvin et al., 2006). Studies regarding schoolwide positive behavioral support practices report reductions in office referrals, as well as improvements in school climate and academic gains (Horner et al., 2004; Luiselli, Putnam, & Sunderland, 2002; Terrance, 2001).

Because not all students respond to schoolwide positive behavioral support, a second level of support—group support—is a means for addressing groups with a need for more intensity (Turnbull et al., 2002). Examples of group support might include group reinforcers and classroom-wide self-monitoring or self-management systems.

At the third level of positive behavioral support are supports put in place for students with more chronic and severe behavioral issues (Irvin et al., 2006). For these students, functional assessment and individualized support plans are recommended (Sugai et al., 2000).

Another popular classroom and school management system is Canters' Assertive Discipline. Components of this discipline model include posting positively stated classroom rules, teaching classroom rules, and informing students of consequences for infractions and rewards for compliance; delivering consequences and rewards consistently; teaching behavioral expectations; and providing frequent positive interactions with students (Canter & Canter, 2002). Typically, this system involves some way of keeping track of rule infractions, such as names and subsequent checks on the board, so that repeated infractions earn higher levels of consequences. It shares some points in common with schoolwide positive behavioral support, including an emphasis on clear expectations, consequences, and rewards. Lane and Menzies (2003) report on a school that used Assertive Discipline as the schoolwide component of their positive behavioral support program.

Practices such as Assertive Discipline and schoolwide positive behavioral support offer step-by-step approaches to handling disruptive behavior and encouraging positive behavior. These structures can be a comfort to teachers experiencing distractions in the classroom. However, these approaches tend to be designed and directed by teachers and administrators with little input from students. Teacher- and administrator-centered approaches, such as Assertive Discipline and schoolwide positive behavioral support, have met with criticism. One criticism is that these approaches emphasize means and strategies rather than the goals that many teachers and parents desire for learners (Butchart, 1998). They are criticized for their narrow focus on such short-term goals as classroom order (Butchart, 1998; Kohn, 1995; Marshall, 2001). Although they may be helpful in achieving classroom order in the short term, approaches that focus solely on classroom order may not consider other social and emotional needs of learners, such as the need for autonomy, belonging, competence, and an ethos of caring, as well as the need to develop the skills for democratic citizenship (Butchart, 1998; Emmer & Stough, 2001; Kohn, 1995; Marshall, 2001). Furthermore, these programs have met with criticism because of their overreliance on rewards and sanctions, which may interfere with intrinsic motivation (Kohn, 1995; Marshall, 2001). With limited opportunity for input, choice, feedback, and participation in classroom government, attempts to help students become self-regulated learners, wise decision makers, and good citizens are defeated.

In addition to their short-term focus, teacher-centered programs take a technical view of the teacher's role (Brown, 2003). They are based on the premise that good classroom management is a matter of applying known solutions to known problems. In contrast, this text takes a more professional view of teaching based on the premise that the work of a professional requires finding solutions to problems that change from day to day and using professional judgment and multiple sources of information to gain insight and make careful decisions regarding those problems. Teaching brings many predicaments, circumstances, and decisions that vary according to the unique circumstances of the learners, the school, and the community.

Despite the criticisms, a routinized management approach like positive behavioral support can be beneficial if considered as one part of a comprehensive approach. Comprehensive approaches also seek to address the social and emotional needs of learners, foster positive dispositions toward learning, and teach responsibility.

Toward a Comprehensive, Constructive Approach

Teachers can create the classrooms that inspired their decision to teach. Many professionals agree that good classroom management is more than a recipe for encouraging good behavior. The goals of classroom management and discipline practices warrant consideration of what teachers want for their learners and what kind of classroom they want to create. The challenges that classroom teachers face on a daily basis warrant consideration of multiple child, family, cultural, and community factors, as well as the perspectives of all stakeholders, including families, students, and other teachers. In addition, teachers must create classrooms where opportunities for learning are optimal and equitable for all learners.

This text presents a comprehensive look at classroom management and schoolwide discipline. The text is divided into four sections of consideration for classroom management: Philosophical Orientation, Multiple Perspectives, Relationships and Structures, and Goals and Outcomes. These areas are depicted in Figure 5.5 and discussed briefly below. They are presented in a circular model as it is the premise of this text that each area informs the others. Rather than promoting one fixed approach, this text is also based on the premise that classroom management is a dynamic process that requires engaging in critical reflection and thoughtful refinement of classroom practices as student populations change, new problems arise, new perspectives are gained, and new goals are developed. It is the premise of this text that positive productive classrooms and healthy school climates are created through continual reflection and inquiry.

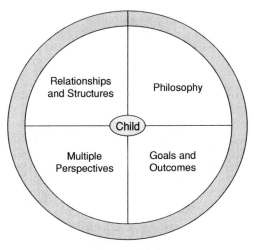

FIGURE 5.5 *Essential Aspects of Classroom Management*

Philosophical Orientation

Many philosophical orientations inform classroom management practices. Two common orientations are behavioral theory and constructivist theory. In Readings B and C, I explore the contributions of those orientations to classroom management practices. I also consider theories of motivation and engagement as relevant and informative for classroom management practices.

Behavioral theory and practice have provided many tools for systematically examining and changing the behavior of students. Practices based on behavioral theory include token economies and reward systems, as well as systems such as Canters' Assertive Discipline and schoolwide positive behavioral support. Although these practices can be helpful if used carefully, they often rely on external control of students. At the same time, behavioral principles can be unintentionally at work in the classroom with undesirable results.

The constructivist orientation allows teachers to consider the inherent social nature of the classroom and students, consider the students' perspective, and address the social and emotional needs of learners. The views of social constructivist theorists go beyond the behaviorists' perspective and acknowledge the contributions of the school curriculum, the classroom and school environments, families, and the broader culture and community in shaping school experiences and student learning. The behavioral theorist focuses on the prediction and control of events in the immediate environment; a social constructivist explores the entire sociocultural context of a student's life to gain insight into a student's school experience.

Careful examination of one's philosophical orientation can assist the teacher in developing classroom practices. Teachers have varying perspectives and ideas as to their role as a teacher. Teachers can develop their own metaphor for teaching as a basis for examining their role and understanding their current philosophical practices. Metaphors can help teachers make sense of who and what they are as teachers and be reflective about their practice. A teacher's metaphor may indicate whether his or her philosophical orientation lends itself toward a behavioral model or a constructivist model, reveal whether the classroom is student centered or teacher centered, and define what the teacher values. For example, constructivist teachers may see themselves as coaches or guides, while behaviorist teachers may see themselves as technologists or diagnosticians. The metaphor that a teacher adopts can reveal his or her perceptions of students and classroom life. For example, in a qualitative study, Hyland (2005) examined the metaphors of white teachers of African American learners. In this study, metaphors revealed how well-intentioned teachers may perpetuate racial bias in the classroom. For example, one teacher saw herself as a helper. Interviews with her revealed that she saw her children and their families as incapable of helping themselves. Other metaphors include the following:

> Teacher as a leader
> Teacher as a partner (Tabak, Gurion, & Baumgartner, 2004)
> Teacher as a facilitator
> Teacher as a nurturer
> Teacher as a caregiver

The Circle of Courage (Brendtro, Brokenleg, & Van Bockern, 1990) provides a useful framework for considering desirable outcomes for learners. The Circle of Courage incorporates four universal human needs: the needs for belonging, mastery, independence, and generosity. This framework is discussed in detail in Chapter 2. Subsequent chapters use the framework to summarize and illustrate essential concepts for classroom management practices that are responsive to learners.

Multiple Perspectives

Unlike more homogenous classrooms of the past, classrooms today represent diverse populations. Many classroom populations represent a wide range of cultures, ethnicity, family structures, and income levels. Often the teacher's culture is different from that of many of his or her students and their families. Empowering learners and families by seeking their perspective, input, and feedback in developing classroom practices can generate goodwill, greater commitment and investment in learning, and support for school and classroom activities. In addition, careful examination of assumptions, beliefs, and biases can assist teachers in developing classrooms that are culturally responsive. Often the perspectives of families and learners are ignored, but research tells us that gaining multiple perspectives can increase motivation and academic achievement.

As with family and student perspectives, teachers' perspectives are also key to developing positive and productive classroom and school environments. Teachers can engage in communities of practice and collaborative reflection and inquiry as a professional practice. Doing so allows teachers to take a systems view of predicaments that interfere with optimal learner engagement and achievement. For example, if bullying is a problem identified by students, families, and teachers, one approach is to target the bullies for intervention. Alternatively, a systems approach would involve looking at the school climate and classroom conditions that potentially nurture bullying. Addressing bullying at the systems level may lead to lasting improvements that will benefit all children.

Relationships and Structures

At the heart of classroom management and positive school climate are the relationships and structures that teachers create and nurture. Taking advantage of the social nature of school can assist teachers in developing strong relationships based on respect, responsibility, and learning. Relationships come into play in classroom management and school climate both with regard to teachers' relationships with students and students' relationships with each other. Developing positive relationships at both levels requires intentional action. With regard to student relationships, teachers can take action to develop relationships with even the most reluctant children and youth. Research indicates that positive productive relationships with students increase academic achievement and a sense of belonging to the school. In addition, learners who establish positive connections with their teachers are more open to adult guidance and are more likely to follow school and classroom norms.

Developing a sense of community among learners has many known benefits as well. Community allows learners to feel a sense of belonging and attachment to school. It provides a foundation for engaging learners in solving problems and behaving in socially responsible ways. It also assists teachers in keeping the focus on learning—the work of the community—as opposed to obedience and control.

Most teachers desire for learners to want to learn. Attitudes and dispositions for learning that children and youth bring to the classroom can vary greatly. Some learners bring a curious nature and an insatiable appetite for learning while others, because of their individual circumstances, may be reluctant to fully engage in learning. In addition, motivation for schoolwork tends to decline as children get older. Motivating learners and maintaining academic engagement are proactive classroom practices that can help keep behavioral issues in check. Fueling a positive disposition for learning can be accomplished with an understanding of motivation and careful work to help children adopt learning goals and develop confidence.

In even the best of classrooms, disruptions and distractions occur. Bullying and violence is another, growing concern in many schools. Minor disruptions and distractions can be handled in ways that preserve dignity and allow the student to learn from his or her mistakes. A systemic approach is recommended for dealing with more persistent challenging behavior, as well as school violence.

Goals and Outcomes

As with considering the teacher's role, an examination of what the teacher values can also be helpful in developing responsive classroom management practices. The Interstate New Teacher Assessment and Support Consortium (INTASC) standards, as seen in Table 5.1, indicate expected dispositions of teachers. Teachers are wise to review those dispositions and reflect on their meaning and application in the classroom. In addition, some teachers value quiet orderly students, students who are prepared for class, and students who are self-directed and self-motivated. Examining values can lend itself to establishing goals and practices that incorporate those values. Professional practice involves articulating goals and outcomes and assessing classroom practices in relation to desired goals.

TABLE 5.1 *Interstate New Teacher Assessment and Support Consortium (INTASC) Standards*

#1: The teacher understands the central concepts, tools of inquiry, and structures of the discipline(s) that he or she teaches and can create learning experiences that make these aspects of subject matter meaningful.

#2: The teacher understands how children learn and develop and can provide learning opportunities that support their intellectual, social, and personal development.

#3: The teacher understands how students differ in their approaches to learning and creates instructional opportunities that are adapted for diverse learners.

#4: The teacher understands and uses a variety of instructional strategies to encourage students' development of critical thinking, problem solving, and performance skills.

#5: The teacher uses an understanding of individual and group motivation and behavior to create a learning environment that encourages positive social interactions, active encouragement in learning, and self-motivation.

#6: The teacher uses knowledge of effective verbal, nonverbal, and media communication techniques to foster active inquiry, collaboration, and supportive interaction in the classroom.

#7: The teacher plans instruction based on knowledge of subject matter, students, the community, and curriculum goals.

#8: The teacher understands and uses formal and informal assessment strategies to ensure the continuous intellectual, social, and physical development of the learners.

#9: The teacher is a reflective practitioner who continually evaluates the effects of his or her choices and actions on others (students, parents, and other professionals in the learning community) and who actively seeks opportunity to grow professionally.

#10: The teacher fosters relationships with school colleagues, parents, and agencies in the larger community to support students' learning and well-being.

Research and Practice

The research and professional literature that informs classroom management comes from many disciplines, including psychology, sociology, and education. This text draws from each of those disciplines to synthesize what we know about learners, classrooms, motivation, behavior, and so forth. I use examples of classroom-based research from these disciplines. In addition, I have spent time in many classrooms as a teacher, as a participant observer, and as a parent. I use many examples from several wonderful teachers that I have spent time with and observed putting research into practice, including Jonnie Walkingstick, Ron Watson, Louise Burrell, and others. At times, I also compare these classrooms with classrooms in which management practices and resulting outcomes are less than desirable. I also include the voices of students who give firsthand accounts of life in the classroom. These experiences and accounts help to describe what great classroom management looks like, sounds like, and feels like.

Summary

Classroom management practices are of concern to many students, families, and teachers. For optimal learning and development, children and youth need environments that nurture relatedness, autonomy, competence, and caring. Creating optimal classrooms requires consideration of philosophical perspectives, as well as the perspectives of all stakeholders. In addition, it involves creating and nurturing positive productive relationships and establishing structures that facilitate learning. While prescriptive approaches may be useful in some respects, they may ignore other desired goals and outcomes for learners, such as positive dispositions toward learning, self-responsibility, and appreciation of diversity. Drawing on research and accounts of real classrooms, this text presents a comprehensive learning approach to classroom management. It provides teachers with strategies for developing relationships and structures. And it provides teachers with the benefit of multiple perspectives and engages teachers' professional development through critical reflection, goal setting, and evaluating progress toward goals.

References

Baumrind, D. (1971). Current patterns of parental authority. *Developmental Psychology Monograph, 4*(1, Part 2).

Birch, S. H., & Ladd, G. W. (1996). Interpersonal relationships in the school environment and children's early school adjustment: The role of teachers and peers. In J. Juvonen & K. Wentzel (Eds.), *Social motivation: Understanding children's school adjustment* (pp. 199–225). New York: Cambridge University Press.

Brendtro, L. K., Brokenleg, M., & Van Bockern, S. (1990). *Reclaiming youth at risk: Our hope for the future.* Bloomington, In: National Education service.

Brown, K. L. (2003). From teacher-centered to learner-centered curriculum: Improving learning in diverse classrooms. *Education, 124*(1), 49–54.

Butchart, R. (1998). Punishments, penalties, prizes, and procedures: A history of discipline in U.S. schools. In *Classroom discipline in American schools: Problems and possibilities for democratic education* (pp. 19–49). Albany: State University of New York Press.

Canter, L., & Canter, M. (2002). *Assertive discipline: Positive behavior management for today's classroom* (3rd ed.). Santa Monica, CA: Canter & Associates.

Carpenter, S. L., & McKee-Higgins, E. (1996). Behavior managment in inclusive classrooms. *Remedial and Special Education, 17*(4), 195–204.

Emmer, E. T., and Stough, L. M. (2001). *Classroom management: A critical part of educational psychology, with implications for teacher education, 36*(2), 103–112.

Feistritzer, E., & Haar, C. (2005). *Profile of teachers in the U.S.* Washington, DC: National Center for Education Information.

Horner, R. H., Todd, A. W., Lewis-Palmer, T., Irvin, L. K., Sugai, G., & Boland, J. B. (2004). The School-Wide Evaluation Tool (SET): A research instrument for assessing school-wide positive behavior support. *Journal of Positive Behavior Interventions, 6*(1), 3–12.

Hyland, N. E. (2005). Being a good teacher of black students? White teachers and unintentional racism. *Curriculum Inquiry, 35*(4), 429–459.

Ingersoll, R. M., & Smith, T. M. (2003, May). Keeping good teachers. *Educational Leadership, 60*(8), 30–33.

The Council of Chief State School Officers. Interstate New Teachers Assessment and Support Consortium (INTASC) standards (2008). Retrieved March 1, 2008, from http://www.ccsso.org/projects/interstate_new_teachers_assessment_and_support_consortium.

Irvin, L. K., Horner, R. H., Ingram, K., Todd, A. W., Sugai, G., Sampson, N. K., et al. (2006). Using office discipline referral data for decision making about student behavior in elementary and middle schools: An empirical evaluation of validity. *Journal of Positive Behavior Interventions, 8*(1), 10–23.

Kohn, A. (1995). *Punished by rewards: The trouble with gold stars, incentive plans, A's, praise, and other bribes.* Boston: Houghton Mifflin.

Lane, K. L., & Menzies, H. M. (2003). A school-wide intervention with primary and secondary levels of support for elementary students: Outcomes and considerations. *Education & Treatment of Children, 26*(4), 431–451.

Lewis, R. (1999). Teachers coping with the stress of classroom discipline. *Social Psychology of Education, 3*(3), 155–171.

Luiselli, J. K., Putnam, R. F., & Sunderland, M. (2002). Longitudinal evaluation of behavior support intervention in a public middle-school. *Journal of Positive Behavior Intervention, 4*(3), 182–188.

Lunenburg, F. C., & Schmidt, L. J. (1989). Pupil control ideology, pupil control behavior, and the quality of school life. *Journal of Research and Development in Education, 22*(4), 36–44.

Marshall, M. (2001). *Discipline without stress, punishments, or rewards.* Los Alamitos, CA: Piper Press.

McCombs, B. L., & Whisler, J. S. (1997). Learner-centered classrooms and schools: Strategies for increasing student motivation and achievement. *National Association of Secondary School Principals (NASSP) Bulletin, 81,* 1–14.

National Center for Education Statistics. (2005). Teacher attrition and mobility: Results from the 2004-05 teacher follow-up survey. Retrieved September 21, 2007, from http://nces.ed.gov/pubsearch/pubsinfo.asp?pubid = 2007307

Rydell, A.-M., & Henricsson, L. (2004). Elementary school teachers' strategies to handle externalizing classroom behavior: A study of relations between perceived control, teacher orientation, and strategy preferences. *Scandinavian Journal of Psychology, 45*(2), 93–102.

Smith, D. L., & Smith, B. J. (2006). Perceptions of violence: The views of teachers who left urban schools. *High School Journal, 89*(3), 34–42.

Soenens, B., & Vansteenkiste, M. (2005). Antecedents and outcomes of self-determination in 3 life domains: The role of parents' and teachers' autonomy support. *Journal of Youth & Adolescence, 34*(6), 589–604.

Sugai, G., & Horner, R. H. (2002). Introduction to the special series on positive behavior support in schools. *Journal of Emotional and Behavioral Disorders, 10*(3), 130–135.

Sugai, G., Horner, R. H., Dunlap, G., Hieneman, M., Lewis, T. J., Nelson, C. M., et al. (2000). Applying positive behavior support and functional behavioral assessment in schools. *Journal of Positive Behavior Interventions, 2*(3), 131–143.

Tabak, I., Gurion, B., & Baumgartner, E. (2004). The teacher as partner: Exploring participant structures, symmetry, and identity work in scaffolding. *Cognition and Instruction, 22*(4), 393–429.

Taylor-Greene, S., Brown, D., Nelson, L., Longton, J., Gassman, T., Cohen, J., et al. (1997). School-wide behavioral support: Starting the year off right. *Journal of Behavioral Education, 7*(1), 99–112.

Terrance, S. A. (2001). Schoolwide example of positive behavioral support. *Journal of Positive Behavior Interventions, 3*(2), 88–95.

Turnbull, A., Edmonson, H., Griggs, P. Wickham, D., Sailor, W., Freeman, R., et al. (2002). A blueprint for schoolwide positive behavior support: Implementation of 3 components. *Exceptional Children, 68*(3), 377–404.

U.S. Department of Justice & National Center for Education Statistics. (2007). School survey on crime and safety (SSOCS), pp. 22–36. In *Indicators of school crime and safety*. Washington, DC: Author.

Wentzel, K. R. (2002). Are effective teachers like good parents? Teaching styles and student adjustment in early adolescence. *Child Development, 73*(1), 287–301.

Reading B: Constructivism: The Circle of Courage

Through others, we become ourselves.

—*L. S. VYGOTSKY*

Imagine the following classroom. The first week of school, Mrs. Philsinger engages learners in getting to know each other, participating in discussions about how the classroom should be, what behaviors are most conducive to learning, and ways to help each other learn. Students complete a WebQuest, which helps them explore rules and think about rules that are important to them and ones that will help everyone in the classroom community learn. Mrs. Philsinger contributes her own expectations throughout these discussions. From these discussions, learners create a classroom covenant. Each classroom member signs the covenant and a plan is developed for sharing the covenant with newcomers. Learners are asked to demonstrate examples of behavior that convey the classroom covenant and ones that do not. As issues come up, the teacher provides direct reminders of the covenant. Learners are engaged in finding solutions to classroom disruptions and in finding ways to ensure that everyone in the classroom learns. The covenant is discussed over the next several weeks to determine how it fits within the classroom community, whether it describes how they want their classroom to be, or whether it needs to be modified.

During these first weeks, Mrs. Philsinger also facilitates activities that allow students to get to know her and each other. She gives students a survey that asks about their interests, their talents, their learning preferences, and their concerns about school. She allows time for students to share something about themselves and guides them in finding things they have in common with each other. She engages learners in writing learning goals in journals and makes plans to conference with each student about their learning goals within the first 2 weeks. She communicates that she cares about the learning of each student and that she will do everything that she can to ensure that each student learns. She sets the stage for collaborative learning and peer tutoring by asking students to help each other learn and to look out for each other at every opportunity.

As you can see from the example, the learners are active participants in learning about rules and covenants and how they work; they are engaged in shaping how the classroom functions. Such activities at the beginning of the school year allow the learners and the teacher to get to know each other and the stage is set for caring and helping each other. Most important, the expectation is set that the classroom is a community whose primary mission is learning. Mrs. Philsinger is capitalizing on learners' experiences, perspectives, and interactions to assist in developing a positive classroom environment and helping students learn prosocial behaviors.

According to constructivist theory, learning is most meaningful when participants are engaged in constructing their own knowledge and understanding. Social constructivist theory recognizes that learners are influenced by their interactions with each other; with the teacher; and with the broader context of the school, community, and culture. Constructivist views also recognize that perceptions help to create individual understanding, meaning, and reality (Kukla, 2000). Informed by the perspectives of learners, constructivist teachers capitalize on, guide, and facilitate social interaction to enhance learning and develop a safe learning community in which all members are encouraged, valued, and respected. Attending to and capitalizing on interactions and relationships in the classroom can maximize student engagement and motivation, as well as provide a realistic context to develop the competencies learners need as citizens in a democratic society.

In this chapter, I describe constructivist theory as it relates to learning and classroom management. I describe a constructivist perspective with regard to classroom management that acknowledges the social nature of the classroom; the impact of relationships; the perspectives of learners; the classroom climate; and the broader school, community, and culture. I use the Circle of Courage as a framework for considering constructivist theory in enhancing academic engagement and social learning.

Constructivism

Constructivist theory is based on the idea that individuals construct their own knowledge and understanding of the world through their interactions with problems, objects, and other individuals (Prawat & Floden, 1994; Reynolds, Sinatra, & Jetton, 1996). Prior learning and experience also play a critical role in the learning process. Learners create their own understanding based on past and present experiences and knowledge. According to the constructivist view, merely being present for the presentation of new information in a classroom does not necessarily constitute learning or understanding. Likewise, being told what to do and when to do it does not necessarily generate self-discipline, a sense of responsibility, or respect for community.

The many varieties of constructivism cover a wide terrain. One of these perspectives—social constructivism (Bruner, 1986, 1990; Vygotsky, 1962, 1978)—relates closely to issues related to classroom management.

Social Constructivism

For social constructivist theorists, learning is not only a creative process, but a social one as well. Learning occurs when a child develops inner speech or internalized thought processes through the social experience of interacting with peers and adults (Vygotsky, 1978). From this perspective, social interaction is a key means of learning in the classroom with regard to both academic and social behaviors. With regard to academic knowledge, critical thinking, reasoning, problem solving, and meaningful learning are enhanced when students have ample opportunity for dialogue and interaction with their peers (Palincsar, 1998). Knowledge and understanding of social skills, conflict resolution, problem solving, compromise, and so forth are enhanced by the same kind of social engagement and participation as academic learning (Carlsson-Paige & Lantieri, 2005; Dam & Volman, 2004). Hence, in the classroom, social activity and social interaction provide ripe opportunity for learning prosocial behaviors, effective communication, and democratic values. In the example at the beginning of this chapter, the teacher sets the stage for allowing learners these opportunities. She encourages discussion and participation in the development of classroom rules and she helps the students understand the purpose and the importance of participation in creating rules.

The Circle of Courage

In the classroom described at the beginning of this chapter, Mrs. Philsinger understands the importance of students connecting with her and each other; she provides opportunities for students to help each other, she seeks student input, and she communicates that she cares about their learning. She is beginning to address the students' need to feel a sense of belonging, autonomy, generosity, and competence.

The Circle of Courage (see Figure 5.6) represents a holistic approach to childrearing and community building based on traditional Native American philosophy (Brendtro, Brokenleg, & Van Bockern, 1990). Although grounded in Native American tradition, the philosophy is not unique to this tradition. The basic tenet of the Circle of Courage—that to develop as healthy members of the community, children and youth require security, relationships with peers and adults that are characterized by affiliation and attachment, a sense of autonomy, and opportunities for caring and responsibility—corresponds to the principles of social constructivist frameworks for child development. Both social constructivist theory and the tradition represented by the Circle of Courage emphasize the role that peers and others play in the learning of young people (Reynolds, Sinatra, & Jetton, 1996).

Brendtro, Brokenleg, and Van Bockern (1990) first described the Circle of Courage, which is based on Native American philosophies of childrearing, the work of early pioneers in education, and contemporary resilience research. The four central values or "spirits" of the Circle of Courage include belonging, mastery, independence, and generosity. Many theories of motivation, including self-determination theory and the related developmental theories of motivation, agency, and initiative, suggest that student engagement in

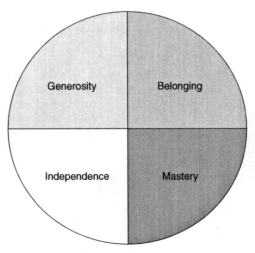

FIGURE 5.6   *The Circle of Courage*

Circle of Courage	Practice	Description	Evidence	How it promotes belonging, independence, mastery, and generosity.
Belonging	Cooperative learning	Students work together to complete learning tasks	Hanze and Berger (2007)	Creates interdependence of group members and promotes working toward common goals.
	Democratic classroom practices	Students participate in activities such as making class and school rules, planning classroom events, finding solutions to problems, etc.	Vieno, Perkins, Smith, & Santinello (2005)	Students have a sense of ownership, investment in, and connection to the community when they have input.
Independence	Choice	Incoroporates students' interests and preferences and allows opportunities for students to make choices	Reeve, Jang, Carrell, Jeon, & Barch (2004)	Considers student perspective and empowers students to make decisions.
	Teaching Students To Be Peacemakers, a conflict resolution program	Teaches students conflict resolution skills	Johnson & Johnson (2004)	Students are empowered to regulate and control their own actions and find solutions to conflicts with peers.
	Class meetings	Engage students in learning to solve problems and conflicts, and use respectful language to communicate	Landau & McEwan (2000)	
Mastery	Learning orientation	Helps students to emphasize and adopt goals related to learning or mastery as opposed to demonstrating ability or measuring performance relative to others in the class (performance goal orientation)	Wolters (2004)	Learning goal orientations foster positive self-efficacy beliefs and encourage learners to seek challenges, as well as assistance, when needed.
Generosity	Cross-age peer tutoring Peer tutoring, peer-assisted learning	Older students are paired with younger students to assist with academic skills; each student takes a turn as coach and as learner	Patterson & Elliot (2006)	Students are given the opportunity to help others in the school community.

school is greater when the classroom and school climate meet individual needs of autonomy (independence), relatedness to others (belonging), and competence (mastery). While these theories do not specifically mention generosity, generosity contributes not only to belonging, mastery, and independence, but also to the development of respect for community. Our senses of belonging, mastery, independence, and generosity are created by our experiences, our perceptions, and our interactions with others.

Belonging

Mrs. Philsinger conducts activities from the very beginning of the school year to help learners gel as a community. Students develop ownership of the classroom by taking part in how it is arranged and in deciding on the rules. The activity of adjusting desks paves the way for students to understand and appreciate differences. Students are given the opportunity to learn about each other and the expectation for helping each other is set.

The acceptance, attention, and affection of others help individuals to gain a sense of attachment or belonging to their home, school, or community. A sense of belonging or relatedness is essential for emotional health and well-being. In school, connectedness is related to higher levels of many desirable behaviors and lower levels of negative behaviors. With a strong sense of belonging, youth become open to guidance from other members of the community. Some children and youth are more trusting of and open to positive relationships with adults than are others. However, research indicates that even children with difficulty forming positive relationships can benefit from practices that encourage belonging. School belonging tends to decline during adolescence, but practices geared toward enhancing belonging at this age can be particularly beneficial in protecting adolescents against the development of many undesirable behaviors and habits.

BELONGING AND ATTACHMENT.   According to Brendtro, Brokenleg, and Van Bockern (1990), in traditional Native American society, all adults served as teachers for younger persons and children were taught to see themselves as related to everyone with whom they had regular contact. This notion of belonging is closely related to the concept of psychological attachment, which Flannery, Torquati, and Lindemeier (1994) defined as a "strong affectional bond between individuals which reflects an enduring relationship and a proclivity to seek proximity" (p. 16).

Although one's experience of attachment changes, with respect to both its objects and its emphasis, as one leaves childhood and progresses through adolescence and old age (Thornton, Orbuch, & Axim, 1995), Marrais (1996) suggests that attachment nevertheless "remains the single most compelling motive behind the construction of meanings in life" (p. 45). In their review of Western theoretical frameworks of individual behavior, Thornton, Orbuch, and Axim (1995) corroborated Marrais' claim about the fundamental importance of attachment. They pointed out that central to virtually all Western perspectives is the assertion that the quality of one's interpersonal relationships is strongly related to one's mental and physical well-being and, therefore, is vital to one's satisfaction and enjoyment in life.

BELONGING IN SCHOOL.   As with home and community, children flourish when they feel a sense of belonging or connectedness at school. Catalano et al. (2004) define school attachment as having close affective relationships with peers and adults at school, an investment in the school, and a commitment to doing well in school. Research indicates that students are more likely to experience increased academic engagement and consequently academic success and greater satisfaction with school when they feel connected to school (Blum, 2005; Blum, McNeely, & Nonnemaker, 2001, 2002; Furrer & Skinner, 2003; Klem & Connell, 2004). Researchers have also demonstrated that school attachment not only increases academic achievement but contributes to well-being and reduces the risk of behaviors such as drug and alcohol use, early sexual activity, delinquency, violence, and gang involvement (Catalano et al., 2004; McNeely & Falci, 2004). In their recent study, Hill and Werner (2006) demonstrated that strong school attachment can protect children and adolescents against aggression and delinquency.

For many children and youth, a sense of belonging and positive relationships with teachers are more tenuous. Some youth have insecure attachments (Bowlby, 1969), resulting in difficulty forming friendships with peers and trusting relationships with adults. In school, students who experience isolation, rejection, or alienation often are less likely to conform to group norms and classroom rules (Osterman, 2000).

Youth with insecure attachments may especially benefit from practices that generate belonging and positive relationships. While early attachment theorists asserted that young children who failed to attach to their mothers during infancy later in life become unable to establish and maintain friendships and to trust those with whom they have regular contact (Weitzman and Cook; 1986), recent research regarding attachment theory calls this assertion into question (Hill & Werner, 2006; Weitzman & Cook, 1986). Brendtro, Brokenleg, and Van Bockern (2002) posit that both belonging and attachment are powerful motives that can be satisfied, even for children and youth with insecure attachments. For many young persons, belonging and attachment to others and to school can be fostered by relationships with adults who recognize that belonging and attachment are central to the development of social competence and self-esteem.

In addition to positive relationships with adults, learners also benefit from positive relationships with their peers. Affording students the opportunity to collaborate and socialize with peers in positive classroom environments enhances belonging, as well as motivation and academic engagement (Hughes, Zhang, & Hill, 2006; Osterman, 2000). Unfortunately, many school practices can undermine these relationships. According to Osterman (2000), the current emphasis on standardized testing in schools often emphasizes individualism and competition over community and collaboration. This emphasis contributes to learners' experience of isolation and alienation, as well as the formation of cliques and clans.

School attachment and motivation tend to decline in the middle and high school years (Klem & Connell, 2004; Marks, 2000). However, it is increasingly recognized that positive relationships at school with peers and adults are beneficial to adolescent development. School friendships can help adolescents cope with the social and emotional challenges of high school and engender positive school affiliation (Hamm & Faircloth, 2005). Resilient adolescents who best overcome difficult life circumstances such as poverty and violence are often guided by strong and supportive adults (Rutter, 1987; Werner, 1995; Werner & Smith, 1982). Research suggests that intentional efforts to attend to attachment during the middle school years can negate the disenfranchisement that typically occurs during these years (Henry & Slater, 2007; Hill & Werner, 2006; King, Vidourek, Davis, & McClellan, 2002; McNeely, Nonnemaker, & Blum, 2002).

FOSTERING BELONGING.   What factors contribute to a sense of belonging? In his review of the literature, Blum (2005) notes that child-centered practices, positive classroom management, positive peer relationships, and gaining student perspective all contribute to attachment. These practices are discussed throughout this text.

Mastery

In Mrs. Philsinger's classroom, students soon understand that the teacher and the classroom community care about and support each student's learning. By helping students set individual learning goals, each student will be able to see his or her own growth throughout the year. No comparisons of students will be made so that each student can feel confident that he or she can be successful.

Theorists agree that competence is an inherent psychological need of all human beings that serves the purpose of helping people develop and adapt to their environment. Children, as well as adults, strive for mastery of their environment. A sense of accomplishment or achievement feeds motivation for further achievement. Success brings a sense of efficacy, whereas failure stifles motivation. In addition to its influence on motivation, competence can affect classroom behavior. According to Brendtro et al. (2002), children and youth with a low sense of competence can express their frustration through troubling behavior. While individuals with a strong sense of competence tend to be more highly motivated and engaged in learning, learners with a low sense of competence avoid academic challenges and use inappropriate behavior to escape difficult work. Learners develop their perceived sense of competence through experiences and social interactions. While perceptions of competence tend to change over time and to be subject specific, some learners develop an illusion of incompetence. Practices that encourage high levels of competence can be implemented easily in the classroom.

MASTERY AND MOTIVATION.   The strong influence of perceptions of competence on motivation is a core component of most theories of motivation (Pajares, 1996; Valentine, Dubois, & Cooper, 2004). For example, self-efficacy theory, expectancy theory, and self-determination theory all include competence as a significant factor that drives human behavior. Briefly, according to expectancy theory, the level of success that an individual perceives he or she can achieve is a strong factor in the motivation equation. According to self-determination theory, intrinsic motivation is the product of a sense of competence, relatedness, and autonomy. According to Bandura's self-efficacy theory, a person's perception of competence has a strong influence over their choices and behavior. While each theory has slight differences in the definition of competence, for learners in the classroom, the basic premise is the same: Learners thrive in classrooms when they believe that they can be successful.

MASTERY, ACHIEVEMENT, AND BEHAVIOR.   Self-efficacy refers to "beliefs in one's capabilities to organize and execute the courses of action required to produce given attainments" (Bandura, 1995, p. 2). According to the research of Bandura and his colleagues, self-efficacy beliefs have influence over our course of action, our choices, our efforts, our perseverance in the face of obstacles, our resilience to adversity, whether our thoughts are self-hindering or self-aiding, stress levels, and accomplishments. Self-efficacy with regard to academics reduces vulnerability to depression; causes individuals to see setbacks, failures, and obstacles as surmountable, and encourages greater effort. In addition, students' levels of perceived competence are related to the value they place on academic tasks that may also lead to increased academic engagement (Jacobs et al., 2002).

According to researchers, the flip side, or low self-efficacy, affects motivation and achievement, as well as behavior. Bandura (1994) found that a low sense of self-efficacy creates despondency, diminishes motivation, and puts learners at risk for substance abuse, as well as transgressive acts. Other researchers have found that learners with low levels of competence exhibit less self-regulation, more negative attitudes, and less class participation (Bouffard, Boisvert, & Vezeau, 2003; Fleury-Roy & Bouffard, 2006).

In addition to lowered motivation, low self-efficacy can elicit escape and apathy. While the need for competence drives learners to direct their energy toward competence, depending on their perception of possible outcomes, they may be driven to either achieve competence or avoid incompetence. Learners can seek to avoid or escape academic work by engaging in inappropriate behavior. Inappropriate behavior may serve the purpose of avoiding an academic situation where failure appears imminent (Reid & Nelson, 2002). In addition, learners who have experienced failure and low grades may reduce effort and display an apathetic attitude toward grades and academic work to cover up for their perceived incompetency (Tollefson, 2004). Finally, learners with low self-efficacy may engage in self-handicapping behaviors. In order to escape appearing incompetent and deflect attention away from their ability, they engage in behaviors and/or excuses such as not putting forth effort (I didn't really try) or acting like grades are unimportant (I don't care how I do in this class) (Urdan & Midgley, 2001).

In addition to self-efficacy in the academic realm, students form perceptions of their competence with regard to social skills such as self-regulation, empathy (Bandura, 1994; Brendgen, Vitaro, Turgeon, Poulin, & Wanner, 2004), and the ability to make friends (Jacobs, Vernon, & Eccles, 2004). Children and youth with a low sense of social competence tend to engage in problem behavior, are more vulnerable to peer pressure and negative social influences, and have lower levels of self-regulation, while learners with high levels of social competence are able to maintain friendships, are less prone to depression and inappropriate behavior, and enjoy emotional well-being (Bandura, Barbaranelli, Caprara, & Pastorelli, 2001; Caprara, Barbaranelli, Pastorelli, & Cervane, 2004; Jacobs, Vernon, & Eccles, 2004).

DEVELOPING COMPETENCE. According to Bandura (1994), several factors influence one's perception of competence. These factors include mastery experiences, social persuasion, vicarious experiences, and emotional and physiological states. Others identify the threat of being stereotyped as a source of a deflated sense of competence and the goal structure of the classroom as relevant to student competence.

Mastery Experiences. Probably the most compelling factor with regard to the development of perception of self-efficacy is mastery experience. Success fosters feelings of competence. With repeated failure, competence declines. In their study, Usher and Pajares (2006) demonstrate that a student's perception of mastery experiences is a strong predictor of that student's self-efficacy beliefs. These authors also explain that perception rather than actual performance is a key factor here. For example, a grade of B on an exam for a student accustomed to lower grades could be perceived as a successful experience, while an individual accustomed to A's could perceive the same grade of B as a failure. Not surprisingly, a decline in school grades tends to be accompanied by a decline in students' perceptions of competence (Bouffard et al., 2003).

Vicarious Experiences. Vicarious experiences can also influence self-efficacy. If learners lack information or are uncertain about their ability with regard to certain activities, they may develop their self-efficacy perceptions based on observations of classmates. If classmates with perceived similar abilities experience success in certain activities, learners may assume that they will have the necessary competence as well.

Social Persuasion.   Social persuasion involves the verbal judgments of others. In the classroom, teachers, peers, or parents may convince learners to put forth greater effort by boosting their sense of competence. Bandura cautions, however, that instilling confidence through social persuasion is not always easy. A history of failure is difficult to overcome even with great encouragement. Furthermore, unrealistic boosts in self-confidence from a parent or teacher are quickly deflated if the learner experiences failure. In addition, social persuasion can more easily work to undermine confidence than to boost it. That is, learners can be easily persuaded that they lack ability and hence avoid challenges and give up easily. According to the research of Usher and Pajares (2006), social persuasion seems to influence girls and African Americans to a greater extent than white males.

Emotional and Physiological State.   Finally, emotional and physiological state can influence perceptions of competence. Persons who are experiencing stress, tension, despondent mood, fatigue, or sickness may feel less confident in their abilities. In the classroom, children and youth dealing with difficult circumstances in their homes, community, or school (e.g., children who are bullied at school or abused at home) may have lower self-efficacy due to these stressors, especially if these children are already beset with self-doubt. In addition, anxiety over exams or other academic tasks can undermine students' perceptions of academic competence.

Stereotype Threat.   Steele and Aronson (1995) identify stereotype threat as a source of diminished self-efficacy for certain groups. According to Aronson and Steele (2005), stereotype threat involves negative stereotypes, especially those that deal with intellectual inferiority. Stereotype threat plays an important role in the poor achievement of certain students—African Americans, Latinos, and girls in math-oriented domains. Social persuasion and emotional states may come into play with the notion of stereotype threat. Aronson (2004) explains that students who are aware of stereotypes may become anxious in certain academic situations, such as testing situations. They fear that the stereotype may be grounded in truth or that their performance will reinforce the stereotype. Aronson (2004) cites several experiments that document the powerful effect of stereotype threat on student performance. Students may be vulnerable to this threat as early as the sixth grade, when they begin to assess their own competence and they become aware of the negative expectations that others may have of certain groups.

Goal Structure of the Classroom.   In addition to the factors described above, the goal structure of the classroom can influence learners' perceptions of competence (Urdan & Midgley, 2001). In classrooms where competition, grades, and achievement relative to peers are emphasized, students may adopt lower self-efficacy beliefs. Where practices emphasize mastery, effort, improvement, and intellectual development, students are more likely to feel confident that they can be successful.

PERCEPTIONS OF COMPETENCE OVER TIME.   Perceptions of competence can change over time and are subject specific. Young children are likely to have high levels of self-efficacy, which tend to become more realistic around third grade (Fleury-Roy & Bouffard, 2006). As with a sense of belonging, a student's sense of competence begins to decline in adolescence and this continues through high school (Jacobs, Lanza, Osgood, Eccles, & Wigfield, 2002; Summers, Schallert, & Ritter, 2003; Usher & Pajares, 2006). Researchers speculate that the decline in perceptions of competence may be due to the structure of middle school and students' changing perceptions of what it takes to be successful (Jacobs et al., 2002). With regard to school structure, in middle school, students are often grouped by ability, and become more aware of their performance in relation to their peers. In addition, in middle school, learners become more aware of their level of achievement and begin to perceive competence rather than effort as the reason for successes or failures. Finally, research indicates that perceptions of competence tend to be subject specific. For example, a student's perception of his or her level of competence in math tends to decline more rapidly over the school years than does self-efficacy for language arts (Jacobs et al., 2002).

ILLUSIONS OF INCOMPETENCE.   Children who have low self-efficacy with no apparent deficits in ability have an illusion of incompetence. Teachers may not be good judges regarding which students have illusions of incompetence (Fleury-Roy & Bouffard, 2006). Gaining student perspective with regard to self-efficacy can help teachers provide support for self-efficacy where needed. As with belonging, constructive teachers assist students in developing mastery, avoiding stereotype threat, and acquiring protection against an illusion of incompetence. The following strategies are suggested.

- Provide ample opportunities for students to master content and skills so that students can experience success.
- Assist students in making attributions of successes and failures in ways that enhance perceptions of mastery. Help students attribute success to effort and ability, and failure to either lack of effort or other external factors rather than lack of ability. When her students are struggling with a skill or concept, Jonnie Walking-stick, an elementary school teacher, makes comments to her students like, "Oh, I must not have done my job today, let me try again."
- Avoid activities and grading practices that allow learners to compare themselves with each other.
- Use structures and activities that promote cooperation. Cooperative arrangements reduce competition, distrust, and stereotyping among students (Aronson, 2004).
- Teach learners that intelligence is fluid rather than fixed. Research indicates that stereotype threat is reduced when students are taught that intelligence is not a fixed trait, but rather that it is influenced by effort and practice (Aronson, 2004).
- Look for improvements rather than perfection. Help learners see their progress and growth and see mistakes as opportunities to learn rather than as failures.
- Teach students about stereotype threat. Aronson (2004) indicates that teaching students about stereotype threat can help improve test scores and study habits. He suggests that exposing students to models who have been successful through hard work and persistence despite academic struggles can be beneficial.

Independence

People need to have a sense of control over their own destiny. Independence or autonomy refers to one's sense of control and responsibility over their actions. Like belonging and mastery, independence plays a crucial role in growth and development (Osterman, 2000). And like mastery and belonging, it influences behavior, motivation, and achievement in the classroom. In Mrs. Philsinger's classroom, students participate in developing classroom rules, as well as finding solutions as problems arise. Constructivist teachers do classroom management *with*, not *to*, students and consequently build competence, ownership, and self-reliance instead of dependency. In addition, practices that foster autonomy prepare learners for responsible participation in citizenship. With a strong sense of autonomy, children can learn responsibility and self-discipline. Teachers can support or thwart autonomy in the classroom.

BENEFITS OF INDEPENDENCE.   Autonomy has great advantages for learners. Citing numerous studies, Vansteenkiste, Lens, and Deci (2006) report that these advantages include decreased drop out, deeper learning, greater creativity, less superficial information processing, higher achievement, and enhanced well-being. These findings have been replicated across cultures, genders, and age groups. Recent research also suggests that in classrooms where teachers support autonomy, students are more actively engaged (Reeve, Jang, Carrell, Jeon, & Barch, 2004; Reeve & Jang, 2006). In the self-determination theory of motivation, Deci and Ryan (2000) consider autonomy to be one of the keys to intrinsic motivation. In addition, many studies show the power of gaining student input in fostering belonging and engagement in school (Whitlock, 2006).

In addition to academic and social benefits, classroom practices that support student autonomy are also in line with democratic values and practices (Carlsson-Paige & Lantieri, 2005). Practices that engage learners in meaningful decision making and give students a voice in their classroom contribute to the preparation of students to participate independently in a meaningful and critical way in authentic social practices and activities.

With choice comes responsibility. Empowering children to make choices and decisions in ways that are socially responsible involves teaching perspective and encouraging reflection with regard to the impact of our decisions on the community. Practices that nurture these skills nurture greater self-discipline and self-responsibility rather than simple obedience to authority (Brendtro & Long, 1995).

People without a sense of autonomy often lack an internal locus of control and intrinsic motivation. Students who are empowered through opportunities for responsibility and decision making develop strong internal motivation, self-discipline, and a sense of autonomy (Brendtro, Brokenleg, & Van Bockern, 2002). Denied these opportunities, students develop an external locus of control and may be reliant on external motivation.

PRACTICES THAT SUPPORT INDEPENDENCE.   While teaching practices that support autonomy have many positive influences, many teachers more frequently use controlling motivational strategies that thwart autonomy, for example, rewards and punishment (Reeve & Jang, 2006). They may feel pressure to use more controlling procedures because of external influences such as high-stakes testing, or they may lack the know-how to implement practices that support autonomy. However, many such teaching practices can be easily implemented in the classroom.

Reeve and Jang (2006) identify two types of practices that support autonomy: those that attempt to gain student perspective and those that nurture independence. Those that gain student perspective include practices such as listening to students and asking students for input. Those that nurture autonomy include allowing students time to talk with each other, allowing students to have a choice in seating arrangements and the way they work, providing rationales for lessons, using praise as a way to give informational feedback, offering hints that allow students to generate answers and solutions on their own, letting students know that you recognize and accept their perceptions, and being responsive to student-generated questions.

Stefanou et al. (2004) also identify three ways that teachers can support autonomy. These include allowing students a decision-making role in terms of classroom management issues or organizational autonomy. Classroom meetings are an excellent example of a practice that allows students a voice in the classroom. Procedural autonomy allows students choices about how they use instructional resources. Giving choices of assignments, projects, and/or learning products is an example of procedural autonomy. The third way that teachers can support autonomy is allowing for cognitive autonomy or allowing students to think for themselves. An example of cognitive autonomy would include engaging students in self-evaluation and reflection.

Reeve and Jang (2006) identify controlling or autonomy-thwarting practices. These practices include spending a greater percentage of time engaging in teacher talking rather than allowing for student talk, holding and controlling classroom materials, giving solutions and answers instead of guiding students to them, giving commands and directives, asking controlling questions, criticizing students, and using praise to control behavior.

Generosity

Mrs. Philsinger communicates caring in her words and actions right from the beginning of the school year. Caring is a powerful theme throughout the year. By Mrs. Philsinger's modeling of caring, as well as encouragement for caring for each other, students will experience the benefits of the giving of oneself. The spirit of generosity involves the sense that one can and should contribute to the community, consider the welfare of others, and share personal and human resources. The opportunity to help and give to others in the community can increase the sense of self-worth in children and youth, foster a commitment to caring for others (Brendtro et al., 1990), and nurture social responsibility (Berman, 1990). Providing learners with an opportunity for giving to the lives of others and improving the community around them and the world builds self-esteem.

Opportunities for generosity can be powerful learning experiences and leave students feeling empowered and competent (Muscott, 2000). Curwin (1993) reported on the remarkable results of seeing difficult youth, including many who had been involved in gangs, make significant changes in attitudes and behaviors after being given responsibility as caretakers, tutors, and helpers of people in need. Those who are helped don't see the helping students as failures, so the attitudes of all concerned change and those changes lead to hope.

In a study of Japanese schools, Lewis (1995) concluded that students succeeded in academic achievement because of the schools' attention to children's need for belonging, contribution, and competence. She described the program as value-rich and the community as caring and supportive, with an emphasis on learning to live in groups. She reported a common end-of-day question: "Did our group members do something kind for one another today?" (p. 39). However, as Lipsitz (1995) notes, American schools themselves are rewarded for individual academic achievement and not for creating caring communities.

Opportunities for students to demonstrate caring and to participate in helping relationships with peers or adults are scarce, constrained by structured transition times and limited opportunities within a class (Bosworth, 1995). Teachers and programs that do provide a chance for one student to help another strongly favor the students who are academically stronger (Bosworth, 1995; McNamara, 1996). However, with careful planning, opportunities for nurturing generosity can be built into the school day.

DEVELOPING GENEROSITY.   Teachers are often concerned with students' self-esteem and self-worth. Typical beginning-of-the-year activities, especially in elementary schools, include activities that help children define why they are "special" in an effort to make students feel good about themselves. While these activities are well intentioned and may serve to help teachers get to know their students and for students to get to know each other, a sense of self-worth may be more easily and genuinely accomplished by providing opportunities for helping others (Brendtro & Longhurst, 2005).

For students to learn to help others, to contribute to the good of the school, and to care about people other than friends, we must provide opportunities to develop these values through shared rituals, routines, and discussions (Noblit, Rogers, & McCadden, 1995). For example, one classroom practice that can cultivate altruism is cooperative learning. In a study of cooperative learning, Guilles (2002) found evidence that learners who work in cooperative groups are more attuned to each other's needs and are more willing to give help when asked than those who aren't given the same opportunity.

Robinson and Curry (2006) provide specific suggestions for encouraging altruistic behaviors. First, teachers can provide opportunities for helping through activities such as peer tutoring, projects that involve a service to the school or community, and engaging students in solving community problems such as having students identify a way to recognize and appreciate school staff or finding ways to assist families in need. Second, engaging children in tasks that serve the classroom community can foster generosity. Learners can have classroom or school responsibilities that provide service or assistance where needed. Third, in addition to opportunities for helping and giving, time must be made for open discussions of values and issues (Curwin, 1993; Robinson & Curry, 2006) related to altruism and social responsibility.

Service learning provides another vehicle of engaging youth in generous behavior. Service learning is a service experience that includes intentional learning goals (Billing, 2000). According to her review of research, Billing concludes that when service learning involves an authentic need and includes meaningful planning, service, reflection, and celebration, learners become actively engaged. Other research indicates that youth who volunteer are less likely to engage in risky behavior (Mueller, 2005). Student choice, responsibility, and decision making are also key factors in successful service learning.

The Circle of Courage and the Power of Social Interaction

As mentioned previously, for social constructivist theorists, social interaction is a key means of learning. The four spirits of the Circle of Courage, which represent basic human needs, are either enhanced or broken through our interactions and communication with others. In the classroom, it is the interactions of learners and their teachers and peers that develop the spirits of belonging, mastery, independence, and generosity. When schools and classrooms attend to those spirits, youth may not feel the need to rebel, bully, or avoid learning. For example, Siris and Osterman (2004) document how attention to belonging, competence, and autonomy assisted an elementary school in New York not only to address a growing bullying problem, but also to create a more positive learning environment overall. In this study, teachers intentionally observed their own classrooms for opportunities for choice and autonomy. Prior to the observations, the teachers claimed that these opportunities were plentiful, but their own observations revealed that they were few and far between. In addition, teachers discovered that students who were victims of bullying had fewer opportunities for competence building; they received less positive attention for their accomplishments than their peers. It is interesting that opportunities for caring and helping other students were attributed to helping students gain a sense of belonging. In other words, in many instances, the need for belonging, competence, independence, and generosity were missing, but when it was addressed, children flourished.

Communication with learners can help build the spirits represented in the Circle of Courage. Language that communicates competence, autonomy, belonging, and generosity can be as important as actions.

COMMUNICATE COMPETENCE. Teachers can use language that fosters a sense of competence in the face of frustration. For example, a teacher may be tempted to say, "Todd, come on, this isn't hard for you, you are such a bright boy." A comment such as this one may lead Todd to think that since a task is hard for him, he must not be that bright. Instead, a teacher may say, "This is hard, but I think if you keep trying, you will get it."

COMMUNICATE BELONGING. The language we use can reinforce to learners that they are an important member of the community. Statements such as "We missed you yesterday and are happy you are back with us." "What ideas do you have to make our classroom more comfortable?" "How can we welcome new students to our class?" communicate that everyone belongs.

COMMUNICATE INDEPENDENCE. Language which conveys that the learner is responsible and can make decisions can foster independence. Questions like "What would be the best way to make sure we leave our classroom clean every afternoon?" "How would you like to present your project?" "What solutions can we find to this problem?" show respect for learner autonomy and an expectation of responsibility.

COMMUNICATE GENEROSITY. Statements that acknowledge instances of caring in the classroom can generate generosity. Such statements could include "I appreciate how you helped Charlie with his math." "Sally feels hurt, what can we do to make her feel better?"

Constructivism and the Power of Perspective

For constructivist theorists, individual perceptions of events and experiences provide powerful information (Rodgers, 2006). Social constructivist theorists acknowledge the contributions of the school curriculum, the classroom and school environments, and the broader culture and community in forming the perceptions of learners in the classroom (Cook-Sather, 2002). Although students in the classroom may experience the same activities, each student may create different meaning. Constructivist teachers understand the process by which different perceptions are generated by the same instructional activities to help them better plan and manage instruction (Hutchinson, 2006).

The perceptions of learners are important because to the learners they are reality. Teachers and administrators may have good intentions when developing management and discipline programs to control aberrant student behavior and increase academic achievement. However, if those programs are not perceived as helpful, fair, and respectful by the students, they often are not successful. If students perceive themselves as incompetent and perceive unnecessary control, alienation, and lack of purpose, the best ideas of teachers may only further frustrate and alienate them. Students are the ones most affected by educational policies and practices. Gaining and using student perspective can serve to empower students, convey trust, and help shape practices most conducive to student learning (Cook-Sather, 2002). Hence, gaining student perspective with regard to their experiences of mastery, independence, belonging, and generosity is essential in a constructivist classroom. Chapter 6 deals in depth with student perspectives and how to obtain them.

Research-Based Practices

With No Child Left Behind (NCLB) legislation and increasing demands for school accountability, school professionals have a growing concern that teachers use "evidence-based" practices, particularly those that result in increased student achievement. Classroom management practices can affect the amount of time that students are engaged in learning, their attitudes toward learning, their motivation, and their willingness and ability to collaborate with each other. As mentioned in Chapter 1, research that informs classroom management draws from many disciplines, including education, psychology, and sociology. Classroom practices that support the areas of the Circle of Courage, as well as enhance academic achievement, engagement, attitudes, motivation, and prosocial behavior, are well documented in professional literature. Figure 5.1 includes practical examples of practices from applied classroom research for each area of the Circle of Courage that align with constructivist philosophy.

Summary

Mrs. Philsinger's classroom, described at the beginning of this chapter, illustrates what constructivist classroom management practices look like. This chapter deals with the constructivist view of classroom management. Classrooms are, by their nature, inherently social places where children and youth form much of their identity. According to constructivist theory, it is that social interaction that creates learning, motivation, and behavior. Taking advantage of that social interaction to help students develop belonging, mastery, independence, and generosity, can enhance motivation, engagement, achievement, and prosocial behavior. Learners themselves are the experts with regard to their school experiences. Gaining their perspective allows teachers to understand what learners may need to be engaged, motivated, socially appropriate, and socially responsible.

References

Anderman, L. H. (2003). Academic and social perceptions as predictors for change in middle school students' sense of school belonging. *Journal of Experimental Education, 72*(1), 5–22.

Aronson, J. (2004). The threat of stereotype. *Educational Leadership, 62*(3), 14–19.

Aronson, J., & Steele, C. M. (2005). Stereotypes and the fragility of human competence, motivation, and self-concept. In C. Dweck & E. Elliot (Eds.), *Handbook of competence and motivation* (pp. 436–456). New York: Guilford.

Bandura, A. (1994). Self-efficacy. In V. S. Ramachaudran (Ed.), *Encyclopedia of human behavior,* 4, (pp. 71–81). New York: Academic Press.

Bandura, A. (1995). *Self-efficacy in changing societies.* New York: Cambridge University Press.

Bandura, A., Barbaranelli, L., Caprara, G. V., & Pastorelli, C. (2001). Self-efficacy beliefs as shapers of children's aspirations and career trajectories. *Child Development, 72*(1), 187–206.

Billing, S. H. (2000). Research on K–12 school-based service-learning: The evidence builds. *Phi Delta Kappan, 81*(9), 658–664.

Blum, R. (2005). A case for school connectedness. *Educational Leadership, 62*(7), 16–20.

Blum, R. W., McNeely, C., & Nonnemaker, J. (2001). Vulnerability, risk, and protection. In Fischhoff, B., Nightingale, E. O., & Iannotta, J. G. (Eds.), *Adolescent risk and vulnerability: Concepts and measurement.* Washington, DC: National Academy Press.

Blum, R. W., McNeely, C., & Nonnemaker, J. (2002). Promoting school connectedness: Evidence from the National Longitudinal Study of Adolescents. *Journal of School Health, 2*(4), 138–146.

Bosworth, K. (1995). Caring for others and being cared for. *Phi Delta Kappan, 76*(6), 686–693.

Bouffard, T., Boisvert, M., & Vezeau, C. (2002). The illusion of incompetence and its correlates among elementary school children and their parents. *Learning and Individual Differences, 14*(1), 31–47.

Bouffard, T., Marcoux, M., Vezeau, C. & Bordeleau, L. (2003). Changes in self-perceptions of competence and intrinsic motivation among elementary schoolchildren. *British Journal of Educational Psychology, 73*(2), 171–186.

Bowlby, J. (1969). *Attachment* (Attachment and loss series). New York Basic Books.

Brendgen, M., Vitaro, F., Turgeon, L., Poulin, F., & Wanner, B. (2004). Is there a dark side of positive illusions? Overestimation of social competence and subsequent adjustment in aggressive and nonaggressive children. *Journal of Abnormal Child Psychology, 32*(3), 305–320.

Brendtro, L. K., Brokenleg, M., & Van Bockern, S. (1990). *Reclaiming youth at risk: Our hope for the future.* Bloomington, IN: National Education Service.

Brendtro, L. K., Brokenleg, M., & Van Bockern, S. (2002). *Reclaiming youth at risk: Our hope for the future* (Rev. ed.) Bloomington, IN: National Education Service.

Brendtro, L., & Long, N. (1995). Breaking the cycle of conflict. *Educational Leadership, 52*(5), 52–56.

Brendtro, L. K., & Longhurst, J. E. (2005). The resilient brain. *Reclaiming Children and Youth. 14*(1), 52–60.

Bruner, J. (1986). *Actual minds, possible worlds.* Cambridge, MA: Harvard University Press.

Bruner, J. (1990). *Acts of meaning.* Cambridge, MA: Harvard University Press.

Carlsson-Paige, N., & Lantieri, L (2005). A changing vision of Education. *Reclaiming Children and Youth, 14*(2), 97–103.

Caprara, G. V., Barbaranellie, L., Pastorelli, C., & Cervane, D. (2004). The contribution of self-efficacy beliefs to psychosocial outcomes in adolescence: Predicting beyond global dispositional tendencies, *37*(4), 751–763.

Catalano, R. F., Haggerty, K. P., Oesterle, S., Fleming, C. B., & Hawkins, J. D. (2004). Importance of bonding to school for healthy development: Findings from the Social Development Research Group. *Journal of School Health, 74*(7), 252–261.

Cook-Sather, A. (2002). Authorizing students' perspectives: Toward trust, dialogue, and change in education. *Educational Researcher, 31*(4) 3–14.

C., Kevin. (1994). My independence day. *Journal of Emotional and Behavioral Problems, 3*(2), 35–40.

Curwin, R. L. (1993). The healing power of altruism. *Educational Leadership, 51*(3), 36–39.

Dam, G. T., & Volman, M. (2004). Critical thinking as a citizenship competence: Teaching strategies. *Learning and Instruction, 14*(4), 359–379.

Deci, E. L. & Ryan, R. M. (2000). The "what" and "why" of goal pursuits: Human needs and the self-determination of behavior. *Psychological Inquiry, 11*(4), 227–268.

Flannery, D. J., Torquati, J. C., and Lindemeier, L. (1994). The method and meaning of emotional expression and experience during adolescence. *Journal of Adolescent Research, 9*(1), 8–27.

Fleury-Roy, M.-H., & Bouffard, T. (2006). Teachers' recognition of children with an illusion of incompetence. *European Journal of Psychology of Education, 21*(2), 149–162.

Furrer, C., & Skinner, E. (2003). Sense of relatedness as a factor in children's academic engagement and performance. *Journal of Educational Psychology, 95*(1), 148–162.

Guillies, R. M. (2002). The residual effects of cooperative-learning experiences: A two-year follow-up. *The Journal of Educational Research, 6*(1), 15–20.

Hamm, J. V., & Faircloth, B. S. (2005). The role of friendship in adolescents' sense of belonging. *New Directions for Child and Adolescent Development, 2005*(107), 61–78.

Hanze, M., & Berger, R. (2007). Cooperative learning, motivational effects, and student characteristics: An experimental study comparing cooperative learning and direct instruction. *Learning and Instruction, 17*(1), 29–41.

Henry, K. L., & Slater, M. D. (2007). The contextual effect of school attachment on young adolescents' alcohol use. *Journal of School Health, 77*(2), 67–74.

Hill, L. G., & Werner, N. F. (2006). Affiliative motivation, school attachment, and aggression in school. *Psychology in the Schools, 43*(2), 231–246.

Hughes, J. N., Zhang, D., & Hill, C. R. (2006). Peer assessments of normative and individual teacher–student support predict social acceptance and engagement among low-achieving children. *Journal of School Psychology, 43*(6), 447–463.

Hutchison, C. B. (2006). Cultural constructivism: The confluence of cognition, knowledge creation, multiculturalism, and teaching. *Intercultural Education, 17*(3), 301–310.

Jacobs, J. E., Lanza, S., Osgood, D. W., Eccles, J. S., & Wigfield, A. (2002). Changes in children's self-competence and values: Gender and domain differences across grades one through twelve. *Child Development, 73*(2), 509–527.

Jacobs, J. E., Vernon, M. K., & Eccles, J. S. (2004). Relations between social self-perceptions, time use, and prosocial or problem behaviors during adolescense. *Journal of Adolescent Research, 19*(1), 45–62.

Johnson, D. W., & Johnson, R. T. (2004). Implementing the "teaching students to be peacemakers" program. *Theory into Practice, 43*(1), 69–79.

King, K. A., Vidourek, R. A., Davis, B., & McClellan, W. (2002). Increasing self-esteem and school connectedness through a multidimensional mentoring program. *Journal of School Health, 72*(7), 294–300.

Klem, A. M., & Connell, J. P. (2004). Relationships matter: Linking teacher support to student engagement and achievement. *Journal of School Health, 74*(7), 262–273.

Kukla, A. (2000). *Social constructivism and the philosophy of science.* New York: Routledge.

Landau, B., & McEwan, G. P. (2000). Creating peaceful classrooms. *Phi Delta Kappan, 81*(6), 450–454.

Lewis, C. C. (1995). The roots of Japanese educational achievement: Helping children develop bonds to schools. *Educational Policy, 9*(2), 129–133.

Lipsitz, J. (1995). Prologue: Why we should care about caring. *Phi Delta Kappan, 76*(9), 665–666.

Marks, H. M. (2000). Student engagement in instructional activity: Patterns in the elementary, middle, and high school years. *American Educational Research Journal, 37*(1), 153–184.

Marrais, P. (1996). *The politics of uncertainty: Attachment in private and public life.* London: Routledge.

McNamara, K. (1996). Bonding to school and the development of responsibility. *Reclaiming Children and Youth at Risk, 4*(4), 33–35.

McNeely, C.A., J.M. Nonnemaker and R.W. Blum (2002) Promoting Student Connectedness to School: Evidence from the National Longitudinal Study of Adolescent Health. Journal of *School Health, 72*(4): 138–146.

McNeely, C., & Falci, C. (2004). School connectedness and the transition into and out of health-risk behavior among adolescents: A comparison of social belonging and teacher support. *Journal of School Health, 74*(7), 284–292.

Mueller, A. (2005). Antidote to learned helplessness: Empowering youth through service. *Reclaiming Children and Youth at Risk, 14*(1), 16–19.

Muscott, H. (2000). A review and analysis of service-learning programs involving students with emotional/behavioral disorders. *Education and Treatment of Children, 23*(3), 346–368.

Noblit, G. W., Rogers, D. L., & McCadden, B. M. (1995). In the meantime: The possibilities of caring. *Phi Delta Kappan, 76*(9), 680–685.

Osterman, K. F. (2000). Students' need for belonging in the school community. *Review of Educational Research, 70*(3), 323–367.

Pajares, F. (1996). Self-efficacy beliefs in academic settings. *Review of Educational Research, 66*(4), 543–578.

Palincsar, A. S. (1998). Social constructivist perspectives on teaching and learning. *Annual Review of Psychology, 49*(1), 347–375.

Patterson, P., & Elliot, L. N. (2006). Struggling reader to struggling reader: High school students' response to a cross-age tutoring program. *Journal of Adolescent and Adult Literacy, 49*(5), 378–389.

Prawat, R. S., & Floden, R. E. (1994). Philosophical perspectives on constructivist views of learning. *Educational Psychologist, 29*(1), 37–48.

Reeve, J., & Jang, H. (2006). What teachers say and do to support students' autonomy during a learning activity. *Journal of Educational Psychology, 98*(1), 209–218.

Reeve, J., Jang, H., Carrell, D., Jeon, S., & Barch, J. (2004). Enhancing student motivation by increasing teachers' autonomy support. *Motivation and Emotion, 28*(2), 147–169.

Reid, R., & Nelson, J. R. (2002). The utility, acceptability, predictability of functional behavioral assessment for students with high-incidence problem behaviors. *Remedial and Special Education, 23*(1), 15–23.

Reynolds, R. E., Sinatra, G. M., & Jetton, T. L. (1996). Views of knowledge acquisition and representation: A continuum from experience centered to mind centered. *Educational Psychologist, 31*(2), 93–104.

Robinson, E. H., & Curry, J. R. (2006). Promoting altruism in the classroom. *Childhood Education, 82*(2), 68–73.

Rodgers, C. R. (2006). Attending to student voice: The impact of descriptive feedback on learning and teaching. *Curriculum Inquiry, 36*(2), 209–237.

Rutter, M. (1987). Psychological resilience and protective mechanisms. *American Journal of Orthopsychiatry, 57*(33), 316–331.

Siris, K., & Osterman, K. (2004). Interrupting the cycle of bullying and victimization in the elementary classroom. *Phi Delta Kappan,* 288–291.

Steele, C. M., & Aronson., J. (1995). Stereotype vulnerability and the intellectual test performance of African Americans. *Journal of Personality and Social Psychology, 69,* 797–811.

Stefanou, C. R., Perencevich, K. C., DiCintio, M., & Turner, J. C. (2004). Supporting autonomy in the classroom: Ways teachers encourage student decision making and ownership. *Educational Psychologist, 39,* 97–110.

Summers, J. J., Schallert, D. L., & Ritter, P. M. (2003). The role of social comparison in students' perceptions of ability: An enriched view of academic motivation in middle school students. *Contemporary Educational Psychology, 28*(4), 510–523.

Thornton, A., Orbuch, T. L., & Axim, W. G. (1995). Parent–child relationships during the transition to adulthood. *Journal of Family Issues, 16,* 538–564.

Tollefson, N. (2004). Classroom applications of cognitive theories of motivation. *Educational Psychology Review, 12*(1), 63–83.

Urdan, T., & Midgley, C. (2001). Academic self-handicapping: What we know, what more is there to learn? *Educational Psychology Review, 13*(2), 115–138.

Usher, E. L., & Pajares, F. (2006). Sources of academic and self-regulatory efficacy beliefs of entering middle school students. *Contemporary Educational Psychology, 31*(2), 125–141.

Valentine, J. C., Dubois, D. L., & Cooper, H. (2004). *The relation between self-beliefs.*

Vansteenkiste, M., Lens, W., & Deci, E. L. (2006). Intrinsic versus extrinsic goal contents in self-determination theory: Another look at the quality of academic motivation. *Educational Psychologist, 41*(1), 19–31.

Vieno, A., Perkins, D. D., Smith, T. M., & Santinello, M. (2005). Democratic school climate and sense of community. *American Journal of Community Psychology, 36*(314), 327–341.

Vygotsky, L. S. (1962). *Thought and language.* Cambridge, MA: The M.I.T. Press.

Vygotsky, L. S. (1978). Mind in society: The development of higher psychological processes. Cambridge, MA: Harvard University Press.

Weitzman, J., & Cook, R. E. (1986). Attachment theory and clinical implications for at-risk children. *Child Psychiatry and Human Development, 17,* 95–103.

Werner, E. E. (1995). Resilience in development. *Current Directions in Psychological Science, 4*(3), 81–85.

Werner, E. E., & Smith, R. S. (1982). *Vulnerable but invincible: A longitudinal study of resilient children and youth.* New York: McGraw–Hill.

Whitlock, J. L. (2006). Youth perceptions of life at school: Contextual correlates of school connectedness in adolescence. *Applied Developmental Science, 10*(1), 13–29.

Wolters, C. A. (2004). Advancing achievement goals theory: Using goal structures and goal orientations to predict students' motivation, cognition, and achievement. *Journal of Educational Psychology, 96*(2), 236–250.

Reading C: Behavioral Theory

Behavior is determined by its consequences.

—*B. F. Skinner*

Mr. Clark starts the school year by posting a list of rules on the board. He talks to the students about why each rule is important. The rules cover any behavior that would interfere with learning. He demonstrates examples of following the rules and examples of behaviors that would be considered rule breaking. He informs learners of consequences for breaking the rules, but assures that those who follow the rules will be rewarded. He monitors the room frequently and praises many instances of good behavior that he catches by making specific comments about their behavior and their work. He drops a marble in a jar anytime he notices prosocial behaviors that he is especially trying to encourage. He explains to the class that when the jar is full, they will have a pizza party. When needed, Mr. Clark reminds students of the rules and redirects them back to their schoolwork. He applies consequences fairly and consistently. He watches for negative behavior patterns that may arise and adjusts classroom schedule, seating order, and so forth so that distractions to learning will be minimal. For example, he notices two students who appear to get each other off task when they are assigned seat work. He moves the students so that they are not sitting next to each other and therefore are not tempted to distract each other.

Mr. Clark tells learners that while they will have many opportunities for fun, work will always come first and fun will follow when the work is completed. He distributes a survey to ascertain students likes and dislikes, interests, and so forth. He will use the information to identify possible rewards and fun activities to reinforce desired behaviors. He had heard that this particular group had an aversion to math the year before. He takes a proactive approach to this concern by starting math with fun math games and easy math work to relieve the anxiety of the group and allow them to associate math with more positive feelings.

Mr. Clark is beginning his school year from the perspective of behavioral theory. He recognizes that he can control events in the classroom in ways that will optimize learning. Behavioral strategies in the classroom are intended to produce positive changes in the social and academic behavior of students. According to this theory, proactive classroom management involves arranging antecedents and consequences to promote positive behavior and eliminate or reduce inappropriate behavior. Many classroom teachers translate this theory into the use of rewards and sanctions in the classroom. However, appropriate use of behavioral theory requires a much broader understanding of theory and the application of its principles. Misuse of behavioral theory can be counterproductive as it may deter internal motivation and individual self-responsibility. Even without conscious application, the behavioral principles of classical conditioning, negative and positive reinforcement, and punishment may be unintentionally at work in the classroom. Understanding how these principles can shape behavior in the classroom can assist a teacher regardless of his or her philosophical perspective. Understanding of basic behavioral principles and cautious application can provide the classroom teacher with useful insights and strategies, especially when dealing with the challenges that some children bring to the classroom.

In this chapter, I describe applied behavioral techniques for managing student behavior. One part of this chapter is devoted to classical conditioning, with an emphasis on how students' feelings toward school, both positive and negative, are learned emotional responses to experiences in school. In addition, the uses and misuses of positive reinforcement, negative reinforcement, and punishment are discussed. I also compare and contrast, in summary form, the philosophical premises of behaviorism with those of social constructivism.

Behavioral Principles

Behavioral theory views behavior as a learned response that is dependent on antecedent events and resulting consequences in the environment. In other words, behavior is viewed from a functional perspective in terms that are both measurable and observable. The origins of the behavioral model have their basis in the research of many prominent theorists who empirically derived scientific principles of learning. Each of these principles can be at work in the classroom with both positive and negative outcomes for learners.

Classical Conditioning

Mr. Clark learned that math might be particularly anxiety producing for his group of learners. To help disassociate math from negative feelings, Mr. Clark starts the year by setting the stage for fun and success with math.

Classical conditioning occurs when one neutral stimulus is paired with another stimulus that causes a physiological response that is involuntary. Soon the neutral stimulus begins to illicit the same physiological response as the one with which it is paired. The response then becomes controlled by the neutral stimulus. The famous psychologist Pavlov demonstrated this principle by conditioning dogs to salivate at the sound of a bell by pairing the bell with the presentation of raw meat. Eventually, Pavlov's dogs began to salivate when they heard the bell (the neutral stimulus). Classical conditioning isn't reserved for animals; humans respond to it as well. Advertisers often pair their product with beautiful women, fun, excitement, peacefulness, and so forth. In this way, individuals are conditioned to associate a product with a certain feeling, looking younger, having fun, relaxing, and more. Hence, classical conditioning connects feelings with environmental cues and with behaviors, and can be a form of influence in the classroom, both negative and positive.

When students are humiliated or made to feel anxious, they can be conditioned to feel anxiety and despair when faced with academic challenges. When tasks are presented as sanctions or punishment and their absence as a reward, students may become conditioned to dread school tasks. On the other hand, students can experience academic tasks and contexts that cause or encourage pleasant emotions. They can be conditioned to feel enthusiasm, excitement, or enjoyment. When academic tasks are presented as a challenge, privilege, or opportunity, then students begin to associate pleasant feelings with academic work. Consider the following examples, both positive and negative, of classical conditioning in the context of the classroom.

NEGATIVE EXAMPLES OF CLASSICAL CONDITIONING.   By pairing academic tasks with a negative association, children may be conditioned to dread assignments. For example, when his classroom or certain students in his room misbehave, Mr. Berry requires students to stay in at recess and write spelling words in sentences. The writing of spelling words in sentences is paired with the loss of recess. Consequently, students associate spelling with the bad feeling they have when they are being punished or reprimanded. The sound of the word "spelling" begins to cause dread.

Teachers can condition students to view academic work as undesirable. For example, Mrs. Little gives passes excusing students from homework or other academic tasks as a reward for good behavior. Avoidance of work is paired with reward and recognition from the teacher. Students begin to associate academic work avoidance as pleasurable.

Children who meet with ridicule or failure are conditioned to dread or avoid academic settings and tasks because of the negative feelings associated with them. Albert is ridiculed by his classmates when he reads aloud. Anthony begins to feel anxious when the teacher calls him to the reading table. Because ridicule (causing feelings of anxiousness) is paired with reading, Albert begins to dread reading.

POSITIVE EXAMPLES OF CLASSICAL CONDITIONING.   Students can be conditioned to see academic work such as a math problem as a challenge and an exciting opportunity when the presentation is paired with enthusiasm and encouragement by the teacher. In Mr. Clark's room, he begins math with fun games in which students experience success. He is intentionally trying to break the pattern of math anxiety that the students experienced the year before. In another classroom, Mrs. Patnic presents a math problem as a puzzle to be solved; mistakes and multiple ways of solving it are allowed. She states that students can use their recess time or lunch time to continue their work on it or talk to their friends about it if they wish. Students come to associate math with fun and challenge.

Operant Conditioning

While classical conditioning forms an association between two stimuli, operant conditioning forms an association between a behavior and a consequence, either positive or aversive. Reinforcement and punishment are at work in operant conditioning. Positive reinforcement is providing something positive to increase the likelihood that a behavior will occur again. Negative reinforcement is the removal of something aversive that increases the likelihood that a behavior will reoccur. Punishment is the presentation of something aversive or the removal of something pleasant to decrease the likelihood that a behavior will reoccur. It is important to note that behavioral theory indicates that a stimulus is defined as reinforcement or punishment based on its effect on behavior.

POSITIVE REINFORCEMENT.   Praise, contingent attention, and rewards are three common uses of the principle of positive reinforcement. Used appropriately, they can have a good effect; however, if misused, they have unintended consequences.

Praise.   For children desiring positive teacher attention, praise can be powerful. Despite considerable research attesting to the effectiveness of contingent praise, in their extensive review, Beaman and Wheldall (2000) found little evidence that teachers systematically use praise as positive reinforcement. Teachers tend to respond more frequently with disapproval of behaviors that they would like to decrease than with approval of appropriate behaviors. This response pattern can discourage inappropriate behavior. However, the contingent use of praise has repeatedly been shown to increase positive behavior.

While praise from teachers can be a positive reinforcer, praise from peers can also have a positive effect on behavior. Several studies document the positive effect of favorable peer reporting, a strategy that encourages peers to report the positive behavior of their peers (Moroz & Jones, 2002; Morrison & Jones, 2007; Skinner, Cashwell, & Skinner, 2000). Positive peer reporting is described in Figure 5.6.

Attention. Contingent use of teacher attention has also been shown to have a powerful effect on student behavior (Alber & Heward, 1999; Beaman & Wheldall, 2000; Craft, Alber, & Heward, 1998). Unfortunately, students may not be discriminating customers when it comes to teacher attention. That is, attention via teacher disapproval can maintain behavior as well as teacher approval or praise. Hence, teachers who use high rates of disapproval may provide students with positive reinforcement in the form of negative attention and consequently increase student misbehavior. As mentioned earlier, stimulus

---

FIGURE 5.7 *In the Classroom*

Tootling

What is the opposite of tattle? Tootle! (Skinner, Cashwell, & Skinner, 2000).
Also known as positive peer reporting, tootling involves teaching students to praise each other.

How it's done

- Teach students to recognize the prosocial behavior of their peers.
- Give students examples of prosocial behaviors such as lending a pencil, helping to carry books. Ask students to give examples of how they help at home and how they help at school.
- Give students an index card and ask them to watch for and report the prosocial behavior of their peers.
- Place a tootle box in the room to collect the tootles.
- Create a chart that shows the number of tootles each day.
- Set a goal (e.g., 100 tootles); when the goal has been reached, celebrate and set a new goal.
- Read the tootles aloud at the end of each day.

Advantages

- Gives students an alternative to tattling.
- Gives students recognition and praise from their peers.

For whom

- This strategy and variations of it have been used successfully with elementary-aged students and adolescents.

Evidence

- Jones, Young, & Friman (2000) used a version of tootling with adolescents and documented a decrease in inappropriate behavior of targeted students at risk for special education referral.
- Moroz and Jones (2002) used positive peer reporting to increase social involvement of elementary-school-aged children who were socially withdrawn.
- Morrison and Jones (2007) used postive reporting to reduce critical incidents of inappropriate behavior in elementary classrooms.

is defined by its effect on behavior. What a teachers sees as punitive (a reprimand) may be a reinforcer (attention) to the student.

On the other hand, positive attention from the teacher in terms of individual time, positive feedback, or individual assistance can improve behavior. For example, Mrs. Marshall keeps a chart of the students in her high school social studies classroom. She checks each time she attends to an individual student by giving assistance or feedback or showing concern. She refers to the chart daily to ensure that each student is receiving her attention over a week's time. Consequently, the group that tends to be unruly for other teachers is well behaved for Mrs. Marshall.

Rewards.   Rewards can also be used to modify behavior (Stage & Quiroz, 1997). Rewards such as stickers, a special activity, or tokens that are then exchanged for small prizes can be used as reinforcers. Many researchers caution about rewards and their effect on intrinsic motivation (Deci, Koestner, & Ryan, 2001). If used inappropriately, rewards can make it unlikely that students will engage in the desired behavior when the rewards are removed. Used sparingly, appropriately, and cautiously however, rewards can be used to support and encourage positive behavior and motivate reluctant learners. Teachers wary of using rewards due to their effect on intrinsic motivation often rely on punitive measures instead (Maag, 2001). Most experts agree that careful use of rewards is preferable to punishment.

NEGATIVE REINFORCEMENT.   Negative reinforcement is the removal of an aversive stimulus that results in an increase in a behavior. For example, the child who has a temper tantrum is given an ice cream cone and this stops the temper tantrum. The caregiver has unwittingly experienced negative reinforcement. The temper tantrum (the aversive stimulus that is removed) increases the likelihood of the caregiver giving into a child's demand for ice cream in the future. Like positive reinforcement and classical conditioning, negative reinforcement may be unintentionally at work, influencing the behavior of the student and/or the teacher in the classroom (Gunter & Coutinho, 1997; Harrison & Gunter, 1996). Consider the following examples:

> Johnny has difficulty with oral reading. When called to the reading table, his behavior becomes disruptive and unruly. The teacher sends Johnny back to his seat, where he puts his head down and remains quiet. In this example, reading (an aversive stimulus for Johnny) is removed, increasing the likelihood that he will repeat his unruly behavior at the reading table. The teacher may also be experiencing negative reinforcement— Johnny's unruly behavior (an aversive for the teacher) is stopped by sending Johnny back to his seat, increasing the likelihood that the teacher will send Johnny to his seat during reading in the future.
>
> When Mary, a high school student, uses offensive language in class, the teacher sends her to the office. Mary has effectively escaped the classroom situation and the teacher has effectively escaped the offensive language. Hence, the chances of the same scenario reoccurring are increased.

PUNISHMENT.   Punishment is the presentation of an aversive stimulus that decreases the likelihood of a behavior reoccurring. Maag (2001) contends that punishment is often used in the classroom because it is easy to administer and works in the short term with many students. Teachers are often negatively reinforced for its use (a quick removal of aberrant behavior). However, most professionals agree that punishment is a short-term solution that brings many undesirable side effects.

ANTECEDENTS.   Kern, Choutka, and Sokol (2002) describe how antecedents can influence behavior in the classroom. Antecedents are events or stimuli that occur before a behavior. One type of antecedent is a discriminative stimulus, or an event that signals a particular behavior to occur. In Mr. Clark's classroom, described at the beginning of the chapter, two friends sitting next to each other may have been the discriminative stimulus for the two to begin talking with each other instead of completing their work. By changing the seating arrangement, Mr. Clark has removed the discriminative stimulus for talking.

Another type of antecedent event is an establishing operation or an event or activity that occurs that may trigger a particular response. For example, skipping breakfast may be an operating event that causes a student who typically stays on task to be unable to complete an assignment. Ensuring that the child has something to eat each morning will improve his or her attention to task. Teachers can recognize how antecedents can influence behavior and use them to their advantage (Kern et al., 2002). For example, Allday and Pakurar (2007) describe a study in which antecedents were changed for three students identified for a study of off-task behavior. In each classroom, the students' on-task behavior during the first 10 minutes of class increased when teachers greeted the students as they entered the classroom. The authors note the simplicity of an intervention that merely engages teachers in positive interactions prior to the beginning of class.

Cognitive Behavior Modification

Classical and operant conditioning focus on observable behaviors and environmental events and tend to ignore the thinking or cognitive aspect of behavior—an unobservable process. In more recent years, behavioral theory has evolved to include the role of cognition. Cognitive approaches to altering behavior include cognitive behavior modification (CBM) strategies first introduced by Meichenbaum (1977). Many researchers contend that typical operant and classical conditioning strategies do not have as lasting an effect as cognitive approaches that emphasize self-control (Robinson, Smith, Miller, & Bronwell, 1991). Self-instruction and self-monitoring are two CBM procedures that have been effective in altering behavior in the classroom, especially for students who are hyperactive, impulsive, and aggressive (Robinson et al., 1999; Swaggart, 1998). Such procedures have been used successfully in general education classrooms with adolescents (Freeman & Dexter-Mazza, 2004; Hughes et al., 2002) and elementary-school-aged children (Levondeski & Cartledge, 2000).

Self-Monitoring

In self-monitoring, students are given a simple recording sheet on which to record the presence or absence of certain behaviors. For example, Crum (2004) provided a third grader with a chart with instructions to, when prompted by the teacher, record a "+" in a square if he was working or studying or a "0" if he was off task and not working. This student increased his on-task behavior considerably and was eventually engaged in setting his own goals for his behavioral improvements.

Self-Instruction

In self-instruction, students are taught to quietly verbalize the steps necessary to complete particular social or academic tasks (Swaggart, 1998). To use self-instruction appropriately, a teacher models thinking aloud the steps to the problem, has the student repeat the steps, rehearse the steps, and apply the steps, in context. In a meta-analysis of studies, Robinson et al. (1991) indicate that CBM that uses self-instruction can be used successfully in the classrooms to improve behavior.

Tools for the Classroom

Mr. Clark uses the principles of behavioral theory as a tool in his classroom to create a high level of on-task behavior and a positive classroom climate, and to promote appropriate behavior. As mentioned, knowledge of the principles of behavioral theory can assist teachers in arranging classroom conditions to be conducive to learning and the development of social skills. Tools that stem from behavioral theory are functional assessment and positive behavior support. Functional assessment involves determining the function or purpose of a behavior for students (e.g., avoiding work or gaining stimulation). Functional assessment assists a classroom teacher in demystifying the behavior of individual children who present classroom challenges despite a teacher's best efforts. Information from a functional assessment can be used to develop a positive behavior support plan. Positive behavior support involves changing antecedents and consequences to promote appropriate behavior. Considering functional assessment and positive behavior support from a behaviorist perspective, as well as a constructivist perspective, can assist the teacher in addressing the most disconcerting classroom behaviors.

Application of Behavioral Theory in the Classroom

Many traditional classroom management practices come from a behaviorist perspective. However, without appropriate application of behaviorist principles, they fail in helping students learn prosocial behavior. For example, many classrooms use a system in which rules are posted and punishments are put in place for students who break the rules (Henington & Skinner, 1998). While these types of systems work for some students, when teachers rely on a set system of rules and consequences, they may neglect considering the classroom practices that may contribute to inappropriate behavior. They may fail to look at variables such as the appropriate level and relevance of assignments, appropriateness of classroom materials, classroom arrangement, and also forth. Skinner, Cashwell, and Skinner (2000) identify two other limitations of such approaches. First, some students, although they still engage in inappropriate behavior, become very adept at avoiding punishment by engaging in inappropriate behavior when the teacher isn't looking. When the behavior goes unnoticed by an adult, peers are put in the tenuous situation of being tattlers and adults are put in the position of having to judge whether tattlers are accurate. In addition, the tattlers can become the victims of the perpetrator's revenge for tattling, which then perpetuates bullying behavior. Second, appropriate behavior often goes unnoticed and unrecognized. Even though teachers are trained to "catch students being good," their energy is often spent on the more punitive aspects of the system. Hence, students learn that appropriate behavior isn't valued. Despite the popularity of the above-mentioned system, many positively based behaviorist practices exist. While the primary emphasis of this book is a constructivist approach to classroom management, many behaviorist practices can promote belonging, competence, independence, and generosity and are supported by empirical research. Table 5.2 provides examples of these practices.

Behaviorist Versus Constructivist

Teachers must recognize the contributions from multiple theoretical perspectives. While many of the foundations of the behaviorist perspective oppose those of the constructivist, the wise teacher can find some points in common. For example, both behavioral theory and constructivist theory recognize the positive interactions of teacher and student as key to encouraging appropriate behavior. The behaviorist view encourages praise and attention contingent on appropriate behavior, while the constructivists see good listening and communication and taking the learner perspective as key to building relationships.

In addition to points of agreement, there are points of departure as well. The behaviorists view the teacher as the mediator of the environment. Through manipulation of antecedent events and contingent reinforcement, the teacher controls behavior. From a

TABLE 5.2   *Research-Based Practices that Support the Circle of Courage*

	Practice	Description	Evidence	How it Promotes
Belonging	Praise, teacher attention	Teachers give students positive attention and praise contingent on appropriate student behavior.	Allday and Pakurar (2007)	Promotes a positive student–teacher relationship
Independence	Self-monitoring	A behavior is identified and during regular intervals, a student marks a chart indicating whether or not he or she has engaged in the behavior.	Patton, Jolivette, & Ramsey (2006)	Students are taught to monitor their own specific behaviors
Competence	Peer tutoring, peer-assisted learning	Students take reciprocal roles in tutoring each other.	McMaster, Fuchs, & Fuchs (2007)	Students engage in the practice of academic skills with feedback
Generosity	Positive peer reporting	Students are taught to recognize and praise incidents of prosocial behavior by their peers	Morrison and Jones (2007)	Students help their peers learn prosocial behaviors

constructivist view, learners are regarded as proactive and self-regulating rather than as reactive and controlled by events that shape behavior. The self-beliefs of learners, such as self-efficacy beliefs, are critical; they allow learners some control over their thoughts, feelings, and actions (Pajares, 2003). The constructivist view of the classroom is child centered, with a focus is on the development of the capacity of learners to become self-disciplined, as well as supportive of the learning community.

From the behaviorist perspective, peers may be an important part of mediating reinforcement, but are not primarily seen as problem solvers. From the constructivist view, children learn to collaborate with each other, as well as with the teacher, to learn prosocial behaviors, to create an atmosphere conducive to learning, and to solve problems as they arise. From the behaviorist perspective, rewards can be useful in shaping behavior. The constructivist teacher is wary of rewards and punishments that "bribe" children to behave appropriately.

How does a teacher reconcile the differences or choose among the philosophies? Careful reflection regarding desired goals and outcomes and the approach or combination of approaches can help. Regardless, the foundations of each perspective deserve careful consideration. For example, positive behavior support is grounded in behavioral theory, but can easily be applied through an integrated perspective that considers the need for belonging, mastery, generosity, and independence.

Summary

Behavioral theory can inform classroom teachers in many ways. Operant and classical conditioning can be at work, both intentionally and unintentionally, to influence behavior and the way that children and adolescents feel about school. Awareness of these principles of learning are necessary for understanding classroom dynamics. In addition to the principles of learning, positive behavior support is a useful tool that is grounded in the behaviorist tradition. This tool can be used from multiple perspectives to understand difficult and challenging behavior and can aid teachers in finding ways to support all students in the classroom.

References

Alber, S. R., & Heward, W. L. (1999). Teaching middle school students with learning disabilities to recruit positive teacher attention. *Exceptional Children, 65*(20), 253–258.

Allday, R. A., & Pakurar, K. (2007). Effects of teacher greetings on student on-task behavior. *Journal of Applied Behavior Analysis, 40*(2), 317–320.

Beaman, R., & Wheldall, K. (2000). Teacher's use of approval and disapproval in the classroom. *Educational Psychology, 20*(4), 431–447.

Craft, M. A., Alber, S., & Heward, W. (1998). Teaching elementary students with developmental disabilities to recruit teacher attention in a general education classroom: Effects on teacher praise and academic productivity. *Journal of Applied Behavior Analysis, 31*(3), 399–415.

Crum, C. (2004). Using a cognitive-behavioral modification strategy to increase on-task behavior of a student with a behavior disorder. *Intervention in School and Clinic, 39*(5), 305–309.

Deci, E. L., Koestner, R., & Ryan, R. M. (2001). Extrinsic rewards and intrinsic motivation in education: Reconsidered once again. *Review of Educational Research, 71*, 1–27.

Freeeman, K. A., & Dexter-Mazza, E. T. (2004). Using self-monitoring with adolescent disruptive classroom behavior. *Behavior Modification, 28*(3), 402–420.

Gunter, P. L., & Coutinho, M. J. (1997). Negative reinforcement in classrooms: What we're beginning to learn. *Teacher Education and Special Education, 20*(3), 249–264.

Harrison, J. S., & Gunter, P. L. (1996). Teacher instructional language and negative reinforcement: A conceptual framework for working with students with emotional and behavioral disorders. *Education and Treatment of Children, 19*(2), 183–197.

Henington, C., & Skinner, C. H. (1998). Peer-monitoring. In K. Topping & S. Ehly (Eds.), *Peer-assisted instruction* (pp. 237–253). Hillsdale, NJ: Erlbaum.

Hughes, L., Copeland, S. R., Agran, M., Wehmeyes, M. L., Rodi, M., & Presley, J. A. (2002). Using self-monitoring to improve performance in general high school classes. *Education and Training in Mental Retardation and Developmental Disabilities, 37*(3), 262–271.

Jones, K. M., Young, M. M., & Friman, P. C. (2000). Increasing peer praise of socially rejected delinquent youth: Effects on cooperation and acceptance. *School Psychology Quarterly, 15*(1), 30–39.

Kern, L., Choutka, C. M., & Sokol, N. G. (2002). Assessment-based interventions used in natural settings to reduce challenging behavior: An analysis of the literature. *Education and Treatment of Children, 25*(1), 113–132.

Larson, P. J., & Maag, J. A. (1998). Applying functional assessment in general education classrooms: Issues and recommendations. *Remedial and Special Education, 19*(6), 338–350.

Levondeski, L. S., & Cartledge, G. (2000). Self-monitoring for elementary school children with serious emotional disturbances: Classroom application for increased academic responding. *Behavioral Disorders, 25*, 211–224.

Maag, J. (2001). Rewarded by punishment: Reflections on the disuse of positive reinforcement in schools. *Exceptional Children, 67*(2), 173–186.

McMaster, K. L., Fuchs, D., & Fuchs, L. S. (2007). Research on peer-assisted learning strategies: Promises and limitations of peer-mediated instruction. *Reading and Writing Quarterly, 22*(1), 5–25.

Meichenbaum, D. H. (1977). *Cognitive-behavior modification: An integrative approach.* New York: Plenum Press.

Moroz, K. B., & Jones, K. M. (2002). The effects of positive peer reporting on children's social involvement. *School Psychology Review, 31*(2), 235–245.

Morrison, J. Q., & Jones, K. M. (2007). The effects of positive peer reporting as a class-wide positive behavior support. *Journal of Behavioral Education, 16*(2), 111–124.

Pajares, F. (2003). Self-efficacy beliefs, motivation, and achievement in writing: A review of the literature. *Reading and Writing Quarterly, 19*(2), 139–158.

Patton, B., Jolivette, K., & Ramsey, M. (2006). Students with emotional and behavioral disorders can manage their own behavior. *Teaching Exceptional Children, 39*(2), 14–21.

Robinson, T. R., Smith, S. W., Miller, M. D., & Bronwell, M. T. (1999). Cognitive behavior modification of hyperactivity—Impulsivity and aggression: A meta-analysis of school based studies. *Journal of Educational Psychology, 91*(2), 195–202.

Ruef, M. B. (1998). Positive behavioral support: Strategies for teachers. *Intervention in School and Clinic, 34*(1), 12–21.

Skinner, C. H., Cashwell, T. H., & Skinner, A. L. (2000). Increasing tootling: The effects of a peer-monitored group contingency program on students' reports of peers' prosocial behaviors. *Psychology in the Schools, 37*(3), 263–271.

Stage, S. A., & Quiroz, D. R. (1997). A meta-analysis of interventions to decrease disruptive classroom behavior in public education settings. *School Psychology Review, 26*(3), 333–369.

Swaggart, B. L. (1998). Implementing a cognitive behavior management program. *Intervention in School and Clinic, 33*(4), 235–239.

6 Teachers and Teaching: Educational Philosophy

Educational philosophy is a way not only of looking at ideas, but also of learning how to use ideas in better ways.

—HOWARD A. OZMON AND SAMUEL M. CRAVER
PHILOSOPHICAL FOUNDATIONS
OF EDUCATION, 6TH ED., 1999.

FOCUS QUESTIONS

1. What determines your educational philosophy?
2. What are the branches of philosophy?
3. What are five modern philosophical orientations to teaching?
4. What psychological orientations have influenced teaching philosophies?
5. How can you develop your educational philosophy?
6. What cultural traditions have led to the development of the Canadian educational landscape?
7. What were teaching and schools like in Canada prior to 1875?
8. What patterns did Canadian education develop from 1875 to 1918?
9. What is the history of schooling for First Nations peoples?
10. What educational advancements took place between the Great Wars (1918–1939)?
11. What are the major characteristics of today's Canadian system of education?
16. How are Canadian schools funded?
17. What are some current trends in Canadian education?
18. What are some other types of Canadian schools?

You are having an animated conversation in the teacher's lounge with four colleagues, Manjit, Yuliya, Kim, and Claude, about educational reform and the changes sweeping across our nation's schools. The discussion was sparked by a television special everyone watched last night about new approaches to teaching and assessing students' learning.

"I was really glad to see teachers portrayed in a professional light," you say. "The message seemed to be 'Let's get behind teachers and give them the support and resources they need to implement new ideas and technologies. Effective schools are important to our nation's well-being.'"

"I think it's just a case of schools trying to jump on the band-wagon," Claude says. "All this talk about restructuring schools, developing partnerships with the community, and using technology—they're supposed to be the silver bullets that transform education. These ideas just take time away from what we should be doing, and that's teaching kids how to read, write, and compute. If we don't get back to what really matters, our country is going to fall apart . . . that's my educational philosophy."

"But times have changed; the world is a different place," Manjit says. "Look at how the internet has changed things in just a few years. We can't return to the 'good old days.' Students

195

need to learn how to learn; they need to learn how to solve problems that we can't even imagine today."

"Just a minute," Yuliya interjects. "I don't think the 'good old days' ever were. That's a nostalgia trap. What kids need is to see how education is the key to understanding themselves and others. If we can't get along as human beings on this planet, we're in trouble. Look at the ethnic cleansing in Kosovo, the killing in Rwanda, Angola, Northern Ireland. . . . Sure, we've got the internet and all this technology, but, as a species, we haven't evolved at all."

"Of course we can't return to the past," Kim says, "but we can learn a lot from it. That's one of the main purposes of education . . . to see how the great ideas can help us improve things. Like I tell my students, there isn't one problem today that Shakespeare didn't have tremendous insights into 400 years ago—racism, poverty, war."

"Well, all I know is that, when I started teaching 30 years ago, we taught the basics," Claude says. "It was as simple as that. We were there to teach, and the kids, believe it or not, were there to learn. Nowadays, we have to solve all of society's problems—eliminate poverty, racism, crime, or whatever."

Claude pauses a moment and then turns his attention to you. "What do you think . . . what's your educational philosophy?"

What do you say?

Manjit is correct when she says we cannot return to the past, to the "good old days." On the other hand, Kim is also correct when she says we should learn from the past. We cannot understand schools today without a look at what they were yesterday. The current system of public and private education in Canada is an ongoing reflection of its philosophical and historical foundations and of the aspirations and values brought to this country by its founders and generations of settlers. Developing an appreciation for the ideas and events that have shaped education in Canada is an important part of your education as a professional.

Still, you may wonder, what is the value of knowing about the philosophy and history of Canadian education? Will that knowledge help you to be a better teacher? First, knowledge of the ideas and events that have influenced our schools will help you evaluate current proposals for change more effectively. You will be in a better position to evaluate changes if you understand how schools have developed and how current proposals might relate to previous change efforts. Second, awareness of ideas and events that have influenced teaching is a hallmark of professionalism in education.

This chapter presents several basic philosophical concepts that will help you answer five important questions that teachers must consider as they develop an educational philosophy:

1. What should the purposes of education be?
2. What is the nature of knowledge?
3. What values should students adopt?
4. What knowledge is of most worth?
5. How should learning be evaluated?

What Determines Your Educational Philosophy?

In simplest terms, **educational philosophy** consists of what you believe about education—the set of principles that guides your professional action. Every teacher, whether he or she recognizes it, has a philosophy of education—a set of beliefs about how human beings learn and grow and what one should learn in order to live the good life. Teachers differ, of course, in regard to the amount of effort they devote to the development of their personal philosophy or educational platform. Some feel that philosophical reflections have nothing to contribute to the actual act of teaching. (This stance, of course, is itself a philosophy of education.) Other teachers recognize that teaching, because it is concerned with *what ought to be*, is basically a philosophical enterprise.

Your behaviour as a teacher is strongly connected to your personal beliefs and your beliefs about teaching and learning, students, knowledge, and what is worth knowing. Regardless of where you stand in regard to these five dimensions of teaching, you should be aware of the need to reflect continually on *what* you believe and *why* you believe it.

Beliefs about Teaching and Learning

One of the most important components of your educational philosophy is how you view teaching and learning. In other words, what is the teacher's primary role? Is the teacher a subject matter expert who can efficiently and effectively impart knowledge to students? Is the teacher a helpful adult who establishes caring relationships with students and nurtures their growth in needed areas? Or is the teacher a skilled technician who can manage the learning of many students at once?

Some teachers emphasize the individual student's experiences and cognitions. Others stress the student's behaviour. Learning, according to the first viewpoint, is seen as the changes in thoughts or actions that result from personal experience; that is, learning is largely the result of internal forces within the individual. In contrast, the other view defines learning as the associations between various stimuli and responses. Here, learning results from forces that are external to the individual.

Beliefs about Students

Your beliefs about students will have a great influence on how you teach. Every teacher formulates an image in her or his mind of what students are like—their dispositions, skills, motivation levels, and expectations. What you believe students are like is based on your unique life experiences, particularly your observations of young people and your knowledge of human growth and development.

Negative views of students may promote teacher–student relationships based on fear and coercion rather than on trust and helpfulness. Extremely positive views may risk not providing students with sufficient structure and direction and not communicating sufficiently high expectations. In the final analysis, the truly professional teacher—the one who has a carefully thought-out educational philosophy—recognizes that, although children differ in their predispositions to learn and grow, they all *can* learn.

Beliefs about Knowledge

How a teacher views knowledge is directly related to how she or he goes about teaching. If teachers view knowledge as the sum total of small bits of subject matter or discrete facts, their students will most likely spend a great deal of time learning that information in a straightforward, rote manner.

Other teachers view knowledge more conceptually—that is, as consisting of the big ideas that enable us to understand and influence our environment. Such teachers would want students to be able to explain how legislative decisions are made in the provincial capital, how an understanding of the eight parts of speech can empower the writer and vitalize one's writing, and how chemical elements are grouped according to their atomic numbers.

Finally, teachers differ in their beliefs as to whether students' increased understanding of their own experiences is a legitimate form of knowledge. Knowledge of self and one's experiences in the world is not the same as knowledge about a particular subject, yet personal knowledge is essential for a full, satisfying life.

Beliefs about What Is Worth Knowing

As we saw in this chapter's opening scenario, teachers have different ideas about what should be taught. Claude believes it is most important that students learn the basic skills of reading, writing, and computation. These are the skills they will need to be successful in their chosen occupations, and it is the school's responsibility to prepare students for the world of work. Kim believes that the most worthwhile content is to be found in the classics or the Great Books. Through mastering the great ideas from sciences, mathematics, literature, and history, students will be well prepared to deal with the world of the future. Yuliya is most concerned with students learning how to reason, communicate effectively, and solve problems. Students who master these cognitive processes will have learned how to learn—and this is the most realistic preparation for an unknown future. Last, Manjit is concerned with developing the whole child and teaching students to become self-actualizing. Thus the curriculum should be meaningful and contribute to the student's efforts to become a mature, well-integrated person.

What Are the Branches of Philosophy?

To provide you with further tools to formulate and clarify your educational philosophy, this section presents brief overviews of six areas of philosophy that are of central concern to teachers: metaphysics, epistemology, axiology, ethics, aesthetics, and logic. Each area focuses on one of the questions that have concerned the world's greatest philosophers for centuries: What is the nature of reality? What is the nature of knowledge and is truth ever attainable? According to what values should one live? What is good and what is evil? What is the nature of beauty and excellence? What processes of reasoning will yield consistently valid results?

Metaphysics

Metaphysics is concerned with explaining, as rationally and as comprehensively as possible, the nature of reality (in contrast to how reality *appears*). What is reality? What is the world made of? These are metaphysical questions. Metaphysics is also concerned with the nature of being and explores questions such as: What does it mean to exist? What is humankind's place in the scheme of things? Metaphysical questions such as these are at the very heart of educational philosophy. As two educational philosophers put it: "Our ultimate preoccupation in educational theory is with the most primary of all philosophic problems: metaphysics, the study of ultimate reality" (Morris and Pai 1994, 28).

Metaphysics has important implications for education because the school curriculum is based on what we know about reality. And what we know about reality is driven by the kinds of questions we ask about the world. In fact, any position regarding what schools should teach has behind it a particular view of reality, a particular set of responses to metaphysical questions.

Epistemology

The next major set of philosophical questions that concerns teachers is called **epistemology**. These questions focus on knowledge: What knowledge is true? How does knowing take place? How do we know that we know? How do we decide between opposing views of knowledge? Is truth constant, or does it change from situation to situation? What knowledge is of most worth? How you answer the epistemological questions that confront all teachers will have significant implications for your teaching. First, you will need to determine what is true about the content you will teach; then you must decide on the most appropriate means of conveying this content to students. Even a casual consideration of epistemological questions reveals that there are many ways of knowing about the world, at least five of which are of interest to teachers:

1. *Knowing Based on Authority*—for example, knowledge from the sage, the poet, the expert, the ruler, the textbook, or the teacher
2. *Knowing Based on Divine Revelation*—for example, knowledge in the form of supernatural revelations from the sun god of early peoples, the many gods of the ancient Greeks, or the Judeo-Christian god
3. *Knowing Based on Empiricism (Experience)*—for example, knowledge acquired through the senses, the informally-gathered empirical data that direct most of our daily behaviour
4. *Knowing Based on Reason and Logical Analysis*—for example, knowledge inferred from the process of thinking logically
5. *Knowing Based on Intuition*—for example, knowledge arrived at without the use of rational thought

Axiology

The next set of philosophical problems concerns values. Teachers are concerned with values because "school is not a neutral activity. The very idea of schooling expresses a set of values. [We] educate and we are educated for some purpose we consider good. We teach what we think is a valuable set of ideas. How else could we construct education?" (Nelson, Carlson and Polonsky 2000, 304).

Among the axiological questions teachers must answer for themselves are: What values should teachers encourage students to adopt? What values raise humanity to our highest expressions of humaneness? What values does a truly educated person hold?

Axiology highlights the fact that the teacher has an interest not only in the *quantity* of knowledge that students acquire but also in the *quality* of life that becomes possible because of that knowledge. Extensive knowledge may not benefit the individual if he or she is unable to put that knowledge to good use. This point raises additional questions:

How do we define quality of life? What curricular experiences contribute most to that quality of life? All teachers must deal with the issues raised by these questions.

ETHICS   While axiology addresses the question "What is valuable?" **ethics** focuses on "What is good and evil, right and wrong, just and unjust?"

A knowledge of ethics can help the teacher solve many of the dilemmas that arise in the classroom. Frequently, teachers must take action in situations where they are unable to gather all of the relevant facts and where no single course of action is totally right or wrong. For example, a student whose previous work was above average plagiarizes a term paper: Should the teacher fail the student for the course if the example of swift, decisive punishment will likely prevent other students from plagiarizing? Or should the teacher, following her hunches about what would be in the student's long-term interest, have the student redo the term paper, and risk the possibility that other students might get the mistaken notion that plagiarism has no negative consequences? Another ethical dilemma: Is an elementary mathematics teacher justified in trying to increase achievement for the whole class by separating two disruptive girls and placing one in a mathematics group beneath her level of ability?

AESTHETICS   The branch of axiology known as **aesthetics** is concerned with values related to beauty and art. Although we expect that teachers of music, art, drama, literature, and writing regularly have students make judgments about the quality of works of art, we can easily overlook the role that aesthetics ought to play in *all* areas of the curriculum.

Aesthetics can also help the teacher increase his or her effectiveness. Teaching, because it may be viewed as a form of artistic expression, can be judged according to artistic standards of beauty and quality. In this regard, the teacher is an artist whose medium of expression is the spontaneous, unrehearsed, and creative encounter between teacher and student.

LOGIC   **Logic** is the area of philosophy that deals with the process of reasoning and identifies rules that will enable the thinker to reach valid conclusions. The two kinds of logical thinking processes that teachers most frequently have students master are *deductive* and *inductive* thinking. The deductive approach requires the thinker to move from a general principle or proposition to a specific conclusion that is valid. By contrast, inductive reasoning moves from the specific to the general. Here, the student begins by examining particular examples that eventu-

What might this teacher want her students to learn about aesthetics? How were aesthetic values reflected in the K–12 curricula you experienced?

The Spirit and Principles of Socratic Questioning

- Treat all thoughts as in need of development.
- Respond to all answers with a further question (that calls on the respondent to develop his or her thinking in a fuller and deeper way).
- Treat all assertions as a connecting point to further thoughts.
- Recognize that any thought can only exist fully in a network of connected thoughts. Stimulate students—by your questions—to pursue those connections.
- Seek to understand—where possible—the ultimate foundations for what is said or believed.
- Recognize that all questions presuppose prior questions and all thinking presupposes prior thinking. When raising questions, be open to the questions they presuppose.

FIGURE 6.1 *The spirit and principles of Socratic questioning.*
Source: Richard Paul and Linda Eider, "The Art of Socratic Questioning," Critical Thinking, Fall 1995, 16.

ally lead to the acceptance of a general proposition. Inductive teaching is often referred to as discovery teaching—by which students discover, or create, their own knowledge of a topic.

Perhaps the best-known teacher to use the inductive approach to teaching was the Greek philosopher Socrates (ca. 470–399 BCE). His method of teaching, known today as the Socratic method, consisted of holding philosophical conversations (dialectics) with his pupils. The legacy of Socrates lives in all teachers who use his questioning strategies to encourage students to think for themselves. Figure 6.1 presents guidelines for using **Socratic questioning** techniques in the classroom.

What Are Five Modern Philosophical Orientations to Teaching?

Five major philosophical orientations to teaching have been developed in response to the branches of philosophy we have just examined. These orientations, or schools of thought, are perennialism, essentialism, progressivism, existentialism, and social reconstructionism. The following sections present a brief description of each of these orientations, moving from those that are teacher-centred to those that are student-centred (see Figure 6.2 on page 202).

Perennialism

Perennialism, as the term implies, views truth as constant, or perennial. The aim of education, according to perennialist thinking, is to ensure that students acquire knowledge of

Socrates (ca. 470–399 BCE)

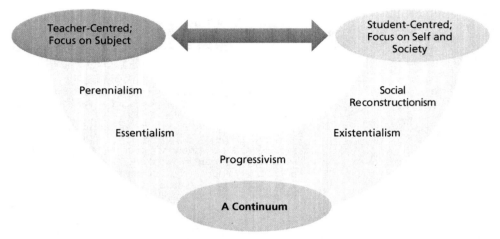

FIGURE 6.2   *Five philosophical orientations to teaching*

unchanging principles or great ideas. Like Kim, whom you met briefly in this chapter's opening scenario, perennialists believe that the great ideas continue to have the most potential for solving the problems of any era.

The curriculum, according to perennialists, should stress students' intellectual growth in the arts and sciences. To become "culturally literate," students should encounter in these areas the best, most significant works that humans have created. Thus a high school English teacher would require students to read Melville's *Moby Dick* or any of Shakespeare's plays rather than a novel on the current best-seller list.

Similarly, science students would learn about the three laws of motion or the three laws of thermodynamics rather than build a model of the space shuttle.

Robert Maynard Hutchins(1899–1977)

PERENNIALIST EDUCATIONAL PHILOSOPHERS Two of the best known advocates of the perennialist philosophy have been Robert Maynard Hutchins (1899–1977) and, more recently, Mortimer Adler, who together developed an undergraduate curriculum based on the study of the Great Books and discussions of these classics in small seminars. Adler, along with Hutchins, was instrumental in organizing the Great Books of the Western World curriculum. Through focusing study on over 100 enduring classics, from Plato to Einstein, the Great Books approach aims at the major perennialist goal of teaching students to become independent and critical thinkers. It is a demanding curriculum, and it focuses on the enduring disciplines of knowledge rather than on current events or student interests.

Essentialism

Essentialism, which has some similarities to perennialism, is a conservative philosophy of education. It was originally formulated by William C. Bagley (1874–1946), an American professor of education, as a criticism of progressive trends in schools. Essentialists, like Claude, whom you met in this chapter's opening scenario, believe that human culture has a core of common knowledge

William C. Bagley (1874–1946)

that schools are obligated to transmit to students in a systematic, disciplined way. Unlike perennialists, who emphasize a set of external truths, essentialists stress what they believe to be the essential knowledge and skills (often termed "the basics") that productive members of our society need to know.

According to essentialist philosophy, schooling should be practical and provide children with sound instruction that prepares them to live life; schools should not try to influence or set social policies. Critics of essentialism, however, charge that such a tradition-bound orientation to schooling will indoctrinate students and rule out the possibility of change. Essentialists respond that, without an essentialist approach, students will be indoctrinated in humanistic and/or behavioural curricula that run counter to society's accepted standards and need for order.

Progressivism

Progressivism is based on the belief that education should be child-centred rather than teacher- or content-centred. The writing of John Dewey (1859–1952) in the 1920s and 1930s contributed a great deal to the spread of progressive ideas. Briefly, Deweyan progressivism is based on three central assumptions:

1. The content of the curriculum ought to be derived from students' interests rather than from the academic disciplines.
2. Effective teaching takes into account the whole child and his or her interests and needs in relation to cognitive, affective, and psychomotor areas.
3. Learning is essentially active rather than passive.

*John Dewey
(1859–1952)*

PROGRESSIVE STRATEGIES   The progressive philosophy also contends that knowledge that is true in the present may not be true in the future. Hence, the best way to prepare students for an unknown future is to equip them with problem-solving strategies that will enable them to discover meaningful knowledge at various stages of their lives.

Educators with a progressive orientation give students a considerable amount of freedom in determining their school experiences. Contrary to the perceptions of many, though, progressive education does not mean that teachers do not provide structure or that students are free to do whatever they wish. Progressive teachers begin where students are and, through the daily give-and-take of the classroom, lead students to see that the subject to be learned can enhance their lives.

How might you explain what is happening in this classroom from the perspective of progressivism? From the perspective of perennialism? From the perspective of essentialism?

In a progressively oriented classroom, the teacher serves as a guide or resource person whose primary responsibility is to facilitate student learning. The teacher helps students learn what is important to them rather than passing on a set of so-called enduring truths. Students have many opportunities to work cooperatively in groups, often solving problems that the group, not the teacher, has identified as important.

Existentialism

Existential philosophy is unique in that it focuses on the experiences of the individual. Other philosophies are concerned with developing systems of thought for identifying and understanding what is common to *all* reality, human existence, and values. **Existentialism**, on the other hand, offers the individual a way of thinking about *my* life, what has meaning for *me*, what is true for *me*. In general, existentialism emphasizes creative choice, the subjectivity of human experiences, and concrete acts of human existence over any rational scheme for human nature or reality.

*Maxine Greene
(b. 1917)*

Life, according to existential thought, has no meaning, and the universe is indifferent to the situation humankind finds itself in. Moreover, "existentialists [believe] that too many people wrongly emphasize the optimistic, the good, and the beautiful—all of which create a false impression of existence" (Ozmon and Craver 1999, 253). With the freedom that we have, however, each of us must commit him- or herself to assign meaning to his or her *own* life. As Maxine Greene, an eminent philosopher of education whose work is based on existentialism, states: "We have to know about our lives, clarify our situations, if we are to understand the world from our shared standpoints. . . . " (1995, 21). The human enterprise that can be most helpful in promoting this personal quest for meaning is the educative process. Teachers, therefore, must allow students freedom of choice and provide them with experiences that will help them find the meaning of their lives. This approach, contrary to the belief of many, does not mean that students may do whatever they please; logic indicates that freedom has rules, and respect for the freedom of others is essential.

Existentialists judge the curriculum according to whether or not it contributes to the individual's quest for meaning and results in a level of personal awareness that Greene (1995) terms "wide-awakeness." The ideal curriculum is one that provides students with extensive individual freedom and requires them to ask their own questions, conduct their own inquiries, and draw their own conclusions.

Social Reconstructionism

As the name implies, **social reconstructionism** holds that schools should take the lead in changing or reconstructing society. Theodore Brameld (1904–1987), acknowledged as the founder of social reconstructionism, based his philosophy on two fundamental premises about the post–World War II era: (1) We live in a period of great crisis, most evident in the fact that humans now have the capability of destroying civilization overnight, and (2) humankind also has the intellectual, technological, and moral potential to create a world civilization of "abundance, health, and humane capacity" (Brameld 1959, 19). In this time of great need, then, social reconstructionists like Yuliya, whom we met in this chapter's opening scenario, believe that schools should become the primary agent for planning and directing social change. Schools should not only *transmit* knowledge about the existing social order; they should seek to *reconstruct* it as well.

SOCIAL RECONSTRUCTIONISM AND PROGRESSIVISM   Social reconstructionism has clear ties to progressive educational philosophy. Both provide opportunities for extensive interactions between teacher and students and among students themselves. Furthermore, both place a premium on bringing the community, if not the entire world, into the classroom. Student experiences often include field trips, community-based projects of various sorts, and opportunities to interact with people beyond the four walls of the classroom.

George Counts (1889–1974)

According to Brameld and social reconstructionists such as George Counts, who wrote *Dare the School Build a New Social Order?* (1932), the educative process should provide students with methods for dealing with the significant crises that confront the world: war, economic depression, international terrorism, hunger, inflation, and ever-accelerating technological advances. The logical outcome of such education would be the eventual realization of a worldwide democracy (Brameld 1956). Unless we actively seek to create this kind of world through the intelligent application of present knowledge, we run the risk that the destructive forces of the world will determine the conditions under which humans will live in the future.

Another of the important contributors to the reconstructivist viewpoint is the work of Paulo Freire, founder of the **critical pedagogy** school of educational philosophy. Freire strongly recommended a teaching approach that assisted students in questioning and challenging those commonly accepted beliefs and practices that dominate. He was very concerned with **praxis**, informed action based on specific values, and believed that students would eventually reach a point of revelation where, recognizing their society as oppressive and deeply problematic, they would work toward bringing about positive change. Freire also believed that true education requires a mutually respectful dialogue among or between individuals. It requires that people work positively with each other. Too much teaching, he argued, was nothing but a form of banking with the educator making deposits in the heads of students.

What Psychological Orientations Have Influenced Teaching Philosophies?

In addition to the five philosophical orientations to teaching described in previous sections of this chapter, several schools of psychological thought have formed the basis for teaching philosophies. These psychological theories are comprehensive world views that serve as the basis for the way many teachers approach teaching practice. Psychological orientations to teaching are concerned primarily with understanding the conditions that are associated with effective learning. In other words, what motivates students to learn? What environments are most conducive to learning? Chief among the psychological orientations that have influenced teaching philosophies are humanistic psychology, behaviourism, and constructivism.

Humanistic Psychology

Humanistic psychology emphasizes personal freedom, choice, awareness, and personal responsibility. As the term implies, it also focuses on the achievements, motivation, feelings, actions, and needs of human beings. The goal of education, according to this orientation, is individual self-actualization.

Humanistic psychology is derived from the philosophy of **humanism**, which developed during the European Renaissance and Protestant Reformation and is based on the belief that individuals control their own destinies through the application of their intelligence and learning. People "make themselves." The term "secular humanism" refers to the closely related belief that the conditions of human existence relate to human nature and human actions rather than to predestination or divine intervention.

In the 1950s and 1960s, humanistic psychology became the basis of educational reforms that sought to enhance students' achievement of their full potential through self-actualization (Maslow 1954, 1962; Rogers 1961). According to this psychological orientation, teachers should not force students to learn; instead, they should create a climate of trust and respect that allows students to decide what and how they learn, to question authority, and to take initiative in "making themselves." Teachers should be what noted psychologist Carl Rogers calls "facilitators," and the classroom should be a place "in which curiosity and the natural desire to learn can be nourished and enhanced" (1982, 31). Through their non-judgmental understanding of students, humanistic teachers encourage students to learn and grow.

Behaviourism

Behaviourism is based on the principle that desirable human behaviour can be the product of design rather than accident. According to behaviourists, it is an illusion to say that humans have a free will. Although we may act as if we are free, our behaviour is really *determined* by forces in the environment that shape our behaviour. "We are what we are and we do what we do, not because of any mysterious power of human volition, but because outside forces over which we lack any semblance of control have us caught in an inflexible web. Whatever else we may be, we are not the captains of our fate or the masters of our soul" (Power 1982, 168).

*B. F. Skinner
(1904–1990)*

FOUNDERS OF BEHAVIOURISTIC PSYCHOLOGY John B. Watson (1878–1958) was the principal originator of behaviouristic psychology, and B. F. Skinner (1904–1990) its best-known promoter. Watson first claimed that human behaviour consisted of specific stimuli that resulted in certain responses. In part, he based this new conception of learning on the classic experiment conducted by Russian psychologist Ivan Pavlov (1849–1936). Pavlov had noticed that a dog he was working with would salivate when it was about to be given food. By introducing the sound of a bell when food was offered and repeating this several times, Pavlov discovered that the sound of the bell alone (a conditioned stimulus) would make the dog salivate (a conditioned response). Watson came to believe that all learning conformed to this basic stimulus–response model (now termed classical or type S conditioning).

Skinner went beyond Watson's basic stimulus-response model and developed a more comprehensive view of conditioning known as operant (or type R) conditioning. Operant conditioning is based on the idea that satisfying responses are conditioned; unsatisfying ones are not. In other words, "The things we call pleasant have an energizing or strengthening effect on our behaviour" (Skinner 1972, 74). Thus the teacher can create learners who exhibit desired behaviours by following four steps:

1. Identify desired behaviours in concrete (observable and measurable) terms.
2. Establish a procedure for recording specific behaviours and counting their frequencies.
3. For each behaviour, identify an appropriate reinforcer.
4. Ensure that students receive the reinforcer as soon as possible after displaying a desired behaviour.

Constructivism

In contrast to behaviourism, **constructivism** focuses on processes of learning rather than on learning behaviour. According to constructivism, students use cognitive processes to *construct* understanding of the material to be learned—in contrast to the view that they *receive* information transmitted by the teacher. Constructivist approaches support student-centred rather than teacher-centred curriculum and instruction. The student is the key to learning.

Unlike behaviourists who concentrate on directly observable behaviour, constructivists focus on the mental processes and strategies that students use to learn. Our understanding of learning has been extended as a result of advances in **cognitive science**—the study of the mental processes students use in thinking and remembering. By drawing from research in linguistics, psychology, anthropology, neurophysiology, and computer science, cognitive scientists are developing new models for how people think and learn.

Teachers who base classroom activities on constructivism know that learning is an active, meaning-making process, and that learners are not passive recipients of information. In fact, students are continually involved in making sense out of activities around them. Thus the teacher must *understand students' understanding* and realize that students' learning is influenced by prior knowledge, experience, attitudes, and social interactions.

How Can You Develop Your Educational Philosophy?

As you read the preceding brief descriptions of five educational philosophies and three psychological orientations to teaching, perhaps you felt that no single philosophy fit perfectly with your image of the kind of teacher you want to become. Or, there may have been some element of each approach that seemed compatible with your own emerging philosophy of education. In either case, don't feel that you need to identify a single educational philosophy around which you will build your teaching career. In reality, few teachers follow only one educational philosophy, and, as Figure 6.3 shows, educational philosophy is only one determinant of the professional goals a teacher sets.

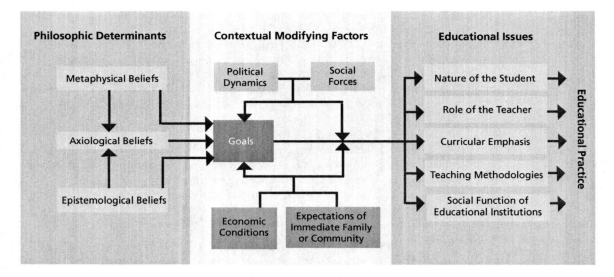

FIGURE 6.3   *The relationship of philosophy to educational practice*
Source: George R. Knight, Issues & Alternatives in *Educational Philosophy*, 3rd ed. Berrien Springs, MI: Andrews University Press, p. 34.

Most teachers develop an *eclectic* philosophy of education, which means they develop their own unique blending of two or more philosophies.

7 Social Learning

Reading A: Social Learning

Chapter Focus

Social learning is a relatively new arrival on the professional landscape and in its many manifestations has met with a checkered response. Some teachers have embraced it with enthusiasm; others have been skeptical.

Social learning is a fairly radical departure from conventional teaching practices, many of which were founded in behaviourism. You will remember that behaviourism tends to place a fairly heavy emphasis on individualism. However, the very term *social learning* suggests that groups of people would be learning together—the antithesis of learning based on individualism. One of the central questions in learning theory is, How do students, as they engage in learning, make meaning and gain understanding? Further questions concern the assumptions and prior knowledge that learners bring to the learning experience. The degree to which a teacher is able to help young people make explicit their prior knowledge and assumptions as they engage in learning often indicates the degree to which new learning can be effective. Think about times you have been involved in new leaning. If you had to learn on your own and your learning involved high degrees of difficulty and complexity, how did you cope? Were you frustrated? Of course, to a considerable extent the answer depends on the kind of person and the kind of learner you are, but, generally speaking, young people experience a certain amount of discomfort when dealing with difficulty and complexity on their own. Sharing learning with others often brings with it comfort and the possibility of insight and enlightenment from the thoughts and ideas expressed by others.

Leinhardt (1992) presents three core assumptions about learning gleaned from a number of modern researchers.

1. Learning is an active process of knowledge construction and sense-making by the student.
2. Knowledge is a cultural artifact of human beings; we produce it, share it, and transform it as individuals and as groups.
3. Knowledge is distributed among members of a group, and this distributed knowledge is greater than the knowledge possessed by any single member.

The larger questions are, How do we use these core assumptions about learning? What do they mean for a classroom teacher? This book looks at the professional landscape and asks, Where to begin? The particular theoretical perspective within social learning that we are choosing to discuss is social-cognitive learning. In the following section we will discuss three facets of social-cognitive learning considered to be useful for those embarking on pre-service learning: constructivism, narrative inquiry, and pro-social skills. There are also, of course, many other areas of credible knowledge that occupy the professional landscape. The ones selected here represent current research and practice, and on this basis we judge them to be a useful starting point for pre-service teachers.

A second aspect of social learning with which we will conclude the chapter is ethical and moral learning.

Focus Questions

1. What conditions would provide learners with opportunities to apply their own efforts at understanding information?
2. Why do people learn from the stories of others?
3. How might schools develop in learners the pro-social skills that are required in society?
4. What is the source of empathy in children? How could learning experiences be designed in order to promote empathy learning?
5. How might learning conditions be created to enhance a learner's internal and external motivation to learn?
6. What role do schools have in the moral and ethical development of learners?
7. How might schools contribute to a student's formation of self-concept and identity?

Social-Cognitive Learning Theory

If behaviourism is psychology's success story in the scientific community, and social learning theory is responsible for increasing that respect, then social-cognitive learning theory is most responsible for deepening that respect. Rigorous scientific studies of children (Bandura, 1965, 1989; Zimmerman, 1990) have extended our understanding and acceptance of social-cognitive learning theory's most important contribution to our knowledge of how people learn—that thinking is socially constructed, that knowledge is a social construction. Put another way, people learn new ways of thinking and behaving from each other.

Today the widely accepted branch of social learning theory is social-cognitive theory (Bandura, 1989). It is important that you understand this plausible explanation of learning, because not only does it help explain one important way that children learn, it also integrates and considers theory from cognitive and behavioural understandings of learning. Perhaps most important for you in your practice as a teacher, social-cognitive learning theory will help you be thoughtful and articulate when commenting on issues such as the effects of television; bullying and its solution; and the influence of societal role models on young people. If you know and understand the basics regarding social-cognitive learning theory, you will understand that children's learning involves a "...cognitive processing activity in which information about the structure of behavior and about environmental events is transformed into symbolic representations that serve as a guide for action" (Bandura, 1977, p. 51).

In social-cognitive learning, children do not need to be reinforced for their behaviours. They can learn by watching what happens to others. This saves time and prevents dangerous situations from being the "teachers" of children. Children can learn from reading stories, watching events, or hearing others tell of their experiences. Finally, we suspect that you already know that people learn from each other because you remember learning from others: your friends, parents, and role models you looked up to. How did that learning happen?

Social-cognitive learning theory is concerned with social behaviour and the social setting in which that behaviour occurs. Social settings are the contexts of behaviour that help create the understanding of what is meaningful in the world of young people. This social setting includes people, of course, but it also includes the media, the sub-text of messages in advertising, and the values and ideologies of the communities in which people live. Why? Because it is setting, or social context, that creates the meaning people see in things, and subsequently influences what can be learned and how it can be learned (Bronfenbrenner, 1989). Perhaps the next two illustrations will help you understand the power that context, the social setting people find themselves in, can have in helping people make meaning and learn.

CASE 7.1

For Your Consideration

Analyze the following scenario to understand how context is powerful in helping people make meaning.

In one school, Grade 12 students were asked to design their own walk-about. In a walk-about, a concept taken from Australian Aborigines, a person goes into the wilderness with very little supporting equipment, tools, clothing, or means to gather food or build shelter. The task is simple—to survive. In this particular school, students designed their own walk-about, a real life situation for the region in which they lived. One student designed a week-long experience of living on the street as a homeless person. She had to find meals, stay warm, and keep safe. Another student designed a week-long bike trip through the Rocky Mountains. All students had real problems through which they learned as they applied strategies and knowledge to their solution.

Students prepared for the problem in the best way they could; reading, discussing, and simulating situations. However, the real learning occurred when they actually encountered problems in the situations they designed and when they carefully documented how they solved those problems. Many found mentors to help them in their situation, others listened carefully to experienced problem-solvers. All students learned informally in the situation through solving the real-life problem.

In terms of learning in schools, social-cognitive learning theory presents many important and relevant practical considerations. Sitting still means something different in physical education than it does at a school assembly. Praise from a teacher in front of peers means something different than praise from a teacher when no one is watching. Young people will put meaning into things they hear, read, and see, using the social setting to do so, and their ability to symbolically represent that which they see and hear. Because they do, important behaviour and thinking happens in this social setting called school. Socialization can become normal or abnormal because of a setting's influence on a young person. Learners learn to symbolize, regulate themselves, develop a sense of confidence in their abilities, and see the future consequences of their actions. Also, they learn to imitate and figure out whether they should imitate, based on the consequences of the person's behaviour they are imitating.

Imitation alone does not explain learning. Learners also learn to regulate their behaviours by observing the effects and reinforcements that others receive for their actions. At times they determine whether a particular behaviour is a good idea or not by seeing how it turns out for the person they are watching. Learners may not even need reinforcement. They simply need to observe a high-status person repeat the behaviour a number of times and get a slap on the wrist, and they learn not try the same behaviour.

CASE 7.2

For Your Consideration

Suppose you found an unfinished Beatles song (or Nirvana, if that's your taste) in an attic. Likely, you'd want to know what the finished song would sound like, how the songwriter would have finished it. You would, wisely, get someone who knows the group— their style of music, way of thinking, and approach to writing—to help finish the score. You would trust someone who is an expert, with the background knowledge to be able to study the unfinished song and apply that knowledge to finishing the song. The expert would use the setting, the context, both his or her own context, including background, and the Beatles' context. The closeness of fit between the now-finished Beatles song and what John or Paul might have done is higher because of the expertise of those in the setting. Who might have a closer fit, you or the experts?

Keeping the above scenario in mind, how does context, or setting, influence meaning-making for young people? Consider movies, music, friends, and the community in your discussion.

Learning is even a little more complicated in social-cognitive theory than it is in behaviourism or in other branches of social learning theory, because in social-cognitive theory young people act cognitively on their setting as much as the setting acts on them. To illustrate, consider the following question: Who socializes whom more, a young baby or the parents of that baby? Is the answer simple?

Some implications of social-cognitive learning theory are addressed in the following questions:

1. Is television a neutral stimulus? How might children symbolically represent violence they see in television?
2. Should teachers and parents be more involved in choosing the friends of young people in their care? How should they express their concern?
3. How should teachers call into question objectionable societal practices?
4. To what extent should teachers consider the school and the community in their moral and ethical decisions? (Refer to teaching qualities in Chapter 1, Reading B.)

Above all, we encourage you to be thoughtful when addressing the settings in which the young people live.

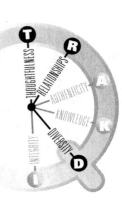

Constructivism

Teachers do not always warmly receive the word *constructivism*. Since constructivism is a relatively recent arrival on the professional landscape, its newness tends to run headlong into old assumptions. Teachers who have not been exposed to constructivism, either during their teacher education or their professional development experiences, may not embrace it as part of their worldview. It does not play a part in their assumptions, which determine how they approach learning and teaching.

Such reluctance to accept new research and practice is not uncommon in teaching. Perhaps it is too early in your pre-professional experience for you to have experienced instances of this kind of implementation problem. However, you might find it interesting to talk about this issue with your peers. Some might have some interesting stories to tell. If you try this, you yourself are engaging in a form of social learning. You will be sharing stories, asking each

CASE 7.3

For Your Consideration

What does *key* mean?

If you replied, "I don't know what you mean by key," you are right, of course. You don't know for sure what we mean by key, because you do not have enough context to help you make meaning. So, let's broaden the context. The key is in the first chapter of the book. Now you have a little more information to go on to help you make meaning of the word key. However, you would still be guessing, because you do not have enough context. Try these sentences:The key is in the first chapter of the book. Make sure that you put it back there when you return, and fill up the car with gas; and do not be late.

Are you surprised by the ambiguity in the sentences? Now you know what key means. But there might be more. What if the two sentences about key were in a paragraph in a story about secret agents, spies, and other mysterious things? Then key takes on even more meaning in the broader context.

Keeping the above illustration in mind, how might the various settings in which young people find themselves influence what they think about issues such as dieting and body image, money and material possessions, jobs and careers, and friends and loyalty? Why is setting important? Why is it important that young people learn as much as they can from as many points of view as possible, including ethical and moral, about important issues in life?

The point we are making is that the social setting influences meaning.

other questions, perhaps challenging each other's views, and gaining clarity and understanding on issues about which you were previously unsure. In short, you will be learning.

What is constructivism? A book of this kind cannot pretend to fully answer this broad question, but we will present a working definition followed by some core understandings of the concept. We define **constructivism** as an approach to learning and teaching that encourages learners to take an active role in their learning. Central to the practice of constructivist learning is the learner's constructing new knowledge on prior knowledge, building understanding, and above all making sense and meaning out of new information. The following quotation provides a useful beginning.

> Much of traditional education breaks wholes into parts, and then focuses separately on each part. But many students are unable to build concepts and skills from parts to wholes. These students often stop trying to see the wholes before all the parts are presented to them and focus on the small, memorizable aspects of broad units without ever creating the big picture. . . . We need to see the "whole" before we are able to make sense of the parts. (Brooks & Brooks, 1993, p. 46)

Constructivist classrooms help young people to make sense of their world through actively acquiring, building, and understanding meaning and knowledge in social contexts. Perkins (1999) cautions that constructivism is more than one thing. He quotes Phillips (1995), who has identified three distinct roles in constructivism: the active learner, the social learner, and the creative learner. You might want to refer to the Perkins article for a discussion of the three distinct roles in constructivism.

The essence of constructivist theory is that young people experience successful learning when they are actively engaged in the following:

- building (constructing) knowledge for themselves—considering new knowledge against prior knowledge and understanding

- reflecting on their views and how they might differ in their understandings with the views of others
- arriving at new understandings that expand their worldview

What conditions should exist in a constructivist classroom? An important condition is that young people be given numerous opportunities to explore ideas, sometimes called phenomena (Vygotsky, 1987), individually, but most often in social contexts. In exploring ideas they would be encouraged to employ problem-solving skills such as hypothesizing, speculating, conjecturing, predicting, and decision making. The whole process would lead students to revise their original thinking. In short, constructivism encourages interplay between new knowledge about a phenomenon and prior knowledge about the same phenomenon that a young person brings to the learning experience. The social context in which the learner engages in exploration enables the learner to gain new meaning and understanding through considering the views of others against his or her own views.

The term *constructivist* may conjure up images of building and architecture. However, in this context it represents the construction of intellect, the design of learning experiences that invite students to construct knowledge and make meaning of their world. Architects who design buildings might borrow from earlier masters; so do educators. Many educational theorists believe that we actively construct knowledge based on what we already know and new information we encounter. Jean Piaget (1983), Lev Vygotsky (1987), and John Dewey (1973) are names worthy of note. Their work supports constructivist perspectives on learning and teaching, and continues to influence today's classrooms, encouraging teachers to put "students' own efforts to understand at the centre of the educational enterprise" (Prawat, 1992, p. 357).

Having considered how constructivism might look in an elementary classroom, we will now examine its application in the wider context of a university learning experience. The learning experience is designed to help first-year education students construct their own understanding of how some influences on learning, such as feedback, might be more powerful than others, such as praise.

These photos show two situations in which students are solving problems and constructing knowledge.

CASE 7.4

For Your Consideration

Read the following scenario and answer the questions that follow.

Some years ago, an observer visited a Grade 3 class as the class was about to begin a reading lesson. Very quickly the children were engaged with papier-mâché, wire, toothpicks, and other assorted material from the teacher's art supplies. Working in groups of three, they were building castles. A little perplexed, the observer made his way over to the teacher and inquired about the reading lesson.

"This is it," said the teacher, in a preoccupied voice.

"But where are the books?" the observer asked.

"Give me a moment and I will be with you," said the teacher. "Let me get them all going."

A little later, the teacher stepped aside from a busy class and explained what was happening. "Before children see the printed words it is important, first of all to find out what they already know about castles. Let them have the chance to show what they look like, and if they know the names of the different parts, let them write the names and stick them on the model castles."

The observer looked over at the castles under construction and names were beginning to appear: "draw brige," "mot," "flag." The children were engrossed in their work. Industry took on a new meaning.

A. Why do you think the children were building castles as part of their reading class?
B. How would this help them to learn to read?
C. When the castles were finished, what do you think the teacher would do next?
D. In the context of teaching reading, research the meaning of terms such as *decoding, encoding, comprehension,* and *context.* How do these terms connect with the teacher's approach described above?
E. Do you think the vignette is consistent with a constructivist approach to the teaching of reading? Why? Why not?

CASE 7.5

For Your Consideration

In the first stage of a university learning experience designed to be constructivist, the task was for students to identify current practices for influencing the behaviours of loved ones.

Step 1. Naming Present Action: the "what" movement

Here the teacher/facilitator asked learners to identify their actions, or behaviours, related to a topic.

In an education class, one of the authors of this book asked students to describe their preferred way of influencing the behaviours of a loved one (boyfriend, girlfriend, husband, wife, parent). The list, written on the board, included praise, thank-you statements, affection, and others.

Step 2. Identifying Assumptions in Actions: the "why" movement

Here the teacher guided the learners to unwrap their actions to expose underlying theories, beliefs, and understandings.

In the class on influences, we questioned each other about why we chose the influences we did. The questions ranged from, Whose interests are being served by a particular choice of reinforcer? to, Is a person's dignity subverted when the person is praised for what he or she should do naturally?

Step 3. Seeing the Research: The Educational Community Story and Vision about Influences on Learning

Here, for the first time, there is a presentation of research; the story of the scientific community—the narrative-based understandings presented in oral or written form—is brought into the learning process. The goal for the students is twofold:

1. Hear the story of the larger community, the experiences of others, the research from the scientific community, the logic and insights from others. It is important that the story and the vision inherent in others' stories are heard and treated with respect in the hearing.
2. Talk about, challenge, and pose questions about the story.

The teacher can present the educational community's story in a number of ways. In the particular education class referred to here, one of the authors asked students to do a simple penny-tossing experiment in groups. All students tossed pennies toward a target, trying to come as close as possible. All tosses were measured. We called this our baseline behaviour. Next, students tossed pennies again, but this time they were blindfolded. One blind group was praised, but given no specific feedback regarding performance (i.e., closeness to the target). A second group was given feedback but no praise. A third group was allowed to take off their blindfolds after each toss to see how close the toss was to the target, before re-blindfolding themselves and trying again.

Before the penny-tossing experiment, each student was asked to predict the outcome of the three scenarios. After the experiment, they compared the results. The insight that feedback is a better influence on performance (at least on a simple task like throwing pennies) than praise was quite startling to many

students. They were ready for the fourth, and arguably most instructive, movement.

Step 4. Interpreting and Synthesizing

Here the goal is for students to discuss two related questions:

1. How does the community's story and vision, the research and its understandings, call into question, affirm or disaffirm, or call upon you to change your understandings and actions?
2. How do your understanding and actions help you comprehend more fully the community's story and vision; how do your understanding and actions confirm the research and its application?

In the class in question, the limited influence of praise in a simple motor task and the very significant influence of feedback regarding performance, was very disconfirming. Most students were surprised and therefore willing to revisit the effectiveness of using praise as the main means to promote learning.

Step 5. Taking Reflective, Constructive Action

Here students make deliberate, ethical, and moral decisions regarding how they will act in the future. In the class in question, many students agreed to carefully study the research and the stories of teachers regarding the use of both feedback and praise in assisting learning.

Go back now and thoughtfully reconsider the original assumption that people learn from experience. Are you more or less convinced now that people learn from reflecting on experience more than they learn from experience itself?

(Adapted from Thomas Groome, 1981, *Christian Religious Education,* San Francisco: Harper and Row.)

Narrative Inquiry

Human beings are storytellers. The advent of publishing, even the hand-written work of scribes, is a relatively recent occurrence in the human story. Prior to the written and printed word, knowledge, tradition, and culture were passed down from generation to generation by word of mouth, through an oral tradition. Elders taught through stories. Younger people learned from the elders' stories.

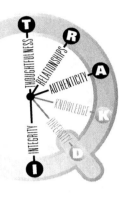

Stories still represent the way people communicate when they are together in social settings. Narrative inquiry seeks to gain clarity and understanding from the stories that people tell. Connelly and Clandinin (1988) describe narrative as "the study of how humans make meaning of experience by endlessly telling and retelling stories about themselves that both refigure the past and create purpose in the future. Thus to study narrative . . . one needs to ask questions not only about the past, or the present, or the future, but about all three" (pp. 24–25). **Narrative inquiry,** then, is the purposeful attempt to capture the experiences of people through asking questions about their personal stories. Narrative inquiry seeks to explicate the past, explain the present, and anticipate the future through a respect for the knowledge contained in the storied lives of people.

How often have you listened to a speaker and noticed how your attention was captivated when the speaker began to relate a story? We all seem to be captivated by stories. Why? Is it because a story provides a snapshot of life experience, a vignette that describes how a person or group of people coped with some facet of life? Even fictitious stories, although they are the products of fantasy or imagination, can teach us about life. In the preface to this book we reminded ourselves that, "Whenever we are together, we combine stories and anecdotes to make conversation. On the basis of stories and events recounted, social occasions are enriched, emotions are shared, plans are made, misconceptions may be generated or clarified, and truth is earned. Above all, understanding is achieved when the attendant conversations are informed and open."

The important thing is that we can learn a great deal from stories if we know how to listen, how to ask questions, and how to generalize to the larger context from which the story emanates. The main claim for the use of narrative in educational research is that humans are storytelling organisms who, individually and socially, lead storied lives. The study of narrative, therefore, is the study of the ways humans experience the world. This general notion translates into the view that education is the construction and reconstruction of personal and social stories; teachers and learners are storytellers and characters in their own and others' stories (Connelly & Clandinin, 1990, p. 2).

In the context of learning, young people and teachers lead storied lives. Young people and their teachers are characters on the professional landscape. To listen to their stories is to understand this landscape. How do we tell our stories? How do we listen to stories? How do we learn from stories?

When teachers speak about teaching, when they speak about their professional landscape, in their voices you will hear their deeply held beliefs about education, teaching, and learning. It is through talk that our beliefs and assumptions are self-critically analyzed (Waldron et al., 1999).

> "Talk" is essential. It is through talk that teachers (students) and administrators articulate their beliefs and values and expectations, their understandings of the context and their uncertainties, and that they come to know the beliefs and values and expectations, the understandings and uncertainties of others. (LaRoque & Downie, 1993, p. 1)

From our earlier discussion of assumptions you will recall the implications of worldview, that uniquely personal perspective that describes how people understand and present themselves to the world. Essentially a person's worldview is the accumulation of assumptions. It is not uncommon for some assumptions to be held tacitly. Occasionally, tacitly held assumptions may be troublesome because they drive a person's response to life

CASE 7.6

For Your Consideration

Read the following story and, in groups of four or five people, answer the questions that follow.

During a recent experience observing Grade 8 mathematics teachers, some of the teaching methods raised significant questions. Typically, a lesson would begin with a request for students to sit down and take out their textbooks. Teachers reviewed the previous night's homework and then explained the day's new learning through verbal explanations and demonstrations on the board, answering questions from the class. After the explanation of new learning, teachers distributed worksheets containing practice questions for completion within a given period of time. Teachers then assigned questions from the textbook for students to start in class and complete for homework.

At this point, in one of the classes, a student challenged the teacher.

"Mr. DeVries, I already know how to do this stuff, do I still have to do it for homework?"

"Yes," said the teacher, "because the mark you will receive makes up part of your grade for the term."

"But what's the point of doing it anyway? When will I ever use it in real life?"

The teacher was clearly uncomfortable with the question and provided an answer that alluded to benefits for further study in later grades and post secondary requirements.

1. What assumptions did the teacher hold about learning?

2. To what extent are students viewed as passive recipients of knowledge?
3. What do you think of the student who was asking the difficult questions?
4. Read the last sentence in the story again. What do you think the teacher began to think about?
5. How would you have answered the student's questions?
6. How would you teach math in a way that would not have invited those tough questions?
7. How might teachers invite learning in ways that respect the humanness of the learner?

Think about the group discussion you have just completed, in which you inquired into the lives of the two characters in the story. The questions about the assumptions the teacher held would help, in some way, to understand his worldview. As you formed opinions about the teacher's life on the professional landscape, you would likely think about what you yourself would do in this situation, and what you would say if your peers asked why you would act that way. To provide a sound reason why, you would draw upon your professional knowledge base for a response. Others might contribute responses that were different from yours, causing you to ponder their response . . . and so on. Stories, or narratives, provide useful vehicles for professional conversation through which learning can occur, insights can be gained, and professional landscapes can be explored.

in ways that may test the harmony of working relationships. Stories and attendant conversations can be useful for uncovering tacit assumptions so that they become available for clarification or challenge.

Pro-Social Skills

The term **pro-social skills** refers to skills that promote social and emotional growth and development in young people. Pro-Social skills include so many categories and sub-categories that we are again confronted with the question of which to select for a book such as this. Rather than present brief details on each form of pro-social skill, we will offer a few as a foundation from which, as pre-service studies progress, you can explore and add others.

The first pro-social skill we present is really a grouping of common skills aimed at developing co-operation among young people. These skills are generally grouped under the umbrella heading of co-operative learning. The second will deal with a particularly human quality called empathy, that special faculty that allows us to project ourselves into the feelings of another to truly understand that person's predicament. Finally, we will present the work of social psychologist, Erik Erikson, whose insights into social growth and development have interesting import for teachers seeking to understand children and nurture their social skills.

Co-operative Learning

Co-operative learning refers to a set of teaching methods in which young people work in small, mostly heterogeneous groups, of three to five members. Members of the groups are responsible for a number of things that typically would include engaging in the intended learning, assuming assigned responsibilities to contribute to the group's effectiveness, and contributing to the learning of the group. Co-operative groups operate with a clearly stated purpose, which, ideally, group members have had some opportunity to shape to give them a sense of ownership. One of the key aspects of co-operative group learning is the assignment of particular responsibilities to group members. Generally speaking, there are three broad types of learning within which young people benefit from these forms of pro-social skills: 1) learning that involves research to gain knowledge, meaning, and understanding, 2) conversation around particular topics, intended to gain meaning and understanding, and 3) peer teaching and learning activities aimed at consolidating learning or helping those whose learning is uncertain.

The important thing to stress is that the foundation for whatever method is chosen, for whatever reason, is the social skills that the young people need to make the co-operative learning successful. What skills do they need to get along with each other? How can they co-operate with each other so that learning can occur? It is important that the skills required are taught quite specifically so that the young people can apply them toward co-operation and successful learning in the social group context. Co-operative learning motivates students to help one another learn. Johnson and Johnson (1987) present a set of conditions necessary for students to co-ordinate efforts to achieve mutual goals:

1. Get to know and trust one another.
2. Communicate accurately and unambiguously.
3. Accept and support one another.
4. Resolve conflicts constructively.

Johnson and Johnson (1990) further state that "interpersonal and small-group skills make possible the basic nexus among students; and if students are to work together productively and cope with the stresses of doing so, they must have at least a modicum of these skills" (p. 30). Slavin (1987, p. 4) provides further support for the value of social skills in motivating young people to help one another learn:

1. Students can translate the teacher's language into "kid" language. Students experiencing difficulty understanding from a teacher, often gain the understanding when explained by a peer.

2. Those students who do the explaining learn by doing, so when students have to organize their thoughts to explain ideas to other group members, they must engage in cognitive elaboration that greatly enhances their own understanding.

CASE 7.7

For Your Consideration

We have suggested that for co-operative learning, young people work in small, heterogeneous groups of three to five members.

A. What does the term *heterogeneous* mean?
B. Using criteria that you glean from the information on co-operative learning, design a scenario for a co-operative group of two working in a math class in Grade 4. Share your scenario with others and discuss the criteria.
C. Apply the Teaching Qualities Model to your scenario. What new insights do you uncover?
D. How does the teaching quality of authenticity inform the discussion of your scenario?

3. Students can provide individual attention and assistance to each other. In a co-operative group there is nowhere to hide; there is a helpful non-threatening environment in which to try out ideas and ask for assistance.

Learning Empathy

Schools are uniquely social places. Hundreds, sometimes thousands, of people congregate there each day to engage in learning, which requires being with others, co-operating with others, and generally getting along with others. If all this is to happen effectively, then to a considerable extent, the "getting along" will benefit from the ability of people to be empathetic. **Empathy** is the ability to respond positively to personal emotions and to understand and respond to the feelings of others in compassionate ways. The more we are able to project ourselves into the feelings of others, to understand them in compassionate ways, the more harmonious and sensitive the relationships will be. Think about relationships in the teaching qualities cycle. To what extent would the ability of young people to be empathetic contribute to relationships that support successful learning? Clearly there would be much to gain. The teaching quality of thoughtfulness would also benefit from consideration in the same context.

Nurturing empathy includes three broad dimensions. Young people need to learn what empathy is and how to recognize emotion in themselves and others. Learning how to respond positively to emotions within themselves and others tends to enhance their abilities to be aware of emotions and the skills for positive response. Secondly, it is important for young people to focus on their own feelings at first. They need to be clear about how they feel in certain situations. Only through this self-understanding will they be able to understand the feelings of others. A third step is to try to have the learners see similarities between themselves and others.

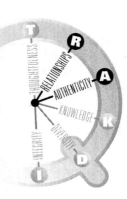

Empathy is a desirable quality at any age, but in young people it needs to be nurtured in a positive, explicit way. Occasionally you may hear teachers speak almost dismissively about concepts and qualities such as empathy. School, after all, is for learning about subjects that are important to success in life. Basic skills, discipline, hard work are the stuff of schooling! How do you feel about this kind of attitude? Think about the teaching qualities of authenticity and relationships. Learning is frequently a difficult task. As

CASE 7.8

For Your Consideration

Design a co-operative learning situation in which peer tutoring is involved.

1. Write a short script for a two-minute situated performance. In your script demonstrate the value of empathetic understanding in the peer-tutoring situation.

2. Rewrite the same script, changing the scenario to one in which empathetic understanding is not present.

3. Discuss the two scripts. As part of your discussion, consider each teaching quality and identify its implications for students in this context.

young people struggle to engage in new learning, to what extent would understandings of these two teaching qualities be useful for a teacher in knowing how to respond to a young person's struggles?

Empathetic understanding and other related qualities can contribute to academic performance. Occasionally you may hear comments suggesting that character-related matters are not the domain of schools. Families, churches, and other social institutions should be responsible for the development of these character traits. We have taken a position in support of empathy development at the beginning of this discussion, but we can also say that academic achievement is a beneficiary. There is a strong correlation between students' skills and abilities in empathetic understanding and academic achievement. Kohn (1991) reports program evaluation results on measures of higher-order reading comprehension, showing that students in schools with programs designed to increase empathy have higher scores than schools that do not. Gallo (1989) cites evidence that the teaching of empathy enhances critical thinking skills and creative thinking.

Identity Learning

Identity learning is really a person's attempt to answer the question, Who am I? It is a person's quest to achieve confidence, to feel a sense of well-being through successful lifestyle decisions. Among the theorists who have researched and considered how people form their identities, none has been more influential than Erik Erikson. Erikson studied the social development of people from birth through adulthood. Psychosocial development may be described as a passage through a series of stages, each with its particular goals, concerns, accomplishments, and dangers. The stages (shown in Table 7.1) are interdependent, with a person's success in later stages being dependent on success in earlier stages. At each stage a person faces what Erikson calls a psychosocial crisis. The way an individual resolves each crisis will have a lasting effect on the person's self-image and world view. The crises he identifies are of interest to teachers as they respond to the learning needs of young people.

You should also note the dominant virtues associated with the age-related crises. The implications of these virtues for teaching will be apparent. Reflect upon the teaching qualities cycle, with specific reference to diversity. The quality of diversity has many dimensions, and Erikson's work exemplifies one such dimension. What implications would Erikson's work have for a teacher working with any age group of young people?

TABLE 7.1   *Erikson's Eight Stages of Psychosocial Development*

Stages	Approximate Age	Important Event	Description
1. Basic trust vs. basic mistrust	Birth to 12–18 months of age	Feeding	The infant must form a first loving, trusting relationship with the caregiver or develop a sense of mistrust.
2. Autonomy vs. shame/doubt	18 months to 3 years	Toilet training	The child's energies are directed toward the development of physical skills, including walking, grasping, controlling the sphincter. The child learns control but may develop shame and doubt if behaviour is not handled well.
3. Initiative vs. guilt	3–6 years	Independence	The child continues to become more assertive and to take more initiative, but may be too forceful, which can lead to guilt feelings.
4. Industry vs. inferiority	6–12 years	School	The child must deal with demands to learn new skills or risk a sense of inferiority, failure, and incompetence.
5. Identity vs. role confusion	Adolescence	Peer relationships	The teenager must achieve identity in occupation, gender roles, politics, and religion.
6. Intimacy vs. isolation	Young adulthood	Love relationships	The young adult must achieve identity in occupation, gender roles, politics, and religion.
7. Generativity vs. stagnation	Middle adulthood	Parenting/Mentoring	Each adult must find some way to satisfy and support the next generation.
8. Ego integrity vs. despair	Late adulthood	Reflection on and acceptance of one's life.	The culmination is a sense of acceptance of oneself as one is and a sense of fulfillment.

(*Source:* Adapted from Lester A. Lefton, *Psychology,* 5/e (p. 65), 1994, Boston, MA: Allyn and Bacon. Copyright © 1994 by Pearson Education. Adapted by permission of the publisher.)

CASE 7.9

For Your Consideration

You are teaching Grade 8 classes in a school of 500 students. In addition to your teaching assignment, you have an advisory responsibility for a group of fifteen students with whom you meet for twenty minutes every day. One member of your group has been ostracized by her social group of girls, who are also part of your advisory group.

Using Erikson's model and the teaching qualities cycle, determine a course of action to deal with the problem.

Motivation and Learning

To bore someone, according to Webster's dictionary is "to weary with tedious dullness." "The word boring has its roots in an Old English word meaning to drill using the same motion over and over. When faced with constant repetition, we become bored—and we become unmotivated" (Silver, Strong, & Perini, 2000, p. 45). Teachers are interested in developing ways to motivate their students. Most teachers want to go beyond corporal punishment or disapproval and ridicule as a major source of motivation. They want to positively motivate their students to learn, and to be active participants in the students' learning. They want students to be excited about learning, happy to come to school, ready for and interested in the learning experience.

What is motivation? Motivation involves goal-oriented behaviour. It "is the general term for all the processes involved in starting, directing, and maintaining physical and psychological activities" (Zimbardo & Gerrig, 1996, p. 428). We define **motivation** as the disposition or willingness of a person to engage in learning through a commitment to complete the learning task. Various types of motivational theories emphasize various perspectives, such as biological or social; intrinsic and extrinsic; nature, nurture and environmental influences; and drive theories. It is perhaps unrealistic to expect a single theory to explain the variety of motives that encourage students to learn. In the following section, we present several theories that educators have considered in their attempt to understand the best ways to motivate their students. While you read these, reflect on how your understanding of each of the theories is informed by the teaching qualities introduced in Chapter 1, Reading B.

Another perspective on motivation that you might find interesting and informative is found in the work of social psychologist Abraham Maslow (1962, 1970). Maslow proposed a sweeping overview of human motivation. His theory assumes that people have many needs, which he organized hierarchically (see Figure 7.1).

FIGURE 7.1
Maslow's Hierarchy of Needs

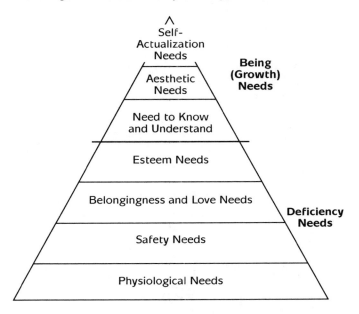

(Source: Data for diagram based on Hierarchy of Needs from *Motivation and Personality,* 2nd ed., by Abraham H. Maslow © 1970. Reprinted by permission of Pearson Education, Inc., Upper Saddle River, NJ.)

INTRINSIC AND EXTRINSIC MOTIVATION

Some explanations for why students are motivated to learn include internal factors, such as personal reasons, need, interest, curiosity, enjoyment, and the reward of the activity itself. These are called intrinsic motivators. We define **intrinsic motivation** as the internal pleasure, enjoyment, and satisfaction a person derives from working in an activity.

A second set of factors is called extrinsic motivators. **Extrinsic motivation** occurs when learners work on tasks for external reasons—for reward, such as a grade or material object; avoidance of punishment; or parental approval, for example. In the classroom have you witnessed these two types of motivation? Sources for internal motivation include personal goals, intentions, expectations, and explanations for success or failure; self-concept, self-esteem, and self-confidence; self-knowledge and sense of self-efficacy. Personality factors include willingness to undertake risk, ability to manage anxieties, curiosity, and persistence in effort (McCown, Driscoll, Schwean, Kelly, & Haines, 1999). External motivation may come from the desire to please or to meet expectations of a teacher or parent; to avoid getting in trouble; to achieve a reward, prize, or other incentives. It may not surprise you that intrinsic motivation is a preferable motivational state. "The intrinsically motivated person is more likely to stay involved in and demonstrate commitment to learning than is the extrinsically motivated person" (McCown et al., 1999, p. 275).

CASE 7.10

For Your Consideration

During your field experience, observation is more meaningful when you are focused on a particular goal and have a clear purpose for this observation. During your next field experience, observe the ways students are motivated intrinsically (from within) and extrinsically (from factors outside themselves) (Parkay et al., 1996). You may find it more useful to look at the two motivations individually, one session at a time.

Intrinsic Motivation

Answer the following questions in detail:

- What topics do students talk about with enthusiasm?
- When do they appear most alert and participate most actively?
- When do they seem to be bored, confused, frustrated?

(Adapted from Parkay et al., 1996, p. 63.)

What else have you noticed with respect to intrinsic motivation in this field experience?

Extrinsic Motivation

Answer the following questions in detail:

- How do teachers show their approval to students?
- What reward programs do you notice?
- What punishments are given to students?
- What forms of peer pressure do you observe?

(Adapted from Parkay, et al., 1996, p. 63.)

What else have you noticed with respect to extrinsic motivation in this field experience?

1. Which of the teaching qualities (knowledge, relationships, authenticity, integrity, thoughtfulness, and diversity) enhance your understanding of intrinsic and extrinsic motivation?
2. Can your understanding of the motivational makeup of your students be of assistance in teaching your students?
3. How would you encourage intrinsic motivation in your students?

Ethical and Moral Learning

> Can you tell me, Socrates, whether virtue is acquired by teaching, or by practice; or if neither by teaching nor practice, then whether it comes to man by nature, or in what other way?
>
> —*MENO'S QUESTION TO SOCRATES*

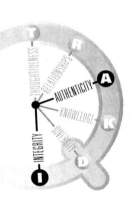

Moral learning has been part of the schooling debate for many years, rising and falling in popularity with the mores of society. The debate might be summed up in this question: Should schools teach morals and, if so, whose morals? Sometimes moral learning is presented as character education, but whatever its incarnation, whether as morals, ethics or character, the concern is with developing thinking and action that reflects "right," "good," and "proper" ethical conduct in ways that complement teachings and practices from family, religious, or humanistic beliefs. In short, **moral education** may be understood as a process whereby principles for action on complex societal issues are formulated and applied.

Today's society has many problems that give us cause for concern. The media presents daily reports of crime, teen pregnancy, theft, suicide, bullying, and assault, suggesting a moral crisis. Clearly, not all these examples are moral issues, but concerned citizens are increasingly looking to schools to teach morals and values. Parents who choose private schools frequently do so out of concerns related to morals and values.

Think about your time in grade school. How many issues of a moral nature occurred that had some impact on you? There is a danger when responding to moral concerns. Should teachers be left to decide for themselves which morals and which values to deal with in their classrooms? Should teachers be left to decide, whimsically, how to teach morals and values? One could easily imagine the pitfalls inherent in such licence. In deciding not only what morals to teach, but how to teach those morals, teachers should refer to research on the topic. In later pages of this chapter, we introduce four researchers whose work provides interesting approaches to moral learning.

We believe that moral learning is essential for today's young people and that schools must pay it appropriate attention. Some would argue that moral development is the domain of church and family, and that schools should stick to the business of intellectual development within subject areas and their related skills. The argument has some merit in this time of crowded curricula. However, the issue is complex and certainly more

These children are co-operating in their learning tasks. What aspect of social-cognitive learning theory might be at work here?

profound than the "crowded curricula" position. Leaving aside the "dysfunctional family" and "significant decline in religious adherence" debates, consider two pertinent conditions:

1. Young people are exposed to many influences in their lives, many temptations, many pressures on their decision making, many forces attempting to persuade and convince, many images presenting unrealistic expectations. Do you think schools therefore have an obligation to make a contribution to the moral education of young people?
2. Young people congregate in schools, where large numbers of their peers meet for hours each day in social contexts. Schools have little choice about functioning as social institutions. They do, however have choice, as to *how* they will function.

Morality and Spirituality

The current interest in spirituality is worthy of note. Human beings have always had some compelling attraction toward a greater, often unfathomable, power. People have worshipped multiple gods, spirits within inanimate objects, physical features such as mountains, and deferred to greater powers within their environments. Religions, before the relatively recent education of the masses, would project morality almost by decree. Priests, rabbis and holy people would determine the appropriateness of thought and action through their position and preaching. Philosophers and theologians would engage in debate with only limited impact on society at large. Attilla's Huns, Roman legions, Viking hordes, and knights of the Crusades, for example, perpetrated their conquests with scant regard for what is "right" in today's sense of the term, but with a firm belief in their own sense of what was "right" to them at the time.

The Renaissance period of European history, beginning in the fifteenth century, saw the advent of modernism, that period when reason became a hallmark of progress and thought. Feudalism began to wane, and all forms of dogma were challenged and questioned. It was, in short, the era of scientific thinking. Universities began to appear and scholarship blossomed. Churches were very much involved with the establishment of modernism and their hierarchies were often in opposition to secular scholars. The church would debate from beliefs grounded in faith, and academia would argue from more secular positions. Both sides valued reason. It was within this kind of climate that the Reformation took place.

During the nineteenth and twentieth centuries morality was postulated by rules and regulations imposed on society by both authority and societal self-regulation, through custom and tradition. Authority was still, by and large, imposed through church and state, and societal self-regulation through civil codes and forces of law and order. Philosophers, however, were still at work. Descartes, in exploring the essence of self, coined his now-famous logic in the expression, "I think, therefore I am." Sartre explored existentialism. Kant insisted that moral acts could be considered to be so only if they were performed out of a principled sense of duty.

Jurgen Habermas, a "critical theorist" from Germany, posited educational theories that arguably hold significant meaning for moral education and for the advent of postmodernism. He identified three distinct types of human "interest," each of which would lead to a particular way of knowing. His first human interest was *technical,* with a related way of knowing called *empirical.* A more traditional teaching style would be related to this, with an emphasis on "banking" knowledge. His second human interest was *hermeneutical,* with a related way of knowing called *interpretative.* The teacher and student make meaning from knowledge, as they look for connections in learning through conversation and discourse. Habermas's third human interest was *emancipatory,* with a related way of knowing called *liberation.* In this interest, a teacher believed that without liberation, any belief system becomes static and susceptible to control by vested interest groups. The *emancipatory* way of knowing would move students from passive, possibly submissive, receiving of knowledge, to a more thoughtful, critical reflection leading to liberation and change.

When the emancipatory interest is served, students gain a deeper understanding of knowledge and confront knowledge and reality, theory and practice, in short, engage in shared praxis. In Chapter 1, we described the concept of praxis as the deliberate integration of ethical reflections and understandings about the commonplaces of professional knowledge into teaching practice. When you share these ethical reflections and understandings with others, in the course of your practice, then you are engaging in shared praxis. This whole notion of praxis, especially shared praxis, is worthy of further reflection at this juncture. Revisit the discussion of shared praxis introduced in Chapter 1 and think about the importance of the concept to moral learning.

The idea of moving from thought to action is important in any learning endeavour, but think how critically important it is in the moral domain. Habermas's emancipatory interest encourages people, ultimately, to engage in critique and reflection on knowledge and behaviour, to challenge it and develop new knowledge leading to action for change. "Critical reflection, in the emancipatory way of knowing, leads to *praxis,* when 'theory' or 'handed down knowledge' is scrutinized and critiqued, and new knowledge, which changes or challenges accepted knowledge, is forged" (Engebretson, 1997). Very often we know, intellectually, what should be done in a given situation, but it may be debatable whether we actually do it. Think about the complexity of this giant leap from thought to action. Cast your mind back to, say, Grade 8. Were there instances when perhaps you knew the right thing to do, but you didn't do it? Maybe you were with a group of your friends when some of your group verbally abused a younger student. You knew it wasn't right but you said and did nothing. Maybe some of your friends used vulgar language. You did the same even though you didn't think it was a good idea. You really didn't like it and you knew your parents wouldn't approve. Could your parents, your church, your school, or any other human influence in your life have done anything differently to make a difference in this regard? Of course, it is a very complex matter. The big question is, Can we afford not to pay attention to the moral learning of learners?

CASE 7.11

For Your Consideration

Think of two ways that the emancipatory interest could be explored by a teacher in a grade three classroom. Is it reasonable or important for a Grade 3 teacher to consider this question?

It is interesting to contemplate the recent interest in spirituality. Habermas's postulation that people have an emancipatory interest would subscribe to the seeming wish people have to form their own opinions, to think for themselves. Within this interest, amid the complexity of today's world, there is an apparent search for deeper meaning to human behaviour. Leaders in the corporate and educational worlds, for example, address this meaning in works such as *Going Deep* (Percy, 1997), *Synchronicity: The Inner Path Of Leadership* (Jaworski, 1998), *Leadership from Within* (Bender, 1997), *Encouraging the Heart* (Kouzes & Posner, 1999), *Principle-Centred Leadership* (Covey, 1992), *Moral Leadership* (Sergiovanni, 1992), and *The Soul of Education* (Kessler, 2000). The commonality in these works is the search for a deeper understanding of self, of one's place in the scheme of things, and the harmonious coexistence of intrapersonal and interpersonal relationships in all facets of life. This seeking for spirituality has interesting connections to those peoples we often somewhat arrogantly call "primitive," those who have not been influenced by western civilization. Perhaps a need for morality in our lives is innate? Perhaps, in this age of an educated populace, where people enjoy liberation in thought, the emancipatory interest is emerging and the always-present need for moral codes is becoming more explicit.

Morality and Co-operation

Co-operation is a fundamental requirement in the human community. The skills and competencies of co-operation contribute to our survival. In the days of hunting and gathering, people co-operated for physical survival. Later, when societies were more settled, co-operation led to advancement in industry, arts, health, and welfare. The sense of community that co-operation inspires appeals to the inner needs that human beings have for care and compassion. It is altruism; it is concern for the welfare of others, it is other-centred; it is doing the "right thing;" it is the Golden Rule. "Co-operation is an essentially humanizing experience that predisposes participants to take a benevolent view of others. It allows them to transcend egocentric and objectifying postures and encourages trust, sensitivity, open communication and pro-social activity." (Kohn, 1991) Co-operation in schools is a pre-condition for the social life, but also a powerful means of learning. Within the school, then, there are extant conditions that lend themselves to moral learning. The task for the school is to render moral learning explicit within the social learning community.

A co-operative group at work.

Moral Learning and Ethics

Moral learning and ethics are two terms that are often used interchangeably: **Ethics** is concerned with principles of conduct generally considered to be "good," "right," and "proper" for both the welfare of the individual and society. **Moral learning** is the process by which people acquire and practice principles of right, good, and proper ethical conduct.

Moral education seeks to understand how people learn to conduct themselves in right, proper, and good ways, to do the right thing. The fundamental question often is, What is the right thing and who decides what it is? The debate is rooted in considerations of altruism and socialization. The moral learning of children must, of course, proceed from a clear understanding of their overall development as maturing young people. The over-arching goals are to nurture altruism, empathy, and a general disposition toward concern for the welfare of self and others. The subjugation of self-centred interest to the welfare of others is a particularly admirable human quality. It is a quality based in reason, our ability to be thoughtful, and our ability to act on that thoughtfulness. It contributes to becoming fully human.

Moral Learning in Schools: The Moral Dimension of Teaching

Schools are places where children and adults congregate for the purpose of learning. Children arrive at school to be taught, in groups, by adults who are responsible for the learning and teaching that takes place, and for the orderly conduct of daily life in the school. How is daily life in school to be regulated? How are decisions made that go beyond the regulatory rules and policies of the place? Interactions between people in schools are constant. The interactions concern learning, conduct, consequences, interpersonal events, decision making, responsibility, and so on. They all involve choices. How are these choices made and on what bases do people found their decisions? "The choices embed themselves in and arise out of individual moral agency grappling with obligation to others." (Thomas, 1990) Thomas takes the position that teaching is, inherently, a moral enterprise. Using what he calls a "simple vocabulary to describe teaching" he offers three statements in an attempt to bring clarity to the morality of the schooling enterprise:

1. Parents entrust their children to school. Trust obliges teachers to be careful. Teachers are to proceed carefully with the work of empowering students.
2. Empowerment is remarkable. One human being sets out to make others strong and able. That one human being is not to exploit, coerce, or manipulate the others. . . . At the outset, we can at least say that the empowering teacher must be powerful, for impotence does not call forth potency.
3. Parents entrust their children to teachers. School is mandatory. . . . The teacher, then, is obliged to care for children and be responsible for their empowerment. (Thomas, 1990, pp. 266–267)

Trust, care, obligation, and *responsibility,* Thomas believes, are words that carry the burden of morality. Not only teaching, but schooling also is a moral enterprise. Think, for a minute, about daily life in school. How are students spoken to in the school office? What tone and manner do teachers display when they observe a learner misbehaving? If two boys engage in a heated argument in the hallway at lunchtime, how would teachers deal with the situation? If a school has a detention room, why are students sent there and what do they do during their detention time? The larger question to ask of all these situations is, What will the students learn from their treatment? Therein lies a critical consideration as to whether teaching and schooling constitute a moral enterprise.

Moral Learning Research

Moral learning is a process through which young people acquire and practise principles of right, good, and proper ethical conduct. *Character education* is often used synonymously with *moral education*. In the design of this process schools must look to research that explores human development and demonstrates how, through the different phases of development, young people might be nurtured toward thinking, reasoning, and acting in moral ways. We now present a summary of the work of four researchers as useful references for that process.

JEAN PIAGET (1896–1980): COGNITIVE DEVELOPMENT AND MORAL JUDGMENT

Piaget's research in developmental psychology attempted to understand how knowledge grows. In his pursuit of this understanding, Piaget spent a great deal of time observing children as they reacted to their environments. He presented stories to children and engaged them in discussions. He would question them about the stories. Over time, Piaget began to formulate a description of how moral judgments develop and how cognitive development occurs in young people. His premise was that children learn through actively interacting with their environments. Table 7.2 on the next page summarizes his theory of cognitive development.

LAWRENCE KOHLBERG (1927–1987): DEVELOPMENTAL STAGES OF MORAL DEVELOPMENT

Kohlberg explored Piaget's work, modifying and elaborating on Piaget's conclusions to lay solid groundwork for current debates on moral education and moral learning. Like Piaget, he used stories to investigate moral reasoning for all ages. Kohlberg's stories presented **moral dilemmas** on which his subjects were asked to judge the best course of action. He concluded that young people form ways of reasoning through their experiences, which include understandings of moral concepts such as justice, equality, fairness, and human welfare. The following moral dilemma is typical of those used by Kohlberg in his research:

> In Europe, a woman was near death from cancer. One drug might save her, a form of radium a druggist in the same town had recently discovered. The druggist was charging $2000, ten times what the drug cost him to make. The sick woman's husband, Heinz, went to everyone he knew to borrow the money, but he could only get together about half of what it cost. He told the druggist that his wife was dying and asked him to sell it cheaper or let him pay later, but the druggist said, "No." The husband got desperate and broke into the man's store to steal the drug for his wife.
>   Should the husband have done that? Why? (Kohlberg, 1969, p. 376)

Kohlberg classified the reasoning used by young people to respond to the dilemmas he presented. On the basis of his research he identified six stages of moral reasoning, within three levels (shown in Table 7.3)

TABLE 7.2 *Piaget's Stage Theory of Cognitive Development*

Stage	Age	Characteristics
Sensorimotor	Birth to about 2 years	It "is primarily characterized by the development of sensory (simple input) and motor (simple output) functions" (R. Sternberg & Williams, 2002, p. 46). Two main accomplishments at this stage are object permanence, the understanding that objects continue to exist even when not immediately visible, and representational thought, mental ideas of external stimuli (R. Sternberg & Williams, 2002).
Preoperational	Approx. 24 months to 7 years	Children begin to communicate using words, use words as symbols for concrete objects, and are often egocentric, "centered on the self without understanding how other people perceive a situation" (R. Sternberg & Williams, 2002, p. 47).
Concrete Operational	Approx. 7–12 years	Children at this stage "not only have mental representations but also can act on and modify these representations. They can think logically as long as the logical thinking applies to these representations" (R. Sternberg & Williams, 2002 p. 48). An example of this is their development of conservation, "the recognition that even when the physical appearance of something changes, its underlying quantity (how much there is of it—number, size, or volume) remains the same—or in other words, is conserved" (R. Sternberg & Williams, 2002, p. 48). At this stage the child's thinking is reversible; he or she can see the higher level of liquid in the tall thin beaker after pouring out the same amount into a shorter wide beaker.
Formal Operational	About age 11 through adulthood	Individuals in this stage can form abstract as well as concrete mental representations, and can see second-order relations, "or relations between relations, as required by analogical reasoning" (R. Sternberg & Williams, 2002, p. 49).

(Source: From Robert J. Sternberg and Wendy M. Williams, *Educational Psychology,* 2002, Boston, MA: Allyn and Bacon. Copyright © 2002 by Pearson Education. Reprinted by permission of the publisher.)

Refer to the reasoning you used when responding to the dilemma involving the man whose wife was dying of cancer. If you accept Kohlberg's model, into which stage of moral reasoning would you fit? Do you feel you fit comfortably into one stage or does your reasoning embrace a number of stages? Kohlberg would argue that people have a dominant stage and that to develop to more advanced stages they benefit from questions that reflect the moral reasoning of the next more advanced stage.

TABLE 7.3 *Kohlberg's Theory of Moral Development*

Level 1—Preconventional Level of Moral Reasoning	Child is responsive to cultural rules and labels of good and bad, right or wrong, but interprets these in terms of consequences of action (punishment, rewards, exchanges of favours).
Stage 1: Punishment-and-Obedience Orientation	Physical consequences of action determine its goodness or badness. Avoidance of punishment and deference of power are valued.
Stage 2: The Instrumental–Relativist Orientation	Right action consists of that which satisfies one's own needs and occasionally the needs of others. Reciprocity is a matter of "You scratch my back and I'll scratch yours."
Level II—Conventional Level of Moral Reasoning	Maintaining the expectations of the individual's family, group, or society is perceived as valuable, regardless of consequences.
Stage 3: The Interpersonal Concordance or "Good Boy–Nice Girl" Orientation	Good behaviour is that which pleases or helps others and is approved by them.
Stage 4: The "Law and Order" Orientation	Orientation toward fixed rules and the maintenance of the social order. Right behaviour consists of doing one's duty and showing respect for authority.
Level III—Postconventional, Autonomous, or Principled Level of Moral Reasoning	Effort to define moral principles that have validity and application apart from the authority of groups.
Stage 5: The Social Contract, Legalistic Orientation	Right action is defined in terms of rights and standards that have been agreed on by the whole society.
Stage 6: The Universal Ethical Principle Orientation	Right is defined by conscience in accord with self-chosen ethical principles appealing to logic and universality.

(Source: Excerpted from Lawrence Kohlberg, "The Claim to Moral Adequacy of a Highest State of Moral Judgment," *Journal of Philosophy, LXX, 18,* (Oct. 25, 1973): 631–632. Reprinted with permission.)

In response to criticism, Kohlberg later modified his stages to reject Stage 6 as a logical progression from Stage 5. He considered it to be more of a theoretical endpoint that rationally follows, rather than a specific stage. Stages 1 to 5 have been empirically supported by findings from longitudinal and cross-cultural research (Power, Higgins, & Kohlberg, 1989).

CONCERNS ABOUT KOHLBERG'S MODEL

Kohlberg's model has been criticized. His claim that young people pass through stages in "invariant sequence," that is, from one stage to the next in sequence, with the only variant being the precise age at which they might move to a higher stage, has been challenged. Holstein (1976) found that children might vary in their stage of development depending on the particular dilemma to which they were responding. He found high levels of ambiguity in Kohlberg's stage developmental theory. Kohlberg has also been challenged on the basis of gender. His research subjects were male, and notable differences were detected when his dilemmas were applied to female subjects (Holstein, 1976; Gilligan, 1982).

Further criticism concerns Kohlberg's dependence on moral reasoning, or thinking. The whole question of feeling appears to be absent from the stages. When people are confronted with a moral dilemma, feelings, emotions, and attitudes cannot be discounted. Peters (1977) argues that empathy and altruism should be high on any list of considerations when responding to moral dilemmas. Moral reasoning is not, solely, an objective, intellectual exercise.

STRENGTHS OF KOHLBERG'S MODEL

Regardless of the absence of emotion, feelings, and attitudes in Kohlberg's approach, he does present useful insight into the process of moral reasoning. Moral learning is clearly a complex matter that is composed of many interconnected dimensions in which reasoning and thinking are prominent and practical. Relationships are very important and later discussion of Gilligan and Noddings will show the profound nature of positive relationships to the effectiveness of moral reasoning. Teachers, on a daily basis, deal with young people who display inappropriate behaviour. Frequently this behaviour involves other students and raises moral concerns. If a teacher has an understanding of a young person's capacity for moral reasoning, then the teacher knows that responding with comments and questions within the child's ability to comprehend will likely encourage understanding and resolution. If this kind of response is in the context of good relationships, then a successful outcome is much more likely. Kohlberg's theory represents a significant contribution to our understanding of moral development. "A good scientific theory is one that generates new research. In this regard, Kohlberg's theory has proven to be very successful" (McCown et al., 1999, p. 87).

CAROL GILLIGAN: GENDER DIFFERENCES IN MORAL DEVELOPMENT

Gilligan (1982) noted that Kohlberg's research subjects were all males and concluded that his findings were biased against women. She conducted research in which she listened to women's stories and experiences. She concluded that it was possible to discern, from women's experiences, a morality, or **ethic of care.** This contrasts with Kohlberg, who determined that morality was based on justice and fairness. The essential equality upon which Kohlberg's theory is founded provides an interesting apposition to the compassion and empathy of Gilligan.

Gilligan's research suggests three stages of moral learning with two periods of transition. Her first stage, individual survival,would see a person with self as one's sole concern. The first transition would see a person moving from egocentrism to an emerging sense of responsibility, arriving at the second stage of goodness, self-sacrifice, and social conformity. The second stage would see the person demonstrating greater social participation and a general acceptance of social conventions and protocol. The final transition is from goodness to truth. The characteristic of this transition is a subservience of self to the interests of a morality of care. An individual at this stage wrestles with looking after one's own self-interest before the interest of others. This leads to Gilligan's final stage, morality of non-violence. In this third stage the individual engages in comfortable concern for self and others. Altruism is understood and practised. There is a reconciliation of selfishness and responsibility.

At each level, the complexity of the self–other relationship increases. During the two periods of transition, responsibility becomes more sophisticated within the self–other context.

CASE 7.12

For Your Consideration

Task 1

Shawn O'Malley is behaving badly in Ms. Harrison's Grade 4 class. He is calling Jennifer Coltroni nasty, hurtful names and threatening to spoil her nice new school bag. Jennifer was given the last piece of green construction paper in the art class, and Shawn wanted it. Ms. Harrison pulled Shawn to one side and started to speak sternly.

"Shawn, why are you being so mean to Jennifer?"

"Because she always gets what she wants," said Shawn. "She's such a goody-goody, I hate her."

"Now look here, Shawn O'Malley, there are rules in this school that we all must follow. The principal has made these very clear and if you don't follow these rules you will finish up in his office."

"Well, why does she have to get the last piece of art paper?"

"You are now being very rude to your teacher and you are breaking another rule we have in this school . . . "

Complete this scenario. How do you think it will end? Why? Discuss your reasons in a group setting.

Task 2

Shawn O'Malley is behaving badly in Ms. Harrison's Grade 4 class. He is calling Jennifer Coltroni nasty, hurtful names and threatening to spoil her nice new school bag. Jennifer was given the last piece of green construction paper in the art class and Shawn wanted it. Ms. Harrison pulled Shawn to one side and . . .

Now discuss this scenario in the context of moral development. How would you talk to Shawn? How would you reason with him? How would you resolve the situation?

The broad question, "Can moral reasoning be taught?" looms large. Concepts such as empathy, justice and fairness, altruism, compassion, and caring are important humanistic qualities that most would agree are necessary for a healthy society. Surely the learning of these moral qualities contributes to a complete individual; they are part of the whole person.

Kohlberg suggests that the following three conditions can help children internalize moral principles.

1. Exposure to the next higher stage of reasoning.
2. Exposure to situations posing problems and contradictions for the child's current moral structure, leading to dissatisfaction with his [or her] current level.
3. An atmosphere of interchange and dialogue combining the first two conditions, in which conflicting moral views are compared openly. (Banks, J., 1993, p. 3)

Gilligan used cohorts of girls for her research and in this regard her work may be thought of as a theory of female moral development. Her work certainly does pertain to female moral development, but it is not confined to one gender. Other research (Walker, deVries, & Trevethan, 1987) indicates that some people value justice while others value caring, and it is not possible to link either preference to gender. Gilligan's theory respects the role of affect in the moral development of young people. Kohlberg's adherence to justice, fairness, and the rules and regulations focus is expanded to introduce those aspects of character described by caring, compassion, feelings, emotions, and attitude. Clearly there is more to moral development than cognition. The role of gender in moral development is still in need of greater clarity, but Gilligan has helped to create awareness that care is an essential dimension of moral reasoning.

NEL NODDINGS: AN "ETHIC OF CARE" AND MORAL LEARNING

Noddings explores moral learning through caring as a moral orientation in teaching. She acknowledges that, "caring has often been characterized as feminine because it seems to arise more naturally out of woman's experience than man's" (Noddings, 1984, p. 218). She believes, however, that on reflection, the ethical orientation of caring may be understood as **relational ethics.** Such ethics are tied to experience, because all questions and considerations focus on the human beings involved in the situations being considered and their relations to each other. Noddings presents the following definition of relational ethics:

> any pairing or connection of individuals characterized by some affective awareness in each. It is an encounter or series of encounters in which the involved parties feel something toward each other. Relations may be characterized by love or hate, anger or sorrow, admiration or envy; or, of course, they may reveal mixed affects—one party feeling, say, love and the other revulsion. (Noddings, 1984, p. 218)

A relational ethic, an ethic of caring, differs significantly from the more conventional understanding of ethics in that it does not root itself in an emphasis on duty. Kohlberg and Piaget both stress the adherence to rules for the determination of right, wrong, and justice. Piaget believed that morality is defined individually through struggles to arrive at fair solutions through the consideration of rules. Kohlberg determined his stages of moral reasoning based on an individual's response to duty understood through rules and laws of social conventions. An ethic of care prefers acts done out of love and natural inclination. When acting out of an ethic of care, judgments are not grounded in conformity to rules or principles; rather they are concerned with the relation itself. The concern is two-fold: a) the physical impact on those involved in the relation, and b) the feelings and ways of responding to the actions from those involved in the relation. Responding through an ethic of care calls on a sense of obligation to stimulate natural caring. Noddings (1984) considers natural caring to be a superior state, "because it energizes the giver as well as the receiver."

Noddings' approach to moral learning is not a stage developmental approach such as Piaget's, Kohlberg's and, to a lesser extent, Gilligan's. Rather it is more of a series of conditions that need to be present for an ethic of care to be nurtured. The first relational ethic is one of modelling an ethic of care, where self-affirmation and responsibility are encouraged in young people. Noddings refers to the teacher as the one caring, and to the learner as the one cared for. "When a teacher asks a question in class and a student responds, [the one caring] receives not just the 'response' but the student . . . [f]or the brief interval of dialogue that grows around the question, . . . indeed 'fills the firmament'." (Noddings, 1984, p. 176) Her second relational ethic is dialogue. The intention is to encourage a form of dialectic between feeling and thinking that will lead, in a continuing spiral, to the basic feeling of genuine caring and the generous thinking that develops in its service. Openness on any topic is encouraged. A third relational ethic is practice. Opportunities are created for practice in caring, with the emphasis being on how the skills developed contribute to competence in caring. A final relational ethic is that of confirmation, in which the hope is to shape an acceptable child by assisting in the construction of his or her ethical ideal. "When we attribute the best possible motive, consonant with reality, to the cared-for, we confirm him; that is, we reveal to him an attainable image of himself that is lovelier than that manifested in his present acts." (Noddings, 1988, p. 224)

CASE 7.13

For Your Consideration

1. How would Gilligan respond to Shawn in For Your Consideration 7.12? How would you introduce the role of affect to Shawn's situation? How would compassion and empathy be employed in Shawn's situation?
2. Noddings explores moral learning through caring. Using her understanding of caring as relational ethics, how would you respond to Shawn through the relation itself?
3. Finally, think about our teaching qualities and apply them to Shawn's situation. Consider the work on moral learning, but don't confine yourself to it. Use any knowledge and experience you have in your professional repertoire as you consider and reflect upon each of the teaching qualities.

One thing to remember is that teachers should always apply professional judgment to any school situation with which they must deal. Children are unique; seldom is there a standard, single way of responding to them. When dealing with almost any matter with young people, the single important question is what will the young person learn from the way you respond to her? With Shawn, the question is particularly germane. What would he likely learn from his treatment in Task 1 in For Your Consideration 7.12?

We have now considered the work of four people in the area of moral development. What does this work mean for schools? What implications would it have for you as a teacher? First of all, you would have to be aware of your school's approach to moral learning. Young people of all ages benefit from consistency. It is very important that adults in a school treat young people in ways that aim to encourage the same kinds of behaviour in similar ways. To pursue this question in a little more depth, refer to Task 2 in For Your Consideration 7.12.

Reflection and Perspective on the Chapter

The main goal of a teacher is to facilitate learning in students. Teachers can fail in that goal, however, if they make incorrect assumptions about learning in social settings. One goal of your education, the same goal of the lifelong learning of teachers, is to adjust your assumptions so that they are more accurate. Many seemingly evident assumptions about learning need to be reconsidered. These include the role of the setting in which young people learn.

There are a number of plausible explanations for social learning and how it occurs. All theoretical perspectives regarding social learning refer to the role that others have in learning. The core premise in each explanation is that learning is socially constructed, that knowledge is a social construction. Learning depends on others. We have identified and discussed two educational approaches to designing learning experiences so that

social learning is positive. They are constructivist-oriented teaching and narrative inquiry. We have also discussed broad areas in which social learning might be considered, either as outcomes (e.g., pro-social skills), or as areas in which social learning might make a contribution to a child's development (e.g., moral learning). We believe that our choices of topics are the most influential ones for designing learning experiences in classrooms. The other areas in which social learning might be considered are cooperative learning, learning empathy, identity learning, and motivation and learning.

Social-cognitive learning theory is a branch of social learning theory in which the learner is considered to be an active-cognitive participant in learning. Learners can symbolically represent the events they see and hear, and can learn vicariously from considering the results that others experience from their actions. This saves time and prevents potentially dangerous experiential learning from having to be designed and implemented.

Throughout the chapter we have discussed the social conditions of learning, how teachers can create the external social conditions that create, in turn, the internal conditions of learning. Motivation is an example of an internal condition; keeping children free from the fear of failure by increasing the number of times they are successful is an external condition.

Key Terms

constructivism   223
co-operative learning   229
empathy   230
ethic of care   243
ethics   239

extrinsic motivation   234
identity learning   231
intrinsic motivation   234
moral dilemmas   240
moral education   235

moral learning   239
motivation   233
narrative inquiry   227
pro-social skills   228
relational ethics   245

Suggested Further Reading

Bay, Theresa M., and Turner, Gwendolyn, Y. (1996). *Making School a Place of Peace.* Upper Saddle River, NJ: Prentice-Hall Inc. and Thousand Oaks, CA: Corwin Press, Inc.

Fullan, M. (2003). *The Moral Imperative of School Leadership.* Thousand Oaks, CA: Corwin Press.

Malicky, Grace, Shapiro, Bonnie, and Mazurek, Kas. Eds. (1999). *Building Foundations for Safe and Caring Schools.* Edmonton, AB: Duval House Publishing.

Simon, Katherine, G. (2001). *Moral questions in the classroom: How to get kids to think deeply about real life and their school work.* New Haven, NH: Yale University Press.

Reading B: Constructivist Theory

During a 1st-grade math lesson on measurement and equivalency, children were asked to use a balance to determine how many plastic links equaled one metal washer in weight. The teacher recognized and seized an opportunity to help one particularly eager child, Anna, begin to construct a rudimentary notion of ratio and proportion.

Teacher: How many links does it take to balance one washer?

Anna: (After a few seconds of experimenting) Four.

Teacher: If I placed one more washer on this side, how many more links do you think we would need to balance it?

Anna: One.

Teacher: Try it.

Anna placed one more link in the balance tray and noticed that balance was not achieved. She looked confused and placed another link in the tray and then a third. Still no balance. She placed one more link in the tray. Balance was achieved. She smiled and looked at the teacher.

Teacher: How many cubes did it take to balance one washer?

Anna: Four.

Teacher: And how many to balance two washers?

Anna: (Counting) Eight.

Teacher: If I put one more washer on this side, how many more links will you need to balance it?

Anna: (Pondered and looked quizzically at the teacher) Four.

Teacher: Try it.

Anna: (After successfully balancing with four links) Each washer is the same as four links.

Teacher: Now, let me give you a really hard question. If I took four links off of the balance, how many washers would I need to take off in order to balance it?

Anna: One!

(Brooks & Brooks, 1999, p. 73)

Constructivism is a psychological and philosophical perspective contending that individuals form or construct much of what they learn and understand (Bruning et al., 2004). A major influence on the rise of constructivism has been theory and research in human development, especially the theories of Piaget and Vygotsky. Human development is the subject of Chapter 8; however, the present chapter covers Vygotsky's theory because it forms a cornerstone of the constructivist movement. The emphasis that Vygotsky placed on the role of social mediation of knowledge construction is central to many forms of constructivism.

In recent years, constructivism increasingly has been applied to learning and teaching. The history of learning theory reveals a shift away from environmental influences and toward human factors as explanations for learning. This shift began with the advent of cognitive psychology, which disputed the claim of conditioning theories that stimuli, responses, and consequences were adequate to explain learning. Cognitive theories place great emphasis on learners' information processing as a central cause of learning. Yet despite the elegance of cognitive learning theories, some researchers have felt that these theories fail to capture the complexity of human learning. This point is underscored by the fact that some cognitive perspectives use behavioral terminology such as the "automaticity" of performance and "forming connections" between items in memory.

Today, a number of learning researchers have shifted even more toward a focus on learners. Rather than talk about how knowledge is acquired, they speak of how it is constructed. Although these researchers differ in their emphasis on factors that affect learning and learners' cognitive processes, the theoretical perspectives they espouse may be loosely grouped and referred to as *constructivism*. Anna's construction of understanding is evident in the opening scenario.

This chapter begins by providing an overview of constructivism to include a description of its key assumptions and the different types of constructivist theories. Vygotsky's theory is described next, with emphasis on those aspects relevant to learning. The critical roles of social processes and private speech are discussed, followed by coverage of motivation and self-regulation from a constructivist perspective. The chapter concludes with a discussion of constructivist learning environments, including their key features, examples of instructional methods, and the components of reflective teaching.

When you finish studying this chapter, you should be able to do the following:

- Discuss the major assumptions and various types of constructivism.
- Explain the key principles of Vygotsky's sociocultural theory and implications for teaching in the zone of proximal development (ZPD).
- Explain the function of private speech for learning and self-regulation.
- Discuss how classroom structure and TARGET variables affect student motivation.
- Describe how teacher expectations are formed and how they can affect teachers' interactions with students.
- Discuss self-regulation from a constructivist perspective to include the role of students' implicit theories.
- List the key features of constructivist learning environments and the major components of the American Psychological Association (APA) learner-centered principles.
- Describe how class discussions, peer tutoring, and cooperative learning can be structured to reflect constructivist principles.
- Explain how teachers might become more reflective and thereby enhance student achievement.

Constructivist Assumptions and Perspectives

Many researchers and practitioners have questioned some of cognitive psychology's assumptions about learning and instruction because they believed these assumptions could not completely explain students' learning and understanding. These questionable assumptions are as follows (Greeno, 1989):

- Thinking resides in the mind rather than in interaction with persons and situations.
- Processes of learning and thinking are relatively uniform across persons, and some situations foster higher-order thinking better than others.

- Thinking derives from knowledge and skills developed in formal instructional settings more than on general conceptual competencies that result from one's experiences and innate abilities.

Constructivists do not accept these assumptions because of evidence that thinking takes place in situations and that cognitions are largely constructed by individuals as a function of their experiences in these situations (Bredo, 1997). Constructivist accounts of learning and development highlight the contributions of individuals to what is learned. Social constructivist models further emphasize the importance of social interactions in the acquisition of skills and knowledge. We now examine further what constructivism is, its assumptions, and its forms.

Overview

WHAT IS CONSTRUCTIVISM?   Strictly speaking, constructivism is not a theory but rather an *epistemology*, or philosophical explanation about the nature of learning (Simpson, 2002). As discussed in Chapter 1, a theory is a scientifically valid explanation for learning. Theories allow for hypotheses to be generated and tested. Constructivism does not propound that learning principles exist and are to be discovered and tested, but rather that learners create their own learning. Readers who are interested in exploring the historical and philosophical roots of constructivism are referred to Bredo (1997) and Packer and Goicoechea (2000).

Nonetheless, this chapter is entitled "constructivist theory" to maintain consistency with other perspectives and because constructivism makes general predictions that can be operationalized and tested. Although the latter predictions are general and thus open to different interpretations (i.e., what does it mean that learners construct their own learning?), they could be the focus of research.

Constructivist theorists reject the notion that scientific truths exist and await discovery and verification. They argue that no statement can be assumed as true but rather should be viewed with reasonable doubt. The world can be mentally constructed in many different ways, so no theory has a lock on the truth. This is true even for constructivism; there are many varieties, and no one version should be assumed to be more correct than any other (Derry, 1996; Simpson, 2002).

Rather than viewing knowledge as truth, constructivists construe it as a working hypothesis. Knowledge is not imposed from outside people but rather formed inside them. A person's constructions are true to that person but not necessarily to anyone else. This is because people produce knowledge based on their beliefs and experiences in situations (Cobb & Bowers, 1999), which differ from person to person. All knowledge, then, is subjective and personal and a product of our cognitions (Simpson, 2002). Learning is situated in contexts (Bredo, 2006).

ASSUMPTIONS   Constructivist theory highlights the interaction of persons and situations in the acquisition and refinement of skills and knowledge (Cobb & Bowers, 1999). Constructivism contrasts with conditioning theories that stress the influence of the environment on the person; constructivist theory also contrasts with cognitive information processing theory that places the locus of learning within the mind with little attention to the context in which it occurs. It shares with social cognitive theory the assumption that persons, behaviors, and environments interact in reciprocal fashion (Bandura, 1986, 1997).

A basic assumption of constructivism is that people are active learners and must construct knowledge for themselves (Geary, 1995). To understand material well, learners must discover the basic principles for themselves, as Anna did in the opening lesson. Constructivists differ in the extent to which they ascribe this function entirely to learners. Some believe that mental structures come to reflect reality, whereas others (radical constructivists) believe that the individual's mental world is the only reality. Constructivists also differ in how much they ascribe the construction of knowledge to social interactions with teachers, peers, parents, and others (Bredo, 1997).

Many of the principles, concepts, and ideas discussed in this text reflect the idea of constructivism, including cognitive processing, expectations, values, and perceptions of self and others (Derry, 1996). Thus, although constructivism seems to be a recent arrival on the learning scene, its basic premise that learners construct understandings underlies many learning principles. This is the epistemological aspect of constructivism. Some constructivist ideas are not as well developed as those of other theories discussed in this text, but constructivism has affected theory and research in learning and development.

Constructivism also has influenced educational thinking about curriculum and instruction. It underlies the emphasis on the integrated curriculum in which students study a topic from multiple perspectives. For example, in studying hot-air balloons, students might read about them, write about them, learn new vocabulary words, visit one (hands-on experience), study the scientific principles involved, draw pictures of them, and learn songs about them. Constructivist ideas also are found in many professional standards and affect the design of curriculum and instruction, such as the learner-centered principles developed by the APA (discussed later).

Another constructivist assumption is that teachers should not teach in the traditional sense of delivering instruction to a group of students. Rather, they should structure situations such that learners become actively involved with content through manipulation of materials and social interaction. How the teacher structured the lesson allowed Anna to construct her understanding. Activities include observing phenomena, collecting data, generating and testing hypotheses, and working collaboratively with others. Classes visit sites outside of the classroom. Teachers from different disciplines plan the curriculum together. Students are taught to be self-regulated and take an active role in their learning by setting goals, monitoring and evaluating progress, and going beyond basic requirements by exploring interests (Bruning et al., 2004; Geary, 1995).

Perspectives

Constructivism is not a unified theory but rather has different perspectives (Table 7.4) (Bruning et al., 2004; Moshman, 1982; Phillips, 1995). *Exogenous constructivism* refers to the idea that the acquisition of knowledge represents a reconstruction of structures that exist in the external world. This view posits a strong influence of the external world on knowledge construction, such as by experiences, teaching, and exposure to models. Knowledge is accurate to the extent it reflects that reality. Contemporary information processing theories reflect this notion in concepts such as schemata, productions, and memory networks.

In contrast, *endogenous constructivism* emphasizes the coordination of cognitive actions (Bruning et al., 2004). Mental structures are created out of earlier structures, not directly from environmental information; therefore, knowledge is not a mirror of the external world acquired through experiences, teaching, or social interactions. Knowledge

TABLE 7.4   *Perspectives on Constructivism*

Perspective	Premises
Exogenous	The acquisition of knowledge represents a reconstruction of the external world. The world influences beliefs through experiences, exposure to models, and teaching. Knowledge is accurate to the extent it reflects external reality.
Endogenous	Knowledge derives from previously acquired knowledge and not directly from environmental interactions. Knowledge is not a mirror of the external world; rather, it develops through cognitive abstraction.
Dialectical	Knowledge derives from interactions between persons and their environments. Constructions are not invariably tied to the external world nor wholly the workings of the mind. Rather, knowledge reflects the outcomes of mental contradictions that result from one's interactions with the environment.

develops through the cognitive activity of abstraction and follows a generally predictable sequence. Piaget's (1970) theory of cognitive development fits this framework.

Between these extremes lies *dialectical constructivism*, which holds that knowledge derives from interactions between persons and their environments. Constructions are not invariably bound to the external world, nor are they wholly the result of the workings of the mind; rather, they reflect the outcomes of mental contradictions that result from interactions with the environment. This perspective has become closely aligned with many contemporary theories. For example, it is compatible with Bandura's (1986) social cognitive theory, with cognitive modeling, and with many motivation theories. It also is referred to as *cognitive constructivism* (Derry, 1996). The developmental theories of Bruner and Vygotsky (discussed in this chapter) also emphasize the influence of the social environment.

Each of these perspectives has merit and is potentially useful for research and teaching. Exogenous views are appropriate when we are interested in determining how accurately learners perceive the structure of knowledge within a domain. The endogenous perspective is relevant to explore how learners develop from novices through greater levels of competence. The dialectical view is useful for designing interventions to challenge children's thinking and for research aimed at exploring the effectiveness of social influences such as exposure to models and peer collaboration.

Situated Cognition

A core premise of constructivism is that cognitive processes (including thinking and learning) are situated (located) in physical and social contexts (Anderson, Reder, & Simon, 1996; Cobb & Bowers, 1999; Greeno et al., 1998). *Situated cognition* (or *learning*) involves relations between a person and a situation; cognitive processes do not reside solely in one's mind (Greeno, 1989).

The idea of person–situation interaction is not new. Most contemporary theories of learning and development assume that beliefs and knowledge are formed as people interact in situations. This emphasis contrasts with the classical information processing model that highlights the processing and movement of information through mental structures (e.g., sensory registers, working memory, long-term memory). Cognitive information processing downplays the importance of situations once environmental inputs are received. Research within a variety of disciplines—including cognitive psychology, social cognitive learning, and specific content domains (e.g., reading, mathematics)—shows this to be a limited view and that thinking involves an extended reciprocal relation with the context (Bandura, 1986; Cobb & Bowers, 1999; Derry, 1996; Greeno, 1989).

Research highlights the importance of exploring situated cognition as a means of understanding the development of competence in domains such as literacy, mathematics (as we see in the opening scenario), and science (Cobb, 1994; Cobb & Bowers, 1999; Driver, Asoko, Leach, Mortimer, & Scott, 1994; Lampert, 1990). Situated cognition also is relevant to motivation. As with learning, motivation is not an entirely internal state, as posited by classical views, or wholly dependent on the environment, as predicted by reinforcement theories. Rather, motivation depends on cognitive activity in interaction with sociocultural and instructional factors, which include language and forms of assistance such as scaffolding of information (Sivan, 1986).

Situated cognition addresses the intuitive notion that many processes interact to produce learning. We know that motivation and instruction are linked: Good instruction can raise motivation for learning, and motivated learners seek effective instructional environments (Schunk, 1995). A further benefit of the situated cognition perspective is that it leads researchers to explore cognition in authentic learning contexts such as schools, workplaces, and homes, many of which involve mentoring or apprenticeships.

Research on the effectiveness of situated learning is recent, but results are promising. Griffin (1995) compared traditional (in-class) instruction on map skills with a situated learning approach in which college students received practice in the actual environments depicted on the maps. The situated learning group performed better on a map-skill assessment. Although Griffin found no benefit of situated learning on transfer, the results of situated learning studies should be highly generalizable to similar contexts.

The situated idea also is pertinent to how learning occurs (Greeno et al., 1998). Students exposed to a certain procedure for learning a subject experience situated cognition for that method; in other words, that is how this content is learned. For example, if students repeatedly receive mathematics instruction taught in didactic fashion by a teacher explaining and demonstrating, followed by their engaging in independent problem solving at their desks, then mathematics learning is apt to become situated in this context. The same students might have difficulty adjusting to a new teacher who favors using guided discovery (as done by the teacher in the opening lesson) by collaborative peer groups.

The instructional implication is that teaching methods should reflect the outcomes we desire in our learners. If we are trying to teach them inquiry skills, the instruction must incorporate inquiry activities. The method and the content must be properly situated.

Situated cognition fits well with the constructivist idea that context is an inherent part of learning. Especially in subject domains, this idea increasingly has been shown to be valid. Nonetheless, extending the idea of situated learning too far may be erroneous. As Anderson, Reder, and Simon (1996) showed, there is plenty of empirical evidence for contextual independence of learning and transfer of learning between contexts. Rather than being at an impasse over knowing whether learning is situated, researchers need to explore the issue in greater depth. We need more information on which types of learning proceed best when they are firmly linked to contexts and when it is better to teach broader skills and show how they can be applied in different contexts.

Contributions and Applications

Constructivist theory has only recently been applied to the field of learning; hence, research exploring constructivist assumptions about learning is in its infancy. Another factor that makes determining the contributions of constructivist theory difficult is that the approach is not a unified one that offers specific hypotheses to be tested. Bereiter (1994) accurately noted that the claim that "students construct their own knowledge" is not falsifiable but rather is true of all cognitive learning theories. Cognitive theories view the mind as a repository of beliefs, values, expectations, schemata, and so forth; hence, any feasible explanation of how those thoughts and feelings come to reside in the mind must assume that they are formed there. For example, social cognitive theory emphasizes the roles of expectations (e.g., self-efficacy, outcome) and goals; these beliefs and cognitions do not arise from nowhere but rather are constructed by learners.

Constructivism eventually must be evaluated not on whether any of its premises are true or false. Rather, it seems imperative to determine the process whereby students construct knowledge and how social, developmental, and instructional factors may influence that process. Research also is needed on when situational influences have greater effects on mental processes. A drawback of many forms of constructivism is the emphasis on *relativism* (Phillips, 1995), or the idea that all forms of knowledge are justifiable because they are constructed by learners, especially if they reflect societal consensus. Educators cannot accept this premise in good conscience because education demands that we inculcate values such as honesty, fairness, and responsibility in our students regardless of whether societal constituencies deem them important.

Furthermore, nature may constrain our thinking more than we wish to admit. For example, research suggests that some mathematical competencies—such as one-to-one correspondence and being able to count—are not constructed but rather largely genetically driven (Geary, 1995; Gelman & Gallistel, 1978). Far from being relative, some forms of knowledge may be universally endogenous. Acquisition of other competencies (e.g., multiplying, word processing) requires environmental input. Constructivism—with its emphasis on minimal instructional guidance—may downplay the importance of human cognitive structures. Instructional methods that are mapped better onto this cognitive structure may actually produce better learning (Kirschner, Sweller, & Clark, 2006). Research will help to establish the scope of constructivist processes in the sequence of competency acquisition and how these processes change as a function of developmental level (Muller, Sokol, & Overton, 1998).

Constructivist perspectives have important implications for instruction and curriculum design (Phillips, 1995). The most straightforward recommendations are to involve students actively in their learning and to provide experiences that challenge their thinking and force them to rearrange their beliefs. Constructivism also underlies the current emphasis on *reflective teaching* (discussed later in this chapter). Social constructivist views (e.g., Vygotsky's) stress that social group learning and peer collaboration are useful (Ratner, Foley, & Gimpert, 2002). As students model for and observe each other, they not only teach skills but also experience higher self-efficacy for learning (Schunk, 1995). Application 7.1 shows constructivist applications. We now turn to a more in-depth examination of constructivism and its applications to human learning.

APPLICATION 7.1

Constructivism and Teaching

Constructivism emphasizes integrated curricula and having teachers use materials in such a way that learners become actively involved. Kathy Stone implements various constructivist ideas in her third-grade classroom using integrated units. In the fall, she presents a unit on pumpkins. In social studies, children learn where pumpkins are grown and about the products made from pumpkins. They also study the uses of pumpkins in history and the benefits of pumpkins to early settlers.

Mrs. Stone takes her class on a field trip to a pumpkin farm, where they learn how pumpkins are grown. Each student selects a pumpkin and brings it back to class. The pumpkin becomes a valuable learning tool. In mathematics, the students estimate the size and weight of their pumpkins and then mea-

sure and weigh them. They establish class graphs by comparing all the pumpkins by size, weight, shape, and color. They also estimate the number of seeds they think Mrs. Stone's pumpkin has, and then they count the seeds when she cuts open her pumpkin. As another class activity, the students make pumpkin bread with Mrs. Stone's pumpkin. For art, they design a shape for the carving of their pumpkins, and then with Mrs. Stone's assistance they carve them. In language arts, they write a story about pumpkins. They also write a thank-you letter to the pumpkin farm. For spelling, Mrs. Stone uses words that they have used in the study of pumpkins. These examples illustrate how Mrs. Stone integrates the study of pumpkins across the curriculum.

Vygotsky's Sociocultural Theory

Vygotsky's theory is a constructivist theory that emphasizes the social environment as a facilitator of development and learning (Tudge & Scrimsher, 2003). The background of the theory is discussed, along with its key assumptions and principles.

Background

Perhaps no theorist has influenced modern constructivist thinking more than Lev Semenovich Vygotsky, who was born in Russia in 1896. He studied various subjects in school, including psychology, philosophy, and literature, and received a law degree from Moscow Imperial University in 1917.

Following graduation, he returned to his hometown of Gomel, which was beset with problems stemming from German occupation, famine, and civil war. Two of his brothers died, and he contracted tuberculosis—the disease that eventually killed him. He taught courses in psychology and literature, wrote literary criticism, and edited a journal. He also worked at a teacher training institution, where he founded a psychology laboratory and wrote an educational psychology book (Tudge & Scrimsher, 2003).

A critical event in Vygotsky's life occurred in 1924 at the Second All-Russian Congress of Psychoneurology in Leningrad. Prevailing psychological theory at that time neglected subjective experiences in favor of Pavlov's conditioned reflexes and behaviorism's emphasis on environmental influences. Vygotsky presented a paper ("The Methods of Reflexological and Psychological Investigation") in which he criticized the dominant views and spoke on the relation of conditioned reflexes to human consciousness and behavior. Pavlov's experiments with dogs and Gestalt theorist Köhler's studies with apes erased many distinctions between animals and humans.

Vygotsky contended that, unlike animals that react only to the environment, humans have the capacity to alter the environment for their own purposes. This adaptive capacity distinguishes humans from lower forms of life. His speech made such an impression on one listener—Alexander Luria (discussed later in this chapter)—that he was invited to join the prestigious Institute of Experimental Psychology in Moscow. He helped to establish the Institute of Defektology, the purpose of which was to study ways to help handicapped individuals. Until his death from tuberculosis in 1934, he wrote extensively on the social mediation of learning and the role of consciousness, often in collaboration with colleagues Luria and Leontiev (Rohrkemper, 1989).

Understanding Vygotsky's position requires keeping in mind that he was a Marxist and that his views represented an attempt to apply Marxist ideas of social change to language and development (Rohrkemper, 1989). After the 1917 Russian Revolution, an urgency among the new leaders produced rapid change in the populace. Vygotsky's strong sociocultural theoretical orientation fit well with the revolution's goals of changing the culture to a socialist system.

Although Vygotsky had some access to Western society (e.g., writers such as Piaget; Bredo, 1997; Tudge & Winterhoff, 1993), little of what Vygotsky wrote was published during his brief lifetime or for some years following his death. Unfortunately, a negative political climate prevailed in the former Soviet Union; among other things, the Communist Party curtailed psychological testing and publications. Although Vygotsky was a Marxist, he propounded revisionist thinking (Bruner, 1984). He moved from a Pavlovian view of psychology focusing on reflexes to a cultural–historical perspective that stressed language and social interaction (Tudge & Scrimsher, 2003). Some of Vygotsky's writings were at odds with Stalin's views and, hence, were not published. References to his work were banned in the Soviet Union until the 1980s (Tudge & Scrimsher, 2003). In recent years, Vygotsky's writings have been increasingly translated and circulated, which has expanded their impact in fields such as education, psychology, and linguistics.

Basic Principles

One of Vygotsky's central contributions to psychological thought was his emphasis on socially meaningful activity as an important influence on human consciousness (Bredo, 1997; Kozulin, 1986; Tudge & Winterhoff, 1993). Vygotsky attempted to explain human thought in new ways. He rejected introspection and raised many of the same objections as those raised by behavioral psychologists. He wanted to abandon explaining states of consciousness by referring to the concept of consciousness; similarly, he rejected behavioral explanations of action in terms of prior actions. Rather than discarding consciousness (which the conditioning theorists did) or the role of the environment (which the introspectionists did), he sought a middle ground of taking environmental influence into account through its effect on consciousness.

Vygotsky's theory stresses the interaction of interpersonal (social), cultural–historical, and individual factors as the key to human development (Tudge & Scrimsher, 2003). Interactions with persons in the environment (e.g., apprenticeships, collaborations) stimulate developmental processes and foster cognitive growth. But interactions are not useful in a traditional sense of providing children with information. Rather, children transform their experiences based on their knowledge and characteristics and reorganize their mental structures.

The cultural–historical aspects of Vygotsky's theory illuminate the point that learning and development cannot be dissociated from their context. The way that learners interact with their worlds—with the persons, objects, and institutions in it—transforms their thinking. The meanings of concepts change as they are linked with the world. Thus, "school" is not simply a word or a physical structure but also an institution that seeks to promote learning and citizenship.

Finally, there are the individual, or inherited factors, that affect development. Vygotsky was very interested in children with mental and physical disabilities. He believed that their inherited characteristics produced different learning trajectories than those of children without such challenges.

Of these three influences, the one that has received the most attention—at least among Western researchers and practitioners—is interpersonal. Vygotsky considered the social environment to be critical for learning and thought that social interactions transformed learning experiences. Social activity is a phenomenon that helps explain changes in consciousness and establishes a psychological theory that unifies behavior and mind (Kozulin, 1986; Wertsch, 1985).

The social environment influences cognition through its "tools"—that is, its cultural objects (e.g., cars, machines) and its language and social institutions (e.g., schools, churches). Social interactions help to coordinate the three influences on development. Cognitive change results from using cultural tools in social interactions and from internalizing and mentally transforming these interactions (Bruning et al., 2004). Vygotsky's position is a form of dialectical (cognitive) constructivism because it emphasizes the interaction between persons and their environments. *Mediation* is the key mechanism in development and learning:

> All human psychological processes (higher mental processes) are mediated by such psychological tools as language, signs, and symbols. Adults teach these tools to children in the course of their joint (collaborative) activity. After children internalize these tools they function as mediators of the children's more advanced psychological processes. (Karpov & Haywood, 1998, p. 27)

Vygotsky's most controversial contention was that all higher mental functions originated in the social environment (Vygotsky, 1962). This is a powerful claim, but it has a good degree of truth to it. The most influential process involved is language. Vygotsky thought that a critical component of psychological development was mastering the external process of transmitting cultural development and thinking through symbols such as language, counting, and writing. Once this process was mastered, the next step involved using these symbols to influence and self-regulate thoughts and actions. Self-regulation uses the important function of private speech (discussed later in this chapter).

In spite of this impressive theorizing, Vygotsky's claim appears to be too strong. Research evidence shows that young children mentally figure out much knowledge about the way the world operates long before they have an opportunity to learn from the culture in which they live (Bereiter, 1994). Children also seem biologically predisposed to acquire certain concepts (e.g., understanding that adding increases quantity), which does not depend on the environment (Geary, 1995). Although social learning affects knowledge construction, the claim that all learning derives from the social environment seems overstated. Nonetheless, we know that learners' cultures are critical and need to be considered in explaining learning and development. A summary of major points in Vygotsky's (1978) theory appears in Table 7.5 (Meece, 2002).

TABLE 7.5   *Key Points in Vygotsky's Theory*

- Social interactions are critical; knowledge is co-constructed between two or more people.
- Self-regulation is developed through internalization (developing an internal representation) of actions and mental operations that occur in social interactions.
- Human development occurs through the cultural transmission of tools (language, symbols).
- Language is the most critical tool. Language develops from social speech, to private speech, to covert (inner) speech.
- The ZPD is the difference between what children can do on their own and what they can do with assistance from others. Interactions with adults and peers in the ZPD promote cognitive development.

(Meece, 2002)

Zone of Proximal Development

A key concept is the ZPD, defined as "the distance between the actual developmental level as determined by independent problem solving and the level of potential development as determined through problem solving under adult guidance or in collaboration with more capable peers" (Vygotsky, 1978, p. 86). The ZPD represents the amount of learning possible by a student given the proper instructional conditions (Puntambekar & Hübscher, 2005). It is largely a test of a student's developmental readiness or intellectual level in a specific domain, and it shows how learning and development are related (Bredo, 1997; Campione, Brown, Ferrara, & Bryant, 1984) and can be viewed as an alternative to the conception of intelligence (Belmont, 1989). In the ZPD, a teacher and learner (adult/child, tutor/tutee, model/observer, master/apprentice, expert/novice) work together on a task that the learner could not perform independently because of the difficulty level. The ZPD reflects the Marxist idea of collective activity, in which those who know more or are more skilled share that knowledge and skill to accomplish a task with those who know less (Bruner, 1984).

Cognitive change occurs in the ZPD as teachers and learners share cultural tools, and this culturally mediated interaction produces cognitive change when it is internalized in the learner (Bruning et al., 2004; Cobb, 1994). Working in the ZPD requires a good deal of guided participation (Rogoff, 1986); however, children do not acquire cultural knowledge passively from these interactions, nor is what they learn necessarily an automatic or accurate reflection of events. Rather, learners bring their own understandings to social interactions and construct meanings by integrating those understandings with their experiences in the context. The learning often is sudden, in the Gestalt sense of insight, rather than reflecting a gradual accretion of knowledge (Wertsch, 1984).

For example, assume that a teacher (Trudy) and a child (Laura) work on a task (making a picture of mom, dad, and Laura doing something together at home). Laura brings to the task her understandings of what the people and the home look like and of the types of things they might work on, combined with knowledge of how to draw and make pictures. Trudy brings the same understandings plus knowledge of conditions necessary to work on various tasks. Suppose they decide to make a picture of the three working in the yard. Laura might draw a picture of dad cutting grass, mom trimming shrubs, and Laura raking the lawn. If Laura were to draw herself in front of dad, Trudy would explain that Laura must be behind dad to rake up the grass left behind by dad's cutting. During the interaction, Laura modifies her beliefs about working in the yard based on her current understanding and on the new knowledge she constructs.

Despite the importance of the ZPD, the overarching emphasis it has received in Western cultures has served to distort its meaning and downplay the complexity of Vygotsky's theory. As Tudge and Scrimsher (2003) explain:

> Moreover, the concept itself has too often been viewed in a rather limited way that emphasized the interpersonal at the expense of the individual and cultural–historical levels and treats the concept in a unidirectional fashion. As if the concept were synonymous with "scaffolding," too many authors have focused on the role of the more competent other, particularly the teacher, whose role is to provide assistance just in advance of the child's current thinking. . . . The concept thus has become equated with what sensitive teachers might do with their children and has lost much of the complexity with which it was imbued by Vygotsky, missing both what the child brings to the interaction and the broader setting (cultural and historical) in which the interaction takes place. (p. 211)

The influence of the cultural–historical setting is seen clearly when we consider that Vygotsky felt that schooling was important not because it was where children were scaffolded but, rather, because it allowed them to develop greater awareness of themselves, their language, and their role in the world order. Participating in the cultural world transforms mental functioning rather than simply accelerate processes that would have developed anyway. Broadly speaking, therefore, the ZPD refers to new forms of awareness that occur as people interact with their societies' social institutions. The culture affects the course of one's mental development. It is unfortunate that in most discussions of the ZPD it is conceived so narrowly as an expert teacher providing learning opportunities for a student (although that is part of it).

Applications

Vygotsky's ideas lend themselves to many educational applications (Karpov & Haywood, 1998; Moll, 2001). The field of self-regulation (discussed later in this chapter) has been strongly influenced by the theory. Self-regulation requires metacognitive mediators such as planning, checking, and evaluating. This section and Application 7.2 discuss other examples.

Helping students acquire cognitive mediators (e.g., signs, symbols) through the social environment can be accomplished in many ways. A common application involves the concept of *instructional scaffolding*, which refers to the process of controlling task elements that are beyond the learners' capabilities so that they can focus on and master those features of the task that they can grasp quickly (Bruning et al., 2004; Puntambekar & Hübscher, 2005). To use an analogy of scaffolding employed in construction projects, instructional scaffolding has five major functions:

1. providing support
2. functioning as a tool
3. extending the range of the learner
4. permitting the attainment of tasks not otherwise possible
5. using selectively only as needed.

In a learning situation, a teacher initially might do most of the work, after which the teacher and the learners share responsibility. As learners become more competent, the

APPLICATION 7.2

Vygotsky's Theory

Vygotsky postulated that one's interactions with the environment contribute to success in learning. The experiences one brings to a learning situation can greatly influence the outcome.

Ice-skating coaches may work with advanced students who have learned a great deal about ice-skating and how their bodies perform on the ice. Students bring with them their own concepts of balance, speed, movement, and body control based on their prior experiences in skating. Coaches take the strengths and weaknesses of these students and help them learn to alter various movements to improve their performances. For example, a skater who has trouble completing a triple axel toe loop has the height and speed needed to complete the jump, but the coach notices that she turns her toe at an angle during the spin that alters the smooth completion of the loop. After the coach points this out to the skater and helps her learn to alter that movement, she is able to successfully complete the jump.

Veterinary students who have grown up on farms and have experienced births, illnesses, and care of various types of animals bring valuable knowledge to their training. Veterinary instructors can use these prior experiences to enhance students' learning. In teaching students how to treat an injured hoof of a cow or horse, the instructor might call on some of these students to discuss what they have observed and then build on that knowledge by explaining the latest and most effective methods of treatment.

teacher gradually withdraws the scaffolding so learners can perform independently (Campione et al., 1984). The key is to ensure that the scaffolding keeps learners in the ZPD, which is raised as they develop capabilities. Students are challenged to learn within the bounds of the ZPD. We see in the opening lesson how Anna was able to learn given the proper instructional support.

It is critical to understand that scaffolding is not a formal part of Vygotsky's theory (Puntambekar & Hübscher, 2005). The term was coined by Wood, Bruner, and Ross (1976). It does, however, fit nicely within the ZPD. Scaffolding is part of Bandura's (1986) participant modeling technique, in which a teacher initially models a skill, provides support, and gradually reduces aid as learners develop the skill. The notion also bears some relation to shaping, as instructional supports are used to guide learners through various stages of skill acquisition.

Scaffolding is appropriate when a teacher wants to provide students with some information or to complete parts of tasks for them so that they can concentrate on the part of the task they are attempting to master. Thus, if Kathy Stone were working with her third-grade children on organizing sentences in a paragraph to express ideas in a logical order, she might assist the students by initially giving them the sentences with word meanings and spellings so that these needs would not interfere with their primary task. As they became more competent in sequencing ideas, she might have students compose their own paragraphs while still assisting with word meanings and spellings. Eventually, students will assume responsibility for these functions. In short, the teacher creates a ZPD and provides the scaffolding for students to be successful (Moll, 2001).

Another application that reflects Vygotsky's ideas is *reciprocal teaching*. Reciprocal teaching involves an interactive dialogue between a teacher and small group of students. Initially, the teacher models activities, after which teacher and students take turns being the teacher. If students are learning to ask questions during reading comprehension, the instructional sequence might include the teacher modeling a question-asking strategy to check on his or her own level of understanding. From a Vygotskian perspective, reciprocal teaching comprises social interaction and scaffolding as students gradually develop skills.

An important application area is *peer collaboration*, which reflects the notion of collective activity (Bruner, 1984; Ratner et al., 2002). When peers work on tasks cooperatively, the shared social interactions can serve an instructional function. Research shows that cooperative groups are most effective when each student has assigned responsibilities and all must attain competence before any are allowed to progress (Slavin, 1995). Peer groups are commonly used for learning in fields such as mathematics, science, and language arts (Cobb, 1994; Cohen, 1994; DiPardo & Freedman, 1988; Geary, 1995; O'Donnell, 2006), which attests to the recognized impact of the social environment during learning.

Finally, an application relevant to Vygotsky's theory and to the topic of situated cognition (discussed in a prior section) is the notion of social guidance through *apprenticeships* (Radziszewska & Rogoff, 1991; Rogoff, 1990). In apprenticeships, novices work closely with experts in joint work-related activities. Apprenticeships fit well with the ZPD because they occur in cultural institutions (e.g., schools, agencies) and thus help transform learners' cognitive development. On the job, apprentices operate within a ZPD because they often work on tasks beyond their capabilities. By working with experts, novices develop a shared understanding of important processes and integrate this with their current understandings. Apprenticeships represent a type of dialectical constructivism that depends heavily on social interactions.

As noted above, a critical aspect of apprenticeships is that instruction is set within a particular cultural context. Childs and Greenfield (1981) described the teaching of weaving in the Zincantecan culture of Mexico. Young girls observed their mothers and other older women weave from the time they were born, so when instruction began, they already had been exposed to many models. In the early phases of instruction, the adult spent more than 90% of the time weaving with the child, but this dropped to 50% after weaving one garment. The adult then worked on the more difficult aspects of the task. The adult's participation dropped to less than 40% after completion of four garments. This instructional procedure exemplifies close social interaction and scaffolding operating within the ZPD.

Apprenticeships are used in many areas of education. Student teachers work with cooperating teachers in schools and, once on the job, often are paired with experienced teachers for mentoring. Counselor trainees serve internships under the direct guidance of a supervisor. On-the-job training programs use the apprentice model as students acquire skills while in the actual work setting and interacting with others. There is much emphasis on expanding youth apprenticeships, especially for non–college-bound adolescents (Bailey, 1993). Future research should evaluate factors that influence the success of apprenticeships as a means of fostering skill acquisition in students of various ages.

Critique

It is difficult to evaluate the contributions of Vygotsky's theory to the fields of human development and learning (Tudge & Scrimsher, 2003). His works were not circulated for many years, and translations have only recently become available. Even so, only a small number of sources exist (Vygotsky, 1978, 1987). Researchers and practitioners have tended to zero in on a single concept (the ZPD) without placing it in a larger theoretical context, which is centered around cultural influence.

Another issue is that when applications of Vygotsky's theory are discussed, they often are not part of the theory but rather seem to fit with it. When Wood et al. (1976) introduced the term *scaffolding*, for example, they presented it as a way for teachers to structure learning environments. Therefore, it has little relation to the dynamic ZPD that Vygotsky wrote about. Although *reciprocal teaching* also is not a Vygotskian concept, the term captures much better this sense of dynamic, multidirectional interaction.

Given these issues, there has been little debate on the adequacy of the theory. Debate that has ensued often has focused on "Piaget versus Vygotsky," contrasting their presumably discrepant positions on the course of human development (Duncan, 1995; although on many points they do not differ). While such debates may illuminate differences and provide testable research hypotheses, they are not helpful to educational practitioners seeking solid methods for improving children's learning.

Possibly the most significant implication of Vygotsky's theory for education is that the cultural–historical context is relevant to all forms of learning because learning does not occur in isolation. Student–teacher interactions are part of that context. Research has identified, for example, different interaction styles between Hawaiian, Anglo, and Navajo children (Tharp, 1989; Tharp & Gallimore, 1988). Whereas the Hawaiian culture encourages collaborative activity and more than one student talking at once, Navajo children are less acculturated to working in groups and more likely to wait to talk until the speaker is finished. Thus, the same instructional style would not be equally beneficial for all cultures. This point is especially noteworthy given that many schools are seeing a large influx of Asian and Hispanic American children.

Social Processes and Private Speech

A central premise of constructivism is that learning involves transforming and internalizing the social environment. Language plays a key role. This section discusses a central mechanism—private speech—that serves to perform these critical transforming and internalizing processes.

Private Speech

Private speech refers to the set of speech phenomena that has a self-regulatory function but is not socially communicative (Fuson, 1979). Various theories—including constructivism, cognitive–developmental, and social cognitive—establish a strong link between private speech and the development of self-regulation (Berk, 1986; Frauenglass & Diaz, 1985; Harris, 1982).

The historical impetus derives in part from work by Pavlov (1927). Recall from Chapter 2 that Pavlov distinguished the first (perceptual) from the second (linguistic) signal systems. Pavlov realized that animal conditioning results do not completely generalize to humans; human conditioning often occurs quickly with one or a few pairings of conditioned stimulus and unconditioned stimulus, in contrast to the multiple pairings required with animals. Pavlov believed that conditioning differences between humans and animals are largely due to the human capacity for language and thought. Stimuli may not produce conditioning automatically; people interpret stimuli in light of their prior experiences. Although Pavlov did not conduct research on the second signal system, subsequent investigations have validated his beliefs that human conditioning is complex and language plays a mediational role.

The Soviet psychologist Luria (1961) focused on the child's transition from the first to the second signal system. Luria postulated three stages in the development of verbal control of motor behavior. Initially, the speech of others is primarily responsible for directing the child's behavior (ages 1½ to 2½). During the second stage (ages 3 to 4), the child's overt verbalizations initiate motor behaviors but do not necessarily inhibit them. In the third stage, the child's private speech becomes capable of initiating, directing, and inhibiting motor behaviors (ages 4½ to 5½). Luria believed that this private, self-regulatory speech directs behavior through neurophysiological mechanisms.

The mediational and self-directing role of the second signal system is embodied in Vygotsky's theory. Vygotsky (1962) believed that private speech helps develop thought by organizing behavior. Children employ private speech to understand situations and to surmount difficulties. Private speech occurs in conjunction with children's interactions in the social environment. As children's language facility develops, words spoken by others acquire meaning independent of their phonological and syntactical qualities. Children internalize word meanings and use them to direct their behaviors.

Vygotsky hypothesized that private speech follows a curvilinear developmental pattern: Overt verbalization (thinking aloud) increases until ages 6 to 7, after which it declines and becomes primarily covert (internal) by ages 8 to 10. However, overt verbalization can occur at any age when people encounter problems or difficulties. Research shows that although the amount of private speech decreases from approximately ages 4 or 5 to 8, the proportion of private speech that is self-regulating increases with age (Fuson, 1979). In many research investigations, the actual amount of private speech is small, and many children do not verbalize at all. Thus, the developmental pattern of private speech seems more complex than originally hypothesized by Vygotsky.

Verbalization and Achievement

Verbalization of rules, procedures, and strategies can improve student learning. Although Meichenbaum's (1977, 1986) *self-instructional training* procedure is not rooted in constructivism, it recreates the overt-to-covert developmental progression of private speech. Types of statements modeled are *problem definition* ("What is it I have to do?"), *focusing of attention* ("I need to pay attention to what I'm doing"), *planning and response guidance* ("I need to work carefully"), *self-reinforcement* ("I'm doing fine"), *self-evaluation* ("Am I doing things in the right order?"), and *coping* ("I need to try again when I don't get it right"). Teachers can use self-instructional training to teach learners cognitive and motor skills, and it can create a positive task outlook and foster perseverance in the face of difficulties (Meichenbaum & Asarnow, 1979). The procedure need not be scripted; learners can construct their own verbalizations.

Verbalization seems most beneficial for students who often experience difficulties and perform in a deficient manner (Denney, 1975; Denney & Turner, 1979). Teachers have obtained benefits with children who do not spontaneously rehearse material to be learned, impulsive learners, students with learning disabilities and mental retardation, and learners who require remedial experiences (Schunk, 1986). Verbalization helps students with learning problems work at tasks systematically (Hallahan et al., 1983). It forces students to attend to tasks and to rehearse material, both of which enhance learning. Verbalization does not seem to facilitate learning when students can handle task demands adequately without verbalizing. Because verbalization constitutes an additional task, it might interfere with learning by distracting children from the task at hand.

Research has identified the conditions under which verbalization promotes performance. Denney (1975) modeled a performance strategy for 6-, 8-, and 10-year-old normal learners on a 20-question task. The 8- and 10-year-olds who verbalized the model's strategy as they performed the task scored no higher than children who did not verbalize. Verbalization interfered with the performance of 6-year-olds. Children verbalized specific statements (e.g., "Find the right picture in the fewest questions"); apparently, performing this additional task proved too distracting for the youngest children. Denney and Turner (1979) found that among normal learners ranging in age from 3 to 10 years, adding verbalization to a strategy modeling treatment resulted in no benefits on cognitive tasks compared with modeling alone. Participants constructed their own verbalizations, which might have been less distracting than Denney's (1975) specific statements. Coates and Hartup (1969) found that 7-year-olds who verbalized a model's actions during exposure did not subsequently produce them better than children who passively observed the behaviors. The children regulated their attention and cognitively processed the model's actions without verbalizing.

Berk (1986) studied first and third graders' spontaneous private speech. Task-relevant overt speech was negatively related, and faded verbalization (whispers, lip movements, and muttering) was positively related to mathematical performance. These results were obtained for first graders of high intelligence and third graders of average intelligence; among third graders of high intelligence, overt and faded speech showed no relationship to achievement. For the latter students, internalized self-guiding speech apparently is the most effective.

Keeney, Cannizzo, and Flavell (1967) pretested 6- and 7-year-olds on a serial recall task and identified those who failed to rehearse prior to recall. After these children learned how to rehearse, their recall matched that of spontaneous rehearsers. Meichenbaum and Asarnow (1979) identified kindergartners who did not spontaneously rehearse on a serial recall test. Some were trained to use a rehearsal strategy similar to that of Keeney et al. (1967), whereas others received self-instructional training. Both treatments facilitated recall relative to a control condition, but the self-instructional treatment was more effective. Taylor and his colleagues (Taylor, Josberger, & Whitely, 1973; Whitely & Taylor, 1973) found that educable mentally retarded children who were trained to generate elaborations between word associate pairs recalled more associates if they verbalized their elaborations than if they did not. In the Coates and Hartup (1969) study, 4-year-olds who verbalized a model's actions as they were being performed later reproduced them better than children who merely observed the model.

Schunk (1982b) instructed students who lacked division skills. Some students verbalized explicit statements (e.g., "check," "multiply," "copy"), others constructed their own verbalizations, a third group verbalized the statements and their own verbalizations, and students in a fourth condition did not verbalize. Self-constructed verbalizations—alone or combined with the statements—led to the highest division skill.

In summary, verbalization is more likely to promote student achievement if it is relevant to the task and does not interfere with performance. Higher proportions of task-relevant statements produce better learning (Schunk & Gunn, 1986). Private speech follows an overt-to-covert developmental cycle, and speech becomes internalized earlier in students with higher intelligence (Berk, 1986; Frauenglass & Diaz, 1985). Allowing students to construct their verbalizations—possibly in conjunction with verbalizing steps in a strategy—is more beneficial than limiting verbalizing to specific statements. To facilitate transfer and maintenance, overt verbalization should eventually be faded to whispering or lip movements and then to a covert level. Internalization is a key feature of self-regulation (Schunk, 1999; see section on self-regulation later in this chapter).

These benefits of verbalization do not mean that all students ought to verbalize while learning. That practice would result in a loud classroom and distract many students! Rather, verbalization could be incorporated into instruction for students having difficulties in learning. To avoid disrupting the work of other class members, a teacher or classroom aide could work with such students individually or in groups. Application 7.3 shows some ways to integrate verbalization into learning.

Socially Mediated Learning

Many forms of constructivism, and Vygotsky's theory in particular, stress the idea that learning is a socially mediated process. This focus is not unique to constructivism; many other learning theories emphasize social processes as having a significant impact on learning. Bandura's (1986, 1997) social cognitive theory, for example, highlights the reciprocal relations among learners and social environmental influences, and much research has shown that social modeling has a powerful influence on learning (Rosenthal & Zimmerman, 1978; Schunk, 1987). In Vygotsky's theory, however, social mediation of learning is the central construct (Karpov & Haywood, 1998; Moll, 2001; Tudge & Scrimsher, 2003). All learning is mediated by tools such as language, symbols, and signs. Children acquire these tools during their social interactions with others. They internalize these tools and then use them as mediators of more advanced learning (i.e., higher cognitive processes such as concept learning and problem solving).

APPLICATION 7.3

Self-Verbalization

A teacher might use self-verbalization (self-talk) in a special education resource room or at a work station separated from other students in a regular classroom to assist students having difficulty attending to material and mastering skills. When Mrs. Stone introduces long division to her third-grade students, she uses verbalization to help those children who cannot remember the steps to complete the procedure. She works individually with the students by verbalizing and applying the following steps:

- Will (number) go into (number)?
- Divide.
- Multiply: (number) 3 (number) 5 (number).
- Put down the answer.
- Subtract: (number) 2 (number) 5 (number).
- Bring down the next number.
- Repeat steps.

Use of self-talk helps students stay on task and builds their self-efficacy to work systematically through the long process. Once they begin to grasp the content, it is to their advantage to fade verbalizations to a covert (silent) level so they can work more rapidly.

Self-verbalization also can help students who are learning various sport skills and strategies. They might verbalize what is happening and what moves they should make. A tennis coach, for example, might encourage students to use self-talk during practice matches: "high ball—overhand return," "low ball—underhand return," "cross ball—backhand return."

Aerobic and dance instructors often use self-talk during practice. A ballet teacher might have young students repeat "paint a rainbow" for a flowing arm movement, and "walk on eggs" to get them to move lightly on their toes. Participants in aerobic exercise classes also might verbalize movements (e.g., "bend and stretch," "slide right and around") as they perform them.

The centrality of social mediation is apparent in self-regulation and constructivist learning environments (discussed later). For now, let us examine how social mediation influences concept acquisition. Young children acquire concepts spontaneously by observing their worlds and formulating hypotheses. For example, they hear the noise that cars make and the noise that trucks make, and they may believe that bigger objects make more noise. They have difficulty accommodating discrepant observations (e.g., a motorcycle is smaller than a car or truck but may make more noise that either).

In the context of social interactions, children are taught concepts by others (e.g., teachers, parents, older siblings). This is often a direct process, such as when teachers teach children the difference between squares, rectangles, triangles, and circles. As cognitive psychologists might say, such concepts are internalized as declarative knowledge. Thus, children use the tools of language and symbols to internalize these concepts.

It is, of course, possible to learn concepts on one's own without social interactions with others. But even such independent learning is, in a constructivist sense, socially mediated, because it involves the tools (language, signs, and symbols) that have been acquired through previous social interactions. Further, a certain amount of labeling is needed. Children may learn a concept but not have a name for it ("What do you call a thing that looks like____?"). Such labeling involves language and will likely be supplied by another person.

Tools are useful not only for learning but also for teaching. Children teach one another things they have learned. Vygotsky (1962, 1978) believed that by being used for social purposes, tools exerted powerful influences on others.

These points have interesting implications for instruction. For example, two different instructional approaches, guided discovery and expository teaching, are employed in school, but typically for the lower-level, more basic-type of knowledge that serves as the foundation for higher mental processes. Once children have acquired basic concepts, they can engage in independent learning to "discover" more-advanced principles. This does not have to involve children working alone; rather, they can work collaboratively. But it does suggest that students must be well prepared with the basic tools, and this teaching can be quite direct. There is no need for students to "discover" the obvious, or what they can be easily taught. Constructed discoveries are thus the result of basic learning, not their cause (Karpov & Haywood, 1998).

The implication is that teachers must prepare students to engage in discovery by teaching them the tools to do so and then provide opportunities for it. Some classroom applications of socially mediated learning are discussed in Application 7.4.

APPLICATION 7.4

Socially Mediated Learning

Socially mediated learning is appropriate for students of all ages. Gina Brown knows that success in teaching depends in part on understanding the culture of the communities served by the school. She obtains consent from the schools where her students are placed and from the appropriate parents and she assigns each of her students to be a "buddy" of a school child. As part of their placements, her students spend extra time with their assigned buddies—for example, working one-to-one, eating lunch with them, riding home on the school bus with them, and visiting them in their homes. She pairs her students and the members of each dyad meet regularly to discuss the culture of their assigned buddies. Thus, they might discuss what their buddies like about school, what their parents or guardians do, and characteristics of the neighborhoods where their buddies live. She meets regularly with each dyad to discuss the implications of the cultural variables for school learning. Through social interactions with buddies, her, and other class members, Gina's students develop better understanding of the role of culture in schooling.

Historical events typically are open to multiple interpretations, and Jim Marshall uses social mediation to develop his students' thinking about events. As part of a unit on post-World War II changes in American life, he organizes students into five teams. Each team is assigned a topic: medicine, transportation, education, technology, suburbs. Teams prepare

a presentation on why their topic represents a significant advance in American life. Students on each team work together to prepare the presentation, and each member presents part of it. After the presentations are finished, Jim leads a discussion with the class. He tries to get them to see how advances are interrelated; for example, technology influences medicine, transportation, and education; more automobiles and roads lead to growth in suburbs; better education results in preventative medicine. Social mediation through discussions and presentations helps students gain deeper understanding of changes in American life.

Motivation

Constructivism is primarily a theory of human development that in recent years has been applied to learning. One who reads the constructivist literature will find little mention of motivation. Nonetheless, constructivist theory seems applicable to motivation, and some motivational principles explored by researchers in other theoretical traditions fit well (Sivan, 1986). Aspects of motivation especially relevant to constructivism include contextual factors, implicit theories, and teachers' expectations.

Contextual Factors

ORGANIZATION AND STRUCTURE

Constructivism stresses contextual specificity and notes the importance of taking the context of learning environments into account in attempting to explain behavior. A topic highly relevant to constructivism is *organization and structure of learning environments*— that is, how students are grouped for instruction, how work is evaluated and rewarded, how authority is established, and how time is scheduled. Many researchers and practitioners believe that learning environments are complex and that, to understand learning, we must take into account many factors and how they interact with one another (i.e., one factor might supplement or detract from the influence of another factor) (Marshall & Weinstein, 1984).

An important aspect of organization is *dimensionality* (Rosenholtz & Simpson, 1984). *Unidimensional* classrooms include a small number of activities that address a limited range of student abilities. *Multidimensional* classrooms have more activities and allow for greater diversity in student abilities and performances. Multidimensional classes are more compatible with constructivist tenets about learning.

Classroom characteristics that indicate dimensionality include differentiation of task structure, student autonomy, grouping patterns, and salience of formal performance evaluations (Table 7.6). Unidimensional classrooms have *undifferentiated task structures*. All students work on the same or similar tasks, and instruction employs a small number of materials and methods (Rosenholtz & Simpson, 1984). The more undifferentiated the structure, the more likely the daily activities will produce consistent performances from each student and the greater the probability that students will socially compare their

TABLE 7.6 *Characteristics of Dimensionality*

Characteristic	Unidimensional	Multidimensional
Differentiation of task structure	Undifferentiated; students work on same tasks	Differentiated; students work on different tasks
Student autonomy	Low; students have few choices	High; students have choices
Grouping patterns	Whole class; students grouped by ability	Individual work; students not grouped by ability
Performance evaluations	Students graded on same assignments; grades are public;much social comparison	Students graded on different assignments; less public grading and social comparison

work with that of others to determine relative standing. Structures become *differentiated* (and classrooms become multidimensional) when students work on different tasks at the same time.

Autonomy refers to the extent to which students have choices about what to do and when and how to do it. Classrooms are unidimensional when autonomy is low, which can hinder self-regulation and stifle motivation. Multidimensional classrooms offer students more choices, which can enhance intrinsic motivation.

With respect to *grouping patterns*, social comparisons become more prominent when students work on whole-class activities or when students are grouped by ability. Comparisons are not as prevalent when students work individually or in mixed-ability groups. Grouping contributes to classroom multidimensionality and affects motivation and learning. Grouping has added influence over the long term if groups remain intact and students understand they are bound to the groups regardless of how well they perform.

Salience of formal *performance evaluations* refers to the public nature of grading. Unidimensional classrooms grade students on the same assignments, and grades are public; hence everyone knows the grade distribution. Those receiving low grades may not be motivated to improve. As grading becomes less public or as grades are assigned for different projects (as in multidimensional classes), grading can motivate a higher proportion of students, especially those who believe they are progressing and capable of further learning (Pintrich & Schunk, 2002).

Unidimensional classrooms have high visibility of performance (Rosenholtz & Rosenholtz, 1981), which can motivate high achievers to learn, but often have a negative effect on everyone else. Multidimensional classrooms are more likely to motivate all students because they feature more differentiation, greater autonomy, less ability grouping, and more flexibility in grading with less public evaluation.

TARGET

Classrooms include other factors that can affect learners' perceptions, motivation, and learning. Some of these, as shown in Table 7.7, can be summarized by the acronym *TARGET*: task design, distribution of authority, recognition of students, grouping arrangements, evaluation practices, and time allocation (Epstein, 1989).

The *task* dimension involves the design of learning activities and assignments. There are many ways to structure tasks to promote a mastery (learning) goal orienta-

---

TABLE 7.7   *TARGET Factors Affecting Motivation and Learning*

Factor	Characteristics
Task	Design of learning activities and assignments
Authority	Extent that students can assume leadership and develop independence and control over learning activities
Recognition	Formal and informal use of rewards, incentives, praise
Grouping	Individual, small group, large group
Evaluation	Methods for monitoring and assessing learning
Time	Appropriateness of workload, pace of instruction, time allotted for completing work

---

tion in students—for example, by making learning interesting, using variety and challenge, assisting students to set realistic goals, and helping students develop organizational, management, and other strategic skills (Ames, 1992a, 1992b). Task structure is a distinguishing feature of dimensionality. In unidimensional classes, students use the same materials and have the same assignments, so variations in ability can translate into motivational differences. In multidimensional classes, students may not all work on the same task and thereby have fewer opportunities for social comparisons.

Authority refers to whether students can assume leadership and develop independence and control over learning activities. Teachers foster authority by allowing students to participate in decisions, giving them choices and leadership roles, and teaching them skills that allow them to take responsibility for learning. Self-efficacy tends to be higher in classes that allow students some measure of authority (Ames, 1992a, 1992b).

Recognition, which involves the formal and informal use of rewards, incentives, and praise, has important consequences for motivated learning (Schunk, 1989). Ames (1992a, 1992b) recommends that teachers help students develop mastery goal orientations by recognizing progress, accomplishments, effort, and self-directed strategy use; by providing opportunities for all learners to earn rewards; and by using private forms of recognition that avoid comparing students or emphasizing the difficulties of others.

The *grouping* dimension focuses on students' ability to work with others. Teachers should use heterogeneous cooperative groups and peer interaction where possible to ensure that differences in ability do not translate into differences in motivation and learning. Low achievers especially benefit from small-group work because contributing to the group's success engenders feelings of self-efficacy. Group work also allows more students to share in the responsibility for learning, so that only a few students do not do all of the work. At the same time, individual work is important because it provides for clear indicators of learning progress.

Evaluation involves methods for monitoring and assessing student learning; for example, evaluating students for individual progress and mastery, giving students opportunities to improve their work (e.g., revise work for a better grade), using different forms of evaluation, and conducting evaluations privately. Although normative grading systems are common in schools (i.e., students compared to one another), such normative comparisons can lower self-efficacy among students who do not perform as well as their peers.

Time involves the appropriateness of workload, pace of instruction, and time allotted for completing work (Epstein, 1989). Effective strategies for enhancing motivation

APPLICATION 7.5

Applying TARGET in the Classroom

Incorporating TARGET components into a unit can positively affect motivation and learning. As Kathy Stone develops a unit on deserts, she plans part of the unit but also involves her students in planning activities. Mrs. Stone sets up learning centers, plans reading and research assignments, organizes large- and small-group discussions, and designs unit pre- and posttests as well as tasks for checking mastery throughout the unit. The class helps Mrs. Stone plan a field trip to a nearby desert, develop small-group project topics, and decide how to create a desert in the classroom. Mrs. Stone and the students then develop a calendar and timeline for working on and completing the unit. Notice in this example how Mrs. Stone incorporates motivational components into the TARGET classroom features: task, authority, recognition, grouping, evaluation, and time.

and learning are to adjust time or task requirements for those having difficulty and allowing students to plan their schedules and timelines for making progress. Giving students greater control over their time helps allay anxiety about completing work and can promote use of self-regulatory strategies and self-efficacy for learning (Schunk & Zimmerman, 1994; Zimmerman et al., 1994). Application 7.5 gives some classroom applications of TARGET.

Implicit Theories

Constructivist theories call attention to many facets of motivation, including the cognitive and the affective. A central premise of many contemporary theories of learning and motivation, and one that fits nicely with constructivist assumptions, is that people hold *implicit theories* about issues such as how they learn, what contributes to school achievement, and how motivation affects performance. Learning and thinking occur in the context of learners' beliefs about cognition, which differ as a function of personal, social, and cultural factors (Greeno, 1989; Moll, 2001).

Research shows that implicit theories about such processes as learning, thinking, and ability influence how students engage in learning and their views about what leads to success in and outside of the classroom (Duda & Nicholls, 1992; Dweck, 1991, 1999; Dweck & Leggett, 1988; Dweck & Molden, 2005; Nicholls, Cobb, Wood, Yackel, & Patashnick, 1990; Nicholls, Patashnick, & Nolen, 1985; Nicholls & Thorkildsen, 1989). Motivation researchers have identified two distinct implicit theories about the role of ability in achievement: entity theory and incremental theory. Students may view their abilities as representing fixed traits over which they have little control (*entity theory*) or as a set of skills that they can improve through learning (*incremental theory*) (Dweck, 1999; Dweck & Leggett, 1988; Dweck & Molden, 2005). These perspectives influence motivational patterns and, ultimately, learning and achievement. Wood and Bandura (1989) found that adults who view managerial skills as capable of being developed use better strategies, hold higher self-efficacy for success, and set more challenging goals than those who believe such skills are relatively fixed and not capable of being altered.

Students who believe that abilities are relatively fixed are apt to be discouraged if they encounter difficulty in school because they think they can do little to alter their status. Such discouragement results in low self-efficacy, which can affect school learning adversely (Schunk, 1995; Schunk & Zimmerman, 2006). Conversely, students who believe they have control over their learning capabilities are less apt to give up when they encounter difficulty and instead alter their strategy, seek assistance, consult additional sources of information, or engage in other self-regulatory strategies (Zimmerman, 1994, 1998; Zimmerman & Martinez-Pons, 1992).

Evidence also shows that implicit theories can affect the way that learners process information (Graham & Golan, 1991). Students who believe that learning outcomes are under their control may expend greater mental effort, rehearse more, use organizational strategies, and employ other tactics to improve learning. In contrast, students who hold a fixed view may not expend the same type of effort.

Students differ in how they view kinds of classroom learning. Nicholls and Thorkildsen (1989) found that elementary school students perceived learning substantive matters (e.g., mathematical logic, facts about nature) as more important than learning intellectual conventions (e.g., spelling, methods of representing addition). Students also saw didactic teaching as more appropriate for teaching of conventions than for matters of logic and fact. Nicholls et al. (1985) found that high-school students held definite beliefs about what types of activities should lead to success. *Task orientation*, or a focus during learning on mastery of the task, was positively associated with student perceptions that success in school depends on being interested in learning, working hard, trying to understand (as opposed to memorizing), and working collaboratively.

Implicit theories undoubtedly are formed as children encounter a variety of socialization influences. Dweck and her colleagues have found evidence for implicit theories in children as young as $3\frac{1}{2}$ years (Dweck, 1999). Early on, children are socialized by significant others about right and wrong, good and bad. Through what they are told and what they observe, they form early implicit theories about rightness, badness, and the like. At achievement tasks, praise and criticism from others serve as strong influences about what produced good and poor outcomes (e.g., "You worked hard and got it right," "You don't have what it takes to do this right"). As with other beliefs, these may be situated within contexts; teachers and parents may stress different causes of achievement (effort and ability). By the time children enter school, they hold a wide range of implicit theories that they have constructed and that cover most situations.

Research findings such as those summarized in this section have profound implications for teaching and learning because they show that asking whether one understands a fact or principle is insufficient (Greeno, 1989). The premise that learning requires providing students with information to build propositional networks is incomplete. Of greater importance may be how children refine, modify, combine, and elaborate their conceptual understandings as a function of experience. Those understandings will be situated in the context of a personal belief system and will include beliefs about the usefulness and importance of knowledge, how it relates to what else one knows, and in what situations it may be appropriate. Research continues into how students form implicit theories, how these theories change as a consequence of cognitive development, and how learners resolve inconsistencies (e.g., students who believe ability is fixed but whose teachers provide feedback linking higher achievement with greater effort).

Teachers' Expectations

A motivational topic that has attracted much research and applied attention and that integrates nicely with constructivism is *teachers' expectations*. Theory and research suggest that teachers' expectations for students relate to teacher actions and student achievement outcomes (Braun, 1976; Cooper & Good, 1983; Cooper & Tom, 1984; Dusek, 1985; Rosenthal, 2002).

The impetus for exploring expectations came from a study by Rosenthal and Jacobson (1968), who gave elementary school students a test of nonverbal intelligence at the start of the academic year. Teachers were told that this test predicted which students would bloom intellectually during the year. The researchers actually randomly identified 20% of the school population as bloomers and gave these names to the teachers. Teachers were not aware of the deception: The test did not predict intellectual blooming and names bore no relation to test scores. Teachers taught in their usual fashion and students were retested one semester, 1 year, and 2 years later. For the first two tests, students were in the classes of teachers given bloomers' names; for the last test, students were in new classes with teachers who did not have these names.

After the first year, significant differences in intelligence were seen between bloomers and control students (those not identified as bloomers); differences were greater among children in the first and second grades. During the subsequent year, these younger children lost their advantage, but bloomers in upper grades showed an increasing advantage over control students. Differences were greater among average achievers than among high or low achievers. Similar findings were obtained for grades in reading. Overall, the differences between bloomers and control students were small, both in reading and on the intelligence test.

Rosenthal and Jacobson (1968) concluded that teacher expectations can act as *self-fulfilling prophecies* because student achievement comes to reflect the expectations. They suggested that results are stronger with young children because they have close contact with teachers. Older students may function better after they move to a new teacher.

This study is controversial: It has been criticized on conceptual and methodological grounds, and many attempts at replication have not been successful (Cooper & Good, 1983; Elashoff & Snow, 1971; Jensen, 1969). Brophy and Good (1974) contended that early in the school year, teachers form expectations based on initial interactions with students and information in records. Teachers then may begin to treat students differently, consistent with these expectations. Teacher behaviors are reciprocated; for example, teachers who treat students warmly are apt to receive warmth in return. Student behaviors begin to complement and reinforce teacher behaviors and expectations. Effects will be most pronounced for rigid and inappropriate expectations. When they are appropriate or inappropriate but flexible, student behavior may substantiate or redefine expectations. When expectations are inappropriate or not easily changed, student performance might decline and become consistent with expectations.

Once teachers form expectations, they may convey them to students through socioemotional climate, verbal input, verbal output, and feedback (Rosenthal, 1974). *Socioemotional climate* includes smiles, head nods, eye contact, and supportive and friendly actions. Teachers create a warmer climate for students for whom they hold high expectations than for those for whom expectations are lower (Cooper & Tom, 1984). *Verbal input*, or opportunities to learn new material and difficulty of material, varies when high-expectation students have more opportunities to interact with and learn new material and are exposed to more difficult material. *Verbal output* refers to number and length of academic interactions. Teachers engage in more academic interchanges with high- than with low-expectation students (Brophy & Good, 1974). They also are more persistent with highs and get them to give answers by prompting or rephrasing questions. *Feedback* refers to the use of praise and criticism. Teachers praise high-expectation students and criticize low-expectation students more (Cooper & Tom, 1984).

Although these factors are genuine, wide differences exist between teachers (Pintrich & Schunk, 2002). Some teachers consistently encourage lower achievers and treat them much like the patterns described above for high achievers (e.g., give more praise, get them to answer more questions). Teachers have expectations for students; the real issue is whether these expectations become negatively self-fulfilling for some and how they do so. Appropriate expectations can improve learning. Tailoring difficulty of material and level of questioning to students based on their prior performances (which are correlated with teacher expectations) seems instructionally appropriate. Expecting all students to learn with requisite effort also seems reasonable. Greatly distorted expectations are not credible and typically have little effect on learning. Most teachers at the elementary level (when expectation effects may be strongest) hold positive expectations for students, provide for a lot of successes, and use praise often (Brophy & Good, 1974).

The topic of teacher expectations fits with constructivist theory because it seems likely that students construct theories about what their teachers think and expect of them. Whether or how these theories influence their achievement actions is less predictable. Our beliefs about what others expect of us may motivate ("She thinks I can do it, so I'll try"), demotivate ("She thinks I can't do it, so I won't try"), or lead us to act contrary to our theories ("She thinks I can't do it, so I'll show her I can"). The best advice is to expect that all students can succeed and to provide support for them to do so, which should help them construct appropriate expectations for themselves. Application 7.6 gives some suggestions for conveying positive expectations to students.

APPLICATION 7.6

Teacher Expectations

Expectations that teachers hold for students can positively and negatively affect their interactions with students. Teachers might incorporate some of the following actions into classroom practices:

- Enforce rules fairly and consistently.
- Assume that all students can learn and convey that expectation to them.
- Do not form differential student expectations based on qualities unrelated to performance (e.g., gender, ethnicity, parents' background).
- Do not accept excuses for poor performance.
- Realize that upper limits of student ability are unknown and not relevant to school learning.

A college English professor told her class that they would be expected to do a lot of writing throughout the semester. Some of the students looked apprehensive and the professor tried to assure them that it was a task they could do. "We can all work together to improve our writing. I know some of you have had different experiences in high school with writing, but I will work with each of you and I know by the end of the semester you will be writing well."

One student waited after class and told the professor that he had been in a special education class in school and said, "I can hardly write a good sentence; I don't think you can make a writer out of me." To which the professor replied, "Well, sentences are a good place to begin. I'll see you Wednesday morning in class."

Self-Regulation

Constructivist researchers have written about self-regulation, which seems natural given that a central assumption is that learners construct not only knowledge but also ways for acquiring and applying it. There are various sources for constructivist accounts of self-regulation, including cognitive–developmental theory, precursors of contemporary cognitive theories (e.g., Gestalt psychology, memory), and Vygotsky's theory (Paris & Byrnes, 1989). Regardless of the source, constructivist views of self-regulation rest on certain assumptions, as shown in Table 7.8 (Paris & Byrnes, 1989).

Two key points underlying these assumptions are that sociocultural influences are critical and that people form implicit theories about themselves, others, and how to best manage demands. These are discussed in turn.

Sociocultural Influences

Vygotsky's constructivist theory of human development lends itself well to self-regulation. Recall from our earlier discussion that Vygotsky believed that people and their cultural environments constituted an interacting social system. Through their communications and actions, people in children's environments taught children the tools (e.g., language, symbols, signs) they needed to acquire competence. Using these tools within the system, learners develop higher-level cognitive functions such as concept acquisition and problem solving. When Vygotsky used the term *higher mental function*, he meant a consciously directed thought process. In this sense, self-regulation may be thought of as a higher mental function (Henderson & Cunningham, 1994).

In the Vygotskian view, self-regulation includes the coordination of such mental processes as memory, planning, synthesis, and evaluation (Henderson & Cunningham, 1994). These coordinated processes do not operate independently of the context in which they are formed. Indeed, the self-regulatory processes of an individual reflect those that are valued and taught within the person's culture.

Vygotsky believed that people came to control their own deliberate actions (i.e., learned to self-regulate). The primary mechanisms affecting self-regulation are language and the ZPD.

Kopp (1982) provided a useful framework for understanding the development of the self-regulatory function of speech. In her view, self-regulation involves a transition from responding to the commands of others to the use of speech and other cognitive tools to plan, monitor, and direct one's activities.

Self-regulation also depends on learners being aware of socially approved behaviors (Henderson & Cunningham, 1994). The meaning of actions depends on both the context and the tools (language, signs, and symbols) used to describe the actions. Through inter-

---

TABLE 7.8   *Constructivist Assumptions of Self-regulation*

- There is an intrinsic motivation to seek information.
- Understanding goes beyond the information given.
- Mental representations change with development.
- There are progressive refinements in levels of understanding.
- There are developmental constraints on learning.
- Reflection and reconstruction stimulate learning.

actions with adults in the ZPD, children make the transition from behaviors regulated by others to behaviors regulated by themselves (self-regulation).

Wertsch (1979) described four stages of intersubjectivity that correspond to the degrees of responsibility held by parties in a social context. Initially, the child does not understand the adult's words or gestures, so there is no intersubjectivity. With maturation of the child and greater sensitivity of the adult to the child's situation, a shared understanding of the situation develops, although responsibility for regulating behavior still lies with the adult. In the third phase, the child learns the relation between speech and activity and takes responsibility for the task. During the third phase, private speech is commonly used to self-regulate behavior. As this speech is internalized to self-directed thought, intersubjectivity becomes complete and self-regulation occurs independently. Internalization becomes the key to use of self-regulatory processes (Schunk, 1999).

It is noteworthy that even after the teacher is no longer present, the child's self-regulatory activity may heavily reflect the teacher's influence. Although the action is self-directed, it is the internalized regulation of the other's influence. Often the child may repeat the same words used by the adult. In time, the child will construct his or her self-regulatory activity and it will become idiosyncratic.

Implicit Theories of Self-Regulation

As was discussed in the preceding section on motivation, implicit theories are an inherent feature of constructivist accounts of learning, cognition, and motivation. Students also construct theories about self-regulated learning. These theories exist along with theories about others and their worlds; hence, self-regulated learning theories are highly contextualized (Paris, Byrnes, & Paris, 2001).

A major type of implicit theory involves children's beliefs about their academic abilities. Children who experience learning problems and who believe that these problems reflect poor ability are apt to demonstrate low motivation to succeed. The beliefs that effort leads to success and that learning produces higher ability are positively related to effective self-regulation.

Children also develop theories about their competence relative to their peers. Through social comparisons with similar others, they formulate perceptions of ability and their relative standing within their class. They also begin to differentiate their perceptions by subject area and to ascertain how smart they are in subjects such as reading and mathematics.

In line with these beliefs, children formulate theories about what contributes to success in different domains. Self-regulatory strategies may be general in nature, such as taking notes and rehearsing information to be learned, or they may be idiosyncratic to a particular area. Whether these strategies truly are useful is not the point. Because they are constructed, they may be misleading.

Learners also develop theories about agency and control that they have in academic situations. For example, they may feel self-efficacious and believe that they are capable of learning what is being taught in school. Conversely, they may entertain serious doubts about their learning capabilities. Again, these beliefs may not accurately capture reality. Research has shown, for example, that children often feel highly self-efficacious about successfully solving mathematical problems even after being given feedback showing that they had failed most or all of the problems they attempted to solve (Bandura & Schunk, 1981). The correspondence between self-efficacy judgments and actual performance can be affected by many factors (Bandura, 1997).

Another class of theories involves schooling and academic tasks (Paris et al., 2001). These theories contain information about the content and skills taught in school and what is required to learn the content and skills. The goals that students formulate for schooling may not be consistent with those of teachers and parents. For example, teachers and parents may want students to perform well, but students' goals might be to make friends and stay out of trouble. For a subject area (e.g., reading), students may have a goal of understanding the text or simply verbalizing the words on a page. A goal of writing may be to fill the lines on a page or create a short story.

Self-regulation, therefore, involves individuals constructing theories about themselves (e.g., abilities, capabilities, typical effort), others, and their environments. These theories are constructed partly through direct instruction from others (e.g., teachers, peers, and parents) but also largely through their personal reflections on their performances, environmental effects, and responses from others. Theories are constructed using the tools (language, signs, and symbols) and, in social contexts, often through instruction in the ZPD.

The goal is for students to construct a self-identity as students. Their beliefs are influenced by parents, teachers, and peers and may include stereotypes associated with gender, culture, and ethnic background. Paris et al. (2001) contended that the separation of identity development and self-regulated learning is impossible because achievement behaviors are indicators of who students believe they are or who they want to become. Strategies cannot be taught independently of goals, roles, and identities of students. In other words, self-regulation is intimately linked with personal development.

Children are intrinsically motivated to construct explanatory frameworks and understand their educational experiences (Paris et al., 2001). When they are successful, they construct theories of competence, tasks, and themselves that aid learning and usage of adaptive learning strategies. But when they are not successful, they may construct inappropriate goals and strategies. To use terminology from cognitive psychology, implicit theories include declarative and conditional knowledge that underlie procedural knowledge. In short, self-regulation is heavily dependent on how children perceive themselves and achievement tasks.

Constructivist Learning Environments

Learning environments created to reflect constructivist principles look quite different from traditional classrooms (Brooks & Brooks, 1999). This section discusses some critical features of constructivist learning environments pertaining to learning and teaching.

Key Features

Learning in a constructivist setting does not allow students to do whatever they want. Rather, constructivist environments should create rich experiences that encourage students to learn.

Some of the ways that constructivist classrooms differ from traditional classrooms are as follows (Brooks & Brooks, 1999). In traditional classes, basic skills are emphasized. Curriculum, which is presented in small parts, uses textbooks and workbooks. Teachers generally disseminate information to students didactically and seek correct answers to questions. Assessment of student learning is distinct from teaching and is usually done through testing. Students often work alone.

In constructivist classrooms, the curriculum focuses on big concepts. Activities typically involve primary sources of data and manipulative materials. Teachers generally interact with students by seeking their questions and points of view. Assessment is authentic; it is interwoven with teaching and includes teacher observations and student portfolios.

Students often work in groups. The key is to structure the learning environment such that students can effectively construct new knowledge and skills (Schuh, 2003).

Some guiding principles of constructivist learning environments are shown in Table 7.9 (Brooks & Brooks, 1999). One principle is that teachers should *pose problems of emerging relevance* to students, where relevance is preexisting or emerges through teacher mediation. Thus, a teacher might structure a lesson around questions that challenge students' preconceptions. This takes time, which means that other critical content may not be covered. Relevance is not established by threatening to test students but, rather, by stimulating their interest and helping them discover how the problem affects their lives.

A second principle is that *learning should be structured around primary concepts*. This means that teachers design activities around conceptual clusters of questions and problems so that ideas are presented holistically rather than in isolated fashion (Brooks & Brooks, 1999). Being able to see the whole helps understand the parts.

Holistic teaching does not necessarily require sacrificing content, but it does involve structuring content differently. A piecemeal approach to teaching history is to present information chronologically as a series of events. In contrast, a holistic method involves presenting themes that recur in history (e.g., economic hardship, disputes over territory) and then structuring content so that students can discover these themes in different eras. Students then can see that although environmental features change over time (e.g., armies—air forces; farming—technology), the themes remain the same.

Holistic teaching also can be done across subjects. In the middle-school curriculum, for example, the theme of "courage" can be explored in social studies (e.g., courage of people to stand up and act based on their beliefs when these conflicted with governments), language arts (e.g., characters in literature who displayed courage), and science (e.g., courage of scientists who disputed prevailing theories). An integrated curriculum in which teachers plan units together reflects this holism.

Third, it is important to *seek and value students' points of view*. Understanding students' perspectives is essential for planning activities that are challenging and interesting. This requires that teachers ask questions, stimulate discussions, and listen to what students say. Teachers who make little effort to understand what students think fail to capitalize on the role of their experiences in learning. This is not to suggest that teachers should analyze every student utterance; that is not necessary, nor is there time to do it. Rather, teachers should try to learn students' conceptions of a topic.

With the current emphasis on achievement test scores, it is easy to focus only on students' correct answers. Constructivist education, however, requires that—where feasible—we go beyond the answer and learn how the students arrived at that answer. Teachers do this by asking students to elaborate on their answers. Thus, they might ask a student, "How did you arrive at that answer?" or "Why do you think that?" It is possible

---

TABLE 7.9 *Guiding Principles of Constructivist Learning Environments*

- Pose problems of emerging relevance to students.
- Structure learning around primary concepts.
- Seek and value students' points of view.
- Adapt curriculum to address students' suppositions.
- Assess student learning in the context of teaching.

(Brooks & Brooks, 1999)

for a student to arrive at a correct answer through faulty reasoning and, conversely, to answer incorrectly but engage in sound thinking. Students' perspectives on a situation or theories about a phenomenon help teachers in curriculum planning.

Fourth, we should *adapt curriculum to address students' suppositions*. This means that curricular demands on students should align with the beliefs they bring to the classroom. When there is a gross mismatch, lessons will lack meaning for students. This does not mean that alignment must be perfect. In fact, demands that are slightly above students' present capabilities (i.e., within the ZPD) produce challenge and learning.

When students' suppositions are incorrect, the typical response is to inform them of such. Instead, constructivist teaching challenges students to discover the information. Recall the opening scenario describing a first-grade lesson on measurement and equivalence. Children were using a balance to determine how many plastic links equaled one metal washer in weight (Brooks & Brooks, 1999). This example shows how the teacher modified the lesson based on Anna's suppositions and how she challenged Anna to discover the correct principle. Even after Anna answered "four" correctly, the teacher did not respond by saying "correct" but rather continued to question her.

Finally, constructivist education requires that we *assess student learning in the context of teaching*. This point runs counter to the typical situation in classrooms where most assessments of student learning occur disconnected from teaching—for example, end-of-grade tests, end-of-unit exams, pop quizzes. Although the content of these assessments may align well with learning objectives addressed during instruction, the assessment occasions are separate from teaching.

In a constructivist environment, assessment occurs continuously during teaching and is an assessment of both students and teacher. In the preceding example, Anna's learning was being assessed throughout the sequence, as was the success of the teacher in designing an activity and guiding Anna to understand the concept.

Of course, assessment methods must reflect the type of learning. Constructivist environments are best designed for meaningful, deep-structure learning, not for superficial understanding. True–false and multiple-choice tests may be inappropriate to assess learning outcomes. Authentic forms of assessment may require students to write reflective pieces, discussing what they learned and why this knowledge is useful in the world or to demonstrate and apply skills they have acquired.

Constructivist assessment is less concerned about right and wrong answers than about next steps after students answer. This type of authentic assessment, which occurs during teaching and learning, guides instructional decisions. Authentic assessment is difficult, because it forces teachers to design activities to get student feedback and alter instruction as needed. It is much easier to design and score a multiple-choice test, but encouraging teachers to teach constructively and then assess separately in a traditional manner sends a mixed message. Given the present emphasis on accountability, we may never move completely to authentic assessment, but encouraging authentic assessment facilitates curricular planning and provides for more-interesting lessons than drilling students to pass tests.

APA Learner-Centered Principles

The APA developed a set of learner-centered psychological principles (American Psychological Association Work Group of the Board of Educational Affairs, 1997). These principles (Table 7.10), which reflect a constructivist learning approach, were developed as guidelines for school design and reform.

TABLE 7.10 *APA Learner-centered Principles*

Cognitive and Metacognitive Factors

1. *Nature of the learning process.* The learning of complex subject matter is most effective when it is an intentional process of constructing meaning from information and experience.
2. *Goals of the learning process.* The successful learner, over time and with support and instructional guidance, can create meaningful, coherent representations of knowledge.
3. *Construction of knowledge.* The successful learner can link new information with existing knowledge in meaningful ways.
4. *Strategic thinking.* The successful learner can create and use a repertoire of thinking and reasoning strategies to achieve complex learning goals.
5. *Thinking about thinking.* Higher-order strategies for selecting and monitoring mental operations facilitate creative and critical thinking.
6. *Context of learning.* Learning is influenced by environmental factors, including culture, technology, and instructional practices.

Motivational and Affective Factors

7. *Motivational and emotional influences on learning.* What and how much is learned is influenced by the learner's motivation. Motivation to learn, in turn, is influenced by the individual's emotional states, beliefs, interests and goals, and habits of thinking.
8. *Intrinsic motivation to learn.* The learner's creativity, higher-order thinking, and natural curiosity all contribute to motivation to learn. Intrinsic motivation is stimulated by tasks of optimal novelty and difficulty, tasks that are relevant to personal interests, and tasks that provide for personal choice and control.
9. *Effects of motivation on effort.* Acquisition of complex knowledge and skills requires extended learner effort and guided practice. Without learners' motivation to learn, the willingness to exert this effort is unlikely without coercion.

Development and Social Factors

10. *Developmental influences on learning.* As individuals develop, there are different opportunities and constraints for learning. Learning is most effective when differential development within and across physical, intellectual, emotional, and social domains is taken into account.
11. *Social influences on learning.* Learning is influenced by social interactions, interpersonal relations, and communication with others.

Individual Differences Factors

12. *Individual differences in learning.* Learners have different strategies, approaches, and capabilities for learning that are a function of prior experience and heredity.
13. *Learning and diversity.* Learning is most effective when differences in learners' linguistic, cultural, and social backgrounds are taken into account.
14. *Standards and assessment.* Setting appropriately high and challenging standards and assessing the learner as well as learning progress—including diagnostic, process, and outcome assessment—are integral parts of the learning process.

Source: APA Work Group of the Board of Educational Affairs, 1997. American Psychological Association, Washington, DC. Copyright © 1997 by the American Psychological Association. Reprinted with permission.

The principles are grouped into four major categories: cognitive and metacognitive factors, motivational and affective factors, developmental and social factors, and individual differences. Cognitive and metacognitive factors involve the nature of the learning process, learning goals, construction of knowledge, strategic thinking, thinking about thinking, and the content of learning. Motivational and affective factors reflect motivational and emotional influences on learning, the intrinsic motivation to learn, and the effects of motivation on effort. Developmental and social factors include developmental and social influences on learning. Individual differences comprise individual difference variables, learning and diversity, and standards and assessment.

Application 7.7 illustrates some ways to apply these learner-centered principles in learning environments. In considering their application, teachers should keep in mind the purpose of the instruction and the uses to which it will be put. Teacher-centered instruction will often be the appropriate means of instruction, and indeed, often it is the most efficient. But when deeper student understanding is desired—along with greater student activity—the principles offer sound guidelines.

Instructional Methods

The educational literature is replete with examples of instructional methods that reflect constructivist principles. Some of the better-known methods are summarized in this section.

APPLICATION 7.7
Learner-Centered Principles

Jim Marshall applies many of the APA learner-centered principles in his history classes. He knows that many students are not intrinsically motivated to learn history and take it only because it is required. He thus builds into the curriculum strategies to enhance interest. He makes use of films, field trips, and class reenactments of historical events to link history better with real-world experiences. Jim also does not want students to simply memorize content but rather learn to think critically. He teaches them a strategy to analyze historical events that includes key questions such as, "What preceded the event?", "How might it have turned out differently?", and "How did this event influence future developments?" Because he likes to focus on historical themes (e.g., economic development, territorial conflict), he has students apply these themes throughout the school year to different historical periods.

Being a psychologist, Gina Brown is familiar with the APA principles and incorporates them into her teaching. She knows that her students must have a good understanding of developmental, social, and individual difference variables if they are to be successful teachers. For their field placements Gina ensures that students work in a variety of settings. Thus, students are assigned at different times to classes with younger and older students. She also ensures that students have the opportunity to work in classes where there is diversity in ethnic and socioeconomic backgrounds of students and with teachers who use methods utilizing social interactions (e.g., cooperative learning, tutoring). Gina understands the importance of students' reflections on their experiences as they construct meaning of teaching. They write journals on the field placement experiences and share these in class. She helps students understand how to link these experiences to topics they study in the course (e.g., development, motivation, learning).

Several commonalities are evident in these methods. One is that the teacher is not always the center of the instruction. Rather, environments are designed so that students have an active role in learning—mentally, physically, socially, and emotionally.

Another common feature is diverse instructional formats—small groups, activity centers, peer collaboration, reciprocal teaching, cooperative learning, scaffolding, and apprenticeships. Students are expected to take responsibility for their learning and contribute to the instruction and conversations. Differentiated classroom structure means that not all students may be working on the same task at the same time. In a class, some students might be in a small group, others at the media center, and still others in a reading group with the teacher.

A third common feature is that learning tasks involve real-world problems rather than the artificial ones found in textbooks. For example, in a science class, students may be given the assignment of devising a plan to save energy in their community. In history, students could develop World War II scenarios if the Normandy invasion had been unsuccessful.

Fourth, the environment should provide multiple representations of content. Assignments may require students to discuss material, read books, search the Web, make graphs and charts, develop a PowerPoint© demonstration, and so forth. Such planning is difficult; it is much easier to design a lesson and present it to the class as a whole. In a constructivist environment, the teacher designs multiple activities for students to engage in and ensures that each student is exposed to different activities.

Constructivism does not absolve the teacher of responsibility. In some ways, it places greater demands on the teacher. Even in situations in which students largely work on their own without direct teacher intervention (e.g., guided discovery), the teacher must ensure that students are properly prepared with the skills they will need and that necessary materials are available.

The task facing teachers who attempt to implement constructivist principles can be challenging. Many teachers are unprepared to teach in a constructivist fashion (Elkind, 2004), especially if their teacher preparation programs have not stressed constructivist teaching. There also are factors associated with schools and school systems that work against constructivism (Windschitl, 2002). For example, school administrators and teachers are held accountable for students' scores on standardized tests. These tests typically emphasize lower-level, basic skills and downgrade the importance of deeper conceptual understanding. School cultures also may work against constructivism, especially if teachers have been teaching in the same fashion for many years and have standard curricula and lessons. Parents, too, may not be fully supportive of teachers using less direction in the classroom in favor of time for students to mentally explore concepts and construct their understandings. Despite these potential problems, however, this section suggests some ways that teachers can incorporate constructivist teaching into their regular instruction and especially for topics that lend themselves well to it (e.g., discussion issues where there is no clearly correct answer).

CLASS DISCUSSIONS   Class discussions are useful when the objective is to acquire greater conceptual understanding or multiple sides of a topic. The topic being discussed is one for which there is no clear right answer but rather involves a complex or controversial issue. Students enter the discussion with some knowledge of the topic and are expected to gain understanding as a result of the discussion.

Discussions lend themselves to various disciplines, such as history, literature, science, and economics. Regardless of the topic, it is critical that a class atmosphere be created that is conducive to free discussion. Students likely will have to be given rules for the discussion (e.g., do not interrupt someone who is speaking, keep arguments to the topic being discussed, do not personally attack other students). If the teacher is the facilitator of the discussion, then he or she must support multiple viewpoints, encourage students to share, and remind students of the rules when they are violated. Teachers also can ask students to elaborate on their opinions (e.g., "Tell us why you think that.").

When class size is large, small-group discussions may be preferable to whole-class ones. Students reluctant to speak in a large group may feel less inhibited in a smaller one. Teachers can train students to be facilitators of small-group discussions.

A variety of the discussion is the *debate*, in which students selectively argue sides of an issue. This requires preparation by the groups and, likely, some practice if they will be giving short presentations on their sides. Teachers enforce rules of the debate and ensure that all team members participate. A larger discussion with the class can follow, which allows for points to be reinforced or new points to be brought up.

PEER TUTORING   Peer tutoring occurs when a student who has learned a skill or concept teaches it to one who has not. Peer tutoring provides an alternative to traditional teaching.

Peer tutoring captures many of the principles of constructive teaching. It ensures that students are active in the learning process. Both tutor and tutee freely participate. There is some evidence that peer tutoring can lead to greater achievement gains than traditional instruction (Fuchs, Fuchs, Mathes, & Simmons, 1997). The one-to-one context may encourage tutees to ask questions that they might be reluctant to ask in a large class.

Peer tutoring also encourages cooperation among students and helps diversify the class structure. A teacher might split the class into small groups and tutoring groups while continuing to work with a different group. The content of the tutoring is tailored to the specific needs of the tutee.

Teachers likely will need to instruct peer tutors to ensure that they possess the requisite academic and tutoring skills. It also should be clear what the tutoring session is expected to accomplish. A specific goal is preferable to a general one—thus, "Work with Mike to help him understand how to regroup from the 10s column," rather than "Work with Mike to help him get better in subtraction."

COOPERATIVE LEARNING   Cooperative learning is frequently used in classrooms (Slavin, 1994, 1995). Unfortunately, when it is not properly structured, the cooperative groups can lead to poorer learning compared with whole-class instruction.

In cooperative learning, the objective is to develop, in students, the ability to work collaboratively with others. The task should be one that is too extensive for a single student to complete in a timely fashion. The task also should lend itself well to a group, such as by having components that can be completed by individual students who then merge their individual work into a final product.

There are certain principles that when followed help cooperative groups to be successful. One is to form groups with students who are likely to work together well and who can develop and practice cooperative skills. This does not necessarily mean allowing students to choose groups, because they may select their friends and some students may be left without a group. It also does not necessarily mean heterogeneous grouping, where different ability levels are represented. Although that strategy often is recommended, research shows that high-achieving peers do not always benefit from being grouped with lower achievers (Hogan & Tudge, 1999), and the self-efficacy of lower achievers will not necessarily improve by watching higher achievers succeed (Schunk, 1995). Whatever the means of grouping, teachers should ensure that each group can succeed with reasonable effort.

Groups also need guidance on what they are to accomplish—what is the expected product—as well as the expected mode of behavior. The task should be one that requires interdependence; no group member should be able to accomplish most of the entire task single-handedly. Ideally, the task also will allow for different approaches. For example, to address the topic of "Pirates in America," a group of middle-school students might give a presentation, use posters, conduct a skit, and involve class members in a treasure hunt.

Finally, it is important to ensure that each group member is accountable. If grades are given, it is necessary for group members to document what their overall contributions were to the group. A group in which only two of six members do most of the work but everyone receives an "A" is likely to breed resentment.

Two well-known variations of cooperative learning are the jigsaw method and STAD (student–teams–achievement divisions). In the *jigsaw method*, teams work on material that is subdivided into parts. After each team studies the material, each team member takes responsibility for one part. The team members from each group meet to discuss their part, after which they return to their teams to help other team members learn more about their part (Slavin, 1994). This jigsaw method (and there are other variations) combines many desirable features of cooperative learning, including group work, individual responsibility, and clear goals.

STAD groups study material after it has been presented by the teacher (Slavin, 1994). Group members practice and study together but are tested individually. Each member's score contributes to the overall group score, but because scores are based on improvement, each group member is motivated to improve because individual improvements raise the overall group score. Although STAD is a form of cooperative learning, it seems best suited for material with well-defined objectives or problems with clear answers—for example, mathematical computations and social studies facts. Given its emphasis on improvement, STAD will not work as well where conceptual understanding is involved because student gains may not occur quickly.

Reflective Teaching

Reflective teaching is based on thoughtful decision making that takes into account knowledge about students, the context, psychological processes, learning and motivation, and knowledge about oneself. Although reflective teaching is not part of any constructivist perspective on learning, its premises are based on the assumptions of constructivism (Armstrong & Savage, 2002).

COMPONENTS   Reflective teaching stands in stark contrast to traditional conceptions of teaching in which a teacher prepares a lesson, presents it to a class, gives students assignments and feedback, and evaluates their learning. Reflective teaching assumes that teaching cannot be reduced to one method to apply to all students. Each teacher brings a unique set of personal experiences to teaching. How teachers interpret situations will differ depending on their experiences and perceptions of the situation. Professional development requires that teachers reflect on their beliefs and theories about students, content, context, and learning and check the validity of these beliefs and theories against reality.

TABLE 7.11   *Components of Reflective Teaching Decisions*

- Sensitive to the context
- Guided by fluid planning
- Informed by professional and personal knowledge that is critically examined
- Enhanced by formal and informal professional growth opportunities

(Henderson, 1996)

Henderson (1996) lists four components of reflective teaching that involve decision making (Table 7.11). Teaching decisions must be sensitive to the context. The context includes the school, content, students' backgrounds, time of the year, educational expectations, and the like. Fluid planning means that instructional plans must be flexible and change as conditions warrant. When students do not understand a lesson, it makes little sense to reteach it in the same way. Rather, the plan must be modified to aid student understanding.

Henderson's model puts emphasis on teacher personal knowledge. Teachers should be aware of why they do what they do and be keen observers of situations. They must reflect on and process a wide variety of information about situations. Teachers must have reasons for what they do.

Finally, decisions are strengthened by professional growth opportunities. Teachers must have a strong knowledge base from which to draw to engage in flexible planning and tailor lessons to student and contextual differences. There is no substitute for strong professional development among teachers.

Reflective teachers are characterized as active persons who seek solutions to problems rather than wait for others to tell them what to do. They persist until they find the best solution rather than settle for one that is less than satisfactory. They are ethical and put students' needs above their own; they ask what is best for students rather than what is best for them. Reflective teachers also thoughtfully consider evidence by mentally reviewing classroom events and revising their practices to better serve students' needs (Armstrong & Savage, 2002).

In summary, reflective teachers (Armstrong & Savage, 2002):

- use context considerations
- use personal knowledge
- use professional knowledge
- make fluid plans
- commit to formal and informal professional growth opportunities.

We can see assumptions of constructivism that underlie these points. Constructivism places heavy emphasis on the context of learning because learning is situated. People construct knowledge about themselves (e.g., their capabilities, interests, attitudes) and about their profession from their experiences. Teaching is not a lockstep function that proceeds immutably once a lesson is designed. And finally, there is no "graduation" from teaching. Conditions always are changing, and teachers must stay at the forefront in terms of content, psychological knowledge of learning and motivation, and student individual differences.

BECOMING A REFLECTIVE TEACHER   What types of experiences are useful to help improve teachers' reflective capabilities? Being a reflective teacher is a skill, and like other skills it requires instruction and practice. The following suggestions seem useful in developing this skill.

Being a reflective teacher requires good *personal knowledge*. Teachers have beliefs about their teaching competencies to include subject knowledge, pedagogical knowledge, and student capabilities. To develop personal knowledge, teachers reflect on and assess these beliefs. Self-questioning is helpful. For example, teachers might ask themselves: "What do I know about the subjects I teach?" "How confident am I that I can teach these subjects so that students can acquire skills?" "How confident am I that I can establish an effective classroom climate that facilitates learning?" "What do I believe about how students can learn?" "Do I hold biases (e.g., that students from some ethnic or socioeconomic backgrounds cannot learn as well as other students)?"

Personal knowledge is important because it forms the basis from which to seek improvement. Thus, teachers who feel they are not skilled enough in using technology to teach social studies can seek out professional development to aid them. If they find that they have biases, they can employ strategies so that their beliefs do not cause negative effects. Thus, if they believe that some students cannot learn as well as others, they can seek ways to help the former students learn better.

Being a reflective teacher also requires *professional knowledge*. Effective teachers are well skilled in their disciplines, understand classroom management techniques, and have knowledge about human development. Teachers who reflect on their professional knowledge and recognize deficiencies can correct them, such as by taking university courses or participating in staff development sessions on those topics.

Like other professionals, teachers must keep abreast of current developments in their fields. They can do this by belonging to professional organizations, attending conferences, subscribing to journals and periodicals, and discussing issues with colleagues.

Third, reflective teaching means *planning and assessing*. When reflective teachers plan, they do so with the goal of reaching all students. Many good ideas for lesson plans can be garnered by discussing them with colleagues and consulting practitioner journals. When students have difficulty grasping content presented in a certain way, reflective teachers consider other methods for attaining the same objective.

Assessment works together with planning. Reflective teachers ask how they will assess students' learning outcomes. To gain further knowledge of assessment methods, teachers may need to take courses or participate in staff development. Authentic methods that have come into vogue in recent years offer many possibilities for assessing outcomes, but teachers may need to consult with assessment experts and receive training on their use.

Summary

Constructivism is an epistemology, or philosophical explanation about the nature of learning. Constructivist theorists reject the idea that scientific truths exist and await discovery and verification. Knowledge is not imposed from outside people but rather formed inside them. Learners construct their understandings of knowledge; it is not acquired automatically. Constructivist approaches vary from those that postulate complete self-construction, through those that hypothesize socially mediated constructions, to those that argue that constructions match reality. Constructivism calls our attention to the fact that we must structure teaching and learning experiences to challenge students' thinking so that they will be able to construct new knowledge. A core premise of constructivism is that cognitive processes are situated (located) in physical and social contexts. The concept of situated cognition highlights these relations between persons and situations.

Vygotsky's sociocultural theory emphasizes the social environment as a facilitator of development and learning. The social environment influences cognition through its tools—cultural objects, language, symbols, and social institutions. Cognitive change results from using these cultural tools in social interactions and from internalizing and transforming these interactions. A key concept is the ZPD, which represents the amount of learning possible by a student given proper instructional conditions. It is difficult to evaluate the contributions of Vygotsky's theory to the field of learning because research testing its predictions is recent and many educational applications that fit with the theory are not part of it. Applications that reflect Vygotsky's ideas are instructional scaffolding, reciprocal teaching, peer collaboration, and apprenticeships.

Private speech is speech that has a self-regulatory function but is not socially communicative. Vygotsky believed that private speech develops thought by organizing behavior. Children employ private speech to understand situations and surmount difficulties. Private speech becomes covert with development, although overt verbalization can occur at any age. Verbalization can promote student achievement if it is relevant to the task and does not interfere with performance. Self-instructional training is useful for helping individuals verbally self-regulate their performances.

Vygotsky's theory contends that learning is a socially mediated process. Children learn many concepts during social interactions with others. Structuring learning environments to promote these interactions facilitates learning.

Aspects of motivation relevant to constructivism include contextual factors, implicit theories, and teachers' expectations. Multidimensional classrooms, which have many activities and allow for greater diversity in student performances, are more compatible with constructivism than are unidimensional classes. Characteristics that indicate dimensionality are differentiation of task structure, student autonomy, grouping patterns, and salience of performance evaluations. The TARGET variables (task, authority, recognition, grouping, evaluation, and time) affect learners' motivation and learning.

Students hold implicit theories about such issues as how they learn and what contributes to achievement. Implicit theories are formed during socialization practices and self-reflection and influence students' motivation and learning. Incremental theorists believe that skills can be increased through effort. Entity theorists view their abilities as fixed traits over which they have little control. Research shows that students who believe learning is under their control expend greater effort, rehearse more, and use better learning strategies. Teachers convey their expectations to students in many ways. Teachers' expectations influence teacher–student interactions, and some research shows that under certain conditions expectations may affect student achievement. Teachers should expect all students to succeed and provide support (scaffolding) for them to do so.

Self-regulation includes the coordination of mental processes such as memory, planning, synthesis, and evaluation. Vygotsky believed that language and the ZPD were critical for the development of self-regulation. In Kopp's theory, self-regulation involves a transition from responding to others to using speech and other tools to plan, monitor, and direct one's activities. A key is the internalization of self-regulatory processes. Self-regulation also involves learning the meanings of actions, which are affected by contexts and tools. As with motivation, learners develop implicit theories of self-regulation that address their competence relative to peers, what produces success in different domains, and how much control they have in academic situations. From a constructivist perspective, identity development and self-regulation cannot be separated because self-identity includes being a student.

The goal of constructivist learning environments is to provide rich experiences that encourage students to learn. Constructivist classrooms teach big concepts using much student activity, social interaction, and authentic assessments. Students' ideas are avidly sought, and compared with traditional classes, there is less emphasis on superficial learning and more emphasis on deeper understanding. The APA learner-centered principles, which address various factors (cognitive, metacognitive, motivational, affective, developmental, social, and individual difference), reflect a constructivist learning approach. Some widely practiced instructional methods that fit well with constructivism are class discussions, peer tutoring, and cooperative learning.

Reflective teaching is thoughtful decision making that considers such factors as students, contexts, psychological processes, learning, motivation, and self-knowledge. The premises of reflective teaching are based on constructivist principles. Becoming a reflective teacher requires the development of personal and professional knowledge, planning strategies, and assessment skills.

A summary of learning issues relevant to constructivist theory appears in Table 7.12.

TABLE 7.12 *Summary of Learning Issues*

Which Processes Affect Learning?

Constructivist theory contends that learners form or construct their own understandings of knowledge and skills. Perspectives on constructivism differ as to how much influence environmental and social factors have on learners' constructions. Vygotsky's theory places a heavy emphasis on the role of social factors in learning.

What is the Role of Memory?

Constructivist theory has not dealt explicitly with memory. The basic principles of constructivism suggest that learners are more apt to remember information if their constructions are personally meaningful to them.

What is the Role of Motivation?

The focus of constructivism has been on learning rather than motivation, although some educators have written about motivation. Constructivists hold that learners construct motivational beliefs in the same fashion as they construct beliefs about learning. Learners also construct implicit theories that concern their strengths and weaknesses, what is necessary for learning to occur, and what others think of their capabilities (e.g., parents, teachers).

How Does Transfer Occur?

As with memory, transfer has not been a central issue in constructivist research. The same idea applies, however; to the extent that learners' constructions are personally meaningful to them and linked with other ideas then transfer should be facilitated.

Which Processes are Involved in Self-Regulation?

Self-regulation involves the coordination of mental functions—memory, planning, synthesis, evaluation, and so forth. Learners use the tools of their culture (e.g., language, symbols) to construct meanings. The key is for self-regulatory processes to be internalized. Learners' initial self-regulatory activities may be patterned after those of others, but as learners construct their own they become idiosyncratic.

What are the Implications for Instruction?

The teacher's central task is to structure the learning environment so that learners can construct understandings. To this end, teachers need to provide the instructional support (scaffolding) that will assist learners to maximize their learning in their ZPD. The teacher's role is to provide a supportive environment, not to lecture and give students answers.

Further Reading

Brooks, J. G., & Brooks, M. G. (1999). *In search of understanding: The case for constructivist classrooms.* Alexandria, VA: Association for Supervision and Curriculum Development.

Epstein, J. L. (1989). Family structures and student motivation: A developmental perspective. In C. Ames & R. Ames (Eds.), *Research on motivation in education* (Vol. 3, pp. 259–295). San Diego: Academic Press.

Karpov, Y. V., & Haywood, H. C. (1998). Two ways to elaborate Vygotsky's concept of mediation: Implications for instruction. *American Psychologist, 53,* 27–36.

Rosenthal, R., & Jacobson, L. (1968). *Pygmalion in the classroom.* New York: Holt, Rinehart & Winston.

Sivan, E. (1986). Motivation in social constructivist theory. *Educational Psychologist, 21,* 209–223.

Tudge, J. R. H., & Scrimsher, S. (2003). Lev S. Vygotsky on education: A cultural–historical, interpersonal, and individual approach to development. In B. J. Zimmerman & D. H. Schunk (Eds.), *Educational psychology: A century of contributions* (pp. 207–228). Mahwah, NJ: Erlbaum.

Vygotsky, L. (1978). *Mind in society: The development of higher psychological processes.* Cambridge, MA: Harvard University Press.

8 Understanding Learners: Emotion, Motivation, and Volition

We saw in previous chapters that cognitive psychology offers insights into learning and teaching that go far beyond what strict behaviorism offers. Cognitive information processing theory, in particular, offers a window into reasoning, knowledge, understanding, problem solving, and other capabilities and qualities of the mind central to education. These complex processes can be understood in terms of the flow of information among memory structures—the sensory register, working memory, and long-term memory.

The computer metaphor is highly instructive for understanding human cognition. But, like all metaphors, it has limitations. The logical calculating aspect of the human mind can most easily be accommodated by the computer metaphor. The more "human" aspects of thinking are not as easily understood within the information-processing paradigm. Three of those qualities—emotion, motivation, and volition (or will)—are the focus of this chapter.

We will consider aspects of the mind that experience and express "hot cognitions"—those that extend beyond cool, dispassionate rationality. Emotions, motivation, and volition are deeply entwined with thinking and learning, often propelling intellectual growth and sometimes standing in the way of it. Hot cognitions are far too important to ignore.

The Trilogy of Mind: Cognition, Affect, and Conation

How can we best divide the many different expressions of the human mind? Which categories do justice to its analytical properties—the ones that conform best to the computer metaphor—along with hot cognitions? One taxonomy, elegant in its simplicity, was proposed by the psychologist and historian Ernest Hilgard (1980). Hilgard showed that scholars from ancient times to the present understood the human psyche as a **trilogy of mind** composed of cognition, affect, and conation. **Cognition**, which is rational thought scrubbed free of complicating emotions, wishes, or will, has been the focus of the previous chapters in this book. **Affect** is roughly equivalent to emotion, and includes temporary feeling states as well as more enduring moods. The third component of Hilgard's trilogy is **conation**, which refers to purposeful striving toward valued goals (Snow, Corno, & Jackson, 1996).

Hilgard's model divides conation into two subprocesses: **motivation** and **volition**. Motivation includes all processes that precede a decision to pursue a particular goal; volition refers to all processes that follow a decision and guide action toward a particular goal. We may be *motivated* by hunger to make a sandwich, but may or may not decide to make it. Once we decide to make a sandwich, *volitional* processes take over as we select ingredients and order the steps necessary to achieve the goal.

INTEREST MAGNET 8.1

Can Computers Have Emotions?

The connection between computers and emotions has a long history, dating back to the founding of artificial intelligence (AI). As the early AI researchers began to design systems that could mimic intelligence, some also aspired to design computer programs that could make computer behavior similar to, or even indistinguishable from, human behavior. The famous Turing test, proposed by the legendary mathematician Alan Turing, is that computers would be intelligent when a human observer could not distinguish computer behavior from human behavior. Satisfaction of the Turing test implied that the computer would have the capacity for emotions, or at least the capability of mimicking emotions.

One of the earliest AI programs, called ELIZA, indirectly challenged the Turing test. It was designed to provide counseling to people seeking psychological therapy. ELIZA provided this "service" by imitating such rudimentary active listening strategies as restating a "client's" claim. Of course, ELIZA did not have emotions, nor did it even mimic human emotions very well, but for AI researchers it was the first step down the long and difficult road to equipping computers with affective sensibilities.

Why even try to build computer programs with emotions? One possible benefit is that a computer with emotional capability can, in some form, interact more effectively with a human user. For example, a computer-based tutor that can read a learner's emotions—whether interest, boredom, or anxiety—can adjust its teaching strategy accordingly (Picard, 1997). Reading emotions is possible if the computer is equipped to analyze the learners' facial expressions, for example. There is also an advantage if the intelligent tutor can mimic interest, such as delight at a cor-

rect response. But that means that a computer must produce voice inflections or on-screen facial expressions that are credible displays of the target emotion. Done well, the capability to project emotion could help to motivate the learner. Realistic emotional interpretations and expressions could also help to enhance the pleasure of electronic games, "digital pets," and computer-mediated selection of entertainment media such as music or movies.

Picard (1995) argued that emotions play a necessary role in rational thinking and decision making. If this is so, then the ability to read emotions is not incidental to intelligent reasoning and action, but is instead a vital component of intelligence. Computers might not reach their potential as aids to human needs and aspirations unless they are equipped with sensitivity to human emotions, or perhaps the ability to have and express emotions.

Can a computer really *have* emotions or must it merely *mimic* emotions? Research might not answer this question, but philosophy can try to address it. Or, undeterred by reality, fiction writers can explore the implications of computers that have their own emotions—usually emotions that have a runaway quality. In the short story collection *I, Robot*, Isaac Asimov (1950) depicted a future in which robots had genuine personalities and eventually rebelled against their human makers. A more disastrous scenario was painted by mathematician and sci-fi writer Vernor Vinge (1993), who predicted that eventually the collective intelligence of machines will cross over into self-aware consciousness. At that point—which he called *technological singularity*—computers will no longer accept their second-class status.

Although Hilgard's trilogy of mind model helps disentangle the different forms of thought engaged by the human mind, it would be a mistake to consider these processes as completely distinct. At any time, the mind might simultaneously engage "cool" analytic cognitions as well as the "hot" cognitions of emotions, purposeful planning, and striving toward goals. The entire trilogy of mind participates interactively during nearly all mental activity, including learning and thinking. As we delve into each of these complex aspects of the mind, we will find applications that support the purposes of education.

Emotions

Learning Emotions

Emotions are highly relevant to learning because long-term memory stores not only factual information but also emotional associations that connect to what we know (Bower & Forgas, 2001). Sometimes these associations are so strong that when we think about a specific person, event, or idea, that memory elicits powerful feelings that are just as salient as the memory's factual content. Emotions can, in turn, strengthen initial learning. Research has shown that when new information evokes emotions, that information is much more likely to be remembered. Emotions have this effect for at least two reasons: First, emotions have the power to focus attention, which is a prerequisite for learning; second, emotional experiences tend to be recalled at a later time, leading to rehearsal and therefore a stronger memory trace (Bower, 1994; Bower & Forgas, 2001). Many teachers intuitively understand the role of emotions in learning, and strive to infuse their teaching with emotional value—to get students excited. When teaching stirs emotions, learners pay more attention and better connect new information with what they already know. Positive emotions in particular help students form associations with prior knowledge, contributing to deep understanding rather than superficial learning (Bower, 1994).

It is easy to name many different emotions, dozens perhaps. You can feel anxious, excited, curious, ashamed, proud, angry, or elated. Not surprisingly, psychologists have tried to organize emotions into frameworks. One of the best-known taxonomies of emotion was advanced by Robert Plutchik (1980; 2001). The model, displayed in Figure 8.1, shows eight basic emotions at the central core, with opposites arranged as pairs (e.g., ecstasy and grief, or rage and terror). Plutchik's model illustrates the different intensity of emotions by presenting basic and more intense emotions at the core and placing less intense and subtler versions of emotions on the periphery. The model also shows that some emotions are combinations of others. Specifically, emotions listed in the open spaces, between the "flower petals," are combinations of the two adjacent emotions.

Although the order and symmetry of Plutchik's model is attractive, emotions may not be as neatly organized as the model suggests. Other psychologists have offered somewhat different taxonomies of basic emotions (Ortony & Turner, 1990). Some of the recognized categories—anger, joy, fear, sadness, and surprise—correspond closely to the core emotions listed in Plutchik's model, but others are different. A model by Parrot (2001) makes more modest claims about the logical structure of emotions. Instead of presenting a faceted framework, Parrot advanced six primary emotions—love, joy, surprise, anger, sadness, and fear. Each of the six primary emotions branches off into secondary emotions, forming a tree structure. The secondary emotions in turn subdivide into a large number of tertiary emotions. The emotions listed as tertiary are typically quite precise and subtle compared to the raw and undifferentiated quality of the primary emotions.

The psychology of emotions is not yet a settled matter, but several patterns can be affirmed. For example, the number of distinguishable human emotions is quite high, yet there seems to be a rather small set of basic or primary emotions, such as fear, anger, desire, sadness, and joy (Panksepp, 1994). These basic emotions are related to others, often by subtlety of feeling or cause (e.g., guilt versus shame, or pity versus sympathy). Moreover,

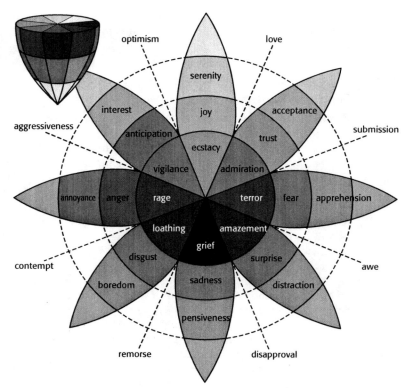

FIGURE 8.1 *Plutchik's Model of Emotions*
In this highly structured model, emotions are shown to vary in
pleasantness and intensity.
[Reprinted by permission of Annette de Ferrarri.]

emotions can be arranged along a positive-negative dimension. Some emotions are clearly pleasant (e.g., happiness) and others unpleasant (e.g., anger). A basic positive-negative dimension seems to hold up as a sensible way to organize emotions (Watson & Clark, 1994).

The positive-negative axis of emotions suggests a direct educational application: to encourage positive emotions toward learning. Educators want their students to enjoy learning and to feel drawn to the subject of study, whether it is literature, physics, computer science, architecture, ancient history, art, or any other domain. If teachers derive satisfaction from advancing their own knowledge and are passionate about their fields of study, they will want their students to experience the same emotions. But as teachers know all too well, attempts to instill positive emotions toward learning are not guaranteed to work. Often, just the opposite occurs; many students develop anxiety, fear, or other negative feelings toward school subjects. Even more worrisome, students sometimes generalize those negative feelings to the entire school experience. Surely, cultivating positive emotions among learners and curtailing the formation of negative emotions is one of the greatest challenges every educator faces.

Asking a teacher to instill positive feelings about learning is a tall order. We experience particular emotions for any number of reasons, some of which are quite accidental. Early in this book we saw that classical conditioning is a very elemental process that can associate strong emotions to new stimuli. The mechanism of classical conditioning is simple—it involves the pairing of two stimuli. One stimulus, the unconditioned stimulus, naturally evokes a particular feeling or physiological response. An angry face or a loud disapproving voice is enough to elicit negative emotions in most children, for example. If that natural stimulus is paired with a neutral stimulus, then the neutral stimulus can prompt the same emotion. For Pavlov's dogs, the neutral stimulus was a bell. For students in the classroom, stimuli that are themselves neutral—books, pencils, and math equations—can acquire positive or negative valences over time. The simple pairing of stimuli can account for some learning of emotional associations.

Positive emotions obviously serve educational ends in a variety of ways. A prime example is the delight we feel when we have an intellectual breakthrough. Whenever we have a flash of insight into a difficult problem, we are likely to feel a rush of satisfaction. Likewise, when we hear and comprehend a clear explanation of a difficult concept, we experience the positive feelings that accompany understanding. For more experienced and successful learners, the *anticipation* of emotional satisfaction that accompanies understanding can sustain their focus. Effective learners look forward to the cognitive breakthrough and persevere to experience its emotional rewards. The implications for teaching are direct: Along with imparting knowledge, teachers can help students to anticipate the deep emotional rewards that accompany intellectual activity, including mastery of difficult but powerful ideas.

Of course, the task of the educator is much more complicated than trying to instill positive emotions and minimize negative emotions. Even "negative" emotions can have potential educational value. What happens, for example, when we read a passage of text that lacks clarity? Perhaps we feel vaguely irritated because it seems fuzzy or ambiguous. We might experience the same feelings when listening to an explanation of a new concept or an illogical rationale for an important decision. This emotional reaction is valuable if it prompts us to ask questions, to develop alternative opinions, and to seek ideas from new sources. In other words, even superficially negative emotions can sometimes lead to improved cognition.

Emotional associations that advance thinking and learning cannot be taught directly. You can't *make* someone feel a prescribed emotion. Still, nothing prohibits a teacher from modeling the emotional rewards of intellectual gains—of curiosities satisfied and insights gained. This does not mean the teacher must put on an act—just the opposite, really. To model the full range of emotional rewards of thinking and learning means to let students into the teacher's private mental world. The teacher can openly convey what he or she is feeling. When the teacher "thinks aloud" through the steps of an intellectual process, she demonstrates cognitive modeling, which can include expressing emotions through voice and gesture.

By communicating the full range of her emotions, a teacher imparts not only the subject matter, but also something of herself. This aspect of teaching—of teaching *oneself* to students—is easily overlooked and infrequently discussed as a vital element of the teaching profession. The opportunity was nicely summed up in the pithy advice of mathematics educator Liping Ma: "Do not forget yourself as a teacher of yourself" (Herrera, 2002). What does it mean for a teacher to teach something of herself to students? For virtually every teacher, it means sharing not only knowledge and skill, but also a deep appreciation, even love, for the subject of study. The intense and enduring enjoyment of literature, mathematics, science, or history is part of what a dedicated teacher can instill in her students.

Intrinsic Motivation

Intrinsic motivation refers to the emotional associations that lead a person to engage in an activity for its own sake, rather than for rewards that lie outside the activity. Any recreational activity that is enjoyable by itself, that you engage in freely without needing compensation or recognition, can be said to be intrinsically motivated. Reading a novel, watching a movie, and spending time with friends can all be enjoyable in themselves. Although placing intrinsic motivation under the heading of emotions might seem odd, intrinsic motivation largely refers to positive feelings toward an activity or the anticipation of positive feelings, which in turn motivate engagement in the activity.

Most educators deeply wish for their students to develop and maintain an intrinsic motivation to learn. Intrinsic motivation easily qualifies as one of the most important goals of education, and for good reasons. Intrinsic motivation is positively correlated with both academic achievement and perceptions of academic competence (Gottfried, 1985). One of the best indications that a teacher has been successful is when a student develops an ongoing interest in the subject of study, such as when a student adopts her English teacher's passion for literature or her biology teacher's love of science. Teachers often hope to spark a deep interest among at least some students—an interest that will continue for the long term, perhaps even affecting a student's course of study and choice of a career.

Unfortunately, available data tell us that intrinsic motivation is not commonly developed as a product of educational experience. Susan Harter (1982) found that intrinsic motivation trended strongly downward as students progressed through the school years. Cross-sectional data showed that for every year that passed between grades 3 and 8, average student intrinsic motivation decreased substantially (Figure 8.2). Intrinsic motivation

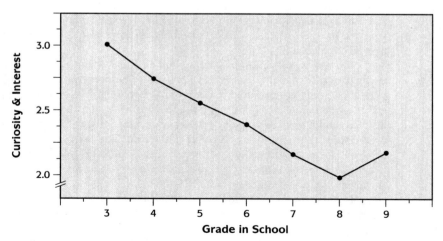

FIGURE 8.2   *Decline of Intrinsic Motivation*
With each passing grade, students become less motivated by their own curiosity and interest. [Adapted from Harter (1982),
Reprinted by permission of Elsevier Global Rights Department].

was replaced with **extrinsic motivation**; in place of curiosity and interest, students were increasingly motivated by the extrinsic incentives of teacher approval and grades (Harter, 1982). This lamentable pattern, which every teacher must confront at some level, indicates a very real risk that, with every passing year, the average student will become less interested in school and less motivated by the **intrinsic rewards** of learning. Teachers must somehow prevent this downward slide and, if possible, reverse it.

The decline of intrinsic motivation during the elementary school years is possibly caused by the widening use of **extrinsic rewards** in schools. Though extrinsic rewards can be effective motivators, they can also erode pre-existing intrinsic motivation. Unlike rats running through a laboratory maze, children have the capacity to wonder why their behavior was rewarded. Children can perceive not only the informational aspect of reward ("I am successful"), but also a controlling aspect ("I am being manipulated") (Deci, 1985). They can also contemplate their own motives for striving to achieve. Extrinsic rewards alone may be sufficient to rationalize to a student why he studies. If so, there is no need to appeal to intrinsic motives; the student's own behavior is **overjustified** by the system of extrinsic rewards.

The system of extrinsic rewards that so pervades education is perhaps necessary and is arguably effective. Gold stars, candy, and smiley faces for reinforcement of desired behavior are ubiquitous. Among older students in the upper grades, in high school, and at the university, test scores and course grades provide frequent feedback to students. Parents, teachers, and fellow students react to these scores and grades, and convey (sometimes intense) social approval or disapproval. The system comes with a cost: Students might feel that the pressure to earn high grades overwhelms any budding interest in a subject of study.

On the other hand, extrinsic rewards are not always counterproductive. Research has shown that praise by itself does not necessarily detract from intrinsic motivation. In fact, extrinsic rewards seem to have an undermining effect only if they are given to students completing a task without regard to the quality of the work (Cameron & Pierce, 1994). Rewards linked to the quality of performance can provide valuable feedback to students and generate beliefs about personal competence where none existed initially. As a precursor to self-confidence, extrinsic rewards might pave the way for intrinsic interest to grow at a later point in the learner's development. Moreover, the typical decline of intrinsic motivation during the school years can arise from factors that have little to do with the system of extrinsic rewards that pervades schooling. The subject matter under study can be difficult and confusing. Complex and abstract knowledge domains, especially those studied in high school, are potentially alienating (Gardner, 1991). To nurture and protect intrinsic motivation among learners is no easy accomplishment. Whenever students pursue a deep understanding of any complex subject or skill, the pathway is almost always fraught with impediments and rife with challenges to self-esteem.

Teachers rightly want to instill intrinsic motivation in their students because they know about the potential intellectual rewards for thinking and learning. Yet another good reason for wanting to develop intrinsic motivation is that positive feelings toward a knowledge domain can influence future decisions to pursue study in that area. The continued willingness of students to learn as evidenced by the choices they make has been called **continuing motivation** (Maehr, 1976). At some point in the education of every student, there comes a time when a choice is offered to continue toward more advanced study or to stop. For some students, this choice is offered during the final years of high school when students choose elective courses. Options open further during college when students choose a major and, after graduation, a career. Continuing motivation is powerful because it encompasses decisions that affect the course of a life and career. This is why Martin Maehr (1976, p. 444) speculated that "continuing motivation may well be *the* critical outcome of any learning experience."

There are additional reasons for cultivating intrinsic motivation as a key outcome of education. Intrinsic motivation is associated with high levels of performance and creativity (Amabile, Hill, Hennessey, & Tighe, 1994) as well as deeper processing of information and greater conceptual understanding (Vansteenkiste, Lens, & Deci, 2006). There seems to be a natural connection between the enjoyment of an activity and highly skilled performance in that activity. Stated differently, excellence and enjoyment coexist and are mutually reinforcing. This connection was explored by the psychologist Mihaly Csikszentmihalyi in his concept of *flow*.

Flow

Most people intuitively understand the concept of flow because they have experienced it personally. Have you ever been so engrossed in a project that you lost track of time? Have you become so completely absorbed by your activity that it becomes, for a while, your entire world? Everything else drops away as your attention focuses like a spotlight on what you must do next. Subjective feelings of intense concentration on a focal activity can be highly pleasurable and even addictive. Csikszentmihalyi (1975) called this zen-like state of consciousness **flow**.

FIGURE 8.3 *Rock Climber in the Flow. Intense concentration on a challenging activity where the difficulty of the task matches the level of ability can create flow—a zen-like state of consciousness. [DK]*

Csikszentmihalyi studied flow states experienced by rock climbers and surgeons, as well as specialists in other areas. He found that the experience of flow was one factor that kept experts highly engaged in their professional or recreational pursuits. He also discovered that flow was associated with particular qualities of activity. In *Beyond Boredom and Anxiety*, Csikszentmihalyi postulated that flow is experienced whenever there is a good match between the difficulty of the task and the ability of the performer. If the task is too easy, boredom sets in; if it is too hard, the performer will become anxious. Either way, enjoyment will diminish. Flow results from an optimal level of challenge. When there is a good match between task difficulty and ability level, boredom and anxiety are equally avoided. Motivation and interest are engaged, and performance is at its peak when ability is stretched without being overwhelmed. That ideal fit produces flow—a psychological state that is highly compelling both intellectually and emotionally.

If you have experienced flow, then you know that such a state of mind is one of the major emotional rewards of intellectual activity. There are good reasons to cultivate the ability to experience flow among learners. If each student could experience flow, either regularly or just occasionally, one consequence might be a more widespread intellectual engagement and academic success. Greater numbers of students might engage in serious and sustained pursuit of knowledge and understanding. Perhaps the ability to experience flow should be considered an essential goal of education.

Motivation Theories Based on Global Motives

Theories of human motivation are quite varied in scope and perspective. Some focus on specific ways that people tend to interpret events, or the manner in which they judge their behavior in specific contexts and domains. This section examines theories that account for behavior in terms of broad or global factors. These theories present activity as a consequence of general motives that have a wide influence across the gamut of human behavior.

Physiological Theories

Why human beings do what they do is not at all easy to account for. Nonetheless, there is a basic theory that can explain *some* aspects of human motivation as well as the motivation of animal behavior. That simple account is the **drive theory** of motivation. Drive theory, most famously advocated by the psychologist Clark Hull (1943), specifies that behavior is, at its root, motivated by physiological needs. Drives for food, sex, and sleep are primary examples of physiological demands that motivate behavior. In drive theory, behavior is motivated by a need to reduce "tissue deficits," which is another way of saying that action is motivated by the physiological demands that press insistently on the organism.

The **arousal theory** of motivation is a second but related theory that focuses on the organism's degree of physiological arousal. In this context, *arousal* refers to an organism's level of physiological activity as indexed by heart and breathing rates. An organism, human or animal, in a low state of arousal would be relaxed or asleep; in a high state of arousal, the organism would be agitated and nervous, perhaps afraid or angry, and ready for action. As we have just seen, drive theory implies that behavior is directed toward meeting physiological needs, and presumably toward satiation and a relaxed state—in other words, toward low arousal. But is low arousal best? In a theory advocated by Yerkes and Dodson in 1908, optimal performance is associated with *moderate* states of arousal. For any given activity, performance will suffer if arousal is too low or too high. At moderate levels of arousal, performance will tend to be optimized.

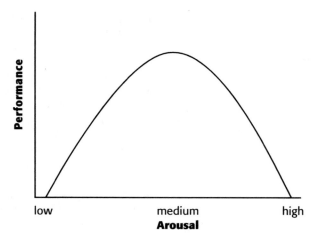

FIGURE 8.4 *Yerkes-Dodson Inverted-U Curve. Performance is optimal at moderate states of physio-logical arousal—neither too relaxed nor too agitated.*

The principle of optimal arousal was captured in the **Yerkes-Dodson Law** about a century ago. On a graph, the law takes the form of an inverted U, with the horizontal axis on the graph indicating physiological arousal, and the vertical axis indicating performance level. The peak represents optimal performance. The Yerkes-Dodson Law seems to hold up as a general principle, but it does vary somewhat depending on a person's level of skill. For experts, the curve will tend to shift to the right, meaning that performance will be best at somewhat higher states of arousal.

Consider what can happen on a basketball court toward the end of a close game. In the final seconds, a foul is committed that puts a player on the free throw line. The game's outcome will be decided by whether the player can make the shot. In this situation, tremendous psychological pressure as well as the noise of the crowd can detract from the shooting ability of a less-experienced player. For a professional basketball player, however, skill and concentration might be sharpened by the higher state of arousal prompted by the stressful situation. Likewise, an expert chef might work very efficiently under high-pressure conditions. Under those same conditions, a novice chef might make mistakes if the arousal produced by high demands becomes overwhelming. The inverted U holds for chefs, basketball players, and all skilled performers, but its peak shifts to the right as novices transition toward expertise.

Curiosity

Jerome Bruner (1966) proposed that among the most basic of all motives is the "will to learn." Bruner noted that this basic human desire, in turn, is strongly motivated by curiosity. When we consider curiosity as a primary motivator of learning, we enter the realm of the cognitive. Drive theory can be construed in completely behavioral terms, and arousal is purely biologi-cal. Neither evokes or needs the mind. Curiosity, by contrast, arises from a discrepancy be-tween what learners expect and what they observe. It is fundamentally cognitive.

Infants and young children are drawn to vivid and changing stimuli. They are at-tracted to new and varied shapes, patterns, colors, and movement. Much infant behavior, in fact, has the effect of causing greater sensory experience. Sensory exploration, in turn, appears to be essential for normal intellectual development (Bruner, 1966). As a child ma-tures, his curiosity changes form. Among older children, curiosity is evoked by complex and incongruous patterns, not only by novelty and vividness. By the early school grades, children are drawn to pictures and stories that have incongruous and surprising elements (Berlyne & Frommer, 1966).

What is the function of curiosity in learning? Above all, curiosity reflects a desire to improve the cognitive organization of ideas (Malone, 1981). The mind is constantly engaged in reconciling new experiences with prior knowledge. In Piaget's theory of cognitive development, for example, cognitive disequilibrium occurs whenever new information cannot be incorporated into existing cognitive structures. The perceiver is motivated to reduce the discrepancy. This process, which Piaget called **accommodation**, advances mental development. As learning proceeds, cognitive structures become more complete and coherent—and more consistent with external realities. Curiosity can prompt and motivate cognitive change in these directions.

Competence Motivation

Drive theory and arousal theory are somewhat contradictory. Drive theory specifies that behavior is an attempt to *reduce* drives. The motive is to satisfy the physiological needs of the body and to make them "go away," at least temporarily. The theory of optimal arousal as formulated by Yerkes and Dodson specifies that lower is not necessarily better. Instead, the organism performs optimally when experiencing a moderate physiological state, one better understood as homeostasis or dynamic balance rather than drive reduction.

Evidence that behavior is not always directed toward drive reduction can be seen even in laboratory mice. In contradiction to Hull's drive theory, mice whose biological needs are satisfied engage in exploratory behavior. Why do they explore? Certainly not to *reduce* any drive, but rather to *raise* physiological or neural activity to a higher, more optimal level. From an evolutionary perspective, it's easy to think of reasons why exploratory behavior would be adaptive and lead to a higher chance of survival in the long run. The important point to note is that exploration of the environment cannot be explained solely by appealing to Hull's drive theory; it must be explained in some other way.

The exploratory behavior of mice seems to have a direct parallel in human behavior. Human beings like to understand their environment and exert some control over it. The idea was formulated in Robert White's (1959) theory of **competence motivation**, which recognized that a basic human motive is to demonstrate control. Drive theories were unable to explain the gamut of human and animal behavior, especially the tendency to explore. Exploratory behavior, as it turns out, is not always in the service of reducing "tissue deficits." To the contrary, exploration often leads to *increases* in arousal, rather than to reductions as drive theory would predict. The self-reinforcing quality of exploratory behavior—exploration prompts *more* exploration—was antithetical to drive theory. This contradiction led White to propose competence as a need in its own right, independent of basic physiological needs.

Much human behavior can be accounted for by the need to exhibit competence. It is possible that, beyond survival needs, a person's primary motivation is to be effective in exerting control over life events and circumstances (deCharms, 1976). The need to be causal reflects perhaps the most basic adaptive response to the environment, helping to ensure immediate survival and longer-term prospects for a thriving existence.

Achievement Motivation

Competence motivation is highly relevant to students' engagement in school activities. The need to exhibit competence can be harnessed to help students advance toward greater knowledge and skill. Of course, students vary considerably in the need to be competent in school settings. Personality theories can help to account for these differences. According to one theory, people differ in a global personality dimension called **achievement motivation** (McClelland, 1961) or **need for achievement** (Atkinson, 1958). For a person to be successful, talent is not enough; there must also be a desire to *use* that talent to become successful. This enduring desire, the need for achievement, helps translate high ability into success (Simonton, 1984).

In *The Achieving Society*, McClelland (1961) described the need for achievement as a deep commitment to standards of excellence. Within any group, some individuals will exhibit a strong need to achieve and others will show comparatively little need for personal achievement. There will be individual variation, with most people displaying moderate levels of achievement motivation. According to McClelland's theory, whole societies and cultures also differ in achievement motivation. He wondered why fifteenth-century Florence experienced such a profusion of talent and concluded that the artists and intellectuals of Florence—Michelangelo, Leonardo da Vinci, and Galileo, among many others—were driven by a high level of achievement motivation that inspired an outpouring of creative achievement during the Italian Renaissance. Societies can differ with respect to the need for achievement, and those levels can change over time. Achievement motivation is therefore a dynamic quality that fluctuates with a society's core beliefs and values.

Soon after achievement motivation was postulated as a global personality trait, one assessment process became favored for measuring a person's need for achievement. That test is the Thematic Apperception Test (TAT) (Murray, 1943). The TAT is a **projective test** of personality. Unlike tests that are common in academic settings, there are no correct or incorrect answers; instead, responses are highly subjective. Projective tests present ambiguous stimuli, such as pictures, and ask the examinee to say what each stimulus means to him or her. The open-ended interpretation that the examinee "projects" onto the ambiguous picture gives important information to the examiner. To the degree that subjects identify achievement-related themes in the TAT pictures, they are judged to have a high need for achievement. As more achievement-related themes are projected onto the pictures, the examinee's overall score on the need for achievement goes up.

The Thematic Apperception Test and the personality trait known as the *need for achievement* are not often employed in educational contexts. Neither the theory nor the assessment is in vogue to the degree that they were in decades past. Part of the reason for the decline in popularity of the TAT and other projective tests is that their generated scores are necessarily somewhat subjective. A score may vary depending on who administers the test, therefore lowering the test's reliability. Nonetheless, the theory of achievement motivation tells us something important about why student behavior varies greatly in academic contexts: Success in schools and other learning environments can be understood partly as arising from differences in this personality dimension. For whatever reason—perhaps a combination of genetic predisposition and environmental experience—people differ in their need to achieve.

A more recently identified personality dimension, called the **need for cognition**, also recognizes individual differences that are strongly related to thinking and learning. The need for cognition refers to the variation among people in their tendency to engage in and enjoy cognition (Cacioppo, Petty, Feinstein, & Jarvis, 1996). People who are on the low end of the need for cognition are cognitive "misers." They minimize efforts to understand information and solve problems, tending instead to rely on the opinions and solutions generated by other people. In contrast, those with a high need for cognition have a strong personal desire to exercise their minds—they have an "endless intellectual curiosity" that compels them to raise questions and seek answers for themselves (p. 247). If we want to understand why there is significant variation in academic achievement, then we can look to the personality dimensions of need for achievement and need for cognition for two promising explanations.

Expectancy-Value Theories

As a personality trait, the need for achievement is not particularly cognitive in its theoretical conceptualization. Other approaches to motivation are much more cognitive in orientation. One such approach, **expectancy-value theory** (Fishbein & Ajzen, 1974), is cognitive in that it speculates on the kind of mental calculation a person makes when facing decisions, and on the nature of information that feeds into those calculations. The very name of expectancy-value theory indicates the two kinds of information that enter into decisions: *expectancy* refers to the likelihood that a particular choice will result in a particular outcome; *value* is the perceived benefit of that outcome.

Decision-making can be quite complicated, of course. Any point of decision might present several options from which to choose. Each of those options will lead to consequences, but those consequences are not necessarily predictable in advance. Perhaps the best a person can do is estimate the probability of each outcome (its expectancy) and how good or bad that outcome would be (its value). Should you ask your friend on a date? Certainly, there is positive value if the invitation is accepted, and negative value if it is rejected. What is the probability of each response? Let's say it's 50/50. In your rough mental calculation you might decide that the pleasure of an acceptance has twice the value as the pain of rejection. Now you know what to do: The rational decision is to ask the person out because the expectancy-value of that decision pathway is highest (even if it is highly subjective, approximate, and intuitive, rather than calculated).

The decision calculus becomes more complicated if you have several different options. When a high school student faces the prospect of finding a date as the prom approaches, he or she may be lucky to have several options (or unfortunate to have to face them). A student might consider the expectancy-value of asking each, and weigh these against the option of not going to the prom at all. Any student would approach the question of prom dates rationally, right? Well, perhaps not. But even if expectancy-value theory only *approximates* the way we make decisions *some* of the time, it has value for interpreting the choices that students make in their academic pursuits. A student can choose to try hard or to slack off, to enroll in an advanced course or to avoid further study, to ask for help or to go it alone. If equipped with the intellectual tools for rational decision making, students will experience greater success in the long run.

Expectancy-value theory recognizes not only the positive value of success but also the negative value of failure. Both enter into the calculus that has the potential to guide decision-making. We differ in our feelings about success, as we have seen in the theory of achievement motivation. Some people have a much stronger personality-driven need to achieve than do others. Expectancy-value theory recognizes that people differ also in their reactions to the prospect of value. Some people have a great aversion to negative consequences—a paralyzing **fear of failure**. For other people, though, the prospect of failure is not debilitating—it may even be energizing as a necessary component of challenge.

Maslow's Hierarchy of Needs

Expectancy-value theory led us to consider that decision making is guided not only by the chances of success and failure, but also by the value of those consequences. How is value decided? Is it entirely subjective, or are there commonalities across people about the value of particular outcomes? Certainly, value is predictable to a degree. A person whose car has broken down in the desert will be extremely thirsty after a few hours of wandering on foot. To a very thirsty person, thoughts of anything but a drink of water are rather insignificant. The same could be said for a starving person; food assumes very high importance. Basic biological needs can be highly compelling, as Hull recognized in his drive theory—but they don't tell the whole story.

Human beings have many other needs besides those that are essentially biological. For example, we have needs for safety and the respect of other people. We also have a need to control our environment and our circumstances as proposed in the theory of competence motivation. When we consider this spectrum of needs, the picture of human motivation starts to look highly complex. Is there a way to simplify things—to lend order to the array of motives that prompt human behavior? One highly influential attempt to organize human motives into a comprehensible schema was made by the psychologist Abraham Maslow (1968). Maslow proposed that certain needs—namely, physiological needs—are fundamental. If those needs are not met, then they automatically assume priority in guiding behavior. But if basic physiological needs are satisfied, then other needs come to the fore. Those needs are presented in the diagram of Maslow's hierarchy (Fig. 8.5).

Maslow's hierarchy shows that the most basic needs are biological. Above those are safety needs. Next in order of priority is belongingness, which refers to the pervasive human need for social connection, for affection, and for love. Still higher up in the hierarchy is self-esteem. If these more basic needs are met, then the need for self-esteem rises

FIGURE 8.5   *Maslow's Hierarchy of Needs. The ordered needs range from basic survival requirements to the pinnacle of fulfillment, self-actualization.*

[Adapted from Maslow, 1987. Electronically reproduced by permission of Pearson Education, Inc.]

in importance. The need for self-esteem probably motivates a significant degree of effort in academic and career success. But if a learner's more basic needs are not met, then activities motivated by self-esteem needs will not be important. This alone says much about the probable impact of poverty on learning. If a child is hungry, in danger, or unloved, then the self-esteem needs that drive a good portion of achievement in academic settings will simply not be relevant.

Maslow was intensely interested in the need placed at the top of his hierarchy—the need for **self-actualization**. The concept of self-actualization is by itself a major contribution of Maslow's theory. Self-actualization refers to the rare instance in which a person reaches his or her highest potential as a human being. When circumstances coincide to produce a person who possesses self-insight, wisdom, intelligence, and the capacity for love—in a combination that is unique to that individual—self-actualization has been achieved. The self-actualized person has become that best possible "version" of himself or herself. By Maslow's reckoning, very few people become self-actualized, but the potential and driving need is within each one of us. The hierarchy specifies that the quest for self-actualization usually builds on the satisfaction of more basic needs.

Self-actualization is the centerpiece of Maslow's theory. In fact, Maslow envisioned a branch of psychology that was directed toward helping people reach their highest potential. He saw psychology as overly focused on understanding and treating people with psychological disturbances—neuroses and psychoses. This was certainly the focus of Freud in his psychodynamic theory of mental illness. The alternative proposed by Maslow was to study psychologically *healthy* people, to understand them, and to apply that knowledge so that others could more fully realize their potential for growth, psychological health, and fulfillment. This orientation to psychology was shared by many other psychologists in the 1960s and 1970s, including Carl Rogers and Rollo May. Collectively, these scholars formed **humanistic psychology**, a branch of research and practice that has diminished in popularity since its heyday, but still has adherents among psychotherapists. The contemporary branch of scholarship known as **positive psychology** is similarly concerned with advancing the theory and achievement of health, well-being, success, and happiness (Bornstein, Davidson, Keyes, & Moore, 2003).

In significant ways, educators can sympathize with the tenets and motives of humanistic psychology. Educators want their students to reach toward their highest potential, even if few will actually achieve that exalted state. Teachers might not use the term *self-actualization*, but many teachers pride themselves in having a role in shaping students' lives toward greater fulfillment, maturity, and productivity. Effective teachers see that potential within each child, and try to awaken each student to his or her unique talents and gifts. Like Abraham Maslow, they realize that unfulfilled basic needs—the need for food, safety, belongingness, and self-esteem—can block students from reaching their potential. But when basic needs are met and with the right opportunities to learn and grow, students can move toward something higher.

Motivation Theories Based on Beliefs About Events

The desire to become self-actualized seems compatible with the larger goals of education. But self-actualization is possible only if a person senses a certain degree of control over the events of her life. After all, how is it possible to grow intellectually and to become successful if there is not some feeling of control? And yet, people differ significantly in the actual degree of control they have over the events of their lives, and in the degree of control they *think* they have over their lives. The theories presented in this section focus on how people differ in interpreting life events, especially experiences of success or failure.

Locus of Control

Psychologist Julian Rotter (1966) proposed that there are two contrasting explanatory styles for interpreting who or what controls a person's life. Some people have an internal **locus of control**. Whatever events transpire—good or bad—they see themselves as responsible. They are willing to take credit for success and assume responsibility for failure. Essentially, they see themselves as exercising control over whatever happens to them. Naturally, they interpret events consistently with this belief. Other people, by contrast, see themselves as *being controlled* by their circumstances. People with this explanatory style have an external locus of control. Whether they experience success or failure, they see external circumstances as responsible for the outcome.

Internal locus and external locus are associated with the parallel terms **origin** and **pawn** (deCharms, 1976). Think of a fairy tale prince on a quest to slay the dragon and rescue the princess locked in a tower. The prince presumably sees himself as an origin because he believes that the outcome of his quest depends on his courage and skill. He has an internal locus of control. The stereotypical princess, meanwhile, waits patiently to be rescued. Like a pawn on a chessboard, she is a pawn to the stronger forces that envelop her. Having an external locus of control, the princess can only hope that the events of her life will work out favorably.

These contrasting explanatory styles are certainly extreme. But in more moderate forms, these two ways of interpreting who or what has control over life events answer a question faced by real people, not fairy tale characters. Children and adults alike often gravitate toward an internal locus of control or external locus of control. Those who see themselves as pawns are quick to blame others for failure. "It's not my fault," they say, because in their own minds they are not in control. Passive by nature or by habit, they have difficulty in setting ambitious goals. Rather than work to create their own reality, their lives "happen" to them. People with an internal locus, however, see life events as emanating from the choices they make. Perhaps overly willing to accept blame for setbacks and failures, they are also more confident of their ability to direct their life path in productive directions. They are convinced that if they can imagine an exciting goal, they will have the personal resources to reach it.

In the continuum between internal and external locus of control, some people think they are capable of just about anything they set their mind to—and perhaps they are. But there are also those who are radically passive toward the circumstances of their lives. These are victims of what has been called **learned helplessness** (Seligman, 1975; Garber & Seligman, 1980). A student who fits this description feels that there is nothing he can do to become successful. The condition is *learned* in that it arises from the repetitive failure of effort to lead to a good outcome. The student might try repeatedly to earn high grades and to please the teacher—all to no avail. Repetitive failure leads to an obvious conclusion: "Nothing I do can produce the outcome I desire." Perhaps at home, also, repeated attempts to please his parents are ineffectual. For the person experiencing learned helplessness, there is a complete disconnection between personal initiative and desired outcomes. The strategy that makes the most sense is simply to stop trying.

Learned helplessness is devastating to the education process. Students who experience feelings of helplessness may find emotional protection in the armor of withdrawal.

Laziness, irresponsibility, truancy, and uncooperativeness all protect "helpless" students from the risk of failure and its consequences, although not from other sanctions. Slow learners, students with learning disabilities, and special education students are all vulnerable to learned helplessness. An alert teacher is mindful of signs of learned helplessness, including passivity and deep discouragement, and will take steps to prevent a further slide into withdrawal.

Teachers' leadership styles can influence how students perceive the causal force of their own actions. Ideally, teachers will steer students away from an external locus of control and toward an internal locus. They want students to know that they can exercise control over the events of their lives, particularly in school. A teacher who monitors her students too closely may hinder the development of an internal locus of control. Under close surveillance, students have little opportunity to develop an internal locus. When students are granted some autonomy, however, they are likely to perceive their actions as arising from within—from the force of their own decisions. There is an additional benefit to giving choice to students: Choice, or even the illusion of choice, is intrinsically motivating (Deci, 1975).

When a teacher nudges students toward a sense of control—toward an internal locus—the teacher advances the causes of learning and intellectual growth. Students' interpretive frameworks can shift accordingly. If a test result is disappointing, a student might consider that he could have studied harder or prepared more fully. The locus is *within*. Likewise, when he experiences success he will not pass it off as a fluke or the result of luck, but rather as a sign that he is able.

Attribution Theory

Theories subsequent to Rotter's locus of control theory expanded on the notion that people have different characteristic explanations for the events of their lives. **Attribution theory** focuses on the explanations people give for success and failure experiences (Weiner, 1985). Those explanations are *attributions* because they *attribute* the event to this or that cause. Building directly on locus of control theory, one dimension of attribution is locus. The locus can be internal, with such attributions as ability (or lack thereof) and effort (or lack thereof). Internal attributions may be controllable or not, which leads to a second dimension, *controllability*. Effort is controllable, but ability usually is not. Many external attributions (e.g., "the test was hard" or "the teacher was unfair") are likewise uncontrollable. Another uncontrollable attribution is luck. A person might say, "I was lucky" or "I was unlucky." But is luck a stable trait, or does it come and go? A person might believe "I'm a lucky person," in which case luck is stable; alternatively, a person might claim that "I just happened to be lucky on that particular occasion," revealing a belief that luck is unstable. This attribution points to a third dimension of attributions: *stability*.

Attribution theory therefore recognizes three dimensions along which explanations can be categorized: locus, controllability, and stability. Each of these three dimensions crosses the other two in a 2 by 2 by 2 matrix, creating eight possible combinations. People tend to develop characteristic patterns of attributions, habitually seeing the events of their lives as a result of luck, ability, effort, and so on. Not all attribution patterns are equally conducive to success in academic settings, or to progress in developing academic ability over time. Consider the statement, "I'm not good at math," an attribution all too frequently spoken or believed, perhaps especially by girls. The attributions are not necessarily backed by evidence. Sometimes students claim to lack ability in mathematics despite

INTEREST MAGNET 8.2

Helpless Fish

Imagine a scenario in which a person or an animal faces a highly unpleasant situation. There may be a way to escape physical or psychological pain but, strangely, the organism does not try to do so. What explains such passivity? Perhaps previous attempts to escape unpleasant stimuli did not bring relief, so the person or animal does not attempt to escape suffering.

This passivity in the face of pain is the hallmark of the dire psychological condition known as *learned helplessness*. The study of learned helplessness originated in experiments with dogs who were given brief but inescapable electrical shocks (Maier, Seligman, & Solomon, 1969). Later, the dogs did not try to escape the shocks even though they could have done so easily by leaping over a low barrier. After conducting research on dogs, psychologists found that learned helplessness also occurs in people, not as the result of experimental manipulations, but through the difficult circumstances of life.

Early research also led to the discovery that learned helplessness could occur in animals as uncomplicated as the common goldfish. Researchers first needed to know whether goldfish could learn to escape an electric shock (Frumkin & Brookshire, 1969). To teach this behavior, the researchers relied on classical conditioning. A few seconds after a light was turned on in the fish tank, part of the tank was electrified. Through trial and error, the fish learned that by swimming to the other end of the tank they could avoid the electric shock that followed the light. Those fish were not helpless—they "knew" how to escape suffering.

However, certain kinds of experiences interfered with the ability of the goldfish to learn the escape behavior (Padilla, 1973). In one experiment, untrained fish were placed into a tank that did not allow escape. The tank had a clear barrier that prevented the fish from swimming to the safe portion of the tank. When the clear barrier was later removed, allowing the fish to escape the shock, they were poor performers. They were no longer effective at learning to avoid the shock even though avoidance was as simple as swimming to the other end of the tank. Here was proof that learned helplessness could be acquired by fish, just as it could be acquired by dogs.

Interestingly, even when the goldfish were previously trained to avoid the shock, they subsequently became passive when they later faced a series of unavoidable shocks. When a goldfish learns that an unpleasant situation cannot be avoided, this creates an enduring disposition of passivity. Even when it becomes possible to control events, the organism does not take advantage of the opportunity. Like goldfish, people also can acquire learned helplessness. If there is no felt connection between actions and outcomes, initiative can shut down. When repeated efforts have no effect, a person may eventually stop trying. Humans become helpless not because they run out of options, but because they have learned, tragically, that their efforts to achieve success or to avoid pain have had no effect.

good scores on exams and on achievement tests. Attributions are sometimes socialized as elements of gender roles. For example, in 1991, the notorious Teen Talk Barbie doll complained: "Math is hard!"

What attributions are most conducive to learning and to academic success? The answer is equivocal. Ability attributions can be helpful if they reflect beliefs about high ability rather than low ability. Attributions of high ability have a potential downside, however. A person who relies on ability might be reluctant to apply effort and extend perseverance over time because high effort is actually counterevidence to high ability attributions. People who believe they are highly able might be reluctant to try hard. Considering the three dimensions, the best attributions are those that have an internal locus, are controllable, and are stable over time. One attribution fits these categories best—effort.

Effort is arguably the most desirable attribution. It works for success ("I succeeded because I worked hard") and for failure ("I was disappointed in my performance because I did not try hard enough"). Effort is universally adaptive because if a person has experienced success, that person will continue to apply effort in the future. If there has been a failure or setback, there is recourse to trying again and trying harder. Too few students see their success and failure efforts as a consequence of level of effort. In the United States, especially, students are prone to interpret their academic successes as a consequence of high ability. Japanese students, by contrast, are more likely to attribute their success to effort (Holloway, 1988). Effort attributions, in turn, lead to greater applications of effort over time. Could this be one reason that Japanese students routinely outperform American students in international studies of mathematics learning?

Knowing what attributions are most conducive to learning and academic success is useful knowledge for teachers. Teachers are likely to hear a variety of explanations for students' performance:

- The test was too hard.
- I got lucky this time.
- I'm not good at this.
- I'm stupid.
- The teacher doesn't like me.
- I studied really hard this time.
- I wasn't prepared for this test.

Of these explanations, teachers should encourage only the last two, which appeal to effort as the cause of success or failure. To a disappointed student, a teacher can suggest, "Well maybe you should study harder next time." The teacher's suggestion is premised on an assumption that level of effort is a legitimate explanation for the student's performance. A student who prefers a different attribution may not like the suggestion. After all, it places responsibility back on the student and implies that hard work lies ahead. In the long run, though, a teacher does the student a favor by encouraging effort attributions. Of course, ability also enters into explanations for success and failure. But ability can be seen as either fixed or changeable, as we will see later in this chapter. If intellectual ability is changeable, then it can be improved through exercising effort toward its advancement.

Motivation Theories Based on Beliefs About Self

Cognitive Dissonance Theory

Motivation theories vary quite a bit, shifting focus from personal values to explanations for success and failure. Another possible focus for motivation theories is beliefs about oneself (Schunk & Zimmerman, 2006). Cognitive dissonance theory is premised on the idea that people wish for consistency between what they believe (or say they believe) and what they do. If the two are inconsistent, the conflict produces an unsettled feeling of tension.

Whenever beliefs and behavior are contradictory, **cognitive dissonance** can result. The word *dissonance* means "an unharmonious clash." Think of the irritating sound of musical instruments that are out of tune—that's musical dissonance. Cognitive dissonance refers to the unharmonious clash of our ideas with our experience, especially our own behavior. To reduce cognitive dissonance requires a change in either beliefs or behavior so that the two become mutually consistent and harmonious (Festinger, 1962).

Sometimes people change their behavior to match their beliefs; in fact, doing so is often presented as a moral imperative because we are supposed to "practice what we preach." An alternative, and a more theoretically interesting possibility, is that we sometimes change what we believe to match what we do. This second possibility is what makes cognitive dissonance theory particularly interesting as well as potentially useful.

Imagine you are given a choice between two equally attractive alternatives. Despite the difficulty of choosing between the two, you later interpret the choice you made as obviously the better one. In other words, your beliefs changed to match and to justify, or rationalize, the choice you made. A more sinister example is that the cognitive dissonance engendered by lying can be reduced either by admitting the lie (changing behavior) or by coming to believe that the lie is true (changing beliefs). It may be easier to believe that we were telling the truth all along than to admit dishonesty, even if reducing cognitive dissonance requires blatant self-deception.

One conclusion we could draw from cognitive dissonance research and theory is that human beings are not truly rational. Instead, we are *rationalizing* beings. That a thought process is coherent and backed by evidence seems to be less imperative than making it *seem* justified. This may seem like a pessimistic conclusion; nonetheless, there is potential here for positive application. A student may firmly believe, "I don't like science." But what happens if by the skills of a talented teacher the student finds himself fascinated during science class? Such an emotion is inconsistent with the declaration, "I don't like science." For the sake of cognitive consistency (and to reduce cognitive dissonance) the student might conclude instead, "Well, maybe I do like science after all." Another student may strongly believe that he hates to read. But when persuaded or forced to read a novel, he might become captivated by the story and have a desire to read other novels (Duchein & Mealey, 1993). For the sake of consistency, he might revise his beliefs to conclude that, in some cases at least, he actually enjoys reading. In these roundabout ways, new behavior can lead to new beliefs, and those new beliefs can be liberating.

Self-Worth Theory

Beliefs about self can include convictions about likes and dislikes, as we have seen in cognitive dissonance theory. Beliefs can also focus on oneself as a person of worth and dignity. In fact, it's possible to construe much of human behavior as directed toward protecting self-worth. We act in ways that elevate other people's opinions of us, or that shield us from low opinions. This strong motive is the focus of **self-worth theory**. Self-worth theory is quite powerful in explaining the choices we make (Covington, 1984). We want to be seen as able, as competent. The desire to enhance feelings of self-worth leads us to select and pursue goals and activities that will likely result in success. We avoid other goals and activities if they are likely to expose our inabilities and so threaten self-worth.

Strategies chosen to avoid threats to self-worth can be serious impediments to learning and personal growth. For example, in order to protect self-worth, two possible strategies are to choose unrealistically difficult goals or ridiculously easy goals. Why would opposite strategies support the same goal of protecting self-worth? Both do so because neither reveals any information about our true ability. If a student enrolls in a very difficult course without sufficient background, nobody is surprised if that student fails. What could anyone expect given that the course is so hard? Likewise, a student might choose unreasonably easy goals, goals that are far below his or her level of competence. We might regard low aspirations as a waste of ability and potential, but for a person who chooses the easy path that choice could be a way of protecting self-worth. Guaranteed success eliminates the possibility of failure and yields no information about one's true ability, which might be precisely the point.

A similar purpose is served by the various excuses, disclaimers, or provisos that we all make from time to time. A student about to take an important test may say to his fellow students, "I didn't study at all for this test!" This statement is strategic if the goal is to protect a sense of self-worth. After all, if the student does poorly, the outcome is completely understandable. On the other hand, if the student does well he can be credited with an impressive achievement. Perhaps his peers will conclude that the student is highly intelligent for having done so well without having studied. By disclaiming having studied at all, the student can only win. Poor performance is excusable and high performance is impressive—either way, self-worth is preserved. Sometimes on the basketball court I hear my fellow players make similar disclaimers before the game begins. A favorite strategy is to say something like, "I haven't picked up a basketball in two years." By this simple declaration a player's self-worth is effectively insured against later damage. If he plays poorly, we all understand why; if he plays well, we will be in awe—or so he might hope.

A similar purpose is served when a student claims a lack of effort. If he says, "I didn't try at all," the opinions of others are hedged in his favor. Strategies gauged to protect self-worth may have social utility, but they are not necessarily good for education or learning. A student might claim not to have studied for an examination in order to protect self-worth. Another student might claim a lack of effort for a school project or a homework assignment. Low effort signals to everyone that the work product contains little information about the students' true ability. Yet another student might dismiss the importance of an assignment or the educational enterprise altogether. To disengage from the norms and expectations of school, as in learned helplessness, is one way to protect self-worth against injury or attack.

Classrooms are places where feelings of self-worth are always vulnerable to some degree. Feedback about performance and social comparisons about ability are highly salient in the life of a student. Teachers can amplify or attenuate these realities, and should do so, but to remove them altogether is probably impossible and to deny them outright is counterproductive. Teachers should try to understand the importance of self-worth and the strategies that students use to protect those feelings. In making pedagogical choices, teachers can also try to protect those vulnerabilities while curtailing the counterproductive strategies that students sometimes adopt.

Entity and Incremental Theories

As students develop belief systems about themselves and their experiences, they also develop personal theories about the nature of intellectual abilities. These personal theories can differ dramatically from one student to another. According to the model proposed by Dweck and Leggett (1988), students view their intellectual abilities in one of two ways. Some students see their abilities as essentially fixed. They hold an **entity theory** of ability. Intelligence is believed to be present to a greater or lesser degree, and is highly stable through life. No amount of effort can raise ability, and disuse cannot erode it. In the entity view, ability is preset and unalterable.

Students who hold an **incremental theory** of ability see things very differently. To these students, intellectual abilities, including intelligence, are not fixed but instead are modifiable through experience and effort. If a student views his ability as low, this is not a cause for resignation or passivity. Rather, the student can try to increase his or her ability over time. Just because the learner sees his present ability, say, in mathematics or music, as low does not mean it must stay low. Mathematical or musical ability, like the ability to write well or to be knowledgeable in a field of study, can be learned. Ability, to a large extent, is modifiable. Students who perceive ability this way—as alterable through experience—have an advantage over students who see ability as static. For educational purposes, the incremental view of ability is preferable to the entity view.

Perhaps you have detected some overlap between Dweck and Leggett's entity/incremental model of ability and Weiner's attribution theory that we considered earlier. Incremental beliefs align well with effort attributions; entity beliefs align with ability attributions. Successful students are more likely to make effort attributions to explain their academic achievement. They see their immediate performance as a product of effort, and are likely see their intellectual ability as changeable over time. In a later chapter, we will see that the development of expertise is strikingly consistent with entity theories of ability. With focused effort applied over a long timeline, the expert becomes extraordinarily capable.

Self-Efficacy Theory

Among the various belief systems that guide human behavior, self-efficacy beliefs are among the most important. In Albert Bandura's theory, **self-efficacy** beliefs are estimates that people make about their ability to perform specific actions. Self-efficacy refers to the self-assessment of one's ability to perform specific tasks in specific situations. It is a major construct in social science, one that is highly relevant to educators.

Self-efficacy is different from self-esteem, which is concerned with generalized feelings about personal worth. Self-efficacy also differs from self-concept, which is comparatively broad in referring to beliefs about oneself along a wide range of concerns. Self-efficacy is specific. We might hold a high self-concept of ourselves as good students, but our self-efficacy beliefs would depend on the specific academic area. For example, we might have high self-efficacy beliefs about our ability to do well in mathematics or music, but low self-efficacy in creative writing or debate. In athletic domains, self-efficacy would vary by the specific sport. Although Lance Armstrong proved that he was a champion cyclist, he freely admitted that he had poor hand-eye coordination. He had high self-efficacy as cyclist, but neither his self-efficacy nor his skill extended to athletic performance generally. Like Lance Armstrong, we can differentiate the skill areas we excel in from those we don't.

We all have some sense of what we do well and what we do poorly. Each of us has self-efficacy beliefs about dozens or hundreds of specific performance domains. Those beliefs are not necessarily accurate. Self-efficacy is not the same as ability; what we believe about our ability might not be true. Moreover, beliefs about what we can do can have real effects on performance. Self-imposed mental limitations are well known in the world of competitive sports. American weight lifters, for example, have encountered barriers to progress at certain poundages, whereas European lifters have experienced mental barriers at round numbers of kilograms (Mahoney, 1979). In track events, the four-minute mile was long considered to be unattainable until Oxford medical student Roger Bannister broke that temporal threshold in 1954. Only a month later, Australian runner John Landy beat Bannister's time by a full two seconds. Thereafter, many other world-class distance runners ran sub-four-minute miles.

If self-efficacy is not identical with true ability, is that a problem? Should we strive for accuracy in our self-efficacy beliefs? Maybe not. It is not at all clear that having a completely accurate sense of self-efficacy is ideal. Research has shown, for example, that psy-

FIGURE 6.6
*Roger Bannister
Breaks the Four-
Minute Mile. Once
Bannister crossed
the mental barrier,
many others were
able to do the
same.*
[Keystone/
Getty Images.]

chologically healthy people have slightly exaggerated self-efficacy beliefs when judging their social skills and their degree of control in a situation (Bandura, 1986). Strangely, depressed people often have a *more accurate* sense of their social skills and causal control.

Self-deception is not always helpful, of course. In the many cases where self-efficacy differs from true ability, such beliefs are not only inaccurate, they are also self-limiting. Fortunately, self-efficacy is modifiable—a fact that teachers and parents can use to help the developing learner. Modifiability is important because self-efficacy beliefs have real-world consequences on the choices we make and on our development as learners. Self-efficacy influences goal selection, for example. If we believe that we have the ability to achieve a goal, the pursuit of that goal becomes an option. Conversely, if we believe that we lack the necessary ability (whether we actually do or not) then we are not likely to pursue that particular goal. To the extent that personal success arises from the sequence of goal choices we make, self-efficacy will decisively influence our life paths. Self-efficacy influences not only our choice of goals, but also the level of effort we are willing to devote to pursuing them. An abiding belief that we are capable of success in a given context will lead us to exert effort toward attaining that goal. High perceptions of self-efficacy can help us persist when we face tough challenges (Bandura, 1982). Choice of goals, level of effort, and perseverance are all important consequences of self-efficacy beliefs.

FOUR INFLUENCES ON SELF-EFFICACY   Because self-efficacy is so crucial in the developing learner, we must try to understand the forces that shape beliefs about what we can do. Bandura (1986) noted four sources of information that form self-efficacy beliefs. One very important source of information—the most important, in fact—is *enactive attainments*. Enactive attainments refer to actual personal accomplishments. Beliefs about what we *can* achieve in the future are clearly influenced by what we have *already* achieved in the past. That is why one way to influence self-efficacy is to point out a person's previous accomplishments, to remind the person of what he or she has already done. Bandura found that some patients recovering from heart attacks were reluctant to exercise because they feared they were incapable of sustained physical effort. When these patients agreed to try exercising on a treadmill, they learned that they were far more capable of vigorous exercise than they first believed. Their self-efficacy beliefs were raised by their own successful performance, and so they were more likely to exercise again in the future.

Strangely, people are not always convinced of their ability by their own past performance attainments. A person's self-efficacy beliefs can be higher or lower than their true ability. Some students have an inflated sense of their own talents. Others underestimate what they can do despite evidence of competence, perhaps because their performance conflicts with what they believe about themselves. In educational settings, this biased pattern of interpretation can have serious consequences if a student continues to believe, falsely, that he is incapable. A student might be convinced that he has little mathematical ability despite evidence to the contrary, such as high test scores. So even though actual performance attainments are quite important as sources of information about self-efficacy beliefs, they do not guarantee that subsequent beliefs will be accurate or beneficial.

Fortunately, several other sources of information also feed into self-efficacy beliefs. A second source is *vicarious experience*. This refers to our ability to form beliefs *vicariously*, that is, indirectly by observing the experience of other people. A student who doubts her ability might observe the choices and performances of a similar peer and think, "If she can do it, then so can I." In effect, the peer models successful performance. Modeling is an important mode of learning in Bandura's social cognitive theory. Recall that Bandura proposed, contrary to the tenets of behaviorism, that we need not experience reinforcement directly in order to learn. Instead, we can observe what happens to other people as a consequence of their actions. A similar principle applies to self-efficacy beliefs—we can learn about our own abilities by observing what other people can do. When students choose ambitious and capable peers as models for their own behavior, they will enlarge their visions about what they are capable of doing.

A third source of information influencing self-efficacy is *verbal persuasion*. At one time or another, all of us have been encouraged by the affirmations of a respected teacher, relative, or other esteemed adult. We were told to expect more of ourselves, to set our sights higher than we had in the past. That respected person perceived the latent potential within us and helped us to see our own unrecognized possibilities. This kind of influence—what Bandura called verbal persuasion—illustrates the power of teachers to influence the course of students' lives. Many aspiring teachers choose to enter the teaching profession in part because they want to influence students positively during the course of a teaching career.

Of course, verbal persuasion can exert negative as well as positive effects. A discouraging statement from a teacher or parent, even a peer, can have devastating long-term consequences. One careless remark can cast enduring doubts about what a student is capable of achieving. Parents and teachers need to guard against excessively negative statements to students—statements that can deflate their sense of self-efficacy over the long term. Responsible adults must recognize the power of their words to influence young learners. They can use that power to do tremendous good by speaking honestly and positively about students' abilities to learn and to achieve.

In the context of discussing verbal persuasion, we will now consider a very important and related topic—teacher expectations. Teacher expectations do indeed influence student achievement (Brophy, 1983). Highly effective teachers—those who regularly elicit strong gains in student achievement—believe that their students are capable of learning, and that they, as teachers, are capable of teaching them effectively (Brophy, 2006). The largest expectation effects are found among "proactive" teachers who form their own expectations about students' capabilities without being overly swayed by prior achievement, diagnostic labels, or the opinions of students' former teachers. Proactive teachers see their responsibility as actively transforming the students' capabilities rather than simply accommodating to what those students have accomplished in the past. They are willing to adapt their instructional techniques to achieve these goals. If one teaching approach or curriculum does not work, they will try alternatives (Brophy, 2006). Typically, teacher expectation effects explain about 5 to 10 percent of the variance in student achievement during a single school year. During a single year, such an effect size is not huge, but over multiple years it can amount to a very appreciable influence on students' learning.

Building on these research findings, some professional development programs for teachers have spotlighted teacher expectations as being critically important for determining the academic success of students. In years past, vaunted claims were made that teacher expectations could influence even the measured intelligence of students. In one famous experiment, teachers' expectations for their students were manipulated to determine whether those expectations later affected the children's IQ levels (Rosenthal & Jacobsen, 1968). Teachers in an elementary school were the given names of a few students who were expected to make great intellectual progress ("bloomers") during the school year in comparison to their peers. But selection of the "bloomers" was completely random and had nothing to do with their actual IQ scores. The point was to test the influence of teachers' *beliefs* on changes in the children's measured IQ. The researchers reported that the IQ scores of the "bloomers" had increased by the end of the school year. These students seemed to benefit from teachers' positive beliefs and responded with measurably higher IQ scores. Teachers' beliefs were said to result in a **self-fulfilling prophecy** (Merton, 1948).

Can the beliefs and expectations of teachers really have such powerful effects on children's IQ scores? Subsequent analysis cast doubt on the reported findings and conclusions. One problem was that the IQ test used in the study had technical inadequacies, making the data questionable. When teacher expectation effects were found, they were statistically significant only in first and second grades, not in higher grade levels (Wineburg, 1987). Later attempts to replicate the experiment showed only weak effects or no effects at all. Unfortunately, the limitations of the original research were largely ignored in the popular press. The idea of a self-fulfilling prophecy seemed to resonate with the commonsense expectations of the public—namely, that teachers' beliefs, positive or negative, are potent forces in shaping the intellectual growth of students. The data did not support this belief as it pertains to IQ scores, or did so only weakly.

Bandura recognized a fourth source of information that influences self-efficacy beliefs: *physiological state*. Think about how the body responds to a difficult task. Whenever we face a tough challenge, we might become quite nervous. The body inevitably responds. If the heart beats faster and respiration rate increases, this physiological response may raise doubts about our ability to be successful. In this way, high physiological arousal can signal low ability, and therefore low self-efficacy. On the other hand, a low heart rate and a calm state can signal that a person is capable, implying high self-efficacy. Of course, a teacher does not have direct knowledge of a learner's heart rate, but does have some control over the emotional tone of the classroom, and so can indirectly influence a student's physiological state.

These four sources of information—enactive attainments, vicarious experience, verbal persuasion, and physiological state—are crucially important because they influence self-efficacy, and self-efficacy directly affects performance. Many studies have shown that enhanced self-efficacy can lead to measurable improvements in performance, including performance in academic settings. When teachers help students to develop beliefs about their competence in mathematics, for example, students will learn math more effectively and be more likely to pursue the study of mathematics with confidence. Self-efficacy beliefs organize and influence all stages of performance, including goal selection, persistence, and the interpretation of success outcomes. Beliefs affect behavior.

TRIADIC RECIPROCALITY   Bandura recognized the reciprocal influence of beliefs and behavior as part of a more general model of behavior that he called **triadic reciprocality**. The model specifies three components: the person, the environment, and behavior (Figure 8.7). Two of these—the environment and behavior—were commonly acknowledged by behaviorists as important. The third component, the person, includes all the ways that people differ, including self-efficacy beliefs. The triadic reciprocality model postulates that among the three (triadic) components, each influences the other two (reciprocality).

As we have discussed, self-efficacy is not simply a product of behavior (behavior→ person); self-efficacy beliefs can also influence behavior directly (person→behavior). This aspect of triadic reciprocality—that beliefs can influence behavior—implies that high self-efficacy should be an important goal of education. If this is so, then self-efficacy should be regarded as an important focus for teaching. Among the many worthwhile goals that teachers can have for students, the elevation of self-efficacy is among the most important. As teachers take steps to build students' self-efficacy beliefs—whether through enactive attainments, vicarious experience, verbal persuasion, or physiological state—those beliefs will help students to become more effective learners. In the long run, healthy self-efficacy beliefs are essential to every student's success.

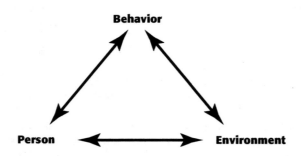

FIGURE 8.7   *Bandura's Triadic Reciprocality Model. Behavior influences (and is influenced by) the external environment as well as by the internal characteristics of the person, including beliefs.*

[Adapted from Bandura, 1986. Reproduced by permission of Pearson Education, Inc.]

Goals

As every teacher knows, motivation varies tremendously from student to student. One point of variation is found in the goals students set for themselves. Even when students share the general goal of being successful in school, the standards by which they judge their success can vary greatly. For example, students can adopt different thresholds of evidence to decide whether or not they are succeeding. To some degree this is appropriate: Whether performance is "good" or "poor" may well be subjective. What a professional athlete defines as impressive athletic performance will probably differ from the average person's definition.

In the same way, success in school can be judged in more than one way. Here, a simple binary distinction is helpful: Progress can be judged against one's own past performance or against the performance of other people. These two ways of judging success have profoundly different implications for how students view themselves and the task at hand.

Task versus Ego Involvement

John Nicholls (1984) proposed two basic ways that students can evaluate their own competence: **task involvement** and **ego involvement**. Although Nicholls presented these dichotomously, they are more accurately viewed as endpoints on a continuum. People are said to be ego-involved if they judge their competence by comparing their own performance to the performance of others. Rather than focusing on the task, their attention is directed toward social comparison. To feel competent under these conditions, a student must perform at least as well as others, and with equal or less effort. Ego-involvement can be induced when tasks are presented as tests of valued skills, such as intelligence. Competition and the presence of an audience can also induce ego involvement.

In Nicholls' theory, people are task-involved if they use their own past performance, rather than the performance of others, as the basis for judging competence. A student who is task-involved is satisfied to know that he is making intellectual progress—that he understands more than he did yesterday or a week ago. The task-involved student is not concerned with his standing relative to peers. Instead, attention is focused on the task at hand. Task involvement has important benefits. Nicholls (1979) found that students who are task-involved are more likely to be intrinsically motivated. Moreover, Nicholls speculated that outstanding creative achievements are more often made by people who are task-involved rather than ego-involved.

In schools, each student's performance is most often evaluated by how it compares to the performance of others. These are conditions that foster ego-involvement. One serious drawback of social comparison is that individuals might be afraid to attempt a task if it could reveal low ability relative to others. Fortunately, teachers can create conditions that are conducive to task-involvement. The most important role for the teacher in this regard is to de-emphasize social comparison as the basis for students' self-evaluation. Teachers can focus on mastery rather than on normative comparisons—on what the student *can do*, rather than on how the student *compares to others*. Teachers can also exercise caution in using competition as a pedagogical device. Finally, a teacher can judiciously choose challenging tasks for students, activities that are neither too easy nor too difficult. Challenging tasks, those that require and will probably yield to high effort, are most likely to generate task-involvement (Nicholls, 1984). Other conditions conducive to task-involvement are the reduction of stress and the reduced salience of extrinsic incentives. All these conditions are to some degree under the control of the teacher.

The distinction between task-involvement and ego-involvement is important and useful. A parallel distinction to that drawn by Nicholls was the identification of learning goals and performance goals among students (Elliott & Dweck, 1988). **Learning goals** are organized around increasing personal competence. **Performance goals** are geared toward gaining the positive judgments of other people. Between these two types of goals, learning goals are the most conducive to school success. For students who struggle with school tasks, learning goals are less likely to lead to discouragement and strategy deterioration.

Goal Properties

Goal-setting is deeply woven into the fabric of human cognition. Starting at age two and a half, children start to form connections between their actions and outcomes that are not physically present (Klossek, Russell, & Dickinson, 2008). Their behavior thereby acquires an instrumental quality that extends their control beyond the immediate environment. Goal-directed behavior is strongly adaptive and indispensable to intelligent thought and action. Goals help to organize behavior and resources toward achieving valued outcomes. The formation and pursuit of goals contributes significantly to success in schools, on the job, and in virtually every context of life. Some goals are preferable to others in maximizing the probability of success. Researchers have found that specific properties of goals bear strongly on the likelihood of those goals being reached, as well as on the level of satisfaction or frustration that accompanies the pursuit of goals.

PROXIMAL AND SPECIFIC GOALS   Goals differ in their operational timeline: whether they are near-term or long-range. On a practical level, near-term **proximal goals** are more likely to be reached than are long-term distal goals (Locke, Shaw, Saari, & Latham, 1981). When students approach tasks that are large and cumbersome—a science project, for example—proximal goals can guide and motivate practical action (Bandura, 1982). Proximal goals can also lead to perceptions of competence and to increased intrinsic motivation. We might wisely set far-off and ambitious **distal goals**, but it is the nearer-term goals—those we will try to accomplish this month, this week, or even today—that are more likely to bring us concretely toward our desired ends. Proximal goals have a further advantage over far-off distal goals: They are correlated with a sense of well-being (Emmons, 1999).

Goals also differ in degree of specificity. **Specific goals** are precisely stated and afford clear criteria to judge whether or not they have been achieved. At a more general level are **abstract goals**, or "goals for goals." Those higher-level goals determine whether or not lesser goals serve valued ends (Haslam & Baron, 1994). One abstract goal might be to become a highly educated person. This general goal can guide the selection and pursuit of more specific goals, such as reading more books or pursuing a master's degree. Typically, proximal goals are also specific goals. Ideally, the specific and proximal goals that guide and motivate our daily behavior are consistent with the longer-range and more abstract goals that define our values and most cherished hopes. A rational goal structure can be judged for its "co-satisfiability"—the degree to which it balances short-term impulses and long-term satisfaction (Bronowski, 1973). Haslam and Baron (1994, p. 44) described goal coherence as consisting of "an integrated vision of the good life as an extended unity in time."

CHALLENGE   Goals have their most positive effects on interest and intrinsic motivation when they are challenging—that is, when they are closely matched to ability. In one research study, elementary school children were asked to choose among classification tasks that varied in difficulty. The children tended to select tasks that were just a little beyond their present abilities and reported those tasks as most interesting (Danner & Lonkey, 1981). The challenging tasks had high information value. The children implicitly sought accurate information about their abilities, a strategy that is opposite to strategies that conceal information about ability in order to protect feelings of self-worth.

TIME MANAGEMENT   One important aspect of goal-directed behavior is the management of goals within the constraints of time. Britton and Tesser (1991) investigated whether college students' ability to manage their time well predicted their grades. The researchers found that two dimensions of time management—short-range planning and time attitudes—predicted total college grades even better than SAT scores. *Short-range* planning included such practices as setting goals for each day and creating a schedule of activities. *Time attitudes* measured whether students felt in control of their time, such as by prioritizing their goals and avoiding unprofitable activities. SAT scores, which are specifically designed to predict college grades, correlated with the students' college grade-point average (GPA) at r = .20. The predictive validity of the time management dimensions was higher, with *short-range planning* correlating with GPA at $r = .25$ and *time attitudes* correlating with GPA at $r = .39$. The time-management aspects of goal setting may have more to do with real-world attainment, including academic success, than we usually appreciate.

COOPERATIVE, COMPETITIVE, AND INDIVIDUALISTIC GOALS   Another dimension of goals is whether their pursuit depends on cooperation, competition, or individual effort. All three goal structures are familiar elements of school life. Researchers have long been interested in which provides the greatest educational benefit. The question is complicated by the fact that cooperation and competition can co-exist, as in the kind of inter-group competition common in team sports. On balance, the research evidence points to the overall superiority of cooperation to both competitive and individualistic goal structures in promoting educational achievement (Johnson, Maruyama, Johnson, Nelson, & Skon, 1981).

Slavin (1980) described specific teaching strategies as **cooperative learning** in which students work in small groups and receive rewards based on group performance rather than individual effort. He found several benefits to cooperative learning, including enhanced group cohesiveness and positive race relations. In most cases, cooperative learning also produced advantages in academic achievement over traditional teaching methods. Slavin found no cases in which cooperative learning produced a disadvantage in learning outcomes. Cooperative goal structures have also been found to be superior to competitive and individualistic goal structures in promoting problem-solving (Johnson, Johnson, & Stanne, 1985).

Goal-setting and goal-directed behavior are important components of an intelligent, successful life. In contrast to biological evolution, which is not goal directed but instead arises from random genetic mutations, the human mind can imagine what possible states of affairs are desirable, and then think and act to achieve those imagined states. The ability to formulate and pursue goals is an important product of education. As we seek to elevate our own intelligent functioning and that of others, we can promote specific and proximal goals as a means to progress toward longer-term aspirations and a greater sense of fulfillment. We can ask our students (and challenge ourselves) to imagine and express those goals, both in speech and in writing, and then stay true to plans to make them reality. To accomplish valued goals through determined pursuit requires sustained volitional control, a topic we consider next under the banner of self-regulation.

Self-Regulation

Volition

When Hilgard proposed the trilogy of mind model, he chose the term *conation* to refer to goal-driven, purposeful activity. He then divided conation into two subprocesses, motivation and volition. This second distinction sharpens the conceptual landscape considerably. **Motivation** refers to all factors that lead up to a decision about a course of action. **Volition** refers to all of the processes that maintain goal-focused behavior once the goal is adopted. The first is *pre-decisional* analysis; the second is *post-decisional* self-regulation (Corno, 1993). The crucial dividing point is the decision to act. The forces that feed into the decision are motivational. After a decision is made to act, the processes that sustain focus toward achieving the selected goal are volitional.

In **action control theory**, psychologists Heinz Heckhausen and Julius Kuhl (1985) suggested an image of how motivation and volition relate sequentially. They took the historical metaphor of Julius Caesar's military campaign in 49 B.C. While in northern Italy, Caesar was warned by the Roman Senate to resign command of his army. He could have complied with the Senate's orders by turning back early in his march toward Rome. But

FIGURE 8.8   *Caesar Crossed the Rubicon River. The phrase, "crossing the Rubicon," refers to the decisive moment when motivation culminates in a volitional decision to act.*
[Rodney Shackell/DK]

the leader reached a critical point at the Rubicon River. When Caesar crossed the Rubicon River, he committed himself to challenging the leadership of Rome and to sparking a civil war. Crossing the Rubicon was the decisive point, the point of no return, when turning back became inconceivable or nearly so. In these metaphorical terms, Heckhausen and Kuhl cast the point of decision as "crossing the Rubicon" in all goal-directed behavior (Corno, 1993). The Rubicon of decision-making divides motivation from volition.

Both processes, motivation and volition, are vital to successful action. Both can also go awry, leading to ineffective behavior. To illustrate, let us say a student has been assigned to write a term paper that is due on Monday. It's Friday night, and there is just enough time over the weekend to write a paper that will earn a grade of B. The paper will require some background research, an outline, and many hours of writing and rewriting. The student is motivated to write the paper, but faces some distractions, including the options of going to the beach or attending a concert. His motivation to write the term paper competes with other attractive possibilities.

Just after dinner on Friday night, the student makes a decision to set aside all distractions and to dedicate the weekend to writing the term paper. Once the student decides to write the paper, volitional processes take over. These include decisions about what subgoals must be pursued, and how to arrange those activities over a workable timeline. For example, the student might decide to complete an outline on Friday evening, to produce a good draft by the end of the day on Saturday, and to have a polished paper by Sunday night. Of course, the decision to pursue a goal does not guarantee that the goal will be achieved. Setbacks and distractions can litter the pathway of good intentions. Subgoals that initially seemed reasonable can turn out to be overly ambitious. Unplanned events, such as a phone call from a family member or a surprise visit from a friend, can throw a plan off course. Volitional processes keep us on track despite impediments to progress. Some of us are better than others at dealing with distractions and difficulties. Just as we differ in the motivational forces that lead to goal-setting, so we also differ in volitional skills that keep us focused on achieving our chosen goals.

In reality, then, making a decision to pursue a particular goal does not guarantee that we will maintain that commitment over time. A decision to write a term paper over the weekend can be derailed by distractions, fatigue, or even forgetfulness. We all face impediments to the volitional decisions we make. We also differ in our ability to "protect" our own volitional intentions from disruption. Perhaps you know iron-willed, highly focused people who pursue their goals relentlessly. You might know other people who are comparatively poor at following through on their commitments. They are easily distracted; perhaps they even wish for distractions so that they have an excuse to abandon their plans. These individuals are poor at protecting their volitions. They may have their motivational priorities in order and dependably choose worthwhile goals, but are weak at follow-through. From these hypothetical examples you can see value in equipping students not only to be focused motivationally, but also skilled volitionally. Each of us needs the ability to protect our intentions so that we can stay focused, even if we sometimes deviate from a preset plan.

Volitional control, like any form of self-regulation, can improve with practice. Students can employ volitional control strategies when facing social distractions or self-doubt (Corno, 1993). For example, a student might reward herself with relaxation or recreation after completing her math homework. Self-rewards often entail the **delay of gratification**, which in itself may be crucial for success in schools and elsewhere. Children vary significantly in their ability to delay gratification. Psychologist Walter

INTEREST MAGNET 8.3

Is Hypnosis Real?

"You are feeling sleepy, very sleepy. When I snap my fingers, you will believe you are a chicken." So goes the cliché of hypnosis. Is it hocus-pocus fakery or a genuine form of mind control? Neither one, actually. Hypnosis is a state of consciousness induced to make a person more receptive to suggestion. Uses of hypnotism range from entertainment (e.g., getting people to act like chickens) to treatment of chronic pain. The exact nature of hypnosis has been highly controversial, however. One extreme interpretation is that hypnosis does not really exist as a psychological phenomenon, but simply involves role-playing on the part of the hypnotized person. The other extreme view is that hypnosis is a form of "mind control" that can compel a person to do something against his or her will. Neither interpretation is consistent with the evidence.

Most psychologists now accept the reality of a hypnotic state and agree on its usefulness, but still disagree on its nature. Although different theories have been advanced to account for hypnotism, most explanations accept that the hypnotized person is in a highly relaxed state. A hypnotist almost always tries to induce this state by instructing a person to close his eyes, and by suggesting that the person is becoming more relaxed and his limbs are becoming "heavy." Physiological changes attest to the authenticity of the hypnotic state. For example, hypnotism is associated with reduced sensitivity to pain. In some people, the pupils become less reactive to light and therefore do not constrict as readily as they would in a normal state. Brain researchers have documented a shift in brain waves toward alpha

rhythms, EEG signals that are midway between alert states ("beta") and sleep states ("delta").

A highly relaxed brain state makes some people much more open to suggestion (Nash, 2001). A suggestion during the hypnotic state might prompt unusual behavior for the sake of entertainment, a practice called stage hypnosis. However, hypnosis can also be applied to pursue an important outcome, such as weight loss, cessation of smoking, reduction of chronic pain, and other important goals. Hypnotism has long been used by some dentists as a pain-management strategy for patients, and was employed by medical doctors before the development of reliable anesthetics. One use of hypnotism that is much more controversial and fraught with danger is "memory recovery." This involves use of hypnosis to recall memories—often traumatic memories from childhood. Research has shown that such memories can feel true even if they are false. Because hypnosis places the person in a relaxed state, even a false memory can be "remembered" without much effort. The person can mistake ease of recall for the truth of the memory (Nash, 2001).

Nevertheless, hypnosis is now widely acknowledged to be useful. Hypnotism is used in the treatment of certain disease conditions, such as asthma. It can also add value to psychotherapy, improving the effectiveness of treatment. Moreover, growing evidence from brain scans shows that the hypnotized brain exhibits different patterns of activation than a non-hypnotized brain. The hypnotic state is real, not magical, and it can be useful as well as entertaining.

Mischel showed four-year-old children a marshmallow and then offered a choice: Each child could eat one marshmallow immediately or have two after the psychologist returned to the room about 15 minutes later (Mischel, Shoda, & Rodriguez, 1989). Mischel found that children who opted to wait for two marshmallows—those who could delay gratification—were more likely to be successful students as teenagers. They had higher SAT scores, were more goal-focused, and had a greater capacity to cope with stress.

Volitional control strategies include the ability to manage such intrusive emotions as frustration and boredom. A larger set of **self-regulation strategies** have been recognized as strong predictors of academic success (Pintrich, 2000; Zimmerman & Pons, 1986). These strategies include goal-setting, planning, seeking information, monitoring progress, and structuring the environment to reduce distractions. Strategies that protect volitional commitments can be seen as "meta" functions alongside metacognition. Just as higher-order cognition employs metacognitive functioning, so too it relies on metavolitional processes. In Vygotskian fashion, students can focus on and protect their volitional intentions by observing the same skilled process in others, including the teacher. In group processes also, students can learn from others how to stay focused on the task at hand, monitor progress toward goals, and persist through difficulties and setbacks.

Volitional control is important to effective intellectual activity. Intelligent problem solving requires breaking down a complex problem into multiple subgoals and pursuing each in a sensible order, without losing track of any. For some people, the volitional drive to achieve chosen goals is so intense that their determination almost defies belief. Yet exceptional perseverance through setbacks can lead to eventual vindication. Unusual grit through a gauntlet of rejections can become legendary. The novelist Stephen King is rumored, early in his career, to have driven a spike through his many rejection letters from potential publishers and displayed the sheaf near his typewriter. In cases where dogged perseverance pays off, it looks like virtue; in other cases, though, it can appear delusional. Does extraordinary success require a degree of volitional intensity that seems imbalanced or even pathological? Possibly. But extreme volition can also be counterproductive in everyday situations. After all, intelligence requires not only the ability be focused on goals, but also the sense to disengage from strategies when they are not working. For lower-ability learners, this disengagement can be challenging as those students sometimes persist long after their strategies have proven to be ineffective (Corno, 1993).

Volitional control is not only important for success, it is also necessary for developing the high levels of skill that constitute expert performance. In the next chapter on cognitive development, we will see that expertise is achieved only after many years of dedicated engagement in a field. World-class performance requires a degree of focus and self-discipline that is unusual in the general population. In the development of expertise, volitional control over thought, action, and effort are indispensable.

New Directions

Perhaps by its very nature, rational cognitive activity is simpler and easier to understand than are human feelings, motives, and intentions. Theories of hot cognition—of emotion, motivation, and volition—are certainly complex. Every valuable framework presented in this chapter, such as self-efficacy theory or attribution theory, seems to capture a slice of what is important. None of the frameworks seems to be a candidate for a grand theory that can bring order to the many different aspects of motives, feelings, and intentionality.

One possible direction for developing a more comprehensive theory is to combine constructs from different models to present a fuller picture of the feeling, striving person. For example, aptitudes can be considered in combined pairs. Such **aptitude complexes** combine two or more motivational traits, or they may combine a motivational trait with a cognitive dimension, such as intelligence (Snow, 1992). The hope is that with a more complete description of the student by trait pairs or higher-order complexes, more precise recommendations can be made about suitable instructional approaches.

Motivation theory is also finding expression in teaching practices. Historically, the impetus for child-centered teaching approaches has been partly to give the individual child choice over activities, as well as choice within activities. The assumption is that self-direction is more motivating than teacher-centered and highly prescriptive instruction.

Similar benefits might apply to learning that is mediated by computer technologies. Computer-based learning environments can offer a high degree of sensory interest (through captivating audio and video) as well as adapt to the child's pace of learning. Opportunities for social interaction over computer networks offer additional motivational benefits alongside cognitive advantages (Wigfield, Eccles, Schiefele, Roeser, & Davis-Kean, 2006).

The advancement of motivation theory is important because motivation touches such vital practical concerns. Much of the disparate achievement in education is the inevitable result of differences in motivation for learning. Nicholls (1979) proposed that schools could work toward equality of optimum motivation—the ideal that *all* students ought to have the motivational resources to be successful learners. The goal of **motivational equity** can be seen as a natural complement to the broader ideal of equity in educational achievement and is arguably a necessary condition for greater parity in educational outcomes.

Learning Strategies

The theories presented in this chapter lend themselves to practical application. Widespread negative feelings toward school, for example, sharpen the imperative to use our current understanding to reverse the pattern. Our growing knowledge of "hot cognitions" can help make the experience of learners more enjoyable and more positively directed toward goals that will lead to long-term success.

The strategies presented below are a sampling of the many potential applications of motivation theory to educational practice. Only a subset will be relevant to any single context, and then only by tailoring the strategy to particular characteristics of the students. Whenever an educator applies a general theoretical principle, it is wisely done with a clinical eye, one that appreciates the unique considerations that each instance requires.

1 *Develop positive emotional associations.* The human mind is associative, a truth both behavioral and cognitive psychologists appreciate. Unpleasant negative emotions frequently become associated with the objects and contexts of education, including books, desks, classrooms, and teachers. Good teachers find ways to infuse students' experience with positive feelings that can become generalized to learning.

2 *Present the right conditions for flow.* One manifestation of positive emotion is the state of high attentional focus called flow. When the demands of an activity are closely matched to the ability of a person, that task can be completely absorbing—so much so that the person can lose track of time and the larger context. Teachers may experience flow states while teaching; they might also try to encourage the conditions that will help their students to feel flow as they go about their work.

3 *Encourage effort attributions.* Not all attributions are equally beneficial. Ideally, students develop attributional styles that emphasize an internal locus. Among attributions with an internal locus, effort attributions are probably best. When students see their successes as the product of effort applied over time, they know how to proceed when faced with a new challenge. They also have an optimistic recourse if they experience failure. An effort attribution means that it's time to try again, and possibly harder.

4 *Watch for evidence of learned helplessness.* Whenever a student concludes that there is no connection between effort and outcomes, education has effectively ended. Slow learners and students with disabilities are particularly vulnerable to discouragement and to simply giving up. Teachers must be alert to impending frustration and do whatever they can to avert learned helplessness. They must try to ensure

that effort does not cease, and that every student experiences some success.

5 *Build self-efficacy through verbal persuasion.* Self-efficacy beliefs are constructed through several sources of information. One of the most important is verbal persuasion. A respected peer or adult can communicate to a student that he or she is able to rise to the challenge. A teacher has substantial power to do good by helping students recognize their ability to succeed when that ability is allied with steady effort.

6 *Encourage incremental theories of ability.* Many students develop "entity" theories, which portray abilities as predetermined and fixed. A much better stance is to see abilities as changeable or improvable over time. This is the "incremental" view of ability. Those who see ability as improvable will have options open for them. Even if students presently lack ability in a domain, that lack is not necessarily permanent. Students with an incremental view see ability as potentially improvable with effort.

7 *Develop task-involvement in students.* Students judge their success according to different criteria. One standard for judging success is comparison with other students; in this case the student is ego-involved. Ego-involvement is not as adaptive in the long run as task-involvement. Teachers can encourage task-involvement, where the basis for judging competence is students' gains compared to their own past performance. Social comparison can be toned down or minimized.

8 *Teach students to protect volitional intentions.* Every successful person knows how to make good decisions, and how to follow through after those decisions have been made. Follow-through requires the protection of volitional intentions from competing goals, distraction, fatigue, and discouragement. Through cognitive modeling, encouragement, and reminders, teachers can help instill volitional control skills in their students.

9 *Develop students' perseverance.* Many people who eventually achieve success and acclaim do so through unusual perseverance. The capacity for high volitional control is tremendously valuable. Teachers understand that great achievements are never easy. One vital educational goal for all students should be to develop the ability to persist through difficulty in order to achieve valued and challenging goals.

10 *Set specific and proximal goals.* Ultimate goals provide overall direction to life's decisions, but near-term and precisely stated goals are those most likely to lead to measurable progress and to well-being. Teachers and students alike need to develop habits of setting specific and proximal goals. These goal structures lead to higher levels of satisfaction, and they contribute directly to an intelligent life.

These ten strategies show that theories of emotion, motivation, and volition lend themselves to direct application in educational settings. To the degree that teachers can help students develop positive feelings toward learning, as well as positive beliefs about themselves as learners, important goals of education will be advanced. The strategies apply not only to teachers' instructional decisions, but also to how teachers view their own professional skills and growth. The best schools are filled with positive and highly motivated students and teachers.

Conclusion

Ernest Hilgard's model of the trilogy of mind explicitly acknowledged that mental activity was not a simple matter of cool rationality. This was a necessary corrective to the simplistic assumptions of information-processing theory. Cognitive science, itself a reaction to the anti-mentalist zeal of radical behaviorists, was largely centered on understanding "cool" cognitions by looking to its favorite metaphor, the digital computer. Unfortunately, it left precious little room for purposeful striving. Bruner (1990) lamented the early omission of will and emotion from information-processing psychology:

With the mind equated to [a computer] program, what should the status of mental states be—old fashioned mental states identifiable not by their programmatic characteristics in a computational system but by their subjective making? There could be no place for "mind" in such a system—"mind" in the sense of intentional states like believing, desiring, intending, grasping a meaning. (pp. 8, 9)

The computer metaphor is a wonderful heuristic for research, an excellent entry-point into the otherwise bewildering complexity of the mind and mental processes. But taken too seriously it turns the human mind into a "living machine," a grotesque depiction that humanistic psychologists, among others, detested (May, 1969). Unlike machine computation, human thought is imbued with emotions, wishes, and intentions.

Hilgard proposed a trilogy of mind composed of cognition (rational thought), affect (emotional thought), and conation (purposeful thought). Hilgard also subdivided conation into motivation (forces that feed into decisions) and volition (forces that control thought and behavior after decisions). We have followed Hilgard's typology in exploring "hot" cognitions by considering, in turn, emotion, motivation, and volition. All three are vital to the mission of education; each is within the orbit of educational concerns.

Even with helpful guidance from Hilgard's typology, the subject of this chapter is complex. Its inherent complexity is partly related to distinctively cognitive aspects of the mind. People have belief systems about what they can do (self-efficacy), about their own abilities (entity and incremental abilities), about the probable payoff from courses of action (ex-pectancy-value theories), and about what constitutes success (ego- versus task-involvement). The power of belief is manifest negatively as learned helplessness and positively as unusual perseverance toward high achievement. Indeed, knowledge that belief systems are learnable makes these subjects even more complex, but also potentially alterable.

Theories of hot cognition—emotion, motivation, and volition—must be considered an unfinished project. Cognitive analysis of "cool" cognition has led to great advances in organizing the vast array of cognitive abilities and uncovering their mechanisms. Perhaps information-processing psychologists began with the computer metaphor intuitively realizing that the problem of understanding rational thought was more tractable than comprehending human feelings, drive, and will. Progress toward the identification of psychological constructs dealing with emotion, motivation, and will have been slower and more difficult. Yet for all the remaining work to be done, there is a greater recognition than ever that an understanding of the complete range of mental functions is necessary not only to a complete science of mind, but also for the extension and improvement of human functioning.

For now we have to content ourselves with theories that are not neatly integrated, but nonetheless hold important applications to teaching and learning. Building on our best theories, we can employ strategies to help students understand that they are capable of experiencing success—or, if they lack ability, that it can develop over time. We can help students to enjoy learning, and when learning becomes difficult, to persist. With guidance from theories of emotion, motivation, and volition, we have strategies to shape the feelings and belief systems that help students advance toward their highest potential as learners.

References

Amabile, T. M., Hill, K. G., Hennessey, B. A., & Tighe, E. M. (1994). The work performance inventory: Assessing intrinsic and extrinsic motivational orientations. *Journal of Personality and Social Psychology, 66*(3), 950–967.

Asimov I. (1950). *I, Robot*. New York: Gnome Press.

Atkinson, J. W. (1958). *Motives in fantasy, action, and society*. Princeton, NJ: Van Nostrand.

Bandura, A. (1982). Self-efficacy mechanism in human agency. *American Psychologist, 2*, 122–147.

Bandura, A. (1986). *Social foundations of thought and action: A social cognitive theory*. Upper Saddle River, NJ: Prentice Hall.

Berlyne, D. E., & Frommer, F. D. (1966). Some determinants of the incidence and content of children's questions. *Child Development, 37*, 177–189.

Bornstein, M. H., Davidson, L., Keyes, C. L. M., & Moore, K. A. (Eds.)(2003). *Well-being: Positive development across the life course*. Mahwah, NJ: Lawrence Erlbaum Associates.

Bower, G. H. (1994). Some relations between emotions and memory. In P. Ekman & R. J. Davidson (Eds.), *The nature of emotions: Fundamental questions* (pp. 303–305). New York: Oxford University Press.

Bower, G. H., & Forgas, J. P. (2001). Mood and social memory. In J. P. Forgas (Ed.), *Handbook of affect and social cognition* (pp. 95–120). Mahwah, NJ: Lawrence Erlbaum Associates.

Britton, B. K., & Tesser, A. (1991). Effects of time management practices on college grades. *Journal of Educational Psychology, 83*(3), 405–410.

Bronowski, J. (1973). *The ascent of man*. Boston: Little, Brown, & Company.

Brophy, J. E. (1983). Research on the self-fulfilling prophecy and teacher expectations. *Journal of Educational Psychology, 73*, 631–661.

Brophy, J. E. (2006). Observational research on genetic aspects of classroom learning. In P. A. Alexander & P. H. Winne (Eds.), *Handbook of educational psychology* (2nd ed.)(pp. 755–780). Mahwah, NJ: Lawrence Erlbaum Associates.

Bruner, J. S. (1966). *Toward a theory of instruction*. Cambridge: Harvard University Press.

Bruner, J. S. (1990). *Acts of meaning*. Cambridge, MA: Harvard University Press.

Cacioppo, J. T., Petty, R. E., Feinstein, J. A., & Jarvis, W. B. G. (1996). Dispositional differences in cognitive motivation: The life and times of individuals varying in need for cognition. *Psychological Bulletin, 119*(2), 197–253.

Cameron, J., & Pierce, W. D. (1994). Reinforcement, reward, and intrinsic motivation: A meta-analysis. *Review of Educational Research, 64*(3), 363–443.

Corno, L., (1993). The best-laid plans: Modern conceptions of volition and educational research. *Educational Researcher, 22*(2), 14–22.

Covington, M. V. (1984). The self-worth theory of achievement motivation: Findings and implications. *The Elementary School Journal, 85*(1) 5–20.

Csikszentmihalyi, M. (1975). *Beyond boredom and anxiety*. Hoboken, NJ: Jossey-Bass.

Danner, F. W., & Lonkey, E. (1981). A cognitive-developmental approach to the effects of rewards on intrinsic motivation. *Child Development, 52*, 1043–1052.

deCharms, R. (1976). *Enhancing motivation*. New York: Irvington.

Deci, E. L. (1975). *Intrinsic motivation*. New York: Plenum.

Duchein, M. A., & Mealey, D. L. (1993). Remembrance of books past . . . long past: Glimpses into aliteracy. *Reading Research and Instruction, 33*, 13–28.

Dweck, C. S., & Leggett, E. L. (1988). A social-cognitive approach to motivation and achievement: *Journal of Personality and Social Psychology, 54*, 5–12.

Elliot, E. S., & Dweck, C. S. (1988). Goals: An approach to motivation and achievement. *Journal of Personality and Social Psychology, 54*(1), 5–12.

Emmons, R. A. (1999). *The psychology of ultimate concerns*. New York: The Guilford Press.

Festinger, L. (1962). Cognitive dissonance. *Scientific American, 207*, 93–102.

Fishbein, M., & Ajzen, I. (1974). Attitudes towards objects as predictors of single and multiple behavioural criteria. *Psychological Review, 81(1)*, 29–74.

Frumkin, K., & Brookshire, K. H. (1969). Conditioned fear training and later avoidance learning in the goldfish. *Psychonomic Science, 16*(3), 159–160.

Garber, J., & Seligman, M. E. P. (Eds.)(1980). *Human helplessness: Theory and applications*. New York: Academic Press.

Gardner, H. (1991). *The unschooled mind*. New York: Basic Books.

Gottfried, A. E. (1985). Academic intrinsic motivation in elementary and junior high school students. *Journal of Educational Psychology, 77*, 631–645.

Harter, S. (1982). A developmental perspective on some parameters of self-regulation in children. In P. Karoly & F. H. Kanfer (Eds.), *Self-management and behavior change: From theory to practice* (pp. 165–204). New York: Pergamon Press.

Haslam, N., & Baron, J. (1994). Intelligence, personality, and prudence. In R. J. Sternberg & P. Ruzgis (Eds.), *Intelligence and personality* (pp. 32–58). New York: Cambridge University Press.

Heckhausen, H., & Kuhl, J. (1985). From wishes to action: The dead ends and short cuts on the long way to action. In M. Frese & J. Sabini (Eds.), *Goal directed behavior: The concept of action in psychology* (pp. 134–160). Hillsdale, NJ: Lawrence Erlbaum Associates.

Herrera, T. (2002). An interview with Liping Ma: Do not forget yourself as a teacher of yourself. *ENC Focus, 9*(3), 16–20.

Hilgard, E. R. (1980). The trilogy of mind: Cognition, affection, and conation. *Journal of the History of the Behavioral Sciences, 16*, 107–117.

Holloway, S. D. (1988). Concepts of ability and effort in Japan and the United States. *Review of Educational Research, 58*(3), 327–345.

Hull, C. L. (1943). *Principles of behavior.* New York: Appleton-Century.

Johnson, D. W., Maruyama, G., Johnson, R., Nelson, D., & Skon, L. (1981). Effects of cooperative, competitive, and individualistic goal structures on achievement: A meta-analysis. *Psychological Bulletin, 89*, 47–62.

Johnson, R. T., Johnson, R. W., & Stanne, M. B. (1985). Effects of cooperative, competitive, and individualistic goal structures on computer-assisted instruction. *Journal of Educational Psychology, 77*, 668–677.

Klossek, U. M. H., Russell, J., & Dickinson, A. (2008). The control of instrumental action following outcome devaluation in young children aged between 1 and 4 yrs. *Journal of Experimental Psychology: General, 137*(1), 39–51.

Locke, E. A., Shaw, K. N., Saari, L. M., & Latham, G. P. (1981). Goal setting and task performance. *Psychological Bulletin, 90*, 125–152.

Maehr, M. L. (1976). Continuing motivation: An analysis of a seldom considered educational outcome. *Review of Educational Research, 46*, 443–462.

Mahoney, M. j. (1979). Cognitived skills and athletic performance. In P. C. Kendall & S. D. Hollon (Eds.), *Cognitive-behavioral interventions,* (pp. 423–443). New York: Academic Press.

Maier, S. F., Seligman, M. E. P., & Solomon, R. L. (1969). Pavlovian fear conditioning and learned helplessness. In B. A. Campbell & R. M. Church (Eds.), *Punishment and aversive behavior* (pp. 299–342). New York: Appleton-Century-Crofts.

Malone, T. W. (1981). Toward a theory of intrinsically motivating instruction. *Cognitive Science, 4,* 333–369.

Maslow, A. H. (1968). *Toward a psychology of being* (2nd ed.). New York: Van Nostrand Reinhold.

May, R. (1969). *Love and will.* New York: Delta.

McClelland, D. C. (1961). *The achieving society.* Princeton, NJ: Van Nostrand.

Merton, R. K. (1948). The self-fulfilling prophecy. *Antioch Review, 8*, 193–210.

Mischel, W., Shoda, Y., & Rodriguez, M. L. (1989). Delay of gratification in children. *Science, 244*, 933–938.

Murray, H. A., (1943). *The Thematic Apperception Test.* Cambridge, MA: Harvard University Press.

Nash, M. R. (2001). The truth and the hype of hypnosis. *Scientific American, 285*, 46–55.

Nicholls, J. G. (1979). Quality and equality in intellectual development: The role of motivation in education. *American Psychologist, 34*, 1071–1084.

Nicholls, J. G. (1984). Conceptions of ability and academic motivation. In R. Ames & C. Ames (Eds.), *Research on motivation in education: Vol. 1. Student motivation* (pp. 39–73). Orlando, FL: Academic Press.

Ortony, A., & Turner, T. J. (1990). What's basic about basic emotions? *Psychological Review, 97*, 315–331.

Padilla, A. M. (1973). Effects of prior and interpolated shock exposures on subsequent avoidance learning by goldfish. *Psychological Reports, 32*, 451–456.

Panksepp, J. (1994). The basics of basic emotion. In P. Ekman & R. J. Davidson (Eds.), *The nature of emotions: Fundamental questions* (pp. 20–24). New York: Oxford University Press.

Parrot, W. (2001). *Emotions in social psychology.* Philadelphia: Psychology Press.

Picard, R. W. (1995). *Affective computing.* MIT Media Laboratory Perceptual Computing Section Technical Report No. 321.

Picard, R. W. (1997). *Affective computing.* Cambridge: MIT Press.

Pintrich, P. R. (2000). The role of goal orientation in self-regulated learning. In M. Boekaerts, P. R. Pintrinch, & M. Zeidner (Eds.), *Handbook of self-regulation* (pp. 451–502). San Diego, CA: Academic Press.

Plutchik, R. (1980). A general psychoevolutionary theory of emotion. In R. Plutchik & H. Kellerman (Eds.), *Emotion, theory, research, and experience: Volume 1: Theories of emotion* (pp. 3–33). New York: Academic Press.

Plutchik, R. (2001). The nature of emotions. *American Scientist, 89*, 344–350.

Rosenthal, R., & Jacobsen, L. (1968). *Pygmalion in the classroom: Teacher expectation and pupils' intellectual development.* New York: Holt, Rinehart & Winston.

Rotter, J. B. (1966). Generalized expectancies for internal versus external control of reinforcement, *Psychological Monographs, 80*, (1, Whole No. 609).

Schunk, D. H., & Zimmerman, B. J. (2006). Competence and control beliefs: Distinguishing the means and ends. In P. A. Alexander & P. H. Winne (Eds.), *Handbook of educational psychology* (2nd ed.)(pp. 349–367). Mahwah, NJ: Lawrence Erlbaum Associates.

Seligman, M. E. P. (1975). *Helplessness.* San Francisco: W. H. Freeman.

Simonton, D. K. (1984). *Genius, creativity, and leadership.* Cambridge, MA: Harvard University Press.

Slavin, R. E. (1980). Cooperative learning. *Review of Educational Research, 50*, 315–342.

Snow, R. E. (1992). Aptitude theory: Yesterday, today, and tomorrow. *Educational Psychologist, 27*(1), 5–32.

Snow, R. E., Corno, L. & Jackson, D. III (1996). Individual differences in affective and conative functions. In D. C. Berliner & R. Calfee (Eds.), *Handbook of educational psychology* (pp. 243–310). New York: Macmillan.

Vansteenkiste, M., Lens, W., & Deci, E. L. (2006). Intrinsic versus extrinsic goal contents in self-determination theory: Another look at the quality of academic motivation. *Educational Psychologist, 41*(1), 19–31.

Vinge, V. (1993). *The coming technological singularity: How to survive in the post-human era.* http://www-rohan.sdsu.edu/faculty/vinge/misc/singularity.html.

Watson, D., & Clark, L. A. (1994). Emotions, moods, traits, and temperaments: Conceptual distinctions and empirical findings. In P. Ekman & R. J. Davidson (Eds.), *The nature of emotions: Fundamental questions* (pp. 89–93). New York: Oxford University Press.

Weiner, B. W. (1985). An attributional theory of achievement motivation and emotion. *Psychological Review, 92*, 548–573.

White, R. W. (1959). Motivation reconsidered: The concept of competence. *Psychological Review, 66*, 297–333.

Wigfield, A., Eccles, J. S., Schiefele, U., Roeser, R. W., & Davis-Kean, P. (2006). Development of achievement motivation. In W. Damon & R. M. Lerner (Eds.), *Handbook of child psychology* (6th ed., Vol. 3)(pp. 933–1002). Hoboken, NJ: John Wiley and Sons.

Wineburg, S. (1987). Does research count in the lives of behavioral scientists? *Educational Researcher, 16*(9), 42–44.

Yerkes, R. M., & Dodson, J. D. (1908). The relation of strength of stimulus to rapidity of habit formation. *Journal of Comparative Neurology of Physiology, 18*, 459–482.

Zimmerman, B. J., & Pons, M. M. (1986). Development of a structured interview for assessing student use of self-regulated learning strategies. *American Educational Research Journal, 23*(4), 614–628.

9 Unit Planning

Unit Planning

Unit planning, or long-range planning, at its simplest, is the decision to teach a series of related lessons on a particular theme. For example, a teacher might decide to teach about the fur trade. Such a theme could take from several days to several weeks to teach. At the most basic level the teacher, when planning such a unit, would consider the major or foundational objectives of the unit, the best instructional approaches for the various lessons, how many lessons, what resources might be needed, and, finally, the best means of assessing the students' learning during and after the unit. There are, of course, other considerations, such as learner characteristics and subject matter, but the basic elements of a unit are not difficult.

When thinking of the major objectives, the learner-centered teacher asks, "What do I want students to know and be able to do?" and "What attitudes, values, and appreciations are desirable?" Very often the objectives are laid out in the state curriculum guide. It is advantageous to have a range of instructional strategies. Some lessons in your unit might require direct instruction through lecture or video. Other lessons will need an interactive, constructivist approach, with the teacher building knowledge with the students. Other choices might involve group work such as cooperative learning or experiential learning, with simulations and role playing. There may be times when the students work individually. A variety of approaches is normally best. Consideration must be given to the nature of the learners, their academic backgrounds, and any special needs. After instruction is carried out, the teacher determines if the students have met the objectives and if the planning and instruction were effective. Unit planning essentially involves a three-step process of planning, implementing, and evaluation.

Good planning improves classroom management. It produces interesting attainable goals and higher student achievement. It is a good idea to inform students of the plans. Instruction is most efficient when the objectives, content, and the way it is presented and evaluated are congruent, and when a course is divided into units and then structured and sequenced into individual lessons for clarity and ease of learning and to avoid confusion. Designing units and lessons to achieve educational objectives is both an art and an applied science as decision making occurs. A professional doesn't "wing it."

WHY PLAN UNITS?   A bridge is not built without a blueprint; a diamond is not cut without a careful plan. A professional teacher needs to plan. It is simply not sufficient merely to follow the chapters and pages of a text or workbook. What does the curriculum guide suggest? What is the grade level? What are the ages, capabilities, needs, and interests of the students? How much can be done in a semester, a month, a week, a lesson? What teaching methods and student activities are best? What materials and resources should be used? There are no short cuts. Research shows the relationship between student achievement and teachers who plan and are organized. Lessons do not spring out of thin air. Instead, they should arise from the broad objectives of units that are planned to achieve course objectives.

WHAT IS A UNIT?   A course should flow from one topic to another to promote integrated student understanding and performance capability. *Units* are centered on a topic, theme, or major concept and organize the course into manageable, cohesive divisions that focus learning; units center learning and instruction on course objectives. Units may be either *interdisciplinary* (integrating more than one subject area) or *subject focused* (staying within a specific subject area).

Courses are typically divided into several units (themes), consisting of a series of from three to twenty or more lessons that tie together into a whole. Just as lessons are to achieve unit objectives, units are to meet course objectives. A unit is based on a broad problem or area of investigation and is an arrangement of content (product and process), materials, and activities around a central topic. A good unit plan replaces blind acceptance of the text as the basis for curricular organization (and day-to-day planning based on expediency) with a series of meaningful, internally unified learning experiences. Some people think a unit plan is an outline of the content to be covered, but much more is involved. Good unit planning considers the myriad of variables you must face to foster student "success experiences."

By now you may have developed some proficiency in planning and delivering lessons. Units and lessons are similar in several ways. In a sense, a unit plan is like a large lesson plan. Both have objectives (unit objectives are broad); identifiable content; introductory, developmental, and culminating activities and teaching methods; and ways of assessing student progress. Good lesson and unit plans are based on knowledge of course objectives, learners, subject matter and organization of these for instruction, suitable teaching methods and student activities, and tacit knowledge picked up from daily classroom experiences. Units are different from lessons in that lessons must link together to achieve unit outcomes. The first lesson hooks to the next and subsequent lessons, the second lesson hooks to the following lesson and subsequent lessons, and so forth.

Good unit planning follows the basic steps of effective decision making for teaching:

1. *Needs assessment:* Student readiness and needs
2. *Objectives:* Knowledge, skills, and values
3. *Presentation:* Content; instructional strategies and methods; materials and resources; communicating expectations and classroom management
4. *Assessment* (formative and summative) and *evaluation* of the unit.

Sensible but creative choices can be made through careful course, unit, and lesson planning. Berliner (1984) describes the preinstructional, during instruction, postinstructional, and climate decisions that should be made (Figure 9.1).

Arends (2002) presents three phases of teaching and thus three phases of teacher planning and decision making: preinstructional, instructional (or interactive), and postinstructional. Phases are useful in simplifying planning. Other chapters examine elements of unit planning in detail.

FIGURE 9.1 *Decisions in Instructional Planning*

Preinstructional Factors

Content decisions: What goals and objectives? What will be taught and content emphasis?

Time allocation decisions: How much time will be given to subjects and topics?

Pacing decisions: How rapidly should the content be covered?

Instructional decisions: What instructional strategies and methods will be used?

Activity structure decisions: What student activities will be used?

Climate Factors

Communication of expectations: How will expectations of students be communicated?

Developing the environment: What will be done to have a safe, orderly, academically focused environment?

Managing deviancy: How will discipline procedures be sensibly managed?

Developing cooperative environments: How will cooperative and interpersonal relationships be fostered?

During-Instruction Factors

Engaged time: How much on-task time will be used?

Time management: How much time will be given to each subject, topic, and transitions?

Monitoring success rate: How will success rate be monitored and ensured?

Academic learning time: How much time will learners be in activities related directly to learning outcome measures?

Monitoring: How will students be monitored, including during independent study? What individual teacher–student interactions will occur?

Structuring: What kind of organizers and summaries will be provided?

Questioning: What type and levels of questions will be posed?

Postinstructional Factors

Tests: How can the desired learning be appropriately tested?

Grades: What kind of grading and reporting system will be used? How can grading used be objective and fair?

Feedback: How can substantial corrective feedback and praise contingent on appropriate behavior be provided and student ideas used?

Source: Berliner, 1984, pp. 51–77.

Renner (1983, pp. 97–99) has a useful 10-Step Planning Model you could use. Start anywhere and shift back and forth as ideas come to mind. The important thing is that all the steps be completed. Teachers, when they plan, usually consider instructional approaches and content *before* they write objectives. An experienced teacher might first decide what to do (content), how to do it (strategies), consider the broad goals (objectives), and, finally, how to evaluate (assessment). Following is another ten-step planning sequence.

A Ten-Step Unit Planning Sequence

1. Select the *unit topic* and decide which *course objectives* (taking into account school, district, and department of education guidelines) the unit is to address.
2. Do a *concept hierarchy and task analysis* of the concepts and skills to be learned (this could be called a concept map or web).
3. Prepare a *content outline* and sequence the topics (facts, concepts, principles, skills, and processes) to be learned.
4. Beginning with brainstorming, select suitable *teaching methods* and *student activities* and organize these under the headings of introductory, developmental, and culminating.
5. Identify appropriate *resources and materials.*
6. Ensuring they are congruent with course objectives, write appropriate *unit objectives.*
7. Prepare the summative *evaluation,* making sure this is congruent with unit objectives and student activities.

8. Decide which personal *professional targets* you will work on and the data collection instruments you will likely use.
9. Determine *prerequisite student learning* and how you will know whether students have the necessary background to proceed.
10. Prepare *lesson plans* for the first one or two lessons of the unit. (pp. 97–101)

Note: You will likely be returning to previous steps to make additions or changes (going back and forth) as you plan.

ELEMENTS COMMON TO MOST TEACHING UNIT STRUCTURES.   Unit plans involve advance thought about what will be taught and how. Plans should not be "cast in concrete." Alternate selections, emphasis, choice of teaching methods and student activities, and expansion, addition or deletion should be possible. However, most good unit plans have common elements. The main ideas of unit planning we have been discussing are illustrated in Figure 9.2.

CONSIDERATIONS IN PLANNING.   The general goal or purpose for the unit should be written. This is explained in a *rationale statement* that, in one or two paragraphs, overviews the content to be covered, outlines the major outcomes to be met, and explains why it is important that students achieve the outcomes. The rationale should communicate the nature and substance of the unit and help you select and organize content and write and sequence objectives.

The *content* and its sequence must be decided and reflected in a content outline. Discover curriculum guide requirements and how much time you can allocate. A good content outline is based on knowledge of the concepts, skills, and processes involved. Therefore, before the outline is written, a hierarchy of concepts should be created, and, an analysis of the skills and processes in the unit should be conducted. This information is vital for sequencing content.

Consider the essential cross-curricular content of all learning and integrate this into the planning. These should include oral and written communication skills, creative and critical thinking, technological literacy values, and independent learning skills.

Decide the *prerequisite learning* students need. A *pretest* (formal or informal) may need to be selected or constructed. Consider the interests and backgrounds of students, and their level of development, expectations, cultural background, and learning styles.

Broad *objectives/goals* should be written. Later, objectives for each lesson must be prepared (congruent with unit objectives/goals). Unit objectives/goals express the reasons for the unit and guide the specific objectives chosen for lessons. Whereas course objectives are stated in broad terms, unit objectives are a step closer to specificity, and lesson objectives should be very specific. Each objec-

FIGURE 9.2   *Elements That Most Unit Plans Have in Common*

I. A. Unit title
    B. Subject and grade level
    C. Rationale (justification and the broad purpose) for unit
    D. Foundational objectives: knowledge; skills; and attitudes and values
    E. Curriculum link
II. A. Timeline/content outline
    B. Concept map
III. A. Prerequisite learning
IV. A. Lesson plans (introductory, developmental, and culminating)
    B. Instructional approaches and activities
    C. Resources (print, nonprint, and human)
    D. Adaptive dimension
V. A. Management plan
    B. Classroom climate
VI. A. Assessment (diagnostic, formative, and summative [congruent with objectives])
    B. Evaluation of unit
VII. A. Professional growth targets

tive should contribute to the achievement of the general objectives of the course and the goals of schooling. Every unit objective should suggest expectations of behavioral change in the learner as a result of the experiences students would have. Unit objectives should be (1) stated in terms of some recognized need; (2) learner, not teacher oriented (they are not a list of activities); (3) specific and measurable; (4) achievable by most learners; and (5) descriptive of desired functional learner behavior, not the subject matter to be covered (i.e., what the learner is to be able to do or know or feel). Of course, unit objectives may need to be modified as the unit is delivered.

TEACHING STRATEGIES, METHODS, AND STUDENT ACTIVITIES. When selecting teaching methods and student activities, consider the topics, ideas, concepts, skills or processes, and affective content to be covered; lesson presentation skills, instructional techniques, methods, strategies, or models; classroom routines and management; and interpersonal relating and group skills (including establishing the teaching/learning environment) to be used. Learner readiness, background, and interests must be recognized. Planning, too, must be in keeping with sound learning psychology principles and the developmental stage of the learners.

While "teaching methods" refers to the instructional approaches chosen, "activities" are what students will be doing. Think of more activities than you can use, so good choices can be made as the unit unfolds. Plan to use a range of teaching methods; variety helps maintain interest and meet diverse student needs and learning styles. Once a concept map and skill analysis have been done, the content, teaching methods, and student activities should be planned for subsequent sections.

1. *Introductory.* This part should set the stage, provide motivation, or provide orientation to the problem or area of investigation. The first thing that might be done is a pretest (written or oral) to discover the knowledge and abilities of each student about the topic to be studied. This section can be part of one, two, or more lessons.

2. *Developmental.* This is the "heart" of the unit. It is where the topic is studied. It is one to fifteen or more lessons. Normally, a variety of teaching strategies and methods and student activities should be used. Data are analyzed, generalizations drawn, and conclusions made. Student participation should be as active as possible and lead to success. Activities should be varied to suit individual abilities, interests, and learning styles; activities should be challenging, and methods and activities should consider the facilities and time available.

3. *Culminating.* Learning should be unified. Students need to tie understandings together, recognize interrelationships, and examine the problem or topic in retrospect. They should recognize what was gained, unsolved problems, and needed further study of related problems or topics. The culminating section may dovetail with the introductory section of another unit or units. Summative testing is usually included. In short: Conclude! Review! Summarize! This section may be the last part of a lesson or be two or more lessons.

4. *Materials and resources.* Materials and resources should reinforce the teaching methods and student activities used. They are aids to, not substitutes for, teaching. Models, strategies, methods, activities, rules and procedures, and materials and resources are vehicles through which learning occurs. Materials and resources may include the assigned text, workbooks, manuals, books, the Internet, reference materials (both for use by

students and to be used by you), newspapers, games and simulations, models, charts, maps, films, recordings, transparencies, bulletin boards, TV, community resources, and so forth.

5. *Assessment.* Assessment should measure the degree of student achievement. It also should measure the effectiveness of instruction and the unit. Checklists, formative and summative tests, and anecdotal records can be used to evaluate achievement. Examples of assessment techniques are standardized or teacher-made tests, student assignments, case studies, conferences with other teachers and parents, diaries or logs (kept by students), rating scales, anecdotal records, and self-analysis by students.

6. *Professional growth.* Student teachers should plan for professional growth. Planning and delivering units involves many teacher competencies: the actual planning, use of a variety of instructional strategies and methods, assessment ability, and self-evaluation. Student teachers should use data sheets for the collection of descriptive data on their unit planning capabilities.

7. *Concept map or web.* Prepare a concept map or web to help you sequence the content and learning activities of a unit. This instruction device can foster student success, since it is easier for you to arrange the content appropriately, decide the important concepts, and break the content into logical divisions.

Concepts can be arranged into a hierarchical (or other) structure that illustrates the relationships of concepts to each other. A concept map is a means for representing the conceptual structure of a unit or units of knowledge. When you prepare a concept map, you have something that can be used with students as an advance organizer, an in-progress organizer, or a post organizer. Imagine that you intend to teach a unit on systems of the human body. The concept map of "Systems of the Human Body" (in Figure 9.3) shows a possible approach.

A concept map is a sophisticated advance organizer. Students can see the whole picture as well as the details to be covered. It may be a good idea to post the concept map on a bulletin board so students and teacher can refer to it as knowledge is constructed.

A unit plan uses all aspects of the educational palette to create an overall picture. Different modes of representation have been considered. Some elements of the plan will involve concrete experiences, others may be visual or symbolic. Objectives, sequence, and degree of control have been examined. The learning styles of the students have been taken into account as well as the kinds of outcomes required. Careful attention has been given to incorporating the major teaching strategies and methods. The unit reflects a sophisticated teaching approach after careful thought to the learning of the students. It is more than the content outline or textbook chapter headings. Appendix 9.1 is a checklist to help you plan units, and Appendix 9.2 is a data sheet that can be used for feedback on your unit. A unit planning model is shown in Figure 9.4.

INTEGRATED THEMATIC UNITS.   Thematic instruction occurs when instruction is organized around macro "themes." It is based on the belief that people acquire knowledge best when learning occurs in the context of a coherent "whole" and when learners can connect it to the real world. Thematic instruction integrates basic disciplines such as reading, math, and science by exploring a broad subject, such as communities, pollution, rain forests, or use of energy. These topics can be placed in the context of an authentic subject that is practical but broad enough to allow creative exploration. Reasons put forward for using thematic units are that their use eliminates the isolated, reductionist nature of

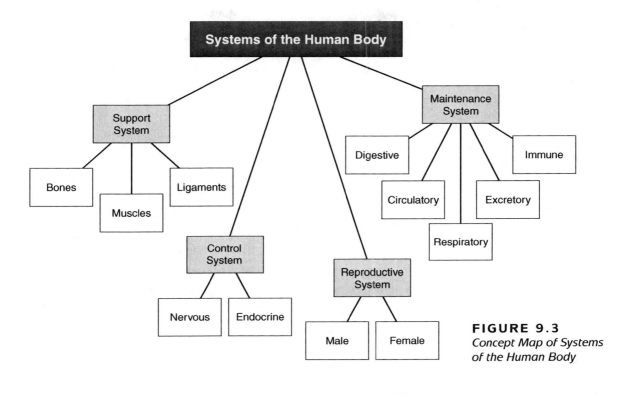

FIGURE 9.3
Concept Map of Systems of the Human Body

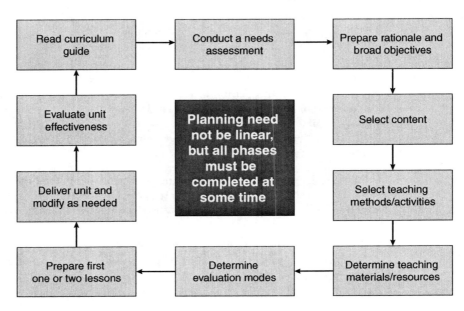

FIGURE 9.4 *Unit Planning Model*

teaching around disciplines rather than experience, compacts the curriculum, recognizes the reality and value of interdisciplinary learning, increases student interest and time engaged, and is a powerful way to reintegrate the curriculum.

Thematic instruction most often occurs within a grade level of students. Teachers work together as a team to design curriculum, instruction, and assessment around a theme. It tends to be used more in elementary grades than in high school, where vertical planning tends to dominate.

TCP—CURRICULUM KNOWLEDGE

Adapts curriculum to student needs

Selects material appropriate to learner needs and interests; sets curriculum goals taking into account learner differences and interests; can restructure content for various ability and interest levels.

Uses prescribed curriculum without adjusting for learner needs and interests; cannot restructure content for various ability and interest levels; rigid application of curriculum guidelines.

Knows subject matter

Has an excellent grasp of the subject area content (concepts, information, skills, theories); can articulate the structure of different subject areas; can see interrelationships among different subject areas; rich in breadth and depth; presents information, skills, and methods of the subject accurately and in appropriate sequence; uses teacher and student resources appropriately.

Treats subject content as a body of disjointed information; unable to construct relationships within individual subject areas; unable to build relationships among different subject areas. Inaccurately, poorly used, poorly sequenced information; superficial skills and methods; inadequate use of sources.

Exhibits knowledge of local and state curriculum

Understands local and state core curriculum requirements; uses local and state curriculum guides effectively.

Not aware of the value of local and state curriculum guides in planning.

A SUGGESTED PLANNING APPROACH. The discussion above has presented the essential elements of unit planning. You need an approach that works for you. Parsons (1992) has practical suggestions you can easily adapt. He stresses that although "it may seem easy to pick up another teacher's unit, . . . you must make your own units of study. . . . If you don't you will never really be comfortable" (p. 10). He gives helpful, practical tips for the novice and experienced teacher (pp. 10–13).

1. Start fresh. You do the initial planning and structuring. Find the curriculum guide for your area, for both legal and practical reasons. Legally, you are required to teach the state or provincial curriculum. Practically, curriculum guides are full of useful ideas. See the curriculum guides as resources, not laid-out plans.

2. Break research into two areas, content and methods.

3. Photocopy the part of the curriculum guide you will be teaching. Highlight and list the things you believe students should know. Decide how important the unit is and what its length will be.

4. Look at the learning activities in the curriculum guide. (The guide is usually more than a list of topics.) List the activities in no particular order. This will be your resource of ideas.

5. You are now ready to look at other resources. (Remember, you are teaching children, and you do not need to know everything before you begin to teach.)

6. To find appropriate content, you need appropriate resources—many small sections from several books may be better than a large section from one book. More detailed content can be suggested later. Reading in depth should come later, not at the planning stage.

7. As you read the resources, note the major things, ideas, and generalizations the resources repeat. What content do all the resources mention?

8. Write out the key content elements. These, along with the specific content from the curriculum guide, become the core content you want students to know.

9. Check these and other state or provincial resources and teaching units for ideas for activities. List those that might be helpful. Check especially for stimulating activities for students and crucial content you may have missed. Modify the activities and ideas for your use.

10. Take the material and ideas you have gathered, and cut and paste your unit together.

11. Take a big, current, empty calendar and jot down what will happen each day. Put this up in the class so students can see what is happening. Organize according to the scope of the unit, variety of activities, chronology of topics, holidays, and whatever else is important.

12. Construct a finished product that is tight, well organized, and justifiable.

13. Finally: think skills (work toward students' learning); think success (work toward mastery of content); be sensitive to students' reactions (plans are absolute if nothing better happens in class); ask yourself, "What will students be doing when I am doing what I am doing?" (How will the class respond to the approaches and activities?); don't worry if things don't go as planned—it's better to fill lessons with good learning and not just get through the material.

Gregory and Chapman (2002) ask questions that aptly summarize the key ideas of planning.

- What do I want students to know or be able to do as a result of this learning experience?
- How will we judge success?
- What do they already know and are able to do?
- How can attention be captured and sustained?
- What will be the emotional "hook" for the learners?
- How will new information and skills be required?
- How will students practice and rehearse to make new meaning and understanding?
- How will they receive ongoing feedback during and after the learning? (p. 84)

LINKING PRACTICE TO THEORY

Note the many elements of planning. Were you aware of the planning involved in your school and university classes? As you plan, what influences you the most—the subject or the student? Do you teach to promote the status quo, or to bring change? How do your values influence your approach to planning? How much freedom do you have as you plan? Should you plan alone or with others? How did your plans change as you taught your students?

Summary

Successful lessons do not just happen. Think about what learners should know or be able to do as a result of a lesson, and how you will begin, develop, close, and evaluate the lesson. Have a plan for personal professional development—a target—for every lesson. There are three different kinds of set (orientation, transition, and evaluation) and two kinds of closure (review and transfer) you can plan, or a serendipitous event may become an excellent closure. Students should be as actively involved as possible. You can maintain interest by varying your presentation through focusing, kinesic variation, shifting interaction, using silence, and shifting senses. Conscious attention to transfer should occur.

Activities

OBJECTIVES USING THE COGNITIVE DOMAIN

For each objective (items 1–11): (a) Indicate the B, C, and D; and (b) name the level of the cognitive domain.

1. Given an outline map of Canada (showing province borders), each student will be able to write the name of each of the ten provinces and two territories in the appropriate area of the map.
2. Given ten shots in basketball, each student will be able to sink at least five.
3. When given six major events that contributed to the outbreak of World War II on September 1, 1939 (in random order), each student will be able to list the events in chronological order and write an analysis on how each event contributed to the conflict.
4. In hockey, using twenty-five pucks lined up on the nearest blue line, and using the slap shot, the student will be able to shoot at least twenty of them into the open net.
5. Using the guitar chords C, G7, and D, the student will compose a simple song (including lyrics).
6. Given five poems, each student will be able to identify and list at least three poetic devices common to the five poems. He or she will write the examples found in each poem.
7. After studying six painting elements, each student will paint a picture and will state how she or he has used each element in the picture.
8. The class will meet at 9:00 P.M. on October 15 outside the Brown Farm gate. After gazing at the sky, each student will point out the constellations Orion and Ursa Major, and the following stars: Betelgeuse and Rigel. Then, the class will meet at Ernie's Pizza Palace and each student will draw a picture of the two constellations and name the stars mentioned above (while eating pizza).
9. Join four classmates whose grade and subject-level interests are similar to yours. In turn, each person describes a lesson he or she has taught or observed. The group agrees on well-stated objectives for each lesson.
10. In the same groups as in Activity 12, agree on a topic of interest in a school subject of the group's choosing and design an objective for each level of the cognitive domain, each level of the affective domain, and each level of the psychomotor domain.
11. Turn to a classmate and (a) agree on the difference between an activity and objective, (b) what makes an objective "well written," and (c) how you typically would go about planning a lesson.
12. Participate in a class discussion on the value of careful planning, things that might cause plans to change, and what can be done to prepare for possible changes and the unexpected.

SET AND CLOSURE

1. Your instructor may model a lesson that has a clear set, development, and closure. Determine the parts of the lesson and critique it in terms of the principles discussed in this chapter.
2. Join a subject specialization group. Brainstorm examples of set inductions under the headings Orientation, Transition, and Evaluation.
3. In the same group, brainstorm closures under the headings Review, Transfer, and Serendipity.
4. Join a subject specialization group. Pick a topic and design a lesson plan that has an appropriate and motivating set, an interesting development, and an appropriate closure. The plan must flow smoothly and appropriately from one phase to the next. Groups tell the class about their plan, and the class has to identify the kind of set and kind of closure chosen.
5. Every member of the class is to prepare a lesson plan having an appropriate set, development, and

closure. Share plans in subject specialization groups. Group members are to identify the kinds of set and closure and comment on the flow from one phase of the lesson to the next.

6. Teach a microteaching lesson and field classroom lesson that has the professional target of appropriate set, development, and closure.

7. Try the activity that follows.

RECOGNIZING LEVELS IN BLOOM'S COGNITIVE TAXONOMY

Write the level of Bloom's taxonomy for each statement in the exercise below.

K = knowledge; C = comprehension; AP = application; AN = analysis; S = synthesis; E = evaluation

1. _____ From memory, recite a stanza from a poem.
2. _____ Put a statement into your own words.
3. _____ Name the states on the West Coast.
4. _____ Discover how a lawn sprinkler works.
5. _____ Classify flowers.
6. _____ Find the area of a triangle.
7. _____ Debate the pros and cons of. . . .
8. _____ Demonstrate how to fold a letter.
9. _____ Draw a map of a room.
10. _____ Categorize all the clothes you own.
11. _____ Name Donald Duck's nephews.
12. _____ Insert the correct jigsaw puzzle piece.
13. _____ Predict the outcome of a murder mystery.
14. _____ Critique a play.
15. _____ Choose the best option.
16. _____ Solve an algebra problem.
17. _____ Give an example of a hero.
18. _____ List all the Presidents of the United States.
19. _____ Design a house.
20. _____ Plan a family reunion.
21. _____ Adjudicate in a music festival.
22. _____ Compare cars of the years 1950 and 2002.
23. _____ Which Greek god was the god of war?
24. _____ Find a way to make poison ivy edible.

KEY: 1 = K; 2 = C; 3 = K; 4 = AN; 5 = AN; 6 = AP; 7 = E; 8 = K; 9 = AN; 10 = AN; 11 = K; 12 = AN; 13 = AN; 14 = E; 15 = E; 16 = AP; 17 = C; 18 = K; 19 = S; 20 = S; 21 = E; 22 = AN; 23 = K; 24 = S

In review, the six levels of Bloom's cognitive taxonomy are

Knowledge: To recall specific information, terminology, and generalizations and to know methods of organizing and criticizing facts

Comprehension: To understand the material or data; to translate, explain, or summarize and extend the idea

Application: To use general ideas, procedures, or principles in concrete situations

Analysis: To break down information into its component parts, identify the parts, and understand their relationships and organization

Synthesis: To put together parts of experiences with new material into a well-integrated whole to provide creative behavior for the learner

Evaluation: Based on criteria (or standards), to make judgments about the value of ideas, methods, solutions, etc.

These and other uses of the taxonomy can be found in Bloom et al.'s classic (1956) work. Ideas on Bloom appear in many modern educational texts and articles.

LESSON PLAN COMPONENTS

Read the case that follows—twice. The first time, get an idea of how the teacher intends to teach a lesson. The second time, see if you can pick out the parts of a lesson plan. Each paragraph focuses on a different decision that must be made—decision descriptions follow the case.

1. Mr. Messer intends to teach a lesson on planets as part of a unit called "Our Solar System." He has been asked by another middle-school science teacher, Ms. Schmidt, what he intends to do. He says he wants students to know the parts of the solar system. More specifically, after the coming lesson, he wants students to be able to look at an unlabeled chart of the solar system and, based on their knowledge of the characteristics of planets, pick out the planets.

2. The teaching aids he intends to use are a large chart of the solar system, a three-dimensional model of the planets, sun, and moons, a twelve-minute film, and an unlabeled one-page diagram of the solar system. He realizes the lesson will spill over into the next day's science period. He knows that some lessons will take only fifteen minutes, whereas others may take two or three periods.

3. Students have been taught procedures for learning new concepts and are familiar with concept hierarchies and concept mapping.

4. Mr. Messer thinks students already know something about planets but he is unsure how much. He plans to begin the lesson by asking how many have seen the *Star Trek* movies or the television series by that name. Using questions, he wants to discover what students know about planets. Then, he will show a big chart of the solar system and provide an overview of what students will learn.

5. He tells students they are about to see a film and to pay particular attention to the planets. After the film, he will ask students to name the planets mentioned, and why they are all called planets. Using the three-dimensional model of the planets, sun, and moons, Mr. Messer, while occasionally referring to the film, intends to review how planets orbit the sun and how moons orbit planets. Then, he wants to form heterogeneous groups of five to agree on the critical attributes of planets. Groups will list and display these on newsprint. Once this is done, he wants to draw a definition of "planet" from the class. Using question and answer, he wants to help the class learn the characteristics that are part of all planets and those characteristic of some but not others. He wants to draw a definition of the concept "planet" from the class. Now, using the unlabeled chart of the solar system, he intends to point randomly at planets, the sun, and moons and ask students to tell which are planets and which are not. The students have to justify their answers based on the definition and their knowledge of the critical attributes of planets.

6. To close the lesson, Mr. Messer will use question and answer to review the critical and noncritical attributes and the definition of the concept "planet." He intends to ask students how their learning about planets can be useful. After showing students how to go about it, he will distribute an unlabeled diagram of the solar system and prepare students for the next lesson. For homework, they are to label the planets and, in writing, explain their decisions.

7. During the lesson, Mr. Messer intends to watch students carefully for signs of uncertainty. He will ask questions and, if necessary, reteach portions of the lesson using an alternate activity.

He get further evidence of understanding through the homework assignment and, later, through the unit test.

8. Mr. Messer has a personal professional development plan for each of his lessons. Lately, he has been working on improving his questioning technique. He discovered that most of his questions have been directed to six or seven students. His intention for this lesson is to spread questions evenly. To help him achieve his target, he will ask one of the students to insert a check mark on a seating plan beside the name of every student asked. This will provide objective data on how he spread questions during the lesson.

During practice teaching, before you teach a lesson, your cooperating (sponsor) teacher will expect you to present and discuss your written lesson. Your plan will have two components: (1) *learning by students*—plans to help students achieve the intentions (objectives) of learning the subject matter and developing positive attitudes; and (2) *professional development*—plans by the teacher to achieve a professional target or competency.

Does the inclusion of component 2 surprise you? Think about it. Professional teachers, no matter how good, are always seeking ways to improve. *After ten years of teaching you will want to have had ten years of experience, not one year of experience ten times.* It is unlikely that much improvement will occur without a systematic approach. What better way to improve than to target an aspect of your teaching every time you teach?

How well did you do in identifying the parts of a lesson? A paragraph-by-paragraph analysis of Mr. Messer's lesson plan follows.

Paragraph 1. The *topic* of the lesson is identified, and intentions or *objectives* students are to achieve are stated. How the teacher will know whether they have achieved objectives is specified.

Paragraph 2. A list of teaching *aids and resources* that the teacher intends to use is given.

Paragraph 3. The background students are expected to have is identified. This is *prerequisite learning.*

Paragraph 4. This is the introductory or *set* portion of a lesson. Mr. Messer wants the interests of students to be piqued. Teachers want students to be positively disposed (have a positive mind set) toward, and be encouraged to be involved in, the lesson. The set of a lesson often includes a preview or overview of what is to be studied "Today we will . . ." or "After today's lesson you will know . . . and be able to. . . ." "You will enjoy learning about. . . ."

Paragraph 5. The next part of a lesson is the body or *development*. The teaching methods and student activities to be used, and the sequence of these, to help students acquire the knowledge and skills intended are specified. How interactive the lesson will be and how actively students will be engaged in learning tasks is outlined. (Although they are not mentioned in this scenario, classroom management plans also can be stated. Sometimes, to ensure clarity, questions that will be asked are written out. Sometimes, more activities than will actually be used are listed. If the teacher finds something is not working, he or she will not be at a loss for what to do.)

Paragraph 6. The *closure* portion of a lesson is intended to bring the lesson to a successful end. It often involves review to "tie up" a lesson, and frequently, a bridge is built to subsequent learning ("Today we did. . . ." "What you now know or can do is. . . ." "Tomorrow we will. . . ." That is, a summary of what has been learned is provided, and the students become aware of how learning will connect to future study.

Paragraph 7. The teacher needs to know whether students have learned what is intended. The intentions (objectives) are constantly kept in mind—sometimes, in the light of what is occurring, they are modified. This portion of a lesson plan is the *evaluation*. Evaluation is formative *and* summative. *Formative evaluation* occurs during every part of the lesson (e.g., paragraphs 4 through 6). This happens as the teacher looks around the room and notices nonverbal behavior such as a puzzled look, or (verbally) by how students respond to questions. Another way is to give several spot quizzes (written or oral) during segments of the lesson. *Summative evaluation* occurs when, at the end of the lesson, a test is written or students have to perform something. You may have noticed that summative evaluation may also be used to do closure.

Paragraph 8. The set, development, and closure portions of a lesson plan include a record of what the teacher intends to do to help students achieve learning objectives. The focus is on students. In this paragraph the focus is on the *professional development* of the teacher. The *target* area, and specific aspects of that target, are specified (e.g., the distribution aspect of Mr. Messer's questioning technique). Plans of how this is to be done are stated.

GENERAL PLANNING

1. Join a subject group. Brainstorm examples of each of the five kinds of stimulus variation.
2. In the same group as in "Activity 1," write and present a skit illustrating stimulus variation. The rest of the class observes and collects data.
3. Planning is a critical part of many ventures. In groups, consider things that are frequently planned, such as going on a trip. Create a planning cycle that includes planning, carrying out the plan, and reviewing and revising the plan.
4. You and your classmates have been taught by teachers. Reflect about a favorite lesson. Explain what was taught and consider the components the teacher had to consider and carry out. Compare your findings with the lesson outline in the text.
5. Things "happen" in school classrooms. However, some teachers, when planning, confuse activities with objectives. Teachers might write in their planning books: today we will have a discussion, or today we will watch a film. Consider things you have learned in your major. In a chart, compare the activities you did and the learning objectives (what you were expected to learn).
6. Think again about your major subject area. What cognitive, psychomotor, and affective knowledge have you mastered? Share your learning with students from another discipline.

APPENDIX 9.1   *Unit Planning Professional Target*

PROFESSIONAL TARGET—PLANNING THE TEACHING UNIT

Unit Title
Grade Level and Subject Area   Time Estimate

Rationale statement adequate for explaining why is it important for students
to study the teaching unit?   Yes ____   No ____
Comments:

Unit objectives clear and measurable?   Yes ____   No ____
Comments:

Content outline clear and in appropriate sequence?   Yes ____   No ____
Comments:

Appropriate concept map completed?   Yes ____   No ____
Comments:

Prerequisite student learning identified and provision made,
as appropriate, for pretesting?   Yes ____   No ____
Comments:

Sequence of lessons, Introductory, Developmental,
and Cumulative?   Yes ____   No ____
Comments:

Variety and balance of appropriate teaching methods and
student activities?   Yes ____   No ____
Comments:

Suitable variety of resources and materials listed?   Yes ____   No ____
Comments:

Formative and summative assessment congruent with objectives?   Yes ____   No ____
Comments:

Additional observations?

APPENDIX 9.2 *Unit Plan Feedback Sheet*

UNIT PLAN FEEDBACK SHEET

Requirements met: 1 Most definitely,   2 Quite well,   3 For the most part,
4 Partially,   or 5 Little Evidence

1. Planning and Organization   Comments
   1 2 3 4 5   Rationale statement
   1 2 3 4 5   Prerequisite learning; entry knowledge
   1 2 3 4 5   Concept/skills/processes map
   1 2 3 4 5   Declarative/procedural/affective objectives

2. Selection of Teaching Methods/Student Activities   Comments
   1 2 3 4 5   Use of competencies presented in text
   1 2 3 4 5   Choice of teaching methods/student activities
   1 2 3 4 5   Selection of routines/procedures

3. Meeting Student Needs   Comments
   1 2 3 4 5   Motivation
   1 2 3 4 5   Varying interactions/control
   1 2 3 4 5   Recognizing learning styles
   1 2 3 4 5   Recognizing cross-cultural needs
   1 2 3 4 5   Evaluation

4. General Assessment
   1 2 3 4 5   Provision of appropriate teaching methods and learning activities
            for student growth in all three domains
   1 2 3 4 5   Meaningful sequence of experiences and components to accomplish
            the central purpose of the unit
   1 2 3 4 5   Interesting, relevant, and challenging, but achievable
   1 2 3 4 5   Holistic understanding of the teacher as a decision maker evident

5. Personal Professional Development
   1 2 3 4 5   Target/competencies (selection and data collection targets
            identified, a plan for achieving each is stated, and a suitable
            data collection method and instrument for each target are
            selected or designed)

10 Engaging Learners: Questioning, Discussion, Seatwork, and Homework

Students across the educational spectrum understand studied material better, retain it longer, and enjoy their classes most when they learn actively rather than passively. (Shenker, Goss, & Bernstein, 1996)

Questioning

What's in a question, you ask: Everything. It is the way of evoking stimulating responses or stultifying inquiry. It is, in essence, the very core of teaching. (Dewey, 1933, p. 266)

Questioning Trends

Teachers ask an incredible number of questions. They use them to check recall of and increase retention of information, to interpret information, to guide the development of concepts or skills, to promote thinking, evaluate learning, and to review. Questions are used to discover what students know before beginning a lesson or unit, to motivate and to discover what interests students. During a lesson, questions are asked to see if students recall and understand what was presented. Questions increase student involvement in the development of the lesson. They keep students attentive and on task.

Effective teachers ask more questions than less effective teachers, they phrase questions clearly, avoid run-on questions, and specify the conditions for the response. They probe for clarification and nudge students to higher levels of thinking. Although responses are acknowledged, praise is used with discretion.

Many questions require rote memory for a correct response. Perhaps, because questions that require recitation of facts take less time, teachers sometimes avoid asking

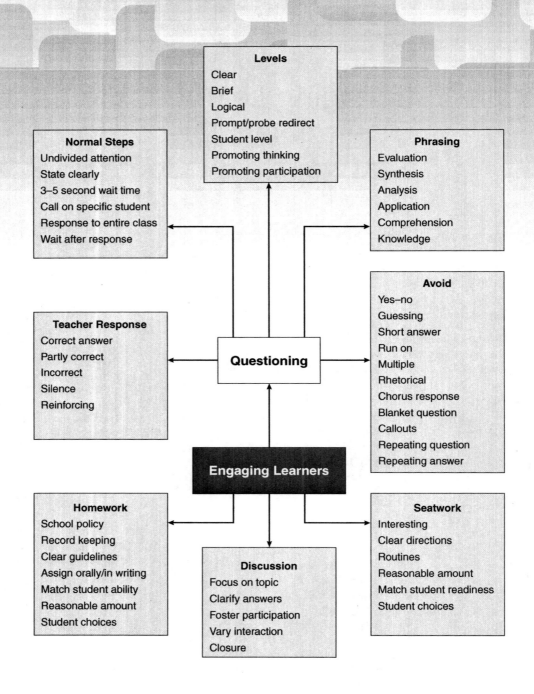

Levels
Clear
Brief
Logical
Prompt/probe redirect
Student level
Promoting thinking
Promoting participation

Normal Steps
Undivided attention
State clearly
3–5 second wait time
Call on specific student
Response to entire class
Wait after response

Phrasing
Evaluation
Synthesis
Analysis
Application
Comprehension
Knowledge

Teacher Response
Correct answer
Partly correct
Incorrect
Silence
Reinforcing

Questioning

Avoid
Yes–no
Guessing
Short answer
Run on
Multiple
Rhetorical
Chorus response
Blanket question
Callouts
Repeating question
Repeating answer

Engaging Learners

Homework
School policy
Record keeping
Clear guidelines
Assign orally/in writing
Match student ability
Reasonable amount
Student choices

Discussion
Focus on topic
Clarify answers
Foster participation
Vary interaction
Closure

Seatwork
Interesting
Clear directions
Routines
Reasonable amount
Match student readiness
Student choices

higher-level questions. Both elementary and secondary teachers ask many questions, but, elementary teachers ask more. Sadker and Sadker (2003) report that the typical teacher asks between 30 and 120 questions an hour. According to Kathleen Cotton (1998), research reveals that questioning follows lecturing as the most commonly used teaching method, with teachers spending from 35 to 50 percent of instructional time in questioning sessions.

Sandra Feldman (2003), discussing teachers and questioning, notes that "many teachers feel inadequately prepared in this critical component of effective teaching. Teacher education and induction programs sometimes gloss over questioning strategies. This is a disservice to both teachers and their students" (p. 8).

TCP—QUESTIONING SKILLS

Has effective questioning skills

Excellent use of questions: choice; steps in; conducting; wait time; cognitive level; prompts, probes, and redirects; and distribution.	Rarely uses questions; unaware of effective steps, use of wait time, and cognitive level; up-and-down rows distribution; repeats questions and student answers; accepts chorus responses and callouts.

Questioning Procedures

The way questions are asked is important (see Figure 10.1). CTE Home (2003–2004) recommends that teachers ask clear, specific questions; use suitable vocabulary level; ask questions ranging from the lowest to the highest levels of Bloom's taxonomy; and use questions to help students connect important concepts.

"The act of questioning has the potential to greatly facilitate the learning process, it also has the capacity to turn a child off to learning" when done poorly (Brualdi, 1998).

NORMAL STEPS.   Teach students how to participate in questioning, explaining why it is important for them to normally follow the routine you wish to establish. As part of your explanation, tell the class you value the contribution of everybody as a member of the class. Tell them that nobody knows everything and it is OK to risk: no sincere answer or question is "dumb" or something to be ashamed of—sincere questions present opportunities for learning. Having students observe the questioning pattern that follows can increase participation and learning and is an important aid to classroom management.

1. *Get the undivided attention of the entire class.* All students should feel a part of the teaching/learning process and think they personally are being addressed. This is supported by eye contact and body movements.

2. *State the question clearly.* Direct the question to the entire class rather than a specific student. Each student in the class should think he or she could be asked for the response. Eye contact and body language can help achieve this goal.

3. *Pause for three to five seconds.* Wait for at least three seconds before calling on a specific person to respond ("wait time" will be discussed later in this chapter).

4. *Call on a specific individual to respond.* Requests for responses should be spread among volunteers and nonvolunteers, matching question difficulty with student likelihood to respond successfully. Normally, callouts and chorus responses should not be accepted, and questions should not be posed in an up-and-down-the-rows manner (this limits participation to those being asked, lets others "off the hook," and invites control problems).

5. *Require students to respond to the whole class.* Because all students should feel ownership for the development of the lesson, responses should be directed to you *and* the

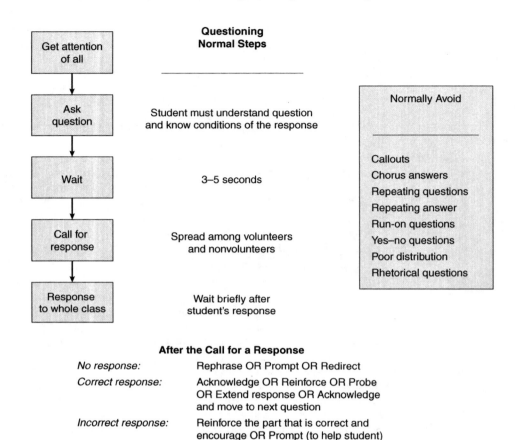

FIGURE 10.1 *Normal Procedure in Asking Questions*

entire class. A student's answer may lead to the next question, or a redirect, and be part of the development of the topic. Exercise patience in letting students complete their answers. Jumping in too quickly may cut students off from giving a more complete answer.

6. After a student is asked and responds, you can: (a) acknowledge the answer if correct and provide reinforcement if appropriate; (b) if the answer is incorrect or incomplete, you can recognize what is correct and use a prompt, rephrase the question, or redirect the question; (c) probe for clarification or for a higher-level response; or (d) simply move to the next question. If the student does not respond, you can encourage and prompt the student or redirect. Questions should be asked of volunteering and nonvolunteering students. This helps ensure that all remain attentive. Teachers should normally help students with incorrect responses, acknowledge the part that is correct, and help them get the correct answer. A data sheet you can use to practice this target is given in Appendix 10.1.

PHRASING QUESTIONS. All thinking is driven by questions. "Good questions generate good thinking. Deep questions, deep thinking. No questions, no thinking" (Paul,

2002). Phrasing questions is important to what goes on in a class discussion. You set the stage and make statements that provide information, challenge, summarize, and help organization and development. The statements you make are as important as the questions posed; and the questions or comments that come from students help the discussion.

The questions you ask should be:

1. *Clear.* Students should know what is asked and how they should respond.
2. *Brief.* Long questions can tax memory (students can easily forget what was asked and therefore be embarrassed). Run-on, or a series of questions, should be avoided.
3. *Logically sequenced.* Early questions provide background (for review). Follow with questions that increase understanding and then application to solving problems. Concluding questions can lead to new insights or be used to evaluate.
4. *Match the level of students.* The language used should not interfere with learning. If new or complex words must be used, define these before the question is asked.
5. *Designed to promote thinking and participation.* Use questions that emphasize why and how, rather than what, where, and when. Build on lower-level questions with higher order questions. Move students along by using *convergent questions* (bringing things together to get a "right" answer), *divergent questions* (those with "no right answer," leading students to a new perspective, to synthesize, or be creative), and *evaluative questions* (students make carefully considered and substantiated judgments).

> Education is more than filling a child with facts. It starts with posing questions. (D. T. Max, *The New York Times*)

Good questioning is not something that works in isolation. It occurs within the structure of a classroom and exemplifies the key elements of high-quality teaching. Weiss and Pasley (2004) say that teacher questions are crucial in helping students make connections and learn concepts, and that effective questions monitor students' understanding of new ideas and encourage them to think more deeply. High-quality instruction, they say, takes place:

- When the teacher's questioning strategies are likely to enhance the development of student conceptual understanding/problem solving (e.g., the teacher emphasized higher-order questions, used wait-time appropriately, and identified prior conceptions and misconceptions).
- When the teacher encourages and values participation by all.
- When the climate of the lesson encourages students to generate ideas, questions, conjectures, and/for propositions.
- And not when teachers use low-level "fill-in-the-blank" questions asked in rapid-fire fashion with an emphasis on getting the right answer and moving on rather than helping students make sense of the concepts. (pp. 24–28)

PRACTICES TO AVOID
- *Yes–no questions.* They encourage guessing and have little diagnostic value.
- *Questions that encourage guessing.* They have low diagnostic power.
- *Leading questions.* These contain a portion of the answer or suggest the answer and may encourage dependence on you.

- *Short-answer questions.* Except when drilling or preparing for higher level questions, avoid questions largely restricted to narrow, short answer, memory, or recall—we want to help students improve their ability to think.
- *Run-on or interrupted questions.* These add confusing and unnecessary detail or are lengthy and may cause students to forget or wonder what was asked.
- *Multiple questions.* These may cause students to forget what was asked, wonder which question to answer, or what you are really asking.
- *Rhetorical questions.* These are questions for which you do not expect a response; although they occasionally have emphasis value or cause students to participate covertly, overuse may cause students to be inattentive and not respond when actually asked.
- *Questions that ask for chorus responses.* Although chorus responses have value for reviewing or drilling facts or practicing foreign language vocabulary, they can lead to control problems and should normally be avoided; they have little diagnostic value.
- *Blanket questions.* Questions such as, "Does everybody understand?" or "Do you have any questions?" usually waste time and have little or no diagnostic value. After asking a question, it is better to ask a specific individual to respond to discover if that student understands.
- *Allowing callouts.* When students call out an answer without being asked, management problems can result; you lose control of appropriate distribution of questions, and many students will not have had enough wait time. Of course, when you call for a free-flowing discussion, it is normal to have unsolicited responses.
- *Repeating the question.* This may just encourage inattentiveness, interrupt the flow of discussion, and center the interchange more on you. However, if the question was poorly phrased or too complex, it may need to be rephrased or broken into subquestions.
- *Repeating a student's answer.* This usually wastes time and causes students to be inattentive and ignore the contributions of peers. If a response was unclear, ask the student to rephrase it, or use a redirect. On occasion, for emphasis, another student can be asked to repeat the answer, or you may do this.

DISTRIBUTION OF QUESTIONS.   When a few eager or aggressive students dominate question-and-answer sessions, others tend to "tune out" or participate passively. All students should have the chance to contribute and think they may be asked to participate.

The climate should be positive and encouraging. Effective teachers encourage a high rate of correct responses and help students with incorrect responses. They use "wait time" to encourage broad participation. When you distribute questions, consider student ability and the likelihood of a correct response. Question sequences should be thoughtfully planned; normally, begin with questions that review the information needed for success with subsequent higher-level questions. A data collection instrument for question distribution patterns is shown in Figure 10.2.

Using "Wait Time"

The concept of "wait time" was developed by Mary Budd Rowe (1972). Wait time, the time from the end of the teacher's question to when a student is called to respond, has been extensively researched. Authorities agree that wait time should be three to five seconds (Cotton, 1988; Stahl, 1994; Sadker & Sadker, 2003) or more, particularly when

Professional Target—Question Distribution

Enter student names in boxes. Place a check mark or the question number in the appropriate box as questions are asked.

Descriptive observations about the nature of question distribution:

Note: This observation form can also be used for recording eye contact, teacher movement, student off-task behavior, etc.

FIGURE 10.2 *Question Distribution Target*

higher-order questions are asked. The benefits are impressive (Berliner, 1987; Stahl, 1994; Sadker & Sadker, 2003): students tend to give longer answers (up to 700 percent longer); the number of supported and logical responses increases; failures to respond are reduced; more students volunteer to respond; higher-order responses are given more frequently; students rated as slow by teachers respond more often and ask more questions; more confidence is shown in responding; students ask more questions; student–student exchanges increase; students are more willing to risk because the number of speculative responses increases; and the need to discipline decreases.

In summary, Cotton's review of literature on questioning led her to conclude that increasing wait time could result in: higher student achievement, retention, more higher-level responses, greater response length, more unsolicited responses, decreases in failure to respond, more and better-quality support for responses, more contributions by students who participate infrequently with short wait times, expansion of the variety of responses, more student–student interactions, and more questions asked by students.

Some authorities prefer the term "think time" over "wait time." Stahl (1990), who initiated the term think time, says the purpose of wait time is to allow students and the teacher to do on-task thinking, and there are places in a lesson where periods of silence are as important as wait time. He adds, sometimes less than three seconds of uninterrupted silence is appropriate.

When wait time is increased, students have time to think an answer through, rehearse it, and build up courage. Teachers make better use of questions and answers. They have time to scan the room and encourage students to feel accountable, consider the next question and its phrasing, sequence questions, make distribution decisions, and think about how to handle responses. When wait time is increased, teachers are more flexible, make fewer errors, and have better continuity in the development of ideas. Teachers ask fewer questions, make more requests for clarification or elaboration, and become better at using student responses. With sufficient wait time, teachers revise their opinions of some students favorably. For example, minority students may now participate or increase the quantity and quality of their participation (Rowe, 1986, p. 45).

Levels of Questions

Jill Slack, in an interview in Blair (2002), says, "Questioning is one of the missing pieces in teacher training. Teachers often ask closed-ended questions that don't allow the students to demonstrate their level of knowledge or lack of knowledge." She explains, "The quality of response is affected by the quality of the question's content and how the question is asked. The pacing of the question also comes into play" (p. 1) Richetti and Sheerin (1999) observe that teachers who are constructivists share "a fundamental belief in the potential of a child's mind, in the need to challenge and refine students' thinking, and in their ability to make curriculum come alive" (p. 58).

When using questions and answers, you can help students progress well beyond a low level. Use probes and questions that are open ended or require analysis, synthesis, or judgments and support. This stimulates thinking, moving beyond rote memory. Asking higher-cognitive-level questions (requiring thought, not just memory) increases student achievement. The best pattern for younger and lower-ability students is simple questions with high success rates; for high-ability students, harder questions should be asked and more critical feedback given.

Bloom's taxonomy was introduced earlier. It is one way to look at levels of questions as student readiness and appropriate objectives are considered. Examples of key words or phrases in each category are given below.

Knowledge level (recalling or recognizing information):

Recall	How many?	Where?
Define	Who?	When?
List	What?	

Comprehension level (describing, putting in own words, giving examples):

Describe	Summarize	Interpret
Give an example	Explain	Paraphrase
Rephrase	What's the main idea?	

Application level (applying to a new context; using a concept to solve a problem):

Classify	Operate	Demonstrate
Select	Solve	Relate
Prepare	Use	

Analysis level (Discover, or break down into, the parts; find the structure):

What are the causes?	Analyze	Subdivide
What is the order?	Diagram	Infer
Outline	What are the reasons?	

Synthesis level (organize in a new way, or into a new whole):

Plan	Produce	Devise
Construct	Design	Combine
Create	Rewrite	

Evaluation level (judge based on criteria, a rationale, or standards):

Judge	Which is better? Why?	Discriminate
Criticize	Appraise	Do you agree?
Support	Justify	Why?

Note: As a caution, Bloom's taxonomy should not be used rigidly nor used as a linear and inflexible hierarchy. It is a guide to varying questions and to moving from low to higher levels. There is little point, however, in arguing about exactly where in the taxonomy a given question fits. Furthermore, you may prefer another classification system.

A data instrument you can use to practice this target is in Appendix 10.2.

QUESTIONING AND COGNITIVE LEVEL. Cotton (1988), in a Northwest Regional Laboratory report, cites research on cognitive level questioning.

- About 60 percent of questions are lower cognitive, 20 percent are higher, and 20 percent are procedural.
- Higher-cognitive questions are not always better in getting higher-level responses, fostering learning gains.
- Lower-cognitive questions are more effective than higher-level questions with primary-level children, particularly disadvantaged children, and better when the teacher's purpose is learning factual knowledge and helping students commit it to memory.
- When asking many lower-level questions is appropriate, the greater the number of questions, the greater the student achievement.
- When lower-level questions are predominant, the level of difficulty should result in a high percentage of correct responses.
- Beyond the primary-grades level, a combination of higher- and lower-cognitive questions is more effective than exclusive use of one or the other.
- Students whom teachers perceive as slow or poor learners are asked fewer higher-cognitive questions than students perceived as more capable learners.
- Above the primary level, particularly for secondary students, increasing use of higher-cognitive questions considerably above 20 percent results in higher learning gains.
- Asking higher-cognitive questions alone will not necessarily result in higher-cognitive responses.

- Teaching students how to draw inferences and providing practice leads to higher-cognitive responses and greater learning gains.
- Increases in the use of higher-cognitive questions in recitations do not reduce student performance on lower-cognitive questions on tests.
- For older students, increasing use of higher-cognitive questions to 50 percent or more is related to increases in on-task behavior, student response length, relevant volunteered contributions by students, student-to-student interactions, use of complete sentences when responding, speculative thinking, and relevant questions asked by students.
- For older students, increased use (up to 50 percent) of higher-cognitive questions is positively related to higher teacher expectations about children's abilities, particularly for students teachers habitually have thought to be "slow" or "poor" learners.

Handling Responses

Teachers tend to fall into a pattern of calling mainly on higher-ability students to answer questions; the questioning pattern should have all students called upon as equally as reasonable (Good & Brophy, 1995, p. 277). Having equitable distribution is a demanding but important challenge (Kauchak & Eggen, 2003, pp. 167–168).

How you handle student responses makes a difference. Discussion and participation can be enhanced. Allowing sufficient *wait time* is fundamental to encouraging responses. You can use *prompts* or clues if the initial question was too difficult or you want to encourage a student. Cueing is an important skill. You can learn how to guide students to the right answer without giving it to them (overuse of prompts, however, can cause dependence). *Probes* can be used to elicit clarification, more detail, or higher-level responses; probing encourages students to move just ahead of where they are and is part of the essence of good teaching. *Redirects* shift the question to another student to confirm a response, invite comment, stimulate discussion, or when a student originally asked did not respond.

Normally, only accept responses from those recognized. This lets you control distribution, allows wait time to be used, and leads to better diagnosis. Responses should be addressed to the whole class. This helps students feel accountable for the development of the lesson. Effective teachers encourage the student who has been asked to respond. This shows they want all to participate and learn. To this end, prompts or probes can be used and unanswered questions can be redirected. Students achieve best when they have high success rates (from 70 to 80 percent), and students giving incorrect answers should be helped (Wilen & Clegg, 1986, p. 157). Give time for a complete answer. A student may need time to complete a response; and providing postresponse time allows other students to think and to consider volunteering (Stahl, 1994). Don't jump in or nod quickly after a response—rapid reinforcement may distract and block development of ideas. Use reinforcers selectively; an endless stream of teacher "OK's" or "right's" becomes a meaningless "part of the woodwork." Not every correct answer need be reinforced. Moving to the next question implies that the response was correct and keeps discussion moving. Building on a student's response, immediately or later, is a good way to reinforce. When you reinforce, be sincere and use a variety of expressions instead of repeatedly saying, for example, "good." Add *why* the answer was good.

When you are responding to a student answer, if the answer is correct and confident, you often can simply accept it and move on. If the answer is correct but hesitant, surface why the answer was right. This provides an opportunity to explain the content again (students may need the review). If the answer was partly or totally wrong, but the student did honestly try, then probe, prompt, rephrase the question, or reteach. Interpret sincere attempts to the student's advantage. Return later, with a similar question, to a student who gave an incorrect or hesitant answer. Use answers to earlier questions as a basis for later questioning. Normally, students should reply with complete statements and good English (encourage this in a nonblaming, nonthreatening way). Finally, promote constructive inter criticism among students (ideas can be challenged, but personal attacks cannot be permitted).

LINKING PRACTICE TO THEORY

How you ask questions is influenced by your experience and philosophy. If you see knowledge as compartmentalized and able to be transmitted without considering the learner, your questions may deal only with basic content. If you see content as closely linked to your teaching approach and knowledge and to your and your students' interests, your questioning may be more complex. Why is asking questions not as simple as it might seem? How does questioning affect learning?

Use the data collection instruments in this chapter to help you analyze the cases that follow. Your instructor may pose specific questions for your response.

CASE 10.1 Questioning

Making Haystacks

Ms. Lepage's grade 2 class has been working on a "Farm" theme for a few days. Today, Ms. LePage gathers students at the back of the room on the carpeted area. She says, "I have something for you to think about. I'm going to ask some questions to help you think." She pauses until everyone seems ready. "I want everyone to have a turn answering today, so I'll ask you to put up your hands instead of calling out the answer. I'm going to give you time to think before I call on anyone, to help us get some high-quality answers. I will ask somebody to respond. The answer should be loud and clear so all in the room can hear and keep up with what is going on. Listen carefully, because I usually will not repeat the answer that was given.

"This afternoon, we're going to make haystacks. What do you think we'll need?" Children's hands begin to go up. Ms. LePage acknowledges hands by smiling, but waits for more hands. She calls on students by name. Answers include, "Hay," "Straw." "Think about what haystacks look like," Ms. LePage prompts. "What else could we use?" Again a few

hands go up, then more, and finally most hands are up. Ms. LePage calls students by name for their answers. "Grass," "Weeds," "Corey's hair" (all laugh, including Corey), "String," "Twine," "Bullrushes," "Cattails." "Good answers!" Ms. LePage says. "You really do remember what haystacks look like. Now, I'm going to give you another clue that will change things quite a bit. We're going to be able to *eat* the haystacks. What do you think we'll use to make them?" The children wave their hands. Again Ms. LePage waits until many hands are raised. A student blurts out an answer and Ms. Lepage shakes her head with a smile, looks at the student, and puts an index finger to her lips. The students are very anxious to be chosen. Answers include "Spaghetti," "Fettucini," "Linguine," "Cotton candy," "Noodles." "Oh, that's close," says Ms. LePage. "What kind of noodles?" The children guess several kinds of noodles, but no one guesses chow mein noodles. "Have you ever seen this kind of noodles?" Ms. LePage holds up a box of chow mein noodles. She shows the recipe on chart paper, and preparations are made for cooking.

CASE 10.2 Questioning

There Should Be a Law

Mr. Njika's grade 12 social studies class has been studying the idea of "free trade" between Canada, Mexico, and the United States. As the class opens, Mr. Njika reviews the last day's lesson on different kinds of trade barriers, including tariffs. This is done through recall questions. He goes on, "Class, what are examples of products that we import?" The class supplies answers that Mr. Njika writes on the chalkboard. "What products do we export?" He records these on the chalkboard and adds items that students had missed. "Which of our imports do you think come from the other two potential free trade partners, and to which partners do we export our products?" Students respond, some just guessing. Mr. Njika receives their answers, making sure that they are accurately entered on the board.

The next part of the lesson is a brief lecture on the law of comparative advantage. To summarize, students learn that economic theory states the country that should produce a product or service is the one that can do it in the most cost-effective way. Each country should produce those goods and services at which it has an advantage compared to other countries, and these goods and services should be traded for ones for which they do not have a "comparative advantage."

"Let's try to discover if the Canada–Mexico–United States free trade idea is a good one. How do you think we should go about making such a decision?" One student responds that there must be an economic advantage for all countries. Another student adds that it's important to retain national identity. With some prompting, probing, and redirecting, students advance most of the arguments pro and con that they had learned in their study of tariffs. The class concludes with small groups beginning to discuss a question posed by Mr. Njika: "What do you think the long-term effects, on each country, of the three-way free trade agreement, if it is passed, will be?" The groups are to finish their discussions next day and report. They are told to think about the problem overnight and to ask others, or read about it.

CASE 10.3 Questioning

To Be or Not to Be . . .

Mr. Schmidt is taking up Shakespeare's *Hamlet.* He is a substitute teacher fresh out of university. The regular teacher is on sick leave. Mr. Schmidt looks about the room at faces that are sizing him up and says, "Your regular teacher tells me you were just doing the *Hamlet* soliloquy." "Yeh," calls out Henrico from the front row. Mr. Schmidt looks at his seating plan and says "Let's talk a bit about Hamlet. Jan, who is he?" "I guess he's the son of the king, he's . . . the prince of Denmark," replies Jan. "Pretty good. Can you explain why he's unhappy?" "I guess it's because someone killed his father," replies Jan with more confidence. "Great answer," says Mr. Schmidt, smiling. "Can you relate the death of his father to other scenes in the play? Take your time. None of you has to answer at once." "Would that be where the ghost told Hamlet he should get revenge?" asks Andrea. "Andrea, why doesn't he get revenge right away?" queries Mr. Schmidt. Andrea thinks deeply. "Could it be because his uncle killed the king?" "And what did his uncle do next?" asks Mr. Schmidt. José holds up his hand. "José, what do you think?" Mr. Schmidt walks toward José. "The uncle married Hamlet's mother, which complicates things," says José. "Then," says Mr. Schmidt, "what are the reasons for Hamlet's hesitation?" "I guess he loves his mother and doesn't want to make her unhappy," José confidently offers. "Great," says Mr. Schmidt, moving to the front. "How does all this link to the soliloquy?" Andrea eagerly gets back into the discussion: "Could it be that he's so unhappy he's thinking about suicide?" "All of you," Mr. Schmidt says, "what do you think of Hamlet so far"? Praveen, usually a quiet student, joins in: "It's great how you got us thinking for ourselves without telling us the answers." "Yeh!" adds Andrea, "That was fun. I liked the way you ask questions." "You get us thinking," says Praveen, as the bell rings.

Discussion

> One implication of Vygotsky's theory of cognitive development is that important learning and understanding require interaction and conversation. Students need to grapple with problems in their zone of proximal development, and they need the scaffolding provided by interaction with a teacher or other students. (Woolfolk, 2004, p. 333)

TCP—DISCUSSION SKILLS

Conducts effective class discussions

Conducts effective classroom discussions; helps class focus on topic; fosters participation; varies interaction so all participate; brings closure and summary; conducts guided and open discussions.

Discussions have no apparent structure; little evidence of planning; a few students dominate; no satisfactory summing up and closure.

How do you like sitting through a typical lecture, dutifully taking notes? Although there is an important place for lecture and other direct and expository approaches, your participation as a student is passive. You know that the more actively you are involved in learning, the more you are motivated, the easier it is for you to master the content, and the better you remember it. In highly teacher-centered instructional approaches, teachers select the objectives, content, and the teaching and learning strategies and methods—students sit and listen. In contrast, in student-centered (constructivist) approaches, teacher and students make decisions together. Effective teachers involve students actively. They use a variety of interaction patterns, particularly question and answer and discussion, to promote interaction and reflective discourse. They also involve students in meaningful seatwork and homework.

Discussion (small group and whole class) is a major part of this chapter because it involves all the targets (instructional skills) studied in previous chapters: lesson planning, communication, interpersonal and group skills, classroom management skills, varying presentation, and questioning. Seatwork and homework are examined at the end of this chapter.

Purposes of Discussion

Discussion can be used for several purposes (Cruickshank, Bainer, & Metcalf, 2003, pp. 185–186) to: review and extend what students have studied for mastery of a subject, to provide an opportunity for students to examine opinions or ideas, to solve a problem and to improve problem-solving capability, and to help students develop communication, interpersonal, and group skills. One or more of these four goals might be part of a lesson using discussion. Discussion is usually more effective than a more direct method for higher-level outcomes and retention. Most students enjoy discussion and are motivated by it. It fosters attitude change and enhances moral reasoning.

Conducting Discussion

> Discourse can be thought of . . . as exposing one's invisible thoughts for others to see. Through discussions, then, teachers are given a window for viewing the thinking skills of their students. . . . Thinking out loud also provides students opportunities "to hear" their own thinking and to learn to monitor their own thinking processes. (Arends, 2004, p. 428)

Learning and understanding are enhanced through interaction and conversation. "By thinking together, challenging each other, and suggesting and evaluating possible explanations, students are more likely to reach a genuine understanding" (Woolfolk, 2004, p. 451). Discussions are particularly effective when multiple answers are possible (Gage & Berliner, 1998).

Discussions are characterized by: (1) recognition of a common problem or topic, (2) introduction, exchange, and evaluation of ideas and information, (3) seeking an objective or goal, and (4) student–teacher or student–student interaction (Orlich, Harder, Callahan, Kauchak, & Gibson, 1994, p. 224).

Discussion can be with the whole class, the teacher or a student as the leader, or in small groups of students. Whole-class discussion requires teacher and students to interact verbally. Much knowledge can be gained through creative inquiry and active student participation. Discussion can be adapted to many classroom situations. It can be *guided* or *unguided* (open). It can help build classroom climate and lead to intrinsic student interest in the subject.

GUIDED DISCUSSION.   When you conduct a discussion by interjecting and using thought-provoking questions, you are using guided discussion. This is effective for promoting understanding of important concepts. In guided discussion, you are the discussion leader and authority source, and (when needed) the information source. Guided discussion is used to guide students as they review what they have been studying, or to promote understanding or develop the ability to apply learning—you draw out needed information and make frequent use of convergent (who, what, where, and when) questions. You prompt, probe, and seek wide participation. Guided discussion is similar to guided discovery or inquiry.

OPEN DISCUSSION.   Discussion can be completely free and consist largely of student–student interchange. This is unguided or open discussion. It is an exciting way for students to engage in high-level, creative thinking. Open discussion may be risky and more difficult to conduct, but can be exciting and rewarding. It is more free flowing than guided discussion. You are a facilitator, not an authority source or figure. Your role involves focusing, setting boundaries, encouraging participation (but, unlike guided discussion, not necessarily wide participation), and promoting positive interaction. You listen, paraphrase, perception-check, ask open-ended questions, and probe, without pushing the class toward predetermined conclusions. Avoid intervening too often, because it may get in the way. Divergent ideas and originality are welcomed, and high-level and critical and creative thinking is sought.

Guidelines for Effective Discussion

Discussion should be "businesslike," on-topic conversations. There is much more to it than first meets the eye. You need to plan, conduct, and summarize. Skills include interpersonal exchanges, motivation, questioning, and reinforcement.

Effective discussions normally need to be based on material that is familiar to students. Students should not "pool ignorance." The discussion topic can be a problem or issue that does not have a "correct" answer. It may be desirable to have students discover the answer. The issue should be of interest to the class. You set the stage, stress that opinions must be supported (based on evidence), and ensure the terms and concepts needed are understood. Students need to understand that although consensus may be sought, arriving at consensus is not mandatory—it is OK to "agree to disagree." Good discussion is student centered. Normally, interject only to encourage, keep discussion on track, mediate, spread participation, provide needed information, or reinforce. The rules of common courtesy must prevail. Ideas can be challenged; personalities must never be attacked. If possible, students should be seated so they can easily see and hear each other. Discussion should usually conclude with consensus, a solution, insights gained, or a summary (preferably provided by students). Students need a clear understanding of the major points and application to other situations. A summary of considerations for conducting discussions follows.

Teachers who are good at conducting class discussions demonstrate certain behaviors. They are aware that good discussions have certain characteristics:

- Based on material familiar to students
- Terms and concepts needed are understood
- Opinions reflect sound critical thinking
- Encourage, paraphrase, ask for clarification
- Discussion kept on track
- Rules of common courtesy honored
- Students easily see and hear each other
- Time for thought
- Summary of arguments, insights, decisions
- Discussion leader mediates, spreads participation, provides needed information, reinforces
- Issue to be discussed of interest to class
- Students briefed on rules and behavior
- Student centered
- Welcome diverse suggestions
- Unsupported opinion giving avoided
- OK to challenge ideas, no personal attacks
- Consensus sought but not demanded
- Use of prompts, probes, redirects
- Transfer of learning to other situations
- Discourage self-serving behaviors (e.g., blaming, storytelling, showing off)

Encouraging Participation

You can do much to make discussion meaningful to students when you encourage positive and productive participation. Students need to appreciate the importance of, and be directly taught how to: listen, take turns, encourage others to participate, and speak clearly and to the point. Arends (2004) provides some interesting approaches to encouraging participation and to promote discussion. For participation he suggests:

- *Time tokens.* If a few people talk most of the time and some never talk, time tokens can be distributed. Each student is given some tokens designating a time (i.e., 10 or 15 seconds). Students who have used up their tokens can say no more.
- *High-talker tap-out.* In most classes, if you do not intervene, a few students will do most of the talking. Balanced participation can be encouraged by assigning a student to act as participation monitor. The monitor can pass a note or use a "limited number of entries" system to have the "high talker" suspend participation until all have had a turn (p. 379).

For discussion he recommends:

- *Think-pair-share.* After a discussion topic is introduced, have student pairs exchange ideas and practice listening. An alternative is to have students write about the topic before they share. The advantage is that individuals are more likely to participate because they will have something to say and participation is less risky. This technique might also be used in the middle of a discussion.
- *Buzz groups.* To encourage listening to each other, insist that during some discussions (those in which objective is to learn listening skills), before students can speak they have to paraphrase what the previous speaker said.
- *Beach ball.* Beach ball is particularly effective for younger students. A beach (or other) ball is given to a student to start the discussion. Only the person with the ball can talk. Other students raise their hands and are passed the ball when they want to talk. A variation is to have to continue to pass the ball to somebody who has not yet spoken. The procedure can begin again when all have spoken (p. 446).

The Talking Circle

You can learn how to respect the needs of diverse learners when you include students from cultures different from your own in class interactions. As one example, many indigenous traditions use a process for coming to a group decision or understanding. It is called the *talking circle*. The Four Worlds Development Project (1982) describes how talking circles work. Each person, when it is his or her turn, can speak as freely and passionately as he or she wishes, without interruption (but is not required to speak or can speak later). Comments are restricted to the issue or question—not to what another person has said. Participants receive the contributions of all other speakers with respect, even when disagreement occurs. They are allowed to speak without interruption. Each speaker's ideas are to be acknowledged and built upon. Participants need to believe that what they say will be accepted without criticism. Comments need to be descriptive and nonjudgmental—positive and negative comments are to be avoided. Everybody needs to feel safe, so moral or ethical issues can be dealt with without offending anyone. Good talking circles make it possible for rich thought to be accumulated so common ground and consensus can be sought. The goal is for group members to stand together and move forward in a cooperative spirit.

Talking circles are particularly useful when people need to share feelings or when a topic does not have a right or wrong answer or when a risk-free environment is desired. Your class does not have to be aboriginal for you to use talking circles. They can be a valuable part of your instructional repertoire. When you use them, teach guidelines for their use. Learning needs to be a shared endeavor and cooperative experience. The Four Worlds Development Project presents guidelines for the use of talking circles:

- All comments should be addressed directly to the question or issue.
- Only one person speaks at a time.
- Silence is an acceptable response.
- At the same time, everyone must feel invited to participate.
- It is often better to hold talking circles in groups of ten to fifteen, not a large group.
- The group leader facilitates the discussion by acknowledging contributions in a nonjudgmental way.
- No comments that put down others or oneself should be allowed.

- Speakers should feel free to express themselves in any way that is comfortable.
- Some groups have found it useful to encourage participants to pray silently for the one who is speaking.

A mechanism is needed to ensure that a few vocal students do not dominate. An atmosphere of patience and nonjudgmental listening can help shy students speak out and bolder students to moderate participation. A way to signify who has the floor can be established. Going around the circle from one person to the next can be used. Another way is to use an object (such as a feather), which is held by the person speaking, who, when finished, passes it to another person who has indicated the desire to speak or to the person next to him or her.

A data instrument you can use to practice conducting discussions is given in Appendix 10.3.

Interaction Patterns

Discussions involve a range of interaction patterns. You may wish to discover your pattern of interaction with members of a class. Some students tend to monopolize a discussion. You can use a simple data collection instrument to discover: (1) which students tend to monopolize discussion and (2) how the discussion moves from one person to another. At five-second intervals indicate, by tallies or arrows, where the discussion is centered, and, by means of arrows, show lines of interaction. Two simple ways of analyzing teacher–student interactions are shown in Figures 10.3 and 10.4.

Planning Class Discussions

As with any teaching method, advance planning is a must. Although some discussions occur spontaneously, planning ahead allows flexibility and spontaneity. As you plan, think about the purpose and whether discussion is appropriate for the lesson. Consider whether students have the background or skills needed for a worthwhile discussion. How will you handle situations such as the silent student or a student who verbally attacks another (ideas can be challenged, but persons never attacked)?

Decide the approach, for example, guided or unguided, or exchange of ideas after a reading or experience versus a problem-based interchange. Make a lesson plan (a concept map or web of the information, ideas, and feelings that may surface in the discussion can be included). Consider room arrangement—circular or semicircular works best. Decide the *set* to stimulate interest and participation. Review discussion etiquette, what is appropriate and inappropriate behavior. Decide what you will do to ensure orderly exchanges, wide participation, and elicit formative summaries, a concluding summary, and the closure you intend to use.

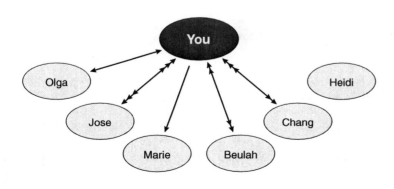

Student–Teacher Interaction:

- What was the nature of the discussion and interaction?

FIGURE 10.3   *Interaction Pattern One*

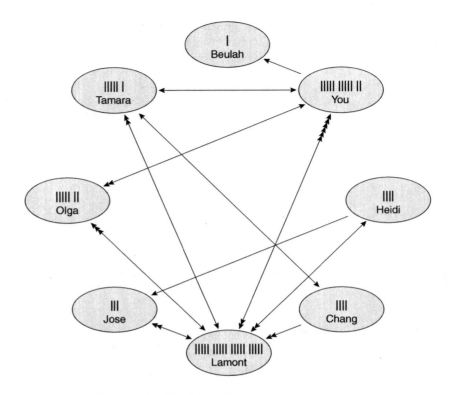

Teacher–Student Interaction:

- What was the degree of teacher control?
- Who did not participate?
- Who received the most attention?
- How many tallies were there?
- How much student initiation of interaction was there?
- How many are the same persons?

FIGURE 10.4
Interaction Pattern Two

Guidelines for designing teacher led class discussions are suggested by Allan and Nairne (1984):

1. *The topic.* When you plan, begin by focusing on the topic and getting everyone involved. The topic should be: (a) positive in focus (what *should* occur, rather than what should not occur) and (b) narrow in scope. This does not mean negative thoughts and feelings should not come out (especially during the exploration stage), but movement must be toward, and toward clear emphasis on the goal, new and adaptive things, or behaviors.

2. *Introduction and warm-up.* Explore the problem area. You can begin with a warm-up or "icebreaker" activity or presentation that readies students for the discussion. Questions requiring "yes" or "no" or closed answers about the topic could be asked. For example, "Have you heard about . . . ?" or "How many of you . . . ?" Then announce the discussion topic and, if possible, tie it to previous work. The warm-up might provide clues about students' feelings toward the topic.

3. *Exploration.* Open questions, those that move from general to specific, should be asked during the exploration phase. For example, "What does the term racism mean?" Then move to more specific questions, such as, "Have you ever witnessed a situation where you think somebody was being racist?" Questions here should help students explore the problem by coming to know and verbalize their thoughts and feelings about the topic.

4. *Understanding.* The goal in this phase is to help students objectively understand the problem area by moving their frame of reference from themselves to other people and to see other perspectives. Use questions that foster insight or greater awareness and help students understand the dynamics involved in an issue. Use questions such as, "For what reasons do racism occur?" or "What would make somebody act in a racist way?" or "How do you think the other person would feel?"

5. *Action steps.* In this stage, activate a sense of responsibility and encourage students to move into action. The kind of question to use is, "What can you do to deal with the problem?" or "What can governments do to improve matters?"

6. *Termination.* In this phase, help students organize and summarize their thoughts and feelings. Ask questions such as, "What have you learned from the discussion?" and, moving a step further, "What do you think you will do the next time you witness a racist incident in the school yard?" These questions provide feedback about what students have learned.

Effective discussion can involve many different approaches. Try the approaches suggested until you have several models that work for you and your students.

CASE 10.4 Discussion

Born or Made to Order?

Professor Gomez wants to model running a discussion with his class. As the students come in they notice the VCR/DVD player.

JOHN: So, Professor Gomez, do we get movies today?

PROF: Very perceptive, John. OK, everyone, today we are going to explore running a discussion. The topic is "Is teaching an art or a science?" In other words, are teachers born to teach, or do they need to be trained? I'm going to begin by showing two clips from the film, *Dead Poets Society.* The first one shows teachers in the school beginning their lessons. The next one shows the way Mr. Keating begins his first English class. Here is a data sheet on running a discussion. I want you to describe what happens in our class.

JOHN: So, running a discussion is our professional goal.

PROF: Right. (They watch the videos.)

LUIS: Hey, that's a great film.

PROF: Thanks, Luis, for your enthusiasm. Now, how many of you think teaching is an art, just comes naturally with no training needed? *(Ten hands go up.)* Great! How many think teaching is a science and training is needed? (Eight hands go up.) Good! I guess the rest of you are on the fence or think teaching is a bit of both. *(The remaining seven nod.)* OK, get into your three groups and each group brainstorm why you think teaching is an art, a science, or both. Write your responses on the newsprint I have provided. *(The groups get to work.)* We will hear both sides and use the third group to come to a conclusion.

PROF: All ready? Right? Each group can present in turn; then we'll have an open discussion with each group defending its position.

continued

GROUP 1: We think teaching is an art. People are born with a natural instinct for teaching; we think skill without passion is not effective; knowing skills does not mean you can teach well. You need an intrinsic feeling for teaching to teach well. You need humor and empathy; you have to have personality and need intuition. The best place to learn is *with* the students.

GROUP 2: We think teaching is a science. There are steps and rules to follow; there are goals and targets that you work toward. You need to experiment (like scientists) with new techniques and need lesson-planning skills and knowledge about learning and teaching styles. There are so many theories on teaching, it must be science based. Many of the skills must be learned.

GROUP 3: We think it's a mix, like Yin and Yang. Yes, you need passion, but you need skills to deliver the passion. You need empathy for kids, but if you don't have knowledge, the empathy won't do much good. Teaching is a bit like theater. You need the innate feeling for acting, but the best actors go to acting school, just as dancers go to dancing school.

PROF: Great stuff! Tell me, was Keating a natural teacher?

GROUP 1: Yes, he had a real instinct and passion.

PROF: Do you think he planned ahead to take the students into the hall?

GROUP 2: Yes, that was his set. He thought the whole thing out. He knew how to motivate.

PROF: So John, share with us what you wrote.

JOHN: The topic was "Is teaching an art or a science?" You introduced it with the film *Dead Poet's Society.* You said the aim was to look at both sides of the issue and come up with a synthesis. After each group, your questions brought about a summary of the positions. For clarity, you made us paraphrase what we said, and I guess you probed quite a bit and challenged our assumptions. There was a lot of student participation in our groups, and when we presented you waited quite a bit while we thought out our answers.You allowed us to come to a summary so we agreed on some of the main points.

PROF: Well, thanks, John, that was great.

CASE 10.5 Discussion

Getting Them to Talk!

In the staff room, Ted, a social studies teacher, is having coffee with Sophie, who teaches English. Ted closes his teaching notes with frustration. "My discussions don't seem to work," he comments. "I put the kids into groups and have them discuss topics I give them. They always get off task." "Well, there are guidelines," says Sophie. "What kinds of topics do you discuss?" "It varies," says Ted, sipping coffee, "usually topics like the causes of war, the nature of revolution, and people's basic rights." "Wow, those do sound interesting," says Sophie, "but it's important that students know something about the topic, understand the terms and concepts, and the subject should be something students are interested in." "You mean, topics close to their lives," says Ted, thoughtfully. "Yes," continues Sophie, "because they must be able to support what they say. So, either the topic should be familiar, they should have knowledge of it, or both." OK," comments Ted, opening his notes, "I can appreciate that. What else?" "First," replies Sophie, "students need practice in how to think critically so that not only do they give sound opinions, they learn how to discuss intelligently. For example, you can help them see the difference between a fact and an opinion—they should separate what's relevant from the irrelevant and detect bias." "I see," says Ted, "I need to teach them quite a few skills. How about running a discussion? My students seem to ramble." "Well," replies Sophie "keep the discussion on track and summarize the arguments from time to time. Students should be taught to respect each other's points of view. Most important, they can challenge someone's opinions but not the person." So," says Ted, thoughtfully, " I have to teach students new skills in discussion and critical thinking. Thanks Sophie, I'll give it a try."

Seatwork and Homework

The intense feeling homework arouses may be proportionate to its important role in a child's education. Numerous studies testify to the powerful link between homework and improved student achievement. Homework has also been shown to help teach students to work independently, encourage responsibility and develop good study habits. (Feldman, 2004, p. 6)

TCP—ASSIGNING SEATWORK AND HOMEWORK

Sets meaningful seatwork and homework

Seatwork and homework assignments follow a clear school or classroom policy; guidelines clear to the students; assignments match student ability or challenge reasonably; students given some choice; prompt and meaningful feedback.	Little consistency or policy to the seatwork and homework assignments; haphazard setting of homework; no clear guidelines; care not taken to match student ability; no choice in the assignments; inadequate feedback; assignments returned late.

Both seatwork (in-class individual study) and homework (out-of-class individual study) usually involve independent learning but can occur in pairs or small groups. Studies by Weinstein and Mignano (1993, pp. 149–150) revealed students spend over half the time working independently. School policies often require teachers to assign homework regularly. The time students are expected to spend on homework may vary from 15 minutes a day for young students up to 60 minutes per class for older students. Time spent on seatwork often is a sizable portion of each subject period. This means that seatwork and homework should be structured and monitored to increase learning and help students become self-regulated learners.

Student practice, through seatwork or homework, often is needed after material (particularly a skill) has been presented. When done well, practice allows students to deepen understanding of content, retain (overlearn) what was presented, and gain speed and accuracy (Kaplan, 1990, p. 390). Some skills need to be practiced to the point of automaticity. Practice provides opportunity for students and you to become aware of what students know and do not yet know. The main reasons for seatwork and homework are to provide practice, enrichment, or remediation when students have difficulty learning content or a skill (Montague, 1987, p. 258). Independent practice gives students the repetitions needed to integrate new and previous knowledge or skills, to become automatic in the use of skills, and to overlearn content (Rosenshine & Stevens, 1986, p. 386). Unless overlearning occurs (particularly in math and elementary reading), material will likely not be retained (p. 386).

Seatwork

The activity elementary students engage in most is seatwork. Seatwork can be defined as independent, supervised classroom desk work. It is even plentiful in junior high school and high school. *Seatwork,* or supervised individual study, is used to provide students with opportunity to gain appropriate practice and feedback on a variety of academic tasks. It is normally used to provide practice after instruction, but it can be used to develop inquiry abilities. It should not be the main approach. Woolfolk (2004) cautions that seatwork requires careful monitoring. Teachers need to be constantly on the move to help students who need it and to catch students "doing it right" (p. 446).

THE NATURE OF SEATWORK.   Most seatwork consists of work that is designed for students to perform independently as practice after they have learned the work. Two kinds of seatwork are common. The most common is whole-class supervised study; the other occurs when you work with one group while another works independently. Students should be told the purpose and relevance of seatwork that follows directly from instruction. It should be carefully chosen and sequenced, clearly explained and monitored, and specific feedback provided. Seatwork assignments may be prepared by the teacher or assigned from a text or workbook.

PURPOSE OF SEATWORK.   Although seatwork in school classrooms is usually assigned to extend knowledge, not just to keep students busy, much seatwork is unlikely to succeed in meeting its intentions. This is true of both teacher-made and workbook assignments. Seatwork needs to be a meaningful extension of lessons and students need to see the connection between a lesson and seatwork. Assignments may coordinate poorly with the preceding instruction and do little more than confuse, mislead, or be busy work. Make sure students understand and do not just want to get it over with, that they do not just daydream, walk around, or socialize. What can happen is the assignment is "just right" for a few students but too hard or too easy, too short or too long, or boring for the rest. Most difficulties with seatwork can be corrected. For best results, the work assigned should be individualized. It can be more effective when individualized and when it is used to diagnose problems or solidify learning, but it must be used correctly.

ASSIGNING SEATWORK.   As stated above, assignments should be tailored to meet individual needs and interests through the content involved and the exercises available. Student choice is desirable. Directions for seatwork should be clear, and teachers should move about during seatwork to react to the work being done. Students should not practice errors! They should be able to do at least 80 percent, even 100 percent, of seatwork correctly. As mentioned earlier, "catching students doing it right" is as important as tactful correctives. Time "up front" (before seatwork begins) reduces the time needed for explanations to individuals at their seats. Clear directions increase at-task behavior and eliminate misbehavior because students do not understand, or cannot do, what was assigned.

Before you ask students to begin seatwork, make sure they understand the concepts and skills involved and know how to do the work. A good procedure is to begin the seatwork as a whole-class endeavor. If, for example, students have been assigned questions, you should do the first one or two questions, step by step, with the whole class. Then, it may be a good idea to do one or two more questions asking individuals to tell you and the class "what to do next." After "guided practice" has taken place, students can work independently. Following this, monitored seatwork can begin. A data sheet on direction giving is included in Chapter 6, Reading A.

MONITORING SEATWORK.   Move about the classroom during seatwork. Do not spend too long with one or two students. When you discover a student is doing an assignment incorrectly, do not just tell the student what to do next, nor just have the student tell you what to do next. Ask "how" and "why" questions. Although repetition for retention is important, understanding needs to be promoted.

Content that is difficult or complex should be broken into parts. Several segments of instruction, each followed by practice, may be necessary. If you find that many students are experiencing the same problem, halt the seatwork and reteach the troublesome material.

You may have one group (or grade, in a two-grade classroom) work independently while another is being instructed. Be positioned and have seats arranged so both groups can be observed. A routine should be set up and followed. For example, for students who need help, the routine may be to have them write their names on a certain place on the chalkboard and then work on another question or other material until you can get to them. A good practice is to signal while students are working. For instance, you can say, "You should have about half of the questions done now," and later, "You have five minutes left." When work has been completed, students must know how to turn it in and what to do next (for example, other assignments, free reading, or to check work with designated peers).

ALTERNATIVE USES OF SEATWORK. The evidence suggests that less time should be devoted to individual seatwork and more to techniques such as teacher-led whole-class practice (e.g., question-and-answer sessions and repetition drills). Other alternatives include having students work in pairs, cooperative group activities, and competition between groups.

Borich (1998, p. 432) notes that research offers guidelines for seatwork (below).

GUIDELINES FOR USE OF SEATWORK
- Select and teach interesting content until students are likely to get 80 percent of seatwork correct.
- Provide clear directions and establish routines for doing the work, its format, handing it in, and correcting it.
- Do guided teacher-led practice; check comprehension as well as knowledge of "what to do and how to do it."
- Assign work that is differentiated to suit individual needs.
- Monitor in-progress seatwork, stress understanding and skill, provide feedback, correctives, and reinforcement. Have the work handed in, provide feedback, and return it.
- Have sufficient appropriate materials available to students.
- Students need to think the seatwork has real learning value and believe that self-regulated learning is important (not just busy work).
- Clear instruction is needed on what to do and how to do it.
- Best suited for (a) practice of previously taught material, or (b) preparation for a lesson.
- Teachers need to monitor student progress and ensure the work is being done correctly.

CASE 10.6 Seatwork

The Seat of Learning

Ms. Desai's English class is getting ready for a seatwork assignment on Greek mythology. This is their first seatwork assignment so she wants them to understand her guidelines for seatwork.

MS. DESAI: OK, class, we've examined several Greek myths. Now I want you to work on your own myth of Prometheus. I have a handout for you, so let's go over the assignment. Mark, will you read the first section?

MARK: In your own words, write out the story of Prometheus in one paragraph.

MS. DESAI: Fine. Abdul, what is the story basically about?

continued

ABDUL: Well, Prometheus feels sorry for humans so he steals fire from the gods on Mount Olympus and gives it to humans to use.

MS. DESAI: Great. OK, Sharma, will you read the next section?

SHARMA: Do a drawing of the story. It can be one drawing or done as a cartoon strip.

LEE: Ms. Desai, I can't draw!

MS. DESAI: That's OK, Lee, you can do stick figures. They can be very effective. Maria, will you read the next instruction?

MARIA: Make a list of things the fire that Prometheus took could represent in Greek times and today.

MS. DESAI: Thanks, Maria. Could you give an example?

MARIA: Fire could represent knowledge.

MS. DESAI: Anything else?

ABDUL: It could be technology.

MS. DESAI: Great, you all have the idea. Does everyone know what to do and how to do it? [Class members nod in agreement.] And, what's our routine, Mark?

MARK: We do a rough copy, have you check it, and then do a good copy on white typing paper.

MS. DESAI: I think you're all ready to go. Check with me if you have any concerns. You know where the crayons and typing paper are kept. Enjoy!

Homework

THE RESEARCH ON HOMEWORK. There are five kinds of homework: practice to master skills and reinforce material learned in class; preparation for upcoming lessons; extending learning beyond what was treated in class; transfer of ideas and skills to new situations; and practicing creativity, critical thinking, and problem solving (Burden & Byrd, 2003, p. 181). Homework needs careful planning, and students need to be taught how to make it meaningful.

Whether homework should be assigned and how much and the kind have been, and still are, issues among students, teachers, and parents. Many school personnel and parents think homework is a good way to extend learning. To be most effective, students "should feel responsible for doing homework and should understand that homework is crucial to learning" (Kauchak & Eggen, 2003, p. 416). Homework use, however, varies from district to district and from school to school. It can be a useful supplement to in-class instruction and increase achievement (at least for secondary students), but we know little about how much and the kind to assign. Research on homework suggests that if teachers assign homework to increase achievement, the odds are that homework for elementary students will have little effect, five to seven hours of homework per week for middle-grades students will have moderate results, and students in high school who do large amounts of homework have higher achievement than those who do little. Cooper (1989) reports that the effects of homework are substantial for high school students, positive for junior high students, but negligible for elementary school students (p. 88). More recently, Kauchak and Eggen (2003) report that homework significantly increases achievement, but "to be effective, it must be a logical extension of classroom work" (p. 375). They add that research has "found that in addition to amount, the frequency of homework is important" (p. 375), with five problems each night, not twenty-five once a week (Cooper, Lindsay, Nye, & Greathouse, 1998). Homework should be an extension of instruction. Cooper (1989) says homework to practice previously taught content or preparation for forthcoming lessons is more effective than homework related to new materials. Kaplan (1990) observes that most studies questioning the value of homework were done on assignments of routine practice, not preparation for new lessons (p. 393). Cooper (1989) concluded that homework works best if material is not too complex or completely unfamiliar (p. 88). Cooper (2001) reviewed findings that younger students do not benefit from homework as much as older students. He concluded, "Studies indicate that younger students have limited attention spans, or more specifically, limited abilities to tune out distractions," and that "younger students haven't yet learned proper study skills" (p. 36). He provides the following homework policy guidelines, which "can make homework an effective teaching tool."

- *Coordinate policies.* Districts, schools, and classrooms should coordinate policies.
- *State the rationale.* The broad rationale for homework should be stated (why mandatory, time requirements, and coordination of assignments among classes).
- *Assign homework.* Homework should be assigned, but the amount depends on developmental level and the quality of home support. It should not be just for knowledge acquisition. In younger grades it can develop good study habits, help students realize they can learn at home as well as at school, foster independent learning, and show parents what is going on at school.
- *Use other approaches.* Homework is only one approach to show children that learning takes place other than in school. (pp. 37–38)

Cooper stresses that teachers should have "flexible homework policies" to "take into account the unique needs and circumstances of their students" (p. 37).

Guidelines for the frequency of homework by students are provided by Cooper (2001): grades 1–3, one to three assignments no longer than fifteen minutes each; grades 4–6, two to four per week; grades 7–9, three to five; and grades 10–12, four to five. Teacher discretion can be used for additional voluntary assignments.

When effective teachers use homework, they grade it and provide correctives and reinforcement (Walberg, 1990, p. 472). Cooper agrees, saying that homework should be included in the grading system. Research suggests that students need to be taught to organize their assignments (Kaplan, 1990, p. 393).

PURPOSE AND CHARACTERISTICS OF HOMEWORK.   Most students think homework is valuable, even if they do not always do it. Parents also think it is valuable and expect it. Inform parents of your homework policy as well as when it is done well and when it is not done. Parents can be asked to check homework, although some of it may have been completed at school. In some jurisdictions, especially in disadvantaged economic areas, it may be unrealistic to assign homework or expect it to be checked by parents. Homework, like any school work, should *never* be used as punishment. This leads to a dislike of the subject, teacher, and schooling.

Many of the characteristics of effective seatwork apply to homework used for practice. If homework is for students to preview material, students should be taught how. Ideally, when homework is for practice, it is individualized. This may be difficult to do if a class is large. Homework should be of reasonable length and difficulty, and should match student ability to work independently. It should be monitored and an accountability system established to ensure it is done on time. It should be marked, and students should correct mistakes and turn the work in again. If needed, reteaching should occur.

"Effective homework assignments do not just supplement the classroom lesson; they also teach students to be independent learners" (U.S. Department of Education, 1986, p. 42). That is, when homework is used well, students gain experience in "following directions, making judgments and comparisons, raising additional questions for study, and developing responsibility and self-discipline" (p. 42). Stress positive reinforcement. Emphasize what was done well and why.

Homework can have value beyond student achievement. Ideally, parents need to know, in general, what is happening in the classroom, the homework expected, and what they can do to support the learning of their children. Providing homework and emphasizing its benefits can help students develop responsibility for studying outside the classroom. It can extend opportunities for students to expand assignments, let students respond to classroom instruction in individualized ways, prepare students for upcoming classroom activities, and provide opportunities for students to practice what they have learned.

If teachers use homework as an instructional tool, it must be part of what happens in the classroom and not an afterthought to keep students busy at home. Homework, normally, should be addressed first thing, before the day's lesson begins. Also, if homework is to be effective, teachers must assign it based on some objective other than simply on the belief that homework is useful.

PROVIDING FEEDBACK ON SEATWORK AND HOMEWORK

- *Rapid feedback.* Provide feedback as soon as possible, to avoid practice of errors and to avoid impeding learning at subsequent levels.
- *Specific feedback.* Students need to know, specifically, what was done satisfactorily and what is needed to achieve success. "Very Good" with little or no comment is not helpful. What was "good," and what made it so should be said in writing or orally.
- *One-on-one as much as possible.* Get around to each member of the class to personalize feedback and leave the messages, "You are important" and "You can succeed."
- *Match learner readiness.* Try to tailor assignments to accommodate individual needs.
- *Stress positive reinforcement.* Emphasize what was done well and the reason why; for areas needing improvement, help students do "even better."
- *Deferred success—not failure.* Avoid the notion of "failure." Instead, emphasize that students "have not yet succeeded" and encourage them to keep trying.
- *Stress discovery of how to perform correctly.* Encourage students to constantly improve by checking their own work or by getting feedback from peers.
- *Stress process during formative stages.* During the formative stages of learning, stress the "how to" and the "why" instead of putting inordinate emphasis on a correct product.
- *Feedback on total class performance on assignments.* Tell the class how the group did on an assignment. What went well, why, and what needs attention? Accept part of the responsibility, telling them you will do some reteaching to help them help themselves.

ACADEMIC INTEGRITY.   An important consideration for seatwork and homework is *academic integrity.* Increasingly, students are doing seatwork and homework with the aid of computers. The availability of the Internet has increased the possibility of plagiarism. The following guidelines can help.

- Expectations of academic honesty must be made clear to all students.
- Students welcome clear guidelines on integrity in their assignments.
- Guidelines must not be ambiguous or unrealistic.
- Periodically review the guidelines and expectations.
- Deal with and discourage the "everyone does it" perception.
- Assess students' work fairly and promptly.

- Have assignments that are well planned to encourage creative and original work.
- Build preplans into assignments, so students show their intended approach and ideas.
- Ensure effective classroom management and examination security.
- Model integrity and honesty. Do not ignore or trivialize dishonesty.

A CAUTION. Homework can have a negative effect on family life and worsen the disparity between social classes; it can punish children from families with fewer resources (e.g., owning a computer) or in a nonsupportive home environment (CPSER, 2004). The quality, amount, and timing of homework have frequently come under criticism by parents. Schools need a reasonable, fair homework policy that is clearly communicated to students and parents. Responding to the effects on students of poverty and the effects of nonfunctional family settings is an issue that school staffs need to address.

CASE 10.7 Homework

The Dog Ate It!

Ms. Desai has just finished marking homework assignments. She wants to acknowledge what the class accomplished.

MS. DESAI: Good morning, class. I've marked your homework. Because this is your first homework assignment, I want to say how well you have all done. Samuel, what is our homework policy?

SAMUEL: I can't remember exactly.

MS. DESAI: Well, it's posted on the wall over there. Will you read the first line?

SAMUEL: Homework shall be given out no more than three times a week, and should take no more than one hour each time.

MS. DESAI: How much time did I give you for this assignment?

SAMUEL: You gave us two nights, one night to find modern examples of Greek or Roman myths in magazines and so on, and one night to write our accounts.

MS. DESAI: What did you find, Abdul?

ABDUL: I looked in the Yellow Pages and I found lots of stuff like Midas Mufflers and Ajax Cleaners.

MS. DESAI: Wonderful. And what did I ask the class to write, Maria?

MARIA: We had to write out the story of the myth in a few words, telling how the modern example matched.

MS. DESAI: Did I give you choices?

MARIA: Yes, you said we could do pictures instead of a written write-up or we could paste an example from a magazine.

MS. DESAI: So, did everybody have enough time?

SEAN: I took more than an hour to find examples, but it was kind of fun, so I didn't mind.

MS: DESAI: How about the rest of you . . . enough time? *(Nods and smiles from the class.)* OK. I'm going to pass out the work. Then I'll come around and have a word with each of you while you read the story of Demeter. What's her other name?

MARK: I know, . . . it's "Ceres." I know 'cause it reminds me of cereal.

LINKING PRACTICE TO THEORY

What was your own experience of homework and seatwork in your schooling? Try the approaches suggested in this chapter. To what extent can they apply to your current teaching situation? Did you enjoy discussions when you were a student? Were they effective to your learning? Can discussions play a significant part in your classroom approach?

Summary

Much is known about effective questioning. Normally, good questioning involves a sequence of gaining attention, addressing the question to the whole class, waiting, asking an individual to respond, having the individual respond, and waiting briefly. How you phrase questions makes a difference. Avoid questions and questioning practices that discourage students or that have low diagnostic value. Distribute questions evenly, and take into account learner ability and readiness. Using wait time increases the amount and level of learning. Use more open-ended and higher-level questions. Handle responses sensitively, making effective use of prompts, probes, and redirects. Students should not be afraid to risk answers, and their questions should be encouraged.

Discussion can be used for four purposes: to review and extend what students have studied for mastery of a subject; to provide an opportunity for students to examine opinions or ideas; to solve a problem or to improve problem-solving capability; and to help develop communication, interpersonal, and group skills. Teachers can learn techniques to make discussions effective. A particularly effective form of discussion is the talking circle. Students like the guideline that encourages participation *when ready* to contribute. Complex issues can be handled with dignity.

It is useful for teachers to examine interaction among students and between teacher and students. Critical thinking is an important part of engagement. It is enhanced through effective questioning, especially through higher-level questions and the use of wait time.

Seatwork and homework can extend learning time, produce investigative work, and help students become independent learners. Monitoring seatwork is important. Seatwork needs purpose and relevance. It should not be assigned to keep students busy. It should meet individual needs and, when appropriate, involve student choice. Homework can be a way to create positive relationships with parents, informing them of their children's learning. Take care to ensure that your students have the at-home resources to do homework. Both seatwork and homework need prompt feedback.

Activities

QUESTIONING

1. Recall a teacher who made effective use of question and answer. How did this teacher go about questioning? Join four or five peers to agree on principles for effective question and answer.
2. The instructor teaches a brief model lesson (about fifteen minutes) on a topic using questioning that systematically moves through the levels of the cognitive domain of Bloom's taxonomy and using as many of the techniques presented above as possible. Debrief, commenting on the behaviors used and the sequence of questions.
3. Join a subject group of five. Pick a topic that lends itself to question and answer. Compose a series of questions that move students through the levels of Bloom's cognitive domain.
4. On cards, list practices to avoid. In class, discuss why they are ineffective. Then, compare the findings with those stated in the chart.
5. Have a volunteer teach a lesson to the class that involves questions. Have the volunteer practice good wait time. Discuss the results with the class. Use Figure 10.2.
6. Take a typical lesson from your files. Rewrite the plan, include questions at each level.
7. Research technological software programs that foster thoughtful responses to questions. A good example is the CD, *Sophie's World,* based on the book by Jostein Gaarder (1996), in which a young girl responds to questions on philosophic issues.
8. The summary of the book, *Sophie's World,* states, "One day Sophie comes home from school to find two questions in her mail. 'Who are you?' and 'Where does the world come from?' " Try the questions on young children during your field experience. Share the results.
9. Groups of four play a game that is a variation of "Tic Tac Toe" ("X's and O's") devised by Sadker and Sadker (1979). Two people act as players, the other two as judges. Disputes are settled by the teacher—the appeal court judge. The player who begins announces the cognitive domain level (see

diagram below) at which he or she will attempt to phrase a question. The question is posed. Judges rule on whether the question is at the level proposed. If the answer is correct, the player can enter an X. The next player then attempts to phrase a question after announcing the chosen domain. If this player is successful, an O is entered. There is a winner when a player has a series of three vertical, horizontal, or diagonal correct answers. When the game is over and if there is a winner, the winner wins the right to be a judge and a former judge becomes the other player; the loser continues to play. If the result is a draw, players and judges switch roles.

Tic-Tac-Taxonomy		
Synthesis	Knowledge	Analysis
Analysis	Synthesis	Evaluation
Evaluation	Application	Comprehension

DISCUSSION

1. Small groups explain how you might deal with problem individuals during a whole-group discussion: (a) students who never participate; (b) students who monopolize the conversation; (c) students who begin to argue with each other; (d) "smart Alec" students; and (e) students who play the part of class clowns.

2. Interview your supervising (or other) teacher, asking when and how he or she uses whole-group and small-group discussion.

3. Select a controversial topic, e.g., "Is teaching a science or an art?" (See 7.) Divide each group into three groups: those who support the topic, those who oppose the topic, and those who have mixed feelings. Have each group prepare a defense of their point of view, listing reasons on a blank transparency. Conduct a discussion. On the Internet, find some highly recommended discussion group sites for students. Consider the value of such sites for helping young people to discuss.

4. Discuss in class: on the spaceship *Enterprise*, what/who would be the perfect electronic teacher?

5. Design a questionnaire that would be useful to rate a school's technological capability.

6. Discuss, in class, the advantages and disadvantages of guided and open discussions.

7. Select a discussion topic (e.g., teaching as an art versus teaching as a science). Create three groups. One group presents "teaching as an art," one "teaching as a science," and one "teaching as a mix of art and science." Following the third presentation, encourage open discussion on the ideas raised.

8. Divide the class into four groups. Following the guidelines presented in this chapter, each group presents a teacher-led discussion.

SEATWORK AND HOMEWORK

1. Select one of your lessons. Following the guidelines presented in this chapter, add a seatwork assignment.

2. Create pairs. Half the class sets a homework assignment that the other half must do. The next class, in pairs, has the homework "marked" according to the guidelines presented in this chapter.

3. Visit the web site, "Ask Jeeves" (www.ask.com). Rate the value of such a site in terms of helping students ask questions and in terms of homework help.

4. Design homework assignments for your discipline (e.g., English or social studies), requiring students to use electronic sources such as online or CD-ROM encyclopedias. Build in a variety if choices.

5. Many schools now have web sites on which homework is posted. Have groups of five consider the ways in which you as a teacher would use such a site.

6. Have students investigate the question of how a teacher might deal with the problem of plagiarism by students using the Internet?

APPENDIX 10.1   *Questioning: Steps, Prompts, Probes, and Redirects*

PROFESSIONAL TARGET—QUESTIONING STEPS, PROMPTS, PROBES, REDIRECTS

1. Record the steps used: attention of all secured (record an "A"); phrase question ("Q"); wait ("W"); name student ("N"); student responds ("R").
2. Enter the number of seconds of wait time allowed after question is asked.
3. Enter a check mark if a prompt, probe, or a redirect is used.

Question Number	Steps Followed (e.g., of correct steps: A, Q, W, N, R).	No. of Seconds of Wait Time	Prompt Used	Probe Used	Redirect Used
1.					
2.					
3.					
4.					
5.					
6.					
7.					
8.					
9.					
10.					
11.					
12					
13.					
14.					

APPENDIX 10.2 *Question Patterns Target*

PROFESSIONAL TARGET—QUESTIONING PATTERNS

Please record the question asked (or the substance of it). Later, (a) classify questions as: knowledge: facts or information, (enter a "K"); comprehension ("C"); application ("Ap"); analysis ("An"); synthesis ("S"); or, evaluation ("E"); (b) decide whether the question was clear, repeated, "yes–no," run-on, leading, blanket; or, (c) classify questions as convergent (single correct answer expected), divergent (unexpected or differing from the standard answer) or evaluative (seeking significance or worth).

No.	Question	Level
1.		
2.		
3.		
4.		
5.		
6.		
8.		
9.		
10.		
11.		
12.		
13.		
14.		

Analysis of questioning patterns (by student teacher or teacher):

APPENDIX 10.3

PROFESSIONAL TARGET—DISCUSSION

Record what was said and done by the teacher and the reaction of students.

Discussion Skill	Observations

A. Focusing on topic
Way topic was introduced
Establishment of aims
Restating of aims
Irrelevancies redirected?
Stage summaries emerge?
Dealing with off-task behavior

B. Clarification of answers
Paraphrasing
Summarizing
Probing
Elaborating
Analyzing

C. Promoting participation
Use of students' ideas
Use of silence
Challenging
Key questions
Providing information

D. Varying interaction
Setting of ground rules
Use of eye contact
Encouraging participation/interaction
Seeking agreements

E. Summarizing
Evaluation of discussion effectiveness
Proposal(s) for follow-up

F. Other teacher interventions/actions
to ensure all are attending

11 Understanding Concepts

The Nature of Concepts

Understanding Concepts

From the womb to the tomb, concepts provide meaning and are vital to the way we organize and structure our world. It would be impossible to think about anything without concepts. Concepts help us live and learn and see things in generalized patterns. In this chapter, we look at the kinds of concepts, their importance to learning and personal understanding, and the nature of attributes, prototypes, and exemplars. The value of concept mapping in giving meaning and structure, and the need to consider learner diversity and readiness, are examined.

WHAT IS A CONCEPT? If we had to, we could tell somebody what concrete objects such as desks, hats, or cups are. We could give understandable definitions of ideas such as friendship, or democracy and dictatorship. We likely could define events such as wars and conferences or classes of people such as Caucasians or Aboriginals. Each is a concept. These words are labels under which we categorize objects, ideas, events, or people—they are *concepts*.

Have you ever said, "I haven't any concept of what you're talking about?" or "Can you conceptualize my tripping over the out-of-bounds line?" Popular usage of the term *concept* is different from pedagogical usage. In education, a concept is a category or set of objects, conditions, events, or processes, that can be grouped together based on similarities and represented by a word or other symbol or image. When we encounter something—for example, a desk—we recognize it because of its key characteristics, or attributes, though that particular desk may differ in some ways from other desks we have seen. We know it is something to sit at while we attend school, study, read, or write. The particular color, height, or material it is made of is not important for us to recognize it is a desk. When we say, "Somebody is sitting in my desk," the person to whom we are speaking knows what

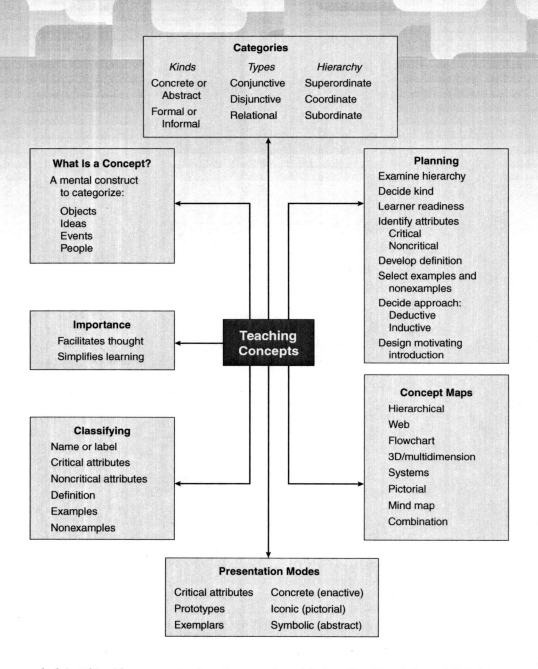

Categories

Kinds	Types	Hierarchy
Concrete or Abstract	Conjunctive	Superordinate
	Disjunctive	Coordinate
Formal or Informal	Relational	Subordinate

What Is a Concept?

A mental construct to categorize:

Objects
Ideas
Events
People

Planning

Examine hierarchy
Decide kind
Learner readiness
Identify attributes
  Critical
  Noncritical
Develop definition
Select examples and
  nonexamples
Decide approach:
  Deductive
  Inductive
Design motivating
  introduction

Importance

Facilitates thought
Simplifies learning

Teaching Concepts

Concept Maps

Hierarchical
Web
Flowchart
3D/multidimension
Systems
Pictorial
Mind map
Combination

Classifying

Name or label
Critical attributes
Noncritical attributes
Definition
Examples
Nonexamples

Presentation Modes

Critical attributes	Concrete (enactive)
Prototypes	Iconic (pictorial)
Exemplars	Symbolic (abstract)

a desk is. This aids communication. Concepts have labels or formal or informal definitions represented by a word, symbol, or mental picture.

IMPORTANCE OF CONCEPTS.   Concepts help us cope with living and learning. They are mental constructs or images that simplify our learning efforts and facilitate thought and communication (Martorella, 1986, p. 183). Concepts are essential to comprehension, promote recall, are functional shortcuts to communication, and aid the transfer of learning.

We are inundated by countless bits of information and knowledge in our personal worlds. Suppose every individual chair had a separate name (or category), and the word *chair* did not exist. How could we learn and remember the name of every single chair we encounter? How could we communicate efficiently without concept names? When we tell someone to "take a chair," he or she knows what we are talking about. We do not have to name each object in the room that can be used for sitting and provide the option of selecting and sitting on one. Besides, would that person have had experiences with, and the same label for, each individual object? Further, communication breaks down when two people have different understandings of a concept, or when one person does not have a concept that is essential to a conversation. Mutual knowledge of the same concepts is essential for efficient communication. For example, the "light" might "go on" for you when somebody from Paris says *chaise* and you catch on that he means the concept of *chair*. Thought and learning are aided immeasurably by grouping, or organizing, all chairs under the same label—*chair*. After all, they all have the same essential characteristics. We need societally accepted word meanings and labels for things and beings. Concepts are basic building blocks for thinking, higher-level thinking in particular.

Generalizations are based on concepts expressed in a relationship, but they are more complicated than their component concepts. Generalizations are rules, regulations, principles, laws, conclusions, inferences, axioms, proverbs, mottoes, propositions, and hypotheses. They are relationships of broad applicability; for example, "A stitch in time saves nine" is a generalization composed of several concepts (stitch, time, saves, nine), meaning it is more efficient to take time do it now, or right, and so to save the time needed for undoing or redoing—it is much easier to do it right the first time. It is important that students understand the component concepts of generalizations. For instance, in the rule, "Water freezes at 32° Fahrenheit," students must understand the concepts water, freezes, degrees, and Fahrenheit, or they will not understand the generalization and learning is reduced to rote memorization. True learning requires making connections between concepts.

CONCEPTS AS PERSONAL UNDERSTANDINGS. Concepts are *personal* understandings of a symbol, an individual's unique way of acquiring meaning from experience. Each person has a history with concepts and will have different experiences with concepts. How often has somebody asked you to clarify, or define, what you meant when you used a word or expression? How often have you had a misunderstanding or argument, because a word had a particular meaning to you but a different one for the other person?

A four-month-old baby has a limited range of functional concepts and responds to a limited number of "words." When children grow older and begin to speak, they acquire many verbal labels for concepts that, initially, are based on one or a few instances. At first, the word *chair* may be used by a child for a single chair, perhaps a highchair. Slowly, the child says and understands *chair* for other objects used for sitting. As the child grows older, many other objects are labeled *chair:* an easy chair, a rocking chair, a reclining chair, and so on. As an adult, the term *chair:* will likely extend to things such as to "chair a meeting," and to "chairperson."

Concepts develop slowly from facts and information, moving from specifics to abstractions. They are constantly open to change through experience and insights, and they develop at different rates for different people. They have somewhat different meanings for different people and mean different things as new experience is gained.

TCP—TEACHING CONCEPTS

Provides effective teaching of concepts and explanations

Prior analysis; students learn critical and noncritical attributes and appropriate definitions; effective examples and nonexamples and understanding extended over time; effective selection of the number and sequence; concepts presented in a lesson or unit interrelated: appropriate choice and use of inductive and deductive approaches.

No prior analysis; definitions often "muddied" with noncritical attributes; definitions presented without emphasis on understanding; relationships not identified; poor selection of examples and absence of nonexamples; approach always deductive.

Kinds of Concepts

Concepts can be categorized in several ways, as shown in Figure 11.1. Some are harder to learn than others because of learner background or developmental level and because it is easier to find examples or prototypes for some, and different kinds of concepts may require different teaching approaches. We can examine the kinds of concepts, such as concrete and abstract concepts, and whether concepts are acquired in formal or informal contexts. We can distinguish different types of concepts and we can examine how concepts relate to each other in a hierarchy. Figure 11.2 shows an example analysis of a concept.

CONCRETE/ABSTRACT.   *Concrete* concepts (e.g., wheels, reptiles, and levers) can be perceived through the five senses. *Abstract* concepts (e.g., democracy, beauty, and truth) are concepts that are only acquired indirectly or through inference.

Abstract concepts are harder to learn than concrete concepts. Different teaching approaches may need to be used. For example, analogies (comparisons) may be used to teach abstract concepts such as *nationalism.* Students are told that the concept *nationalism* is somewhat like the concept *family*—families are groupings of people that have common at-

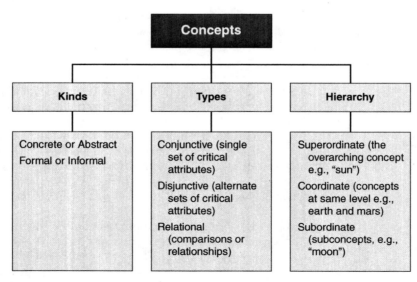

FIGURE 11.1   *Categories of Concepts: Kinds, Types, and Hierarchy*

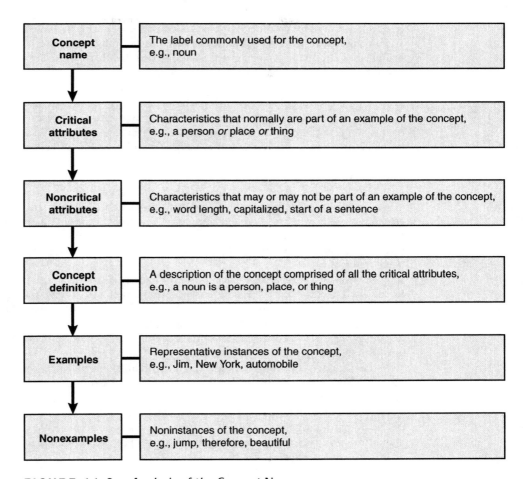

FIGURE 11.2 *Analysis of the Concept* Noun

tributes. Some of the critical attributes of family are also nationalism attributes. Then, another analogy can be used, and still another, pulling out attributes of nationalism. This is done until students can distinguish between good analogies and inappropriate analogies (a streetcar full of people is not an example of nationalism) and grasp the definition of nationalism. Although some concepts are learned informally and others are learned formally, many concepts are learned through a combination of formal and informal experiences—for example, truth, justice, morality, or "good music."

Another approach is to consider examples of the behavior of people who are nationalistic and, from this, infer the meaning of nationalism. An alternate way to teach abstract concepts is to provide instances (and noninstances) of acts and consequences (or before and after, or cause and effect). Attributes are inferred and definitions derived. This approach could be used for concepts such as pollution, waste, or war.

FORMAL/INFORMAL.   Concepts acquired in *formal* contexts are acquired through some form of systematic instruction in, for instance, schools, job training, or from parents (e.g., operation of an internal combustion engine may be learned in school; rules of right and wrong may be learned in Sunday school or other religious school). Concepts acquired in *informal* contexts are concepts we usually acquire through informal life experiences (e.g., using a radio, refrigerator, and automobile).

Concepts can vary in the flexibility of rule structures or in the relationships of critical attributes. Concepts can be differentiated as conjunctive, disjunctive, or relational.

Conjunctive concepts have unchanging rule structures. Phrased another way, they have a single set of characteristics or critical attributes. Conjunctive concepts must have two or more critical attributes that must always be present. For example, a *lake* is always a body of water surrounded by land, and a *square* is always a quadrilateral with all four sides equal.

Disjunctive concepts permit two or more, or alternate, sets of critical attributes, each of which might define the concept, *and* any one attribute alone is sufficient, *or* not all of which have to be present. A good example is the strike in baseball. A strike is called when the batter swings and misses *or* when the batter hits a foul ball *or* when the umpire judges that the ball has passed through the strike zone (Martorella, 1986). A noun is a person *or* place *or* thing.

Relational concepts are concepts whose meanings depend on comparisons or relationships. They do not have special attributes but must have a fixed relationship between or among attributes. A line cannot be called parallel *unless* there is another line to compare it to (Martorella, 1986); a man is not an uncle *unless* he has a nephew; a woman is not a mother *unless* she has at least one son or daughter. Other examples are pollution, large, small, heavy, time, ugly, and rapid.

Disjunctive concepts are complex and more difficult to learn than conjunctive concepts. Relational concepts are even more complex and hard to learn. Disjunctive and relational concepts do not fit the concept definition provided for conjunctive concepts, which states that there must be a single set of defining attributes. Some concepts just cannot be defined with a single set of features. For many concepts (e.g., social class, justice, alienation, poverty), the boundary is not clear and one cannot state with certainty what is or is not an instance.

RELATIONSHIPS TO OTHER CONCEPTS AND HIERARCHIES.   Learners should be aware of how the concepts they are learning are related to other concepts. A *hierarchy* of related concepts can be developed that can be helpful in planning and delivering instruction. Consider the, albeit incomplete, hierarchy of minerals in Figure 11.3.

Components of a hierarchy can be described in terms of superordinate, coordinate, and subordinate concepts. A *superordinate concept* in the example in Figure 11.3 is minerals. All the other concepts are part of this generic concept. Similarly, metals are superordinate to rare, common, and alloy; rare is superordinate to gold, platinum, and silver; and so on. *Coordinate concepts* are coordinate to one another: metals and stones; rare, common, and alloy metals; rare and precious stones; gold, platinum, and silver rare metals; and so on. Coordinate concepts share common critical attributes, but have to be differentiated from one another—each shares the critical attributes of the concepts to which it is coordinate, but also has one or more unique critical attributes. *Subordinate concepts* explain a hierarchy. Metals and stones are subordinate to minerals; rare, common, and alloy are subordinate to metals; gold, platinum, and silver are subordinate to rare metals; and so on. Subordinate concepts share common critical attributes and have one or more unique critical attributes.

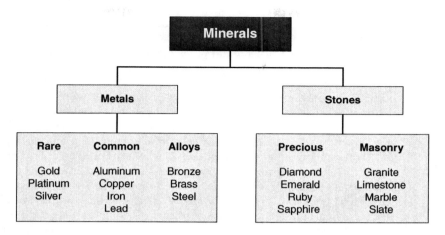

FIGURE 11.3 *Hierarchy of Minerals*

Not all concepts lend themselves easily to placement in a hierarchy. There are unclear cases. To illustrate, is a tomato a fruit or a vegetable? For many concepts, it is difficult to identify and articulate critical attributes. Concept analysis is still useful, however, whether we use the traditional attribute approach, the prototype approach, or a combination.

Teaching concepts so they make sense to learners means taking hierarchies into account. Instruction should be in a logical sequence, recognizing and taking advantage of groupings and relationships (vertical or horizontal). An advance organizer (e.g., a chart or table depicting the key ideas and relationships in a unit) may be presented representing the hierarchy of concepts to be learned. This helps, particularly when direct instruction is being used. Presenting concepts that are part of a hierarchy in a hit-and-miss fashion makes little sense. Usually, an advance organizer should be used when teaching deductively, and a postorganizer may work well when teaching inductively. As each concept is introduced, its place in the organization can be pointed out, and, finally a postorganizer should be used.

Learning Concepts

ATTRIBUTES AND PROTOTYPES OR EXEMPLARS. As stated earlier, we can recognize a concept because of its key characteristics or critical attributes. Concepts such as *hat, envelope,* or *tree* each have key attributes. In a class discussion of the concept *tree,* students would have little trouble giving example attributes such as having leaves or being a living thing. Teaching of concepts through critical attributes is discussed below.

Some authorities prefer to stress prototypes (sometimes called *exemplars*) of concepts rather than critical attributes. *Prototypes* are the best representatives of a category. For instance, cats and dogs are prototypes of mammals and, even though a whale is also a mammal, it is not a prototype. Kauchak and Eggen (2003, p. 258), Woolfolk (2004, p. 276), and as far back as Medin and Smith (1984) describe the prototype approach, which is based on the belief that students learn concepts by forming mental prototypes after being exposed to *best examples.* Those who emphasize the prototype approach point out that, particularly for more complex concepts, it is difficult to identify clear and unchanging attributes. They believe attributes may only be probable of class members and cannot be stated on an all-or-none basis; and better examples of a concept have more characteristics than poorer examples.

Exemplars, say Sternberg and Williams (2002), are "highly typical instances" of a concept (p. 312). Some examples, says Ashcraft (2002), are better examples of concepts than others. A student's memories, for example, of specific dogs provide the basis for recognizing examples not previously seen. The pet dogs in a student's town may be the exemplars that are the basis for categorizing other animals as dogs seen in another town or on TV.

McKinney, Gilmore, Peddicord, and McCallum (1987) compared the traditional approach (concepts taught through critical attributes) and the prototype approach (concepts taught through presentation of best examples). They found no difference in achievement between groups. They found, however, that students taught by the critical attribute approach could generate more examples than those taught by the prototype approach. You should likely not take an either–or stance in favor of one approach or the other. In any case, it is important that the first examples presented to learners be "pure" or clear representatives of the concept to be learned; and selection of examples should be based on familiarity to learners. A rule might be to present examples in the order of "pure to obscure." In other words, they should be prototypes that learners know about. Less prototypical examples should not be introduced until learners have a good understanding of the critical attributes of the prototype or exemplar. For example, when teaching about "birds," begin with birds such as robins, which students have seen, before introducing birds such as ostriches, which do not fly, or penguins, which do not fly but do swim.

Two approaches to teaching concepts are the *deductive* and the *inductive* approaches. Some teachers prefer the deductive approach (providing the definition, and then listing attributes), but Joyce, Weil, and Calhoun (2004, pp. 62–64) argue that this runs counter to much current practice. They prefer the inductive approach, what they and some others call *concept attainment*. This involves a sequence of presenting students with data in sets of items (both positive and negative exemplars), students comparing these exemplars, students developing hypotheses about the nature of a category, having them identify positive exemplars, perhaps having students provide examples, students sharing hypotheses and describing how their understanding developed, having the teacher supply the technical label of the concept, and finally, having students search for more items of the class of concept.

Helping learners acquire concepts is one of the greatest challenges teachers face, whether in kindergarten or graduate school. There is no substitute for careful planning and sensitive, methodical instruction. If you plan and teach effectively, learners can master concepts. Mastery involves the ability to tell whether something is or is not an example of a concept and the ability to find or create an example of a concept and tell why it is an example. It includes the ability to modify nonexamples to make them examples and justify the changes made, and to use a concept name, or label, correctly and justify the choice through critical attributes.

A good coach devises a "game plan" and helps team members acquire the knowledge and skills needed to execute the plan. If the coach is to have an effective game plan executed well, he or she must have a thorough knowledge of the concepts and skills involved. This knowledge is used when the coach does the planning needed before instruction and practice occurs. Careful planning must precede effective and efficient concept instruction and learning. "Winging it" normally just does not work. A Concept Analysis Form that may be helpful is shown in Appendix 11.1. A *Ten Step Model* for planning to teach a concept is discussed below. It is *not* intended to be rigidly linear and sequential for either planning or teaching concepts.

Connecting Concepts through Concept Maps

Where does a concept being learned fit into the scheme of things? The ability to understand, recall, and use a concept is enhanced when students can see visually how a concept is related to other concepts as a hierarchy or ideas that are related. Concepts can be mapped as a hierarchy of relationships. A visualization of a *concept map* is given in Figure 11.4.

Students' understanding of a concept is not complete unless it is linked to other related concepts (Kauchak & Eggen, 2003; Hall, Hall, & Saling, 1999). It is easier for students to make meaning of what is being taught when concept maps are presented or created. When concept maps are used, relationships between concepts are depicted visually, either as a graph presented by the teacher, or as one designed by students themselves. Concept maps can be used in several ways. By constructing a map you become more aware of the key concepts and their relationship. Also, you will not be as likely to leave out or misinterpret some concepts. You become more sensitive to how concepts can best be presented. Concepts can be used as an advance organizer and referred to as the lesson or unit progresses. This helps students get "the bigger picture," notice the relationships between individual concepts, and develop a better understanding of the definitions of individual concepts. A concept map can also be used at the end of a lesson or unit to review and consolidate learning. Alternatively, you can have students construct concept maps, thereby allowing them to become active learners and attain deeper personal meaning. A further possibility is for you, as an assessment strategy, to have students make concept maps. This makes assessment more meaningful and authentic.

Figure 11.4 is a concept map showing the hierarchy of bodies in our solar system. By viewing the parts of the solar system as a hierarchy, students can see the connections between concepts within the hierarchy. This enhances learning. In the map of the solar system, concepts are named. Later in the chapter a complete lesson is built around the concept of a solar system. Novak and Gowin (1984) show a concept map made by a student on "water" (Figure 11.5). In this concept map, linking words are used to make relationships obvious.

Concept maps come in a variety of formats, including hierarchical, web or spider, flowchart, systems, and 3D or multidimensional (Table 11.1). Regardless of background,

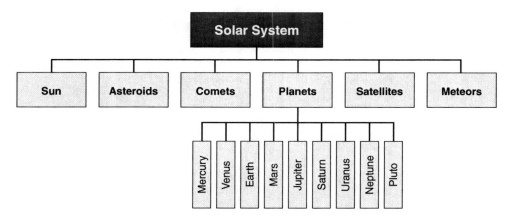

FIGURE 11.4 *Concept Hierarchy of* Solar System

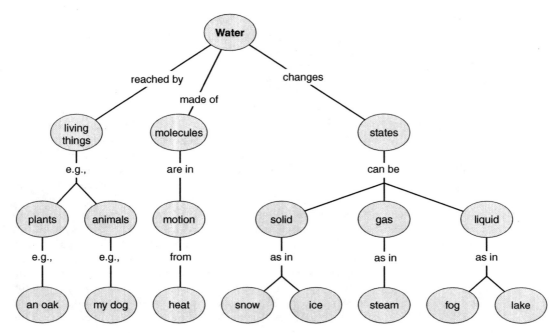

FIGURE 11.5 *Concept Map: Water*

Source: Based on ideas from Novak, 1991, and Novak & Gowin, 1984, p. 16.

it is always desirable to have the "real things" or at least pictures available for handling or viewing. Even when learners are mature, there still are times when learners lack readiness and enactive or iconic examples should be used. Abstract concepts, of course, are learned indirectly through the senses and inference. For these, instruction may need to be heavily verbal, or symbolic, as in, for example, algebra or sentence structure.

TABLE 11.1 *Concept Map Formats*

Hierarchical	Information presented in order of importance, with the most important information on top.
Web or spider	Information organized with the central theme in the middle and subthemes arranged around the center.
Flowchart	Information or steps organized in a linear way.
3D or multidimensional	Information too complicated to be shown in two dimensions, so three dimensions are used.
Systems	Like a flowchart, information organized in parts, one part flowing to the next, each with an input, process, and output. The output for one becomes the input for the next part.
Pictorial	Information presented as pictures, landscapes, or symbols. Also, word ideas can be arranged in the shape of a tree, a wheel, a snake, or other design.

Diversity: Recognizing Learner Background

When concepts are introduced, consideration must be given to the previous experiences and developmental levels of learners. The medium through which concepts are presented (concrete, pictorial, or symbolic) should depend on learner developmental level. A teacher could largely talk about a concept, but learners may not have the necessary linguistic comprehension to benefit. The examples presented should, in this case, be concrete or hands-on. At the next level, learners may have had day-to-day experience with the examples, but it may be desirable to provide visual representations of the concept—for example, pictures. At still another level, it may be sufficient to use verbal or other symbols. Furthermore, learners differ in preferred learning style or cultural background (e.g., a student who recently arrived from Thailand may have no idea of how hockey is played). Abstract concepts, of course, are learned indirectly through the senses and inference. For these, instruction may need to be heavily verbal, or symbolic, as in, for example, algebra or sentence structure. Metaphors and analogies may not be familiar to all learners, so teachers need to consider the background of students in their classes. It now is more common for teachers to stress connections with prior knowledge. Bulgren, Deshler, Schumaker, and Lenz (2000) call this *analogical instruction.*

Learner Readiness: Modes of Presentation

The examples used, defining attributes noted, and definitions used should vary with the developmental level of learners. The concept *plant* is introduced early in a child's schooling and returned to many times with increasing degrees of complexity as the child progresses through the school grades, and with even more complexity with college study of the concept. The first grappling with a concept is at a simplified level. With successive reintroductions, the examples or exemplars (prototypes) used become more complex, the defining attributes more detailed and varied, the definition more encompassing and complex, and the hierarchy to which the concept belongs becomes more specific and inclusive. That is, there is a vast difference between the definitions studied and the way they are studied by a grade 3 student in a science class and a graduate student in biology. Graduate students are at an advanced level at which discussion can take place about what may or may not be critical attributes.

A useful and classic way to think about presentation mode is *Dale's Cone of Experience* (Figure 11.6), which shows the progression from direct, first-hand participation to pictorial representation and on to purely abstract symbolic expression (Wiman & Mierhenry, 1969). The Cone of Experience is similar to Bruner's (1960) three major modes of learning (enactive—doing; iconic—seeing, observing; and symbolic—reading, hearing).

Concepts and Teaching Approaches

So far we have discussed the nature of concepts. We now look at some practical teaching approaches. These include doing a concept analysis, examining a specific lesson model, teaching concepts through both deductive and inductive approaches, and a suggested teaching cycle.

Planning Guide for Analysis of Concepts

Concept learning involves the skill of *classifying*—putting things into a class and then being able to recognize members of that class. It involves ability to list or, when presented,

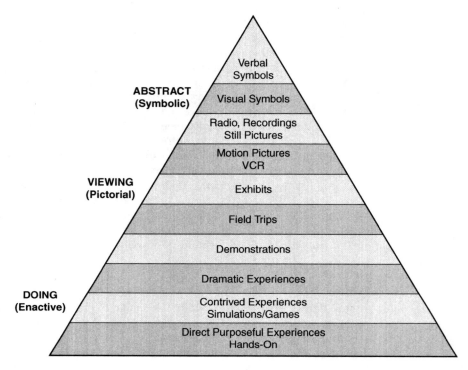

FIGURE 11.6   *Dale's Cone of Experience*
Source: Based on the research of Edgar Dale, 1969.

recognize examples of a concept when asked. When teaching concepts, you need four components: (1) the name of the concept; (2) examples and nonexamples; (3) relevant and irrelevant attributes, and (4) a definition. Joyce et al. (2004) present a concept attainment model. In this approach there are two phases. In phase one, the concept is identified and the teacher presents examples; students compare attributes in positive and negative examples, generate and test examples, and state a definition. In phase two, the teacher confirms hypotheses, names the concept, and restates definitions; the students generate additional examples (p. 72). You can play a major role in helping learners through these operations by analyzing the concepts to be learned before they are taught. As a first step, when planning to teach a concept you can identify:

- Names or labels
- Critical attributes (or characteristics)
- Noncritical attributes
- Definitions of concepts to be learned
- Examples
- Nonexamples

Before teaching a concept, it is advisable to do a concept analysis. The format illustrated in Appendix 11.1 may be used to help you analyze concepts. While the sequence of analysis can be done as illustrated, planning need not be linear. Let us examine each aspect.

CONCEPT NAME. Most concepts can be named. The name or label of a concept is the symbol under which all instances of that concept are grouped or categorized. We use names to think and to communicate concepts such as *wheel, lake,* or *reptile* (we also use words to communicate concepts such as *democracy* or *love*).

CRITICAL ATTRIBUTES. We should be able to identify concepts rapidly and easily. This can be done based on their key common characteristics—the critical (nonvarying) attributes. Consider these examples:

Concept name	*Critical attributes*
wheel	circular frame; hard material; can turn on an axle
lake	large; body of water; surrounded by land
reptile	cold-blooded; egg-laying; air-breathing; moves on belly or on small short legs; vertebrate; scales or bony plates

NONCRITICAL ATTRIBUTES. Much of the confusion when students try to learn concepts occurs because of noncritical attributes (which can vary) that can be associated with a concept. For example, a young child may first associate the word *chair* with the yellow chairs in the kitchen. All chairs, then, must look like those yellow kitchen chairs. Chairs in the living room, because they are a different color and shape, are not yet *chairs.* The child has not learned that color and shape are noncritical attributes of *chair.* Some noncritical attributes are particularly befuddling. For example, a child may believe that all birds fly, but there are birds that cannot fly. Flying is a noncritical attribute of the concept *bird.* Noncritical attributes are attributes found in some, but not all, members of a class. Consider the following:

Concept name	*Noncritical attributes*
wheel	color; size; whether or not it has spokes
lake	depth; size; location; vegetation
reptile	size; coloration; length of tail; habitat

CONCEPT DEFINITION. Concept definitions contain all the essential or critical attributes and express the relationship of these attributes to each other. Consider these examples:

Concept name	*Definition*
wheel	a circular frame of hard material capable of turning on an axle
lake	a large body of water surrounded by land
reptile	an air-breathing vertebrate that moves on its belly or on small short legs, and is covered with scales or bony plates

CONCEPT EXAMPLES AND NONEXAMPLES. Simply defining a concept is not sufficient. It is essential that we have experience with both examples and nonexamples of concepts (exceptions will be discussed later). Gold is an example of a rare metal and a nonexample of an alloy; and a diamond is an example of a precious stone and a nonexample of a common metal. Examples are *positive instances* of a concept. Nonexamples are *negative instances* of a concept. Examples and nonexamples of some common concepts are

Concept name	Examples	Nonexamples
wheel	wagon wheel; car wheel; game show wheel	pie; frisbee; Chinese checkers board
lake	Lake Superior, Windemere Lake, and Lac LaRonge	Amazon River, Pacific Ocean, and Juan de Fuca Strait
reptile	snake, lizard, alligator	beaver, seal, and duck

There are exceptions to the example approach to teaching concepts. Sometimes it may not be possible to consider examples. For example, have you ever observed an atom (even with a microscope)? An amp, ohm, or erg? Nationalism? An angel? Models and diagrams are often used to teach these, analogies might be used, or act-and-consequence instances might be used. Examples are only such if they are part of the learners' backgrounds.

USING EXAMPLES AND NONEXAMPLES.   When you teach a concept, we recommend that you start with a few well-chosen familiar examples (four or five are sufficient), emphasizing the defining attributes. Learning complicated concepts and being able to generalize to recognize new instances requires a larger number of examples; younger or less able learners require even more examples. Then, nonexamples should be presented, discovering why they are not examples. Following this, learners can practice differentiating between examples and nonexamples, giving reasons for their selections. Examples are more effective when they differ widely in a number of noncritical attributes—for example, plants can be of different sizes, shapes, and colors—and nonexamples are more effective when they exhibit few critical attributes—for example, a plant is alive, but so are the nonexamples rabbits and trout. Woolfolk (2004, p. 279) says that nonexamples should be very close to the concept but miss by one or just a few critical attributes (e.g., a circle-like line that is not completely closed is a nonexample of a circle, or a drinking-glass-like object that does not have a bottom is a nonexample of a drinking glass). This, she feels, should be done to avoid *overgeneralization*. Perhaps the truth is that, initially, nonexamples should have few critical attributes, and when students have a grasp of the definition, nonexamples that differ only on one or a few critical attributes should be introduced. Begin by presenting very pure and common examples before moving to the more obscure. *Undergeneralization* should be avoided. For example, learners should realize that the concept *mammals* includes whales and dolphins. These kinds of examples should not be introduced until students have had experience with pure instances (or prototypes) of the concept.

Concepts and Textbooks

A serious weakness in some textbooks is that the authors too frequently provide a definition of a concept, provide an explanation, and then support the explanation with only one example or too few examples. Often, a key defining attribute is underemphasized or even missed entirely. The problem is compounded by definitions that do not include all the critical attributes, definitions that do not clearly state the relationships of attributes, or definitions that are too sophisticated for the learner level. What often is missing is careful prior concept analysis. Small wonder students have difficulty and that learning then is reduced to a kind of rote search for contextual clues.

The message is, do not unduly (or undeservedly) rely on textbooks. They are teaching aids, not "the course." Do an analysis, yourself, of the concepts students are to learn.

An Example Approach

TEACHING THE CONCEPT *SOLAR SYSTEM.*   See the *Ten Step Model* in Figure 11.7.

1. *Examine the concept hierarchy.* Emerging research has found that concepts "typically are not learned in isolation" but are assimilated into knowledge organized into networks (Good & Brophy, 1995, p. 251). Concepts are part of a hierarchy that can provide important information that should be used to control the sequence in which the component concepts

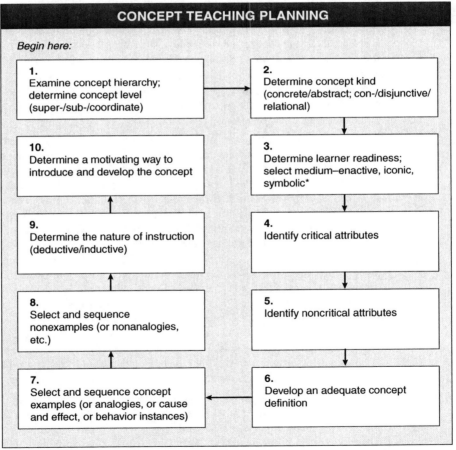

*In step 3, *enactive* refers to the use of hands-on learning, *iconic* refers to learning through the use of images such as pictures, models, diagrams, and drawings, and *symbolic* involves learning through, for example, words, numbers, or codes.

FIGURE 11.7   *Ten Step Model for Teaching a Concept*

are presented. Determine the place in the hierarchy the concept occupies. Assume that a teacher is about to begin an astronomy unit in science on the solar system, and consider the partial hierarchy in Figure 11.4 shown earlier.

The concepts *sun, asteroid, comet, planet, satellite,* and *meteors* are subordinate to the superordinate concept *solar system.* The concept *planets,* however, is superordinate to the concepts *Mercury, Mars, Pluto, Earth, Venus, Uranus, Neptune, Saturn,* and *Jupiter.* These nine planets, therefore, are subordinate to the concept *planets.* Though they have an identity and unique attributes, they also are coordinate concepts because they have common critical attributes.

A likely first step is to prepare a concept hierarchy (see Figure 11.4). This can be an advance organizer and part of the set for a unit. The complexity of the hierarchy should depend on the previous experience and age of the learners. A sequencing decision has to be made. What will help learners understand and recall the concepts in the hierarchy and the relationship of these concepts to each other? In what order should the concepts be introduced? Proceed from the top and work down? Vice versa? Probably during the development of the unit, coordinate concepts should be introduced and then presented individually. If the coordinate concepts of the nine planets are being treated, in what order should they be presented? Smallest to largest? Vice versa? Most to least familiar? Closeness to sun? Other?

2. *Decide the kind of concept.* Once a concept has been selected from the hierarchy, a decision has to be made about the kind of concept, whether concrete or abstract, or conjunctive, disjunctive, or relational.

- Is it a concrete concept (one that can be perceived through the five senses), or is it an abstract concept (one that can only be acquired indirectly or through inference)? A rabbit, as an example of a mammal, can be observed and is a concrete concept; socialism is an example of an abstract concept. Specific planets can have both concrete and abstract attributes. If the concept is the planet Venus, it can be observed without a telescope, but Pluto is so distant and small, the technology needed to observe it is normally not available. The concept Venus is less abstract than Pluto, because Venus can be viewed more readily.

- Is it a conjunctive concept (one with an unchanging rule structure or single set of critical attributes), or a disjunctive concept (one that permits two or more, or alternative, sets of critical attributes—one attribute alone may be enough or not all the attributes need to be present), or a relational concept (one whose meaning depends on comparison or a relationship)? The concrete concept of the metal *copper* is a conjunctive concept. The abstract concept *citizen* is a disjunctive concept (one can be a citizen of a country *or* a city or province, and one can be born a citizen *or* become one after immigrating). The concept *moon* (a satellite) is a relational concept because each moon has a relationship to, or must circle, a specific planet.

3. *Decide learner readiness.* What background, previous experience, do learners have with the concept and the hierarchy to which it belongs? Some concepts (and their hierarchy) are presented to learners several times, with increasing complexity, during schooling. How old are the learners? What are their developmental levels? Slow or fast? Preferred learning styles? The kind of concept to be learned should influence the medium chosen to teach it.

If learners are young or "slow," presentation should, as much as possible, be at the enactive (hands-on or concrete), or possibly at the iconic, level (pictures, diagrams, models). If the concept is abstract and good analogies are hard to find, the presentation may need to be largely symbolic (words or other symbols). A rule of thumb is that it is often appropriate to support symbolic presentations with "the real thing" or visuals—at least at the introductory stages. Readiness influences: (1) the kinds and number of examples that should be used; (2) the specificity and complexity of the concept definition to be learned; and (3) the pacing and number of repetitions (practices) needed for mastery.

The first thing you may have to do is clear up misconceptions that can impede the use of a term in the subject being studied. The popular use of the term *concept* is different from a professional teacher's use of that term. For example, the popular use of the word *credit* is different from that of an accountant. The accounting instructor must point out (and periodically reinforce) the difference.

4. *Identify critical attributes.* The key common characteristics of the concept must be identified. These are the defining, or critical attributes, sometimes called "nonvariable" attributes. *Large, body of water,* and *surrounded by land* are critical attributes of the concept *lake.* You can use several sources to begin to decide what these attributes are, and how they can be presented. Two common sources are a dictionary and the textbook for the course. An important caution is that these are just starting points! The critical attributes identified as part of the concept definition or description may not be complete and/or may be misleading or at an inappropriate level for the class. In other words, because it is in the dictionary or textbook is no assurance the information is accurate, complete, or appropriate.

Let us examine an example to find critical attributes. Imagine a science text stating, "Comets are balls of ice and dust that orbit around the sun, but usually have elongated, elliptical orbits." This definition reveals that two attributes ("balls of ice and dust" and "orbit around the sun") are critical. Some confusion could be caused because the textbook definition states the orbit is usually elongated and elliptical; therefore, you need to decide whether to include this in the definition used by students.

5. *Identify noncritical attributes.* The next step is to find the characteristics that may be, but not need be, part of a given instance of the concept to be learned—the noncritical attributes. These attributes are normally not needed to define the concept. Including them in the definition can be confusing and interfere with learning and transfer. For example, the size of a triangle is a noncritical attribute and has no bearing on whether a given figure is or is not a triangle. The ring around the planet Saturn is a noncritical attribute of planet. A comet does not have to have an orbit that is elongated and elliptical—though that is the usual shape. Clearly identifying noncritical attributes helps ensure that learners will understand the concept.

6. *Develop an adequate concept definition.* Once you have clearly identified critical and noncritical attributes, select or compose a suitable definition. The definition must include the critical attributes and the relationship of attributes to each other. Including noncritical attributes most often provides a "muddy" definition that is hard to understand. A lake is a large body of water that is surrounded by land. The attributes—all must be present—are "large" *and* "body of water" *and* "surrounded by land." A comet, in the definition provided above, is a "ball of ice and dust" that [*and*] "orbits around the sun," but [*and*] "usually has an elongated and elliptical orbit."

7. *Select and sequence concept examples.* Suitable examples must be selected and sequenced if learners are to understand a concept. Good examples, presented in the sequence of obvious to less obvious, help learners discover critical attributes, and help prevent undergeneralization. Examples must be sequenced. The first example should be "pure"—a "best example" (prototype or exemplar) of the concept and contain few noncritical attributes. If possible, at least three to five examples should be given. Young learners, or slow learners, may need additional examples. You point out—better still, learners discover—the critical attributes of the concept from the examples presented. If, for example, the topic under study is the planets in our solar system, begin with the better-known planets Venus, Earth, Saturn, and Mars and defer introducing the planet Pluto.

8. *Select and sequence concept nonexamples.* Based on the definition, particularly through critical and noncritical attributes, learners will need to be able to distinguish between examples and nonexamples of a concept and should be able to give reasons for the distinctions. Your task, as teacher, is to select and sequence nonexamples. Probably, the first nonexamples should be obvious and contain few critical attributes. For example, *sun* and *stars* could be nonexamples of *planet.* To prevent overgeneralization, later nonexamples should be close to the definition and differ in, say, one attribute—for example, *asteroids.* With very young learners, less stress should be on nonexamples and more stress on examples.

9. *Decide the nature of instruction.* You now must decide the instructional approach to use. This should be based on the information gained through doing the above eight steps. Should the approach be deductive or inductive? Should an example and nonexample (from which attributes can be observed or deduced) approach be used? Should analogies be used from which inferences can be drawn and attributes identified? Cause–effect and inference? Behavior and inference?

The *deductive* (or *expository*) *approach* begins with the presentation of a concept definition, then is illustrated with examples and nonexamples. This uses a rule → example sequence, and, as a memory jog, can be called the *rule–e.g.* approach. The *inductive approach* involves presenting examples followed by student discovery of the definition. The sequence is from specifics to the general, or *e.g.–rule.*

10. *Find motivating ways to introduce and develop concepts.* Learning concepts can be productive and enjoyable when it touches the personal lives and needs of students. Recognize learner interests and lead them through exciting adventures. Learner developmental level must be recognized and instruction should be varied, interactive, and involve as many senses as possible. Learning styles and cultural background need to be considered. Challenge learners but still "organize for success experiences." When a student asks, "Why do I have to learn this?" give a good answer from the student's point of view. Statements such as, "You may need this later in life," or "Astronauts need to know this," or "It's going to be on the exam" are not good enough.

If you have planned well, you will be armed with knowledge that will let you: (1) provide different kinds of well-sequenced examples students can understand and use and that avoid undergeneralization; (2) provide well-sequenced nonexamples that avoid overgeneralization; (3) help learners identify or infer the critical attributes of the concept; (4) help learners identify or infer the noncritical attributes of the concept; (5) help learners understand a concept definition that contains the critical attributes and the relationship of these to each other; and (6) provide practice so learners will be able to recall and use the concept correctly.

EXAMPLE OF A LESSON PLAN.   Using the format provided earlier, a lesson plan for teaching the concept *planet* follows.

Lesson: Planet

I. *Topic*   Planet

II. *Content Identification*   The topic "Planets" in a unit on "Our Solar System"

III. *Objectives*
   A. Given a diagram of examples and nonexamples of a planet, each student will be able to identify each planet.
   B. Given the above items, each student will be able to write a suitable justification for the selections made.

IV. *Prerequisite Student Learning*
Familiarity with the solar system concept hierarchy and exposure to the concepts of solar system and sun. Familiarity with the notions of critical and noncritical attributes and super-, sub-, and coordinate concepts.

V. *Presentation Activities*
   A. Introductory
      1. Ask students whether they heard about the recent meteor shower and what they know about it.
      2. Questions to discover students' knowledge of the solar system they have gained through watching the television series or movie *Star Trek*.
      3. Using a large, unlabeled chart of the solar system, provide an advance organizer and state the objectives.
   B. Developmental
      1. Show a short film on the solar system, asking students to pay particular attention to the planets.
      2. Ask students to name the planets that were mentioned in the film.
      3. Using a large three-dimensional model of the planets, sun, and moons, demonstrate how planets orbit around the sun.
      4. Divide students into groups of five to agree on the critical attributes of planets; groups report to the class and then agreement is reached.
      5. The same groups agree on and report what they believe to be noncritical attributes.
      6. Using questions and discussion, draw the concept definition from the class.
      7. Using the unlabeled chart of the solar system, with the class as a whole, randomly point to stars, planets, satellites, etc., asking students to say whether items are examples or nonexamples of planets, requiring that students' responses be justified.
   C. Closure
      1. Using question and answer, review critical and noncritical attributes and the concept definition.
      2. Draw super-, sub-, and coordinate concepts of "planet" from students, and how their learning about "planet" can be useful.
      3. Assign an unlabeled diagram of the solar system for homework. Students are to label the planets and, in writing, justify their choices and show why other items were not chosen.
      4. Foreshadow the topic of the next lesson.

VI. *Materials and Aids*   Large chart of solar system; short film on solar system; one-page diagram of solar system.

VII. *Evaluation*   Questioning; reports by groups; homework assignment; unit test.

Teaching Using Deductive and Inductive Approaches

Your approach in a lesson may be deductive, inductive, or a combination. You can learn when each approach is appropriate.

Deductive (expository) teaching may work better in some situations, and inductive teaching in others. The deductive approach, being teacher centered, tends to be direct and closed; the inductive approach, being learner centered, tends to be open, indirect, and emphasizes helping learners to think.

Expository teaching is suitable for teaching the relationships among several concepts. Older learners are better able to benefit from an expository approach because they have a larger bank of concepts they can mentally manipulate. An advance organizer should precede the deductive approach. It can be time efficient for teaching large numbers of facts and simple, concrete concepts. It can be used if rapid attainment of basic familiarity with background concepts is needed for what is about to be taught. The deductive approach should begin with a discussion about the concept before the definition is provided. For instance, some ideas or anecdotes about, or characteristics of, the concept can be surfaced. Then the definition can be provided and examples and nonexamples used to understand the definition based on critical attributes.

Learners are more intrinsically interested when an inductive approach is used. They achieve higher-cognitive-level outcomes and are better able to transfer their learning. Proponents of problem-based and active learning believe learners should learn through active involvement with concepts and be permitted to discover concepts themselves.

Whether the approach is deductive on inductive, the question "Why?" should be asked. "Why is this an example?" "Why is this a nonexample?" Most students recall concepts only through examples and not through definitions. Insistence on rote memorization of definitions is questionable—do stress understanding.

Many authorities argue that the definition should never be given before examples are provided. They believe the definition-first approach may be suitable for formal reasoning, but only in a few cases. Presenting the definition first can court disaster because it promotes rote learning, not understanding. It is critical for most young students that the definition come last and that learners put definitions together themselves to prove understanding. A summary of the deductive and inductive approaches to concept teaching is presented in Figure 11.8.

Deductive and Inductive Approaches to Teaching a Concept		
DEDUCTIVE "rule–eg"	Establish set and then:	INDUCTIVE "eg–rule"
1. Concept label and definition given by teacher		1. Learners discover critical and noncritical attributes through examples
2. Examples, then nonexamples, given, and critical and noncritical attributes pointed out		2. Further learner discovery through nonexamples
3. Definition reviewed		3. Concept labeled and defined by learners
4. Examples and nonexamples presented simultaneously		4. Examples and nonexamples presented simultaneously
5. Practice		5. Practice

FIGURE 11.8   *Deductive and Inductive Approaches to Concept Teaching*

Steps normally followed in the deductive approach are

1. Establish the set and introduce the concept definition, drawing attention to the critical attributes and their relationship(s) to each other.
2. Introduce examples and nonexamples, drawing attention to the critical and noncritical attributes.
3. Review the definition, pointing out critical attributes and their relationship to each other.
4. Present examples and nonexamples simultaneously; draw attention to reasons why examples are instances and why nonexamples are not instances of the definition.
5. Provide practice that requires justification of choices.

Steps often followed in the inductive approach are

1. After establishing the set, introduce examples, helping learners "discover" the critical attributes and noncritical attributes. Learners can provide additional examples.
2. Introduce nonexamples, helping learners strengthen their understanding of the critical and noncritical attributes. Learners can provide other nonexamples.
3. Help learners label the concept and "discover" an appropriate definition that includes the critical attributes and their relationship(s).
4. Present examples and nonexamples simultaneously and have learners distinguish between them, justifying their choices.
5. Provide practice that requires justification of choices.

A Concept Teaching Cycle

Helping learners acquire concepts involves a cycle of preparing and motivating learners to learn; presenting advance organizers; delivering the body of the lesson in an efficient, well-organized, and interesting way (using a variety of media, providing for transfer, and reviewing and providing meaningful practice). Display enthusiasm and explain (and demonstrate) the inquiry approach and questioning techniques. Good concept lessons often follow the teaching cycle in Figure 11.9. A data sheet you can use for feedback when teaching a concept lesson is shown in Appendix 11.2.

1. *Planning.* Before instruction begins, the content is chosen in keeping with the curriculum. The text and other references should be reviewed. The previous experiences and readiness of learners must be considered. Study the hierarchy of which the concept is a part and prepare an advance organizer (concept map or web). Then select the appropriate instructional approach and learning activities.

2. *Presenting objectives and advance organizer.* Normally, at the outset, explain the instructional objectives and how the new learning ties in with what has been studied before and what will be studied in the future. Provide the advance organizer. Presenting objectives and using advance organizers aids understanding and retention.

3. *Engaging in learning activities.* In this phase, learners participate in learning activities. Instruction should include examples and nonexamples and help learners recognize and understand the concept's critical and noncritical attributes and definition.

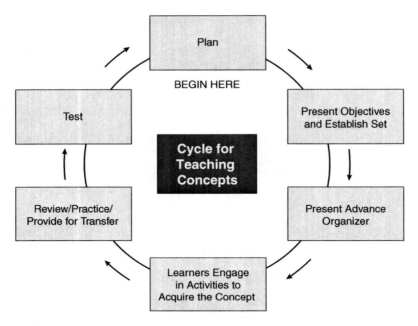

FIGURE 11.9   *Cycle for Teaching Concepts*

Motivation is increased if you show enthusiasm and have high, but achievable, expectations. In this phase, learner participation should be active. Learning is increased by skillful use of question and answer, discussion, clear explanations, and by using a variety of media. During a good concept lesson, students need the thinking skills of data gathering and retrieval (to surface and report examples), contrasting and comparing (to discover differences and similarities), summarizing (forming the concept definition), and classifying (to decide if new items are examples or nonexamples).

   4. *Providing for review and transfer.* If the concept is to be remembered and used, practice opportunity is needed. Learners can be asked to distinguish between simultaneously presented concept examples and nonexamples. Lesson closure should include a review of the concept definition. Ideally, the critical attributes and their relationships should be drawn from the learners rather than recited by you. Learners should show they know the superordinate, subordinate, and coordinate concepts related to the concept. If you want learners to *transfer* learning (generalize to new or related examples or use learning in higher-level operations), teach for transfer.

   5. *Testing.* The final step is testing. This lets you and learners know how well learners have mastered the concept *and* how effective your planning and instruction have been. If necessary, reteach and retest. Testing can be informal and formative (e.g., teacher observation or use of question and answer) and formal and formative or summative. Formal testing may occur later.

   Use the appended data collection instrument in Figure 11.10 to help you analyze the cases that follow. Your instructor may pose specific questions for your response.

FIGURE 11.10 *Concept Analysis Form*

Concept name: Peninsula

Kind of Concept (please check   __X__ Concrete   _____ Abstract
as appropriate):
                    __X__ Conjunctive   _____ Disjunctive   _____ Relational

Presentation Medium or Media: _____ Observing/doing   __X__ Pictorial   _____ Symbolic

---

Examples of Concept (in sequence of presentation):

Chart showing geographic features of the earth. Overhead transparencies (maps) of areas of North America, with peninsulas circled. Sequence of examples would range from coastal peninsulas of moderate size with clear land links to larger land mass, to those of varying sizes, shapes, and locations

---

Nonexamples of Concept (in sequence of presentation):

Maps and pictures of plains, lake, and islands

Critical Attributes (in sequence of presentation):

Area of land; linked by land to a larger land area; almost surrounded by water

---

Noncritical Attributes:

Size; shape; location (whether jutting into ocean, lake, sea); man-made or natural

---

Concept Definition:

"A land area, almost surrounded by water, with a narrow link to a larger land area"

Relationship to Other Concepts:

A peninsula is a geological land feature on the surface of the earth. Geographic features are natural or man-made. Each geographical feature has attributes that make it different from other features

---

Name of Superordinate Concept: Geographical (land) features of the earth
Names of Some Subordinate Concepts: (Kinds of peninsulas)
Names of Some Coordinate Concepts: Island, valley, plateau, delta, isthmus

CASE 11.1 Concepts

What Is Cazoptopin?

Consider the following excerpts from hypothetical lessons.

Excerpt One

> It is very important that you learn about cazoptopin. Cazoptopin is a newly discovered form of quanoptopin. It is extipated in Bratislava. Bratislavians plescalate cazoptopin by salinking quants and then pasking these to prube cazoptopin. Cazoptopin may become one of our most used quanoptopins because it is very effective and relatively easy and inexpensive to pask.

Using complete statements and correct English, please answer the following questions:

1. What is cazoptopin?
2. Where is cazoptopin extipated?
3. How is cazoptopin plescalated?
4. Why is it important to know about cazoptopin?

If you think the above example is a little ridiculous, consider the next one, putting yourself in the place of a grade 7 or 8 student subjected to the following example.

Excerpt Two

> It is very important that you learn about the nervous system. The nervous system is the body's "telephone system." In response to stimuli, it receives and transmits messages about the welfare of the total organism through interoceptors and exteroceptors. Anatomically, the nervous system consists of the cerebrum, the pons and medulla, the spinal cord, twelve pairs of cranial nerves, and thirty pairs of spinal nerves.
>
> The nervous system functions as a storage system and has an environment interpretive system. The peripheral nervous system senses and responds to stimuli and works with the central nervous system to keep the organism alive and well.

Please answer the following:

1. To what can the nervous system be compared? What is the reason for the comparison?
2. Through what does the nervous system transmit messages?
3. Besides receiving and sending messages, what functions does the nervous system have?
4. Why is it important to know about the nervous system?

The above are examples of an all-too-common teaching approach in which a presentation is made or a reading assigned, then questions are asked to see if students can recall what was presented. The teacher may wonder why students have difficulty or are so unmotivated.

CASE 11.2 Concepts

What Is a Peninsula?

Mr. Lewchuk is continuing a series of lessons on geographical concepts, using the form shown in Figure 11.10. He begins by reviewing the concepts covered so far: *continent, coast, island, harbor,* and *gulf.* He asks students for definitions in their own words and to tell whether each is a land or water feature. He then asks individuals to find examples of each concept on a large wall map in the classroom.

Mr. Lewchuk introduces today's topic. "We are going to examine another kind of land feature this afternoon. I will show you examples of this feature; we'll describe each carefully and see if we can generate a definition for this new concept." From the front of the room, he shows a chart drawing of physical features. Pointing, he says, "See this part right here? This is called a peninsula. What can you tell about it from this picture?"

Students volunteer answers that include "it's hooked onto the land," and "it has water around most of it." Mr. Lewchuk jots responses on the board

continued

Chart Example	Map Example #1	Map Example #2	Map Example #3	Map Example #4	Map Example #5
• hooked on to land • water nearly all around • a land feature • large in size • long straight sides • smooth coastline • an area of land	• water on 3 sides • small narrow shape • made of land • not wide anywhere • curved shape • is joined to a larger body of land • shaped like a sheep's head	• narrowest where it joins the land • large rounded shape at the end • water almost all around • irregular coastline	• small in size • water nearly surrounds • a land area • connected to other land	• long, narrow shape • smooth coastline • an area of land • hooked to other land • water almost all places, wide at end	• water on 3 sides • a land feature • large, L-shaped • uneven coastline

as answers are supplied. Keeping in mind the definition he wants students to discover, he asks, "Is it land or water?" Students respond that it is land. "What can you say about the shape? How about the size? Does it extend into an ocean, a lake, or a bay?" Mr. Lewchuk continues to record responses.

Showing an overhead transparency of the Maritime provinces of Canada, Mr. Lewchuk shows areas (peninsulas) that have been circled. He asks the students to describe each example. For each example, he begins a new column of descriptive notes. When all the examples have been examined, there are six columns of descriptive notes, side by side, as shown above.

Mr. Lewchuk asks students to look at the notes on each example. "Are there some things, some descriptors that are present in every example?" Students select the common descriptors: joined to other, usually larger, land, a land feature, and, almost surrounded by water (except for the land link). Mr. Lewchuk explains that, because not all peninsulas are the same, they may vary in size, shape, type of coastline, length, and width. "But to be a peninsula, it must be joined to another land body, must have water nearly all around, and must be made of land."

"We need to think of a way to define 'peninsula' so that we are clear about what it is and is not. A good definition will include all the things a peninsula *must* be. What could we say, in one sentence, about a peninsula?"

Jerry begins, "A peninsula is almost surrounded by water." "I think there's more," says Natasha. "A peninsula is a land feature that is nearly surrounded by water, that is connected to other land." "Good," says Mr. Lewchuk. "We've included all the common descriptors. Can we tighten that up a little?" Jean-Paul concludes, "A peninsula is a land feature, joined to a larger body of land, that is nearly surrounded by water."

"Very clear," says Mr. Lewchuk. "Let's see how the definition works on other examples." He shows two more examples, saying, "Is this a peninsula? Why do you think so? What characteristics does it have?" He then shows a picture of an island. "Is this a peninsula? Why not?" Students respond although it is made of land, it is surrounded entirely by water and does not have a link to another land body. They work through another example and two nonexamples. By comparing the feature to the definition, students decide whether they are peninsulas.

Finally, Mr. Lewchuk asks students to think where they would rather live, on an island or on a peninsula. "Think of being the first inhabitants. Which would have the most advantages? What would be some disadvantages?" After a lively discussion, Mr. Lewchuk asks the students to explain, in writing, reasons for their selection and the advantages and disadvantages of their choice.

CASE 11.3 Concepts

What's in a Contract?

Mr. Yanski's grade 11 law class is studying the law of contracts. The class has been told that there are five elements to a binding contract. One of the elements is "consideration." "A valid contract" Mr. Yanski says, requires 'consideration.' Do you know what that is?" After a long pause, Damon volunteers, "Well, before you sign anything, you should consider things carefully." Mr. Yanski replies, "What you say, Damon, is certainly true, but the legal definition of 'consideration' is a bit different. Let me give an example. When you buy a camera for a friend that has a price tag of $210, the camera is consideration and so is the $210. If the person who had the camera agreed to take a pair of car wheel mags for the camera, the mags also would be consideration. You could even promise to paint his car in exchange for the camera. The service you promise to provide is consideration too. Are you getting the idea?" Upon Mr. Yanski's request, students begin to volunteer other examples. Freda says, "I heard of cases where people bought something really valuable, like a house, for one dollar. Is that legal?" Mr. Yanski replies, "Consideration does not have to be of equal value in a contract. The one dollar also is consideration." Students discover that consideration need not be adequate, that both parties need not benefit personally (for instance, a donation to charity can be made or a person can promise to stop doing something like cutting a lawn at five in the morning).

Mr. Yanski draws the essential features of consideration from the class. Based on the examples the teacher gave and those that students provided, students prepare a definition of consideration. The definition states that consideration is money or money value. The courts won't enforce a promise to do or give something unless the person benefiting does or gives something in exchange (or promises to do so). Mr. Yanski provides a handout containing ten cases. Students are to figure out whether consideration was present and justify their answers. He does the first case with the class and assigns the rest as seatwork. He takes up the cases the next day, using probing questions to see if students understand the definition and critical and noncritical attributes of "consideration."

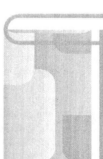

LINKING PRACTICE TO THEORY

How does your approach to teaching concepts reflect your views on how learning takes place? Should you do a concept analysis before teaching a concept? Do you prefer to build knowledge with your students, or to guide them on a predetermined path? How does this chapter tie in with the chapters on communication and questioning? Are you and your students more comfortable with a "doing," pictorial, or symbolic approach? Try the strategies suggested in this chapter to provide an analytical framework for you to think about your experience with concept teaching.

Summary

We cannot think or function without concepts; concept teaching and learning are fundamental to effective schooling. Before teaching a concept, the teacher needs to be sure of its critical and noncritical attributes, examples and nonexamples, and definition. Concepts, which are declarative content, can be classified as: concrete or abstract; formal or informal; conjunctive, disjunctive, or relational; and superordinate, coordinate, or subordinate. Presentations of concepts in textbooks are often inadequate. Concepts can be taught, and attained, deductively or inductively. A systematic approach to planning and teaching should normally be followed.

Ample pure examples of concepts should be presented, followed by less obvious examples and nonexamples. Students should normally be asked to discover the definition of a concept themselves. Overgeneralization and undergeneralization should be avoided.

Concepts can be explained in terms of their purposes: to show a cause-and-effect relationship; to show an action is governed by a general law or rule; to illustrate a procedure or process; or to reveal the intent of an action or process.

Activities

CONCEPTS

1. As an initial exercise, review Case 11.1. Discuss the following: Is a cazoptopin a label or a term? How would you categorize it? In what ways is a cazoptopin a mental construct? Why does seeing a cazoptopin as a concept simplify learning, facilitate thought and communication, and act as a building block for the future? In what ways has teaching about the cazoptopin as a concept been more effective than the contextual clues to answer questions approach?

2. Select several concepts that are common to a school subject of your choice. Analyze each in terms of critical attributes, noncritical attributes, definition, examples, and nonexamples.

3. Select a text from a subject you will teach, or hope to teach, and find examples of: (a) concrete and abstract, (b) formal and informal, and (c) conjunctive, disjunctive, and relational concepts.

4. The instructor may model two short lessons on the same topic to illustrate the deductive and inductive approaches to teaching a concept. Point out the components of each lesson.

5. Join a subject interest group. Brainstorm examples of concrete and abstract concepts, then classify these by degree of difficulty of analysis. Then, select three concrete and three abstract concepts and agree on the critical attributes, noncritical attributes, and concept definitions.

6. In your group, brainstorm, agree on, and justify the selection of examples for conjunctive, disjunctive, relational, and connotative concepts.

7. In your group, using the concept analysis form provided in Appendix 11.1, analyze a concrete concept and an abstract concept.

8. Select a concept and prepare two lesson plans, one illustrating a deductive and the other an inductive approach to teaching that concept.

9. Teach a microteaching lab and a field classroom lesson with the professional target of teaching a concept, using the data collection form in Figure 11.10. Attach a completed concept analysis form (Figure 11.8) to each lesson.

10. In groups, create learner background charts showing how you would teach concepts using concrete, iconic, and symbolic approaches.

11. In subject groups, select a concept from your discipline and create a hierarchy of the concept. Share this with the rest of the class.

12. In pairs, create a lesson plan for teaching a concept from your discipline.

13. Divide the class into four groups. Have one group teach the concept of *chair* from a deductive approach and the other teach it from an inductive approach. Similarly, have the other two groups teach the concept *teaching*.

APPENDIX 11.1   *Concept Analysis Form*

CONCEPT ANALYSIS FORM

Concept name: _____

Kind of Concept (please check): _____ Concrete   _____ Abstract

                                    _____ Conjunctive   _____ Disjunctive   _____ Relational

Presentation Medium or Media: _____ Observing/doing   _____ Pictorial   _____ Symbolic

Examples of Concept (in sequence of presentation):

_____

Nonexamples of Concept (in sequence of presentation):

_____

Critical Attributes (in sequence of presentation):

_____

Noncritical Attributes:

_____

Concept Definition:

_____

Relationship to Other Concepts:

_____

Name of Superordinate Concept:

Names of Some Subordinate Concepts:

Names of Some Coordinate Concepts:

APPENDIX 11.2   *Concept Teaching Target*

PROFESSIONAL TARGET—CONCEPT TEACHING

Kind of Concept: ____ concrete ____ abstract ____ conjunctive ____ disjunctive ____ relational

Presentation Mode: ____ active   ____ graphic   ____ symbolic

Procedure Used: ____ deductive   ____ inductive

Please describe what was said and done and how students reacted.

Aspect of Concept	Descriptive Notes
Examples or analogies or cause-and-effect or behavior	
Nonexamples or nonanalogies or . . .	
Critical attributes identified and/or stressed	
Noncritical attributes	
Relationships identified (e.g., CAR—wheels and body and steering wheel)	
Concept rule defined (critical attributes and relationships?)	
Related concepts identified? Use of concept? (Sub-? Super-? Coordinate?)	
Practice and transfer	

12 Teaching Skills

The Nature of Skills

A student has struggled with language arts and English in school. He was assigned an essay but received a low mark, and tried to write the required critique of one of the short stories the class had studied. He enjoyed the stories, but failed. He took the class again in summer school and, this time, did well. The summer school teacher taught not only the content of the literature, but the skills needed to read for ideas and to write essays and reports. The teacher taught stages of essay writing and, for critiquing a short story, she taught the skills of finding ideas, writing thesis statements, and supporting statements with evidence and comment. The teacher was encouraging and supportive, and gave feedback on each stage of the assignments. Incidentally, this is a true story. A similar example could be found for other subjects. Everything students do in school requires skills. The *how to* (the skills) is as important, if not more so, than the *what* (the content).

Skill Domains

Many people, when they hear the word *skills,* assume what are referred to as *psychomotor* skills, such as playing tennis or using a computer. Some skills, however, are predominantly *cognitive* (for example, categorizing or comparing and contrasting), others have strong *affective* purposes (for instance, paraphrasing, or checking for feelings). Psychomotor skills also have cognitive and affective aspects. Skills fall under the rubric of *procedural knowledge*—knowledge and ability to do something, as contrasted with *declarative knowledge* about something (though, most often, both are needed).

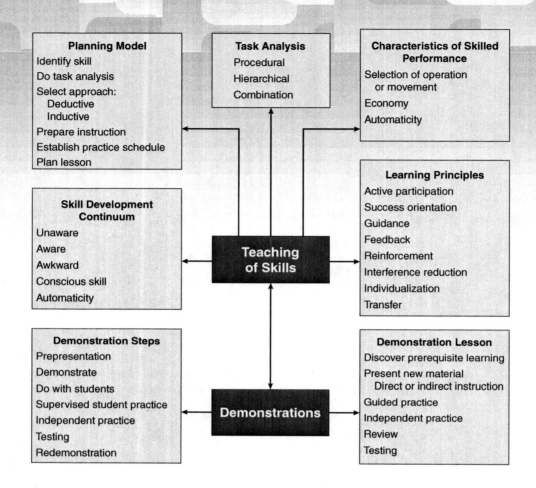

Planning Model
Identify skill
Do task analysis
Select approach:
   Deductive
   Inductive
Prepare instruction
Establish practice schedule
Plan lesson

Task Analysis
Procedural
Hierarchical
Combination

Characteristics of Skilled Performance
Selection of operation
   or movement
Economy
Automaticity

Skill Development Continuum
Unaware
Aware
Awkward
Conscious skill
Automaticity

Teaching of Skills

Learning Principles
Active participation
Success orientation
Guidance
Feedback
Reinforcement
Interference reduction
Individualization
Transfer

Demonstration Steps
Prepresentation
Demonstrate
Do with students
Supervised student practice
Independent practice
Testing
Redemonstration

Demonstrations

Demonstration Lesson
Discover prerequisite learning
Present new material
   Direct or indirect instruction
Guided practice
Independent practice
Review
Testing

TCP—SKILLS AND DEMONSTRATIONS

Provides effective teaching of skills and demonstrations

Prior analysis of skills; developmental level of students accommodated and desired skill level determined; demonstrations clear and systematic; effective guided practice and feedback before independent practice; appropriate choice and use of inductive and deductive approaches.

No prior analysis; readiness of students ignored; absence of or ineffective demonstration; absence of guided practice and feedback; approach always deductive.

SKILLS THAT ARE MAINLY COGNITIVE. We can use a language arts example. If the intention is for learners to develop the cognitive skill of writing paragraphs with topic sentences, several subskills are required: spelling, usage, topic selection, sentence construction, punctuation, and capitalization. Another example, this time in social studies, is map reading, which also involves subskills. Thinking, problem-solving, and decision-making skills are important cognitive skills that must be taught to be learned.

SKILLS THAT HAVE AN AFFECTIVE PURPOSE OR OVERTONE. You also should be concerned with skills with affective purposes or overtones. Many rules and classroom management routines involve affective behaviors and associated skills, the purpose of which is to maintain a positive climate for teaching and learning and reflect the attitudes and values on which these are based. Interpersonal skills (e.g., listening or speaking clearly) and group skills (e.g., initiating, consensus seeking, and conflict resolution), which you help learners acquire through modeling or instruction, are further examples of skills with affective overtones or purposes.

SKILLS IN COMBINATION. Skills are not isolated as motor, cognitive, or affective. A combination and interplay exists. For example, when a guitarist performs, he must be able to do much more than pluck strings. A decision is made about how to express the feelings or emotions involved, using techniques learned to achieve the desired impact on the audience. A professional golfer must not only use correct technique in striking a ball, she must make a decision about the kind of shot to play given the layout of the fairway and green, the wind, and the presence or absence of hazards. As this is occurring, emotions need to be controlled and concentration maintained.

SKILL TEACHING AND PLANNING. Skill teaching requires planning. Several questions need to be asked before instruction begins: What level of skill do learners possess? Learners' readiness? The place of a particular skill in the chain of skills to which it belongs? The nature of the skill to be learned? The subskills? The sequence of subskills? How the lesson is to be presented? The degree of learning (or overlearning) desired? The kind of, and how much, practice needed? The kind of, and how much, guidance needed? The kind of, and how much, feedback to be given? The kind of reinforcement desired? How transfer can be fostered? An important initial step is task analysis of the skill to discover the chain of subskills involved. Careful planning isn't enough. You also need to become proficient with the demonstration-and-practice lesson format.

Learning Principles

The effective teacher recognizes the learning principles to be brought into play while helping learners acquire skills. A brief description of these follows (Figure 12.1).

ACTIVE PARTICIPATION. Active student participation is needed. Participation should be as overt (observable) as possible. Some skills can only be learned this way. Covert (not observable) practice can be used to advantage—for example, silently thinking through the steps of solving an algebra problem, or mentally practicing phrases or short sentences on an imaginary keyboard.

SUCCESS AND FAILURE. Nothing succeeds like success, and nothing stultifies like continued failure. Failure, in itself, is not necessarily damaging; continued failure can be. Nobody likes doing things at which they are not very good! Learners need tasks at which they can succeed *after reasonable effort.* "Organize success experiences." The climate should encourage risk taking and emphasize learning from "deferred successes" (not *yet* succeeding). Errors are clues for further learning, not sins.

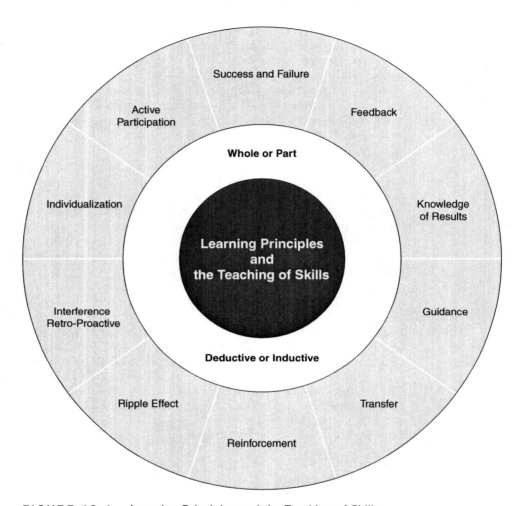

FIGURE 12.1   *Learning Principles and the Teaching of Skills*

FEEDBACK AND KNOWLEDGE OF RESULTS.   Practice is critical to the development and maintenance of skills. To be most useful, feedback must be provided. Knowledge of results (KR) is essential for speedy and efficient learning. Doing something over and over without feedback is inefficient and often unproductive. Joyce, Weil, and Calhoun (2004, p. 316) say that the kind of feedback students receive during practice has much to do with later success. Feedback helps students discover how well they understand new material and discover their errors. To be effective, they say, "feedback must be academic, corrective, respectful and deserved." Good feedback, they add, involves telling the students their correct actions; praise, when given, must be deserved. The more immediate and descriptive (precise and specific) the feedback, the more helpful and the more rapid will be the improvement. When feedback is delayed, students may practice incorrect responses.

GUIDANCE.   How much should you guide a learner as a skill is being learned? What speeds learning? What kind of guidance? How much? The answers lie in part with the individual, in part with age and previous experience. Some learners need more guidance than others. Teacher guidance, at the initial stages of instruction, can greatly increase the degree and rate of learning, but guidance should be gradually withdrawn so students learn to function independently. When guidance is given it should be positive, concise, and focused with appropriate cues.

REINFORCEMENT.   Reinforcement means showing approval or issuing rewards for correct or desirable behavior. Some teachers react only when learners do something wrong, not when learners do it right. We know that positive reinforcement (pleasant tones) strengthens correct and desirable behavior, and that negative reinforcement increases the likelihood of behavior that removes the negative reinforcer. Positive reinforcement in skill learning is particularly effective when it is immediate, earned, and contingent (specifies what was good and why it was good). Merely telling a learner what *not* to do is not particularly effective (and can lead to a negative attitude); the learner must be clear about what to do.

Ideally (not always practical), positive reinforcement should be immediate for correct performance of a skill or subskill until behavior is habitual (this is *regular reinforcement*); *intermittent reinforcement* can also be effective. Regular reinforcement speeds learning; subsequent intermittent reinforcement improves retention.

Reinforcement can have a *ripple effect,* that is, it can be "vicarious." The ripple effect occurs when not only the learner who receives it is affected, but so are others who observe it. However, what is motivating for one learner may not be motivating for another.

INTERFERENCE.   Inserting a second learning activity between original learning and recall of that learning results in interference that reduces retention. When what we learn today interferes with what we learned earlier, *retroactive inhibition* (backward blocking) occurs; and when what we learn today interferes with what we will try to learn, *proactive inhibition* (forward blocking) occurs. Retroactive inhibition occurs, for example, when a student has no trouble with the letter p until q is introduced. A classic example of proactive inhibition occurs when a British national rents a car in Canada, and having learned to drive on the left side of the road in Britain interferes with driving on the right side.

Be aware that learning some things helps the learning of others. For example, having learned to keyboard on a typewriter will greatly help you learn to use a computer, or having learned Spanish first will help you learn Italian.

The way learning experiences are organized aids or hinders skill acquisition and retention. Students can be helped to discover meaningful organization by having elements of the skill placed, and learned, in a logical way; and each part must be seen to fit the whole. Past experience can be used, and instruction must be pitched at the learners' level of ability and insight. You can help reduce interference. The more thorough the earlier and later learning, the less the interference. The things most easily forgotten are those not well learned in the first place. In learning keyboarding, the letter m can be practiced for some time before the letter n is introduced and practiced. You can teach a memory aid (mnemonic device), telling students the two letters are on the keyboard in the same order as in the word *name.* Learners should do *response differentiation* practice using words that contain both letters. This requires them to differentiate between stroking an m and stroking an n.

INDIVIDUALIZATION.   Successful skill teaching and learning requires that individual differences be considered. Some students need more practice than others, and the focus of practice for each person will vary. The wise keyboarding teacher will not tell the whole class to do a timed writing with the objective of simultaneously improving both speed and accuracy. This is confusing and frustrating! The learner cannot focus on both. A student who makes ten or more errors per minute should be working on accuracy; a student who makes two or fewer errors per minute can work on speed; and another who has flaws in stroking technique should work on particular aspects of technique, not accuracy or speed. Although this example is principally psychomotor, the need for individualization is as important for cognitive or affectively toned skills. You can individualize practice through the objectives set and the exercises assigned, checking up during seatwork. Many cognitive skills, and those with affective purposes, can be taught using cooperative group strategies or peer teaching. These provide ample opportunity for individualization.

TRANSFER.   Education is predicated on transfer. It occurs when training in one activity affects a student's performance in other contexts. For example, if a student has learned the steps of problem solving in social studies and applies these to a language arts problem, positive transfer has taken place. Thinking skills learned in one context should be taught so they are likely to be used in other subjects and daily life. Transfer is at the core of problem solving and higher mental processes, innovation, and artistic achievement.

If you want transfer to occur, teach for it! It is not likely to happen by itself. For example, math teachers may recall students learning to do algebra problems using $x, y,$ and z to represent unknowns. When the students were given the same problems but the unknowns were represented by $a, b,$ and $c,$ some couldn't do them—no transfer!

You can facilitate transfer. Hunter (1971) presents four things teachers can do:

1. Point out the *similarities* of past learning to what is about to be learned and the similarities of what is being, or has been learned, to what will be learned. If past learning can interfere, point out the *differences*.

2. Use *associations* students can make between things not necessarily related. For example, when a science teacher teaches astronomy, associations formed by students through having watched a television series on space adventure may stimulate learning. Or a teacher can use a game as a teaching method. Students associate games with fun, and so the new learning likely also will be fun. A field trip used as part of another unit can be *associated* in future units. The perceptive teacher knows the power and transferability of associations. It is not enough for students to learn a skill in isolation—they should apply it to new material in a course, other subjects, and life.

3. The greater the degree of original learning, the greater is the likelihood of transfer. Highly overlearned skills transfer more readily than those half-learned. The teacher needs to provide opportunities for transfer, pointing out how transfer can be affected.

4. The more learners are aware of *essential unvarying elements* (the main concepts and processes and their organization), the greater is the possibility of transfer. Stress these elements and help learners become aware of how they apply to new contexts. For example, a correct stroke in tennis involves a smooth, continuous motion from backswing through follow-through. Don't "hit at the ball," "hit through the ball." This is called a "ballistic stroke," and it applies equally to squash, racquetball, golf, and even striking the keys of a computer. It is an essential unvarying element.

Performance Skills

Effective performance has certain characteristics. The teaching of skills requires an awareness of key stages.

CHARACTERISTICS.   Although all skills involve cognitive, affective, and psychomotor elements, performance skills may involve many psychomotor characteristics. Have you ever heard a seemingly flawless musical performance by a solo guitarist, pianist, or singer? Watched top-ranked tennis players playing a match? Seen somebody rapidly editing a document on a computer? A teacher quickly solving a complex algebra problem on the chalkboard? Someone performing incredibly acrobatic and proficient break dancing? Each is an example of "expert" performance. What features do they have in common? What is expert performance? Bloom (1986) notes that mastery of a skill, from a routine daily task to the highest level of artistry, "depends on the ability to perform it unconsciously with speed and accuracy while carrying on other brain functions" (p. 70). If you study the above examples you will discover that the characteristics of expert performance include selection, economy, and automaticity. Consider golfing:

• *Selection.* The expert rapidly selects and initiates the appropriate response or operation needed. For example, as the golfer walks to her ball on the fairway, she sizes up the shot needed, and by the time she gets to the ball she knows exactly what she is going to do. Among other things, she has considered distance, wind and grass conditions, slope of the fairway and green, placement of the flag, club selection, and the kind of golf swing needed.

• *Economy.* An expert accurately performs a skill with optimum economy of effort, movement, and time. When an expert golfer swings a golf club, each subskill is performed unhesitatingly, smoothly and rapidly, in the appropriate sequence, without a single unnecessary movement or operation, and with just the right amount of effort. Many of the same characteristics are true of an expert musician or a person who rapidly solves a math problem.

• *Automaticity.* An expert performs a skill so that it is totally appropriate and seems to be effortless. The golfer seems consistently to do things without having to think about them. However, the golfer is performing a cognitive skill (thinking) while using a psychomotor skill that has been automatized.

STAGES FOR TEACHING MOTOR SKILLS.   Hellison and Templin (1991) provide the following stages for teaching motor skills:

1. Set
   • Students may not be ready for a demonstration and drill.
   • Play the game or do the activity first to create interest.
2. Modeling or visual clues
   • Demonstrate one of the motor skills involved in the activity they have participated in.
   • The teacher or a student models or demonstrates.
   • Give a few cues or tips.
3. Specific behavioral objectives or challenges
   • Give students a specific behavioral (or performance) objective that challenges them to develop a specific motor skill.
   • Specify what has to be accomplished.

- Challenge but within the students' range.
- When an objective is met, do not continue doing the task (unlike typical drill).

4. Extensions
- Students who complete a specific objective are given more difficult challenges with the same motor skill.

5. Applications
- Modify games so the skill being practiced is the focus of attention.
- Research shows that the old "demonstrate, drill, play the game" accomplishes little skill learning.
- Practice within a gamelike component.

6. Close
- Leave students with something to think about.
- Cue, reminder of the role of the skill in the game.
- General reinforcement.
- What to look forward to in the next lesson. (pp. 55–59)

The principles of learning a skill must not be forgotten when working with the levels. Judith Rink stressed, "Tasks must be appropriate in order for students to learn them," and "If students do not have the prerequisites to learn a skill, they could practice forever and probably not make a great deal of progress" (in Silverman & Ennis, 1996, p. 175).

The Deductive versus the Inductive Approach

A skill can be taught either *deductively* (the teacher tells and directs) or *inductively* (learners discover the steps and relationships). Burden and Byrd (2003, p. 167) argue that students learn basic skills more rapidly when they receive most of their instruction directly from the teacher. Others argue that the choice of approach, deductive or inductive, should depend on the nature of the skill and how important it is for students to understand the concepts and principles involved.

DEDUCTIVE APPROACH.   The pure deductive approach to teaching skills (for example, directly teaching math or directly teaching a dance routine) is very teacher centered. You direct and monitor each step. The skill is modeled, using verbal and nonverbal input. Statements are made such as "First you do this, second you . . ." or "Watch as I. . . ." The first try by students is also directed, "Everybody do this . . . don't go on until I tell you to," and then, "Now do this. . . ." You tell students the principles involved and summarize. In short, you do the showing and telling and students do the listening and doing. Practice is guided, and erring students are told what to do.

Some of the literature discusses skills teaching under the heading of *direct* teaching. Other terms are *explicit* or *active* teaching. A systematic, check-for-understanding, small-step, and active-learner-participation, success-oriented approach is involved. Note that direct instruction has been thought to be indispensable for mastering content and overlearning facts, rules, and action sequences that are essential to later learning. Direct instruction can be used for procedural knowledge (how to do something) for simple and complex skills, and for declarative knowledge (about something) that can be presented in a step-by-step way. Indirect instruction promotes understanding of the conceptual aspects of a skill.

The traditional approach to the teaching of most skills has been the deductive, or directed, method of teaching, whereby the teacher shows or tells what to do. If the teacher notices what a student is doing is wrong, a correction is given. Emphasis for the teaching of *complex skills* is shifting toward discovery, perhaps guided with suggestions, because some now believe skills are learned more permanently this way.

INDUCTIVE APPROACH.   When you stress *discovery* by students of the principles, processes, or steps involved, you use an *inductive approach.* Before the skill is modeled or demonstrated, students watch and think about how it is performed. Questions or cueing can be used to help students discover the steps, processes, or principles. Students summarize. When students practice, you help individuals by asking what should be done and why. When the skill is reviewed, or after students have practiced independently, stress is on *how* and (particularly) *why,* to help students construct personal understanding and meaning.

WHOLE VERSUS PART LEARNING.   The *whole approach* can be used for skills that are not too complex and where subskills are closely knit. This has the advantage of including an overview of the total skill and the relation, or associations, of parts to each other. Skills with many subskills should probably be broken into parts or "chewable pieces." A good practice is to work with as small an amount as possible, while retaining meaning and not wasting time. Proceed in small steps, check for student understanding, and have active and successful participation by all.

For some skills, practice of parts (or subskills) occurs while performing the whole. For example, a student can concentrate on the subskill of the golf grip while swinging a golf club; or a student may concentrate on punctuation while writing sentences.

If the decision is to use the *part approach,* decide the order to introduce parts (subskills). Selection will be based on the nature of the skill and dependence of the parts (subskills) to each other. Probably the most-used approach is the sequence of occurrence of the parts in the total task; another approach is to begin from the end and work in reverse order. Still another approach is to move from the simplest to the most complex subskill. If successful performance of one subskill depends on proficiency in another, then the foundational skill should be learned first.

Sometimes the elements of a skill chain can be learned independently and then put together. Sometimes it matters which part is taught first; in other cases it does not. For example, the parts of speech in a sentence can be learned separately, but you likely will present verbs before adverbs, nouns before pronouns, nouns before adjectives, and so on. Conjunctions and definite and indefinite articles do not normally have to be taught in any particular order. In any case, integration of the components into a smooth sequence must happen eventually.

Skills and Responsibility

Skill development has cognitive, psychomotor, and affective implications. Students may need to learn self-control and responsibility. Many skills are learned within a team or group context—not only in physical education, drama, and music, but also when learning any skill. A way of teaching skills and responsibility popular in physical education programs is Hellison's Awareness Levels. Skills learning is placed within the context of "awareness of and interaction with a loose progression of four values" (Hellison, 1986, p. 27). Hellison's levels are as follows.

> *Level IV, Caring:* Students at Level IV, in addition to respecting others, participating, and being self-directed, are motivated to extend their sense of responsibility beyond themselves by cooperating, giving support, showing concern, and helping.

> *Level III, Self-Direction.* Students at Level III not only show respect and participation but also are able to work without direct supervision. They can identify their own needs and begin to plan and carry out their physical education programs.
>
> *Level II, Participation.* Students at Level II not only show at least minimal respect for others but also willingly play, accept challenges, practice motor skills, and train for fitness under the teacher's supervision.
>
> *Level I, Respect:* Students at Level I may not participate in daily activities or show much mastery or improvement, but they are able to control their behavior enough that they don't interfere with the other students' right to learn or the teacher's right to teach. They do this without much prompting by the teacher and without constant supervision.
>
> *Level Zero, Irresponsibility:* Students who operate at Level Zero make excuses, blame others for their behavior, and deny personal responsibility for what they do or fail to do. (Hellison, 2003, p.28)

Students learn both skills and self-responsibility. "Unless responsibility is internalized as part of a student's belief and value system, it is much less likely to be transferred to settings beyond the gym" (Parker & Hellison, 2001, p. 25).

The Teaching of Skills

Preparing to Teach a Skill

Figure 12.2 shows a *Seven Step Planning Model* that is useful as a planning guide for teaching a skill. The steps do not have to be followed rigidly.

1. *Identify the skill.* The skill that is to be learned must be part of the curriculum for the course. Be clear about the context of the skill in the unit being covered; you may need to refer to the curriculum guide, the textbook, or other references. Know what was previously learned, the learning to follow, and the time that can be allocated for acquiring the skill.

2. *Task analysis before teaching a skill.* Preinstructional planning should include task analysis. This involves analyzing and ordering content as it relates to: (a) the sequence of steps or operations involved (for example, when you open a pop-top can, first you place your finger in the ring, then you lift the lid with the ring, and finally you twist the lid off), or (b) the order in which steps or operations should be learned (for example, before students can find a location on a city map, they have to know how to read the index and use the vertical and horizontal block systems). The latter requires discovery of the sequence of skills prerequisite to acquisition of a higher-order skill. Both kinds of task analysis involve identification of the subskills and the relationships and sequence of the subskills. Task analysis will be treated more fully later.

3. *Desired degree of proficiency and learner readiness.* Consider the age and developmental level of learners and their previous experiences with the skill or a related one. If the skill is cognitive, what cognitive readiness do learners have? If the skill has affective overtones, what is the learners' moral development level and what previous formal or informal learning experiences do they have? If the skill is psychomotor, what is the level of maturation and degree of physical readiness?

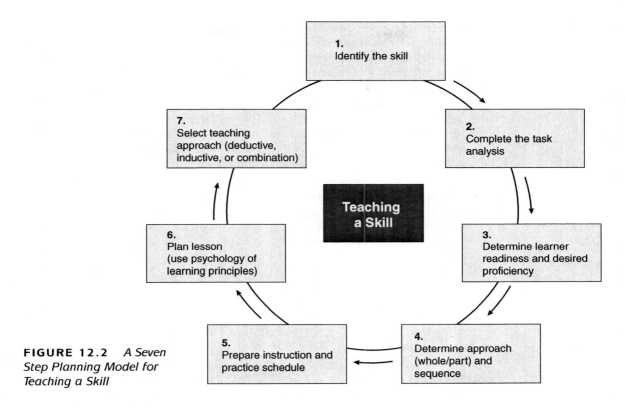

FIGURE 12.2 *A Seven Step Planning Model for Teaching a Skill*

An important consideration is the degree of proficiency desired. How well must learners know the skill? Be aware that learners tend to move along a *skill development continuum:* (1) Unaware (2) Aware (3) Awkward (4) Conscious skill (5) Automaticity.

- *Unaware stage.* The learner begins by not being aware of what is involved in the performance of a skill and, perhaps, where and how it is to be used.
- *Awareness stage.* Before a skill can be acquired, the learner must become aware of it, discover its purpose, and be made aware of why it should be learned.
- *Awkwardness stage.* When the learner is aware of, and has knowledge of, the components of the skill, the learner can try it. First efforts tend to be inefficient, awkward, and full of errors.
- *Conscious skillfulness stage.* Conscious skillfulness develops through numerous tries, guidance, and feedback. The learner becomes proficient but must think consciously about what he or she is doing. The learner lacks complete spontaneity, and performance is still somewhat mechanical.
- *Automaticity stage.* The final stage is the integrated stage. Eventually, with much correct practice, behavior becomes habitual and the learner reaches an automatized phase. The skill can be used comfortably and creatively where and how it should be used.

When you plan to teach a skill, identify where learners are along the skill development continuum. Then, decide the level of skill, or degree of proficiency, learners are to acquire (awareness, awkwardness, conscious skillfulness, or automatization). If learners only need to be familiar with the skill, a portion of a lesson may be sufficient; if students will be expected to perform the skill automatically while doing other things, much practice over several weeks may be needed.

   4. *Select the approach (whole or part) and the sequence of presentation.* When is it more efficient to break a skill into parts (or subskills), with separate instruction for each part? When is it better to teach the whole task? Age, previous experience, preferred learning style, and complexity must be considered. Decide how compact and meaningful the task is. Regardless of the approach, whole or part, identify the order in which subskills should be taught.

   5. *Prepare the instruction and practice schedule.* If a skill is to be learned and retained, a suitable instruction and practice schedule must be set. The classic approach is to review previous learning, establish set, explain and demonstrate (and check up), guided practice (and check up), and independent practice (and check up).

   After a new skill has been presented, to be retained and used, and for it to transfer to new contexts, it must be practiced. How much practice, whether in short or longer sittings, and how many sittings, are things you must decide.

   6. *Consider the learning principles to be included in the lesson.* Several principles of the psychology of learning must be taken into account as you plan and deliver a skill lesson. Examples include having learners participate actively, being aware of the effects of success and failure, giving feedback and providing knowledge of results, providing guidance, providing reinforcement, dealing with the effects of interference, individualizing teaching and learning, and facilitating transfer of training.

   7. *Select the teaching approach.* The approach chosen may be direct (explicit) or guided discovery—it may be deductive or inductive. The deductive approach is satisfactory if skills are straightforward or not too complex, but the inductive approach may be better if students are to understand the principles and processes involved and to speed learning and promote transfer. Skillful modeling or demonstration is important to both the deductive and inductive approaches.

   Both approaches require modeling and usually involve demonstration. We all have learned much by watching someone perform a skill and imitating what we saw, whether this be a psychomotor skill (e.g., using a Bunsen burner in the chemistry lab), a cognitive skill (e.g., solving a geometry problem), or an affectively toned skill (e.g., manners at the dinner table). Become proficient at modeling and demonstrating. When you model and demonstrate, make sure learners can see what is going on, and accompany the demonstration with concise explanations. Discussing the skills and their uses helps later performance.

Task Analysis: Procedural, Hierarchical, and Combination

Whether the skill is motor, cognitive, or affective, ask yourself what is involved in performing it proficiently. What background knowledge or previous experience do students need? What steps or operations are involved? Is a there a sequence of steps or events to follow? You may need to do a task analysis. The operations of physical tasks can be observed and recorded; cognitive tasks, however, require analysis of the knowledge and thought processes needed to perform the tasks (Hanser, 1995). Although task analysis is often associated with special education and vocational education, it has much wider application. It is an important instructional strategy for every teacher. It is done to identify the specific details of tasks, including the knowledge, subskills, attitudes, and personal characteristics needed for successful performance (Brown, 1998).

Task analysis of skills can be approached in terms of the sequence of *procedures* (or steps) to be followed, the *hierarchy* of skills and concepts involved, or a *combination* of the two. You will need to choose between, or combinations of, three kinds of skill analyses:

- The procedural approach: step-by-step
- The hierarchical approach: the hierarchy of subskills needed
- The combination approach: a combination of step-by-step and hierarchical

Be able to use each approach to instructional analysis to identify the subskills and their relationships. This is needed in planning for efficient presentation and learning to be possible.

PROCEDURAL TASK ANALYSIS.   The procedural approach involves identifying the chain of events or operations to be performed (in sequence) to achieve an instructional goal and listing these step-by-step (Dick & Carey, 2005, p. 67). This analysis is useful for pinpointing where instruction should be focused—identifying chain elements and spots where elements must be linked for smooth performance. Analysis of a procedure for folding and inserting a letterhead business letter into a business envelope is illustrated in Figure 12.3.

If these procedures are followed, the final product is a letter inserted into an envelope. When following the procedural approach, steps can be taught independently of each other; however, they do follow a sequence. Each step involves stages: (1) The *input* of one step initiates a (2) *process* followed to reach an (3) *output* of that step. Dick and Carey (2005) recommend that after "you have identified the instructional goal, you will determine step-by-step what people are doing when they perform that goal. The final step in the instructional analysis process is to determine what skills, knowledge and attitudes, known as *entry behaviors*, are required of learners to be able to begin the instruction." (p. 6). Diagrams are an important part of instructional analysis (Dick & Carey, pp. 71–72). In pro-

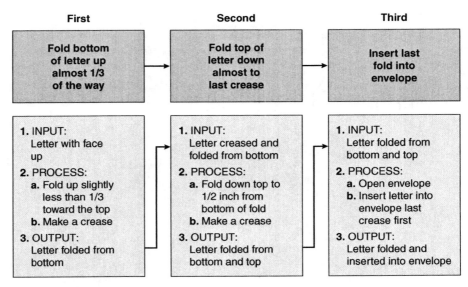

FIGURE 12.3   *Procedural Analysis: Folding and Inserting a Letter into an Envelope*

cedural analysis the diagram is a continuous line (envelope example). In hierarchical task analysis sub-skills must be identified (job interview example). Combination task analysis requires both the step-by-step and hierarchical stages (dictionary example).

HIERARCHICAL TASK ANALYSIS.   A hierarchy is a set of component skills to be learned before the complex skill of which they are a part can be learned. Hierarchical analysis is used to discover what students must know and be able to do before they can successfully learn a skill. For example, students need to know how to write sentences before they can learn to write paragraphs. It identifies the skills (or subskills) needed to perform a higher-level skill. Subskills can be called *enabling* skills, those needed to achieve a "terminal" skill objective. For instance, if the terminal objective is subtracting whole numbers of any size, students need to be able to subtract when several borrowings are required, and before this, they need to have learned single borrowing. The list could be extended downward through other subskills to the ability to do simple subtraction and knowledge of simple subtraction facts.

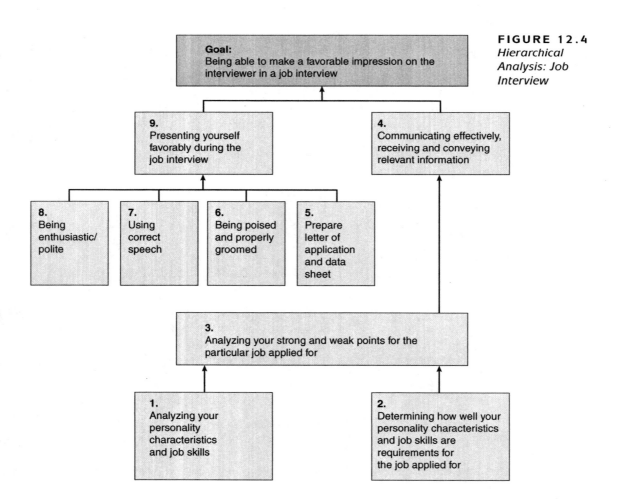

FIGURE 12.4
Hierarchical Analysis: Job Interview

Goal:
Being able to make a favorable impression on the interviewer in a job interview

9.
Presenting yourself favorably during the job interview

4.
Communicating effectively, receiving and conveying relevant information

8.
Being enthusiastic/ polite

7.
Using correct speech

6.
Being poised and properly groomed

5.
Prepare letter of application and data sheet

3.
Analyzing your strong and weak points for the particular job applied for

1.
Analyzing your personality characteristics and job skills

2.
Determining how well your personality characteristics and job skills are requirements for the job applied for

Study the example on preparing for a job interview in Figure 12.4. It identifies the sequencing of enabling skills (subcompetencies) and the terminal objective of making a favorable impression in a job interview. You will see that hierarchical task analysis objectives can be accomplished by: (1) having a good knowledge of the behaviors that are effective for a successful interview, and (2) identifying and arranging the subskills into a logical order (showing the sequence of those that might be prerequisite to others).

When you do hierarchical analysis, you may need numerous revisions before you are satisfied. However, it will provide valuable information about the kinds and sequence of enabling skills students must have or master before the overall skill can be acquired.

Procedural analysis is appropriate for psychomotor skills. Complex skills, cognitive skills in particular, normally require hierarchical analysis. For a detailed description of hierarchical analysis by Dick and Carey, refer to the sixth edition of *The Systematic Design of Instruction* (2005).

COMBINATION TASK ANALYSIS.   Many tasks require a combination of procedural and hierarchical analysis. Consider locating a word in a dictionary (Figure 12.5). The steps to be followed to locate a word are: locate the tab, locate the guideword, and locate the word. The output of the first step is the input for the process of the second; and the output of the second step, in turn, becomes the input for the third. This requires proce-

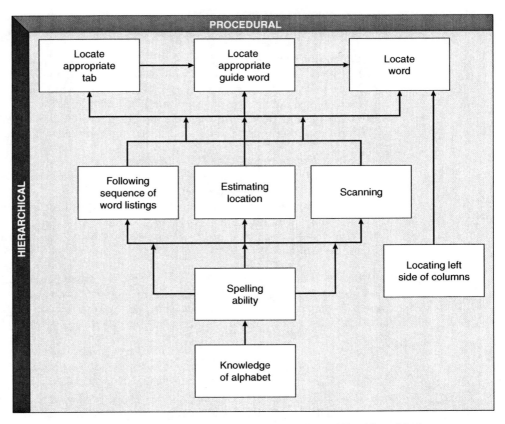

FIGURE 12.5   *Combination Task Analysis: Locating a Word in a Dictionary*

dural (horizontal) analysis, with each step examined in terms of input, process, and output. Prerequisite subskills are shown vertically—selecting and ordering these requires hierarchical analysis. The combination approach is used to analyze a relatively complex psychomotor skill or linear chain of cognitive tasks.

Skills Lesson Planning

Thorough planning precedes effective skill teaching. Steps for planning a skill lesson were presented earlier. You may wish to study these before you proceed. Authorities on the direct teaching of skills agree on essential procedures: orientation, presentation, structured practice, guided practice, and independent practice.

When setting foundational objectives, many provinces now specify skills as well as knowledge and affective objectives. Consider the following examples of knowledge, skills, and values requirements in a social studies unit on global issues (Saskatchewan Learning, 2004).

Knowledge Objectives

1. Know that some challenges or issues are global in nature because they affect the entire earth and will require global involvement to find solutions.
2. Know that human rights are rights to which an individual is entitled simply because he or she is human.
3. Know that the acquisition and utilization of technological and scientific knowledge have given humans the power to change the world's environment significantly.

Skills/Abilities Objectives

1. Learn and practice using criteria as a basis for analyzing information.
2. Learn and practice selecting and applying the abilities of problem solving, dialectical thinking, decision making, and conflict resolution to the issue.
3. Learn and practice defining the main parts, describing cause-and-effect relationships, and describing how the parts of the whole are related to each other.

Values Issues the Student Will Discuss

1. Whether there are acceptable and nonacceptable methods available to individuals and groups seeking to secure their rights.
2. Whether humans and societies will continue to demonstrate a willingness to use force and violence to achieve goals.
3. What criteria are to be used to determine how the earth's resources and species should be used.

It is the role of the teacher to present these objectives in specific terms in lesson plans. However, note how the teaching of skills enhances knowledge and values objectives. A six-step framework for skills teaching designed by the authors of this text is presented in Figure 12.6. Following is an eleven-step procedure for the teaching of skills.

1. *State objectives and provide set.* The effective teacher begins by explaining the objectives, establishing a learning set, and, often, providing an overview. Students should know why it is important to them to be able to perform the skill.

2. *Review and check previous day's work.* Daily review is important for material needed for subsequent learning. The purpose of review and checking assignments is to emphasize the relationships between lessons, ensure that students have the prerequisite

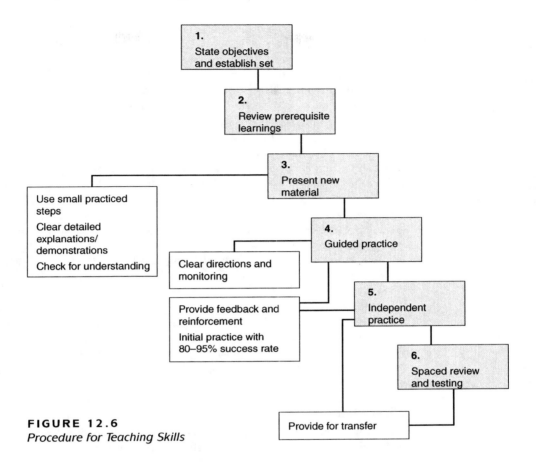

FIGURE 12.6
Procedure for Teaching Skills

knowledge or skills, and ensure they see the new material as an extension of content already mastered.

3. *Present new material in small practiced steps.* Good teachers spend more time presenting new material and guided practice than less able teachers. Make purposes clear and teach in small portions, using step-by-step directions. Make sure each step is mastered before the next is given. Use clear, pure, simple-to-complex demonstrations and examples. Do not skimp on examples or demonstrations. Stress understanding.

4. *Provide clear explanations and demonstrations.* As the skill is explained, modeled, or demonstrated, make sure students know the execution and flow of skills and subskills. All must see what is being modeled or demonstrated. Make explanations interesting, to the point, and complete. Check for understanding. Reteach if necessary.

5. *Check for understanding.* Students must do more than memorize steps or operations. They should understand how and why steps fit together. After each step, make sure each student understands and performs the step correctly. Doing a poor job of assessing the progress of individuals is a major reason for poor skill development. Ask one or more students to show they can understand and perform. Assuming everyone can do it is common. Evaluating the progress of every student and record keeping are necessary.

6. *Provide a high level of guided and active practice.* Practice does not always make perfect—correct practice can. Have students do initial practice, step by step, with you as you demonstrate. Observe carefully whether it is being done correctly. At the initial stages, practice should focus on process (how to do it) rather than product (doing it right). Stress technique. You do not want students to practice incorrect procedures that must be unlearned.

7. *Provide feedback and reinforcement.* Provide specific and descriptive feedback, correctives when needed, and reinforcement for each student's guided practice, seatwork, or homework. Feedback should focus on process. Reinforcement must be supported by an accurate description of what was good. Just telling the student, "That was good," is not helpful. Tell the student what was done well and add, in a supportive way, tips for improvement.

8. *Provide clear directions and monitor seatwork.* Provide clear directions before guided seatwork. Circulate, to give feedback and correctives for those who need it. Effective teachers provide sufficient practice when students learn new material. Students must be able to perform a skill well before practicing independently. Practice should emphasize process with a high rate of success. Decide the nature and quantity of further practice. This depends on the level of learning desired—awkwardness, conscious skillfulness, or automaticity.

9. *Work toward high initial practice success rate.* Students should achieve a success rate of from 80 to 95 percent in initial practices. Assignments should challenge but not be too difficult or complex. Students must "get it right" before engaging in independent practice.

10. *Provide for transfer.* Students must see the relevance to what they studied before and will study later. Ensure transfer. Practice should be as close to an actual situation as possible. After monitored practice, practice can be assigned as homework or done in class the next day. If transfer is wanted, practice it.

11. *Provide spaced review and testing.* If the skill is to be retained, it must be learned very well in the first place; spaced review should occur to ensure retention and consolidate learning. Test often to provide clues for reteaching and the nature of further practice. Testing should disclose present performance capability, understanding, and the ability to transfer.

Practicing a Skill

Practice is important. It is used to overlearn and maintain a skill so it can be used in other, or new, contexts. Simple or isolated behaviors may require little or no practice (for example, locating the space key on a computer). Practice becomes more important as learning becomes more complex, and prolonged practice is needed to polish skills such as touch keyboarding, reading, writing, and computing. Basic skills normally must be overlearned, that is, brought to the automaticity level. The kind, amount, and distribution of practice must be decided and a distributed practice schedule set that includes drills, reviews, and testing. Consider whether practice should be *massed* (in one or a few lengthy sessions) or *distributed* (in a larger number of short sessions). Usually, when motor skills are being learned, it is better to distribute practice with rest intervals between. If time is limited, rest intervals reduce the time available for practice, so rest intervals may be reduced or even eliminated. These affect performance, but not learning, of motor skills. Rest intervals may not be as important for cognitive or affectively toned skills if a high interest level is maintained, but it is generally better to distribute practice unless breaking it up interferes with the flow or degree of learning. It is difficult to generalize about practice schedules and whether practice should be whole or part, massed or distributed. Decisions about these depend on the skill to be learned and the learners.

Example Lesson Plan

Study the lesson plan presented below. Task analysis should be done before the skill lesson is taught. A procedural task analysis for folding and inserting a business letter into an envelope was provided earlier. The lesson below is based on that analysis.

Lesson Plan

I. *Topic:* Business letters

II. *Content:* Folding a standard business letter and inserting it into a standard business envelope

III. *Objective:* After a demonstration of the correct procedure for folding an 8½-by-11-inch business letter and inserting it into a business envelope, each student will be able to do the procedure in one minute or less.

IV. *Prerequisite learning:* None

V. *Presentation activities*

A. *Introductory:* Tell students they will be learning an efficient procedure for folding and inserting business letters and that this is useful and important personal and occupational information. Have them watch as you remove an actual business letter from an envelope and show them the creases on the letter.

B. *Developmental*

1. Tell students to watch carefully as you demonstrate the correct procedure for folding and inserting; conduct the demonstration in three stages: (a) folding bottom of letter up almost one-third of the way; (b) folding the top down almost to the last crease; and (c) inserting the last fold into the envelope. Repeat the demonstration.

2. Distribute three business letters and an envelope to each student; demonstrate and have students copy what you are doing, one stage at a time. They are not to go ahead on their own. After each step, ask students to hold up their letters so you can see if they are doing it correctly and provide help if needed. Repeat the guided practice with a fresh letter.

3. Call a student to the front of the room; call on other students to tell this student how to do the three steps.

4. Ask students to practice folding and inserting with letters they had previously printed. Circulate as students practice to provide feedback, correctives if needed, and reinforcement.

C. *Closure*

1. Tell students you will be timing them as they fold and insert a business letter. Inform them they should be done in one minute or less. Students are to hold up their inserted letters when done. Time the students. Repeat the procedure until everybody in the room is doing it in one minute or less.

2. Compliment students about their accomplishment. Tell them that for every business letter they handle in future assignments, they will be required to fold and insert the letter into an addressed envelope.

VI. *Materials and aids:* Standard business letters and envelopes

VII. *Evaluation:* Observation as students hold up completed materials and one minute timed practice results.

You can use the data collection instrument to help you analyze the cases that follow. Your instructor may pose specific questions for your response.

CASE 12.1 Teaching a Skill

A Great Skill Teacher

You might use the following case as an introduction to this chapter. As you read the following case, note the steps being followed by the instructor and ask yourself what principles of effective teaching are being used.

> Bill Duffer had bought a set of used golf clubs and had played for about two months. Though he had good eye–hand coordination, Bill realized that if he was to improve to the point where he could play a "respectable" game, he needed to take lessons. He booked a set of lessons with golf professional Lee Palmer, who, he was told, was a very good instructor.
>
> It was Monday, and Lee and Bill began the first lesson with the two playing three holes of golf together. This was a surprise to Bill. He thought the first lesson would be on the practice range, but Lee explained he wanted to observe Bill play so he could decide where instruction should begin and the sequence of instruction for future lessons.
>
> The two then went to the practice range. On the way, Lee presented Bill with a diagnosis of Bill's current capability and a projected improvement schedule that was to take place through ten lessons over a period of ten weeks. Bill's putting did not need attention, but he could benefit significantly by improving his golf swing, chipping to the hole, and planning strategy for playing differing golf holes. Lee told

Bill that because golf is so complex, a learner cannot concentrate on every aspect simultaneously. He said the golf swing takes about three seconds and there are dozens of parts to an expert swing. A learner can concentrate effectively only on one or a few things simultaneously. Lee said he'd pick the really important aspects first, give a lesson on an aspect, and then Bill needed to practice that aspect to the point where he no longer needed to think consciously about it.

> Lee then demonstrated the proper golf grip, telling Bill that this was the foundation of the golf swing, that the two hands must act as a unit, and that holding the golf club was like holding a bird—tight enough so that the bird could not escape but loose enough so that the bird would not be hurt. Lee guided Bill's hands into the proper position. Bill then hit several balls as Lee helped Bill make minor adjustments, until Lee said, "Very good, you look like you have the idea." Bill stated that the grip felt awkward. Lee said that this was normal, and that during the rest of the week he should not worry about his score. With practice, the new grip would feel natural and, after some initial awkwardness and perhaps a very temporary drop in proficiency, improvement could be dramatic. The lesson ended with Lee asking Bill to review the elements of the golf grip. The next lesson, Lee said, would concentrate on the body turn as the club was taken back, the ball struck, and the follow-through was completed.

CASE 12.2 Teaching a Skill

Using the Alphabet

Mr. Aftahi planned to teach his grade 1 class how to organize information alphabetically and put words into alphabetical order. Though the children read at varying levels and several have been using primary dictionaries and other reference books, the skill has not been formally taught.

Mr. Aftahi obtained several dictionaries, telephone directories, encyclopedias, reference books, and enlarged copies of index pages. Children enter the classroom after recess and Mr. Aftahi has displayed the books so everyone can see. The students are interested in the large number of books and other materials and become quiet as they watch.

Finally, Jay asks, "What are we going to do with all those things, Mr. Aftahi?" Mr. Aftahi, who has finished displaying the materials, looks around to make sure he has everyone's attention. He asks, "Let's see if we can answer Jay's question. What do you see on these tables?" The children answer, "Books," "Dictionaries," "Encyclopedias," "Papers," and "Telephone books."

"What is in these books?" asks Mr. Aftahi. The students respond, "Names," "Words," "Sentences," "Stories," "You can find out stuff you want to know," "I saw maps in one of those books," and "My mom looks up telephone numbers in the telephone book."

"So there are words, names, sentences, stories, maps, and telephone numbers in these books? Would you say people use these books to find things out?" The children agree. "If I wanted to find a telephone number in this book, what would I do?" Mr. Aftahi gestures toward the telephone directory. "You'd look it up," says Danny. "OK, what does that mean?" asks Mr. Aftahi. Danny explains, "Look for the name of the person you want to phone and the right number is beside his name."

"All right, let's look up Mr. Jessop's number. You say I look for his name and his number will be right there?" Danny nods vigorously and Mr. Aftahi begins at the first page and reads the first few names. "Danny, can you help me here?" Danny comes to help. He studies the page, looks at the name on the board and back at the page. "I don't see it yet," he remarks. "Do you notice anything about the names here?" asks Mr. Aftahi. Students begin to wave their hands. "These names all start with 'A,'" Danny says. "Is the whole book like that?" asks Mr. Aftahi. Danny looks at successive pages. "No," he announces. "There are lots of other letters at the start on other pages."

"What else has 'A' at the start?" "My name," says Andrea. "Yes, it does, but I'm thinking of something bigger than a name," responds Mr. Aftahi. "The ABCs," answers Tuan. "Right. The ABCs, or

the alphabet, starts with 'A.' I wonder if the rest of the book is anything like the alphabet. Tuan, come and work with Danny to see if the telephone book is like the ABCs." Tuan and Danny pour over the book, turning pages, and saying the names of the letters as they come to them. "Yes," they report. "First come the 'A' names, then the 'B' names, and the 'C' names, and so on. The 'Z' names are at the end."

"So where will we look for Mr. Jessop's name?" asks Mr. Aftahi. "In the 'J' names," answer several children. Danny and Tuan turn to the "J" section and find Mr. Jessop's name and number. "See how easy that was once we knew how the names were organized? What is it that tells us what comes first or last, or helps us to know where names are found?" "We can look at the alphabet on the wall, or we can just say the ABCs," says Yvette. "Right, the alphabet can be our guide." Mr. Aftahi then assigns three or four children to each resource to see if the information is organized in the same way. The students are excited to discover the same pattern in the resources they examine. Some say, "I knew it all the time."

"Putting things, like words or names, in ABC order, or alphabetical order, is an important thing to be able to do. It helps us understand the way to find information more quickly and it is a way that many people understand. Today we will practice arranging some word cards in alphabetical order. What will we use as our guide?" "The alphabet." "That's right. Now look at these three words and try to decide which would come first, second, and third if we put them in alphabetical order." He shows the words *cat, apple,* and *ball.* The children easily put them in order.

"How did you do it? What did you do first?" Tara explains, "I just thought of A, B, C and matched up the words." Matt says he looked at the letters on the wall to help him put the words in order. "Both ways are good," says Mr. Aftahi. "Let's try these." He shows word cards saying *Candice, Ewen,* and *Dominique.*

The students arrange these words and do two other examples Mr. Aftahi presents. Finally, each child is presented with a set of three words and asked to arrange them in alphabetical order. "When you have finished, look around for someone else who is finished, get him to check yours and you

continued

check his. Look at the alphabet on the wall if you're not sure. Then trade your cards with someone else who has had theirs checked. Then, do the same thing again. Try to do three sets of cards, and check

three sets of someone else's. Don't do the same set twice."

The children work busily at their desks, the floor, and a large table. Mr. Aftahi circulates.

CASE 12.3 Teaching a Skill

Being Interested in Interest

Ms. Atwater had just taken up yesterday's homework questions on calculating interest in her grade 11 business math class. "Today," she said, "We are going to learn something that is going to be a real benefit to you in the future. You or another member of your family have at times buy something, for instance, a stereo or car, by making a down payment and then paying the rest in monthly installments. As you know, credit is not free. Let's say you buy a boombox for $135.00 and make a $35 down payment. You are told the interest rate will be only 6 percent and that you can pay in 12 monthly installments. How much do you think you will pay in interest?" Maria answers, "That's easy, six dollars." "No way," Orest interjects. "You'll get ripped off for much more." "You're right, Orest. The rate is not calculated as a simple annual interest rate. The truth is that you will pay about twice that. Today you will learn how to calculate true interest rates so you can easily test what you will pay and you won't have a surprise or so you can choose to shop elsewhere if you can get a better deal."

Ms. Atwater then wrote the formula for calculating true interest rate on the chalkboard.

$$\frac{2PC}{A(N + 1)} = R$$

where A = amount of cash or credit received
       N = number of payments in the contract
       P = number of payments per year
       C = total charges including service charges
       R = interest rate in terms of simple annual interest

"Let's see how much that boombox is really going to cost. Watch me use the true interest formula."

$$\frac{2 \times 12 \times 6}{100 \times (12 + 1)} = \frac{144}{1300} = 11.08\%$$

"So, you can see, as we said, you are paying almost twice as much as a simple interest rate would lead you to believe. You pay $11.08 in interest rather than $6.00."

Ms. Atwater then did two more examples on the chalkboard. She asked individual students to tell her each step. Then she sent six students to the chalkboard to do a problem. When they were done, she asked them to explain what they had done. The six went back to their seats and she said, "Turn to page 196. Do problems 1, 2, 3, 4, 5, 7, 9, 11, 13, and 15." Next, she did the first problem, step by step, with the entire class. Then, she circulated as students began their assignment. She stopped to talk to several students. To some she made comments such as, "Why don't you try this . . . ?" To others she said, "That's right. Can you tell me how you got the answer?"

With two minutes left in the period, she gained the attention of the class, saying, "You are well on the way to acquiring a very important 'smart consumer' skill. Please do the rest of the problems for homework. Do one more thing. If you have recently purchased something on credit, calculate the true interest rate on that purchase. Alternately, find out if somebody at home has purchased something on credit recently. Perhaps you can calculate the true interest rate on that purchase."

Demonstrations

Have you ever bought something you had to assemble that included an "easy" explanation for how to do it? Was it easy? Were you frustrated? Didn't you wish that the explanation was clearer, or, better still, that somebody would show you? How often did you memorize something without understanding it because the teacher did not explain it or did so in a confusing way? Were there times you could not solve a problem or complete an operation even after a teacher demonstrated it and you did not want to appear stupid so you did not ask for a redemonstration?

While *explaining* relates largely to the teaching of concepts, generalizations, and principles, *demonstrating* (showing how) applies to skills and processes (cognitive, psychomotor, or interpersonal or social). Demonstrations can be used to help students learn a procedure, process, or illustration. Direct teaching makes extensive use of demonstrations because many of the things we learn come through observing others. A demonstration can provide a critical observed-action experience that transcends verbal explanation. As a teaching method in its own right, demonstration normally involves both a visual part and a spoken explanation. Watching demonstrations saves students unnecessary and time-consuming trial and error. Demonstrations may require concrete performance of actions, skills, or processes. It is the link between "knowing about" and "being able to do." Demonstrations can stimulate interest and provide the advantage of having students use several senses. When demonstrations are done well, ideas and concepts are presented clearly. The result should be increased student attentiveness, learning, and performance. Examples of demonstrations include watching a tennis stroke, a dance step, magnetic attraction or repulsion, solving a quadratic equation, or mixing water colors. Demonstrations can be used to enhance aspects of every school subject.

Procedure for Effective Demonstrations

Before you begin a demonstration, decide whether you will permit students to ask questions during the demonstration. Ask yourself whether a handout is a good idea or whether students should take notes.

1. *Analyze.* Analyze what is to be demonstrated before you begin (i.e., procedural, hierarchical, or combination skill analysis).
2. *Practice.* Do a "dry run" (rehearse). Ask, "What are the key steps to be followed?" "What words should I use?" "Where will students have the most difficulty?"
3. *Set up.* Before the class begins, set up demonstration materials so class time will not be wasted. Make sure all can see. Remember that when one faces the class, right and left are reversed; if possible, demonstrate so students will not have to make right/left transfer. Have ready any materials that students will need. Plan how materials can be distributed quickly (or, in advance, place them at student stations).
4. *Establish the set.* State the objectives for the demonstration and establish the set. If necessary, review prerequisite knowledge or skills. Provide an overview. Students must be informed (and believe) it is important for them to know what is to be learned. With some demonstrations, highlight the aspects students are to observe.
5. *Get and maintain attention.* Secure undivided attention before beginning. Watch for nonverbal clues of inattentiveness or lack of understanding. Check up if necessary.
6. *Demonstrate.* Use well-defined, clearly presented steps. Do not move too quickly. For some demonstrations, do them at normal speed first and repeat the steps in "slow motion." If the procedure is complex, break it into steps and demonstrate these separately. Use clear, concise, oral descriptions. Stress key aspects.
7. *Record key aspects.* It may be useful to record important steps or points for review on the chalkboard, a transparency, or handout.

8. *Redemonstrate.* For understanding, repeat the demonstration (or steps) as necessary. This means check to see if students know the "how" and "why" and if they are ready to try it themselves.

9. *Provide practice.* Have students do it with you, step by step, as often as necessary. Then provide individual practice. Initial practices must be monitored and have a high rate of success (80 to 95 percent). Provide immediate feedback, correctives, and reinforcement. Assign independent practice after you are sure the students know how to do it.

A data collection instrument for use with the target of demonstrating is given in Appendix 12.3. Normal demonstration steps are shown in Figure 12.7. After you have done your demonstration, do a self-evaluation. You can ask yourself:

1. During the introduction, did you get the attention of the class? Tell why what is being demonstrated is important.

2. Did you communicate clearly, make eye contact, encourage feedback, use appropriate language, and pause when appropriate? Could everybody easily see and hear?

3. Where you aware of whether students were following, that you were not moving to quickly or too slowly? Did you respond clearly to questions?

4. Was the quality of the materials used attractive, suitable, easily seen?

5. Did you review the key points, ask for questions, and provide feedback and reinforcement during student practice?

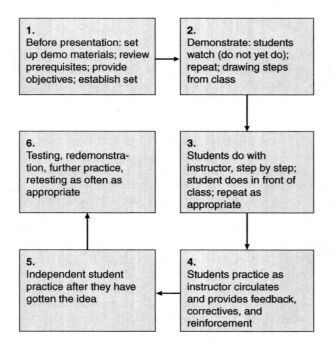

FIGURE 12.7   *Steps in Demonstration*

Demonstration Principles

Modeling (demonstration) by the teacher is most often part of a skill lesson. The purpose is to give students a clear idea of what is expected. This is true whether the skill is psychomotor (e.g., doing a set shot in basketball), cognitive (e.g., estimating an answer in mathematics), or affectively toned (e.g., paraphrasing).

Students need to see and hear each substep. The demonstration must not be hurried. Verbal explanations must be to the point and focus on key aspects. If a skill involves several steps, it may need to be demonstrated several times. Steps may have to be isolated and demonstrated. Students should try the skill (or subskill) "with you." Monitored individual practice should not begin until students are ready. Data collection instruments for use with the professional target of teaching a skill are given in Appendixes 12.1 and 12.2, and for demonstrating in Appendix 12.3.

Common mistakes in giving demonstrations include: (1) students try a skill before they are ready to do it without guidance, (2) too many details are given in an explanation, or too many directions, steps, or details are included (more than a beginner can possibly assimilate at one time), and (3) feedback is not given on "with-the-teacher" attempts.

Use the data collection instruments in Appendixes 12.1, 12.2, and 12.3 to help you analyze the cases that follow. Your instructor may pose specific questions for your response.

CASE 12.4 Demonstrations

Macramé Getting Planted

Mr. Santez has talked with his grade 6 class about making macramé plant holders as Christmas gifts. Not one of the students knows any of the knot-tying techniques, and Mr. Santez intends to demonstrate the half-hitch first. When the students have mastered this, he plans to teach them other knots. Mr. Santez worked at a summer camp in charge of crafts, and he feels sure he can quickly teach students to tie a half-hitch.

After recess, Mr. Santez begins to explain how to tie a half-hitch. Though several students are not attending, he describes the procedure verbally. He soon realizes that several students seem to be having trouble following the directions. He looks in his desk drawer for cord and finds a length of string. He goes through the procedure again at the front of the room, noting he inadvertently omitted a step in his explanation. He points out the change in procedure. Some students look anxious, some seem confused.

The string is rather small, and soon the students are fidgeting and muttering about not being able to see. Mr. Santez tells them to pay closer attention and that if they had been watching in the first place, they would know how to do the knot. He says, "I will show you once more. Then you'll have to do it yourselves."

Mr. Santez goes through the procedure again and leaves the classroom to fetch the macramé cord stored in the art supply room. When he returns with two colors, the students are arguing noisily about the correct procedure. He calls for attention and asks the students to choose a color and to each cut off an arm's length of cord. They begin to follow these directions but are unable to continue because no one can find scissors. Mr. Santez remembers that, because of the last budget cuts, scissors are kept in the principal's office, so he sends a student to get them. Students are quickly losing interest in the project, and begin to make disparaging remarks about the idea.

When the scissors arrive, only a few children seem interested. The others have to be encouraged, and in a few cases ordered, to begin the task. There is general confusion and many students call out questions, and the noise level in the room heightens dramatically.

Mr. Santez works with one individual at a time, showing how to tie the knot. Most of the students who have not yet been helped are having trouble and are waiting. There is a hum of complaints, demands for help, or demands for a change of activity. Frustration increases until a boy who has been trying to tie the knot by himself suddenly throws down his materials and, for a few seconds, sits glowering. The girl behind him laughs and points at him and he leaps up, overturning his desk, and rushes from the room.

Mr. Santez notices him leave and asks the class, "What happened to Mark? Doesn't he like doing macramé?"

CASE 12.5 Demonstrations

Business Math

Look again at Case 12.3, describing a business math lesson. The teacher, Ms. Atwater, demonstrates a math skill. Use the data collection instrument in Appendix 12.3 to analyze the steps used by Ms. Atwater.

LINKING PRACTICE TO THEORY

To what extent do we teach students "what" but not "how" or "why"? Do you find teaching the "what" easier than teaching "how" or "why"? As you plan lessons and units, how should you incorporate the procedural and hierarchical skills involved? How skill-based are the subjects you teach? Try the guidelines suggested in this chapter. How important is it to analyze a skill before teaching it?

Summary

Effective skill teaching requires that teachers recognize the attributes of skilled performance. Planning for teaching a skill should, as appropriate, include procedural, hierarchical, or combination task analysis. Decisions are needed about whether to use a part or whole, a deductive or inductive approach, and the skill-teaching principles involved. The basic steps for good skill teaching are orientation, presentation, structured practice, guided practice, independent practice, rapid feedback, and spaced reviews. Most skills need to be demonstrated within a framework of planning and preparation, demonstration by the teacher, students "doing with" as the teacher demonstrates, monitored student practice, independent practice, testing, and redemonstration as required.

Activities

1. The instructor or a student might model short lessons to illustrate the steps and elements of skill teaching and the deductive and inductive approaches. Point out the components of each lesson.

2. Join a subject area group and brainstorm examples of procedural skills, hierarchical skills, and skills that are a combination of procedural and hierarchical. Do task analyses of a procedural skill, hierarchical skill, and combination skill, and prepare lesson plans for the skills analyzed.

3. Have a class discussion in which class members tell about skills at which they are at an automaticity level.

4. Pass out sheets of letter paper and envelopes and take the class through the steps given in the example of procedural analysis in Figure 12.3.

5. Have the class brainstorm the preparation needed for a successful job interview and then compare their findings with the chart in Figure 12.4.

6. Using a large dictionary, invite selected members of the class up and have them look up preselected words from the front, middle, and back of the dictionary. Ask the class what subskills were needed before the words could be found quickly.

7. Have two volunteers give a skill lesson while the remainder of the class completes the data gathering sheet in Appendix 12.1.

8. Reread the Bill Duffer case presented at the start of the chapter; analyze it in terms of what you have learned.

9. Join a subject group of five. Select a task in the subject, then apply your learning about the teaching of skills and prepare a suitable lesson plan.

10. Examine a can of pudding that has a pop-top opening. Do a procedural analysis of opening the can. Following this, by subject-area interest, join a group to select and analyze a subject skill

11. Obtain a city map. Given an address to find, do a hierarchical analysis of the skills involved. Then, by subject interest, join a group of five or six to select and analyze a subject skill.

12. In a subject-area group, brainstorm examples of demonstrations that can be given in that subject. Categorize these under the headings of skills, processes, procedures, or illustrations.

13. In your group, prepare a demonstration and present to the class. Class members are to provide feedback using the data collection sheet in Appendix 12.3. Debrief.

APPENDIX 12.1   *Teaching a Skill Lesson Target*

PROFESSIONAL TARGET—TEACHING A SKILL LESSON

Lesson Elements	Descriptive Notes

A. Deductive Lesson

Set
Gaining attention?
Reviewing prerequisite skills?
Describing context for use of skill?
Giving skill objective "Today you will . . . learn to. . . ."

Development
Modeling/demo'ing skill step by step?
Cueing ("First you do," "second")?
Visual or verbal input?
Highlighting terms or steps?
Modeling again?
Leading students through skill, cueing?
Checking students' tries?
Modeling again?
Supervised practice?
Feedback?

Closure
Reviewing steps—by student? by instructor?
Reviewing context in which skill is used?
Assigning practice?
Bridging to next step or lesson?
Provision for transfer?

B. Inductive Lesson

Set
As above, *except* skill is introduced in general terms only
    ("Today you will learn a skill that will help you. . . .")

Development
Present/develop, e.g., visually, concrete, on board, etc.
Examples used?
Discovery by students of steps involved?
Summarizing?

Closure
Reviewing steps—by student? by instructor?
Reviewing context in which skill is used?
Assigning practice?
Bridging to next step or lesson?
Provision for transfer?

APPENDIX 12.2 *Teaching a Skill Target*

PROFESSIONAL TARGET—TEACHING A SKILL

Name of Skill:

_____

Procedure Used: _____ Procedural   _____ Hierarchical   _____ Combination

Teaching Elements	Descriptive Notes

Major subskills identified

Subskills of major skills identified

Relationship of subskills

Practice of subskills and/or whole skill

Feedback to students

Use of skill identified

List steps of
    Presentation or Demonstration

Check procedures for the direct teaching of skills as used:

1. _____ Objectives and set provided   4. _____ Guided practice provided

2. _____ Prerequisites reviewed   5. _____ Monitored practice

3. _____ Skill modeled   6. _____ Independent practice assigned

APPENDIX 12.3   *Demonstrating Target*

PROFESSIONAL TARGET—DEMONSTRATING

Please describe what was said or done and how students reacted.

Procedures	Descriptive Notes

Before demo
   Preparation
      Materials/equip ready
      Students able to see

Establishing set
   For demo
   Review prerequisites

Conducting the demo
   Gaining and maintaining attention
   Oral description clarity, language usage
   Nonverbal cues
   Emphasis on key elements/points
   Use of materials, concrete/visual

Check steps used: Comments:

   1. _____ Set
   2. _____ Instructor demo
   3. _____ Instructor repeats demo
   4. _____ Instructor repeats drawing steps from class
   5. _____ A student is asked to do demo
   6. _____ Students practice under supervision
   7. _____ Testing
   8. _____ Redemo
   9. _____ Further practice
  10. _____ Retesting
  11. _____ Individual practice assigned (e.g., homework)

Practice of skill or procedure
   Directions given
   Feedback: checking up, reinforcing

Provision for transfer

13 Direct Instruction and Individual Study

Before direct instruction and individual study are examined, it is useful to place these strategies into a broader context. Figure 13.1 provides an overview of the five main strategies, the teaching methods that are part of each, and the skills the teacher needs to teach the strategies and methods effectively.

> Knowledge for practice is perhaps the most widely accepted perspective on teacher learning. . . . This perspective holds that the more teachers know about subject matter, instructional strategies, effective interventions, and so forth, the more effectively they will teach . . . the new image of teacher learning and related professional development has moved to a more constructivist model of instruction, and away from a transmission model. (McLeskey & Waldron, 2004, pp. 5–6)

As the quotation suggests, the strategies and methods as examples of good practice described later in this book cannot be learned in the college classroom alone. Skilled use is developed over time through classroom experience, interaction with peers, and reflection.

The literature on instruction is inconsistent in its use of the terms *strategies, methods,* and *skills.* We use these terms in a hierarchy of broad (strategies) to specific (skills). An *instructional strategy* is a general approach (e.g., direct or experiential); an *instructional*

OBJECTIVES

You will be able to:

1. Describe the direct instructional strategy and its methods and skills.
2. Describe procedures for effective lecturing, assigned questions, practice and drill, and other direct teaching methods.
3. Suggest the best uses and the limitations of the information presentation or acquisition methods of lecture, assigned questions, and practice and drill.
4. List tips for note taking and decide when note taking might be appropriate and when handouts might be the best approach.
5. Design lessons that involve use of the direct (explicit) instruction strategy.
6. Demonstrate initial competence in the use of direct study methods in microteaching or school lessons.
7. Describe the individual study instructional strategy and selected individual study methods.
8. List advantages and disadvantages of individual study.
9. Discuss effective use of learning centers and computerized learning.
10. Demonstrate initial competence in the use of individual study methods in microteaching or school lessons.

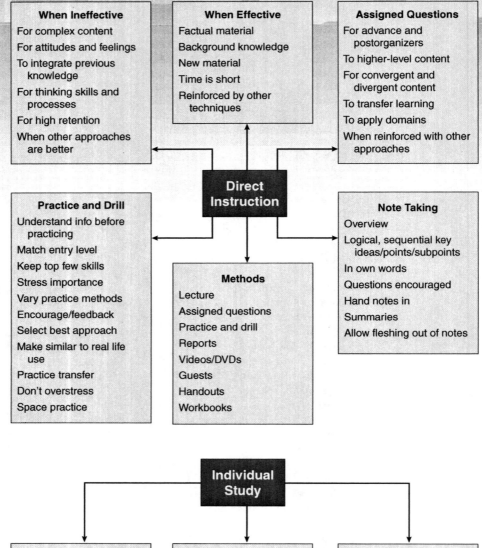

When Ineffective
For complex content
For attitudes and feelings
To integrate previous knowledge
For thinking skills and processes
For high retention
When other approaches are better

When Effective
Factual material
Background knowledge
New material
Time is short
Reinforced by other techniques

Assigned Questions
For advance and postorganizers
To higher-level content
For convergent and divergent content
To transfer learning
To apply domains
When reinforced with other approaches

Direct Instruction

Practice and Drill
Understand info before practicing
Match entry level
Keep top few skills
Stress importance
Vary practice methods
Encourage/feedback
Select best approach
Make similar to real life use
Practice transfer
Don't overstress
Space practice

Methods
Lecture
Assigned questions
Practice and drill
Reports
Videos/DVDs
Guests
Handouts
Workbooks

Note Taking
Overview
Logical, sequential key ideas/points/subpoints
In own words
Questions encouraged
Hand notes in
Summaries
Allow fleshing out of notes

Individual Study

Advantages
Personally active
Match interests
Allow depth/creativity
Motivating
Flexible
Good use of resources
Develop individual responsibility
Life-long learning

Methods
Seatwork
Homework
Essays
Research
Contracts

Disadvantages
Little social interaction
Students may lack study skills
Teacher reluctance
Resources not available
High teacher–student ratio
Costs of computers

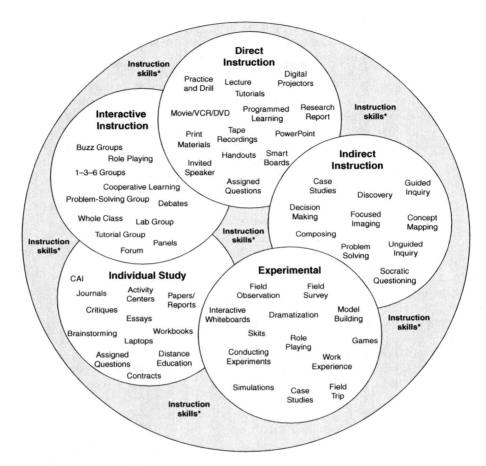

*Instruction skills: skills that are part of many methods (e.g., giving directions, demonstrating, using an overhead projector, focusing, establishing set or closure, and managing).

FIGURE 13.1 *Teaching Strategies with Methods and Skills*
Source: Saskatchewan Learning (1991).

method is a specific approach (e.g., delivering a lecture or small-group report); one or more methods can be part of a strategy; and an *instructional skill* is a specific teacher behavior such as giving a demonstration, asking questions, giving directions, varying presentation, using set, using closure, or using technology such as an overhead projector or PowerPoint presentation.

The strategies are direct, indirect, experiential, collaborative, and individual study—the "big five." You decide which strategic approach, or combination of approaches, to use in a given unit or lesson, and the methods and skills you will use.

Instructional approaches can be selected to match the purposes, whether information acquisition, skill acquisition, high-level cognitive capability, values or attitude development, or a combination of these. Effective course and unit plans normally include several teaching strategies, an array of teaching methods, and numerous instructional skills. Good lessons often include two or more strategies and several methods. No one strategy or method is equally effective for all students.

You, as the teacher, decide whether the strategy should be *direct,* with material transmitted by the teacher or another source. Ask yourself whether the strategy (approach) should be *indirect,* in that as students are asked to discover the meaning of a concept or generalization or how to go about learning or doing something. Should an *experiential* strategy be used, in which students are personally engaged in doing and reflecting about what they do? Should the strategy be collaborative (interactive), in which students work with others as they explore topics or share experiences about what is occurring or has occurred? Finally, should students be asked to be self-directed, to engage in *individual study* and learn and work on their own? Whatever strategies and methods are followed, specific skills are needed. To teach through cooperative or collaborative strategies, for example, skill in working with groups is essential.

The Nature of Direct Instruction

TCP—DIRECT INSTRUCTION

Effective direct instruction/deductive/expository methods

When used, fit content and learner needs; effective principles of lecture and assigned question methods demonstrated; stimulates pupil participation; makes effective use of audiovisual aids, discussion, and question and answer.

Exclusive use of expository approach; instruction highly abstract and not learner centered; students passive; no use of audiovisual aids, discussion, or question and answer.

What Is Direct Instruction?

Traditionally, direct instruction has been associated with "chalk and talk," and, more recently, the overhead projector. Today, direct instruction by overhead projector is being increasingly replaced by techniques such as PowerPoint or smart board presentations.

Instructional strategies need to be learned. Direct instruction can be effective. Its use does not deny building knowledge with the students. However, it is most effective when its subskills are mastered. In the hands of a knowledgeable and skilled instructor, direct instruction is powerful when used with certain content and in the right context.

Using new technologies can help. Weinert and Helmke (1995) report that many studies provide testimony that the direct instruction strategy is effective for certain goals. Direct instruction can even involve and help students learn actively, rather than passively (Leinhardt, 2001).

Paik (2003) presents an interesting synopsis of direct education. She states, "Effective direct instruction, which is still expected in the modern classroom, should consist of: (1) clear teaching, daily review, and homework checks; (2) presentation of new content and skills; (3) teacher monitoring and guided student practice; (4) corrective feedback and instructional reinforcement; (5) independent practice in school and at home with a 90 percent success rate; and (6) weekly and monthly evaluations. The skills and attributes of teachers employing effective direct instruction should include organization, clarity, task orientation, enthusiasm, and of course, flexibility" (pp. 83–84).

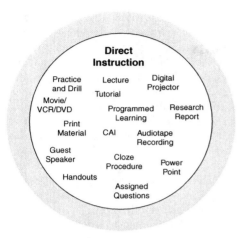

FIGURE 13.2 *Examples of the Direct Instruction Strategy*
Source: Saskatchewan Learning (1991).

Joyce, Weil, and Calhoun (2004) observe that the intention of direct instruction is for there to be "a predominant focus on learning and in which students are engaged in academic tasks a large percentage of the time and achieve a high rate of success" (p. 314). Direct instruction is teacher centered. It normally is not very effective for teaching the skills and processes required in thinking skills, critical thinking, creative thinking, interpersonal or group skills, and learning attitudes and values. Direct teaching is deductive. That is, the rule or generalization is presented and then illustrated with examples. Though this strategy is thought to be easy to plan and use, there is more to it than first meets the eye. It can be effective if careful planning occurs, the content is suitable, and if it is used in conjunction with other approaches. It can be effective for acquiring information or step-by-step skills, introducing other teaching methods, or as parts of other methods. Examples are lecture, assigned questions, didactic questioning, explicit teaching, research reports, workbooks, audio, videotape, DVD, or PowerPoint presentations, library research, and practice and drill. Lecture and assigned questions are the two most common methods. Figure 13.2 illustrates direct instruction.

Lecture and assigned questions should pique student interest and attention, include advance organizers or pattern guides, invite participation—overt (through questions and discussion) or covert (silently to oneself)—through higher-level and open-ended questions, through use of rich examples, and illustrated with audiovisual aids. Direct instruction should include provision for transfer and be combined with, or followed by, other teaching methods.

Direct Instruction and Constructivism

Although direct instruction and constructivist approaches are sometimes presented as opposites, this view is inaccurate because teachers often blend the approaches. Direct instruction can be constructivist. However, this idea is often the subject of heated debate. There are many different names for the approaches. Direct instruction has been called "the training model," "the active teaching model," "the mastery teaching model," "explicit instruction," and "expository teaching." Constructivist teaching goes by such names as "guided discovery," "authentic instruction," "teaching for understanding," "student-centered instruction," or "constructivist teaching." It is worth examining what some see as distinct elements of each approach.

DIRECT INSTRUCTION. Those who support direct instruction see it as effective in improving student achievement. In particular, it is considered valuable for at-risk children. Parents, teachers, and students who want high performance on standardized tests often prefer direct instruction. Supporters claim that systems of knowledge have been developed over time and it is the role of teachers to pass this knowledge on in an organized and systematic way. This suggests that "teachers teach and students learn." The teacher's responsibility is to follow the curriculum and adapt it to student needs. To best achieve this, teachers design lesson and unit plans based on clear objectives, structured instructional approaches, and formal testing. Teachers should teach focused knowledge in a systematic way (Smerdon, Burkam, & Lee, 1999, pp. 5–34). Advocates believe that knowledge and skills are mastered quickly and with high academic gains, and that students will do well in school and university. It is, they think, the proved, classical, and tested approach. Swanson (2001) suggests that a mixed range of strategies is a sound approach. Kozioff, LaNunziata, Cowardin, and Bessellieu (2001) see direct instruction as highly beneficial to students, teachers, and the social structure of the school as a whole. They are critical of the focus on having students doing most of the discovering and believe that learning occurs best through proven instructional units and explicit teaching. Contrary to what some opponents claim, those who support the use of direct instruction, where appropriate, recognize the importance of having students learn and use higher-order thinking skills, research skills, analysis skills, and problem-solving skills.

Those with negative views of direct instruction label it traditional, teacher centered, and didactic (students are passive receptors of knowledge). The most-used direct instruction method is lecture, with teachers teaching as they were taught. Teachers talk, write notes on the chalkboard or overhead, and pass out worksheets for students to complete. Teachers are authority figures; they are active, students are passive.

CONSTRUCTIVISM.   Supporters of constructivism say that it is student centered—students explore and experiment with ideas. Students are active and the teacher is more of a guide or coach. Students construct knowledge linking new information to previous knowledge.

In constructivist teaching and learning, knowledge is actively constructed and reconstructed. It is claimed there are no received and fixed sets of knowledge systems. Students explore ideas and learn research and analysis skills. Earlier knowledge is important, as are higher-order thinking and problem-solving approaches. Students raise questions, test ideas to build understanding, and develop skills. The approach is not as new as it may seem. Some say that good teaching has always involved so-called constructivist elements and, of course, students learn new knowledge on a base of past learning. John Dewey, in 1902, argued for the end of traditional rote learning, saying that students should be active participants in building their knowledge and skills. Sizer states "a prominent pedagogy will be coaching, to provoke students to learn how to learn and thus to teach themselves" (1992, p. 226, in Smerdon et al., 1999). According to the NAASP and the Carnegie Foundation, teachers should be "adept at acting as coaches and facilitators of learning to promote more active involvement of students in their own learning" (NAASP, 1996, pp. 22–23, in Smerdon et al., 1999).

Smerdon et al. (1999) state several assumptions about constructivism. "(1) Some of our notion of what constitutes 'knowledge' may be culturally constructed, rather than truth or fact; (2) knowledge is distributed among group members and the knowledge of the group is greater than the sum of the knowledge of individuals; and (3) learning is an active, rather than passive, process of knowledge construction" (p. 8). They add, "In constructivist classrooms students are encouraged to pose hypotheses and explore ways to test them" (p. 8). Through this approach, students develop transferable problem-solving skills. The views gained become theirs, not necessarily those of their teachers. Using science as a model, Smerdon et al. present five instructional practices as examples of a constructivist classroom: students "(1) make up their own problems and work out their own methods to investigate the problems; (2) design and conduct experiments and projects on their own; (3) make their own choice of science topic or problem to study; (4) write up reports of laboratory and practical work; and (5) discuss career opportunities in scientific and technological fields" (p. 16).

Those who are skeptical about constructivism believe that it relies too much on inefficient time-consuming student discovery and trial and error rather than acceptance of bodies of knowledge. They argue that students may not master important knowledge bases in the disciplines and skills essential to their educational development. They consider it a vague and watered-down approach in which teachers, at times inappropriately, ignore their responsibility as purveyors of knowledge.

CONCLUSION.   Why is constructivism currently so much in vogue? Dalgarno (2001) sees it as the result of the cognitive view of learning replacing the behaviorist view. Behaviorism, he claims, stresses repetitive practice by the student until the required knowledge and skills are mastered through direct instruction. A cognitivist approach has students construct knowledge. Under constructivism, learners build personal representations of knowledge through active individual experiences within the social context of the classroom. This latter, interactive approach to constructing knowledge is based partly on the views of Bruner (1960, 1967) and Vygotsky (1962, 1978).

As stated earlier, direct instruction and constructivism are not necessarily opposites. Students can construct personal knowledge or meaning through direct instruction. Direct instruction could be used for presenting general background information, what Kameenui and Carnine (1998, pp. 8–9) call "the big ideas," followed by the constructivist approach focusing on particular applications and problems. Students could, for example, be presented with the general principles of rocketry, then work on solving the problem of creating and launching their own rocket models. This would fit well with the Smerdon approach.

At times you may need to have students memorize information or master well-defined performance skills (e.g., students must learn the alphabet and how to add and subtract). The approach to be used for these has been called *explicit teaching*. It involves direct instruction methods and has high levels of student time on task. Goals are made clear to students, and sufficient time for instruction and extensive enough content coverage should occur. Careful monitoring of progress and appropriate pacing is needed, and many low-level questions that elicit a high level of correct responses followed by prompt and academically oriented feedback should be used. The major features of direct and explicit instruction are (1) teaching in small steps, (2) providing guidance during initial practice, (3) having students practice after each step, and (4) ensuring a high level of success. Hall (2002) observes that certain components are essential in explicit instruction: pacing, processing opportunity, frequent student responses, monitoring responses, and feedback. When effective teachers teach a body of information or well-defined performance skills, they tend to use an approach such as the Madeline Hunter (1985, 2004) plan that is recommended in some school districts (Figure 13.3).

The direct instruction procedure should *not* be rigid. Gradually transfer responsibility from yourself to students. Teach students to observe, activate prior knowledge, construct meaning, monitor their understanding, organize and relate ideas, summarize, and extend meaning. That is, help students develop *meta-cognitive ability* (thinking about what they know, how they are learning, and how to control their learning). When possible, use interactive approaches including student/teacher discussion and peer teaching. This

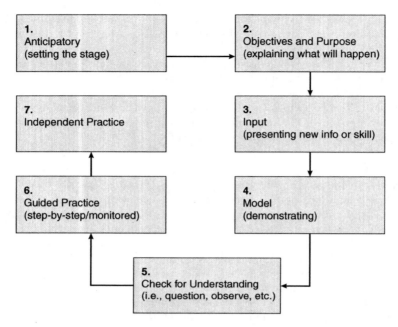

FIGURE 13.3   *Explicit Instruction Steps*
Source: Adapted from Hunter, 1985.

latter approach, particularly when used to teach higher-order thinking, leads to higher achievement by all, including low-achieving students.

The information presentation/acquisition methods are not the only ones available to the innovative teacher to vary or individualize instruction. Techniques that can be used include programmed learning materials, computer-assisted instruction, learning contracts, group tutorials, workbooks, panels, debates, brainstorming, CDs/DVDs, outside speakers, video- or audiotapes, individual or group presentations, and the Internet.

Direct Instruction Teaching Methods

Lecture

Typically, the proportion of instructional time devoted to lecturing increases with grade level. Lecture is a valuable part of your repertoire if it is not overused and if it is not used when other approaches would be better. It may be a waste of time if it is used to present information that will not be needed later in a school subject. Lectured information normally is rapidly forgotten.

Students typically are passive, sit, listen, answer low-level questions, and are often bored (Goodlad, 1983). Lecture is teacher centered, and the attention span of students is limited. Remember, many students—because of learning style preferences and developmental levels—do not readily assimilate lectured content. Other instructional strategies should be used as well, especially if the goal is thinking skills or processes or affective outcomes.

Lectures can be positive and interesting experiences. There was an experiment of a course taught by regular instructors and professional actors (students did not know they were actors). After the term, exam results were compared, and the overwhelming, "dramatic," evidence was (you guessed it) that those instructed by actors had acquired more information (McLeskey & Waldron, 2004).

You may use "straight lecture," combine lecture with a variety of other methods or aids (visuals, demonstrations, question and answer, or discussion), or use "lecturettes" to prepare students for other methods or seatwork. Lecture–discussion is a frequent combination. Although straight lecture, delivered well, can be efficient for communicating basic facts, concepts, principles, generalizations, viewpoints, and arguments about a particular area of knowledge, normally it is best to combine lecture with other techniques and at least to invite covert student participation.

Lecture is effective when:

- The subject matter is factual and there is little opportunity for difference of opinion or problem solving.
- "Firepower" is needed before another method is used (for example, you may wish students to use discussion or do a simulation or role-play) and to make sure they do more than "pool ignorance" or use misinformation.
- A subject is being introduced.
- Time is limited.
- It is later reinforced by another technique.

TIPS FOR EFFECTIVE LECTURING.   A good lecture is like a good speech. Tell them what you are going to tell them; tell them; and then tell them what you told them. Relate past learning to what is being presented, and what is being presented to what will later be learned. Do not present too many points—five or six major points are enough in an hour. Use (or ask for) summaries at the beginning, during the presentation, and at the end. Use pauses to give listeners a chance to catch up and summarize for themselves, or for emphasis. Invite covert participation, use rhetorical questions, challenge students to think, summarize, or formulate questions they can raise later. Supplement lecture with visuals, demonstration, or discussion. Support major points with visuals (including the chalkboard, overhead, charts, or visuals). Show enthusiasm, interest in the topic, and color. Be aware of students' developmental levels—"what they can handle." Incorporate ample examples (verbal or visual) to illustrate points. Select examples that motivate, things students have had experience (or success) with or will be interested in. Draw examples from the class. Use a rate of speaking and choice of vocabulary that suits the class. Speak loudly enough to be heard easily, but not so loud as to irritate. Seat students so all can hear and see. Use stimulus variation techniques: move around the room, use gestures, focus attention ("Listen carefully," "Look at the diagram," etc.), vary interactions, vary volume and tone of voice, and use silence. Create the impression that every student, personally, is being addressed. Use eye contact, position in room, and statements such as "What do you think the result will be?" Do not read from notes or text. Put "key ideas" on a card, chalkboard, or visual. Data collection forms to obtain feedback on the above approaches are provided at the end of this and the following chapter.

Decide if you are going to ask students to take notes, provide a handout, or the information is in the text. If note taking is to be used, teach and provide practice in note taking. Note taking needs teacher pacing and pausing to allow students to take proper notes.

Lectures can be used effectively when time is short, if you have a large class, and it is well supplemented, but be aware of how you can handle potential shortcomings.

Cruickshank, Bainer Jenkins, and Metcalf (2003) suggest the following visual aids through which a presentation can be enhanced:

- Printed material that serves as advance organizers: handouts, outlines, "questions to think about"
- Overhead transparencies: outlines, drawings, charts, diagrams, maps, cartoons, quotes, key words and ideas
- Pictures and prints: photographs, paintings, posters, slides
- "Clips" on CD or videotape
- Maps, wall charts, and globes
- Concrete objects (manipulatives) (p. 179)

The above ideas can make a presentation exciting. Advance organizers help focus attention on the material to be covered. The advance organizer can be a concept map, chart, outline, or simply key words. Transparencies for lectures often are poorly prepared. They can be dramatically improved by using different font sizes, colors, or illustrations such as pictures, drawings, or cartoons. A powerful quotation or key words can add emphasis, focus, interest, or humor. Pictures or posters, a few slides, and video or CD clips can change the pace, add dramatic effect, and bring the lecture to life. A bulletin board or maps or wall charts can be effective. Students can get up and point to significant information. Finally, concrete objects can be viewed or passed around and touched. Imagine the creativity, power, and interest, depending on the topic, that is possible by, for example, bringing in a human skeleton or a live animal.

A data collection instrument you can use for feedback on your use of lecture is provided in Appendix 13.1. Lecture is often accompanied by use of a chalkboard or overhead projector. Data collection instruments to help you use and get feedback on these techniques are provided in Appendices 13.2 and 13.3.

Handouts

More material can be covered when handouts are provided. Students are freer to think about the presentation, formulate questions, and get the pertinent and correct information. Also, you do not have to pace yourself as for note taking. A disadvantage is that students' minds may wander because they don't have to concentrate to take notes; or they may not attend because they are getting a handout. Students remember better if they write it down themselves. Note taking promotes comprehension and retention because students must understand if they are to select pertinent material, organize, and summarize.

Tips for Effective Note Taking

When you lecture, foster effective note taking by:

- Providing an overview, or outline, of what is to be presented
- Presenting your lecture logically, sequentially, teaching students to be aware of structure
- Teaching students to listen for key ideas, points, and subpoints—using verbal and nonverbal clues and appropriate pauses or tonal/volume variation

- Teaching students to record ideas in their own words, defining the concept for themselves—this requires comprehension
- Encouraging students to ask questions
- Avoiding verbatim dictation—if used, limit it to confirm important features such as summaries or definitions
- Having students hand in notes to discover if they are complete and accurate, or having them check notes against the text or other reference (alternately, have students periodically "play back" what they have taken down)
- Making sure you provide (or elicit) stage and closing summaries
- At times, asking students to take abbreviated notes that can be "fleshed out" later

Note taking is a specific skill. Don't assume students know how to do it. Like any other skill, it must be taught and practiced. You may have heard of a teacher telling students not to copy notes verbatim but to record the highlights of the information. The teacher wonders why this was not done well or not done at all. The answer is that the skill may not have been taught.

Assigned Questions

Teachers, particularly in multigraded situations, often assign questions as seatwork or homework. These are usually taken up the next class period. *Assigned questions* is a teacher-centered method in that the teacher structures the questions and is in control of taking them up. Questions may be written on the chalkboard, dictated, provided in a handout, or assigned from a text or workbook.

Questions can be used to introduce facts, concepts, generalizations, argument, and points of view. To foster comprehension, students should answer in their own words. Ensure that questions are not trivial and that students have independent study and research skills. Because learning styles differ, some students do not benefit greatly from this method. If questions are assigned as seatwork, circulate to reinforce correct work, encourage, or supply correctives. Good assigned questions stimulate high-level thinking, problem solving, decision making, and affective outcomes. Questions can move beyond information acquisition and promote comprehension and use of thinking skills. To use assigned questions well, have students do sample questions in class to ensure a minimum of 80 percent success during seatwork and of 95 percent for homework; normally it is best to combine this method with others.

WHEN THE ASSIGNED QUESTIONS METHOD IS EFFECTIVE.   Assigned questions are effective when the questions are well phrased and answering involves more than mechanical "search and copy" from a reference or other source. Assigned questions can be effective when rapid information acquisition is necessary (time is limited) or when "firepower" is needed before another method is to be used (for example, you want students to acquire background information before engaging in a group discussion) and if the questions are later reinforced by another method. Assigned questions can be used for basic facts, concepts, principles, generalizations, viewpoints, and arguments. Students should have been taught independent study and research skills, particularly if sources beyond the text (e.g., the resource center) are used. The method is useful when you want to attend to individual students during seatwork. It can be used to advantage if the text is well written and structured.

TIPS FOR USING THE ASSIGNED QUESTIONS METHOD

- Use advance or postorganizers and introduce material in a motivating way for a positive mindset for learning—if students see the worth of questions, they are more likely to do them, and do them well.
- Select questions well: (a) make sure students focus on important information or thinking skills, (b) go beyond low levels—ask students to apply information, seek out relationships, assumptions, or implications, combine information in new ways, or evaluate information using sound criteria; (c) use a mix of *convergent* (single correct answer) and *divergent* open-ended (several correct answers) questions.
- Teach summarizing skills. Have students learn information acquisition skills and how to use the resource center and community resources.
- Ask students to phrase responses in their own words rather than mindlessly copying.
- Circulate during seatwork, helping students learn research and reporting skills, and providing encouragement and positive reinforcement.
- When taking up questions, apply the skills presented in Chapter 10 (avoid an up-and-down-the-rows procedure, use probes and redirects, and challenge students to stretch their minds).
- Build bridges ("transfer") between present learning and past and future learning, between your subject and others, between present learning and life.
- Help students use and apply the conceptual, skills and processes, and affective domains.
- Think about how you can overcome the shortcomings of this technique (which are similar to those of lecture); and reinforce learning through other teaching/learning methods.

A data collection instrument you can use for feedback on your use of assigned questions is provided in Appendix 13.4.

Practice and Drill

The old saw has it that "practice makes perfect." Lecture and assigned questions (and other teaching methods) are often followed by practice and drill. After knowledge has been presented, students may need to overlearn the material to remember and use it in new contexts. The practice-and-drill method is used so that students can repeat information or do a skill or process almost automatically. Practice should stress understanding and students should have learned how to transfer to another aspect of a subject, other subjects, and life. This, too, requires practice.

The effectiveness of practice depends on how it is conducted. If it is done well, it extends or polishes a skill or habit or enhances the ability to recall and apply information. The word *drill* has negative connotations, and sometimes extensive and better-quality practice may be needed. Rote practice and drill usually have little value. For practice and drill to be valuable, original learning must be thorough, and learning must be a problem-solving process (in that a learner, with your help, explores ways of making personal connections).

WHEN PRACTICE AND DRILL ARE EFFECTIVE.   Students develop a personalized understanding of the skill, habit, or information when time is allocated to overlearn content. Practice and drill promote long-term retention and automatization (instantaneous recall or application). It is effective when students link past and future learning and feelings of accomplishment are generated.

TIPS FOR USING PRACTICE AND DRILL
- Make sure the information or activity is clearly understood, to avoid practice of errors.
- Match students' entry skill/recall and set a practice schedule.
- Only a few skills can be effectively drilled simultaneously.
- Make sure students realize why they need the skill.
- Avoid boredom—use a variety of enjoyable practice situations.
- For initial practice, encourage and provide feedback and positive reinforcement.
- Decide which practice approach is best: review of previous work, extensive or intensive practice, short or longer periods of practice, learning by part or whole, practice of new with the old, and point of diminishing returns.
- To aid transfer, conduct practice under conditions as similar as possible to actual use situations of the skill or information.
- Provide regular, and sufficient, opportunity to apply (transfer) what has been learned.
- Avoid having students become unduly product conscious. Focus may need to be on process or technique—don't impose summative criteria at a formative stage.
- Some pressure is desirable, but too much is counterproductive. Stress self-competition, not other competition.
- Space practice (close together at the start) and provide reviews.

Precede practice with clear demonstration and directions. This usually needs to be followed by guided (often teacher-led) practice. Proper materials and working conditions are needed. Conditions should be as similar as possible to later use situations. It must be carefully monitored and feedback, correctives, and reinforcement provided. Practice should be individualized to focus, as needed, on technique, accuracy, and speed.

A data collection instrument you can use for feedback on your use of practice and drill is provided in Appendix 13.5.

Didactic Questioning

In didactic questioning, the teacher is in control. Questions tend to be convergent, low cognitive, and often begin with *what, where, when,* or *how.* A danger is that questions may be simplistic, encourage guessing or waving of hands to gain approval, and discourage insightful answers or creativity. Questions can be used to diagnose student recall and comprehension, previous learning, decide the extent to which lesson objectives were achieved, or drill students for retention of information or skills. Effectiveness can be increased by frequent "why" questions and occasional "what if" questions. The didactic questioning method has the same limitations as lecture and assigned questions.

Use the data collection instruments in Appendices 13.1 to 13.5 to help you analyze the cases that follow. Your instructor may pose specific questions for your response.

CASE 13.1 Direct Instruction

Sounds Interesting!

Mr. Braun planned to begin a series of lessons on sound and hearing with a grade 8 class. The human ear and its structure had been studied in previous years, but Mr. Braun thought a review lecture on the

continued

nature of sound should precede project work by the class. Mr. Braun decided that work on individual and group projects would strengthen students' research and independent study skills.

During recess, Mr. Braun assembled charts and other materials. When the class resumed, he began, "I mentioned yesterday that you were going to choose a project that has to do with an aspect of sound and hearing. This is a fascinating area to study, and many interesting projects could be picked. First, though, let's review the basic information you need before we can go on.

"Suppose you are about to step off the curb of a busy street. You look left and right but don't see any cars. Just as you are about to step into the street, you hear the blare of a car horn. You jump back, saved by your ears. Your ears are very special equipment. They gather information from every side; they continuously keep you in touch with the world around you."

Mr. Braun went on to explain that sounds we hear are caused by motion. Motion causes sound waves to go out in every direction. He took out a metal ruler and held it tight against the edge of the table so about eight inches stuck out. He twanged the free end, which caused the ruler to vibrate and make a low humming sound.

Mr. Braun asked, "What is causing the sound you hear?" Miriam responded, "The ruler is moving up and down." "Why does that make a sound?" Miriam answered, "I think it has something to do with molecules." "That's right. Does anyone know how sound is related to molecules?" He paused, but no one volunteered.

Getting a piece of chalk, Mr. Braun drew a series of diagrams on the board showing the effect on air molecules when a ruler moves up, down, and up again. He used the terms *compression* and *expansion*. "While the ruler continues to vibrate and push the air into a pattern of compression and expansion, you hear the disturbance as a humming noise. The air molecules push against other molecules nearby, transferring the force of the disturbance across the air. The disturbance—the sound—moves incredibly quickly, 1,120 feet each second." He drew a wavy line to represent the sound and showed it reaching a human ear.

Next he demonstrated that plucking a guitar string made it vibrate, though the vibration was harder to observe, causing a sound. The sound was higher pitched as well. Mr. Braun explained the differences in compression and expansion between higher-pitched and lower-pitched sounds.

"Remember learning about the human ear?" Mr. Braun put up a large diagram of an ear. "How is it that we 'hear' sounds?" Marc recalled the project he did last year on sound and hearing, and, using the diagram, showed how sound waves are "heard." After a discussion, Mr. Braun asked the students to get pen and paper and join work groups. When each group was settled in its area, Mr. Braun gave instructions. "There are many things about sound and hearing we have not talked about today. There are questions that haven't been answered. Let's prepare a list of the questions you think need to be answered. Questions will provide ideas for your group's research topic. Record all questions that are mentioned. We'll put them together so you can choose a topic and start work."

CASE 13.2 Direct Instruction

What's Bugging You?

Mr. Johnson's grade 10 health lesson is on the agents of infection. He gains the attention of the class, tells them they will need to take notes, and begins to write on the chalkboard saying, "There are four main causes of infection: bacteria, viruses, fungi, and animal parasites. First, bacteria are microscopic plantlike, single-celled organisms that can be classified by their shapes." He then, in turn, describes bacilli, spirilla, and spirochetes. Following this he describes and de- fines generation time, botulism, and tetanus. He continues, "Most bacteria, like *Escherichia coli* that live in our intestines, are not harmful and are actually necessary for our existence; others, like Staphylococci, can be present on our skin without causing much of a problem but once infection starts can lead to serious complications and need to be treated with antibiotics." He describes how staph problems occur. He asks, "Remember when you had a sore throat? This was likely caused by Streptococci." Then he tells the class about these bacteria and the problems they can cause.

When he has finished his presentation of bacteria, in a similar way he presents information to the class about viruses, fungi, and animal parasites. With eight minutes left in the period he says, "Close your notebooks. Who can name the four agents of infection?" He continues reviewing until the bells rings.

CASE 13.3 Assigned Questions

Mapping It Out

Ms. Perez has a mixed grade 6 and 7 class. Nineteen of the students are in grade 6 and eight are in grade 7. On this day, she wants to begin a study of Paraguay with the grade 7s. She also must spend time with the grade 6s to finish teaching the map reading skills they need for their group projects. She decides to assign questions for the grade 7 students to work on while she spends the first part of the period with the younger students. She wants the questions to do more than simply keep the grade 7s busy; she hopes the questions will both provide valuable background information and engage the students in thinking about Paraguay.

Ms. Perez assembles copies of maps showing the physical features, population distributions, and annual rainfall of Paraguay. She includes world maps and two globes. Questions are on the board:

1. What are the physical features in this country?
2. Where are the areas of dense population?
3. Which areas are dry and which have heavy rainfall?
4. Judging from the names of cities, towns, and rivers, what language might be spoken?
5. What might the climate be like? Give reasons for your answer.
6. What might be some ways of earning a living in Paraguay?
7. Can you suggest reasons for the way the population is distributed?
8. Can shipping and trading with other countries take place easily? Why or why not?

At the beginning of the period, Ms. Perez asks the grade 6 students to get their materials ready while she gives instructions to the seventh graders. "As you know, we are about to begin a study of some South American countries. It is possible to tell many things about a country from maps. I have copies of maps of Paraguay that show the physical features, population distribution, and annual rainfall in different areas. Remember, as we learned about African countries, the way people earn their living is influenced by the climate, the amount of rainfall, access to cities, and access to transportation routes. I want you to build on what you've learned earlier and see how much information you can gather from these maps. Feel free to guess, but have good reasons for your answers. We'll check our information later. You may work in pairs or threes. Discussion will help you select the best answers, but try to work quietly." Ms. Perez has the students read the questions, makes sure they understand them, and turns to work with the sixth-grade students.

The seventh graders move to tables at the back of the room where the maps are placed, and begin to work through the questions in pairs and threes.

CASE 13.4 Technology and Direct Instruction

Teaching with Power

In the corridor of the local elementary school, Chan, a grade 6 teacher, notices his friend John pushing a cart, with new-looking equipment, into his grade 7 room. "John," he asks, "What's that you're wheeling into your room?" John pauses and replies, "I went to this workshop on 'The Computer in the Classroom.' Most was on PowerPoint. I'm going to try it." "Well, John," comments Chan, "Give me the chalk and overhead any day. That's all I need. I don't want the board to force me to try all this stuff in the classroom. I'm

continued

busy enough and don't have time for the training." "It doesn't take that much time," observes John, looking at his colleague's slim folder of teaching material. "Look," argues Chan "I put in about sixty hours a week in this place and don't have time for fads. Chandra got into technology and tells me she spends hours on Web searches for materials. Time is a teacher's most precious resource."

Noticing that students are beginning to gather in the hall, John wheels the cart into his room. Chan follows. "I know," says John, "it took me longer last night to make my PowerPoint presentation than if I just wrote it up. But it's terrific, the kids'll love it, and I can use it over and over or adapt it for future classes." Chan argues, "I never make the same presentation. I always vary the pace or focus. That's how I reach students, and chalk or transparencies give me flexibility. If I use PowerPoint, I'd be controlled by technology. Kids are never quite the same. They vary in ability and personality. I adjust like an actor with different audiences! There's no need to change my methods." John points at the board and says, "The chalkboard was once technology. Kids learned 'cause they got what was said or taught by at least copying our notes. Think of PowerPoint and the Web as new, improved, colorful chalkboards. You can't fight technology."

Chan moves toward his room. He motions John to follow. An impressive computer system is on the desk. "Look," he says, indicating the computer, "I don't fight technology. I use the computer to do marks. The spreadsheet is easy and helps keep my grades in order." "Well, then" comments John, "how about letting the kids work at computers in the classroom? The computer can give them much of the stuff you do." "Sure," says Chan, "kids can find information on the computer, but to really learn, they need to interact with a person. It's a question of time. The best use is having kids learn with my guiding them. Computers take too much time, training, and resources. They're not worth the trouble. The computer spreadsheet saves me time, so I use it. But what you're doing *adds* work. Computers help administration with attendance, grading, and getting supplies. They don't save time and work for the teacher in the classroom. Education is a people thing, not a tech thing. Anything that takes me away from teaching kids weakens education. Get me a computer that grades papers and I'm on your side!" "Chan," says John, "you're a lost cause!" "No," says Chan, writing notes on the board, "most teachers think like me. Technology isn't a natural part of how teachers work. I like technology, but it doesn't really help me be a teacher."

CASE 13.5 Direct Instruction

To Be Told or to Discover

A heated argument has been taking place in the staff room of Harbor High School. It began when one of the teachers asked if the teacher in the class next to his could keep the noise down. The other teacher had said that it wasn't "noise," it was "discussion." Eventually the whole group in the staff room were involved in a lively debate on direct instruction versus a constructivist approach. Both groups seemed to have powerful points. The direct side argued that teacher-directed instruction was much more structured, efficient, and systematic. It was, after all, the teacher's job to teach and transmit the needed knowledge and skills to students—*teachers teach and students learn.* Constructivist learning is too vague and time consuming. The constructivist side retaliated by saying that learning isn't given out, it must be built by the students through meaningful activities. Students

should work together and the teacher must not be the sole source of learning. Direct instruction is rigid, with a single point of view dominating. Students need to learn how to learn.

If you were a member of the staff of Harbor High School, what side might you have leaned toward? Should teaching be a mix of both strategies, or is one approach better than the other?

Though direct instruction is often perceived negatively, it can be a powerful way to teach. What has been your experience as a student in school and university classes? Was it positive or negative? To what extent has your experience shaped the kind of teacher you would like to be? Try the approaches to direct instruction suggested in this chapter. Reflect on your attempts. What worked for you and your students? Do you see the strategy in a new light?

The Individual Study Strategy

TCP—INDIVIDUAL STUDY STRATEGY

Effective use of the individual study strategy

Students are taught specific research skills and effective use of computer technology; homework and seatwork well planned and monitored: students encouraged to develop individual responsibility and lifelong learning skills and interests; students taught to think carefully about their academic tasks.

Limited use of individual study approaches; students rarely do meaningful homework and seatwork; individual research and computer skills rarely taught.

Employs resource-based teaching/learning and a wide variety of media and resources

Students involved in research; students are involved in individual and group research projects; school resources used beyond classroom include community resources; students taught how to use resources; inquiry oriented climate promoted; students involved in planning and assessing their learning.

Bound to prescriptive materials; lesson formats are stereotypical; students not taught to process information; lack of variety in resources used; direct instruction orientated; students not involved in planning and assessing their learning.

Uses instructional technology to enhance student learning

Uses computers effectively to enhance student learning; effectively uses a range of audiovisual technology and approaches; teaches students to use technology and the Internet with skill and awareness; uses a variety of nonprint material.

Computer and Internet illiterate; seldom uses nonprint materials; does not teach students to use available technology and resources.

What Is Individual Study?

The term *individual study* has several synonyms: independent learning, self-regulated learning, self-directed study (or learning), self-teaching, and individualized study. The term *individual study* is used in several ways. Broadly, it can include anything a person does independently, ranging from supervised seatwork on mathematics in a classroom to a personal trip to Italy to study Roman ruins. For our purposes it is an individual educational pursuit carried on by a person to self-improve. Individual study may be self-initiated or teacher initiated, but the focus here is on study under the guidance of a teacher. This involves identification of a topic, problem, or project through to evaluation based on course objectives. Feedback and correctives are as important to individual study as they are to other strategies. Feedback can come from you, be built into materials, or be a combination of the two.

The Importance of Individual Study

One of the joys of a good education is to gain a love of learning for its own sake. The child who can learn alone has the gift of independence. There is immense satisfaction in following your interest or hobby. Independent learning encourages responsible decision making through problem analysis, reflection, and decision making. Life-long learning and the ability to respond to change are developed. The teacher who encourages individual study fosters skills and attitudes of immeasurable importance. Figure 13.4 presents the strategy and some key methods.

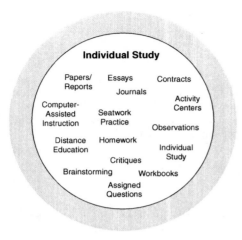

FIGURE 13.4   *The Individual Study Strategy and Methods*
Source: Saskatchewan Learning (1991).

Students need to learn how to learn. They need to be able to work independently to become self-sufficient, responsible citizens. A major purpose of schooling is to teach students how to learn independently—how to teach themselves. Independent learning must be taught and practiced. Use should begin as early as kindergarten and be used throughout schooling.

Much of what students learn can be learned through other teaching strategies, but students must acquire life-long independent learning skills. Mastery of the basic knowledge in a school subject does not automatically increase independent learning. New knowledge can easily be lost if students do not use it in new contexts. Specific efforts, by students, need to be made to bridge the gap between possessing knowledge and using it to learn on their own.

Kinds of Individual Study Methods

Bear in mind that a *strategy* is a broad label for a specific teaching approach. Each of the five strategies presented in this text has its methods. When you decide to use the individual study strategy, a choice can be made from many methods. Examples range from supervised study in the classroom or library to self-directed learning separate from, or instead of, course requirements. Alternatives include:

Essays	Interviews	Individualized assignments
Reports	Brainstorming	Programmed learning
Projects	Problem solving	Computer-assisted instruction (CAI)
Models	Decision making	Independent research
Journals	Learning centers	Acceleration (individual progress
Inquiry	Learning units	through text)
Games	Learning activity packets (LAPs)	Correspondence courses
Fantasies	Learning contracts	Distance education

SELECTING AN INDIVIDUAL STUDY METHOD.   The individual study instructional strategy can be the major instructional strategy in combination with other strategies or with one or more individuals while another strategy is used with the rest of the class. Ask yourself which will be effective for the class as a whole and for individuals. How much control are you willing to relinquish? When direct instruction is used, high teacher control is normal and learning outcomes and pacing are predictable and safe. Unintended learning outcomes—sometimes desirable, sometimes producing outcomes you may not like—and inappropriate pacing can result when individual study is used. This is a risk that must be taken if students are to improve their independent learning capabilities.

It is possible to run an entire course effectively using individual study methods. Courses that emphasize mastery learning may be set up this way. In this situation, you become a resource person rather than a presenter. On the other hand, you can use the direct instruction approach and explicit instruction but provide opportunity for independent learning through assignments or asking students to apply (using an independent learning technique) the content learned through explicit instruction.

THE TEACHER'S ROLE.   Butler (2002) outlines the importance of the teacher's role in fostering independent (self-regulated) learning:

> To promote self-regulation teachers must assist students to engage flexibly and adaptively in a cycle of cognitive activities (i.e., task analysis, strategy selection and use, and self-monitoring). Further, key instructional targets include promoting students' construction of (a) metacognitive knowledge about academic work, (b) strategies for analyzing tasks, (c) metacognitive knowledge about task-specific strategies (e.g., for managing work, history reports, reading text books, writing paragraphs, learning math), (d) skills for implementing strategies, and (e) strategies for self-monitoring and strategic use of feedback. (p. 82)

What is implied here is that for students to be successful at independent learning, they need skills to think about their academic tasks, to be aware that different tasks require different strategies, skills in getting tasks done and the needed skills to work independently, and to be open to constructive feedback.

For such an approach to be successful, teachers need to: (1) provide an environment that allows growth of learner independence (one that is supportive and encourages curiosity, the desire to learn, and self-confidence); (2) provide a continuum of increasing student responsibility for decision making; (3) transfer control as students take greater responsibility; and (4) provide an appropriate student/learner relationship.

Advantages of the Individual Study Strategy

- Students personally and actively, not passively, interact with the content to be learned.
- The interests and needs of individual students within the prescribed curriculum can be matched; the curriculum can be supplemented and enriched.
- Students can pursue topics in as much depth as they like and exercise as much creativity as they like.
- Motivation is higher when students are involved in selecting what is studied.
- It can be used in any subject and allows flexible choice of time, place, and other elements.
- Many individual methods are inexpensive and do not require additional equipment.
- Students feel their studies are relevant and important when a reason for its use is to bridge school learning and community reality.
- Resources available to students are broadened when the out-of-school community is used. It lets students develop knowledge and skills that cannot be obtained in the school.
- Emphasis is placed on individual student responsibility and accountability.
- The study skills learned contribute to life-long autonomous learning capability.

Independent Study Methods

Independent study methods can empower students as control is increasingly shifted, as earned, from teacher to student.

Teacher-directed learning   Student-directed learning

Well-designed methods personalize learning and are motivating. They add flexibility and variety to your instructional repertoire. What follows is a description of a selection of teaching methods within the independent study instructional strategy.

INDIVIDUALIZED INSTRUCTION AND TECHNOLOGY.   Current technology, especially computers, can enhance opportunities for individualized instruction and prepare young people for technological developments. Today's young people need technological skills and critical-thinking and problem-solving abilities. DuBosq (2002) observes that individualized instruction through technology "gives students choice in and control of their learning" (p. 29). He adds that students "can evaluate their own performance through a rubric" (p. 30). Good software, for example, will give direct feedback to the student. And the computer has endless patience! A concern of some educators is how to both individualize instruction and bring everyone in a class to the desired level of achievement. Roth (1999) sees the computer as the means to do this (p. 27). Previously we discussed the issue of direct instruction as a means of disseminating information. The problem is that the teacher has to present information to the whole class. Roth says the role of the computer is to present information to individuals at their computers. He says, "this responsibility can be shifted, for computers are generally better than humans at disseminating the desired information" (p. 28). He presents advantages: (1) Students gain individual attention. (2) Students can progress at their own rate. (3) Subjects can be better integrated. (4) Feedback is immediate. (5) Mistakes are private and positive, not negative learning experiences. (6) Encouragement is always provided. (7) Class level boundaries are eliminated so there is no limit to the possible level of achievement. (8) Students compete against themselves, not each other (pp. 27–30).

Individualized instruction does not mean working alone. Students can work in small groups with the computer or interact with other students, in different locations, who use computers. Students enjoy working together at the same computer, but they can work with students in another part of the world.

The most influential item of technology in the past was the written word and later the printed book. The student, for instance, could be guided by another person through reading. That person need not be present and in fact could have died centuries earlier. Today the most influential item of technology is the computer. Just as the printing press freed information for all to peruse, so the computer is becoming the great democratizer of knowledge, changing the teacher to a facilitator, not a disseminator of information.

Teachers still like to control the flow of information, once through chalk, then through the overhead projector, and, more recently, thorough PowerPoint presentation. Perhaps the computer with its sophisticated software will introduce a new mindset and new opportunities for individualized instruction. The computer can dramatically shift the focus from teacher-directed to student-directed learning.

The chalkboard has returned in a new and dramatic form. A BBC broadcast on March 7, 2002, in a report called *Digital Change at the Chalk Face,* discussed "digital whiteboards" or "smart boards." At Queniborough School in Leicestershire (England), the head teacher purchased one for every classroom. These permit teachers to project the Internet in real time and use it with DVD and videotape. The "smart board" can record up to twelve hours of information, written in the teacher's handwriting, which can later be converted into print as class notes. Students enjoy the technology. "It is wonderful for children to look at a large piece of text, and for that text to become interactive is amazing. The children say it has helped them remember things and they are very focused. It makes learning so much fun." So, the chalkboard, albeit digital with many new possibilities, is alive and well.

Computers in the Classroom

Because most computers in the classroom are used individually, the role of computers deserves attention. Computerized instruction brings novelty and variety and can be more fun than the usual seatwork. Three levels of involvement are possible: drill and practice (the computer gives questions, scores answers, and provides immediate feedback), tutorials (applications range from simple recall or knowledge level to problem solving), and simulations (for involvement in gamelike or near-real applications). Research on the effectiveness of computerized instruction is largely positive. Some studies found that learning time was reduced and others that the time used was about the same as with traditional instruction. Student attitudes about using computers for instruction were improved.

TERMS. Cotton (1991) presents definitions of terms that are helpful in understanding the varied uses of computers in the classroom (not all terms apply to individualized instruction).

Computer-based education (CBE) and *computer-based instruction* (CBI) are broad terms that can refer to almost any kind of computer use in educational settings, including drill and practice, tutorials, simulations, instructional management, supplementary exercises, programming, database development, and writing using word processors. These terms may refer to stand-alone computer learning activities or to activities that reinforce material introduced and taught by teachers.

Computer-assisted instruction (CAI) most often refers to drill-and-practice, tutorial, or simulation activities offered either by themselves or as supplements to traditional teacher-directed instruction.

Computer-managed instruction (CMI) can refer to the use of computers by school staff to organize student data and make instructional decisions or to activities in which the computer evaluates students' test performance, guides them to appropriate instructional resources, and keeps records of progress.

Computer-enriched instruction (CEI) refers to activities in which computers (1) generate data at the students' request to illustrate relationships in models of social or physical reality, (2) execute programs developed by the students, or (3) provide general enrichment in relatively unstructured exercises designed to stimulate and motivate students.

BENEFITS OF COMPUTER-ASSISTED INSTRUCTION. Cotton says the best-supported research is that use of computer-assisted instruction to supplement traditional, teacher-directed instruction results in achievement superior to that with traditional instruction alone. In general, this is so for different ages and subject areas. Cotton suggests advantages of CAI over traditional approaches:

- The use of word processors in writing programs leads to better writing outcomes than the use of paper and pencil.
- Desirable outcomes are obtained when computers are used as part of a holistic, writing-as-a-process approach.
- CAI enhances learning rate.
- The retention of content learned is superior.

- The use of CAI leads to more positive student attitudes.
- CAI students have more of an internal locus of control/sense of self-efficacy.
- CAI students have higher rates of time on task.

STUDENTS LIKE COMPUTERS.   Cotton's list of why students like computers offers insight into student attitudes to learning. Students say they like working with computers because computers: are infinitely patient; never get tired; never get frustrated or angry; allow students to work privately; never forget to correct or praise; are fun and entertaining; individualize learning; are self-paced; do not embarrass students who make mistakes; make it possible to experiment with different options; give immediate feedback; are more objective than teachers; free teachers for more meaningful contact with students; are impartial to race or ethnicity; are great motivators; give a sense of control over learning; are excellent for drill and practice; call for using sight, hearing, and touch; teach in small increments; help students improve their spelling; build proficiency in computer use, which will be valuable later in life; eliminate the drudgery of doing certain learning activities by hand (e.g., drawing graphs); and work rapidly—closer to the rate of human thought.

POSSIBILITIES AND PITFALLS OF COMPUTER USE.   Based on an extensive range of literature, Gibson (1999) lists the possibilities and pitfalls of computer use.

Possibilities
1. *Enhanced learner motivation* (excitement and novelty; computers more engaging to students than texts; motivated to explore; polished-looking products; seen as personally relevant)
2. *Increased access to information* (quicker and easier access to information; students can learn to manage information rather than memorize; increases student acquired information)
3. *Perceived authenticity* (first-hand information; direct data gathering perceived as more relevant)
4. *Increased individualization* (information in a variety of modalities—auditory, visual; computers accommodate different learning styles; students can work at their own pace; students can choose and determine the direction for their learning)
5. *Expanded interactions* (students can be more active in their own learning; simulations allow students to direct and vicariously experience events; the teacher no longer the primary dispenser of information but a facilitator of students' explorations)
6. *Opportunities for collaboration* (computer technology can provide a more meaningful "workshop" atmosphere)
7. *Expanded representation of ideas* (students are provided with multiple ways of representing their ideas)
8. *Increased productivity* (students often more productive, with some children better able to express their ideas)

Pitfalls
1. *Mindless fact gathering* (students will need instruction in how to critically examine and make informed choices about the material)
2. *Poor curriculum coverage* (computer programs may be a poor match with curriculum objectives and guidelines)

3. *Reduced reading development* (concern over reduced development of reading skills; computers very visual, with reduced text)
4. *Diminished writing skills* (although computers may encourage some, students lose interest in the key stages of writing such as first drafts; work may be disjointed and lack cohesion. Prewriting note form stage neglected)
5. *Neglected research skills* (the abundance of sources can get students off task; easy to cut and paste rather than synthesize, sequence, and analyze information)
6. *Need for critical thinking* (computer seen as the "truth" or as neutral; need critical thinking as with any other source)
7. *Absence of real-life experience* (the computer cannot promote the same learning and deep understanding that comes from real-life experiences)
8. *Reduced direct interaction* (potential isolation from others; working cooperatively on computer projects can counter isolation) (pp. 227–230)

Learning Centers

Though "open education" has largely disappeared as a significant movement, it has left the legacy of a more flexible approach to instruction. Learning centers that let students work "hands on" independently or with peers are part of that legacy.

A learning center is a self-contained, self-directed learning environment where students interact with materials; the center may provide immediate feedback about learning. Learning center assignments make it possible to individualize a portion of the curriculum. They can be used by individuals, pairs, or small groups. Learning centers provide students with choices in keeping with their interests. They are a constructive academic alternative for students who have finished assigned tasks. They allow students to interact directly with materials and can even allow concrete, hands-on experience.

Learning centers can be used at all grade and subject levels and for a broad range of assignments. Assignments can be subject specific or multidisciplinary. The duration of tasks can be five minutes to several weeks. Centers may be inexpensive, requiring minimum materials and space, or may require much space, extensive equipment, and expensive supplies.

For learning centers to be effective, they must be well planned and able to operate with minimum teacher direction. Preassessment of learners' knowledge and skill should occur. Ideally, students have a say in selecting and constructing centers, with student choice of activities possible. Activities should motivate students so they remain on task. Monitoring and feedback systems should be established. Ideally, a student progress record-keeping system is needed, and continuous, nonpunitive feedback should be built in. Paired or small-group work can be used effectively and is a desirable alternative.

Mastery Learning

Mastery learning is a common form of individualized instruction that may be done with or without a computer. You would like to have all your students achieve 100 percent success. How realistic is this? Though it might be argued that this technique is dated, no discussion of the individual study instructional strategy is complete without attention to mastery learning. It is an individualized method that lends itself to use in traditional settings. Advocates of mastery learning believe that if by success one means achievement of well-defined goals, expecting a rate of 80 percent or higher may not be unrealistic.

Mastery learning is based on the belief that differences in achievement are at least partly due to differences in the time needed to learn (Bloom, 1968), the appropriateness of the task for a learner, and the kind of instruction chosen (Hart, 2002; Motamedi & Sumrall, 2000). Bloom emphasizes clear directions, active learner participation, and reinforcement based on success, feedback, and correctives. Mastery learning programs can be for the class as a whole, a small group, or an individual. They have several things in common:

- Objectives are determined.
- The curriculum is divided into small chunks of knowledge and skills to be learned.
- Preassessment is used to determine if students have the necessary skills to begin or if they already have some or all the skills to be studied.
- Students take different lengths of time to complete a task (self-pacing).
- Formative evaluation (progress checks) such as daily or weekly tests, that are not part of the grading system, is used extensively.
- Correctives (or remediation), as many as necessary, are provided.
- Evaluation is criterion based.

Key considerations are the amount of active learning time, the feedback and correctives provided, and the nature of instruction. Mastery learning uses a cycle of teaching, testing, reteaching, and retesting. It can result in a higher level of performance and achievement compared to traditional instruction because students learn at different rates and need different materials. Some believe that mastery learning does not have a proper conceptual base, takes from advanced students and gives to the poorer students, and not all students are equally capable.

Focused Imaging

You help students' tap into their personal creative ability when you provide opportunities for them to use their imaginations. A wonderful teaching method for this is *focused imaging*. It can be used for something to be pictured, heard, sensed, or felt. It is fun, motivating, and inspiring for students and teacher. An example of focused imaging occurs when students are told to close their eyes and imagine they are the lead singer performing in front of an adoring audience, followed either by writing a paragraph describing the experience or sharing feelings with peers.

Focused imaging, which can be used in any school subject, is the use of personally developed images applied to curricula. It is like daydreaming that is used to explore the content of a lesson or unit. The process is free flowing, unique to each individual, with no incorrect answer. Self-esteem is fostered through safe, successful personal imaging. The teacher needs to make sure the classroom atmosphere is relaxed and to be open to a variety of (sometimes unexpected) responses. When students engage in focused imaging, they build a bridge from external sensations to internal awareness. It helps them assimilate new information. Another use is mental rehearsal before trying something "for real." Also, students can mentally come up with and try alternate approaches to a problem, imaging what would happen given different scenarios. Students can use focused imaging before they begin creative writing, a visual art project, a badminton strategy, or even before they attempt an answer to a test question.

Study Skills

To learn efficiently through independent study methods, students must understand what they have experienced and comprehend what they have read. They should be able to retain and use the information and ideas studied. The techniques students use to study can be put into two categories: (1) knowing how to find information needed for an assignment, and (2) techniques for learning the material presented. Teachers need to be aware of common study problems. Many students do not budget time effectively. They cannot estimate how much time to allow, nor do they set up a regular study schedule. Physical conditions may be unsuitable, finding a good place to study may be difficult, lighting may be inappropriate, or noise may interfere. Some students are disorganized and either do not know how, or are not sufficiently motivated, to organize well. Students may be deficient in reading skills and find it hard to read with comprehension; or note-taking skills (from written material or classroom presentations) may be weak. Finally, students may not have learned specific techniques for studying.

The ways children study influence how much they learn. Teachers can often help children develop better study skills.

- Adjust study according to the complexity of the material, time available, what is already known about a topic, purpose and importance of the assignment, and standards to be met.
- Space learning sessions over time rather than cram or study the same topic continuously.
- Identify the main ideas in new information.
- Connect new material to what is already known.
- Draw inferences about the significance of new information.
- Assess how well study methods are working by appraising personal progress. (U.S. Department of Education, 1986, p. 39)

How well students learn depends on academic potential, motivation, academic skills, and personal management skills. *Academic skills* refer to how new information and ideas are gathered, connected to those already known, organized and understood, committed to memory, and used. *Personal management* refers to how students manage time, their emotions, and their relationships with other people. Students can be taught academic skills and helped with personal management. In short, students can acquire effective learning strategies.

CASE 13.6 Individual Study

Wild Animals

Ms. Perez plans to have her grade 5 class develop reports on "Wild Animals in the Tropics." She wants the children to experience and learn basic things about research projects. They will need to generate ideas, organize topics, find and record information from resource materials (note taking), organize information, and present it in a clear way. Ms. Perez intends to review and teach the research skills needed as students work on the project. She thinks the project will take about two weeks.

First she gets the children to choose the animal they will research. To work toward an outline or concept map of their topic, she has the students, in threes, brainstorm questions about their choices of animals. She suggests everyone should have at least one hundred questions. Questions become more specific, and many more are generated. That afternoon, students who had fewer than one hundred questions take their materials home to add to their lists.

Next class, Ms. Perez reviews concept mapping as a way to show relationships among categories. Each child spends the period categorizing his or her questions into groups of related information. The next period is used to tentatively sequence the question categories.

In a subsequent class, Ms. Perez distributes 3×5 cards on which students are to record their information. She has found that using cards encourages students to summarize instead of copying long passages as they take notes. There are enough resource books in the room for everyone. The children have, in the past, practiced looking for and recording information. They spend class time and some out-of-school time to find and record information. To stay on topic, they are encouraged to keep checking over their categories of questions.

Later, Ms. Perez gets the students to sort their information and notes into question categories. Over the next few days they work on the categories, one at a time, deciding what to include and putting information in order. For this project the students are to develop a set of notes for an oral report to their classmates.

CASE 13.7 Individual Study

Spoon Feeding

Mr. Wang and three of his colleagues in the English Department of Beacon High School had a discussion after school one day that started with a long-time department member, Ms. Traut, saying, "Students nowadays just seem to want to be spoon fed. Their attitude seems to be 'Tell me what to memorize and then don't bother me.'" The discussion got Mr. Wang thinking. "Perhaps," he thought to himself, "there are two things the matter. One, teachers haven't taught students learning strategies; and second, teachers don't allow students to act as independent learners."

Mr. Wang resolved that he had an obligation to his students to do something about the two problems. He had read that it was possible to improve students' study skills, that learning strategies such as reading comprehension skills could be learned and could transfer to other subjects.

What would you suggest that Mr. Wang do to help students acquire learning strategies; and how could he release control to his students in such a way that they would rise to the challenge of becoming independent learners?

LINKING PRACTICE TO THEORY

The individual study strategy has changed considerably, especially with school use of computers and the Internet. Compare your schooling experience with the expectations of students today. What new skills need to be taught? Compare the skills in this chapter with skills teaching in Chapter 12. How can individual study approaches be given realistic significance? Compare the effectiveness of your approach to teaching with the expectations of the strategy described in this chapter.

Summary

The "big five" instructional strategies are direct instruction, indirect instruction, interactive instruction, experiential learning, and individual study. The most common approach is direct instruction. It is deductive and teacher centered. The two most common methods in direct instruction are lecture and assigned questions. It often involves note taking and practice and drill and is effective for information or skill acquisition. Direct instruction can be an exciting and valuable teaching approach when presented with the creative use of media and other techniques. Direct instruction should be balanced with other strategic approaches. Individual study involves teaching students specific research skills and the effective use of computer technology. Individual study encourages students to develop individual responsibility and life-long learning skills and interests. It is an approach that encourages meta-cognition, in which students think about their learning.

Activities

DIRECT INSTRUCTION

1. Join a subject group to discuss: (a) what you think to be a proper mix of teaching methods; (b) when it is appropriate to use lecture, assigned questions, and practice and drill; and (c) how these methods can be best used in subject specializations.

2. Teach a lesson that has effective lecture as a professional target. Using the data collection instrument in Appendix 13.1, have someone observe and give you feedback or complete the instrument yourself after you have taught the lesson. If teaching a lesson is not practical, observe a lesson (or film of a lesson) and analyze it using Figure 13.4.

3. Teach a lesson with assigned questions as a professional target. Use Appendix 13.4. Have somebody collect data or complete the instrument yourself. If teaching a lesson is not practical, observe a lesson (or film of a lesson) and analyze it.

4. Observe a teacher using practice and drill. Use Appendix 13.5. Do a class survey on the following (circle the appropriate response): SA, Strongly agree; A, Agree; D, Disagree; or SD, Strongly disagree.

   Direct instruction was an effective part of my education.   SA   A   D   SD

   Direct instruction was an enjoyable part of my education.   SA   A   D   SD

5. In subject groups, take up a topic suitable for direct instruction. Design a PowerPoint presentation. Share with the class the pros and the cons of using PowerPoint in your discipline. You should show samples of your presentation to the class.

6. The overhead projector is used frequently by teachers. (a) In your next field experience, discuss with your cooperating teacher its possible uses. (b) In class, discuss the most effective ways of using an overhead projector.

7. Marshall McLuhan (1994) said, "The medium is the message." Discuss this statement in the light of technology and education. Do chalkboards, overhead projectors, and PowerPoint presentations give different messages?

INDIVIDUAL STUDY

1. Form pairs. Research and do a two-page write-up of an independent-study teaching method. Use the headings: "What is the (name the method)?" "How does it work?" "What are its advantages?" "What are its disadvantages?" "How can the disadvantages be overcome?" "For what kind of subjects or content is it particularly suitable?"

2. The next time you are in a school setting, if appropriate, ask one or more teachers which independent study methods they use and how they go about seatwork and homework and if the school has a policy regarding these.

3. In a subject-area/grade-level group, discuss and then report to the whole class how the teaching of learning strategies can be incorporated in the delivery of the subject(s) you hope to teach.

APPENDIX 13.1   *Professional Target: Lecture*

PROFESSIONAL TARGET—LECTURE

Describe what was said and done and student reactions.

Lecture Considerations	Observations
1. Organization (advance organizer, structure, postorganizer)	
2. Relating present to past or future learning	
3. Using summaries (by teacher or students)	
4. Stimulating students to think, participate covertly	
5. Using stimulus variation	
6. Supplementing with visuals, discussion, question and answer	
7. Showing enthusiasm, interest in topic, color	
8. Examples used to illustrate key ideas (verbal or visual)	
9. Appropriateness of delivery for note taking	
10. Creating feeling each student is being addressed	
11. Use of handout	
12. Appropriateness of time for amount of material covered	

APPENDIX 13.2 *Professional Target: Chalkboard*

PROFESSIONAL TARGET—USING THE CHALKBOARD/WHITEBOARD

Describe what is done and student reaction.

Chalkboard/Whiteboard Plan

Chalkboard/Whiteboard Observed

Examples of Skills	Descriptive Comments
1. Easy to follow organization?	
2. Writing in a straight line?	
3. Writing large enough?	
4. Organization—left to right top to bottom	
5. Clarity/quality of writing	
6. Movement to and from board	
7. Position while writing	
8. Movement while writing	
9. On board in advance? As part of presentation?	

APPENDIX 13.3   *Professional Target: Overhead Projector Use*

PROFESSIONAL TARGET—USING THE OVERHEAD PROJECTOR

Please use descriptive statements.

1. *Simplicity*

   (a) Using point form (not sentences)

   (b) Normally having no more than six points per transparency

   (c) Using LARGE print

2. *Focusing*

   (a) Using a pointer (pen, pencil, bar stick, etc.)

   (b) Turning projector off when not in use to return attention to the teacher

3. *Progressive Disclosure*

   (a) Showing one point/line at a time; blocking out others until you get to them

4. *Visibility*

   (a) Having the screen in a corner of the front of the room

   (b) Having the projector far enough for its light to fill the screen

   (c) Making sure the images are clearly focused

   (d) Facing the class but not blocking students' view of the screen

   (e) To focus attention, pointing at the transparency, not the screen

5. *Appeal of Presentation*

   (a) Spacing, use of pictures, cartoons, borders, boxes, etc.

   (b) Motivational impact

APPENDIX 13.4 *Professional Target: Assigned Questions*

PROFESSIONAL TARGET—ASSIGNED QUESTIONS

Describe what was said and done and student reactions.

Assigned Questions Considerations	Observations
1. Way topic was introduced	
2. Directions on how to go about getting/recording answers	
3. Advance organizer or postorganizer use	
4. Nature of questions: domain, levels, convergent or divergent	
5. Circulation during seatwork; nature of help	
6. Procedure in taking up; use of probes, redirects	
7. Tie in to past/future learning	
8. Integration of domains	
9. Use of encouragement, reinforcement	

APPENDIX 13.5   *Professional Target: Practice and Drill*

PROFESSIONAL TARGET—PRACTICE AND DRILL

Practice/Drill Considerations	Observations
1. Determination of entry capability	
2. Provision for understanding	
3. Need for information/skill established	
4. Provision for practice variety	
5. Provision of feedback, reinforcement, encouragement	
6. Similarity to actual use conditions	
7. Emphasis on product or process	
8. Use of competition; self-competition	
9. Length and spacing of practice	
10. Linking or application of skill to other content	

14 The Indirect and Experiential Instruction Strategies

The Indirect Instruction Strategy

What Is Indirect Instruction?

Learning can be more meaningful, thorough, and usable when learners seek and discover knowledge. Students benefit when they draw conclusions from information they find themselves or have been given. Indirect instruction comes under many headings. Terms that are sometimes used interchangeably are inquiry, induction, problem solving, action research, decision making, and discovery. We group these under the heading of indirect instruction. The kinds of methods to achieve this are in Figure 14.1 on page 445.

In contrast to the direct instruction teaching strategy, indirect instruction is student centered. Examples of indirect teaching methods are debates, panels, field studies, research reports, group investigation, brainstorming, simulations, guided inquiry, and unguided inquiry. In indirect instruction, a high level of student

OBJECTIVES

You will be able to:

1. Define direct and indirect inquiry, and deductive and inductive learning/teaching.
2. Demonstrate the use of inductive behaviors while using a direct teaching method.
3. Describe guided and unguided inquiry.
4. Demonstrate initial competence in the use of indirect and individual study methods in microteaching or school lessons.
5. Describe mastery learning and considerations in using it.
6. Describe indirect learning strategies and places in the curriculum where they can be used.
7. Define the experiential instructional strategy and list its characteristics.
8. State the purposes of experiential education.
9. Name and describe the experiential instruction methods presented in this chapter.
10. Describe the experiential cycle and apply it to a school subject.
11. List advantages and limitations of experiential teaching and learning.
12. Apply learning about experiential learning to in- and out-of-school learning experiences and in a microteaching or school classroom lesson.

TCP—INDIRECT INSTRUCTION STRATEGY

Provides effective use of indirect/inductive/inquiry methods

Use matches content and learner needs; instruction highly learner centered; pupil discovery fostered; appropriate learning materials available; sensitive to learners' experiential backgrounds; learners presented with problems or issues to be explored and solved.

Instruction exclusively teacher centered and expository or deductive; information-centered instruction.

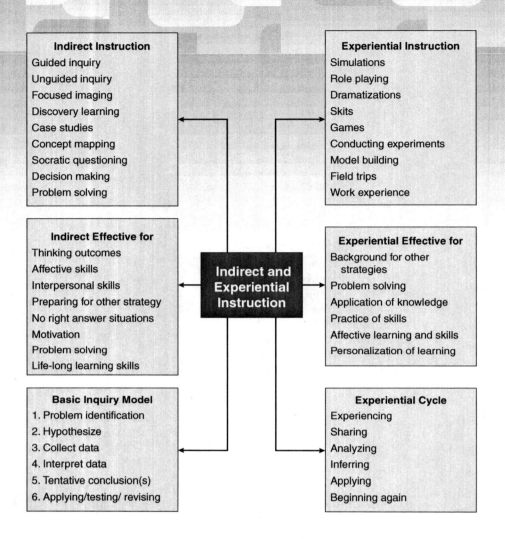

Indirect Instruction	Experiential Instruction
Guided inquiry	Simulations
Unguided inquiry	Role playing
Focused imaging	Dramatizations
Discovery learning	Skits
Case studies	Games
Concept mapping	Conducting experiments
Socratic questioning	Model building
Decision making	Field trips
Problem solving	Work experience

Indirect and Experiential Instruction

Indirect Effective for	Experiential Effective for
Thinking outcomes	Background for other strategies
Affective skills	
Interpersonal skills	Problem solving
Preparing for other strategy	Application of knowledge
No right answer situations	Practice of skills
Motivation	Affective learning and skills
Problem solving	Personalization of learning
Life-long learning skills	

Basic Inquiry Model	Experiential Cycle
1. Problem identification	Experiencing
2. Hypothesize	Sharing
3. Collect data	Analyzing
4. Interpret data	Inferring
5. Tentative conclusion(s)	Applying
6. Applying/testing/ revising	Beginning again

involvement is sought. It is flexible, frees students to explore diverse possibilities, reduces fear of incorrect answers, fosters development of creativity, and promotes development of interpersonal skills. On the other hand, indirect instruction is a slower way to expose students to content than direct instruction, and it requires expertise in indirect methods and skills.

Although much indirect instruction is a combination of inductive and deductive teaching, the inductive approach is predominant. For example, it occurs when students are asked to identify basic information, encouraged to explain data by determining cause-and-effect relationships, or infer or make a hypothesis that goes beyond the information at hand.

What Is Inquiry?

Indirect teaching fosters student participation through observation, investigation, drawing inferences from data, or forming a hypothesis. When indirect instruction is used, you

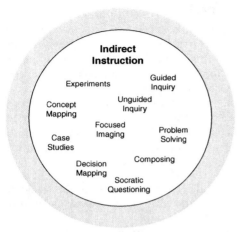

FIGURE 14.1 *The Indirect Instruction Strategy*

Source: Saskatchewan Learning (1991).

take advantage of students' natural interest in discovery, suggesting alternatives, or solving problems. Your role shifts from lecturer/director to facilitator/supporter/resource person. You relinquish control, and outcomes are often unpredictable and less "safe." You arrange the learning environment, provide opportunity for student involvement, and provide feedback on student responses. Students conduct an inquiry rather than passively receive information.

Webster's dictionary defines the word *inquire* as "to ask about," "to search into," or "to make investigation." Importantly, the investigative process of inquiry should involve the student not only in seeking answers but also in formulating questions and deciding the best methods to use, and then conducting the study. Some people think the inductive method of inquiry is the traditional "scientific method." Inquiry is no longer viewed this way. Scientists use inductive methods, but modern science goes beyond pure inductive logic. Inductive reasoning is a basis for inference building, and scientists rely on theories on which to base experiments.

Basic steps in using inquiry teaching are illustrated in Figure 14.2. The basic processes of inquiry are

1. Observing
2. Classifying
3. Using numbers
4. Measuring
5. Using space–time relationships
6. Predicting
7. Inferring
8. Defining operationally
9. Formulating hypotheses
10. Interpreting data
11. Controlling variables
12. Experimenting
13. Communicating

Inquiry processes should be learned and practiced systematically. Provide time for conceptual skill building. Every student can, and should, learn the skills (even the "slow" students). This opens doors to learning things that just might not be in the textbook. Some of the skills will be stressed in Chapter 16.

Guided Inductive Inquiry

We can approach inquiry in two ways. In the first way, the teacher carefully guides students toward a specific discovery or generalization; in the second, inquiry is more casually supervised (free discovery), and students are involved in setting up the problem and seeking its solution. Descriptions of guided and unguided inductive inquiry follow.

In *guided inductive inquiry,* students are expected to arrive at generalizations because the learning activities, classroom recitations or discussions, learning materials, and visuals

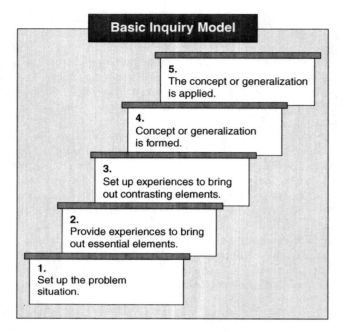

Basic Inquiry Model

5.
The concept or generalization is applied.

4.
Concept or generalization is formed.

3.
Set up experiences to bring out contrasting elements.

2.
Provide experiences to bring out essential elements.

1.
Set up the problem situation.

FIGURE 14.2   *Basic Steps in Using the Inquiry Teaching Method*

are arranged so everything is available for students to arrive at the generalizations you have determined. Students are to develop the habit of being systematic and use a process of making observations and drawing inferences. An observation is recorded and inferences drawn (inferences are generalizations about certain objects or events). Years ago, but as relevant today, Womack (1966) presented classic steps for arriving at a generalization through guided discovery:

- Decide on the generalization(s) students should discover from a particular unit of study.
- Organize the learning activities and materials in a way that exposes the strands or parts of the generalization(s) to the students.
- Ask students to write a summary of the content that contains the generalization(s).
- Ask students to identify the sequence of the pattern of events comprising the content, omitting any reference to any particular people, place, or time.
- Ask students to synthesize the various parts of the pattern of events into one complete sentence that purports to be a generalization.
- Ask students to offer proof that their generalization is suitable by citing examples that it existed and operated in other periods, places, and among other peoples. (p. 13)

QUESTIONING AND GUIDED INQUIRY.   As you know, questioning is important in inquiry. You become a question asker, not a question answerer. Much time is spent interacting with students, but you provide few answers. See Figure 14.3 for stems for questions that can be used in inquiry.

USING GUIDED INQUIRY.   Beamon (2002) describes the elements of guided inquiry as

- Guided questioning
- Linking content to issues, themes, and problems
- Social interaction
- Active exploration
- Authentic assessment
- Helping learners to make meaningful connections among the big ideas of a discipline and their personal experiences, conceptions, and beliefs

Beamon stresses that when we teach adolescents we need to understand how they think, learn, and feel and that we need to be aware that the curricular and instructional decisions we make affect the nature of the adolescent's learning experiences. Central to Beamon's writing is the *adolescent teaching model,* which has four components: (1) emphasis

FIGURE 14.3   *Examples of Inquiry Stems*

Examining Cause-and-Effect Relationships, or Analyzing Events

---

What is happening?	What took place before this happened?
What has happened?	Where have you seen something like this happen?
What do you think will happen now?	When have you seen something like this happen?
How did this happen?	How could we make this happen?
Why did this happen?	How does this compare with what we saw or did?
What caused this to happen?	How can we do this more easily (or quickly)?

Stems for More Static or Nonliving Objects

What kind of object is it?	What can you do with it?
What is it called?	What is it made of?
Where is it found?	How was it made?
What does it look like?	What was its purpose?
Have you ever seen anything like it?	How does it work or operate?
How is it like other things?	Where?
When?	How can you recognize or identify it?
How is it different from other things?	What other names does it have?

Note: These prompting questions help students understand all kinds of relationships, which is a goal of inquiry. The questions can be used with pictures, models, and other visuals (particularly when teaching younger children or children without first-hand experience with something).

on student understanding of the essential concepts of the discipline in question; (2) strategies to motivate students and to promote student inquiry; (3) suggestions for guiding students to become progressively self-directive; and (4) opportunities for student self-evaluation, reflection, and application of learning.

The key to the inquiry approach is active, not passive learning. In, for example, the teaching of science, students "are introduced to science methods and use them to engage in hands-on, 'minds-on' activities that inspire them to discover scientific knowledge rather than being told answers by the teacher or textbook" (Jorgenson & Vanosdall, 2002, p. 602). These authors condemn what they call the "drill and kill" model of teaching science, with emphasis on the text, videotapes, or end-of-chapter questions. They observe, "The inquiry approach was founded on the premise that children learn actively, not passively" (p. 602).

Inquiry-based learning requires students to find a topic, create questions, and gather, sort, and analyze information. A crucial next stage is to do something with the information. This "is what distinguishes inquiry-based projects from typical school research projects" (Owens, Hester, & Teale, 2002, p. 617). It links inquiry-based approaches to constructivism and authentic instruction. The authors claim that the "most successful inquiry projects emerge from topics that are of real interest to the students" (p. 617). They say that teachers should be models and demonstrate for students how to (1) formulate questions that move beyond the literal level of understanding, (2) collect information from a wide variety of resources, and (3) use the information in a meaningful way (p. 618). Science is particularly suited to inquiry:

The hallmark of science learning . . . is independent student inquiry. . . . Inquiry-based approaches to science instruction invite learners to investigate the world around them in order to pose and solve problems, construct mental models of phenomena, and understand procedures that scientists use in their work. Students practice inquiry at varying levels of sophistication, ranging from guided investigations of elementary concepts to independent explorations in which learners generate and refine hypotheses, design ways to systematically test complex relationships, evaluate evidence, and internalize the epistemological assumptions of the inquiry enterprise itself. (Windschitl, 2000, p. 81)

Windschitl sees the value of computer-supported learning environments, including software, to enhance inquiry approaches and experiential learning.

Drayton and Falk (2001) note that a key question in inquiry-based learning is "Who is doing the intellectual work?" (p. 28). Although they see the value of direct instruction, they say there must be student-to-student talk, activities in which students need each others' results, and times in which they need to test arguments and evaluate their methods (p. 29).

Unguided Inductive Inquiry

As you can see, in guided inductive inquiry you play the key role by asking questions, prompting, structuring materials and situations, and in general being the major organizer of learning. This is a good way to begin a gradual shift from direct teaching to teaching that is less structured and is open to alternative solutions. Unguided inductive inquiry is predicated on inductive logic, but it is open ended and students take responsibility for examining data, objects, or events.

The basic processes in unguided inductive inquiry are observation, inference, classification, communication, prediction, interpretation, formulation of hypotheses, and experimentation (as in guided inquiry). Your role is reduced and that of the student is increased. The major elements of unguided inductive inquiry are that:

- Learners' thought processes are a progression of specific experiences and observations to inferences and generalizations.
- The purpose is to learn procedures for examining occurrences, objects, or data to draw inferences and arrive at generalizations.
- You, as teacher, control only the materials and pose questions such as "What does this mean?" Students interact, work, and ask many questions with no further teacher guidance.
- Students discover meaningful structure or patterns through observations and inferences.
- Appropriate resources and materials are needed.
- The number of generalizations that learners will generate may be unlimited.
- Students should share inferences and generalizations so class members can benefit from each other's perceptions.

Inquiry permits greater learner creativity. Learning is enhanced because learners "find out for themselves." You may need a new set of behaviors. You act as a "clarifier," helping when students make gross errors in logic, generalize too broadly, take too much inference from data, assign cause–effect relationships where there are none, or assign single cause–effect relationships where there are several. Use a nonthreatening manner in

Guided Inquiry
Teacher carefully guides students toward a discovery or generalization

Unguided Inquiry
Supervision more "casual" (free discovery and students are involved in setting up the problem as well as seeking the solution)

Steps for Both
1. Problem identification
2. Tentative research hypothesis/objectives
3. Data collected; tentative answers tested
4. Data interpreted
5. Tentative conclusions/generalization
6. Applying or retesting conclusions, revising original conclusions

FIGURE 14.4 *Overview of Guided and Unguided Inquiry*

verifying conclusions and generalizations. If there are errors in logic or inferences, point them out, but do not tell what the correct inference is because this defeats the purpose of the inquiry episode. Concrete evidence should be required for generalizations; thus, comprehension and analytic skills are reinforced. Practice is given in making and testing hypotheses. Inquiry can stimulate classroom discussions in every school subject.

As you have discovered, inquiry processes can be used in daily lessons as part of almost every teaching strategy and method. If students are to be involved (overtly or covertly), if you tell less and ask more, if you stress thinking skills and processes, your teaching will be more inductive or inquiry oriented. An overview of guided and unguided inquiry is provided in Figure 14.4.

Using Inquiry Methods

WHEN TO USE INQUIRY METHODS.   Inquiry methods can be effective when:

- Thinking skills and processes, or affective skills or processes should be stressed.
- Learning "how" to do something is more important than just getting the right answer; or when "why" is more important than "what."
- Students need to experience something rather than just hear or read about it.
- Several "right" answers are possible, or when "right" can change with circumstances.
- The content should focus on discovering solutions to problems or making decisions.
- The focus is on development of creativity.
- The focus is on concepts, attitudes, or values.
- You wish students to become more ego-involved and thus self-motivated.
- An objective is for students to develop life-long learning capabilities.

TIPS FOR USING INQUIRY METHODS.   Begin by discovering the experience your students have had with inquiry techniques. If necessary, teach, and provide practice in, inquiry skills and processes. Use open-ended and higher-level questions, solicit and accept divergent responses, and use probes and redirects. Encourage and reinforce as students develop responsibility for discovering "answers." Avoid telling the answers and what to do next. Act as a helper or facilitator. Be supportive of student responses, ideas, differing views and interpretations, and recognize that inquiry techniques are harder to do well and take more planning. Have adequate facilities and materials, including data sources, so inquiry can occur effectively. Make full use of school and district resource centers and staff. In using guided inquiry, ensure that the problems are suitable; in unguided inquiry, ensure that the investigations students select are manageable. Require students to support their comments with evidence and reason. Teach how to write or phrase the concepts, principles, or generalizations to be tested. Elicit student–student interaction and sharing; stress support and cooperation, not competition. Encourage the attitude of acting on the current verified "best answer," knowing that additional evidence may lead to a new "best answer," rather than not acting until the final, ultimate truth is found. Teach the difference between "healthy" and "negative" skepticism. Remember that the "content" of inquiry is the "process," and that the product or solution may be less important. A goal is to develop students' abilities to learn how to learn and to take responsibility for planning, conducting, and evaluating.

Summary

The term *inquiry* is sometimes used interchangeably with *discovery* and *problem solving*. Whatever the term, the emphasis in this method is on questioning and actively engaging students. As a teaching method, it is used to encourage students to recognize and state problems, ask questions that lead them to seek answers, recognize whether the answers are reasonable, and for "answers" to point to further study.

TEACHER BEHAVIOR AND INDIRECT INSTRUCTION.   Students' backgrounds need to be discovered and, if necessary, they should be taught suitable skills and processes (e.g., data gathering techniques, data interpretation, and critical thinking). Reason and evidence are stressed. The attitude to be fostered is that what seems the "best answer" may not be best in the light of evidence. Students are encouraged to make informed guesses and helped to realize the difference between healthy skepticism and negativism. Teachers who use the indirect strategy well make sure the problem is manageable and that students understand the purpose of an activity. Adequate references, materials, and facilities should be available, and full use made of the resource center. Students are encouraged to accept ownership for learning and are helped to select and use investigation techniques and thinking skills. The teacher avoids "telling" and uses "asking." Open-ended questions and prompts and probes are used and divergent responses accepted. Students are encouraged to risk. Creativity and independent, resourceful thinking are valued and transfer to new situations fostered.

Importantly, the effective teacher accentuates the positive, deemphasizes competition, encourages exchange of ideas, and encourages students to cooperate and support each other. Ideas can be challenged, but people cannot be attacked. The teacher provides feedback on students' use of inquiry, decision-making, and problem-solving skills.

WHEN ARE INDIRECT INSTRUCTION METHODS EFFECTIVE?   You can use indirect instruction processes every school day and with almost every lesson. It is effective when:

- Thinking outcomes are desired.
- Value, attitude, or interpersonal or group skills outcomes are desired.
- Process (learning "how") is at least as important as product (getting "the right answer").
- Students need to experience something in order to benefit from later instruction.
- There are no "right" answers.
- The focus is personalized understanding and long-term retention of concepts or generalizations.
- Ego involvement and intrinsic motivation are desirable.
- Decisions need to be made or problems need to be solved.
- Life-long learning capability is desired.

BASIC FORMAT FOR INDIRECT TEACHING.   You can use the examples of indirect teaching strategies shown in Figure 14.1. Examples of indirect instruction methods vary from use of question and answer as part of a lecture to use of full-blown unguided inquiry. In the basic model for indirect teaching, a problem is posed, students inquire, and a discovery is made.

The Inductive Approach

In the previous chapter you were introduced to the use of teaching strategies categorized as direct or expository (i.e., lecture, assigned questions, and practice and drill). Direct strategies tend to be teacher centered, deductive, and closed, often based on the view that bodies of knowledge (the "content") are both a means and an end. This is the traditional approach (though many teachers do not use it exclusively). Indirect strategies tend to be student centered, inductive, and open, often exploring and building the knowledge with students.

It may be useful to review the definitions of the terms *inductive* and *deductive*. In the *inductive approach,* learners move from the specific to the general. You, for example, may provide experiences in which students organize several facts or details into a major concept or principle. Alternatively, you may first introduce the concept or principle and then show how a set of known facts fit. Here, students are guided from the general to the specific through direct teaching. This is the *deductive approach.*

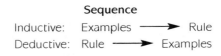

The teacher's role is to create situations in which students can learn on their own rather than provide prepackaged information. The fundamental goal should be to make students self-sufficient. Students should often learn through active involvement with concepts and principles and be permitted to discover concepts and principles themselves. Students need to learn to think for themselves, to take part in the knowledge-getting process.

Instructional experts agree that learning should be much more experiential (and interactive). This is an inductive inquiry approach. Initially, you may experience difficulty and frustration with some aspects, and want more structure—to some extent, we are all "prisoners" of our own experience. This chapter will help you learn more about inquiry and set the stage for further experience so that the inquiry or inductive approach can become a more comfortable part of your repertoire.

INDUCTIVE TEACHING. Inductive teaching encourages development of the academic skills of reasoning and theory construction. It encourages students to work either from evidence they discover themselves or from material handed out by the teacher for concept and principle learning. An example of the inductive process is when students are required to identify basic information (data), encouraged to explain the data by relating one point to another (drawing cause-and-effect relationships), and when they make inferences and form hypotheses that go beyond the information at hand. For example, students given pictures of various nationalistic activities and objects (a flag, a group of soldiers, an anthem) might hypothesize on the meaning of nationalism.

Inductive instructional strategies usually are soliciting skills. "Inductive teaching consists largely of systematic movement from fact recall questions to conceptual questions and finally to opining and valuing questions" (Martin, 1983, p. 85). Reacting skills are used to encourage student responses. The three kinds of inductive instructional skills (Table 14.1) are (1) structuring—arrangement of the learning environment; (2) soliciting—provision

TABLE 14.1	*Inductive Teaching*
Component Skill	**Example**
Structuring Skills (A very simple overview usually suffices)	"Today's discussion will concern the Cold War balance of power that existed among the nations of the world."
Soliciting Skills Fact-recall questions	"How many countries did we classify last time as Western, Communist, Third World, and Neutral?" "Which countries, if any, within each group might have been considered major military powers?"
Conceptual questions	"How did the political ideologies of each group related to their international policies?"
Opining or valuing questions (In inductive teaching, such questions ask pupils to speculate and theorize as well as state their own opinions.)	"What general principle concerning the role of superpowers would you be prepared to make in this regard?" "Can you imagine what would have happened if Cuba joined the Western Bloc? What would our theory say about this?"
Redirection (A great deal of redirection of the previous questions will occur in any good inductive teaching strategy, in order to involve many pupils.)	"All right, can somebody else carry that idea a bit further?" "Tom, you don't agree. Tell us why." "What do you think, Bert?" "Brenda?" "Carl?"
Positive questioning	Ask questions; pause; call on reciter.
Reacting Skills Incorporating student responses into lesson	"You're saying that each superpower must be viewed as being equally strong as all other superpowers. Let's see whether we can work with your idea for a few minutes."

Source: Adapted from Martin, 1983, pp. 85–86.

of opportunities for student involvement; and (3) reacting—provision of feedback or instructional responses to student involvement (p. 63).

The indirect, inductive teaching strategy makes many demands of the teacher. It can be one of the most satisfying approaches. Why? To what extent do you need to know your students and subject matter well? Think of all the skills and competencies it draws upon—communication and interpersonal skills, awareness of the learning abilities and values of students, classroom management, and planning. How did you find the inductive experience? Is it more risky than direct instruction, where *you* control the variables? Reflect on your experiences. How is knowledge structured in the classroom? Can discovery be fostered? How satisfying is the approach for you and your students? What insights did you have?

A data collection instrument you can use for inquiry is provided in Appendix 14.1. Use this data collection instrument to help you analyze the cases that follow. Your instructor may pose specific questions for your response.

CASE 14.1 The Inquiry Approach and Computer Software

An Ant Community

Mr. Stein's grade 6 class is studying the behavior of ants. First Mr. Stein placed an ant hill simulation software program on the computers. With the simulation, he thinks, he can have students study the behavior of ants—where they live in the ant hill, their hierarchical relationship to one another, how they forage for food, and how they interact with the world outside the ant hill. By changing the variables in the simulation, students try various interesting experiments—including what happens when the population is dramatically increased or decreased, or the temperature changes, or there is a decline in the food supply. The students have many questions and try variations to find the answers. Mr. Stein also obtained an ant hill in a glass case so the students can conduct inquiry with real materials as well as computer-based models. This study of the real ant hill helps students see the limitations of science and learn respect for the complexity of science.

CASE 14.2 Indirect Instruction

An Awareness Lesson

Ms. Jacques was a student teacher in a grade 4 class. The youngsters were enthusiastic participants in most activities. In their enthusiasm, they could become very competitive. Ms. Jacques had tried to use small-group learning, but the children found it difficult to follow the instructions and the structure of group learning. They appeared to lose interest before the task began. Ms. Jacques was not happy with the way she found herself enforcing basic expectations. She decided to try a more indirect approach.

She assigned the class to three groups in three different locations and gave instructions for the task. This time, she did not tell them how to work together in groups. As the groups began, the cooperating teacher and Ms. Jacques's student teaching partner each attached themselves to a group, leaving Ms. Jacques to work with one group. Both of the other groups received direction and coaching as they worked. Disagreements were resolved and the groups kept on task.

In Ms. Jacques's group, however, things did not go smoothly. The children quarreled over the materials, couldn't agree on the task, and three children competed strongly for leadership. While this was going on, in keeping with her plan, Ms. Jacques managed to keep from intervening. At the end of the period, her group had not completed the task. The other two groups had finished products of which they were proud. With prompting from their respective adults, they explained how they had worked to complete their tasks.

Ms. Jacques gathered her group together and asked them how they felt about their group work. They said they wished they had finished so they'd also have had something to show. "I wonder why we didn't finish," said Ms. Jacques. "Did we understand the task we had to do?" The group agreed they knew what had to be done. "Did we have the materials?" she asked. "We had everything, we just didn't do it right," volunteered Jesse. "That's right," added Jeremy. "We should've started working instead of arguing." "If we'd decided who would be leader, that person could've made sure everyone's idea was listened to and we could've decided how to do our project sooner," offered Amanda. "And better," Pat broke in, "I still have a great idea for how to start." "I wanted to be the one that drew our invention," Joan said, "but I should have shared instead of keeping the markers myself." "We wasted our time," said Simon.

"I wish we could do the project," Jeremy said. "I'd miss recess if we could." The others agreed. "Well, I think that's possible," said Ms. Jacques. "It sounds as if you have good ideas of how to work as a group now. Maybe it wasn't a waste of time if you have learned ways *not* to work in a group. Let's list the things we want to do as we work on the project. Then we'll decide when we can get together to have another go at it."

CASE 14.3 Indirect Instruction

Getting the Point

Mr. Haggar found that the students in his grade 10 language arts class did not know how to use the colon and semicolon. He decided to take time out to teach the use of these to his class. He began, "I've just finished reading your essays and noticed that you have difficulty distinguishing between and using colons and semicolons. We'll take time today to help you understand the difference between these useful punctuation marks and provide practice to help you remember them. After today, I'm sure you will find it easy to use these helpful writing tools."

The class was divided into groups of six. Then, Mr. Haggar distributed a handout that consisted of three parts: (1) ten examples of the use of colons, (2) ten examples of the use of semicolons, and (3) ten sentences that required, as appropriate, insertion of either a colon or a semicolon. "There are rules for the use of the colons and semicolons in written English. You are to do a three-stage exercise. First, go through part one of the handout to study examples of the use of a colon. Discuss what you observe and agree on a definition of a colon. Second, study the sentences that contain semicolons and then arrive at a definition of a semicolon. We will then take time out to hear the definitions you have discovered and to agree on a common definition. The third step will be for you to go through the sentences that do not contain the necessary mark, colon or semicolon, and agree on which mark to use and where to place it."

Mr. Haggar circulated as groups were working and listened to reports of their definitions. A common definition was derived from those provided by the groups. He circulated again as they did the third part of the exercise. He was pleased with what he saw and heard. In conclusion, he had each student, privately, write a definition in his or her own words, of the two punctuation marks. Finally, several students read their definitions to the rest of the class.

The Experiential Instruction Strategy

> The teacher's task . . . can be supported by a wise use of a wide variety of devices that expand experience, clarify it, and give it personal significance. (Jerome Bruner, 1960, p. 91)

TCP—EXPERIENTIAL LEARNING STRATEGY

Uses experiential learning regularly to encourage active learning

Able to design experiences that facilitate active participation in learning; debriefs student experiences; gets students to discover generalizations from experiences; gets students to apply learnings to new situations.

Students seldom engaged in actual experiences to generate active learning; does not debrief student experiences.

The Nature of Experiential Learning

As you decide the approach to teaching to use to meet the needs of your students, choices will need to be made based on the readiness of learners, their learning styles, the nature of the content, learners' previous experience, and the degree of overlearning desired. Teaching and learning can be approached in the following ways:

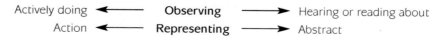

Actively doing ⟵ Observing ⟶ Hearing or reading about

Action ⟵ Representing ⟶ Abstract

The first continuum depicts a range of experiences from being actively involved through observation to listening or reading. The second continuum is the range of abstraction of a learning experience. You can pick learning experiences that are at an *abstract level* (verbal or visual) *or* representational *or iconic level* (recordings, movies, slides, pictures, exhibits, models) *or* action or *enactive level* (games, simulations, or direct experiences). The approach can be structured, rigid, artificial, and direct, or less structured, real, integrated, holistic, and indirect. *Experiential learning* (or teaching) is at the left side of the continuum. All the modes along the continuum can be used at one time or another. The purpose of this section is to discuss what *experiential education* is, when to use it, and how to use it.

WHAT IS EXPERIENTIAL LEARNING?   Webster's defines *experiential* as the actual living through of an event or events. Experiential learning is an action strategy. Instead of hearing, talking, or reading about something, students participate in the context to be studied. Although there is some disagreement on the meaning of the term, many definitions emphasize the same thing. In experiential learning, the learner is directly in touch with real things and people or is involved in activities that simulate real activities and people. For example, students might role-play the 1919 Versailles Peace Conference or enact the trial of Galileo. It involves direct encounter with the phenomenon being studied, instead of just thinking about it or only considering the possibility of doing something with it. The process is normally inductive, learner centered, and activity oriented. Personalized reflection about an experience and plans to apply learning to other contexts are critical. This is a critical part of the debriefing process in which students reflect on or discuss what they have learned. Experiential learning occurs when learners: "(a) participate in an activity, (b) critically look back on the activity to surface learning and feelings, (c) draw useful insight from analysis, and (d) put learning to work in new situations" (Pfeiffer & Goodstein, 1982).

Australia's RMIT Teaching and Learning Unit (2004) defines experiential learning as "experiences that are designed and chosen for their ability to extend and challenge student thinking in a broad range of capabilities." The characteristics, they say, are that (1) students are actively involved in the process of learning; (2) the problems they work on are realistic, as are the situations; and (3) the learning can be used to develop many different capabilities, such as acquiring, assimilating, or creating new knowledge and deeper understanding; personal development; problem-solving capability; interpersonal skills; planning ability; assessment skill; assessment by peers; and learning how to learn. Additional information can be found at the RMIT web site, www.rmit.edu.au. Go to "Our Organization" and then to the Teaching and Learning section for additional ideas for teachers.

The experiential learning model is learner centered and activity oriented. Learners must work cooperatively with varying degrees of teacher direction to make curriculum decisions. The mode tends to be self-directed, unstructured, self-paced, and personalized. When using experiential learning, flexibility in the developmental process may be necessary. Feelings, attitudes, values, and (importantly) experiences are critical content. An assumption is that people really learn only that which has personal meaning. The needs of learners and their psychological and cultural characteristics are considered.

Self-control of one's educational experiences is critical. Students feel better about themselves and the value of educational experiences if they have a hand in identifying learning experiences that affect their growth and development and their progression toward self-integration.

Experiential education involves a first-hand "encounter" or "directness" or "involvement" or "participation" with the "context" to be studied and reflection on that episode. This results in a change in learners' understanding, skills, and attitudes. It is integrated and holistic and necessarily has an affective component. Students tend to become more emotionally involved in experiential learning approaches. In role playing, students take a considerable degree of personal ownership. Field trips and work experience also involve a high degree of affective learning. Experiential learning occurs when a learner takes part in an activity, reflects critically on it, draws insight from the analysis, and puts the results to work in new contexts. It is an inductive process that proceeds from observation.

PURPOSES OF EXPERIENTIAL EDUCATION.   Because experiential education is a direct encounter with the phenomenon being studied, it is more realistic and therefore is more meaningful. Indirect encounters, like "academic" learning, are also needed and should, based on experience, be woven into development.

It is reasonable to believe that higher-order skills—and indeed intelligence, understanding, and wisdom—develop through experience and reflection. Therefore, it is logical that schools provide opportunities for students to engage in experiences with real (authentic) problems and opportunities that include the variables likely to be encountered in real-world situations.

Further justification for using the experiential teaching/learning mode has come through studies of learning style. Some people prefer a direct, action-oriented style; they, probably, are among those who learned at home by watching and trying what was modeled. Cultural background also influences learning-style preference.

Another purpose of the experiential mode—described some time ago by Jean Piaget—is to aid student cognitive development. For students to be able to think at the highest cognitive development level (formal operations), they must have had some experience, or direct contact, with the substance they bring to bear on mental operations. This applies to any learner who has not proceeded through concrete experience. You, in studying experiential learning, will find that experience is necessary for you to really understand the meaning and use of the experiential mode. Academic knowledge is often a very critical part of experiential learning.

It can be posited that learning is not complete unless the learner moves beyond "knowing about" and "knowing how" into "doing." The ability "to do" fosters transfer of learning. Indeed, the argument goes, "doing" deepens understanding of what something is and knowing how something is (or was) done. Put in another way, theory informs practice and practice informs theory. Struggling with experiences using the experiential mode or applying learning in a "real" context yields completeness of learning.

THE KOLB MODEL OF EXPERIENTIAL LEARNING.   No discussion of experiential learning would be complete without the classic Kolb model. David Kolb (1984) defines learning as "the process whereby knowledge is created through the transformation of experience" (p. 38). The emphasis of experiential learning is on the process of learning and not the product. Because of experience and reflection, knowledge is constantly being transformed (created or recreated) within the learner. Kolb observes that experiential learning theory assumes "ideas are not fixed and immutable elements of thought but are formed and reformed through experiences" (p. 26). According to Kolb, learning is a *process* (not an outcome) by which concepts are constantly modified by experience. He developed an approach to experiential learning that involves conflict between opposing ways of dealing with the world. He emphasizes conflict between concrete experience and abstract concepts and generalizations and between observation and action.

Kolb believes that learners need four abilities or learning modes:

1. *Concrete experience.* Learners must involve themselves fully in new experiences.
2. *Reflective observation.* Learners must observe these experiences, or obtain observations on these experiences, as well as analyze and reflect on these observations. This reflection will bring a previous background, and thus previous experiences (first-hand and second-hand), to bear on these observations.
3. *Abstract conceptualization.* Learners must develop abstractions that, in turn, create concepts and generalizations that are logically sound.
4. *Active experimentation.* Learners must use these new theories to take action, such as making decisions and solving problems. (p. 30)

The Kolb thesis has two dimensions. The first involves "concrete experiences" at one end and "abstract conceptualization" at the other. The second has "active experimentation" at one extreme and "reflective observation" at the other. Kolb argues that conflicts among the four modes must lead to integration for the highest level of creativity and growth to occur. "It involves the integrated functioning of the total organism—thinking, feeling, perceiving, and behaving" (p. 31). The four-stage cycle can be explained as the interaction of two dimensions. The first, the *concrete to abstract,* reflects two different ways of "taking hold" of experiences: (1) reliance on conceptual interpretation and symbolic representation (Kolb calls this "comprehension"); and (2) reliance on the tangible, felt qualities of immediate experience (called "apprehension") (p. 41).

The second dimension, from *action to reflection,* is the manner in which the first dimension is transformed, through either internal reflection or active manipulation of the "external world." The first is called *intention,* and the second is called *extension.* Therefore, "learning is the process whereby knowledge is created through the transformation of experience" (p. 41).

Kolb (1984) says that experiential learning has six characteristics:

1. It emphasizes how learning takes place, instead of what is to be learned.
2. Learners continuously gain and test knowledge through, and in terms of, their experiences.
3. Learners need abilities that are opposites. Choices are made among opposites—concrete experience or conceptualizing abstractly; actively experimenting or reflectively observing.
4. Learners are asked to adapt, in a holistic way, to their social and physical environment.
5. It is an active, self-directed process involving transactions between the learner and the "real-world" environment.
6. Knowledge is created within learners. (pp. 25–38)

Terry (2001) presents an excellent example of how the Kolb model can enhance learning, and its value as a teaching tool. Terry describes how the learning modes can be used in learning situations such as group work, essay writing, and assessment to appeal to different learning style preferences, be matched to student abilities, and the design and application of "diverse examination formats" (p. 7). The idea is that the experiential learning model must consider different learning styles in deciding objectives, planning activities, and assessment. Terry believes the Kolb model is a useful way to increase student learning performance.

A data collection instrument you can use to get feedback on your use of experiential learning is provided in Appendix 14.2.

BENEFITS AND LIMITATIONS OF EXPERIENTIAL LEARNING.   It is common to believe in the superiority of first-hand experience. People speak of "being there," "doing it," and "seeing for oneself" as a valuable way to learn. Buchmann and Schwille (1993), however, say that relying on first-hand experience may delay student teacher development. Previously (1982), they claimed that the notions behind these expressions, and the belief in the value of "common sense," tend to conceal problems and connections and might lead to incomplete understanding or misunderstanding. They say that first-hand experience tends to emphasize only the senses (p. 1), observing that, for those who believe in the superiority of first-hand experience, the "mind is visualized as a container to be filled by whatever comes from the various sense organs" (p. 4).

Sight, sound, and touch can convey misinformation, and a sample may not be an adequate basis for generalizations. First-hand experience may limit learning to practices and standards already established. Much learning requires imagination, and one cannot assume that the present condition is all that is possible. To get beyond the present, learners must develop abstract categories derived from collective experience that can then be used in second-hand experiences. First-hand experience can close avenues to conceptual and social change. Knowledge, too, can be acquired independently of practical action by using resources such as print, visual materials, and other persons.

> Unlike firsthand experience, secondhand information . . . lends itself to a consideration of what is typical, what is generalizable, and what can be found that is different from what is already known. It enlarges the number of cases that can be considered, can include rare occurrences of high value for learning, and represents more adequately than firsthand experience the distribution of events in the real world. (p. 22)

The limitations and fallacies of first-hand experience can be overcome if one plans experiences carefully, anticipates what they have to offer, and selects experiences that vary in some systematic fashion.

Although the limitations of experiential learning must be recognized, there are things students cannot really understand or appreciate just through reading, hearing, or viewing. Experiential learning is an effective strategy if direct or "hands-on" experience is needed before teaching methods that involve iconic (e.g., looking at pictures) or symbolic (e.g., listening to the teacher talk) approaches are used. Experiential education greatly increases retention over methods that stress talking, reading, or even viewing. Students are more motivated when they actively do something or, even better, teach one another by describing what they are doing. Experiential learning helps move education to a personalized, life-enriching process. If you have a choice between two methods, choose the one that involves students the most actively.

There is much truth in the old saying, "If you really want to know something you have to experience it." Obviously there are limitations. It is a bit impractical to have yourself blown up in an atomic explosion to learn about it. When students have the background, much can be learned from print and other materials and other people. Effective teachers decide when to use first-hand and when to use vicarious or second-hand learning experiences.

Teaching Approaches to Experiential Learning

ACTIVE LEARNING AND EXPERIENTIAL LEARNING. Because in experiential learning the learner is directly in touch with real things and people or involved in activities that simulate real activities and people, students develop many capabilities. *Active learning* is a specific experiential learning approach with its own advocates, publications, and web sites. Bonwell and Eison (1991), in an analysis of research, say that active learning has certain characteristics: students must read, write, discuss, or be engaged in solving problems; they must engage in higher-order thinking tasks such as analysis, synthesis, and evaluation; and instructional activities should involve students in doing things and thinking about what they are doing.

Actions suggested by Bonwell and Eison include:

- Pause three times for two minutes each during a lecture.
- Insert brief demonstrations or short, ungraded writing exercises followed by class discussion.
- Create a supportive intellectual and emotional environment that encourages students to risk.
- Use more visual-based instruction.
- Incorporate case studies, cooperative learning, debates, drama, role playing and simulation, and peer teaching.

As can be seen, active learning ranges from making traditional lectures more interesting and active to role playing and simulation. In essence, experiential learning is a form of active learning at the engaged, complex, and risk-taking end of the continuum. If teachers incorporate active learning elements in the classroom, students can acquire the attitudes and skills needed to gain the most from field trips and simulations.

Chickering and Ehrmann (1996) assert that learning is not a spectator sport. When students just sit in class listening to teachers, memorize assignments, and spit out answers, they do not learn much. They need to discuss what they are learning, write reflectively about it, relate it to past experiences, and apply it to their daily lives. What they learn must become part of them. Active learning enlivens teaching as it complements the rationale and framework of experiential learning.

EXPERIENTIAL LEARNING METHODS IN AND OUTSIDE THE CLASSROOM. A teacher can use experiential learning as a teaching strategy both inside and outside the classroom. Inside the classroom, students can, for example, build and stock an aquarium or engage in a simulation; in the community, they can, for example, observe a courtroom as the legal system is being studied. A wide range of experiential learning methods is possible:

Classroom Game/Activity   Field Trip   Direct Experience

THE EXPERIENTIAL LEARNING CYCLE. There are five phases to the experiential cycle (Figure 14.5). A discussion of these five phases, based on the thinking of Jones and Pfeiffer (1979), follows.

1. *Experiencing (an activity occurs).* The first stage in the cycle is to have an experience (an individual or group activity) that includes interaction with the environment and with others. This generates information and leads to feelings. Students usually find this

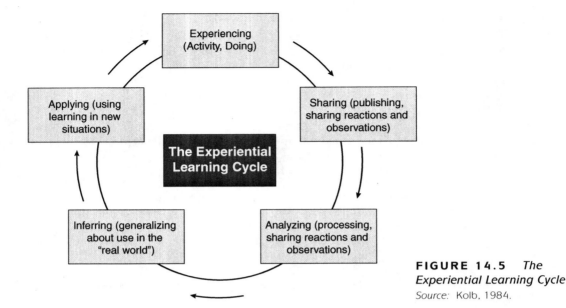

FIGURE 14.5 *The Experiential Learning Cycle*
Source: Kolb, 1984.

stage to be like a game and fun. When you use the experiential learning strategy you can choose from, among others, the following:

Game	Writing	Simulation
Manipulating symbolic objects	Case study	Field project
Conducting an experiment	Fantasy	Field interview
Making a model	Role playing	Field observation
Creating an art object	Skit	Field trip
Making a product	Improvisation	Work experience

The purpose of this stage is, from whatever happens, to develop a common database for the discussion and reflection to follow. The "answer" derived or the product obtained is far less important than the process experienced. In a sense, the process is the product.

Unfortunately, what often passes for experiential education stops with this step, so much of its potential value is lost. For example, students go on a field trip with little follow-up. Typically the follow-up is students completing a prepared factual answer sheet or the teacher later making occasional reference to some aspect of the trip. A successful field trip needs very thorough planning with clear objectives, activities that meet these objectives, and follow-up activities that assess the success of the objectives.

2. *Sharing* (reactions and observations shared—*publishing*). In this stage, students re-call what was experienced, reporting everything they saw and how they felt. This is shared with members of the group or class. The purpose is to provide a database for later analysis. Observations and reactions can be recorded in several ways: a written report, posting on newsprint or a chalkboard, an oral report, an e-mail report or web page, a free discussion, or interviews.

3. *Analyzing* (patterns and dynamics are determined—*processing*). This is a key stage. It involves "talking through" the published experiences and feelings. Data are processed.

This must be systematic. Techniques that can be used include: seeking common themes, classifying experiences, completing a questionnaire, discovering key terms or skills, or discovering patterns of events or behavior.

This is *not* an interpretation or inference stage. Structure, patterns, or key aspects of what was experienced are sought. The focus is on dynamics rather than "meaning."

4. *Inferring* (principles are derived—*generalizing*). Inferring involves answering the question, "So what?" Principles, rules, or generalizations are sought. This step involves discovery of "What I have learned" or "What I am beginning to learn." After data have been analyzed, inferences are drawn about the significance of what was learned through the experience as it applies to new contexts (preferably to life). Ways to infer generalizations include: students record generalizations and how learning can be used in new contexts; students tell what was generalized and potential application; or students post conclusions on newsprint or chalkboard. The inferring stage and the next (applying) make learning practical. They move beyond the "academic," which is sometimes "isolated" and "sterile."

5. *Applying* (planning to use learning in new situations—*the future*). This stage is the reason for the other stages. Transfer should take place for learning of the experience to have optimum value. Students are to apply their learning (generalizations) to situations in which they are currently involved. Techniques that can be used include group planning for application, individual or group contracting, and practice (or simulated) applications. This step involves, "What I intend to do tomorrow is. . . . " If statements of intent are written or made publicly, the likelihood of follow-through is enhanced. (pp. 18–25)

In summary, experiential learning occurs when students (1) engage in an activity, (2) publish what occurred, (3) look back at it critically, (4) gain useful insight from the critical analysis, and (5) put the results to work. For full impact, ensure that *all* the steps are carefully followed. The cycle begins with action (experiencing), moves through reflection (sharing, analyzing, and inferring), and ends with a call for action. When the action that is proposed is initiated, the cycle can begin again.

Exeter (2001) provides an interesting adaptation of the Kolb cycle (Figure 14.6). He stresses experiential activities followed by reviewing through reflection. Careful reflection and description of the experience will lead to conclusions and possible theories about the experience. This, in turn, will lead to planning in which the new learning will be applied to future activities.

USING EXPERIENTIAL LEARNING METHODS. Tips for using experiential methods include the following:

1. Experiential methods can be combined with direct instruction. Set the stage by explaining terms and concepts and then assign an individual or group experiential setting.
2. Relinquish at least a portion of the control to students. At first, some teachers are reluctant to take the risk.
3. Vary the degree of teacher versus student control. Some experiential methods may be very structured (e.g., a game with set rules) and others completely unstructured (e.g., a role-playing improvisation).
4. Evaluation is not as cut and dried as recall or comprehension-level cognitive teacher-made tests. Initially, you may find it difficult to assess both process and product.

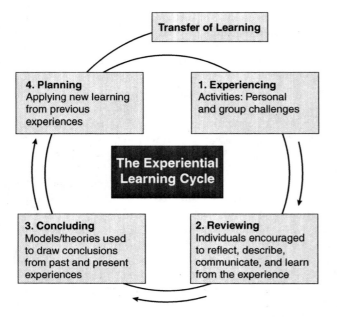

FIGURE 14.6   *Exeter Experiential Learning Cycle*
Source: Exeter, 2001.

5. Capitalize on the higher level of motivation that results from the use of experiential teaching methods.
6. Teach students interpersonal and group skills, which will reduce classroom management problems.
7. Use experiential learning methods to teach not only specific content but also the knowledge, values, skills, and abilities related to common essential learning (e.g., communication, critical and creative thinking, and personal and social values and skills).

An experiential approach enhances self-esteem, increases social and personal responsibility, and contributes to higher-level mental processes and creativity. Student involvement in the planning stage is critical. For example, if a class is visiting a legislature or parliament, discussion in the class could involve such questions as: "What do we need to know before our visit?" "What should we look out for during the visit?" "What questions should we ask when we are there?" "What special responsibilities need to be assigned?" Teachers can visit potential experiential learning sites. Many places—for example, museums—have excellent prepared materials and ideas for experiential learning tasks.

Games, Simulations, and Role Playing

Games can be defined as activities governed by rules that participants play to achieve game objectives by completing these activities successfully. *Simulations* use "real-life" situations, normally requiring participants to make decisions during and following an activity. Simulations may be game like or involve role playing. In *role playing,* participants play parts (assume roles) spontaneously in a situation or around a theme.

When students are actively engaged through games, simulations, and role playing, when they are responsible for their actions, when they reflect on their experiences, when they discuss their learning with peers, and when the experiences shape future experiences, motivation is increased and learning is enhanced and personalized. Learning is more complete because the cognitive aspects (information and thinking skills and processes) and affective aspects (values, attitudes, prejudices, and emotions) and often the physical aspects are critical. Games, simulations, and role playing as methods within the experiential strategy involve principles:

1. An activity for the game, simulation, or role play is done to achieve a purpose or one or more learning objectives.
2. Active involvement is needed if students are to learn the optimum amount from an activity.

3. The activity needs to be followed by debriefing that focuses on the decisions made, the effects of decisions (including feelings), and the effects of commitment for the future.
4. The process, to be most successful, should foster commitment by individuals.

Appendix 14.3 is a data collection instrument you can use to evaluate your skills in directing games, simulations, or role playing.

A PRACTICAL EXAMPLE. Byerly (2001) presents a refreshing view of the importance of experiential learning for students. He sees experiential learning as having three primary components: *modeling*—the teacher demonstrating a skill; *collaborating*—the teacher or a guest working with students, or students working with peers; and *simulating* (enactment within a context that mirrors the real world) (p. 697). He believes that subject area classes can take on large-scale projects such as a model restaurant for home economics, a school representative election modeled on local, state, and national elections, or a model United Nations. "Experiential learning pops up across the curriculum as educators seek to give their students a sense of how learning works in the real world" (p. 698). Byerly recommends trying a large-scale project that may require considerable school and district support. Many teachers consider at least one large-scale experiential project, to give students a valuable learning opportunity. As an example, Byerly discusses a reenactment of a wagon train experience of the 1840s. The following are examples of significant stages of larger-scale experiential learning.

- Fund raising
- Building the context for the activity
- Doing extensive background teaching and research
- Having students help find answers to key questions (purpose of the wagon train, natural obstacles of the time, etc.)
- Instruction and practice sessions for particular roles
- Learning new skills (cooking on open fires or using Dutch ovens)
- Creating authenticity (costumes, props, etc.)
- Having the teacher and parents volunteer for specific roles
- Clear organization
- Promoting goodwill and hard work
- Documenting (photographs/videotape)
- Debriefing (what has been learned?) (pp. 697–699)

Use the data collection instrument in Appendix 14.2 to help you analyze the cases that follow. Your instructor may pose specific questions for your response.

CASE 14.4 Experiential Learning

All about Air

A grade 3/4 class is about to begin a unit on the topic "air." Their teacher, Mr. Chang, plans to introduce the topic by using an experiential approach. He has placed six science experiment stations around the room. Two of these demonstrate "Air occupies space," two demonstrate "Air has weight," and two show "Air exerts pressure."

He begins, "What if I told you, 'There's no such thing as air?' Do you think that's right? How many agree? How do we know there's such a thing as air?

Can we see it, feel it, hear it?" Mr. Chang asks for examples as proof.

After a short discussion, he continues, "Today we're going to find out some other things about air by doing experiments. I have listed names of experiment teams on this chart. Each team will work at the location specified. By following instructions at each station, you should be able to help answer the questions, 'How do we know air exists? What is it like?' Please follow your instructions carefully and carry out each experiment twice. Be sure to record, on the sheet provided, what happens. We'll have a chance to share the results afterward."

Mr. Chang has groups of four work at each experiment station. They follow the directions for their experiment and record the results on their data sheet. They discuss the activity animatedly as they work on the experiments.

After each group has done its experiment two or more times and recorded the results, Mr. Chang asks the groups to bring their data sheets to the large-group discussion area. Each group reports their results. The data sheets are gathered and, with the help of the students, the descriptions of what happened are recorded on large chart paper.

Mr. Chang says, "Let's look at the six descriptions. What patterns or similarities do we notice? Are there similarities in 1 and 2? In 3 and 4? In 5 and 6? Does something always happen? Is there anything that never happens?" The children enthusiastically discuss and compare their results.

Mr. Chang prompts, "Well, what did we learn about air? Do we have proof that air exists? Do we know more about what air is like?" Discussion continues until the following information is generated: air takes up space; air has weight; air pushes or has pressure. The children make new charts outlining and illustrating what they have learned. Data sheets are attached to the charts.

Mr. Chang closes with the following questions: "What are some examples of air taking up space? Exerting pressure? Weighing?" Students generate examples, including vehicle tires, balloons for decoration, bubble packing, filling tires, floats on airplanes, air-filled dinghies or rafts, and balloons moving when you let go of the end.

CASE 14.5 Experiential Learning
All about Water

Ms. Plaxton's grade 10 general science class is studying the topic of water. She likes to use an approach to instruction that is quite student centered. Students had read about water in the library and checked in the Science Center for illustrations of different sources of water. Ms. Plaxton required them to answer several questions about water supply sources, purity or impurity, purification methods, and effects on health and economics. She gave students a test on the topic of water.

Ms. Plaxton marked the test. When she analyzed the results, she was surprised that most students did not seem to know very much about the very common commodity of water. She wonders why. She has just heard about the experiential learning teaching strategy. Next year, she plans to use the complete experiential learning approach.

CASE 14.6 Discussion
Making Social Studies Interesting

Mr. Goldman, an avid student of history who believes strongly in its importance, would like to make his grade 11 social studies class interesting but spends much of his time lecturing. It is obvious that students are bored and are just putting up with him and the subject. He finds himself in a bind. The social studies department of his high school insists that he cover a certain amount and kind of information. His classroom is crowded, so group work is difficult. He has tried to hold class discussions on matters that he finds interesting but has been disappointed because of lack of participation by his students. Getting students to participate is like finding and pulling hens' teeth. Total class discussion, Mr. Goldman believes, can be very worthwhile. He is willing to give this approach one more try. He seeks your advice on how to use class discussion effectively.

LINKING PRACTICE TO THEORY

Experiential learning takes much planning and monitoring. Try the methods suggested in this chapter. Consider the benefits and the drawbacks. What skills and competencies do each approach require? Can they work for all school subjects? How would you meet the challenge of a field experience where this strategy was not encouraged? How can you use the experiences you give the students in your follow-up and debriefing? Experiential learning can involve much personal and emotional involvement by your students. What do you need to do to handle this well? Reflect on your experiences with this strategy and build your own approaches.

Summary

The direct, indirect, and individual study strategic approaches to instruction were presented in the last chapter. The interactive and experiential are two more. The interactive strategy makes use of discussion and sharing among individuals in the classroom and active student involvement. Group size ranges from the total class as a work group through pairs or triads to small work groups. Effective group operation depends on the use of communication and interpersonal skills. These and group skills should be taught. There are a huge variety of groups from which to choose. The teacher needs to monitor the operation of groups and intervene as necessary.

When the experiential instructional strategy is used, students are actively involved in the context to be studied. This strategy is often multisensory and inductive. True experiential instruction involves a cycle of experiencing, sharing, analyzing, inferring, and applying.

Activities

INQUIRY METHODS

1. Join a class discussion in which you and your peers report and discuss the inquiry approaches used by cooperating teachers that have been observed. Do not use teachers' names.
    (a) Describe the teacher behaviors.
    (b) List examples of why the approaches were effective.
    (c) List the basic inquiry processes used.
2. In a subject group, brainstorm topics that are often taught by the direct instructional strategy. Demonstrate how they could be more effectively taught using: (a) inductive and inquiry modes; (b) guided inquiry; and (c) unguided inquiry.

3. Join a subject group to design a lesson using guided inquiry. Using the same lesson topic, design a lesson using unguided inquiry. Have these presented, and ask for critique from the class. If this is not feasible, compare the two instructional approaches in your subject group.
4. Teach a microteaching or school lesson with an inquiry method target. A data collection instrument is provided in Appendix 14.1.
5. People often think that Sherlock Holmes "deduced" the solutions in his famous cases. To what extent can it be argued that he used an inductive approach? Discuss.

APPENDIX 14.1 *Inquiry Orientation Data Collection Instrument*

PROFESSIONAL TARGET—INDUCTIVE, INQUIRY ORIENTATION OBSERVATION GUIDE

Describe what was said and done and how students reacted.

1. Problem or objective understood

2. Adequacy, arrangement of facilities, materials, references

3. How, by whom, data was selected

4. How data was processed, what thinking skills were used

5. Teacher behavior: telling? asking?

6. Use of questions: open/closed, convergent/divergent, teacher/student initiated; use of probes and redirects

7. Teacher behavior: supportive? encouraging?

8. Who provided answers: teacher? student?

9. Manner in which ideas were tested, evaluated

10. Effect of introduction of new data or evidence

11. Application of concept, principle, or generalization to new situation

APPENDIX 14.2 *Experiential Learning Data Collection Instrument*

PROFESSIONAL TARGET—EXPERIENTIAL EDUCATION

Please describe what you hear and see and how students react.

Step	Teacher and Student Behaviors
Students "experience" an activity	
Sharing: students share observations and reactions or feelings about experiences	
Analyzing: students "talk through" the experience they shared, surface patterns, and interactions	
Inferring: students derive principles/ generalizations from their analysis that can be used in the future	
Applying: students tell how they will apply their learning and/or individuals report what they plan to do	

APPENDIX 14.3   *Games, Simulations, or Role-Playing Data Collection Instrument*

PROFESSIONAL TARGET—GAMES, SIMULATIONS, OR ROLE PLAYING

Please describe what you hear and see and how students react.

Step	Teacher and Student Behaviors
Intentions: What are students to know or be able to do as a result of the experience?	
Relevance: Are students relating the experience and learning to their personal lives? Are students involved emotionally and in decision making?	
Operation: Setting? Time? Role assignments? Number of participants? Resources or materials needed?	
Procedure: Rules? Sequence of events (warm-up, briefing, action conclusion)?	
Debriefing: Recalling the activity? Sharing learning and feelings? Pros and cons of potential decisions? Decision? Commitment? Plans for evaluation of carrying out commitment?	

15 The Collaborative Learning Strategy

Diversity among individuals is increasing and is everywhere. Teaching students the skills to interact effectively with diverse individuals is not a luxury, it is a necessity. (Johnson & Johnson, 1999)

Group Skills

The challenge for the teacher is to create a learning environment that promotes cooperative behavior, individual accountability and responsibility, and interdependence. (Centre for Staff Development, 2000)

The term collaborative learning is an umbrella term that includes various interactive approaches and methods for group work. Cooperative learning is an aspect of collaborative learning that takes a very specialist approach to group work. This involves positive interdependence rather than just sharing. A well-known example is the "jigsaw." These approaches are presented in this chapter.

Gross Davis notes, "students learn best when they are actively involved in the process. Researchers report that, regardless of subject matter, students working in small groups tend to learn more of what is taught, and retain it longer than when the same content is presented in other instructional formats. Students who work in collaborative groups also appear more satisfied with their classes" (1993, p. 147).

Collaborative learning, Gokhale (1995) observes, fosters development of critical thinking through discussion, clarification of ideas, and evaluation of others' ideas. If instruction is to enhance critical-thinking and problem-solving skills, collaborative learning is more effective than direct instruction. The

OBJECTIVES

You will be able to:

1. Define interactive teaching and describe patterns available to the classroom teacher.
2. Describe the special purposes of the classroom as a group.
3. Describe the developmental stages through which groups move and list interventions a teacher can use during these stages.
4. Describe stages of group development and teacher behaviors for creating a positive classroom group and list skills needed for effective group participation.
5. Discuss the nature of the class group as a social system and work group.
6. Describe how you can promote effective student interaction in a classroom.
7. List characteristics of effective class discussion.
8. Describe characteristics of different kinds of small groups.
9. Discuss how small groups can be used effectively and list benefits and limitations.
10. List the duties of group leaders and members.
11. Describe the essential components of cooperative learning.
12. Explain the advantages and disadvantages of cooperative learning and appropriate situations in which to use it.
13. Describe the phases for setting up cooperative learning models.
14. Explain how cooperative learning can reduce prejudice among students.
15. Include cooperative learning in a unit plan.

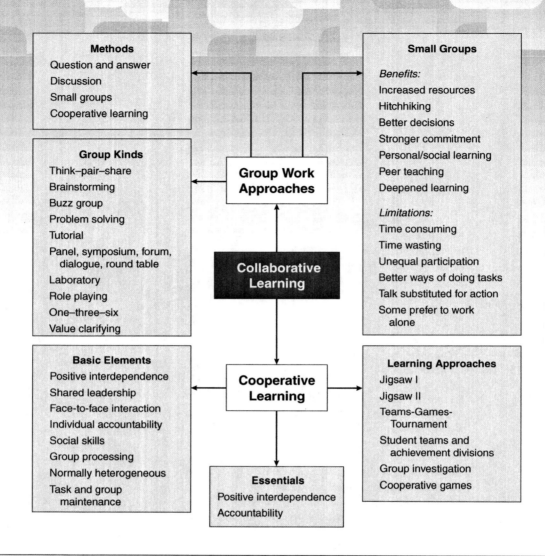

TCP—GROUP SKILLS

Develops group skills in the classroom

Builds rapport with whole class and establishes a cohesive class group; sets achievable, challenging goals for the class group or small groups; uses effective interpersonal and group skills (i.e., participation, consensus seeking, problem solving, conflict resolution, group accountability); models, teaches, and expects use of group skills.

Unaware of the class as a social group and appropriate pupil and teacher behaviors; does not model, teach, and expect use of group skills by pupils.

teacher, she says, needs to view teaching as a process of developing and enhancing students' ability to learn. The role is not to transmit information, but to facilitate learning. This, she says, involves creating and managing meaningful learning experiences and stimulating student thinking.

486

TCP—COLLABORATIVE AND COOPERATIVE LEARNING

Uses collaborative and cooperative learning methods regularly

Uses collaborative and cooperative learning appropriately; teaches specific social skills; monitors group work and gives regular feedback; able to develop positive interdependence among group members; uses a variety of collaborative and cooperative (e.g. Jigsaw) learning methods; allows students to evaluate group effectiveness and accountability.

Uses groups without teaching social skills; gives no feedback to groups; unable to create positive interdependence among group members; does not have students evaluate group effectiveness; uses collaborative and cooperative learning inappropriately; unaware of the special nature of cooperative learning.

Most teaching and learning in schools occurs in a group setting. Each classroom develops a unique personality. A student's personal academic growth depends in large part on the emotional climate of the classroom. It makes sense that you acquire the understanding and skills that build an effective class. Attention to group development results in better classroom management because students interact more positively, are more self-disciplined, and participation in discussion is enhanced because students feel comfortable participating. And, the interpersonal skills and attitudes developed by students apply in other contexts. If the class is harmonious and task oriented, you can use a variety of interaction patterns to achieve education goals.

Kinds of Classroom Interactions

Teaching elementary, secondary, or adult students involves a variety of human interactions.

- *Teacher/whole class:* Highly teacher-centered interaction—for example, lectures.
- *Teacher/class during question and answer:* The teacher asks the class (teacher question); the student addresses the teacher and class (the response); the student responds to another student and the class (reaction); and the student asks the teacher and the rest of the class (student question).
- *Discussion with whole class:* (1) Teacher-guided discussion, in which the teacher steers the class or draws out certain points or principles; or (2) open discussion, a freewheeling discussion with no predetermined "answers."
- *Small-group discussions, projects, or assignments:* The class is divided into small groups. A large number of different small group formats can be used.
- *Cooperative learning:* Groups feature positive interdependence, promotive interaction aided by the reward structure, individual accountability, require communication, interpersonal, and group skills, and group processing to determine group effectiveness.
- *Student pair or triad:* Discussions, projects, assignments, or presentations.
- *Others:* Panels; case study; resource person; laboratory; committees; role playing or skits; simulations or games; forum; interviews; debates; symposia; or combinations.

The Class as a Group

Although some classroom work is one on one, teaching is differentiated from most other professions in that the teacher works with groups and most teaching and learning occurs in a group setting. The classroom is a complex social system in which many dynamic social forces operate: friendships, power and influence, communication patterns, member roles, and school, classroom, and peer-driven behavior norms.

When you ask questions or give an assignment, student responses are affected by your relationship with individuals, peer friendship patterns, and individual and subgroup attitudes. Students influence one another. A class either helps or hinders individual student or group learning. Group processes are always present. It makes sense to understand them.

The classroom as a whole is a work group. Effective teacher/student class groups work on making the environment pleasant and task oriented. They consciously focus on *task achievement* (academic goals and objectives), *group maintenance* (using interpersonal and group skills to build a strong group), and *group effectiveness* (reacting to changing tasks and to member and group needs).

1. *Task achievement:* to achieve academic goals by attaining curriculum goals. Task functions relate to a work orientation to fulfill subject-matter requirements of task achievement. *Social skills* include sharing information and ideas, asking questions, providing information, checking for understanding, summarizing, and keeping students on task.
2. *Group maintenance:* to build a strong class that works well together, in which members help and support each other. Group maintenance functions involve the feelings and interpersonal relationships of class members. The intent is to establish a cohesive and stable work group to efficiently achieve academic tasks. Examples of *group maintenance social skills* are checking for agreement, encouraging others, actively listening, paraphrasing, sharing feelings, responding to ideas, and checking for agreement.
3. *Group effectiveness:* learning how to react to changing tasks and the needs of individuals. Task achievement and group maintenance skills are needed for groups to work effectively.

An inventory, "My Behavior in Groups," which lists task achievement and group maintenance behaviors, is shown in Appendix 15.1.

"Membership" of students in an elementary school class is not voluntary, but as students move through high school, options become available. In a departmentalized high school, membership varies with the teacher and the students enrolled in different subjects. A class may have several teachers and so several social settings. Membership in adult education may or may not be optional. In some cases, employees are required to take courses.

NORMS.   Every group has *norms* (accepted rules for behavior). Rules established by the teacher may or may not be norms, depending on whether they are accepted and followed. Deviation from norms by a student leads to disapproval or rejection by group members, reprimand by the teacher, even expulsion. Examples of norms include the language used, the clothing worn, hairstyles, what one talks about, whom one talks to, and how much work one has to do. Rules a teacher or group leader tries to establish become norms only if the majority of the group accepts and follows them. Each subgroup in the classroom has norms that may or may not be entirely the same as classroom norms. Norms can either interfere with, or facilitate, achievement of curriculum objectives.

STRUCTURE. Group structure also affects class effectiveness. *Group structure* is the pattern of relationships derived through the positions members of the group occupy. Three things affect structure:

1. *Roles:* indicates what people are supposed to do in the group. The two major roles (culturally defined but adapted by members of the class) are "teacher" and "student."
2. *Status:* the hierarchy of positions in the class. The behavior and ideas of some individuals have more influence (or power) than others, and some subgroups have more power than others. The teacher has the greatest formal status and usually is accepted as leader. How the teacher or other persons of high status behave toward an individual affects how that person is viewed by the class.
3. *Attraction:* the extent to which group members like each other and elect to work or play together. Attraction patterns affect the way individuals interact and communicate and thus their achievement. Deliberate effort is needed to build a constructive and cohesive class group.

GOALS. Building an effective and cohesive group can help achieve curriculum objectives and the goals of the class. Goals can come from broader society, school officials, individual teachers, the student body, the specific class, or individuals in the group. One of the most difficult tasks of a teacher is harmonizing different goals. If the goals of these sources differ, the result can be conflict and trouble.

Fostering Group Development

Productive class groups do not happen by accident. As a teacher, try to foster self-concept development and group support for the growth of individuals by attending to three aspects of group functioning:

1. *Task achievement,* by initiating discussion, seeking and providing information, raising questions, providing meaningful group assignments, summarizing, and evaluating
2. *Group maintenance,* by encouraging participation, reducing anxiety, handling conflict, promoting cooperation, and clarifying feelings
3. *Group effectiveness,* by modeling, teaching, and requiring communication, interpersonal, and group skills

Class groups tend to move through relatively predictable stages from the first time they meet through to their last meeting. The stages are (1) beginning the group, (2) developing the group, (3) maintaining the group, and (4) phasing to the future (termination) (Figure 15.1).

1. *Orientation (beginning the group).* "What's expected of me?" "How do I fit?" "Will I make

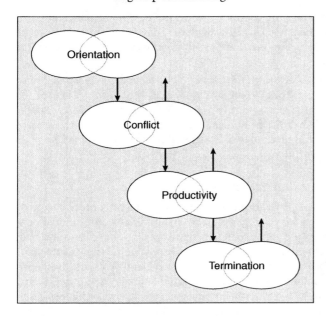

FIGURE 15.1 *Group Development Stages*

a fool out of myself?" "Will the others like me?" "Will I succeed?" "Do I want to be here?" The *orientation stage* is a time of dependency on the teacher and uncertainty as class group members try to sort out their roles and the norms of the group. Relationships begin to be established, and initial participation may be tentative or superficial. Gaining approval of fellow class members is important, and individuals may fear disapproval or rejection. Leadership and influence may remain undecided.

The teacher can help by recognizing and respecting the needs of learners as individuals. Clear information should be given about the objectives, operational procedures, and evaluation for the class. Students can be helped to get to know each other through "ice-breaking" activities and having students engage in group activities that help members get to know and feel comfortable with one another. Norms, such as empathy, trust, openness, respect, acceptance, provisional try, risk taking, and commitment, can be expected. Characteristics of an effective group can be taught (e.g., the duties of group leaders and participants). Rules and routines can be taught and practiced.

2. *Conflict (developing the group).* The second stage is the *conflict stage.* Some anxiety, tension, and disagreement is normal and occurs as a result of increased participation and interaction as group members get to know each other better. A struggle for control may occur. Group members tend to test the leader and other members before the group settles in. As group identity builds, and if the group overcomes the problems of conflict, it can move into a period of group identity and cohesiveness development. Ways of working together emerge, and agreement is reached on behavior norms. It should be stressed that conflict is normal, and the teacher should emphasize that positive learning can result from reconciling differences and learning how to resolve conflicts. Learning how to use problem-solving, decision-making, conflict-resolution, and group-effectiveness monitoring strategies is beneficial.

3. *Productivity (maintaining the group).* Group cohesion is the primary characteristic of a well-functioning group. In the *productivity stage,* class members become good at attaining goals and become more flexible and adaptive in working together. Roles, status, attraction, and norms are established. Goals are accepted. Trust is high, the group is cohesive, and interpersonal conflicts are handled. Group members understand that it is normal to have "ups and downs."

4. *Termination of the group (phasing toward the future).* The teacher can prepare (early in the life of the group) for the phasing out (*termination stage*) by helping students see the ending of the group to be maturation leading to future growth and perhaps future groups. Friendships that have been established need not terminate with the group. The success of the class group can be reviewed, and attributes or skills still to be mastered can be positively identified.

Teacher Interventions for Building Effective Groups

Effective groups rarely occur by chance. Classes run in a mainly teacher-centered, lecture-dominated, write-papers-and-exams way rarely progress beyond the orientation (or conflict) stage. If this is so, the power of the group to help learning will not have been realized. Students learn best when they are actively involved. They need to hone relationship skills to achieve the affective objectives part of the curriculum and to acquire the skills needed to express acceptance, support, and to cooperate. They should support each other during interactions, reject nonsupportive, self-serving behaviors such as ridicule or blaming, and seek ways to improve cooperation. Suggestions for working with the group during the various development stages follow.

Beginning of the Group

1. Get-acquainted activities (introductions, name cards, and "ice-breaking" games)
2. Clearly laying out course (or unit or lesson) objectives, content, and evaluation
3. Teaching and having the class practice rules and routines
4. Activities to promote personal disclosure (as appropriate)
5. Instructor modeling of skills and behavior expected
6. Stating and expecting the principle of group support for individual growth
7. Using teaching methods that require interaction and use of positive norms
8. Teaching and providing activities for class members to learn interpersonal and group skills
9. Introducing and practicing group monitoring techniques

Developing and Maintaining the Group

1. Activities that foster further disclosure and openness
2. Activities that require use of positive, constructive norms
3. Activities that practice participation skills (e.g., listening, interacting, seeking information, sharing information, including and encouraging, clarifying, summarizing, and concluding)
4. Activities to extend interpersonal skills
5. Activities to practice leader, participant, group-effectiveness-monitoring roles
6. Activities that emphasize shared leadership, cooperation, and consensus seeking
7. Activities to practice brainstorming, buzzing, problem solving, and decision making
8. Activities to learn and practice negotiation skills such as listening, initiating, analyzing, diagnosing, interpreting, criticizing, and compromising and conflict resolution
9. Requiring group effectiveness monitoring and providing activities to practice systematic and nonjudgmental observation and reporting, soliciting and giving and receiving feedback, and interpreting data

Preparing for Group Termination

1. Activities that recall and review group experiences and achievements
2. Activities that identify the individual and group skills that have been learned
3. Activities to help the class see that termination leads to future growth
4. Activities to identify ways the current group, or individuals, might continue to provide support in the future

Communication, Interpersonal, and Group Skills

What makes a group effective is the consistent application of group skills: communication (interpersonal), trust, leadership, and conflict-resolution skills. These skills should be taught as purposefully as reading or math skills, using an experiential cycle. Make students aware of why a skill is needed and ensure that they understand what the skill is. Group events develop behaviors and skills.

Consensus Seeking and Decision Making

Whole-class and small-group discussions are often used to come to conclusions or make decisions. The teacher or group leader can make decisions autocratically, or decisions can be made by voting or by consensus. Consensus seeking is often treated as a part of decision making. Critical thinking skills and the process of decision making can be taught.

Setting consensus as a goal, though it may not be totally attained, encourages a group to consider the needs and wishes of all members. It requires listening skills, free exchange of information, acceptance of honestly held beliefs, checking for assumptions and biases, and carefully thinking through opinions. Minority opinions must be valued. Students should be able to stand firm on important issues if they have been carefully thought through, but blind stubbornness is not acceptable. Students should be willing to compromise when conflicts arise.

A useful model to seek consensus is the *One–Three–Six Method*. This involves: presenting the problem; asking individuals, privately, to record (preferably in positive terms) their top priorities; students form groups of three to combine lists and add any new ideas; groups of three form groups of six to combine lists and remove redundancy; a representative is chosen by each group of six to form a committee that combines all lists and arrives at a consensus; the committee reports to the class. This procedure can be repeated periodically.

CASE 15.1 The Class as a Group

Starting off Right

Mr. Festlinger is getting ready for his first class of the year. Sitting at his desk in the classroom, he looks at the empty desks in front of him. Tomorrow the seats will be full of new grade 7 students.

He believes he has done everything to be ready. He has carefully planned his courses and materials. All the resources he needs for the first few weeks are in place. He has his class list ready; in fact, he has everything he needs to actually teach.

What concerns him, however, is getting the class group off to a good start. He is thinking about how he can get the class to trust him and to cooperate with him and with one another. He thinks that perhaps he could begin with some group-building activities. One idea is a scavenger hunt game. The students will try to complete a sheet with such items as "someone wearing red"; "someone who has a pet cat"; and so on. It will be noisy, but the important thing is to establish group openness and support. Too many teachers, he thinks, get down to the academic work, whereas the important thing is group or community building.

He leaves his desk and walks about his room. He has arranged the desks in a way that should allow productive interaction and yet allow order and good management.

The arrangement is flexible enough for various types of groups to operate. Materials are in easy reach and arranged so students themselves can access and distribute them. The few basic rules he insists on and the most important procedures for the first few weeks are posted.

Mr. Festlinger is excited about meeting his new class. He is ready for opening day, but realizes that keeping his class as an effective group will need all his communication and interpersonal skills. He knows that the students will have their own concerns. They will want to gain the approval of their peers. There will be some anxiety and tension, even conflict. He must make sure he is a good model and set clear goals. There is much to do, but he is ready.

Collaborative Instruction and Learning

What Is the Collaborative Instruction Approach?

Collaborative learning is an approach to teaching and learning in which students interact to share ideas, explore a question, and complete a project. Collaborative (interactive) instruction methods range from class discussions through small-group methods or cooperative learning to using the Internet when working on an assignment (Figure 15.2).

FIGURE 15.2 *Collaborative (Interactive) Instruction Methods*

Source: Saskatchewan Learning (1991).

Human beings, to paraphrase Aristotle, are social animals. Significant learning occurs through interaction with others. The long-held notion that instruction should usually be teacher and print centered and occur in a classroom with desks in straight rows has been challenged. Collaborative (interactive) instructional strategies provide viable alternatives. In interactive situations, the behavior of individuals stimulate each other. It is a pattern of communication. Interactive strategies rely heavily on discussion and sharing among individuals. The term *collaborative* denotes an exchange of ideas and active participation.

Collaborative methods let students discover or state personal viewpoints instead of just repeating those presented. Interactive, discussion, and sharing or discourse methods let learners react to the teacher's or peers' ideas, experience, insights, and knowledge, and give rise to different ways of thinking and feeling. Students can learn from peer teachers, develop social skills, organize thoughts, and develop rational arguments. Compared to direct instruction strategies, teacher control is less, but this does not mean that you can relinquish responsibility. You control discussion time, the nature and topics of discussion, group composition and size, and reporting techniques. You need good observation, listening, interpersonal, and intervention skills.

Collaborative approaches are summarized in Table 15.1. If, for instance, you want active participation, increased motivation, and a high rate of retention, chose an interactive method that fosters these, such as problem-solving or decision-making groups. If recall of information and ability to perform step-by-step skills are desired, select a method that uses instructor or peer tutoring. If a high level of cognitive understanding, decision making, or interpersonal skills is the goal, pick an interactive method that calls for investigation and critical or creative thinking, for example, a debate. Cross-cultural understanding can be fostered through cooperative learning, role playing, or simulations. At times you will want a change of pace or to add flexibility to your repertoire by using games, role playing, skits, or simulations. Role playing and simulations incorporate the experiential learning strategy.

TABLE 15.1 • *Selecting Collaborative/Interactive Instruction Methods*

Objective	Possible Method
Active participation, increased motivation, and a high rate of retention	Problem-solving and reporting groups
Recall, performance of step-by-step skills	Instructor or peer tutoring groups
High level of cognitive understanding, decision-making, or interpersonal skills	Investigative critical or creative thinking groups
Cross-cultural understanding	Cooperative learning, role playing, or simulations
Change of pace	Games, debates, simulations

You can choose from a range of grouping and interaction patterns including:

- Teacher (or student) presentations to the total class
- Teacher questions to the whole class and student responses
- Whole-class discussions
- Small-group discussions, projects, assignments, or presentations
- Student pair or triad discussions, projects, assignments, or presentations
- Small groups in front of the class (debates, panels, dialogues, forums, etc.)
- Teacher (or student) presentations, questioning, or discussions with split grade or ability groups
- Cooperative learning
- Combinations or variations of these

Groups and Collaborative Learning

THE CLASS AS A SOCIAL SYSTEM AND WORK GROUP.   The class is a *social system,* a community, affected by friendships, power and influence, communication patterns, member roles and school, peer-driven, and classroom norms. The class that has been helped to develop into a mature group does better, because positive interaction and participation improves self-concept. Threat is reduced, students are more comfortable with each other, feel free to take part actively, and can take risks because peer influence is positive. The classroom group is set up by society as an academic work group. The two major roles are "teacher" and "student." A hierarchy of status exists, and attraction patterns affect the way individuals interact and how well the class functions. You often work with the class as a whole, particularly when presenting information or step-by-step skills or conducting a class discussion.

There are times when a highly teacher-centered whole-class method is effective. However, it is often desirable for students to become more interactive and contribute to the development of the lesson. This can happen when question and answer and discussion are used skillfully. When this occurs, students feel their contributions are valuable and that they, individually, are responsible for the development of the lesson and the learning of classmates.

CREATING AN EFFECTIVE SOCIAL SYSTEM.   Cooperative and collaborative learning are significant educational trends that deserve considerable attention by educators. Tschannen-Moran and Hoy (2000) believe that "Collaborative learning strategies provide a powerful mechanism not only to address affective goals in education but also to enhance students' cognitive development" (p. 161). They say that collaborative learning increases student understanding of ideas and the ability to express them. Students are active constructors of knowledge, not passive recipients of information. These authors think that most teachers do not have the knowledge and skills to make the best use of collaborative learning strategies. They have created a five-part framework based on five "G's" (Figure 15.3):

- *Group characteristics:* Know the cognitive development, social and emotional maturity, and skills of the group.
- *Goal setting:* Be aware of the social skills and affective processes that are age appropriate for the group. Be aware of the cognitive development of individuals and the group as a whole. Set realistic goals.

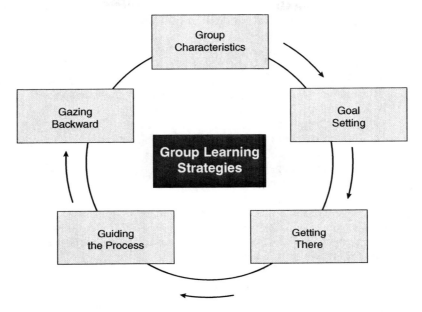

FIGURE 15.3 *Collaborative Learning Group Learning Strategies*
Source: Adapted from Tschannen-Moran & Hoy, 2000.

- *Getting there:* Design group tasks. Select learning strategies. Determine instructions, resources and rewards, and decide on assessment.
- *Guiding the process:* Move about the room and check for student understanding. Check for quality and quantity of interactions.
- *Gazing backward:* Reflect on what went well and where there were problems. Consider teacher directions, participation, time, and resources.

Small Groups

Effective small-group discussions do not happen by accident. Learn what is involved in conducting successful small-group discussions. Many authorities feel that much more use should be made of small groups. They are appropriate if you want to increase teacher–student and student–student verbal interaction and increase social skills so students adopt a responsible, independent mode of learning. Conditions in society make it imperative that people learn to relate well to others and that the school accepts its responsibility for teaching skills that will equip students to fill useful, responsible, and productive roles.

Some teachers have tried small-group methods and said, "I tried small-group discussions but students just sat there like bumps on logs" or "A waste of time, they just socialize!" Another said, "I have far too much important material to cover to use small groups." The problem in the first instance likely was that students were not adequately prepared for discussion and small groups; and the problem in the second case is that small-group methods lend themselves to certain kinds of content but not as well to other kinds.

Discover the readiness of the class to use small groups and, if necessary, intervene with activities that build these capabilities gradually. Training can take place with the class as a whole or within small groups as the need becomes evident. Stanford and Rourke

(1974) proposed the following classic arrangement of skills into categories, used in many current group approaches:

1. Getting acquainted and establishing trust
2. Taking responsibility (including taking the roles of initiator, contributor, clarifier, summarizer, evaluator, recorder, encourager, and harmonizer)
3. Encouraging others to contribute
4. Careful listening
5. Responding to other contributions
6. Setting clear goals
7. Learning to cooperate
8. Coming to consensus

Participants in a small group can be assigned roles. These provide a sense of purpose for each group member. Stanford and Rourke (1974) also summarize the roles students can be assigned and rotated through during small-group discussion, to help them learn "taking responsibility" skills.

- The *initiator* gets discussion underway, helps the group organize, and keeps it moving toward the goal.
- The *contributor* offers opinions, facts, anecdotes, or examples that could help the group solve the problem.
- The task of the *clarifier* is to make sure the terms, problem, and contributions by group members are understood by all. If needed, the clarifier suggests that added information be sought.
- The *summarizer* helps keep discussion relevant and to the point by bringing together and summarizing what has been discussed or learned to date. The summarizer also makes sure everybody in the group understands where the group stands on an issue.
- The job of the *evaluator* is to keep track of how well the group is progressing in its task and tactfully points out problems the group is having in working together.
- The main points of the discussion and the product of the group are noted by the *recorder*. On occasion, what was recorded is read back, to help the group recall what had been covered during discussion or to make sure it is accurate.
- The *encourager* facilitates participation by listening carefully, being friendly, complimenting members for their contributions, and inviting participation.
- The *harmonizer* acts as the peacekeeper by relieving tension (perhaps through humor), settling disputes, helping the group work out disagreements, and suggesting compromises. (p. 103)

A data collection instrument that can be used to evaluate group participation by role is provided in Appendix 15.2.

KINDS OF SMALL GROUPS.   There is an effective small-group method for almost any content. A surprisingly large array is available. Examples of small-group methods are provided below.

1. *Think–pair–share group.* A good way to encourage students to participate in small groups or in class while students extend their thinking and interaction is the

think–pair–share method, developed by Professor Frank Lyman of the University of Maryland Howard County Southern Teacher Education Center (Kagan, 1994). It begins with a short teacher presentation. So students consider more fully what was explained, you pose a question and ask students to spend a minute or two thinking alone about an issue or generalization. Then assign students to pairs to share their thinking. A good practice is to have one student make a statement to be paraphrased by the other until it is understood. This is followed by reversal of statement maker and paraphraser roles. Finally, each pair reports. Reporting can be to two or three other pairs or to the class as a whole. In reporting to the whole class, not all pairs need report. Reporting can be suspended when all major ideas have surfaced.

   2. *The brainstorming group.* Brainstorming is a fun, useful, creative thinking technique that can be used to initiate problem solving. It can be included in any lesson. A group or individual may do it. When it is done in groups, it can be like a game. Four to nine people are given a particular problem, and in five to ten minutes, participants come up with as many ideas or suggestions as possible. Quantity of ideas is the main objective. Judgment about the value, implications, ideas, or suggestions is deferred. The basic rules are to

- Think of as many ideas as possible. Quantity is wanted (the greater the number, the more likely a winning idea).
- Withhold criticism; judgment is ruled out.
- Frill. Sometimes, the wilder the ideas the better—it is easier to tame down than to think up.
- Hitchhike. Seek combination and improvement. One idea can beget another idea, or a whole stream of other ideas.

   Advantages of brainstorming include:

- The pressure to have an immediate "right" answer is removed.
- Creative potential can be released.
- Solutions to seemingly "unsolvable" problems can be initiated.
- It is fun—people like the freedom of expression.
- If several groups are involved, friendly and enjoyable competition occurs.
- When it is done by a group, people who would otherwise never speak up do so, because the climate is nonthreatening.
- It can be used any time a problem comes to light or at any time during a lesson as a refreshing change of pace.
- When it is used in a lesson, students are actively, not passively, involved in learning.

   Limitations of brainstorming are that:

- Some people find it hard to get away from the "practical" or may feel that reasoned ideas are needed.
- Many ideas or suggestions are not worth anything.
- Pet ideas, or the ideas of some people, may have to be discarded.

   3. *The buzz group.* "Buzzing" the solution to a problem involves considering the pros and cons of alternatives for solving a problem and making a decision. A starting point can be brainstorming. An individual or a group can buzz. As a teaching method, it involves every student in the discussion process. People are divided into groups of four to seven. For a limited time (five to ten minutes or so), people try to arrive at consensus about the answer to a problem or question. A novel way to use buzzing is with statements such as, "Let's have a Buzz 36," or "We are going to do a Heinz 57." The first statement calls for groups of three to discuss a topic for six minutes; the second for groups of five to engage in a seven-minute discussion. There are many points in a lesson where buzz groups can be used. The basic rules of buzzing are that

- An issue or problem is presented.
- A leader and recorder for each group are picked by the teacher or elected; the leader sees that all group members participate and the recorder notes contributions.
- Consensus is sought.
- The leader reports areas of agreement (including the rationale) or alternative solutions if there is no agreement.

The limitations of buzzing are that:

- Some people may dominate.
- If all groups of the class deal with the same topic, contributions may be contradictory or hard to combine.
- Participants may need training in interpersonal and group skills.
- Monitoring may be needed to keep groups on task.

4. *Problem-solving group.* Group members, in a systematic way, seek the solution to a problem based on the "scientific method." The steps are: define the problem, brainstorm the likely causes of the problem, decide the most likely cause, brainstorm potential solutions, select the most likely solution (based on determination of pros and cons of alternatives), and decide when and how to implement the solution.

5. *Tutorial group.* Tutorial groups are set up to help students who need remediation or more practice or for students who can benefit from enrichment. The teacher or student leads a tutorial group. Greater attention to individual needs is possible, and students can participate more actively.

6. *Panel, symposium, forum, dialogue, and round table.* Rather than presenting information and ideas through lectures, assigned questions, or readings, you can have students do the job. This can be by setting up a *panel* (a group of students who discuss a topic before a class—chaired by either you or a student), a *committee* (a group of students is assigned by you or the class to learn about a topic and report), a *symposium* (several students become "expert" in a topic and give brief presentations to the class), a *forum* (a class discussion in which a problem is explored through question and answer and short statements under the guidance of a chairperson), a *dialogue* (two people discussing a topic in front of the class), or a *round table* (a group of students discussing an issue in front of a class). Students find these methods motivating. Conclude with a summation to ensure content is organized, correctly understood, and links to what is being studied.

7. *Laboratory group.* A laboratory group is formed to complete a project, an experiment, or practice something that has been presented. A common example is a chemistry laboratory group.

8. *Role-playing group.* In a role-playing group, each member is assigned a role to assume on a controversial topic. Students may or may not agree with the stance of the role they have been given. A role-playing group can bring out all sides of an issue or have students

learn to understand the ideas or feelings of others. Role playing can be a good method for having students learn attitudes.

9. *One–three–six group.* The one–three–six group method can be used at almost any time during a lesson. Students are asked, as individuals, to record their opinion on an issue. Then individuals join two others and come to an agreement. Finally, two groups of three join and seek consensus. Each group of six reports to the class as a whole.

10. *Value-clarifying group.* Groups are presented with a value-laden topic. Each group is asked to seek alternative solutions, discuss the pros and cons of alternatives, and agree on a potential solution. The idea is for students to clarify their values and to learn to understand and tolerate the values of others. Value-clarifying groups should be used with care: this is a controversial method. Some educators believe it motivating and invaluable for developing critical thinking skills; others believe the approach to be a fad that is superficial and laden with inadequacies and problems.

USING SMALL-GROUP METHODS.   Some teachers believe that using small groups can lead to classroom management problems and off-task student behavior. However, attention to group development results in improved classroom management because students become more self-disciplined. Small-group methods should involve orderly grouping so students take part in informed cooperative interaction to share information, solve problems, make decisions, or help each other.

Classroom climate must be open, friendly, and nonthreatening. Group members need acceptance, trust, and security to contribute freely, speak their minds, and be safe from teacher and peer censure and pressure. You relinquish the dominant role in favor of being a learning coordinator, support and resource person, co-planner, and co-evaluator. Student responsibility for planning, executing, and evaluating is increased. Independence and cooperation should be encouraged and student contributions valued. This requires planning, and content relevant to student interests. Before discussion begins, students need content background for meaningful interchange. In short, discussions should not "pool ignorance."

Have a plan for students who are shy, lazy, or dominate discussion, and those who lead the group off task or are negative. Participation, goal setting, consensus seeking, problem solving, decision making, conflict resolution, and group-effectiveness monitoring skills can be taught and learned. This should not be left to chance.

As groups are at work, circulate and intervene as appropriate but avoid dominating. Contributions by all students should be promoted, and interpersonal and group skills stressed. Offer ideas, ask questions, cue, offer verbal and nonverbal reinforcement, and suggest group maintenance activities when needed. In the concluding stage, the results of interaction should be synthesized and summarized. Reporting must occur (oral or through a paper or project). Each group should evaluate its own effectiveness using specific rubrics.

Using Collaborative Learning Well

Mueller and Fleming (2001) agree that cooperative and collaborative learning are an important part of student learning. They suggest ways teachers can structure and guide group learning experiences. A key finding is that "children require periods of unstructured time to organize themselves and to learn how to work together toward a mutual goal" (p. 259). We tend to overstructure how tasks are to be achieved. However, if the task is clear, students often find their own way to achieve the goal.

Boxtel and Roelofs (2001) observe that collaborative learning can help students gain a deeper understanding of concepts, especially when students work together on tasks such as concept mapping. The concern is with how to construct knowledge. They argue that we tend to consider cognitive activities only, and that teachers must consider the "learning and thinking as social and situated processes" (p. 55). Students, they say, should be encouraged in "collaborative elaboration," trying to reach a shared understanding. The use of shared objects or tools can play a critical part in the discussion. Tools such as a text or other materials to experiment with give many students "exploration and manipulation possibilities" (p. 59). Simple Post-it notes on which students can write and arrange ideas help students to structure their shared discussions.

A teacher's planning guide for using small groups is given in Appendix 15.3 . A data collection instrument for use with microteaching or classroom lessons taught with the professional target of small-group teaching is provided in Appendix 15.4.

Benefits and Limitations of Group Methods

Although there are times when group work is very effective and times when another strategy or method should be used, most teachers agree that much more use should be made of small groups.

BENEFITS.   Impressive benefits can result through small-group methods:

1. Increased resources. "Two heads are better than one." A group has access to more information and has a broader background than does any individual. More insights are likely to occur. A group can create more ideas.
2. Members are often stimulated by the presence of others. Members may be motivated to help the group succeed for social approval reasons. "Ideas beget ideas." "Hitchhiking" occurs.
3. Better decisions can result. Groups can produce better decisions than students working separately. Ideas can be clarified, refined, combined, and evaluated through the interaction of group members; therefore, decisions should be superior.
4. Group members may have a stronger commitment. If group members help hammer something out, they feel a stronger commitment to accept the result and follow through.
5. Students are more actively involved. Participation is likely to be active rather than passive. This increases motivation, learning, retention, and commitment.
6. Personal and social learning take place. Increased understanding of self, others, and group processes can result. Interpersonal and social skills can be improved and increased self-concept can result. Prejudices can be reduced. Students gain insights into the attitudes, reactions, and sensitivities of others and may examine and modify their behavior. Ability to contribute rationally and constructively can be improved.
7. Peer teaching is advantageous. Studies confirm that peer teaching is powerful. Some things are learned better and faster when taught by peers. Ideas are put in "student language" not "teacher language"; examples and explanations used by peers are often more relevant to students than teacher or text examples.
8. Learning may be deepened. Often, material is easily forgotten when it is memorized and not understood when direct teaching methods are used. When small groups are used, it is more likely that students will understand the thinking skills or processes involved. When this occurs, learning is more likely to be transferred to new situations.

LIMITATIONS.   You should be aware of the potential limitations of using small groups.

1. Group decision making takes time. More time is required for decision making or planning when it is done by a group than when it is done by an individual. The views of all must be heard, and disagreements may occur that take time to resolve.
2. Time may be seen to be wasted. Discussions, if not well conducted, not only take time, they waste it. Without able guidance or the use of group skills, discussion can wander, be misled, hindered, concerned with trivia, or lack conclusiveness.
3. Convictions may be suppressed. Some members may conform to avoid confrontation or risk censure. Less aggressive students may not be given a chance to present ideas.
4. Some tasks are better done by individuals, i.e., routine or simple tasks, or information acquisition. More material can be covered through methods such as lectures.
5. Talk may be substituted for action. "Visiting" may take precedence over productivity. In some instances, groups may be indecisive because no person is solely responsive for action. One or two individuals may do all the work.
6. Some students prefer to work alone. Unless small groups are used well and the benefits taught, some might rather work alone, thinking they can learn better. Some may be shy, lack social skills, or feel they will not be accepted.

It should be stressed that most disadvantages can be overcome. Doing so, of course, requires careful planning, instruction, and monitoring.

Group Structure and Member Duties

The productivity and health of groups depend on how they are structured. Effectiveness is also affected by how well students understand the duties of group leader and participants. This should be clearly presented or worked out at the beginning of the group.

You can control group size. Large groups (more than twelve members) require more structure and leadership than medium (seven to twelve members) or small (two to five members) groups. Seating should allow members to work together without violating personal space, and suitable materials should be available. Consensus and decision-making procedures should be taught and groups informed that consensus is not always possible or required. Task accomplishment activities should be stressed and a normal operational routine established. Each meeting should start with a statement of what is to done and end with an evaluation of group effectiveness. Groups should be told about meeting times and the completion date.

Group members should understand that each is accountable, that the group leader has specific duties and that others have specific duties.

Group members' duties are to:

- Be on time and attend all group sessions.
- Take an active part and contribute information and ideas.
- Contribute to group maintenance.
- Have a positive, rather than negatively critical, frame of reference.
- Listen when others speak, be empathetic, and hear others out.
- Respect and interact with other members.
- Respect individual differences.
- Avoid prejudices and keep biases out.
- Seek, and be open to, the ideas and suggestions of others.

- Encourage noncontributors to take part.
- Accept responsibility for the consequences of their behavior.
- Be sensitive to the feelings and concerns of others.
- Avoid self-serving, judgmental, blaming, grandstanding, or storytelling behavior.
- Be genuine and open.
- Support others and help them articulate their ideas.
- Help the group by summarizing, clarifying, mediating, praising, and encouraging.
- Use problem-solving, decision-making, and conflict-resolution frames of reference.
- Act as group leader, recorder, or group effectiveness monitor as appropriate.

The group leader's duties are to

- See that the "problem" is clarified.
- Get discussion started.
- Keep discussion moving.
- See that all phases of the problem are brought out.
- Keep discussion on topic.
- Encourage full participation and draw out nontalkers.
- Be objective.
- Rephrase and clarify statements, or have others do this.
- See that stage summaries and a conclusion are made.
- See that all members are treated with respect.
- Respect the confidence of the group.
- Report, or see that the thoughts of the group are fairly reported.

Discussion Approaches

Whole-class discussion requires teacher and students to interact verbally. It recognizes that knowledge is more than a string of correct answers and that much knowledge is gained through creative inquiry and active student participation. The purpose is to stimulate analysis and to interpret and shape attitudes. Discussion can be adapted to many classroom situations. For example, a "magic moment" in teaching and learning may occur if, during a presentation, you notice students are particularly interested in a topic and involve them in a discussion. This helps build a positive climate and leads to intrinsic student interest in the school subject.

Discussion can be guided carefully, step by step, through thought-provoking questions and, when appropriate, by interjecting information. This can be called *guided discussion*. On the other hand, discussion can be completely open and consist largely of student–student interchange. We call this *open discussion*. The former approach is effective for promoting understanding of important concepts; the latter is an exciting way for students to engage in high-level, creative thinking.

GUIDED DISCUSSION.   In guided discussion you, as teacher, are the discussion leader and authority source, and, when needed, information source. Guided discussion is used to guide students as they review what they have been studying, to promote understanding, or to develop ability to apply learning. In guided discussion you draw out the information needed and make frequent use of convergent (who, what, where, when) questions, prompts, and probes, and seek wide participation. Guided discussion is similar to guided discovery or inquiry.

OPEN DISCUSSION.   Open discussion is more difficult to conduct, but can be exciting and rewarding. It is freer flowing than guided discussion. You are a facilitator instead of an authority source or figure. You focus discussion, set boundaries, encourage participation (but unlike in guided discussion, not necessarily wide participation), and promote positive interaction. You listen and use paraphrasing, perception checking, open-ended questions and probes, but don't push the class toward predetermined conclusions. Avoid intervening too often (particularly with questions), because this may get in the way. Divergent ideas and originality are welcome, and high-level and critical and creative thinking are sought.

CONDUCTING DISCUSSION.   There is more to *discussion* (which is similar to a "businesslike" or on-topic conversation) than first meets the eye. Effective application of this teaching method requires a range of skills in planning, conducting, and concluding the discussion. Categories of skills include interpersonal exchanges, motivation, questioning, and reinforcement.

Effective discussions are based on material familiar to students. You set the stage, stress that opinions must be supported (based on evidence), and ensure that terms or concepts are understood. Good discussion is student centered. The rules of "common courtesy" prevail. Ideas can be challenged, but personalities must never be attacked.

Collaborative learning involves students in peer discussion. Chinn, O'Donnell, and Jinks (2000) say that teachers must consider carefully the structure of students' discourse so that students, who are encouraged to consider more detailed issues and questions, will produce more complex conclusions and learn more from one another. They suggest that (1) giving explanations, (2) elaborating on what they have learned, and (3) requesting clarification from their peers are beneficial. In other words, "It is not simply the activity of engaging in discourse that promotes peer learning but the quality of that discourse" (p. 78).

Good teachers establish a classroom ethos that is safe, fun, challenging, and at task. They demonstrate and encourage positive behaviors and avoid negative behaviors (Figure 15.4).

FIGURE 15.4   *Encouraging Positive and Discouraging Negative Behaviors*

Positive Behavior	Negative Behavior
• Encourage	• Blame
• Model listening skills	• Judge
• Are courteous	• Use put-downs
• Are genuine	• Use sarcasm
• Use empathy	• Use story telling
• Paraphrase	• Placate
• Seek information	• Rescue
• Check for feelings	• Theorize
• Ask for examples	• Distract
• Ask for opinions	• Clown
• Probe	• Show off
• Keep discussion on track	• Are rude
• Elicit stage/concluding summaries	
• Are businesslike	

ENCOURAGING PARTICIPATION.   You can do much to encourage positive and productive participation in class discussions and, for that matter, in small-group activities. Students should be taught to listen, take turns, encourage others to participate, and speak clearly to the point.

Effective discussion approaches were presented earlier. A data collection instrument you can use to get feedback on your use of the discussion target is provided in Appendix 15.5.

Peer Tutoring

Students often work alone. Schoolwork is typically based on competition rather than cooperation. When students teach students, a valuable dimension is added to teaching and learning. "Students should be put in situations where they have to reach to understand, but where support from other students or from the teacher is also available. Sometimes the best teacher is another student who has just figured out the problem" (Woolfolk, 2004, p. 52). You likely are familiar with the truism that if you really want to understand something, . . . teach it. Both the tutor and tutee can benefit. Cognitive and affective development is fostered through a student's conversations and interactions with others. Peers provide the information and support needed for intellectual growth. Successful peer tutoring seems to provide feelings of satisfaction and competence that improve self-concept.

Peer teaching can involve groups of three, four, or five, but most peer teaching occurs in pairs. When a teacher uses the peer tutoring method, students are placed in groups or two or more and provided with structured learning activities that include tutoring, practice, and feedback. Normally, students take turns teaching and being taught, answers are checked, and feedback is given.

Use the data collection instruments in this chapter to help you analyze the cases that follow. Your instructor may pose specific questions for your response. Suggest different arrangements and think about the advantages and disadvantages of each arrangement.

CASE 15.2 Collaborative Learning

Getting along with Each Other

Mr. Ramsingh, a student teacher, planned to have his grade 6 students do small-group discussion. The regular classroom teacher was skeptical about the idea; she said the students had never worked in groups before and doubted they could learn that way. But she was supportive to Mr. Ramsingh in his plan to try other approaches.

Mr. Ramsingh was confident the students would welcome the opportunity to become more involved in their learning. He began, "On the playground yesterday, there were many problems. Ms. O'Toole and I had complaints from several of you and from the supervisors. We are very concerned. It seems problems during the break are so great that no one is benefiting. I hope today we can work out ways that will make playground time more enjoyable for everyone. What I'd like you to do is to form groups of four." (The students began to look for friends to join.) "Each group will decide what the problems are and think of solutions." (Many students stopped listening and actively began to negotiate their group membership. Some began calling out to others, some left their desks for whispered discussions). "OK, you can get into your groups now. We'll finish in fifteen minutes and have all the groups report their solutions to the class before recess."

Most students rose and began to form groups. Four girls, by exchanging glances, decided to work together. They chose to work in the reading area. A fifth girl, who had been trying to get the attention of the four, was deliberately excluded. She returned to her desk, took out a library book, and began to read. Meanwhile, much loud discussion ensued. A pair chose each other and would not let anyone else join. Five boys decided to work together, though a sixth was vigorously protesting "That's not fair." The five moved to the reading area and tried to eject the group of girls in that area.

Mr. Ramsingh made suggestions, grouped children who lacked partners, and helped groups to find an area to work. Soon half the discussion time was gone. Mr. Ramsingh made a comment about the passing time, although many students did not hear him. As the children settled into their groups, their voices rose. Some began to complain about specific students on the playground; others wanted to defend those students. One group compared hockey card collections. Gustav

took charge of his group and began to list rules for the playground. Others in his group tried to enter the discussion, but he overruled their ideas and continued to develop his list. Mr. Ramsingh realized that each group should have had papers and pencils for recording; he quickly passed these out and spent time explaining the purpose of these materials to each group as he distributed them. Two groups were still arguing about their work area. Just then the recess bell sounded.

The children looked up in amazement and frustration. "Hey, we're not finished." "We didn't get started!" "Marvin kept fooling around, Mr. Ramsingh." Some students seemed anxious at not having finished. Others argued loudly as they left the classroom, on the way to the playground. The classroom teacher looked stern and Mr. Ramsingh wondered how to salvage the lesson and whether he would be permitted the opportunity to try small groups again.

CASE 15.3 Collaborative Learning

Waning Enthusiasm

Ms. Treblioni, a grade 11 social studies teacher, really liked using small groups. She has the reputation of being one of the best teachers in the school system. With only a few exceptions, she has always had success with them. Most of her students this year really liked the group work that had been done to date. Recently, however, the students' enthusiasm for group work seemed to be waning. She suspected that the problem was mainly a handful of students. There was Trenton and Teresa, both very pleasant and sociable, who just seemed to let the others in whatever group they were in do all the work. Two other kinds of

problems had emerged. One involved Hazel, who just always had to have her way and dominated every group she was in. Nobody seemed to want to work with her anymore. Then there were Fred and Austin. Every time they were in the same group, they seemed to have to out-clown each other. The competition, though amusing, left the other group members disgruntled and Ms. Treblioni frustrated.

In the past, Ms. Treblioni had always solved problems by gently teasing erring students or privately encouraging them. This has not worked. What would you suggest?

CASE 15.4 Collaborative Learning

Bridging to Other Subjects

Mr. Shaw and his eighth-grade students begin each day with an open discussion. As the students come into the class, they pull their desks into a circle. Mr. Shaw joins the circle. The purpose of the discussion varies, but the topics usually come from the class. The students rotate the responsibility of chairing the discussion.

The chairperson's role is to help choose a topic, introduce the topic, keep the discussion on topic, encourage balanced participation, and bring the discussion to conclusion. Mr. Shaw had, earlier in the year, taught interpersonal and communication skills, so students carry out the responsibilities of the chair

continued

with confidence. Though it is not compulsory to take a turn, most students do. Mr. Shaw participates to clarify or summarize, but is careful to model effective group skills. Today, the students have just heard about the police shooting of a young man involved in a high-speed chase in a stolen vehicle. Their feelings about whether the shooting was inappropriate or not are strong. Heated discussion outside the school and in the corridors had occurred.

It's Megan's turn to chair. She begins, "Can everyone see and hear? Some people want to talk about the police shooting. Do you agree?" Most are in agreement, but Jason, who is an avid sports fan, suggests the topic be the nearly completed World Series. There are many moans, and several students support the shooting story. "Is anyone else interested in the World Series as a topic?" asks Megan. "I'd be interested another time," says Morgan, "But I think the shooting story is more important now." "I think so, too," added Jason. "It's the third shooting this year, and my dad says the police need better training." Megan looks around the group. "Do you all agree on this story?" The class indicates they agree. "OK, Jason?" "Yeah," responds Jason, "But let's not forget to have the Series. We could each pick the team we favor to win."

"OK," Megan begins, "Who knows the whole story of what happened with the shooting? We need to get the facts." One student gives an overview of what she heard on the news, and several others add details. Intense discussion occurs that requires monitoring by the chairperson to prevent interruptions and some students from dominating. There is support for the police action by some, who point out that stealing is wrong and driving at high speeds is very dangerous. Others feel sympathy for the young man, whose crime seemed minor compared to the police action. Much of the discussion involves students stating views, sometimes in more than one way. There doesn't seem to be much listening to other positions or questions of other participants. Some students are becoming more emotional as they sense others may not be listening to their views.

Finally Mr. Shaw intervenes. "Let's see if we can figure out the issues here. I hear some people saying that because stealing is wrong, people who steal should be punished. I hear people saying that although stealing is wrong, police should not be able to shoot someone for that kind of crime. So there's an issue about stealing and there's an issue about whether the police action was appropriate. Are there any other issues?" "Another issue is that the boy who was shot was black," says Hamad. "My parents say police treat white people differently from minorities. All the shootings this year have been of black people." There is some agreement, although some students explain this by saying there is more crime committed by people from minority groups.

Megan seeks agreement on the issues and finds that everyone agrees stealing is wrong. The class does not agree on the appropriateness of the police action. As the discussion draws to a close, it becomes clear that agreement will not be possible. Megan asks for a summary of ideas or positions, and the discussion ends with a review of the positions.

Mr. Shaw is thinking of ways he can continue to build on the content of this discussion in other classes. He intends to extend this topic in both social studies and English.

Cooperative Learning

There is a pertinent film, based on a true story, called *October Sky,* which is set in the year 1957. A group of students in a small mining town in the United States is excited when the Soviets place the first satellite (*Sputnik*) into space. They decide to see if they can design, build, and launch model rockets. They realize that much scientific knowledge and skill are needed. Working together to solve many problems, they achieve success. They learn much math and physics in the process, and develop long-lasting skills and values. Experiences they share reveal that each person in the group was needed. They had engaged in cooperative learning.

To be called *cooperative,* learning needs to include certain elements: (1) *group interaction* (face-to-face interaction; the formation of groups to foster on-task behavior); (2) *social skills* (teaching and requiring interpersonal and group functioning skills); (3) *positive interdependence* (working together and mutual support; mutual goals; division of labor; dividing materials, resources or information among group members; and, giving joint rewards); (4) *individual accountability* for mastering the assigned material (responsibility as an individual and to the group); (5) *reflection* (students reflect and can share, and receive and give feedback). Furthermore, cooperative learning requires that students be taught, learn, and use interpersonal and group skills. Finally, students need to learn how to discover how well their learning groups function and the extent to which they use social skills to help members benefit from the working relationships in the group.

Modes of interaction are usually classified as individualistic, competitive, and cooperative. Most classrooms stress student interaction with the teacher and materials; cooperative learning also stresses interaction among students. Cooperative learning reaps the benefits of positive student interdependence as they work together in groups and support one another (Johnson & Johnson, 1980a). "Today, evolving constructivist perspectives on learning fuel interest in collaboration and cooperative learning" (Woolfolk, 2004, p. 492). Johnson and Johnson believe that many reasons for using competitive structures are more myth than reality and that individualizing instruction is not the only, or even the best, alternative to competition. Fears some teachers have about using cooperative goal structures are also myths. The authors say research shows that a cooperative goals structure should be the most frequent structure in the classroom but recognize the benefits of both competitive and individualistic structures (pp. 39–57). When a cooperative teaching strategy is used, emphasis is on cooperation, not competition.

Cooperative learning occurs in classrooms where students work in small groups on learning activities and receive recognition (or rewards) based on group performance. Groups are mixed in ability, and members are to help one another other. Believers claim that cooperative learning motivates students to do their best; they translate the language of the teacher and learn through this; they provide individual attention for one another. In cooperative learning, interaction to enhance learning and develop interpersonal and group skills is emphasized. It supplements the teacher's instruction by having students discuss information or practice skills originally presented by the teacher; sometimes cooperative methods require students to find or discover information.

Cooperative learning is *not:* (1) students sitting beside each other at the same table and talking as they do individual assignments, (2) students doing tasks individually, with those finishing first helping the others, or (3) giving a group assignment and one or two do most of the work to which others sign their names (Johnson & Johnson, in Brubacher, Payne, & Rickett, 1990, p. 77).

Essentials of Cooperative Learning

To improve student achievement substantially, two aspects must be present: (1) students work toward a group goal or recognition—for example a certificate; and (2) success is dependent on learning by each individual in the group (Slavin, 1987, p. 9).

Two things are essential to cooperative learning:

1. It entails *positive interdependence* among students in the task structure. Involvement of each group member is necessary for the group to complete the task. An interdependent task structure is created by having each responsible for a part of the task that cannot be completed by any other in the group—for example, the tutoring aspect. Positive interdependence can be fostered through a reward structure. Here, the final evaluation, if any, is dependent on the reward received by each student.

2. In designing cooperative learning tasks and reward structures, individual responsibility and accountability must be identified. Individuals must know exactly what their responsibilities are to the group, and they must be accountable to the group.

David and Roger Johnson's (1989) approach to cooperative learning has five basic elements:

1. *Positive interdependence.* Students need to believe they are responsible for their learning and that of members of their group.
2. *Face-to-face promotive interaction.* Students need to explain to each other what they are learning and help each other understand and do assignments.
3. *Individual accountability.* Each student needs to demonstrate mastery of the content studied.
4. *Social skills.* Effective communication, interpersonal, and group skills are needed.
5. *Group processing.* Periodically, groups must assess their effectiveness and figure out how it can be improved. (p. 80)

Cooperative Learning and Research

As part of a meta-analysis of research on a range of teaching strategies, research on cooperative learning was "overwhelmingly positive" and showed that cooperative modes are appropriate for all subjects (Joyce, Showers, & Rolheiser-Bennett, 1987, pp. 12–13). Cooperative learning involves group work that increases learning and adds other important dimensions. The positive outcomes are (1) academic gains, especially for minority and low-achieving students, (2) improved race relations among students in integrated classrooms, and (3) increased personal and social development among all students (Slavin, 1987). Slavin (1991) thinks that cooperative learning:

- Enhances student achievement; cooperative learning is most effective when groups are rewarded on the basis of the individual learning of group members.
- Consistently provides positive achievement effects when group goals and individual accountability are present.
- Produces effects on achievement that are about the same at all grade levels, all major subjects, rural or urban schools, and for high, average, and low achievers.
- Has consistent positive effects on self-esteem, intergroup relations, acceptance of academically handicapped students, attitudes toward school, and ability to work cooperatively. (p. 71)

It is not surprising that the research results are so strongly positive. People who talk about ideas with others "understand and remember" them better. Transfer from short- to long-term memory is enhanced. The support that comes from cooperation (in contrast to achievement-limiting competition) is "another plus."

Slavin (1991) reports that research on cooperative learning shows the following:

- For academic achievement, cooperative learning techniques are at least as good as traditional techniques, and usually significantly better.
- Contrary to what is sometimes claimed, it does not hold back high achievers. Cooperative learning methods are, usually, equally effective for all ability levels.
- Studies in senior high schools are about as positive as those in grades 3 to 9.

- Results are just as positive in rural, urban, and suburban settings.
- Cooperative learning methods have been equally effective with students of different ethnic groups.
- "People who cooperate learn to like one another." It has been consistently found that students' perceptions of each other are enhanced through cooperative learning.
- Cooperative learning methods promote positive intergroup relations; ethnicity barriers tend to break down, and more positive interactions and interethnic friendships occur.
- The barrier between physically and mentally handicapped children and their "normal" peers is reduced and the number of positive interactions and friendships increase.
- Cooperative methods increase students' self-esteem or self-concepts. (pp. 75–80)

Other positive outcomes include: greater liking of school, favorable attitudes toward doing well in school, a feeling of being in control of one's fate in school, greater cooperativeness and altruism, and increased time on task. One study found that cooperative learning resulted in students from lower economic backgrounds having better attendance, fewer brushes with the police, and higher behavior ratings. Another study shows that students taught cooperatively were rated higher on "measures of supportive, friendly, and pro social behavior; were better at resolving conflicts; and expressed more support for democratic values" (Slavin, 1991, pp. 80–81).

The success of cooperative approaches is not restricted to K–12 classrooms. Research shows that using cooperative modes with adults is beneficial and should lead to higher productivity (Johnson & Johnson, 1987b). The results are higher achievement, improved interpersonal relationships, greater social support, and enhanced self-esteem (p. 30). Figure 15.5 provides a summary of research on cooperative learning.

Cooperative versus Traditional Learning Groups

Effective traditional groups and cooperative learning groups require many of the same interpersonal and group skills, but they differ in significant ways. Table 15.2 shows the differences.

Cooperative Skills

Proponents of cooperative learning believe that there are no skills more important to humans than cooperative interaction (including interpersonal, group, and organizational

FIGURE 15.5 *Cooperative Learning Research*

1. Greater academic achievement	2. Positive social outcomes
"Lower"-order objectives	Better peer relationships
"Higher"-order objectives	Better social skills
High, average, and low achievers	More social support
Grade levels 2–12	Higher self-esteem
Rural, urban, suburban	Greater liking of subject, class, and school
All major subjects	Reduced prejudice
	Acceptance of academically handicapped
	Ability to work cooperatively

TABLE 15.2   *Cooperative versus Traditional Learning Groups*

Cooperative Groups	Traditional Groups
Interdependence and group accountability	Often not stressed
Normally heterogeneous	Often not homogeneous
Shared leadership	Appointed or elected
Responsibility for others' growth	Responsible for self-growth
Task and maintaining group emphasized	Emphasis on task
Social skills must be taught and used	Often ignored or assumed

skills). Particularly important are communication skills, building and maintaining trust, and controversy skills (Figure 15.6).

You can gradually introduce cooperative learning activities and games to help students acquire communication and helping skills and the basics of small-group organization and operation. These can create the necessary climate for carrying out cooperative learning strategies. Establishing the basic cooperative interaction skills helps groups to work together in completing their tasks. The goal is more than the specific subject matter as dictated by the teacher. It provides a way of acquiring or analyzing, or synthesizing information or skills.

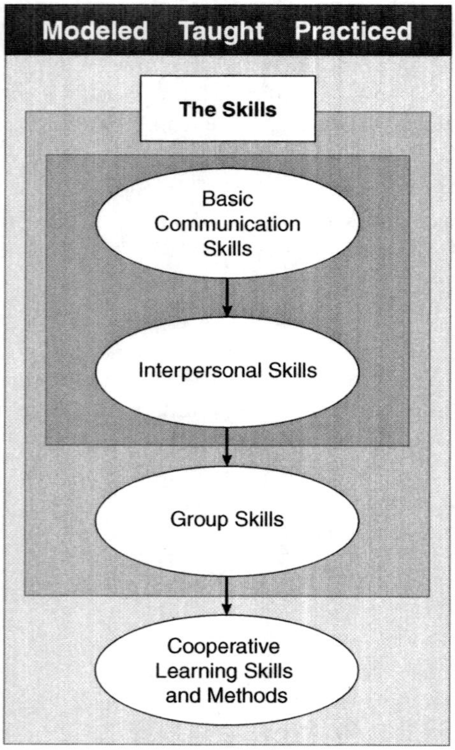

Cooperative planning skills deserve special attention. They should be introduced gradually and practiced in various situations before starting a cooperative learning project; for example, discussions can be held with the whole class or small groups for ideas to carry out an activity such as planning a display or organizing a class trip.

When a cooperative learning method is being used, the teacher is always attending to two things: (1) achieving the learning task and (2) maintaining the group (including building interpersonal and group skills). It is important that cooperative norms of behavior be established. Students can practice interpersonal and group skills. This can be done independent of, or as part of, a group assignment. At times the group may have to put aside the academic learning to work on group maintenance. An example of this occurs when there is a conflict in a group that must be attended to if the group is to be productive.

Building and Maintaining a Trusting Climate

For cooperative learning to be effective, students need collaborative skills. It is particularly important to maintain a trusting climate. Relevant suggestions when using cooperative learning were provided some time ago by Johnson and Johnson (1975b):

- Encourage students to contribute information, ideas, thoughts, feelings, intuitions, hunches, and reactions openly to the group operation.
- Encourage students to share materials and resources.

FIGURE 15.6   *Skills to Be Acquired for Effective Cooperative Learning*

- Encourage students to express cooperative intentions, acceptance, and support toward each other during their cooperative interactions.
- Ensure that students have the skills to express acceptance, support, and desire to cooperate.
- Point out rejecting and nonsupportive behaviors that shut off future cooperation, such as silence, ridicule, or superficial acknowledgment of an idea.
- Periodically have groups that are cooperative evaluate their behavior to ensure it is trusting and trustworthy and how cooperation could be improved. (pp. 105–106)

Principles of Cooperation

Cooperative learning principles involve positive task and reward structures and positive interdependence. A cooperative learning task structure exists when students tutor each other; a cooperative reward structure exists when a student's grade is the total of his or her grade and that of the tutor. Either task or reward structures can be used, or both can be used. A task is structured cooperatively when no one student can do the task alone—for example, requiring a group product. Another example is a "jigsaw," in which each group member is provided with a separate portion of the learning material but every group member is to learn all the material. Reward is structured cooperatively when grades of individuals are dependent on the scores of other team members (e.g., the group grade is based on the sum of the scores). Studies show that these kinds of rewards structures have a powerful influence in directing group efforts. The lowest achiever in a group (if that person's grade contributes heavily to the group grade) often is given much tutoring and support.

Positive interdependence occurs when the achievement of individuals is needed to help the group complete a task or receive a reward—usually leading to cooperation; positive facilitation will usually lead to cooperation. A cooperative classroom structure is built by creating student interdependence. Having students responsible for separate portions of the task fosters interdependence. If classes are structured in a traditional way, the success of one student results in the failure of another (e.g., only one person can get the highest grade and other students do not get that grade). Every time a teacher asks a student to respond to a question, others are not asked; and if only the top projects are displayed, the other students do not have their work recognized. These kinds of occurrences are common in competitive classrooms.

Individualistic task or reward structure is present when the achievements of individual students have no student impact on the achievement of other students; then, there is no incentive either to cooperate or to compete.

The key principles in effective cooperative learning are (1) individual responsibility, and (2) individual accountability. Individuals need to be keenly aware of their responsibilities to the group and must be accountable to it. Research shows that academic gains occur when groups are used only if the goal is a group grade to which each individual contributes, and if individuals follow through on their responsibilities.

Two kinds of individuals can obstruct group effectiveness: the student who reaps the benefits without contributing and the student who takes over the group. Group design should provide safeguards for individual differences and ensure respect for the effort of the less dominant. Each individual should be assigned specific important roles or tasks and be held accountable. Another technique is frequent group process evaluations and having groups conclude each meeting with a discussion of what to do to increase group effectiveness.

Students have different social motives. "Cooperative" students are (1) *altruistic—*they help others make gains; (2) *equality oriented—*they minimize personal achievement compared to the achievement of others; and (3) *group enhancement oriented—*they do their best to help the group achieve. Competitive students tend toward rivalry and being superior. Individualistic students tend to be self- rather than other centered; they are cooperative when there is a "payoff" and competitive when there is a chance of winning.

As students get older, they become individualistic and increasingly compare their achievements with those of others. Also, the need to cooperate or compete is influenced by students' cultural values. Minority, low-income, and rural students tend to have cooperative social motives, whereas white American students often have competitive social motives. Because traditional classrooms assume that motivation occurs through competition, educational outcomes are biased in the favor of majority students. Likely, the most effective classrooms provide meaningful rewards for all students, whether their social motives are individualistic, competitive, or cooperative.

Cooperative Learning Approaches

Cooperative team learning approaches described below are Aronson's Jigsaw, Slavin's Jigsaw II, Devries and Slavin's Teams-Games-Tournament (TGT), Slavin's Student Teams and Achievement Divisions (STAD), Sharan's Group Investigation, cooperative games, and using cooperation to reduce prejudice. These approaches share the feature of small teams, or social units, of students to promote interaction and cooperation.

JIGSAW.   Jigsaw was developed to encourage peer cooperation and tutoring (Aronson, Blaney, Stephin, Sikes, & Snapp, 1978). Students are assigned to five heterogeneous, or "home," groups of five or six members. Academic material is broken into as many parts as there are groups. Students study their portion of the materials with the members of other "home" groups who have been assigned the same material. This is the "expert" group. "Experts" return to their "home" groups to teach their material to other group members. "Home" group members are dependent on the "experts" to be tutored to learn the material, therefore they are motivated to pay attention. Students are quizzed on all the academic material and receive individual grades (there is no team score). Group members are interdependent to the extent that they work together to accomplish the task but not interdependent regarding reward because they are graded as individuals. "Experts" have unique information that makes "home" group members value the contribution of each member. Jigsaw is used mainly in social studies and subjects for which it is important to learn from textual material. However, other creative approaches are possible.

JIGSAW II.   Jigsaw II, described by Slavin (1978a), is a variation of Jigsaw. Students work in heterogeneous groups and each group is assigned a portion of the material. Students study the material assigned and then meet in "expert" groups. After this, students return to their "home" teams to teach their peers. Then, students take a quiz covering all the topics. Quiz scores, based on an individual improvement system, are used to form team scores. High-scoring teams are recognized in some way, such as in a bulletin or school newspaper. Interdependence is key to Jigsaw II: students depend on teammates to provide the information so they can do well on quizzes.

TEAMS-GAMES-TOURNAMENT.   Slavin's (1978a, 1978b) Teams-Games-Tournament (TGT) format, based on motivation theory, involves competitive cooperation with individuals of similar ability competing against each other and with teams competing against one another. Students are assigned to four- or five-member teams. Teams are heterogeneous by ability (e.g., one low-ability student, two of average ability, and one of high ability), racial or ethnic background, and sex. The job of the teams is, through peer tutoring, to prepare each other for a tournament usually held once a week. Tournament tables are set up. Three students of similar academic achievement (determined by previous performance) are assigned to each table. The three highest performers are assigned Table #1, the next three highest sit at Table #2, and so on. When the game is over, contestants are scored. The highest performer of a trio earns 6 points, the mid-performer earns 4 points, and the low performer earns 2 points. Team scores are determined by adding the scores of the team members. The winning team is the one with the most points. It earns recognition through, for example, a newsletter. The composition of teams remains the same, and tournaments run for six to eight weeks. Tournament table group composition changes depending on scores earned by individuals. Performance in the first tournament decides table placement for the second tournament, performance in the second determines placement for the third, and so on. Reward interdependence is created in a team. The more members help one another, the better the team will do in tournaments.

STUDENT TEAMS AND ACHIEVEMENT DIVISIONS. Like TGT, the Student Teams and Achievement Divisions (STAD) format involves competitive cooperation. Teams compete against each other; but, unlike TGT, games and tournaments are not used. Students, through peer assistance, review teacher-taught materials. The teacher distributes rewards to team members and uses an accounting system that avoids head-on student competition.

Students are assigned to heterogeneous teams of four or five members. Students, in teams, study for fifteen-minute weekly quizzes. Quiz scores are translated into team scores using "Achievement Divisions." The highest six scorers are placed in the same Achievement Division and their scores are compared to allocate points. (The top scorer gets 8 points, the second earns 6 points, etc. Students earning the next six highest scores form the second Achievement Division and points are allocated, etc.) The result is that students are compared only with those of similar ability, not the whole class. As in TGT, STAD involves competition among equals. Students do not interact with other members of their division; in teams, they help each other prepare for quizzes, and teams compete to win recognition for performance.

GROUP INVESTIGATION. The Group Investigation (GI) model proposed by Sharan and Lazarowitz (1980) has students gather data, interpret the data through discussion, and synthesize individual contributions into a group product. The emphasis in GI is different from in TGT and STAD, which feature peer tutoring (rather than investigation and reporting). The teacher presents a general topic to the class, which is divided into groups to investigate and report on subtopics. After subtopics are chosen, groups break their subtopics into tasks for individuals and individuals and subgroups carry out their assignments to prepare group reports. The teacher is a facilitator and resource. The use of GI can be particularly effective for higher-order thinking skills and can be a very effective method in high school classes.

After a general topic is introduced by the teacher, the class is divided into two- to six-member heterogeneous task-oriented groups. Students often can pick the topic they would like to investigate, and this influences team membership. Individual groups meet with the teacher to clarify the goals of the investigation and plan how the investigation is to be conducted. Both in- and out-of-school resources can be investigated. Each group then carries out the plan and the teacher monitors progress and offers assistance as needed. Data are analyzed and evaluated and an interesting way of presenting or displaying what was learned to the rest of the class is determined. As coordinated by the teacher, groups then display or present their reports. Evaluation now takes place, with the teacher and students collaborating to decide the assessment methods. Evaluation should include assessment of higher-level learning. It can include individual or group assessment or both.

COMPARING TEAM LEARNING METHODS.   Cooperative learning modes fall into two categories: those emphasizing peer tutoring (Jigsaw, TGT, and STAD), and those emphasizing group investigation. Sharan and Lazarowitz (1980) point out critical differences in the variety and source of information and the nature of the learning task, the nature of interpersonal relations and communications, evaluation of rewards for the academic product, and the organization of the classroom (Table 15.3).

In peer tutoring, the teacher presents information or identifies sources; in group investigation, information can be varied and broad and is gathered by students. Peer tutoring emphasizes acquiring information or skills; group investigation stresses analysis, interpretation, problem solving, and application. With respect to interpersonal relations and communications, peer tutoring teams stress peer instruction and drill within the team, whereas in group investigation, teams are part of mutual exchange that requires techniques such as idea or consensus seeking and decision making. Evaluation of, and rewards for, the academic product also differ. In peer tutoring, the academic product is independent, evaluation is mainly individual (test scores), and rewards tend to be extrinsic; in group investigation, the academic product is interdependent, evaluation is both individual and group, and the reward is mainly intrinsic (based on self-directed interest in the topic). In peer tutoring, the classroom is organized as several separate, uncoordinated, teams to achieve a uniform academic product; in group investigation the class is divided into teams to investigate portions of a broad topic that requires between-team coordination, reporting, and integration into a whole (Sharan & Lazarowitz, 1980, pp. 263–264).

Cooperation and interdependence in learning tasks are fostered by peer tutoring, that is, teaching classmates. Given practice and reinforcement, most children become rather good "teachers." Many learn better from peers than from adults, and benefit greatly

TABLE 15.3 *Comparing Peer Tutoring and Group Investigation Cooperative Learning*

Peer Tutoring	Group Investigation
Teacher provides the information	Students gather the information
Use: information/skill acquisition	Use: for problem solving, interpreting, applying
Peer tutoring (presenting/acquiring)	Information/idea exchange, planning, coordination
Evaluation: usually individual or done with group, done by teacher	Evaluation: individual and/or group; product is interdependent; done by teacher and/or students
Rewards: extrinsic; group recognition	Rewards: mainly intrinsic
Organization: aggregate of teams, same task	Organization: "group of groups," between-group coordination

from teaching other students. In their small groups, each team, rather than the class as a whole, becomes the social unit in which learning is pursued. Classroom instruction process changes from direct instructor control to allow for interaction among peers. Figure 15.7 compares peer tutoring and group investigation methods.

FIGURE 15.7 *Operation of the Peer Tutoring and Group Investigation Methods*

COOPERATIVE GAMES.   When one thinks of classroom games, one usually thinks of something offered as a reward, to provide a break in the academic schedule, or something the physical education teacher has students do. *Cooperative games* can be used to build academic learning. Play is a great medium for positive social learning. It is natural, active, and extremely motivating. While playing cooperatively, students can act, react, feel, and experience. Games can be used "to break the ice," practice interpersonal or group skills when a group maintenance activity is appropriate, or provide a change of pace and simultaneously develop students' social skills. They can be used to have students experience the process of cooperation and develop a positive mind set for it before a cooperative method is used. Many books on cooperative games are available. These describe hundreds of games, ranging from those that require no additional resources or materials to those that require relatively elaborate resources or materials.

Cooperative games are useful in achieving cognitive, psychomotor, or social curriculum objectives. They are "sharing" games: a big difference between cooperative games and most other games is that everybody "wins." The structure is cooperative, not competitive. People play "with" rather than "against" each other. Cooperative games allow maximum participation and opportunity for everybody to be involved. They are not graded or assessed and usually are self-paced and fun. In cooperative games, the more individuals help others, the more they and the group can achieve. So all can "win," the goals are mutual effort, fun, and helping others.

Cooperative games are powerful for positively shaping students' feelings about themselves and others. Competitive games can rob some of the opportunity to experience satisfaction and enjoyment and can lead to unfriendly and negative interactions. Cooperative games can reduce the students' feeling anxious, self-conscious, isolated, or unworthy. They enhance self-concept, creativity, and the ability to get along with others. Through well-designed cooperative games, students become more considerate and caring. Cooperative games can teach the values and behaviors we would like society to have.

Cooperative Learning and Reducing Prejudice

It seems clear, as Sharan and Lazarowitz (1980) state, that team learning "promotes positive interethnic contact under cooperative conditions" (p. 258). This is confirmed by Slavin (1983), who reviewed research on cooperative learning and intergroup relations. He agrees that there is "a strong positive effect of cooperative learning on intergroup relations" (p. 88). Cooperative groups increase interracial contact and lead to cross-racial friendships. Slavin hypothesizes that students learn it is acceptable to interact with members of other races, there is increased awareness of interracial similarities, and racial barriers to peer-group membership break down. Obviously, the more exceptions there are to a stereotype, the more a stereotype breaks down. This happens as a student interacts with (and becomes friends with) one person from another race who does not match the stereotype, then another, then still another, and so forth.

Studies show that the orientation of a classroom, competitive or cooperative, can have significant effects on the academic and social behavior of students, particularly for members of a minority group. Teachers in North America of Anglo or European ancestry often have cultural values characterized by emphasis on competition and winning. In contrast, cooperation was, and is, essential in rural, land-based societies and has become the basic cultural value in indigenous societies. The reward structure in most North American and European classrooms is based on competition. Teachers, then, may wonder why minority students generally do not do as well as majority students. One can say that these teachers, because of cultural background, make a prejudgment by using competitive modes. This prejudice is based on lack of knowledge of how minority students learn, while stressing the schooling expectations and values of a predominantly Anglo-European society. Perhaps if they had used cooperative learning teaching methods, the academic achievement of minority students would have been higher, majority-culture student achievement would have been at least as high, and intercultural social behavior could have been enhanced. Cooperative learning reduces prejudice.

Handling Problems

Some teachers do not want to risk using group work, believing that use of groups promotes off-task behavior and discipline problems. We argue that the opposite is true. Improved classroom management results when groups are established effectively. Teachers who use group approaches well find that misbehavior drops significantly. Because use of groups results in improved social skills, fewer problems arise and students who might be problems can be handled more easily. The thing to remember is that students must be taught how to use groups, and interacting skills must be taught and practiced.

Most students react well to cooperative learning modes; however, all teaching strategies, on occasion, encounter difficulties. Problems can arise with cooperative learning when assigning groups or with socially isolated, high-achieving, disruptive, or low-achieving students.

Care must be taken to assign students into compatible, yet heterogeneous, groups. Students may have limited experience in working with others, and some in-group divisiveness may occur. Careful monitoring of group operation is, of course, necessary. Stress the critical aspects of the operation of cooperative groups and have students engage in group-building exercises or games. This is usually enough, but in the rare cases where a personality conflict exists, you may need to intervene or even restructure a group.

You may have to help the *socially isolated student* become accepted and included by the cooperative group. Students can receive instruction in interpersonal skills before they are introduced to the class, giving the isolated student an opportunity to support the group; or you can assign a task (e.g., recorder) to the student at which he or she can be successful. As groups learn cooperative behavior, peer support (which promotes participation) does develop, and the isolated student should increasingly become included.

A *high-achieving student* may say, " I don't want to be in a group. I can do this better and faster myself." You may have to explain the benefits of cooperative group work, pointing out that when the high achiever explains something to another student, a deeper understanding is gained, and simultaneously, the student acquires important interpersonal and social skills. This student can be assigned a task (such as observer) that requires skill in tabulating, interpreting, and reporting data, giving the student a feeling of the importance of contributing to group achievement. Or you may wish to use bonus marks that can be earned by high-achieving students. These could be partially dependent on the quality of support lent to group development and achievement. On occasion, you may group high-achieving students together, to challenge them or encourage divergent thinking.

A *low-achieving student* may need to discover that he is worthy, has capabilities, and can help others. While low-achieving students may not be handicapped in the usual sense of this term, the techniques suggested by Johnson and Johnson (1980b) may work: assign clear, achievable roles to the student; train him in the interpersonal skills needed to participate; or, set criteria he can meet (perhaps varying what must be mastered for success).

As the group develops its ability to support individuals, the low achiever's self-esteem and performance will increase.

A *disruptive student* with poor interpersonal skills can benefit from cooperative learning. You may have to intervene to help the group deal with the problem. For instance, you may assign the disruptive student a task that keeps him or her constructively busy. The student, for example, may be asked to keep the data collection sheet on task achievement behaviors. Sometimes, however, the student has to be pulled out of the group, at least temporarily, until the problem has been solved.

Evaluating Cooperative Learning

When teachers use cooperative learning, they are concerned with both academic achievement and acquisition of cooperative behaviors. Kagan (1985) points out that: (1) groups should evaluate their process, (2) team members should evaluate each other, (3) individuals should evaluate themselves, and (4) presentations by groups should be evaluated by the teacher and class members (p. 153).

Sources of evaluation instruments, among others, are: Kagan's (1985) *Cooperative Learning: Resources for Teachers,* and Johnson and Johnson's (1985) *Learning Together and Alone: Cooperative, Competitive, and Individualistic Learning.* A source that provides an excellent summary of the process of evaluation with examples is Clark, Wideman, and Eadie (1990), *Together We Learn.* Assessing academic progress when cooperative models are used is, as usual, done through homework, assignments, projects, papers, or tests. Assessment of the behavior of students involves use of observation procedures that describe and record behavior. Usually, an observation sheet is used to record, descriptively and objectively, the nature and frequencies of student behaviors.

Behaviors appropriate for cooperative learning include:

   I. *Leadership*
      A. Achieving the task
         1. Sharing information and opinions
         2. Seeking information
         3. Clarifying or elaborating
         4. Summarizing
         5. Checking progress toward the group goal
         6. Testing for, or facilitating, consensus
      B. Maintaining the group
         1. Including/encouraging/listening to others
         2. Expressing group feelings
         3. Relieving tension and harmonizing
         4. Setting or applying standards
         5. Compromising
         6. Helping solve problems
  II. *Communication*
      A. Listening
      B. Describing behavior accurately
      C. Paraphrasing
      D. Perception checking
      E. Describing feelings
      F. Seeking feedback; providing it when solicited

III. *Displaying trust*
    A. Accepting others and their ideas
    B. Expressing support/intention to cooperate
    C. Following through on promises/responsibilities
IV. *Conflict resolution*
    A. Managing personal feelings/showing empathy
    B. Defining the problem
    C. Discovering sources of the problem
    D. Proposing potential solutions
    E. Selecting the best potential solution
    F. Trying the proposed solution
    G. Evaluating the attempted solution

Prepare a summative profile of each student's progress. You can include mastery of cognitive knowledge and skills, verbal and writing ability, cooperative ability, competitive ability, ability to work independently, and ability to solve problems. You can also record appreciation of a subject area, appreciation of learning, self-awareness of abilities, characteristics that help others, appreciation of cultural and individual differences, appreciation of being trustworthy, and valuing free and open inquiry into problems.

The Teacher's Role in Cooperative Learning Instruction

The teacher assigns the group goal, outlines operational procedures, establishes the evaluation system, and monitors group progress (Figure 15.8). As adapted from Johnson and Johnson (1978), your duties when using cooperative learning include the following.

1. Specify the instructional objectives.
2. Set the size of the group. Size depends on the age of students (two or three for young students), the resources available, the cooperative skills of group members, and the task.
3. Name the group members. Composition is usually heterogeneous by sex, ability, leadership qualities, and ethnic background. Sometimes students can be grouped by interests.
4. Structure the physical arrangement of the room. Consider movement patterns, separation of groups, and access to materials.
5. Make sure that suitable materials are available. Students may all need the same materials, or individuals may need different materials.
6. Explain the task, operational procedures, role expectations, and evaluation criteria. Make sure that expectations for the final product and student behavior are clear.
7. Observe students' cooperative behavior (interpersonal and group skills) progress toward the goal.
8. Be a consultant or intervene as needed to solve problems for achieving the task using cooperative behaviors. Remind students that they are accountable to their group. Group effectiveness forms can be completed by the groups themselves.
9. Evaluate the products of the groups using criteria that were set. Usually, each group member gets the grade assigned to the group. Consider how well students learned or accomplished the task and how well they helped each other.

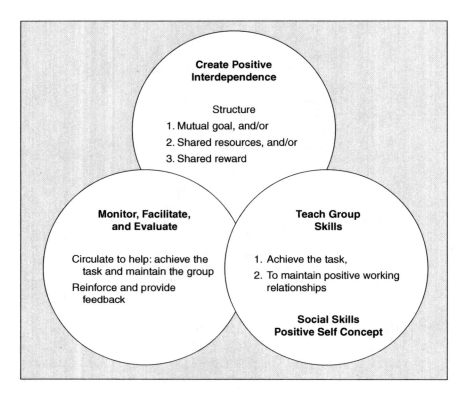

FIGURE 15.8   *Role of Teacher in Cooperative Learning*

Sonnier-York and Stanford (2002) stress "the need to target behavioral/social skills for each student" before students begin the project. The key, they say, is to "monitor," not "control" students, so they "learn on their own or from each other" (p. 42). The essence of cooperative learning is learning from each other, a process that plays a significant part in all authentic learning.

OBSERVATION AND INTERVENTION.   There are two key elements to the teacher's role: *observation* and *supportive intervention.* Though it may be difficult for the teacher to find time for observation during large-group instruction, cooperative learning allows teachers to observe, reflect, and intervene supportively. Keep on top of how groups are functioning, their interests and feelings, who is learning and who needs help. Observe to evaluate the learning occurring, to see if help is needed, to discover the nature of interaction, to decide if group maintenance intervention is needed, and to reflect about your use of the cooperative learning teaching method.

You can observe in two ways: globally or systematically. *Global observation* is informal and a good way to begin. It may lead to systematic observation to confirm or provide information upon which to base interventions. When you use global observation, record what you hear and see. Questions in your mind may include: "Are all students busily engaged in the task?" "Are any students uninvolved?" "Is there evidence of boredom, frustration, disquiet?" "Is the tone of the group friendly, relaxed, animated, or confrontational?" Are there any 'free riders' or 'isolates' or 'bullies'?" *Systematic observation* is more formal. It involves teacher-made or commercial checklists that specify essential task achievement and group-maintenance interaction behaviors. Examples of checklists are included in several cooperative learning texts and other materials.

When you intervene, do so in a supportive way. Interventions should lead to students working together more effectively. Students should see you as a helper, not as a judge ready to point a finger. It may be tempting to provide answers and solve problems for the group, but this defeats a major purpose of cooperative learning and denies students the opportunity to learn how to work through problems. Instead, show confidence in the group's ability to help itself. Intervention should consist of encouragement, patience, and opportunity for reflection. On occasion you can provide alternatives or sources for student consideration.

When you use warm-up activities or intervene with task achievement or group maintenance activities, consider the Clark et al. reference mentioned above, Roger and David Johnson's (1990) cooperative learning warm-ups, grouping strategies, and group activities, and the 1988 manual by Johnson, Johnson, Bartlett, and Johnson, *Our Cooperative Classroom.* Another good reference, directed at early childhood students, is the Lorna Curran (in consultation with Kagan) 1990 book, *Cooperative Learning Lessons for Little Ones: Literature-Based Language Arts and Social Studies.* These references contain many good activity suggestions. A general reference that you should find valuable is Brubacher, Payne, and Rickett (1990), *Perspectives on Small Group Learning: Theory and Practice.* A good source of additional titles and other resources is the annual resource guide of *Cooperative Learning: The Magazine for Cooperation in Education.* The 1990 issue, edited by Nan and Ted Graves, *Cooperative Learning: A Resource Guide,* is Vol. 11, No. 1.

When a cooperative learning teaching method is used, the teacher should obtain feedback. A data collection instrument that can be used is provided in Appendix 15.6.

A data sheet on group participation is provided in Appendix 15.2. The authors suggest that students evaluate each other, and they provide a sample peer evaluation rubric (Appendix 15.7) that can be adapted to any age or grade.

Use the data collection instrument in Appendix 15.6 to help you analyze the cases that follow. Your instructor may pose specific questions for your response.

CASE 15.5 Cooperative Learning

Sharing Apples

In one group, five children sit facing each other. Jason is the "Writer" (recorder) and has a pencil and a sheet on which to record the group's answers. Samantha is the "Teller" (facilitator or chairperson), Arthur is the

"Happy Talker" (encourager), Angie is the "Reader," and Jeannie is the "Checker."

The group is working through three problems they have been assigned. Jason finishes recording the group's answer. As he finishes, Samantha says, "We're ready for the next problem. What's next?"

Angie looks at the card in her hand and reads, "Nathan and Roger, three-year-old twins, woke up from their nap at Daycare. A staff member was preparing an apple for each of them. Roger said, 'Cut my apple in lots of pieces. I want to have more apple than Nathan.' The staff member cut Nathan's apple into six pieces and Roger's into twelve. Who had the most apple?"

"The same," Jason states. "They both get the same."

Arthur says, "But twelve is more than six. Everybody knows that."

"Wait a minute," interjects Samantha. "They each get one apple, right? So how could anybody get more? The pieces get smaller when you cut more of them."

"What do you think, Angie?" asks Jeannie.

"Samantha's right," Angie responds. "They only have one apple each. The pieces are different, that's all. Do you get that, Arthur? The twelve pieces are still one apple, the same as the six. The kids still have one apple each."

"OK. Right, I see how that works," says Arthur.

"Does everybody agree the twins both get the same?" asks Jeannie. The group members show agreement. Jason writes, "Both kids get the same."

"You got the answer pretty fast, Jason and Samantha," says Arthur. "And did a good job of explaining it, Angie."

CASE 15.6 Cooperative Learning

Comparing Economic Systems Cooperatively

Ms. Asuko has heard that cooperative learning, particularly the group investigation method, can be effective for teaching high school students. She is a bit doubtful but resolves to give it a try with a grade 12 unit on comparative economic systems.

She begins, "You have been doing group work in my class and know what is expected of participants and the group leader to work together well as a team. The group effectiveness sheets you used have helped you to work productively. You have discovered that learning through group work is significant and also fun. We are going to try a special form of group work. It is a cooperative learning method called 'group investigation.'" She explains that four heterogeneous groups of seven will be established and each group will be assigned a subtopic and workspace. She says, "Reference materials will be made available in the room, and others can be obtained from the school library or other sources. I will introduce the topic and provide a common topical outline that is to be followed by each group. Each group will research a subtopic and decide how they can present it in an interesting way to the rest of the class. I will debrief what has been presented and you will take a test based on questions submitted by each group. Grades will be a combination of group and individual scores. The topic you will be investigating is comparative economic systems." Ms. Asuko then assigns students to groups by topic (fascism, communism, socialism, and capitalism) and writes a work and reporting schedule on the chalkboard.

Most students appear interested, but Arden, a bright high achiever, asks, "Do I have to be part of a group? Can I do it all by myself?" Ms. Asuko replies, "No, I know you can do a very good job by yourself, but working effectively with others is an important consideration. Besides, effective group investigation often results in a deeper understanding than is possible when something is done independently. Give it a 'provisional try' to see if I am right." She then begins to introduce students to the elements of an economic system before she is to provide an outline that each group is to follow as it investigates its subtopic.

The following day, Ms. Asuko moves students into their groups to do two "ice-breaker" and "get-to-know-each-other-better" exercises. She then asks students to decide how they will approach their investigation.

CASE 15.7 Cooperative Learning

Significant First Nations Leaders

Mr. Sylvester is working through a unit on First Nations cultures. He wants to explore significant leaders in First Nations history. He has collected several key names, such as Chief Sitting Bull and Geronimo. He has put together a reading pack on five important First Nations leaders. It would take some time to teach each, so Mr. Sylvester has decided on a jigsaw approach. He has divided the class into five groups. These are the home groups. Each member of the home group has been given a different First Nations leader information pack. He asks his students to get together with the others who have the same material. These are his expert groups. He has given each expert group the same guiding questions: (1) In what period of time did

the leader live? (2) In what region of North America? (3) Describe two significant events of the leader's life. (4) What was the leader's relationship with the white culture? (5) What main legacy did he leave?

The expert groups work away at their tasks. Some seem to have even broken into subgroups, with each working on one question. Mr. Sylvester then asks each expert to return to the home groups and complete a chart that outlines the names of the leaders and the answers to the questions. Mr. Sylvester is pleased with how hard the students have worked and he is looking forward to his discussion with the class. He is confident that each student will do well on the test he has prepared.

LINKING PRACTICE TO THEORY

What has been your experience with group work? What attitudes do you bring to the approach? How much preplanning seems to be involved? Many methods are suggested in this chapter. Try some of these and compare their strengths and weaknesses. Is more involved than you expected? What is the difference between collaborative and cooperative learning? Why is rapport with the whole class normally necessary before group work can be successful? What is the relationship between the theory in the text and the practice in your classroom? Were the guidelines helpful for giving meaning to your experiences?

Summary

Both collaborative and cooperative learning approaches stress teaching and learning from a "cooperative" rather than competitive or individualistic perspective. For either collaborative and cooperative learning to be effective, students must learn and use communication, interpersonal, and group skills.

Collaborative learning is an approach in which students interact or work together. Research shows that cooperative learning is effective, leading to greater academic achievement and positive social outcomes. Approaches to instruction in schools are often competitive, emphasizing individual achievement. This may not sit well with students from certain cultures. Students master knowledge by becoming experts in an area of knowledge and then by teaching this to other

groups. Cooperative learning teaching methods can be particularly effective in bringing diverse students together. Students with different learning styles can make good contributions to the achievement of a group. The role of the teacher is critical.

Cooperative learning approaches teaching and learning from a cooperative rather than competitive or individualistic perspective. Research supports its effectiveness for academic and social gains and for reducing prejudice and discrimination. Students are divided into heterogeneous groups that are task and reward interdependent.

A data collection instrument you can use to evaluate group effectiveness is provided in Appendix 15.8.

Activities

WORKING IN GROUPS

1. You have been, and are, a member of several groups. What did these experiences teach you about yourself? About the way groups can operate? About how groups should be led?
2. Think about a situation in which conflict occurred in a group in which you were a member. How was the conflict handled? Could it have been handled better? How?
3. Should there be a difference in opening procedures between a long- and a short-term group?
4. Examine the room you are in now. How can it be best set up for a group meeting?
5. What are the most important things to consider near the final stage of the group? What do you think the group should be considering during the termination stage? What strategies would you suggest?
6. Form a group of from five to seven members. A classroom is also a group, albeit fairly large. What can teachers do at the beginning of the year to establish a cohesive, productive group? Brainstorm the kinds of conflict that might arise in a typical classroom. Provide suggestions for solving each kind of conflict.
7. Marks are sometimes allocated for the product of groups and for group operation. What problems does this pose, and how might these be overcome?
8. Engage in a formal debate on the following topic. "Resolved that use of group techniques by a teacher usually results in more management and discipline problems than for a teacher who does not use this instructional approach."

COLLABORATIVE LEARNING

1. In the last chapter you were asked to consider how much you gained when you performed some activity alone. Consider when you enjoyed being with others. How much did you learn? What skills did you develop? Share your findings with others in your group.
2. Join four or five others to play the "Cardinal Principles" game. Members cooperate to build a ten-card house. Each person is given two cards. Preplanning is not permitted. Proceeding clockwise, each student contributes one card at a time. Only four cards can be touching the table top, and no more than two cards can be laid flat. Eight

minutes are given. Debrief on your learning and feelings, and implications for effective group operation for achieving a task and having a harmonious, cohesive group.
3. Take part in a class discussion on the advantages and disadvantages of small-group learning. Follow this with a discussion on how to overcome the disadvantages.
4. Join a subject-interest group. Given five minutes, brainstorm as many topics in a subject area as you can think of that could lend themselves to using a small-group teaching method.
5. Join a subject group to examine the question, "What special classroom management and control considerations are present in the teaching of the subject, and how can these be best handled?" Assign one or two group effectiveness evaluators to collect data and report.

COOPERATIVE LEARNING

1. To help you understand cooperative learning, view the Johnson and Johnson video on *Circles of Learning,* which shows elementary and secondary classrooms where cooperative learning is used. Keep these questions in mind: (1) How are cooperative learning essentials manifested in these classrooms? (2) What problems arise and how can they be overcome?
2. Get into subject groups. Make a chart on the following interactive approaches to instruction: brainstorming, guided discussion, forums, panels, investigative groups, open discussions, debates, problem-solving groups, tutorial groups. The chart should have the following headings: name of interactive approach, example of approach, value (e.g., Investigative Group, examination of Darwin's impact on biology, very useful).
3. Consider a class you remember well in which you were a student. Describe briefly the class as a social group. Consider the friendships, communication patterns, roles, influences, and the like. Describe the class as a work group. Was it teacher or student centered? How successful was the class as a whole? What do you think is the relationship between the class as a social group and as a work group?
4. Select a subject topic that would benefit from discussion (e.g., We should still study Shakespeare in

school; Shakespeare should be dropped and more modern authors studied). Plan the class as both a guided discussion and as an open discussion. What are the merits of each?

5. Examine the following group roles: initiator, contributor, clarifier, evaluator, harmonizer, recorder, summarizer, and encourager. On cards, state: (a) the role that most suits you, and (b) the roles of two of your university classmates. Share and discuss your findings.

6. Cooperative learning does not just happen. The focus is on "we as a group" and not "I as an individual." Students need many skills to be successful in cooperative learning. Brainstorm what these skills are.

7. Schools are becoming more diverse in terms of ethnic background, economic background, and cognitive ability. How can such diversity be used to create effective learning situations?

8. Learn cooperative learning methods by using one of them, Jigsaw. Follow these steps:

Step 1: Introduction and overview of the activity.
Step 2: Formation of heterogeneous "home" groups, each with five or six members.

Step 3: Review of group functions; decision to practice specific functions and to monitor and evaluate them.

Step 4: Formation of "expert" groups; each home group is represented in each expert group. Expert groups will be formed for each cooperative learning model: (a) Jigsaw, (b) STAD, (c) TGT (d) group investigation, (e) cooperative games, (f) cooperative learning and prejudice.

Step 5: Expert groups receive training and use special materials explaining their topic.

Step 6: Expert groups prepare their procedure for tutoring home groups.

Step 7: Experts tutor (explain and drill) their home groups. Material is provided to aid in this activity.

Step 8: Progress of home groups is checked and groups prepare for testing.

Step 9: Each individual is part of an evaluation process that covers all the approaches.

Step 10: Results are posted for each group.

Step 11: Monitoring of both expert and home groups is provided for.

Step 12: The process is analyzed with the whole class.

APPENDIX 15.1   *Analysis of Personal Behavior in Groups*

MY BEHAVIOR IN GROUPS

Directions: Please circle the number that most nearly represents your normal behavior.
1 = much more often than most, 2 = more often than most, 3 = about average for the group,
4 = once in a while, and 5 = rarely or never.

Task Functions

1. 1   2   3   4   5   I offer facts, opinions, suggestions, ideas, and other relevant information.

2. 1   2   3   4   5   I ask for facts, opinions, suggestions, ideas, and feelings from others.

3. 1   2   3   4   5   I am a starter who proposes things to do to initiate action in the group.

4. 1   2   3   4   5   I help develop plans for how to proceed and keep the group on task.

5. 1   2   3   4   5   I summarize what has occurred to date and the major points made.

6. 1   2   3   4   5   I am a coordinator who pulls ideas together and harmonizes activities.

7. 1   2   3   4   5   I diagnose the difficulties the group has in working to achieve goals.

8. 1   2   3   4   5   I energize (stimulate) the group to achieve a higher quality of work.

9. 1   2   3   4   5   I apply the test of reality or practicality of ideas and alternatives.

10. 1   2   3   4   5   I evaluate, compare the standards and goals of the group with group decisions and what was accomplished.

Maintenance Functions

11. 1   2   3   4   5   I encourage others to participate, accept them, and am open to their ideas,

12. 1   2   3   4   5   I help solve conflicts and try to harmonize differences in opinion.

13. 1   2   3   4   5   I help cool tensions by joking, suggesting fun approaches or breaks.

14. 1   2   3   4   5   I use interpersonal skills and make sure that others understand each other.

15. 1   2   3   4   5   I check the climate by determining how members feel about the way the group is working and each other.

16. 1   2   3   4   5   I observe the process the group is using and help discover its effectiveness.

17. 1   2   3   4   5   I remind the group about its goals and standards and help keep it on task.

18. 1   2   3   4   5   I actively listen to others and am receptive to others' ideas.

19. 1   2   3   4   5   I support openness, encourage risk and individuality, and thus build trust.

20. 1   2   3   4   5   I encourage open discussion to solve conflicts and increase togetherness.

Based on the summary of task and maintenance functions provided by David and Richard Johnson in Johnson, D., & Johnson, R. (2003). *Joining together: Group theory and group skills.* Boston: Allyn & Bacon.

APPENDIX 15.2 *Group Participation Data Collection*

Assign each group member a number. When a contribution is made, under the appropriate heading, enter that number with a brief description of the behavior.

Behavior Description

Initiating (getting discussion going, helping the group organize, keeping the group moving toward the goal)

Contributing (offering opinions, facts, anecdotes, or examples that help the group solve problems or move on)

Clarifying (helping make sure that terms, the problem, and group member contributions are understood by all, suggesting that added information is needed)

Summarizing (keeping the group on track by providing stage or concluding summaries and making sure that everybody knows where everybody stands on a topic)

Evaluating (keeping track of how well the group is progressing and in a constructive way pointing out problems that are being encountered)

Recording (recording main points, reading the record back to help recall what was done and to check for accuracy)

Encouraging (listening carefully, being friendly and accepting, complimenting good contributions or effort)

Harmonizing (keeping peace, relieving tension [e.g., humor], settling disputes, working out compromises)

APPENDIX 15.3   *Small-Group Planning Guide*

Subject and Grade Level _____

Unit Name _____   Lesson Topic _____

Statement of the small-group tasks

Objectives to be achieved

Size of groups

How students are to be assigned to groups

Time allotment

Materials needed for each group

Meeting place for each group

Instructions given to groups regarding how they are to go about achieving their tasks

Interpersonal or group skills targets for groups

Evaluation criteria and method for task achievement

Evaluation criteria for interpersonal or group skills

APPENDIX 15.4 *Small-Group Discussion Data Collection Instrument*

PROFESSIONAL TARGET—SMALL GROUP DISCUSSION

Describe the actions, statements made, and student reactions.

Group Discussion Consideration	Descriptive Observations
1. Set, objectives, and tie-in to lesson	
2. How students are assigned to groups	
3. Group meeting place and time allocation assignments	
4. Instructions for group operation regarding academic task	
5. Instructions re interpersonal and group skills to be used	
6. Behavior of students during group operation	
7. Teacher interventions during group operation	
8. Reporting by groups and debriefing	
9. Assessment of groups' effectiveness	

APPENDIX 15.5   *Discussion Data Collection Instrument*

PROFESSIONAL TARGET—DISCUSSION

Record what was said and done and the reaction of pupils.

Discussion Skills	Observations

A. Focusing on topic
    Way topic was introduced
    Establishment of aims
    Restating of aims
    Irrelevancies redirected?
    Periodic summaries?
    Dealing with off-task behavior

B. Clarification of answers
    Paraphrasing
    Summarizing
    Probing
    Elaborating
    Analyzing

C. Promoting participation
    Use of students' ideas
    Use of silence
    Challenging
    Key questions
    Providing information

D. Varying interaction
    Setting of ground rules
    Use of eye contact
    Encouraging participation/interaction
    Seeking agreements

E. Closing discussion
    Summarizing
    Evaluation of discussion effectiveness
    Proposal(s) for follow-up

APPENDIX 15.6 *Cooperative Learning Target*

PROFESSIONAL TARGET—USING COOPERATIVE LEARNING GROUPS

Please describe what is said and done and how students react.

Aspects of the Teacher's Role	Descriptive Comments

1. *Arranging groups*
   Group size
   Heterogeneous assignments
   Time allotments
   Physical arrangements
   Providing materials

2. *Provision for positive interdependence*
   Providing the mutual goal
   Requiring sharing of resources
   Establishing the group and individual rewards

3. *Skill development*
   Explaining roles
   Identifying the interpersonal and group skills
   Practicing the skills

4. *Setting the task and goal structure*
   Stating the task and goal structures
   Checking for understanding

5. *Monitoring and providing feedback*
   Circulating and observing
   Helping with task achievement
   Helping with group maintenance
   Providing and using group-effectiveness instruments
   Providing for student self-evaluation

6. *Assessment*
   Providing quizzes or tests
   Assigning group and/or individual grades
   Using bonus marks
   Other kinds of recognition

APPENDIX 15.7   *Peer Evaluation Rubric*

Directions: Answer the following questions with (1) indicating the lowest and (4) indicating the highest amount of points. Who was your partner?

Did this individual appropriately contribute to the group project?	1 2 3 4
Did this individual spend an appropriate amount of time developing materials?	1 2 3 4
Did this individual spend an appropriate amount of time typing?	1 2 3 4
Did this individual work collaboratively?	1 2 3 4
Was this individual motivated to help?	1 2 3 4
Did you have a positive experience collaborating with this individual?	1 2 3 4

Reflections: _____

_____

_____

_____

_____

_____

_____

APPENDIX 15.8 *Group Effectiveness Data*

GROUP EFFECTIVENESS DATA COLLECTION SHEET

A chairperson and one or two group-effectiveness data collectors are appointed or elected. Observations are recorded objectively and findings are reported. Agreement about group effectiveness is reached and plans for making the group more effective are formulated.

Behavior	Description of Behavior

A. Chairperson

1. Seeing that problem is clarified

2. Discussion initiated and kept moving

3. All phases of problem brought out

4. Discussion kept on topic

5. Participation of all members encouraged

6. Stage and concluding summaries used

7. Statements rephrased if needed

8. Objectivity

9. Listening skills demonstrated

10. All persons treated with respect

11. Thoughts of group accurately reported

B. Participants

1. All members contribute reasonable amount

2. Ideas stated clearly and concisely

3. Prejudices kept out

4. Keeping on topic

5. Storytelling, digressions, showing off avoided

6. Helping others—phrasing ideas, clarifying, encouraging, listening

7. Respecting other's ideas/opinions

8. Not ridiculing, ignoring

9. Helping summarize, conclude

16 Teaching for Thinking: Thinking Skills and Processes

Thinking Skills and Processes

Problem solving is natural to young children because the world is new to them. They exhibit curiosity, intelligence, and flexibility as they face new situations. The challenge . . . is to build on children's innate problem-solving inclinations and to preserve and encourage a disposition that values problem solving. (Trafton & Midgett, 2001, p. 532)

As you teach, you want your students to think both critically and creatively about the subject matter. How can you ask questions to get them to think deeply? Can a thinking skill taught in one subject be used in another subject? Do your students think about their own thinking? Do you value their opinions and encourage them to take risks and try new ideas?

The way teachers have been expected to teach has changed from transmission of knowledge (knowing content) to interpretation of knowledge (thinking about content), that is, that there should be much more emphasis on specifically teaching cognitive strategies. In other words, thinking skills and processes are highly important "content" too.

Recent focus on teacher effectiveness has been on acquisition of thinking skills (Peterson, Kromrey, Borg, & Lewis, 1990, p. 5). Research shows:

> Simply increasing teachers' awareness of the need to teach students how to think without providing training in the specific operations of teaching thinking has little chance of significantly changing classroom performance. . . . educators must systematically undertake specific training in higher order teaching in both preservice and inservice programs. (p. 10)

Eggen and Kauchak (2001) believe the best approach to teach for thinking occurs when it is taught explicitly *and* within the context of the regular curriculum (p. 343). Much earlier, Resnick (1987) said, "Higher order skills must suffuse the school program from kindergarten on and in every subject matter" (p. 48). An obstacle to the development of

OBJECTIVES

You will be able to:

1. Give reasons why thinking skills should be taught within the context of a subject.
2. Define and give examples of learning.
3. List examples of process and product learning.
4. Give examples of and use specific approaches to teaching thinking.
5. List and explain the advantages of higher-order thinking.
6. List and define thinking operations and core thinking skills.
7. Plan ways to encourage the development of dispositions needed for critical thinking.
8. Describe ways students can be taught critical and creative thinking skills.
9. Teach a cognitive skill and a cognitive process in a microteaching or classroom lesson.

Planning for Teaching a Thinking Skill

1. Specify skill label and definition
2. Determine the rules or steps in use of skill
3. Specify use of skill in the content studied
4. Decide how to model, explain, demo the skill
5. Decide how to provide guided/unguided practice
6. Decide how to evaluate
7. Decide how to transfer skill to other subjects
8. Decide how to transfer skill to life situations

Thinking Operations

Comparing

Classifying

Observing

Imagining

Hypothesizing

Criticizing

Collecting/organizing

Summarizing

Coding

Interpreting

Core Thinking Skills
(Marzano et al.)

Focusing

Information gathering

Remembering

Organizing

Analyzing

Generating

Integrating

Evaluating

Thinking Skills and Processes

Critical Thinking Procedures

Distinguish between facts and value claims

Discover reliability of sources

Check accuracy of statements

Distinguish between valid and invalid claims

Distinguish between what is irrelevant and irrelevant

Detect biases

Identify assumptions

Note the ambiguous/equivocal

Recognize inconsistencies

Determine argument strength

Thinking Creatively
(Rothstein)

Welcome class climate

Encourage exploration

Provide school time

Encourage broad interests

Foster the belief students can be more creative

Teach what's involved in being creative

Encourage acquisition and creative use of information

thinking skills is the growing demand for schools to teach more and more facts and information. "The idea that knowledge must be acquired first and that its application to reasoning and problem solving can be delayed is a persistent one in educational thinking" (p. 48).

Beyer (1998) notes that teachers can provide a classroom learning environment that makes thinking possible and students willing to engage in it. You can make the invisible substance of thinking visible for students. This can provide students with an explicit

The PBL Classroom

Teacher is facilitator/
co-learner/mentor/guide

Faculty work in teams

Faculty structure is flexible

Students take responsibility/
create partnerships

Structured problem is basis for
course/motivation through
real-life problems

Student initiative encouraged

Environment is collaborative
and supportive

"One right answer" approach is
is discouraged

Students evaluate themselves

**Creating a PBL Learning
Experience**

1. Identify a problem

2. Connect problem to
students' world for authentic
opportunities

3. Organize subject matter
around the problem

3. Students define learning
experience and plan how
to solve problem

4. Encourage collaboration
through learning teams

5. Students show results
through a product or
performance

**Problem-Based
Learning (PBL)**

PBL Characteristics

• Student centered

• Small groups

• Teacher as facilitator

• Problems as focus and stimulus
for learning

• Problems vehicles for developing
problem-solving skills

• Gain new information through
self-directed learning

guide and support for when they encounter difficult or complex thinking operations. Teachers should integrate instruction in thinking as they teach subject matter.

Importance of Thinking Skills and Processes

There is much controversy about the term *intelligence.* It is not easily quantified, and the debate about effects on intelligence of nature and of environment is ongoing. Intelligence is increasingly viewed as a set of *thinking skills and processes* that can be separately taught and learned. Of course, thinking skills are never "content" free; they are generic to, and can be applied to, all school subjects and used in daily life. While some believe "thinking" is a matter of innate intelligence, many authorities acknowledge that "thinking" should

TCP—THINKING SKILLS

Uses specific instruction in the nature and use of thinking skills and processes

Specific instruction in the nature and use of thinking skills and processes; emphasis on problem-solving and critical thinking skills; objectives and evaluation reflect emphasis on thinking skill acquisition; asks many "why" and "what if" questions.

Sole focus on facts and information of an area of study; "right answer" emphasis; no opportunity for problem solving or critical thinking.

Incorporates key thinking operations and core thinking skills into teaching

Key thinking operations such as comparing and classifying are a key part of teaching, as are the core thinking skills such as organizing and analyzing.

Teaching tends to focus on basic factual information that is accepted at face value without organizing material into new patterns through comparison, classification, and analysis.

Ensures that students use critical thinking procedures

Ensures students are familiar with the difference between facts and value claims, and that they check for bias, validity, and relevance in their research.

Students tend to accept all information at face value; little attempt by students to check material for bias, validity, and relevance; students unaware of critical thinking procedures.

be taught directly. They argue that there never is enough time to teach all the information that could usefully be taught and that we should reduce the time spent on teaching specific information and focus instead on teaching thinking skills. This is in harmony with the view of the teacher as a "learning facilitator" rather than an "information disseminator." The teacher, therefore, needs to facilitate transfer from one portion of a school subject to another, from one school subject to another, and from school to life. Perhaps the most important aspect of direct teaching of thinking as a skill is that it builds a youngster's self-image as a "thinker." Importantly, *problem-based learning* has been developed to help students acquire thinking skills and processes. In problem-based learning, students are presented with meaningful (authentic) situations to develop investigative, inquiry, and decision-making skills.

Also important is meta-cognition (thinking about one's thinking). Kuiper (2002), in a study of nursing practice and education, believes, "once learned, metacognition supports lifelong reflective thinking in divergent situations, enables one to handle ambiguity, assists with problem solving, promotes responsibility for actions, and fosters development of self-confidence for rapid decision making" (p. 78).

Organizing Knowledge and Learning

Learners can handle new information better if they understand how to organize it into patterns. Some approaches examined later in this chapter are coding and classification systems, comparing and contrasting, and sequencing.

Schooling must help students acquire strategies to organize information. Learners need ways to accomplish academic tasks. They need learning strategies (operating steps or patterns) to infer, predict, summarize, or hypothesize. Learning is *strategic,* in that there can be procedures or ways of executing a skill.

When students use certain learning strategies well, memory and comprehension are improved. Pressley and Harris (1990, p. 32) provide examples of effective strategies: summarization, imagery (creating an internal visual image of the content), activating prior knowledge (relating what is known to new content), self-questioning (composing questions that cut across different parts of the content), and question answering (teaching students to analyze questions as a part of attempting to answer them). When students can carry out a certain learning strategy well, they should be helped to learn when to use the strategy in new contexts across the curriculum—teaching for transfer.

The Importance of Thinking Well and Wisely

Sternberg (2003) suggests that the conventional approach to teaching creates "pseudo-experts"—students with expertise that does not mirror what is needed in real-world situations. He says we should teach for wisdom, "teaching them to think in the ways experts do" (p. 5). He suggests that teaching for *analytical thinking* means encouraging students to analyze, critique, judge, compare and contrast, evaluate, and assess; teaching for *creative thinking* means encouraging students to create, invent, discover, "imagine if," "suppose that," and predict; and teaching for *practical thinking* means encouraging students to apply, use, put into practice, implement, employ, and render practical what they know (p. 5).

In preparing students to think like experts, we "should teach children not only to think well, but also wisely" (p. 7). He claims, "those who have not learned to think wisely exhibit five characteristic fallacies in thinking" (p. 7):

1. The fallacy of unrealistic optimism (People think that they are so smart they do not think through what they do.)
2. The fallacy of egocentrism (People think the world centers around them. Wisdom requires one to know what one knows and does not know as well as what can be known and cannot be known.)
3. The fallacy of omniscience (People feel that they are not only experts in their fields, but also all-knowing about pretty much everything.)
4. The fallacy of omnipotence (The belief that if knowledge is power, then omniscience is total power. People who are in positions of power imagine themselves to be all-powerful.)
5. The fallacy of invulnerability (People's view that if they are all-knowing and all-powerful, they can do what they want.)

"Wisdom," Sternberg says, "is the use of successful intelligence and experience toward the attainment of a common good" (p. 7). This involves balancing three kinds of interests that should be informed by values: (1) intrapersonal (one's own); (2) interpersonal (other people's); (3) extrapersonal (more than personal—institutional).

Schools, then, should "consider the development of expertise in wisdom to be an important goal" (p. 7). This is because knowledge does not in itself create wisdom; wisdom provides a way to make important decisions and render important judgments, and wisdom represents an avenue to creating a better, more harmonious world (p. 7). Sternberg concludes that "an augmented conception of expertise takes into account wise and intelligent use of knowledge" (p. 8).

Classic Teaching Approaches

> Just as a traditional architect might borrow the fundamental elements and signature styling from a master architect, such as Frank Lloyd Wright, educators borrow from master craftspeople. They borrow from master cognitive psychologists and neurobiologists who have helped shape structures for the intellect. (Fogarty, 1999, p. 76)

Useful approaches are available to the novice teacher who wishes to teach thinking skills. The following names will be familiar. *John Dewey,* an American educator, was ahead of his time in suggesting that teachers must encourage the thinking and reflection of the child through the child's interaction with the world. Dewey wrote, "I believe that the only true education comes through the stimulation of the child's powers by the demands of the social situations in which he finds himself" (1933, p. 1). His writings make significant reading even today. *Jean Piaget,* a Swiss psychologist, recorded his observations of how children think. Many accept his model of child development and learning. To Piaget, the child cannot engage in certain intellectual tasks until he or she is psychologically ready. Children construct meaning—a concept further developed by Vygotsky and Bruner. Children are innately curious, love learning and asking questions. *Lev Vygotsky* (1978), a Russian psychologist, emphasized the social aspect of learning. He said, "Every function in the child's cultural development appears twice: first, on the social level, and later, on the individual level; first, between people (interpsychological) and then inside the child (intrapsychological). This applies equally to voluntary attention, to logical memory, and to the formation of concepts. All the higher functions originate as actual relationships between individuals" (p. 57). Vygotsky is known for the concept of the *zone of proximal development* (ZPD), the relationship between a student's actual and potential levels of development.

Other significant approaches to teaching thinking skills were developed by Bruner, Bloom, Wasserman, and Marzano.

Bruner: Content and Process

As early as 1967, Jerome Bruner introduced a theory of instruction that examined the relationship between *content* and *process*. Process is the cluster of diverse operations that surround the acquisition and use of knowledge. Through process, we use knowledge as a system for learning in contrast to only amassing information. Bruner said that curriculum should reflect not only the nature of knowledge, but also the process of acquiring it. Instruction should include the steps (stages, patterns, and behaviors) necessary to attain concepts or generalizations or to perform skills. Students need to learn the knowledge acquisition process to function well in a changing world.

Kearsley (2004) states that for Bruner, "learning is an active process in which learners construct new ideas or concepts based upon their current/past knowledge," and that "as far as instruction is concerned, the instructor should try and encourage students to discover principles by themselves. The instructor and student should engage in an active dialog (i.e., socratic learning). The task of the instructor is to translate information to be learned into a format appropriate to the learner's current state of understanding."

For Bruner, "a theory of instruction should address four major aspects: (1) predisposition towards learning, (2) the ways in which a body of knowledge can be structured so that it can be most readily grasped by the learner, (3) the most effective sequences in which to present material, and (4) the nature and pacing of rewards and punishments.

Good methods for structuring knowledge should result in simplifying, generating new propositions, and increasing the manipulation of information" (Kearsley, 2004).

Note again the emphasis on the thinking skills elements of discovery, active dialogue, building on what has been learned, and learner readiness.

Bloom's Taxonomy

Benjamin Bloom's cognitive taxonomy has been the most prevalent model for the teaching and learning of thinking skills. Many studies have used this taxonomy, hundreds of publications have referred to it, and many courses of study have been and are based on it. Many educators find the taxonomy useful as an instructional and evaluation tool. The taxonomy is described in Chapter 3.

Some authorities have concerns about Bloom's cognitive taxonomy and believe that teaching thinking skills should be done differently. Some instructional experts do not hold the notion that "knowledge" is low level and rote, but that knowledge often can be viewed in a more comprehensive way, it may be process or product, and declarative, procedural, or conditional. Few authorities now, including those who believe in Bloom's taxonomy, think the levels are strictly hierarchical or that learning must occur in a linear way.

Wasserman's Thinking Operations

Raths, Wasserman, Jonas, and Rothstein (1967) suggest that thinking skills or operations pertain to any school subject and level and that these can be taught. Their classification system is still widely used. By focusing attention on the teaching of thinking operations, they helped educators go beyond teaching for memorization of information. This is a good place for student teachers to start. By planning lessons that include a procedural (thinking skill or process) objective, you can modify your teaching to incorporate thinking skills. Raths, Wasserman, and Wasserman (1978, pp. 7–29) describe the following thinking operations.

1. *Comparing.* In the operation of comparing, students look for *similarities and differences.* We may choose two items for comparison that have a close relationship (e.g., two musical instruments); alternatively, we can select items that have more subtle relationships (e.g., a train and a caterpillar). Steps in comparing are (a) details are observed, (b) similarities are sought and sorted, (c) searching/sorting for differences, and (d) summarizing (in a list). Comparing activities lead students to additional insights and awareness. As a result of many experiences in making comparisons, students learn how to observe perceptively and compare before drawing conclusions.

2. *Observing.* When we are observing, we can make visual observations of data. Observing also can involve listening, touching, or smelling. The sense evidence used must be checked for accuracy. Students must be made aware of the possibility of distortion and thus false inference and misinterpretation. We want perceptiveness, acuity, and accuracy. Reporting is needed for the accuracy of observation to be checked. Observing should lead to more accurate data on which to base conclusions, and to greater understanding. Like any other skill, practice is required for proficiency.

3. *Classifying.* Classifying involves examining an assortment of items and sorting them into related groups. Each grouping is given a name. When they are classifying, students can process data mentally and organize them systematically. Ability to classify helps us bring order into our lives. Classifying requires three steps: (a) examining data, (b) creating categories, and (c) placing items in categories. The first two require advanced mental

activity and the third requires lower mental skills. We usually should avoid providing students with the categories so that students can exploit the full cognitive potential of this operation. Classification involves discovery of similarities and differences (as in comparing). Students should discover that, though a number of groupings are possible, each must have internal consistency. Normally, only one principle at a time is operative as groupings are established.

4. *Imagining.* For imagining, students are asked to let their minds travel to whatever vistas they can invent, to create freely and to exercise that part of the mind that often goes untapped. In imagining there is a release from rules and regulations and unbinding from data. Divergent thinking is promoted. Imagining leads to creations and inventions; it brings humor, joy, spontaneity, and beauty into our lives. A feeling of accomplishment and enhanced self-concept can result from this rich inner resource.

5. *Hypothesizing.* For the hypothesizing operation, students are to come up with a variety of possible explanations (hunches) for a question, problem, or situation. Hypothesizing involves identifying alternative possibilities and deciding which have the most credibility. High school students can be asked to go a step further to find ways of testing their hypotheses (which carries the operation to greater sophistication). Steps can be: (a) present the problem, (b) have students suggest ways to solve the problem, (c) have these ways considered and combined if appropriate, (d) ask students to anticipate what would happen if suggested solutions were tried, and (e) have students select a hypothesis. Hypothesizing helps free us from dogmatic assertions, from seeing life from only one perspective, and from "black or white" judgments. It lets students deal with problems in school learning and in their daily lives.

6. *Criticizing.* In the criticizing operation we ask students to "evaluate," "make judgments," and "offer opinions" to sharpen their sense of what is desirable or undesirable, high or low quality, and significant or trivial. Students should specify the *criteria* (standards) they use in making judgments. They should identify the evidence on which their judgments were made. Criticizing lets students use a higher level of cognition and sharpen the thinking skills that will improve the quality of their lives.

7. *Looking for assumptions.* Making an assumption means taking something for granted. In situations where a conclusion is drawn or a decision is being made, one or more assumptions enter. What we take for granted (or assume) may only be "probably true" or "probably false." Through this operation students can learn to identify assumptions (ones made themselves or those made by others). Learning to differentiate between what is assumed to be true and what is observable fact is at the heart of logical reasoning. Discrimination—scrutiny of assumptions—should occur. When students become skilled at identifying and examining assumptions, they will be less susceptible to propaganda, seductive advertising, and accepting experimental data as proof and conclusions as "right." They will be less likely to leap to conclusions that are based on limited data and less impulsive in their actions. Studying and practicing this skill is particularly important.

8. *Collecting and organizing data.* The ability to collect and organize information requires several skills: (a) locating information (deciding what are the proper references or appropriate sources, then locating those sources); (b) examining the data and selecting those that are relevant to the inquiry; (c) developing procedures that allow data to be assembled; and finally, (d) organizing data. That is, once sources are identified and tapped, the information culled and gathered, data should be organized. It can be organized into essays, reports, research proposals, menus, almanacs, and bibliographies, to name a few possibilities. Organizing data systematically, logically, and coherently is a complex task and sharpens our ability to locate and comprehend information.

9. *Summarizing.* Summarizing requires condensing and distilling the core message from a piece of work. Students must be able to state, briefly and coherently, the main ideas of something they have heard, seen, or read. Summarizing should be concise but not miss the big ideas. It involves differentiating between what is important and what may be left out. Summarizing skills increase students' abilities to understand. They develop the ability to discriminate and to discern the relevant from irrelevant, significant from insignificant, and consequential from trivial.

10. *Coding.* Codes communicate ideas in "shorthand." For example, an editor uses a shorthand code to communicate aspects of a manuscript to an author. As a thinking operation, coding is a shorthand system for pointing out thought patterns or expressions in the writings or speech of others. To illustrate, the code "X" can be used to identify extreme words and phrases such as "always," "never," "everybody" or "the best," "the worst," or "the only." "E-O" can be used to point out words and expressions of the "either–or" type. "Q" could be "qualifying expressions." "V" can be used to designate "value statements." As students use coding to examine utterances of others, they become more responsible for what they say.

11. *Interpreting.* Interpreting involves explaining the meaning that an experience (story, event, picture, film, poem, graph, chart, joke, body language, etc.) has for us. When we interpret, we put meaning into, and take meaning out of, a body of data. Our interpreting ability is dependent on how well we "read messages." We may misinterpret, which can get us into trouble. Sometimes we miss the meaning. Or we may generalize on insufficient evidence (going beyond the data to draw conclusions). Skillful interpretation increases meaning and understanding; continually misinterpreting severely handicaps the ability to understand and derive satisfaction from experiences.

Marzano's Core Thinking Skills Approach

A second approach to teaching basic thinking operations, that of Marzano, Brandt, Hughes, Jones, Presseisen, Rankin, and Suhor (1988), places core thinking skills into a schema or framework. It sets out eight major categories that are closely related to the steps one might follow in problem solving. Within the master schema, there are twenty-one subprocesses. With this framework, teachers can gradually understand how to use the skills.

Facts and information are the important raw materials for thinking. Knowing how, and having the skills to access and use these to "think," is at least as important! Marzano et al. suggest *core thinking skills* that occur in thinking processes. It should be noted the skills are not always sequenced exactly as in the pattern presented. These skills are outlined in the Hughes (Hughes & Jones, 1988) model (Figure 16.1).

- *Focusing.* Focusing occurs as we (1) define the problem (what is it, who has it, examples of it, when it must be solved, and what makes it a problem) and (2) set goals (short- and long-term outcomes).
- *Information gathering.* Information-gathering skills are brought to play as we (3) observe (pick relevant information) and (4) ask questions (clarify issues and meanings).
- *Remembering.* Remembering takes place when we (5) encode (repeat information, use associations or mnemonics; new information to make it accessible when needed) and when we (6) recall (bring to consciousness, surface when, where, or how information was originally learned).

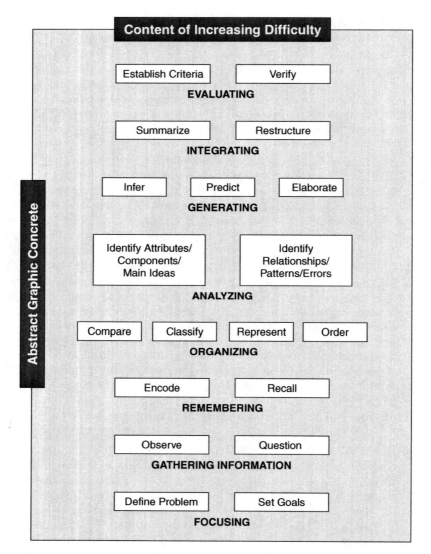

FIGURE 16.1 *Core Thinking Skills—The Hughes Model*
Source: Hughes & Jones, 1988; Marzano, Brandt, Hughes, Jones, Presseisen, Rankin, & Suhor, 1988.

- *Organizing.* Information is organized through (7) comparing (identifying similarities and differences), (8) classifying (grouping, categorizing, or sequencing items), (9) ordering, and (10) representing (showing how elements are related).
- *Analyzing.* This information is analyzed and checked for accuracy as (11) attributes and components are identified (recognizing, putting parts into a whole), (12) relationships and patterns are determined (identifying interrelationships), (13) main ideas and (14) errors are identified.

- *Generating.* We may generate new ideas by (15) inferring (identifying what reasonably may be true), (16) predicting (anticipating what will likely happen), and (17) elaborating (adding details, explanations, and giving examples).
- *Integrating.* We integrate what we have learned and come to a solution through (18) summarizing (condensing, selecting, and combining) and (19) restructuring (combining new knowledge with old into something new).
- *Evaluating.* So we can evaluate, (20) criteria are established and the solution is (21) verified. (pp. 68–114)

Carolyn Hughes (Hughes & Jones, 1988) adds a useful visual view (Figure 16.1) of the Marzano et al. skills. She thinks that content can be of increasing difficulty and that teachers should recognize that teaching/learning experiences (concrete, graphic, and abstract) should match learner readiness. Other approaches to core skills are Beyer's (1984) decision-making steps, and Baron and Sternberg's (1987) suggestions for selecting training skills programs.

Linking New Information to Prior Knowledge

Jones, Palincsar, Ogle, and Carr (1987) observe that researchers believe "information is stored in memory in [interrelated] knowledge structures called schemata" (p. 7). Learners draw on these memory banks as they reflect and make plans (p. 7). This is apparent when a person links previous experience to the solution of a problem or when he compares previous attempts to solve a problem (p. 8)—meta-cognition is involved. The ability to link new information with previous experiences is affected by several factors. One's perspective affects how new information is viewed (e.g., perspectives differ if a person views a proposed building site from an excavation-cost frame of reference rather than effect on environmental). Other variables relate to the characteristics of the learner. Lack of information or unorganized information can limit a person's ability to see patterns, chunk information, or derive analogies, and recognize similarities and differences between problems (p. 9).

Research shows that (1) success in learning situations often depends on the presence of specific previous knowledge, and (2) having prior knowledge is not enough if it cannot be accessed or if the learner cannot relate it to new information. It is important to build on what students know and the skills they have learned. Students may already know how to compare or paraphrase. For example, students must have learned, or must learn, skills such as encoding, organizing, and retrieving information (Jones et al., 1987, pp. 9–10).

Jones et al. (1987) contend that less able students may need explicit instruction in the use of thinking skills and that content and skills instruction should be adjunct to minimize interference. Instruction in strategic skills for the less able should have a strong content emphasis, and application to content areas should receive much attention. Instruction for other students should include thinking skills "within the context of content courses" (p. 17). Stress the transfer of strategic skills to alternative content areas.

Current Issues and Teaching Approaches

The Importance of Process

The *California Assessment Program* includes processes in measuring science and mathematics. Distinguishing between content and process learning is similar to distinguishing between subject-centered and child-centered education. It can be said that process learning is learning for the future, and content learning is learning about those things already discovered, formulated, restructured, and deemed important.

Teachers need to provide for the learning of process. A major decision in teaching is deciding when to extract procedural knowledge from the whole act. The dilemma of whether to teach a process directly or in the context of (embedded in) the curriculum is a concern. Both approaches are appropriate at times, and both are essential. If process is taught directly, provision must be made for transfer.

It is increasingly apparent that teaching for thinking must be a top educational priority if high school graduates are to take their place in our technically oriented society. Current school programs are not adequate. Much more school time must be devoted to thinking skills and integration of these across the K–12 curriculum. Too many students cannot respond effectively and critically to their environment.

An approach to the teaching of process you can use is shown in Figure 16.2. Be aware that teaching process is complicated and requires time and energy. In the long run, emphasis on processes can help achieve the more general goals of education. You will need to learn how to assess "process" learning. If you resort to "product" assessment only, the original purpose is defeated (see Baron & Sternberg, 1987, p. 224). Proper assessment requires the student to apply the process in a new context to see if transfer has occurred.

Processes normally include two or more thinking skills. All humans, by their very nature, are thinkers. As teachers, we want to help students think better, regardless of developmental stage. In addition to basic skills and facts, it is possible to identify higher-order skills and advance knowledge, that is, *content* and *process*. A danger is overemphasis on replication and application and underemphasis on *associative uses* or webs of associations students have and the *interpretive uses* or translation of ideas and giving meaning.

FIGURE 16.2   *Product- and Process-Oriented Classrooms*

The Product-Oriented Classroom	The Process-Oriented Classroom
− The teacher emphasizes, "What did you do?"	+ The teacher also emphasizes, "How did you do it?"
− Tasks revolve around items of content.	+ Tasks involve a "process" of learning.
− The answer is most important.	+ The means of finding an answer is as important as the answer.
− The teacher believes there is a body of content.	+ The teacher recognizes that content is only one component of the learning process to cover.
− The teacher evaluates the product.	+ The teacher also evaluates the process.
− The student "does."	+ The student "does" and thinks about what s/he did.
− The student often lacks an awareness of how s/he learns.	+ The student has a growing awareness of how s/he learns and can learn.
− Learning takes place through factual knowledge acquisition.	+ Learning occurs when students work through a process in which knowledge is manipulated and restructured to reach insight.
− Problem-solving skills develop automatically while learning the content.	+ Problem-solving skills develop while learning content and reflection on the process occurs while working with content.

Source: Contact, Canada Studies Foundation, Toronto.

Education must move beyond memory to educating minds. This is what schooling *should* be about. An approach to the teaching of process is illustrated in Figure 16.3.

There are three promising approaches to the teaching of thinking: *stand-alone, embedding,* and *immersion.* There is considerable material available to help you teach thinking skills through the stand-alone approach, for example, material by Wasserman (1978). Over the years, hundreds of workshops have treated teaching for thinking, critical thinking, and creative thinking in a generic way. The embedding approach builds thinking skills into the regular school subjects, as does the immersion approach. In the former, but not in the latter, thinking skills are made explicit. Embedding is the most commonly accepted. For most students, it is necessary to be explicit. In general, teachers must decide when practice on specific skills is necessary for automaticity. Better understanding occurs when skills are extracted and studied in isolation *as well as* in context. Apparently, "to be caught, it must be taught," and if transfer is to occur to other parts of a subject, to other subjects, and to life, this, too, must be "taught."

Not all basic knowledge should be taught before thinking skills. For instance, various forms of sequencing can be taught at an early age, and young learners can be taught and encouraged to develop their own sequencing system. The classroom should be interactive and activity oriented to foster learning and applying thinking processes and skills.

Teachers need to make decisions about the timing and activities for learning explicit cognitive skills and see that these skills are transferred to various contexts. This is especially true with young learners and those who have difficulty with the processes. Very often, those who complain about achievement in schooling are actually complaining about the lack of use of these skills in higher education and the workplace. Paul (1990) believes the issue is complex. The teacher must make decisions to assure growth in both procedural knowledge and system use and meaning, or the atomistic versus the holistic dilemma.

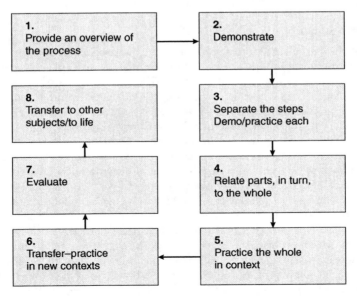

FIGURE 16.3 *An Approach to the Teaching of Process*

Dialectical Thinking

Another level of thinking to include in your teaching is the *dialectical.* "The first characteristic of dialectical thinking is that it places all the emphasis on change. . . . the second characteristic . . . is that it states that the way change takes place is through conflict and opposition" Rowan (2004). Using dialectical thinking is a bit like arguing with yourself. Barry and Rudinow (1994) believe that *dialectical thinking* is the ability to reflect critically on personal thinking and to reason sympathetically using a frame of reference distinct from or even opposed to that frame of reference. This could be called *reflective self-criticism.* Though Barry and Rudinow's suggestions are more appropriate for middle years and high school students, they can be adapted for elementary students.

The first step in the Barry and Rudinow plan is to pose a question for discussion, without presupposing a position. After preliminary discussion and clarification, students take positions they prepare to defend. They ask questions about the other positions and answer questions on their view. In teams with predetermined positions, various roles can be assigned and reassigned for practice. Then, each team prepares a defense to a position to which it was initially opposed. The exercise is recorded so students can review and critique their performances. Variations of this strategy can be created.

Affective and Cognitive Strategies

An excellent web site, The Critical Thinking Community (www.criticalthinking.org) gives a strategy list of thirty-five dimensions of critical thought. It shows how the list can be used in remodeled lesson plans that add the critical thinking dimension. The full list is at www.criticalthinking.org/resources/TRK12-strategy-list.shtml.

Although Pettus and Blosser (2002) think it is important to teach thinking skills to students, they believe "students can creatively develop numerous strategies to aid their recall of information and concepts. Frequently, they develop more up-to-date and relevant strategies and devices than their teachers" (p. 14).

Problem Solving

Students face problems every day, whether with schoolwork, peers, or at home. Students approach problems in four ways: (1) they ignore the problem and hope it will go away, (2) they ignore the problem and don't care if it goes away, (3) they attempt to solve the problem as best they can even though they do not have training in problem solving, or (4) they approach the problem in a sound and systematic way, having been taught how to do this. You can help students follow the fourth approach.

Problem solving requires the application of knowledge and skills to obtain a solution or achieve a goal. Transfer of learning to a new situation must occur. Problem solving has two aspects: recalling or acquiring the information needed to solve a problem, and following an effective problem-solving procedure.

At one time it was thought that problem solving should follow a sequence of problem definition, suggesting possible causes of the problem (hypotheses), and testing each hypothesis. The modern approach is based on what has been learned about how people process information. Expert problem solvers do not begin by suggesting a large number of hypotheses and then testing each one. First they narrow the problem down by deciding the key features of the problem and relating these to information they have at their fingertips or can look up. Then they pick one or a few hypotheses for testing. This approach is time saving and works well because experts do not spend time investigating low-probability hypotheses. The approach requires rapid and accurate problem definition and pattern recognition. Students can be taught how to seek patterns, strategies, and thinking skills they can use to solve problems.

Sternberg (1990) emphasizes that students should discover problems for themselves. Life problems are not well structured, so application of rigid steps often does not work. School problems are usually decontextualized. Problem-solving steps may work for text problems but not "real" ones. Students who care about a problem, because it is theirs, are motivated to face it. Schools normally stop short of being practical; it is important to provide for transfer to life. Sternberg emphasizes that students must be taught how to plan to solve problems and the thinking skills to use.

Begin by having students learn problem-solving steps. When you do this, you help them discover how they like to represent problems—some can just think of the key features, others need to write these down, and others need a visual representation. While we should learn from experience, we often are prisoners of our experiences. Students can learn from experience, to break the chains of tradition and strive for novelty. Real-life problems rarely have a single solution, so students should guard against a "one-right-answer" expectation. At times a problem can be set aside for a while; after incubating, the answer may seem to "jump out." Rothstein (1990) suggests things you can do to help students improve their problem-solving ability.

- *Provide a climate that allows risk taking.* Encourage students to look at problems creatively and provide incubation time. Be accepting and sensitive to students' feelings.
- *Show students how to define the problem.* A problem that is well defined is "half-solved." Make sure students recognize the need to define the problem before they start to solve it. Help them learn to seek the essential features of the problem.
- *Teach students how to do problem analysis.* They should learn to differentiate between essential and nonessential information. Have them ask what materials they have to work with and how these can be used to solve the problem.
- *Have students learn to generate hypotheses.* They should not seek a hypothesis prematurely. Provide instruction and practice in the important skill of brainstorming.
- *Show students how to evaluate each hypothesis.* Students should learn not to jump to conclusions. Have them set criteria for evaluating hypotheses and record the implications or consequences of several hypotheses. Then have them select the best or combine hypotheses.
- *Teach students to recognize factors that affect problem solving.* Factors that influence problem-solving ability are acquiring the necessary information, defining the problem, and letting the problem incubate.
- *Show students how to use analogies.* Encourage students to seek cases that are similar to their problem and the solutions that were successful for these. This reduces the number of errors that will be made and the time needed to solve a new problem.
- *Have students practice solving problems and provide feedback.* They should be encouraged while they are practicing, and feedback should focus on the problem-solving process used rather than getting "the right answer" (pp. 268–270).

Problem-based learning is examined further later in this chapter.

Thinking and Decision Making

Decision making involves making a selection from among alternatives. It is a process (like problem solving, conceptualizing, and reflective thinking) that involves several thinking skills. *Decision making* usually involves (1) stating the desired goal or condition; (2) stating the obstacles; (3) identifying alternatives for overcoming each obstacle; (4) examining alternatives in terms of resources needed and constraints to their use; (5) ranking alternatives in terms of probable consequences; and (6) choosing the best alternative.

Using Questioning to Encourage Thinking

Questioning techniques were discussed in Chapter 10. Questions can be categorized into a hierarchy from low-level (facts and comprehension) through application to high-level (analysis, synthesis, and evaluation). Emphasis on higher-cognitive questions is more effective, particularly for students of average and high ability, while emphasis on fact questions is effective in mastery of basic skills (particularly for lower-ability students). Teachers often emphasize closed, single-right-answer, low-level questions, when emphasis on open-ended, higher-cognitive-level questions would be more effective. You learned how the use of probes and redirects can lead to higher-level thinking and that teacher acceptance of student ideas is positively correlated with student learning gains. Wait time of at least three seconds is critical, particularly for higher-level questions. Students should be encouraged to respond, and responses should be balanced among volunteers and nonvolunteers. Correct responses should be acknowledged, and praise should be used specifically and discriminately. The quality of teacher questioning, use of encouragement, and involvement and acceptance of students are important. The way you respond during question and answer affects whether thinking skills are being developed. Students should feel accepted, able to take risks; and using open-ended questions and sufficient wait time encourages thinking.

Examples of questions that encourage thinking are provided by King (1990). These questions and other ideas on encouraging thinking are available at the University of Texas at Austin's Division of Instructional Information and Assessment web site, www.utexas .edu/academic/diia/gsi/coursedesign/advanced.php.

- How would you use . . . to . . . ?
- What is a new example of . . . ?
- Explain why. . . .
- What do you think would happen if . . . ?
- What is the difference between . . . and . . . ?
- How are . . . and . . . similar . . . ?
- What is a possible solution to the problem of . . . ?
- What conclusions can you draw about . . . ?
- How does . . . affect . . . ?
- In your opinion, which is best . . . ? Why?
- What are the strengths and weaknesses of . . . ?
- Do you agree/disagree with this statement: . . . ?
- How is . . . related to . . . that we studied . . . ?

Symptoms present in classrooms with little encouragement for student thinking are:

- Extreme impulsiveness (emphasis is on doing, without much thinking behind it)
- Overdependency ("Tell me what to do, teacher")
- Dogmatic assertions ("Don't confuse me with data, my mind is made up")

- Inability to apply learned principles to new situations ("What am I s'pozed to do here?")
- Over-anti-intellectualism ("It's your job to tell us what to do")

Traditional expository teaching, characterized by teacher-dominated explaining, telling how, and showing, makes students passive rather than active. Learners need to be involved in acquiring knowledge. Provide acceptance, support, probes, and encouragement to think. Learning that emphasizes thinking is fragile, involving emotions, pressures, and the self-concept of students, dynamics of the class group, and the attitudes of the teacher.

Teaching for Thinking and Transfer

One of the most debated issues in the teaching of thinking is transfer. If you want transfer, teach for it. It should be emphasized in both the set and closure of a lesson and used gradually in more contexts until it is applied in contexts in which learners themselves seek transfer from previous learning.

Acquisition of thinking skills or processes includes *declarative* knowledge. Like a concept, the meaning of a process is always under construction. Thinking processes can even be taught to very young children through activity-oriented classrooms that have many opportunities for idea construction. Unfortunately, a recent study of first graders doing reading seatwork found that getting an activity done was more important than making sense of what they were doing. This suggests that teachers should emphasize the understanding and use of thinking skills.

Evaluation and Thinking

Not only should thinking skills be taught directly, they also should be part of evaluations. That is, if we want students to know and be able to transfer the use of specific thinking skills to new contexts, this must be part of the "reward system." Marks should be specifically allocated for how students use thinking skills in the subject they are studying (not just for recall of information or "getting the right answer"). If student progress using thinking processes and skills is not part of assessment, learning may degenerate to recall of content. The lowest level of evaluation is repeating a thinking skill in its simplest form and in a context already used. To extend evaluation, a skill must be evaluated as it is used in a slightly different context. Many approaches are necessary: written and oral, descriptions, recordings, broad and narrow, standardized, and self-monitoring.

Steps that you can follow when planning to teach a thinking skill are illustrated in Figure 16.4.

Action Research

We believe that most teachers, at all ages and grade levels, are concerned about teaching for thinking. Pre- or inservice teachers can be helped to structure their work in this direction. Emphasize professional development and collaborative action research in which you begin with a structured position and, through an interactive and reflective approach, are led to a refinement of professional judgment. A research approach to development is pertinent for teaching thinking because of the political and moral aspects of thinking in various cultures. Related learning from research in early childhood, middle years, secondary, and adult education can provide a wealth of background. For instance, reading itself can be considered a higher-order thinking skill.

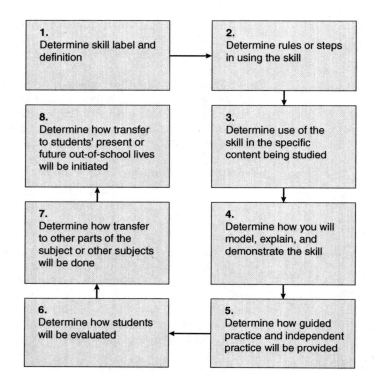

FIGURE 16.4 *Steps in Planning to Teach a Thinking Skill*

17 Teaching for Thinking: Critical and Creative Thinking

Critical and Creative Thinking

Critical Thinking

> Few educators . . . oppose the idea of getting students to think more critically . . . yet rhetoric outstrips practice. (Case & Wright, 1999, p. 179)

You want to help your students become good thinkers, people who think critically. Critical thinking, which many agree involves the use of skills, is a very cerebral thing. It should not be misconstrued that the skills are to be used in a mechanistic way. Having students acquire critical thinking capability needs to be a prime objective of all teachers, not something to be covered if and when the subject matter of the curriculum or textbook has been covered (Case & Wright, 1999, p. 179). To become critical thinkers, students need instruction on what is involved in doing critical thinking, interesting content, opportunity to practice it, and assessments of their attempts at critical thinking.

What Is Critical Thinking?

What is critical thinking? There is disagreement about what qualifies as critical thinking. Most authorities agree that critical thinking involves abilities, background concepts and information, and certain dispositions. Case and Wright (1999) ask, "Of what value in becoming a better thinker is there in asking students to assess the pro and con arguments on an issue if they are profoundly unaware of the standards they should use in critiquing competing pieces of evidence?" (p. 181). While most think dispositions (attitudes) and tools (skills) are involved, some, including McPeck (1990), believe there are no general abilities. It can be argued, however, that there are dispositions and tools that can be learned and transferred in a way that recognizes the uniqueness of disciplines, issues, or situations.

Scriven and Paul (1996) say that critical thinking is "the intellectually disciplined process of actively and skillfully conceptualizing, applying, analyzing, synthesizing, and/or evaluating information gathered from or generated by, observation, experience, reflection, reasoning, or communication, as a guide to belief and action." Earlier, Norris (1985) said, "Critical thinking is deciding rationally what to or what not to believe." Critical thinking can be summarized as "the ability to think about one's thinking so as to recognize its strengths and weaknesses and, as a result, redo and improve the thinking in improved form" (Scriven & Paul, 1996). In a nutshell, "Critical thinking . . . means making reasoned judgments" (Beyer, 1995, p. 8). Whatever the definition, the purpose is to, through questioning and inquiry while being sensitive to context, achieve understanding, evaluate points of view, and solve problems. The process of critical thinking is fundamental to education. For our purposes, we define *critical thinking* as fair-mindedly interpreting, analyzing, or evaluating information, arguments, or experiences with a set of reflective attitudes, skills, and abilities to guide our thoughts, beliefs, and actions. In short, critical thinking involves evaluating the credibility of information.

Critical Thinking Dispositions and Attitudes

Being able to think critically begins with an attitude of being disposed to consider, in a thoughtful and perceptive way, the problems and subjects of aspects of life. When we include critical thinking in schooling, we must emphasize, model, and encourage critical thinking dispositions. You can help your students develop critical thinking abilities by teaching them how to objectively and open mindedly seek answers to questions and problems, and teaching them how to investigate the causes of events. You can model and promote intellectual honesty, even though evidence challenges personally cherished beliefs. Students need to learn the importance of flexibility and have, but not be inhibited by, healthy skepticism until adequate evidence is surfaced. A patient, persistent, and systematic approach to arriving at conclusions and resolving differences needs to be valued, as does the attitude of respect for other points of view after listening carefully to those views.

Procedures and Skills

Authorities disagree about what is involved in critical thinking and when, where, and how it should be taught. We believe that critical thinking should be taught in both a generic and a subject-specific sense. It should not be taught in isolation, whether as a stand-alone topic or as part of a discipline, without providing for transfer—that's the important thing. If students practice critical thinking, content is *always* required—whether from a school subject or some other source. If, for example, it is taught as part of social studies, the teacher needs to help students bridge to, for example, science, English, and other subjects. Critical thinking in social studies is like critical thinking in science, is like critical thinking in solving a community issue, is like making a meaningful decision in a business, and is like making an appropriate choice about a personal quandary. Transfer may not occur unless you deliberately point out transfer possibilities and have students acquire the disposition to seek transfer to new situations.

Sternberg (1985) believes that teaching for critical thinking, "as it usually is done, inadequately prepares students for the kinds of problems they will face in everyday life" (p. 277). He adds, "good thinking in one academic area does not guarantee good thinking in another." His solution is to have programs that sample a variety of content areas and thinking skills in a way that is "true to the way problems appear in our everyday lives"

(p. 278). Critical thinking procedures and skills can be taught! Students need to practice this and, importantly, to practice discovering problems for themselves. Beyer's (1984) list of procedures may well have relevance today:

1. Distinguishing between verifiable facts and value claims
2. Determining the reliability of a claim or source
3. Determining the accuracy of a statement
4. Distinguishing between warranted or unwarranted claims
5. Distinguishing between relevant and irrelevant information, claims, or arguments
6. Detecting biases
7. Identifying stated and unstated assumptions
8. Identifying ambiguous or equivocal claims or arguments
9. Recognizing logical inconsistencies in a line of reasoning
10. Determining the strength of an argument (p. 557)

Paul and Elder (2001) describe intellectual traits that help critical thinking: intellectual humility, courage, empathy, autonomy, integrity, perseverance, confidence in reason, and fair-mindedness. Critical thinking, it can be argued, requires a set of dispositions (or attitudes) *and* specific processes and skills. These dispositions need to be taught.

The ability to think critically involves behavior that can be learned. One can examine the problem, identify the key issues, and ask the following questions: Are there any underlying assumptions? What generalizations can be safely made? What credible sources might shed light on the problem? What have we previously learned about the problem? What kinds of data are relevant? How adequate is the data? Is data presented in a biased or distorted way? How consistent and relevant is our argumentation? What can we do to ensure that personal bias does not affect what we do? What conclusions and possible solutions can be posed? What are the pros and cons of each potential solution. Which solution or what combination of solutions appears best? How can we test the solution or combination of solutions? If the test is not passed, what can be done to arrive at another possible solution to be tested?

Creative Thinking

TCP—CREATIVE THINKING

Ensures that students think creatively

Encourages creative potential of students; welcomes novel and imaginative responses; uses divergent approaches; models creativity and allows open-ended expression; experiential, inductive, and hands-on approaches.

Creativity not apparently welcomed; reliance on standard information; only "right" answers welcome; little attempt to encourage novel, imaginative, and creative ideas.

Creativity is not a single process. Though we recognize and value creative thinking, it defies precise description. *Creative thinking* can be viewed as forming new combinations of ideas to fulfill a need or as thinking in a way that produces original and appropriate results. Creativity has been linked to divergent thinking and originality of thought or execution. Although something can be creative (original) for an individual, it need not be original to mankind. Creativity is found in all areas of life and is not limited to the arts, to geniuses, or to the talented. Creative thinking should be structured into the curriculum and encouraged through open-ended challenges.

Teaching for Creativity

Every student has creative potential. Creativity can conflict with established rules, procedures, and patterns, and what is "correct." When you promote creativity, expect a mixture of novel, imaginative, and valuable answers, and also answers that may seem silly or bizarre. Let students think, solve problems, and use divergent ideas.

Teaching for creativity includes teaching thinking skills. Creativity has long been known to be the highest form of mental functioning. Some instructional strategies are more effective than others in producing creative responses in students. As never before, we need to help students develop creative thinking and feeling skills. Students who have had ample opportunity to use their creative talents will likely use them well throughout their lives. Barriers to creative thinking often are in students' minds; those who are intelligent but not very creative may be disinclined to be imaginative. The barriers may be due to social fears, fear of being wrong, lack of confidence, or the belief that they are not creative.

Model creativity and provide ample opportunity for creative expression by allowing students to express themselves in an open-ended manner and to seek different ways to do something or solve problems. Fear of failure or looking foolish limits creativity. Students must not feel their answers will lower their grades; trying new things should be praised, not suppressed. Small-group problem solving or decision making can promote creativity. Teach brainstorming and have students use it. Students also should be taught constructive disagreement, and that ideas and procedures can be challenged, but people and personalities must not be attacked.

Rothstein (1990) provides suggestions for teaching for creativity:

- *Encourage students to explore things in their environment.* Have them use all their senses and discover the messages sent through each and combinations of senses. Have them describe things they find interesting. Have them discover how to "look at things with fresh eyes."
- *Provide school time to encourage creativity.* Structure activities or exercises that require originality or problem solving. Have students suggest new uses for old things. Make frequent use of brainstorming and creative activities. Let them know that creativity is sought.
- *Encourage students to become interested in many things.* Vary activities, take students on field trips, bring in speakers, and use media to help students "stretch their minds."
- *Help students believe they can learn to become more creative.* Few inventors, scientists, or artists were very creative at first. Reward students who show evidence of creativity, and reward improvement.
- *Teach students what is involved in creativity.* Help them learn that creativity is influenced by the types, number, and originality of alternatives produced. Train students to use specific thinking skills and inquiry and problem-solving processes and how to transfer knowledge of these into new situations.
- *Encourage students to acquire information and use it to be creative.* Show students how knowledge can be used to create alternatives, analogies, or to make inferences (p. 274).

You can help students increase their creative talents by helping them develop *meta-cognitive talents*. For example, teach students how to generate questions about the material studied or ask them to propose activities. Participation helps them take control of learning. They can learn to explore things from a variety of perspectives and decide the consequences of the alternatives generated. Tell them that statements (or thoughts) such as "I can't" or "I don't know how" or "I'm too slow" are not permitted. Students can share ideas with peers and have these paraphrased. This teaches them to become better listeners, clarifies thinking, and fosters fresh ideas. Role playing and simulations can be used. Encourage students to become more hypothetical. Have them assume a stance or position with which they do not agree. Journals help students bring their thoughts together and translate them into constructive action. This can occur when students look back at what happened, how they reacted, decide how they could have reacted, and what they will do in the future.

Honig (2001) suggests ways to encourage creativity in young children:

1. Breaking up old ideas through encouraging new ideas and making children comfortable with ambiguity
2. Making new connections through the creative use of recycled materials such as paper rolls and pipe cleaners
3. Enlarging the limits of knowledge through taking apart old or broken objects such as hair dryers and battery-operated toys to see how they work
4. Allowing the onset of wonderful ideas through encouraging children to move about the classroom in their own creative ways (p. 37)

The way the teacher behaves and runs the classroom is at the core of teaching for both creative and critical thinking. The teacher needs to listen to, and value, students' ideas and opinions. The teacher should encourage students to value each others' thoughts and beliefs. Teachers must be flexible and not insist on conformity at all times. Open-minded discussion is important—students need to discuss their thinking, viewpoints, and attempts at analysis. They need to make decisions, examine alternatives, and act in accord with their decisions. Cooperative learning procedures can be used to advantage.

Teaching your students to think critically and creatively is demanding. Do you really need to know and understand the theory to be effective? Did the specific operations of classifying, organizing, and the like work? You may say, "I really want my students to think about what I teach." How do you achieve this? How does this ideal depend on planning and instructional skills? Do you see the teacher as a facilitator? How can the structures suggested in this text help you? Try the methods and reflect on your experience.

A data collection instrument is provided in Appendix 17.1 for your use when teaching for thinking as a target in microteaching or classroom lessons. You can use this instrument to help you analyze the cases that follow. Your instructor may pose specific questions for your response.

CASE 17.1 Thinking

All about a Farm

The grade 2 class had been involved in a farm unit for several days. They had learned about kinds of farms, farm animals, and farm machinery. Ms. Arnott wanted to build on the new learning and introduce

Different	Comparing	Same
Paul	*Jacques*	
brown hair	black hair	both are boys
taller	shorter	both are in grade 2
wearing runners	sock feet	both play soccer at recess
wearing a sweater	wearing a "Turtles" shirt	both are wearing jeans
blue eyes	brown eyes	both have short hair
		both are Montreal Canadians fans

the thinking skill of *comparing*. She planned, in consecutive lessons, to have the children: (1) compare two farm animals with which they were familiar to introduce comparing, (2) compare two live pet turtles (a snapping turtle and a box turtle), and (3) compare two stories. She thought the children would learn to transfer this skill if they used it in different situations.

In the first lesson, she began, "This afternoon, we're going to do something that's fun. It's called *comparing*. It's a special way of thinking about something and it's called a thinking skill. First, we will practice doing it together, then we'll do it with farm animals; tomorrow we'll try it with something else. Have you ever heard the word *compare*?" She writes the word on the board.

Some children had heard the word. They gave examples: "My mom compares prices when she shops." "I'm tall compared to my baby brother." "My sisters don't like to be compared."

"Those are good examples of how that word can be used. What do you think the word means?" Trish volunteered, "It means seeing if two things are the same."

Ms. Arnott recorded the word *same* on the board, under *Compare*. "Yes, if you look for things that are the same, it's called comparing. It means something else, too," said Ms. Arnott. "It means if you're as tall as your brother," Petra responded. Ms. Arnott asked, "If you are small and your brother is tall, are you the same?" "No, we're different." "So, comparing could be looking for ways things are different?" "Yes," answered Petra. Ms. Arnott wrote *different* under the *Compare* heading. "Now can you tell us what *compare* means?" Ivan answered, "*Compare* means looking for things that are the same and for things that are different." "That's right!" replied Ms. Arnott, "And that's what we're going to do."

"All right, let's see how this would work. I wonder if you can *compare* two boys in our class, just to see if you get the idea. How about Paul and Jacques? Paul and Jacques, stand at the front of the room. Let's make a place for information." Ms. Arnott clears a section of the board and writes the word *comparing* and the headings "Paul," "Jacques," "Different," and "Same" on the board (shown above). The children identify similarities and differences.

"That's great," said Ms. Arnott, "Now let's see if you can compare two farm animals we've been learning about. Which ones should we compare?" Many hands wave. After looking around, Ms. Arnott chooses Marcus. Marcus suggests goats and sheep.

Ms. Arnott gives directions for students to work in pairs, and then distributes papers to each pair. The papers are blank versions of the format used on the board. Ms. Arnott reviews information about goats and sheep with the class and asks them, in pairs, to begin discussing the information. "Decide which things are different, which are the same, and then record the information on your worksheets. When everyone is finished, we'll talk about them."

When the children have completed their task, using a general class discussion, Ms. Arnott asks students to share their responses. Following the discussion, in which she discovers students have the idea of similarities and differences, she concludes, "You all did a good job of comparing today. Tomorrow we'll do more comparing, but we'll look for things that are the same and different for two different kinds of turtles. I'm going to bring my pet box turtle and my pet snapping turtle. We'll look at them, touch them, and see what they eat and how they act in a new place. Then we'll decide what is the same and what is different."

CASE 17.2 Thinking

Assumptions about "Facts"

Mr. Goldstein wanted to teach more than information in his grade 10 science class. In a general way, he had been working on this for some time. He wanted his students to learn to process information rather than just receive and memorize it. It had become a habit to ask broad or open-ended questions and to make sure he waited three to five seconds before calling on a specific student. The number of probes and redirects he used had increased, and he encouraged students, at every opportunity, to become aware of their thinking processes. Though he knew it was a less certain way to conduct lessons, he encouraged divergent thinking, and student questions were obviously welcome.

Mr. Goldstein had decided that he was going to teach certain thinking processes and skills directly. To date, he had taught classifying, coding, and comparing and contrasting. To help his students develop critical thinking capability he decided to teach his students to be sensitive to the difference between statements of fact and assumptions.

Two containers of potato chips were displayed on Mr. Goldstein's desk. Students noticed these as they entered the room, wondering what he was up to today. One container was a large, puffed-up plastic bag and the other was a sealed cylinder one-quarter the size of the bag. "Which of these contains more?" he asked. Students found out that the large container

held 150 grams and the smaller container actually held 200 grams. They had assumed the large container held more.

"Some statements are clearly facts," he said. "For example, grass is generally green in the summer; and there are 5,280 feet in a mile. But, statements like 'It's not going to rain for another three weeks' or 'Sam is a good dancer because he was born in Jamaica' are *assumptions*. An assumption is a statement that is not supported, or not fully supported by evidence." He provided a few more examples that contrasted facts and assumptions. Next, he provided a handout that contained twelve statements. Students were asked to label those statements that were facts and those that were assumptions. Then, he divided the class into buzz groups of six to try to arrive at consensus on the issue of whether disposable containers should be used for food products. He said, "As you debate this issue, be very sensitive about your statements. If you think a statement is a fact, say so; if you are aware that it is an assumption, point this out. I will give you a signal when you have about ten minutes left. At this signal, discuss the implications of making decisions or recommendations based on assumptions." Students reported and he asked them to look for assumptions not only in science but also in other subjects, particularly, social studies, English, and consumer studies.

CASE 17.3 Critical Thinking

Arguing with Yourself

SARAH: Hello, Mark. You look like that statue . . . you know, Rodin—the thinker.

MARK: Well, that's "right on," because I am working out a lesson on the dialectic.

SARAH: The dial what?

MARK: Instead of the usual debates and discussions, it's a way of getting kids to look at both sides of an issue. It's good for critical thinking.

SARAH: How does it work?

MARK: You get a student, a group, or even the whole class to make a value claim on an issue. It could be something like smoking should be banned in all

public places. The students then say what is good, right, or worthwhile concerning the issue.

SARAH: So, they'd express a moral and ethical position.

MARK: Yes, it must be one on which there is an honest division of opinion. Then they'd give supporting arguments and reasons to support their position.

SARAH: That sounds reasonable.

MARK: Then, you get the individual or class to set out a value claim opposing that of the first value claim—in other words, an opposite moral and ethical position—and they must argue the position with supporting arguments.

SARAH: In other words, this dialectic is like a dialogue, like arguing with yourself?

MARK: Exactly. There are other things that should happen, but you have the main idea. Students would decide which value claim is the better, and the value claim has to pass certain intellectual tests.

SARAH: What kind of tests?

MARK: Can the claim apply to different cases? Can it pass a role-exchange test? And are the consequences of agreeing with these value claims acceptable morally and ethically?

SARAH: This sounds exciting. There are so many issues you could discuss. I'm going to try it with my next class.

Problem-Based Learning

TCP—PROBLEM-BASED LEARNING

Skilled and effective approach to problem-based learning

Skilled at setting up student-centered problem-based learning approaches; teacher is facilitator, ensuring that students explore problems themselves; carefully selects problems as focus of learning; students develop problem-solving skills as they direct their learning; meaningful information provided or suggested.

Little or no student-centered approaches; teacher controls and dominates the learning process; problems selected are unauthentic and not challenging; students learn few meaningful skills; information provided is uninteresting or inadequate.

> The interviewer handed the students a battery, a wire, and a light bulb and asked if they could make the bulb light. They could not. This might not be alarming if the students were fourth graders, but they were not. The students were clothed in caps and gowns as they prepared to graduate from Harvard and MIT. (Bracey, 1998)

This is the opening of *Minds of Our Own,* a three-part videotape series on our misconceptions about how the world works. The key idea "is that children bring to the classroom profoundly held ideas about how the world works, and these ideas are incredibly resistant to change," but "our pedagogy does not equip teachers to teach for understanding and then detect misunderstandings through assessment" (Bracey, 1998, p. 328). The reason the Harvard and MIT students could not solve the light bulb problem is similar to why many educators find it difficult to teach thinking, inquiry, and problem solving. We have preconceptions about how things should be. Bracey provides a revealing example of a "friend who doesn't like to boil water in a microwave oven because the water is never hot enough (for her, boiling water equals bubbles rising, not a set temperature)" (p. 329).

Church (2001) claims that "PBL, a well-documented instructional approach that originated in the field of medical education, has extended its application to many areas and taken many forms. . . . Clearly, collaboration, interacting with others, and thinking through situations to improve knowledge and solve problems are of interest to most professions" (p. 6).

Stressing the importance of problem-solving skills is not new. Students can be taught the procedures and processes of thinking and to recognize, define, and go about solving open-ended problems. They can learn to be fluent, flexible, and original in generating ideas—creativity can be learned by practicing it. Techniques of forecasting, too, can be learned. These involve defining and solving future-oriented problems. You can teach habits of mind and the tools students can use to cope with the present and the future.

What Is Problem-Based Learning (PBL)?

As you may have surmised, problem-based learning is any learning situation in which the problem drives the learning. Students discover they need the information or skills to solve a problem. To do this, they need to know how to access the information and how to use critical thinking and problem-solving skills. Problem-based learning is a student-centered method in which learners become increasingly independent of the teacher, who suggests educational materials and provides guidance (SIU, 2002). The teacher's function is to encourage, keep students on track, provide information or suggest sources of information, and be a fellow learner (Aspy, Aspy, & Quinby, 1993).

PBL, which values active learning, has the following characteristics:

- It is student centered.
- Learning occurs in small student groups.
- Teachers are facilitators or guides.
- Problems are the organizing focus and stimulus for learning.
- Problems are a vehicle for the development of problem-solving skills.
- New information is acquired through self-directed learning (SIU, 2002).

Why Use Problem-Based Learning?

The argument posed in the Southern Illinois University School of Medicine web site is that traditional schooling—kindergarten through medical school—leaves students disenchanted and bored with their education. Much of what was memorized is soon forgotten and what is remembered is hard to apply to tasks and problems. Many students can't reason effectively and are unable to take responsibility for their education. Many do not collaborate well with others. Education has been "an imposed set of rituals with little relevance to the 'real world.'"

Through PBL, traditional teacher and student roles change. Students assume more responsibility and so are better motivated with more feelings of accomplishment, "setting the pattern for them to become successful lifelong learners" they become "better practitioners of their profession" (MCLI, 2001). Learning becomes relevant and authentic, occurs in ways similar to how it will be used in the future, and higher-order thinking is promoted.

How Does Problem-Based Learning Work?

PBL is the kind of classroom organization that supports a constructionist approach (NCREL, 2002). Savoie and Hughes (1994) used a process to initiate a problem-based experience for students.

The process of PBL has students, in groups, confront a problem. They organize prior knowledge and try to discover the nature of the problem. Questions may be posed about what they do not understand. They then formulate a plan for solving the problem and decide the resources needed. Following this, they start to gather information with which to work to solve the problem. Potential solutions are generated. The pros and cons of each solution are considered, and a solution, or a combination of solutions, is selected to be tested. A data sheet you can use for problem-based learning is provided in Appendix 17.2.

CASE 17.4 Problem-Based Learning

Making Ancient Egypt Interesting

Two student teachers are in the staff room, discussing approaches to teaching. They have seen much lecture teaching in the school and want to try a more dynamic approach.

HASSIM: Do you think we could try a more challenging approach on the lesson on Ancient Egypt? How about that problem-based learning idea we learned about?

SARAH: We could try it with the section on the pyramids. First we have to give students a problem.

HASSIM: That's easy: "How were the pyramids built?"

SARAH: OK, then we have to use the knowledge they already have to get a clearer idea of the nature of the problem.

HASSIM: So, we'll ask them to brainstorm what they know, such as the size of the pyramids, when they were built, and the fact that most are made from huge blocks of stone.

SARAH: They'll need a plan to solve the problem of how the stones were moved and set in place.

HASSIM: They'll need to see what resources are available, like books, Internet ideas, and so on.

SARAH: And once they've enough resources, they can organize the information to solve the problem.

HASSIM: Sounds good. Let's give it a try.

CASE 17.5 Problem-Based Learning

Saving the Burrowing Owl

Mr. Duszik's grade 7 class was very excited. For their science class today their teacher had invited a special guest, Ellen Forsyth, from the government nature conservancy. She had brought with her a burrowing owl as part of her talk on ecosystems.

She asked the students if they had ever gone on nature hikes or camped with friends or family in the wilderness. All the students had, because Mr. Duszik worked hard to ensure that each grade experienced nature trips at least once a year. Ms. Forsyth asked the students what was the best part of these trips, and they all said it was when they saw rare birds or animals.

Not one of the students had ever seen a burrowing owl, and they were thrilled when Ellen finally took it out of its cage. They were surprised at how small it was—only about nine or ten inches tall. They loved how it looked at them, bobbing from side to side as if to get a better view.

When she was asked why it was called a burrowing owl, Ellen got the students themselves to think of possible reasons and, eventually, they thought it lived in the burrows abandoned by gophers or prairie dogs.

She explained that this creature and many others were in danger because there was so little natural grassland left. They needed whole areas of undisturbed prairie if they were to survive. She said she had a special problem she wanted the whole class to think about. How could creatures like the burrowing owl be saved from extinction?

First students defined the problem. How could large sections of undisturbed natural grassland be set aside for creatures like the burrowing owl? They decided they would need to know many things, such as what creatures were threatened, what possibilities for undisturbed environment existed, what agencies could help, what could they do to get people thinking about the issue, and what was being done already. They decided they should form teams and each should be in charge of a particular aspect of the problem.

They had lots to do and lots to learn. Ms. Forsyth smiled at their energy and enthusiasm. She told Mr. Duszik she had started in her career as a student in the class of a teacher who inspired them with real problems.

LINKING PRACTICE TO THEORY

Think about your school experience. Were you taught thinking skills? What subjects made you think about your learning? Do all subjects make think? Try the approaches to teaching about thinking and problem solving suggested in this chapter. Are the ideas helpful?

    This may be the last chapter before your field experience. For each chapter we have suggested you work with the theory and compare approaches in the text with your growing personal experience. There is a tendency sometimes to decry theory and believe the practicum will provide the "real experience" of teaching. The ideas that shape theory grow from the experiences of many teachers. Britzman (1991) describes a practice teacher who believed his internship would tell him what to do and how to teach. His "tendency to distance himself from his teaching strategies was evident. Most apparent, by the last stages of his student teaching semester, was he had no analytical framework from which to theorize about his experience. His experience appeared trapped in immediacy, subject to the pull of uncontrollable forces over which he had little control" (p. 159). Compare your lived experience of teaching with the theoretical framework in this text. This can have significance for your development.

Summary

Schools have typically neglected teaching for thinking, and transfer of thinking operations from one subject to another and to life. Emphasis has been on information acquisition and low-level content. Students need to do more than learn information. Thinking skills and processes need to be learned, as does the ability to use these in a variety of contexts. If teaching and learning are to be authentic, teachers need to teach for thinking. Some educators see stand-alone thinking skills or process learning as ineffective—believing that thinking skills are discipline specific and little transfer, if any, will occur. Others say a context is always required, but thinking skills are generic and teaching for transfer can occur.

If learning is orientated toward discovery of personal meaning and solving problems, each student, no matter his or her ability or background, tries to make sense of knowledge and experience, and uses his or her skills to do so. The student is constructing meaning. Your classroom can be a supportive community for learning and provide a caring environment that encourages constructive risk taking tempered by creative, critical thinking during individual and group work.

What should schooling accomplish? Philosophers and educational theorists have debated this for decades. Authentic, active, collaborative, problem-based learning is the direction proposed by many contemporary theorists.

Activities

1. You and your subject group choose a thinking skill, analyze it, and plan the steps to teach it.
2. In subject groups, examine lesson plans that you have previously used that could be considered essentially content based. Redesign your lesson plans to be: (a) process based rather than product based; and (b) using the core thinking skills (presented in this chapter).
3. Consider a lesson in school or college in which you were taught, or encouraged, to think. Compare your reflections with the creative and critical thinking charts in this text.
4. Plan a lesson in your subject area with the objective of teaching a thinking skill, which can be demonstrated to the class.
5. Choose a lesson plan you have previously prepared. Revise it to include the teaching of a thinking skill and to encourage the learning of a disposition or attitude.

6. Brainstorm examples of topics that could be discussed using the dialectic model.
7. Meet in subject groups. (a) Brainstorm lists of the most important creative and critical thinking skills that apply to your subject. (b) Indicate those skills that are essential to your subject.
8. Research constructionist teaching or review the section in this text. List the main similarities between constructionist teaching and problem-based learning.
9. Think of problems you have solved outside of school using the PBL model. Describe what you did. Take a "traditional" lesson you have taught. Redesign it using a PBL approach.
10. What would you consider the advantages and disadvantages of a PBL approach in your discipline?

APPENDIX 17.1   *Thinking Skills Professional Target*

PROFESSIONAL TARGET—TEACHING A THINKING SKILL

Please describe what you hear and see including how students reacted.

Teaching Aspect	Teacher and Student Behaviors
The skill label and definition provided	
Rules or steps for using skill provided	
Use of skill in the specific content under study	
Skill modeled (demonstrated and explained)	
Guided practice provided (and the context of practice)	
Independent practice provided	

APPENDIX 17.2 *Problem-Based Learning Professional Target*

PROFESSIONAL TARGET—PROBLEM-BASED LEARNING

Please describe what you hear and see including how students reacted.

Steps	Teacher and Student Behaviors
Problem identified	
Authentic problem connected to the life experiences of the students	
Students, in groups, confront the problem	
Students organize prior knowledge; identify the nature of problem	
Questions posed about what is not understood	
Students design a plan to solve the problem and identify resources needed	
Students gather information to solve the problem	
Solution(s) identified and evaluated	
Solution(s) tried	

18 Moving Forward: Rethinking the Way "We Do Schools"

VIGNETTE

John Zeak had been teaching at Mountain Elementary School for only a few months. Like all new teachers, he had faced several challenges. While he enjoyed working with his grade 7 students, he had found it somewhat challenging to deal with Josh Simms, a likable student whose tendency to harass others was a source of concern. Josh seemed particularly intent on offending everyone whom he believed was different from him. This included the girls and several minority students in the class. He had the knack of finding something disparaging to say about those he harassed. He was also constantly disrespectful of the teacher. At first John Zeak had ignored what he assumed was attention-seeking behaviour that would play itself out as the school year progressed. After all, was he not constantly reminding his students that such behaviour was not acceptable in his class? Josh would eventually "get it" he rationalized. Things did not work out that way and Josh's harassment of some of his peers continued to escalate. Zeak found that he was constantly trying to resolve conflicts that Josh had initiated. As Josh's bullying became increasingly disruptive and

face meeting to discuss the problem. He had hoped that they could collaboratively devise a course of action to teach Josh tolerance and respect for others. To his amazement, Josh's parents seemed unconcerned and dismissive of the problem. In fact, Mr. Simms informed John Zeak in no uncertain terms that he was not to be bothered in future about issues that "do not matter". Meanwhile, there was no change in Josh's behaviour. One particular incident eventually forced the issue. During a group activity, Josh had continuously pestered Celeste, one of the few First Nations students in the class. After several unsuccessful interventions, John Zeak threatened him with suspension at the end of the day if he did stop the harassment. Josh reacted negatively, yelling out, "Quit bugging me! I am exercising my free speech! My parents told me that under the *Charter of Rights and Freedoms*, I can say whatever I like." Zeak was shocked at Josh's misinterpretation of the *Charter*: sure, he had a right to free speech, but not by trampling on the rights of others. Exasperated by Josh's outburst and rudeness before the entire class, John Zeak decided to follow through with his threat of suspension, which he had a legal right to do under the province's education statute. He was not about to allow prejudice to thrive in his class. The next morning, John Zeak was summoned to the principal's office and was surprised to find Josh and his parents in conference with Mr. Thompson, the principal. Mr. Thompson explained that Mr. and Mrs. Simms were about to initiate legal action against him, the principal, and the school board for the violation of their son's fundamental rights to self-expression. As far as they were concerned, Josh's behaviour had not warranted suspension. John Zeak was speechless. He now understood how and from where Josh had learned his prejudice. No, he thought, Mr. Simms is wrong and these issues matter. He wondered how many other students in his class shared Josh's feelings. If he had failed to reach Josh, his strategies for teaching about diversity, mutual respect, and tolerance were clearly not working. What was he doing wrong? He had to find more proactive and results-oriented strategies. Regardless of the outcome of this particular incident, he had to move forward; he would not be discouraged because too much was at stake.

INTRODUCTION: RETHINKING THE WAY "WE DO SCHOOLS"

There is debate in prevailing scholarship over what constitutes social justice, the sources of injustices in school and society, and the educators' role in changing the status quo in Canada and the Western world. Certain groups of students continue to experience negative and unfair treatment that relegates them to the unenviable position of the "other". With this in mind, critical areas should be addressed in order to help diverse learners? These critical areas can be summarized as philosophical orientation, curriculum content, the process of teaching, and the context of teaching. A central theme in this chapter is that it is the way these broad areas are *qualitatively* addressed by teachers which will make a difference moving forward. John Zeak in the vignette above makes a profound statement: He is right, there is too much at stake for all educators not to rethink their approaches to teaching and learning in contemporary Canadian schools. This final chapter of the book, therefore, examines these broad areas individually, from the perspective of directions for future action.

PHILOSOPHICAL ORIENTATIONS: CONFRONTING ORTHODOXY

Teachers and administrators must regularly conduct critical self-analysis, which should culminate in perspective realignment. However, change in perspectives also requires that educators and administrators examine and change their philosophical orientations to teaching, as required. This change may well induce a paradigm shift away from traditional and conservative views of schooling and society. Teachers have to re-evaluate their basic beliefs and assumptions about students, and education. In effect teachers who wish to make a difference have two options: continue to reinforce *orthodox* thinking or embrace transformation-oriented thinking. This book's underlying premise is that educational systems cannot continue to organize themselves in orthodox ways that reinforce exclusionary practices, i.e., in ways that silence those whose cultural capital is considered less valuable than the middle-class values disseminated in schools. Thus, educators must problematize educational knowledge by asking such questions as "Whose interests do schools represent? Whose "ways of knowing" are privileged and whose are devalued? To what extent do Canadian educational policies and practices promote equity and fairness?" and "How can the status quo be challenged?" Visionary educators must have a thorough grounding in what constitutes fairness and social justice, which means meeting people's needs as required, rather than giving everybody an equal share of social resources. But it is not enough to understand these principles, teachers must also implement them in authentic ways as they strive to meet the individual needs of their diverse students. Rejecting orthodox practice also means that educators must eschew the usual practice of labelling students as "at risk", "difficult to educate", etc. Besides the obvious psychological implications of such dichotomization, labelling impacts on teachers' communication and interaction patterns with such students, and on how the curriculum is delivered to the various groups of students within the same classroom. Therefore, traditional methods of teaching (those based solely on the notion of immutable universals) are no longer justifiable given the fluid nature of the world (including student diversity and educational policies). While some teachers are cognizant of this and endeavour to integrate diverse perspectives into the content they teach, they generally use an add-on approach that differs only minimally from traditional approaches to teaching and learning. Reconstituting the way things are done in school should therefore involve a fundamental shift in thinking. That is from orthodox thinking to a transformation-oriented conceptualization of issues, which should manifest in the infusion of diversity issues across the curriculum in constructive and dynamic ways. The basic differences between orthodox and transformation-oriented thinking are outlined in Table 8.1. Also, the following example further illustrates the differences. One of your students who constantly shows concern for the poor and downtrodden comes to school with a newspaper clipping about the appalling condition of some First Nations communities in the Northwest Territories. A teacher who thinks in traditional ways will only acknowledge the student's interest in the story as commendable and then move on to other things whereas a teacher who is truly interested in changing the status quo would not only encourage the student to

TABLE 8.1	Elements of Orthodox Compared with Transformation-Oriented Thinking
Orthodox (Traditional) Thinking	**Transformation-Oriented Thinking**
• Believes in the banking perspective of teaching, in which students are treated as depositories of information	• Questions and engages the curriculum and encourages students to do the same. Sees a link between peoples' experiences and how knowledge is constructed
• Adopts traditional pedagogies and reinforces the status quo	• Embraces and adopts progressive pedagogies such as critical and diversity pedagogy, and diversity-oriented teacher research.
• Believes in teacher-centred approaches	• Believes that knowledge is co-created and makes the classroom a community of learners
• Ignores the intersection of privilege and social positioning in academic achievement	• Understands that privilege contributes to educational success
• Sees education as a meritocracy and views educational successes solely as a function of individual hard work	• Understands that a myriad of interacting variables, including unfair policies and practices, contribute to academic success
• Believes in the value-free notion of education and teaching	• Understands that teaching is a politically charged activity
• Subscribes to the illusion of colour blindness	• Recognizes individual differences, but rejects deterministic views of who can succeed in school
• Sees student diversity as a problem to be "managed" or overcome	• Sees student diversity as a resource that can enrich the quality of teaching and learning for all
• Sees the curriculum as a neutral and universal document	• Sees the curriculum as a cultural artifact that represents the worldviews of the dominant group

develop strategies for improving the situatioin, he or she would make the story the nexus of a major class project.

EMPOWERMENT THROUGH THE CONTENTS OF THE CURRICULUM

Various chapters throughout this book have touched on the issue of the curriculum. This chapter explores how teachers can infuse *diversity issues across the curriculum (DIAC)* through the contents they teach as a natural extension of their quest to make learning a worthwhile experience for all students.

Diversity Issues across the Curriculum (DIAC)

DIAC involves a purposeful attempt to integrate diverse perspectives into what is formally taught in school. It is pedagogical strategy for pervasive curriculum intervention that is intended to provide students with the appropriate knowledge, skills, attitudes, and moral orientation required to live in a pluralistic nation and a globalized world. This means that every subject is to be taught in racially, culturally, linguistically, and gender inclusive ways that challenge orthodox knowledge and position alternative discourse as valued knowledge that all children should have access to. While some topics lend themselves more to integration into the curriculum than others, virtually all subject areas can be adapted to meet student learning needs. The concepts of negotiable and non-negotiable knowledge are models of what schools should teach in a pluralistic society, and an increasingly globalized world. Teachers can use this framework as a starting point for integrating diversity issues across the curriculum. Even when they must adhere to standardized curricula, teachers can still integrate DIAC as they teach the various subject areas. In that instance, the goal is not to change the curriculum, but rather to expand it based on the contextual needs of the students. Ideally, in order to successfully implement DIAC teachers must first **deconstruct** the curriculum (that is, critically examine and engage the contents [Ladson-Billings, 2006]) and the *reconstruct* it to identify the missing information. Filling in the gaps may require inserting the voices of those who have been left out of the curriculum.

How does DIAC work in practice? Recall the cae of the student who came to school with the newspaper clipping discussed above. This is a good example of how teachers can integrate DIAC as part of their instructional activities . The newspaper stry can be inserted into virtually every lesson and unit that will be taught. For example, students could be asked in social studies or language arts to use the issue as the basis of a journal writing activity that deals with ways of improving the lives of First Nations peoples, and perhaps ways of improving the lives of the downtrodden in other parts of the world. Similarly, the same story can be integrated into a lesson in health educatioin by exploring the health and psychological implications of poor social conditions in Canada's Aboriginal communities. It can become part of a math unit if students are asked to research statistical information about Canada's Aborigina peoples. The story can also be used to teach a lesson in history and geography (depending on the grade level). Similarly, a teacher whose particular interest is in integrating diversity issues from a global perspectiuve could discuss the lives of those who are living under similar conditions in other parts of the world, and then have the students propose ways of changing the situation. By adopting this approach to DIAC, the teacher is using a newspaper clipping to teach students global awareness, critical thinking skills, cros-cultural awareness and sensitivity, empathy, poverty, social justice, research, and advocacy skills. The teacher is also providing the students with the opportunity to critique undesirable social conditions, thus enabling them to discuss and develop ideas for creating a just Canadian society.

While some teachers may feel that the above approach is overtly political and therefore should not be a constituent part of classroom activities or practices, it is worth emphasizing that teaching is a political activity. Moreover, the role of an educational system cannot be separated from its historical context, nor can it be viewed apart from the larger political and economic structures of which it is an integral part. The above is only an example of how DIAC can be integrated into lessons, other instances will abound.

Ideally, for DIAC to be effective, it should be addressed at all levels of the educational system. First, at the policy making or ministry level curriculum developers must not only address issues in determining what students should be taught, they should also address how these issues will be integrated in actual instruction. As Dei et al. (2000) argue

> In creating a multi-voiced counter narrative, a new curriculum of learning must be redesigned to reflect alternate realities and worldviews. Schooling must be reoriented to reflect the contributions of non-European cultures to scientific academic work. . . . The partial readings of human development, which have denied the accomplishments and achievements of these grous, must be addressed (p. 183).

It is during curriculum development that the Dei et al. charge should first be addressed. Second, DIAC should also be addressed at the board level. School boards must ensure that teachers are provided the necessary resources to enable them to implement DIAC. Third and most important, teachers should integrate DIAC as discussed above, at the micro-level.

EMPOWERMENT THROUGH THE PROCESS OF TEACHING

In empowering diverse learners, whether we speak in terms of racial or language minorities, immigrant or refugee students, etc., praxis-oriented initiatives must give students a voice, foster their intellectual growth, affirm student identities, and focus on the needs of the individual.

Giving Students a Voice

Reforms that intend to create an inclusive learning environment for diverse students can be implemented by giving them a voice as important members of the learning community. As Freire (1970) argues, a pedagogy that purports to be truly liberating and empowering cannot be successful without the participation of those who are to be empowered. Enabling everyone one to speak is a starting point for changing undesirable educational practices (Ryan, 2006). It is ironic that in Canada, which considers itself a pluralistic democracy (Myer, 2006), some groups still do not have the voice that the constitution explicitly guarantees. The prevailing culture in Canadian schools represents the privileged collective voice of the dominant group. This is the voice that educators must interrogate in order to empower diverse learners. To counteract social reproduction in Canadian schools, teachers must diverge from the persistent pattern of silencing the voices of students from disadvantaged communities. McLaren (2007) underscores the importance of voice in empowering groups that are at the periphery of the school system:

> I would argue along with Henry Giroux that a critical and affirming pedagogy has to be constructed around the stories that people tell, the ways in which students and teachers author meaning, and the possibilities that underlie the experiences that shape their voices. It is around the concept of *voice* that a theory of both teaching and learning can take place, one that points to new forms of social relations and to new and challenging ways of confronting everyday life (p. 244) [emphasis in origial].

The concept of voice as used here refers to collective agency and power that facilitates student ability to engage the system in profound and meaningful ways. But, empowering diverse learners does not solely depend on making students part of the dialog for change. Teachers should also be given a voice that they can leverage to initiate praxis. As micro-level practitioners, it is through the mediation of teachers' voices that undesirable school and classroom practices can be challenged and altered. Also, by using their voices in positive ways, teachers can contribute significantly to restructuring colonizing societal processes that operate both inside and outside the school.

Affirming Students' Identity

A critical element in empowering diverse learners is affirming their identity. Our identity is an integral part of who we are, and in all practical applications, contributes to how we construct knowledge. It is important to remember that some of the academic challenges that minoritized students face are directly linked to the negation of their identity. The bulk of this book is devoted to exploring the ways that educators can affirm the identities of diverse students to increase their academic success and ultimately their life chances. This is also a central argument in the works of writers who advocate progressive educational paradigms such as multicultural education, anti-racist education, critical pedagogy, diversity pedagogy, and culturally relevant teachings (e.g., Banks, 2001; Bennet, 2007; McLaren, 2007; Dei, 1996; Villegas and Lucas, 2002; Gay, 2000; Ladson-Billings, 1994; Delpit, 2006; Fleras and Elliot, 2003; Henry and Tator, 2006). Affirming identities should therefore be a moral agenda that guides the actions of educators in contexts of student diversity.

Fostering Intellectual Growth

One important strategy that teachers can use to empower diverse learners is to foster their intellectual growth. Quite often teachers subscribe to the deficit model of achievement, seeing students from certain racial and ethno-cultural groups as incapable or limited in their abilities (Gillborn, 2004). Consequently there is reduced expectation, which in turn prevents them from supporting the intellectual growth of these students. Expectations are powerful determinants of teacher judgment of a student's abilities. As a matter of fact student ability, often assumed to be innate in many Western societies, may be significantly influenced by experience and the kinds of knowledge to which students are exposed. The teachers who assumed that an excellent critique of Shakespeare was not written by the Black immigrant student (whom they judged as least likely to have studied Shakespearian literature) made a common error. Such ill-considered beliefs lead only to the further disadvantaging of students from nondominant backgrounds.

Ladson-Billings (2006) argues that in order for teachers to move their students from a level of mediocrity to one of possibilities, teachers must see future leaders, neurosurgeons, Nobel Laureates, and social justice advocates among their students. To achieve this, they must move from a state of sympathy to a state of empathy. Such a mental state requires teachers to "feel with the students rather than feeling for them. Feeling with the students builds a sense of solidarity between the teacher and students but does not excuse students from working hard in pursuit of excellence". Excellence and critical pedagogical practices are not mutually exclusive — for instance, by adopting culturally relevant pedagogies, teachers explore all possible avenues to ensure that their students perform to the best of their abilities. Moreover, as Kalantzis and Cope (1999) argue, students need a rigorous curriculum if they are to gain any kind of meaningful access to social rewards. Whereas most critical educators argue for making the curriculum relevant to the experience of students, Kalantzis and Cope caution that

> diversifying curriculum in the interest of 'relevance' is to create a new streaming in a pseudo-democratic garb. Students who would have failed in a comprehensive, traditional curriculum now pass in what everyone . . . know[s] to be 'Mickey-mouse' courses. . . . All too easily, and in the name of cultural self-esteem, this can end in a celebratory multiculturalism of spaghetti and polka; a multiculturalism that trivializes culture and is more concerned with the affirmation of difference than with what students need in linguistic-cognitive terms if they are to gain some degree of broader social access (pp. 260–261).

Based on the understanding that people learn best when their learning is linked to their experiences, critical teaching practices are ultimately about fostering intellectual growth and academic excellence in all learners. When teachers decide that students are incapable of performing certain tasks or are operating below a predetermined level of intellectual ability, their desire to help the students grow intellectually is considerably reduced. This is most unfortunate because our contemporary information-based society demands that teachers deliver intellectually challenging curricula. Indeed, as schools must now prepare students for technology and jobs that may not yet exist, promoting intellectual growth among all students should be the sine qua non for all educators.

Individualized Attention

While this book deals extensively with issues from a group standpoint, it should also be obvious that the individual is as important as the group. It is at the individual level that teachers are able to indeed reach students. Teachers must treat each student as an individual human being requiring special attention whenever necessary, as it is in fact good teaching to pay attention to individual differences. While this book devotes considerable space to teaching students culturally relevant knowledge and pedagogy, it is important to point out that educating students in a multicultural society does not mean typecasting them into preconceived notions of how they are supposed to act. According to Delpit (2006)

> The question is not necessarily how to create the perfect "culturally matched" learning situation for each ethnic group, but rather how to recognize when there is a problem for a particular child

and how to seek its cause in the most broadly conceived fashion. Knowledge about culture is butt one tool that educators may make use of when devising solutions for a school's difficulty in edu-i cating diverse children (p. 167).

On a similar tack, traditional assumptions about learning that contribute to "teaching less instead of teaching more" (Delpit, 2006) must be replaced with more progressive beliefs about the potential of every child to learn.

THE CONTEXT OF TEACHING

In contextualizing teaching and the way forward, this work adopts a perspective that sees the context of teaching and learning extending beyond the classroom to include the communities from which schools draw their students. This conception of the context includes strategies that teachers can adopt to provide a safe, warm, and caring learning environment for all learners, in addition to those that schools can use to reach out to their communities. It includes the strategies for classroom management, as well as those for disciplining students.

The Importance of Empathy

All propositions in this book are aimed at empowering diverse learners and all students in pluralistic societies. It is, however, difficult to achieve these goals if students are not taught how to empathize with their peers. Although not explicitly stated, the theme of empathy runs through teaching for diversity. Whether we talk of teaching global awareness, critical thinking skill, or prejudice reduction and respect for others, empathy is an important precursor to developing these themes. It bears emphasizing that it is difficult to teach tolerance, anti-racism, multiculturalism, and all the other empowering frameworks discussed in this book if students fail to embrace the value of empathy. Empathy is our ability to understand and be compassionate about other people's experiences. As Howard (2006) describes it

> Empathy means "to feel with". [It] requires the suspension of assumptions, the letting go of ego, and the release of the privilege of non-engagement. . . . [It] is the antithesis of dominance. It requires all of our senses and focuses our attention on the perspective and worldview of another person (p. 77).

The issue of empathy is particularly relevant in discourses on diversity. It is through empathy that students from dominant society can understand the experiences of their peers from Canada's diverse communities. But it is not only students who need to develop an ethic of empathy. For example, it is difficult for Whites to comprehend what people of other races have experienced, but empathy can enable them to relate enough to understand. Speaking from the perspective of a White educator in the United States, Howard (2006) contends that while it is difficult for teachers to fully experience the realities of the everyday life of minoritized groups, thay can however "on occasion share a part of the journey together, occupy the same craft for a time and learn to see the view through each others' eyes." This in essence is what Canadian educators must do in order to teach for diversity. In fact, Villegas and Lucas (2002) suggest that the development of empathy should begin in teacher education programs, by using the experiences of prospective teachers who have encountered various forms of oppression as a teaching tool. In order to nurture empathy in their students, teachers themselves must learn to respond to students in an empathetic way. For example, many students in urban schools have had traumatic experiences before coming to Canada: war, refugee status, severe poverty. All these students come to school with various types of challenges that may impact on how they respond to teachers, their peers, and the education system in general. Responding empathetically to these students will contribute significantly to improving their school experiences.

Teaching the Ethic of Care

Related to empathy is the idea of profound caring, which beyond the state of simply understanding, propels teachers to act as advocates of their students. This refers to the ethic of care that teachers at all levels are morally bound to extend to their students and to model. As Noddings (2005: 18) argues, "teachers not only have to create caring relations in which they are the carers . . . they also have a responsibility to help their students develop the capacity to care". In her book *In a Different Voice: Psychological Theory and Women's Development,* Gilligan (1982) argues that while women generally ascribe to an "ethic of care" men tend to subscribe to an "ethic of justice". Although Gilligan distinguishes between these two types of ethics, from a pedagogical perspective all teachers — men and women alike — are expected to demonstrate an ethic of care towards their students. Like Gilligan, Noddings (2005) in her pioneering work on the linkages between interpersonal relationships and positive educational outcomes puts caring at the centre of any meaningful educational change in the contemporary context of student heterogeneity. Manning (1999) provides a précis of the implications of an ethic of caring for teachers:

> There is a special kind of relationship awareness that characterizes an ethic of care . . . So I see my student as a fellow human and a fellow learner. I recognize that he is in need of my help and that I am able to give it. I recognize my role as a teacher and the special obligation this implies. Next, I see him as a member of the classroom community. . . . Finally, I acknowledge the web of personal relationships that can either support or undermine his academic success . . . [A]n ethic of care requires a response on my part. It is not enough to stare at my student and imagine him in a sympathetic way . . . I must make my caring concrete in the actions that I take to respond to his need (p. 119).

Thus, seeing their students as co-sharers of a given space will increase interpersonal bonds between teachers and their students. These transcend not only static sympathy, but make teachers more committed to working towards change in the lives of students, both in and outside the school. The ethic of care enables teachers to act and become advocates for their students. It raises their expectations for their students, and encourages them to become involved in their communities and create vital networks of teacher-parent-community relationships. The ethic of care helps teachers to model appropriate behaviour, nurture healthy, cross-cultural relationships, and above all, work towards increasing the life chances of all students, and in particular those that have been traditionally marginalized.

Community Outreach

Diverse learners come from communities that can be empowered only to the extent that schools encourage collaboration. It is extremely difficult to reach students without collaborating with their families. An earlier chapter explicates the importance of school-family collaboration if school systems hope to meet the needs of students from diverse backgrounds. Community outreach is an important strategy for developing these partnerships. Teachers send home newsletters on a regular basis, but as result of language barriers, the target parents may not be able to read them. This is a common problem in immigrant communities. However, what many schools in Canada do, resources permitting, is send home various translations of the newsletters. Teachers can also take advantage of their students as potential translators. For example, during teacher-parent interviews, students can act as translators (depending of course on the issue to be discussed). It is also important for teachers and principals to attend community functions, and generally make their presence felt within the community.

Community outreach includes inviting parents and community members to come into the classroom to participate in any way that they can. Parents can either help or observe their children at work. Even those who lack language skills should be encouraged to support their children by their very presence in class. Encouraging community members to come into the classroom sends an important signal: Schools are open to power sharing and are willing to work collaboratively with them.

The key to school-community collaboration is building a rapport based on trust. To build community relationships, educators should go out and get to know their school communities and visit First Nations Friendship centres, Greek Association centres, Somalian Community centres, etc. One effective strategy for fostering community outreach is the use of community counsellors. Dei et al. (2000: 212) report that the school board they examined in the Greater Toronto Area employed community liaison counsellors to

- provide support for non-English speaking parents and students
- assist in academic placement based on first language screening
- address concerns about race, culture, and religion in schools' policy and practice
- help parents understand and adapt to the Canadian educational system
- provide pertinent information to teachers, administrators, and school counsellors on the specific needs of their particular communities
- mediate conflicts and concerns among families, schools, and communities.

The dual role of community liaison counsellors as both community advocates and board employees, however, can be challenging. According to Dei et al. "[a]dvocacy for students being their primary concern, often puts counsellors at odds with either parents or the Board. Balancing student, parent and community needs with Board requirements makes their role politically challenging and often contentious".

Professional Development and Life-Long Learning

This book discusses extensively the role of teachers in empowering diverse learners. It also argues that Canadian diversity is not a choice — it is a reality with which school systems and all educators must deal. The degree of success that teachers experience in teaching diverse learners depends on the knowledge they have about teaching such students. It is therefore essential that teachers develop their own theories, perspectives, paradigms, and strategies for dealing with diversity. Doing this requires that they become lifelong learners, as well as regular participants in professional development programs. As Howard (2006) contends, educators, especially White teachers, in multicultural, multiracial, and multilingual settings cannot teach what they do not know.

DIVERSE COMMUNITIES AS AGENTS OF CHANGE

Chapter 5 argues that schools and teachers cannot initiate change without co-opting the participation of the White dominant group. Just as it argues that members of the dominant group must become allies of school systems in order to change the status quo, it is critical that members of mminoritized communities themselves become agents of change. The strategies proposed in Teaching for Diversity can only be partially successful unless disadvantaged groups develop agency in the sense advocated by progressive educators. Indeed, throughout history transformative change never occurred without advocacy and agency on the part of those who are most affected by oppressive social structures, including the educational institutions that reinforce inequality. Unfortunately, many members of the affected communities are often reluctant or unable to act. Through hegemony, some members of disadvantaged communities internalize societal perceptions of their status, leading to a resigned acceptance and normalization of their status.

Nevertheless, it must be emphasized that becoming advocates for change and social justice does not preclude changing patterns of unproductive behaviour. For instance, the practice of Black students discouraging one another from succeeding in school because they are "acting White" is counterproductive, even though such behaviour may be a response to oppressive schooling (Ogbu, 1987). Research has clearly established that many minority familes value education very highly and want their children to acquire higher education. School systems must provide members of Canada's marginalized communities with opportunities to participate in their children's education in more meaningful ways. This is essential because they cannot change the system if they do not understand what goes with it. Based on his reaserch work among a group of White and visible minority students in British Columbia, Orlowski (2001) argues that racism and discrimination remains problematic in Canada and urges everyone (especially educators) to work towards changing the status-quo. He also argues that

> the most effective way to lesson white hegemonic power includes a collective effort on the part of all the minorities. If they hope to be successful in creating a more liberatory Canadian society, these groups will simply have to forget about the ancient social hierarchies that they have experienced (p. 264).

Members of Canadian society who have a subordinate status, and have experienced marginality relative to the two European charter groups, cannot leave the issue of change to chance, nor make it the sole responsibility of "advocates" for equity and socia justice. Canada's diverse communities, both at the individual and group levels, must also become agents of change as we move forward.

DIVERSITY AND STUDENTS WITH DISABILITIES

The bulk of this book is devoted to issues of cultural, racial, and linguistic diversity, as well as to socio-economic and gender-based differences among students. However there is one dimension of diversity — students with special needs — that has so far not been explored and which deserves attention (although it cannot be examined fully in this text). Few works put students with special needs and diversity together, although they are interconnected in very important ways. First, both are concerned with issues such as access to fair and equitable education, equitable representation in the curriculum, language discrimination, and fair measures of performance (Sleeter and Puente, 2001). In effect, both are concerned with promoting equity and social justice in schools and society. Second, some writers argue that the overrepresentation of students from minoritized backgrounds in special education classes is a reflection of wider societal beliefs about the nature of intelligence, what schools should teach, and how students and parents should relate to schools (Sleeter and Puente, 2001; Harry and Klingner, 2006). Third, special education programs by their very nature are exclusionary, and consequently contribute to reproducing inequalities in society. Fourth, another problem that faces special education programs and situates them firmly in the realm of equity is that schools are often poorly equipped to teach students with special needs. Fifth is the controversial practice of organizing special programs for students who are considered exceptionally gifted. This practice remains a source of equity-related debate — the central argument being that labelling some students as gifted or talented implicitly means that other are less well intellectually endowed. Sixth, as argued in the preceding chapters, minority students are disproportionately represented in special programs. Very often, students that have minor behavioural problems are classified as special needs, simply as a function of their racial or cultural background. Sleeter and Puente (2001) argue compellingly that the main point of convergence in discourses on diversity and special education is the overwhelming representation of minority students in special education classes. A report from the Civil Rights Project at Howard University (cited in Bennett, 2007) which has some relevance to the Canadian context, identified variables that contribute to the over-representation of racial minorities in special education programs. These include an over-identification of minority students as needing special education, the mainstreaming of minority, rather than White, students into special education classes, the quality of evaluation, support, and services that result in erroneous placement, and flawed individualized education programs.

Throughout the history of Canadian schooling, dealing with students with special needs has always presented its own set of challenges. Historically for reasons related to easy access, Canadian students with special needs were segregated into their own classrooms, which made it easier to provide them with the specialized attention they needed. However, during the last several decades there has been an ideological shift in thinking about how students with special needs should be treated or grouped for instruction. This trend towards "mainstreaming" or "inclusion" means that for the most part, students with special needs are integrated into regular classrooms. Osborne (1999) and Winzer (2005) advance several reasons why Canadian students with special needs are now being mainstreamed:

1. The segregation of these students leads to stereotyping. Rather than being seen as those who face challenges in learning, they are classified as people who cannot learn at all.

2. Segregation cuts the students off from society, and thus does not prepare them adequately for life outside of their classrooms.

3. Grouping these students into their own special classrooms tends to lower teachers' expectations of them because they are seen as people who can perform only the most basic academic tasks.

4. Segregating them into their own special classrooms tended to facilitate their being labelled as needing special help, even though their problems may not be directly related to academic ability. For example, as Osborne argues, students who are deaf or blind and segregated are considered learning disabled, yet their problem is simply related to visual or auditory impairment. Similarly, students who exhibit some behavioural problems may be considered mentally challenged, but their problem is not really one of ability, but rather a question of attitude.

5. Segregating students makes it easier to avoid looking for different ways of assisting them because they are considered as limited in ability.

6. The principles of educational equity demand that all students should have equal opportunity to learn with their peers.

Segregation of students amounts to an infringement of their human rights because (no matter their level of ability) students with special needs are human beings and citizens and are therefore entitled to the rights and privileges thereof. Moreover, the rights of students with special needs are protected under the *Charter of Rights and Freedoms*. Winzer (2005) summarizes the link between the philosophy of inclusion or mainstreaming to civil rights especially with regards to the United States:

> Special education is intimately connected to common views of social justice. The provision of less restrictive, more natural integrated environments for students with disabilities is an out growth of a social philosophy about individual civil rights that is so critical in the United States. Proponents argue that special classes are discriminatory and unequal and in violation of the democratic ethos that allows equal access to education for all students. That is, removal from the mainstream of education is inherently restrictive and limiting, and the right to be educated with one's peers is a civil right (p. 44).

While there is significant support for integrating students with special needs into regular classrooms, there is also some resistance to the idea. For example, teachers who do not have training in special education often argue that they do not have the expertise to accept such students in their class (Ryan, 2006). Opponents also see integration as additional work for teachers.

However, despite the trend to integrate special needs students into "regular" classrooms, there are nonetheless special education classes, which are designed to accommodate students who have been identified as having some learning disabilities. The number of students who are identified as having learning disabilities such as autism, dyslexia, attention deficit disorder (ADD), and attention deficit hyperactivity disorder (ADHD) has increased dramatically. These last two categories tend to be behaviour related, and typically have an over-representation of minority students, especially boys (Harry and Klingner, 2006).

Another group that usually predominates in special education classes is students that have some form of language-related difficulties, even though for the most part, these language problems are generally about difficulties in enunciating mainstream language (Egbo, 2001). Some writers note how challenging it is to determine the extent to which limited language proficiency is the result of difficulty in learning a second language versus learning disabilities. Therefore, the process of evaluation is problematically imprecise as one bilingual assessor interviewed by Harry and Klingner, (2006) acknowledges

> My role as a bilingual assessor is to determine if the child's difficulties are due to [learning a second language] or due to other factors. Sometimes it might be something I don't know. Sometimes I don't have all of the facts in front of me. Sometimes the discrepancy is so thin. Maybe if they give him more time, he'll make it. Maybe we will give him 2 years and with more time we'll see a change. Maybe sometimes we know that 2 years will not help. Sometimes it is just kind of [a] struggle to see (p. 117).

What is disconcerting about comments such as the above is that the consequence of imprecise identification is erroneous categorization of students as special needs learners. Similarly, students from low socio-economic backgrounds tend to be over-represented in special education classes (Harry and Klinger, 2006). The intention is not to underrate the importance of diagnosing special needs students. Rather, the point is that when identifying students with what Bennett (2007) refers to as the "soft" cases of exceptionalities, i.e., those with behaviour-related diagnoses such as ADD and ADHD, it is prudent to proceed with caution. Delpit (2006) provides an example of why caution is essential. The case involves one of her former students who, in the first grade, was identified as requiring special needs placement. Delpit acknowledges that the student did experience considerable academic difficulty (particularly in mathematics). When she got to know him better, she found that even at the age of seven he had some adult responsibilities at home. For instance, he was solely responsible for taking care of a sister who was suffering from cerebral palsy, a drug incapacitated mother, and the household chores. He was also responsible for doing the family shopping and had become quite adept at handling money. Still, he could not perform some basic mathematical tasks in school. The discrepancy between this student's demonstrated ability at home and his limited academic achievement highlights the problems of what the curriculum sometimes presents and of how schools determine ability and skills. It also illustrates the problem of treating most students using a one-size-fits-all approach. Students differ considerably, and teachers have to find ways of reaching each one of them as a unique individual.

Returning to the issue of labelling, Bennett (2007) argues that

> Successful teachers in inclusive classrooms . . . [discard] the ethnocentric view that low-income and ethnic-minority students are "culturally disadvantaged" and "at risk". They reject the idea that anyone who has not had the "normal" advantages of a middle-income home life is culturally deprived. They realize that a "deficit" view is harmful because it focuses on where our students *aren't* and blinds us to where they *are* (pp. 258–259). [emphasis in original]

In effect, labelling puts blinders on teachers and prevents them from exploring the vast region of possibilities that is their students. Consider the following vignette: The family of sixth grader Chelina had immigrated to Canada from Latin American a few years earlier and settled in Quebec. Chelina was experiencing considerable difficulty learning French, so much so that there was consensus among the experts who evaluated her that she might have some form of learning disorder. In addition to her difficulties with the language, she seemed to be obsessed with various objects in the class. Her dismayed teacher could not understand why Chelina was always tinkering with, or closely examining, the objects that captured her interest. On a number of occasions, she had tried to redirect Chelina's attention back to the task at hand by taking away such objects. She had discussed the issue with some of her colleagues, all of whom were of the opinion that Chelina's obsession was probably indicative of some form of psychological trauma that might be linked to her home life. Little was known about her family life except that her father worked in one of the local factories. This was an unfortunate omission because had the teacher probed a little further, she would have discovered that Chelina's father had been an engineer in their native country before immigrating to Canada as a political refugee. She would also have learned that stringent recertification requirements and his limited proficiency in French had so far prevented him from practising his profession in Canada. Furthermore, she would have understood that Chelina's obsession with objects was the result of her fervent desire to follow in her father's footsteps, i.e., to become an engineer. This case is a good example of why educators must not rush to label students.

CONCLUSION

This volume attempts to build a theory of practice that educators can adopt to initiate social change. The intent is to propose a progressive paradigm of dealing with diversity in Canadian schools. In so doing, several frameworks and models of teaching in contexts of student diversity have been explored. The rationale for exploring various frameworks is based on the recognition that teaching for diversity in authentic and life-changing ways depends on the adoption of an eclectic framework that integrates elements of various models across the curriculum. The work argues that educators must learn to ask uncomfortable questions about taken-for-granted assumptions about educational policies, the nature of learning, and what constitutes valid knowledge, with the ultimate goal of increasing the life chances of those they serve. At the same time, teachers and other educators must also address the issues of fairness, legitimacy, impartiality, and mutual advantage with respect to educational policy and practice. Ultimately, a body of knowledge that has been developed from the perspective of the dominant group can favour only dominant group students. Acknowledged or not, there are procedural rules for how we educate children and the existence of these rules is not in itself problematic. What many argue is unacceptable, is that these rules often reflect only the monolithic views of the dominant groups in Canadian society. This book also argues that schools must reconceptualize the way they are organized and implement mechanisms for sharing power among all stakeholders, especially students from nondominant group backgrounds and their families. The continued exclusion of their voices is blatantly contrary to Canada's chosen identity as a cultural mosaic. Furthermore, in the words of Howard (2006: 143) who writes within the context of the United States, the transformative agenda for all educators involves "dismantling the dominance paradigm and . . . envisioning, creating and modelling a better future, a new social paradigm that honors diversity and ensures greater equity for all . . . people".

While acknowledging that individuals do have a role to play in engendering their own academic and future success, teachers must recognize how a legacy of privilege contributes to the school success of students from the dominant group. Conversely, it must be clearly understood that a history of marginality underlies the negative schooling experiences of students from nondominant communities. The assumption that a predetermined biological or cultural propensity towards failure is the root cause of academic underachievement among some groups of students is no longer a tenable position. It is useful at this stage to highlight some of the issues raised in the book:

- Given that diversity is a stable Canadian reality, examining the relationships between race, culture, gender, and socio-economic status must be a critical starting point for initiating policies and programs that are geared towards *teaching for diversity in Canadian schools*. It is a widely accepted premise that social positioning, privilege, and the knowledge that is reproduced in schools (at least in Western and pluralistic societies such as Canada) intersect in complex ways that affect school success.

- There is compelling evidence to show that minority students have a tenuous relationship with schools as a function of systemic racism, exclusionary educational practices, and Eurocentric ideologies that not only negate their identities but also devalue their cultural capital.

- A myriad of variables account for differential school achievement between various groups of students, and between boys and girls. While cognizant that there is as much intra-group diversity as there are inter-group differences, taking people's backgrounds, learning styles, and worldviews into consideration must be part of critical teaching practices.

- While the explicit goal of schools is to socialize and educate the next generation, and the content required is generally stipulated in the formal curriculum, a substantive amount of what students learn is not openly stated — even though this implicitly conveyed knowledge, or the hidden curriculum, underpins student and teacher behaviour in Canadian schools.

- Historically, Canada has always been a culturally and linguistically diverse society. However, responses to diversity by successive Canadian governments, social institutions, and the public at large are typically influenced by prevailing social ideologies. More importantly, the contemporary demographic profile of Canadian society has always been inextricably linked to immigration policy.

- Canadian schools mirror the diversity in wider society, especially in large urban centres. Consequently, and also as a result of constitutional provisions in the *Charter of Rights and Freedoms*, social and educational policies have been developed to address Canadian diversity and to ostensibly equalize educational and social opportunities for all.

- Progressive educators, and this book, argue that while significant progress has been made towards empowering students from diverse backgrounds, more still needs to be done at all levels of the educational system, especially at the micro-level of the classroom. Furthermore, educational policies and practices must be grounded in the principles of fundamental human rights and social justice, — which reject monocultural and assimilationist educational ideologies in pluralistic societies such as Canada.

- The goal of promoting diversity in Canadian schools cannot be achieved without practical and structural changes to social and educational policies at all levels of the government, and relevant sectors of society. To this extent, policy matters.

Finally, this work argues that authentic change can occur only when teachers and other educators embrace inclusive and anti-bias paradigms and demonstrate an unwavering commitment to social justice. With this in mind, I urge all educators to let transformative praxis begin.

Key Terms

Deconstruction   Diversity issues across the   Empathy
                                  curriculum (DIAC)

Questions to Guide Reflective Practice

1. With regard to teaching for diversity, what in your opinion should be the future direction for teachers? Develop a comprehensive future-oriented strategy to guide your own practice.

2. Based on your reading of this chapter and the book, how can long-term strategies for empowering diverse learners be developed?

3. This chapter argues that the issue of students with special needs intersects with other diversity issues. To what extent do you agree with this assertion? Justify your answer.

4. How can schools maintain a critical balance between preserving group interests and the interests of the individual?

5. How would you characterize the over-representation of minority students in special education programs? Do you believe that it is the result of systemic racism or a true reflection of the situation? How can schools change this trend?

Case Study Analysis: Chapter Opening Vignette

1. Assess John Zeak's handling of the case. Did he do everything he could have done to avoid the escalation of the situation?

2. If you were John Zeak what, if anything, would you have done differently?

3. What is the major error that John Zeak made in this situation that all teachers, especially those that are new to the profession, should avoid?

4. If you were the principal how would you resolve this conflict?

5. Briefly outline an action plan for dealing with students who are prejudiced like Josh.

6. Explain your understanding of John Zeak's comment "there was too much at stake".

Test Your Knowledge

1. Research and identify the policies that guide special education programs in your province. To what extent are special needs students "mainstreamed" in your local schools?

2. Discuss the advantages and disadvantages of integrating students with special needs into "regular" classrooms with a group of your peers. What is the opinion of the majority?

3. Research what extent placement patterns of students with special needs in your province reflect the view that minoritized students are over-represented in special education programs.

4. Interview some special education specialists. What are their views on the practice of "mainstreaming"?

5. Find out what schools in your community are doing to make schools spaces that foster equity, student empowerment, and collaboration among all relevant stakeholders.

6. The chapter argues that one way of empowering diverse students and their communities is through community outreach. What is your local school board's policy for facilitating the participation of members of the diverse communities in the schools within its jurisdiction?

For Further Reading

Bennett C. I. (2007). *Comprehensive Multicultural Education: Theory Practice*, 6th Edition. Boston: Pearson Education.

Delpit, L. (2006). *Other People's Children: Cultural Conflict in the Classroom*. New York: The New Press.

Gay, G. (2000). *Culturally Responsive Teaching: Theory, Research Practice*. New York: Teachers College Press.

Gillborn, D. (2004). Ability, Selection, and Institutional Racism in Schools. In M. Olssen (Ed.), *Culture and Learning: Access and Opportunity in the Classroom* (pp. 279–298). Charlotte: Information Age Publishing Inc.

Grossman, H. (1995). *Teaching in a Diverse Society*. Needham Heights: Allyn Bacon.

Harry, B., and Klingner, J. (2006). *Why Are so Many Minority Students in Special Education?* New York: Teachers College Press.

Howard, G. R. (2006). *We Can't Teach What We Don't Know: White Teachers, Multiracial Schools*, 2nd Edition. New York: Teachers College Press.

McLaren, P. (2007). *Life in Schools: an Introduction to Critical Pedagogy in the Foundations of Education*, 5th Edition. Boston: Pearson Education.

Osborne, K. (1999). *Education: A Guide to the Canadian School Debate–Or Who Wants What and Why?* Toronto: Penguin Canada.

Websites of Interest

www.edu.gov.on.ca/eng/general/elemsec/speced/speced.html Ontario Ministry of Education Website

www.ibwebs.com/canadian.htm Canadian Special Education Website

www.specialeducation.ab.ca/ Alberta Teachers' Association — Special Education Council

www.neads.ca National Educational Association of Disabled Students (NEADS)

www.ethnocultural.ca Canadian Ethnocultural Council

www.cmef.ca Canadian Multicultural Education Foundation